Tecumseh

John Richardson

Matthew Elliott

Roger Hale Sheaffe

Augustus John Foster

The Invasion of Canada

The Invasion

The conquest of Canada is
in our power. I trust I shall
not be deemed presumptive when
I state that I verily believe
that the militia of Kentucky
are alone competent to place
Montreal and Upper Canada
at your feet.

Henry Clay, to the
United States Senate,
February 22, 1810.

Pierre Berton

of Canada
1812~1813

McClelland and Stewart

ISBN 0-7710-1235-7

The Canadian Publishers
McClelland and Stewart Limited
25 Hollinger Road, Toronto M4B 3G2

Endpapers by Tom McNeely

*Printed and bound in Canada by
T. H. Best Printing Company Limited,
Don Mills, Ontario*

Books by Pierre Berton

The Royal Family
The Mysterious North
Klondike
Just Add Water and Stir
Adventures of a Columnist
Fast, Fast, Fast Relief
The Big Sell
The Comfortable Pew
The Cool, Crazy, Committed World of the Sixties
The Smug Minority
The National Dream
The Last Spike
Drifting Home
Hollywood's Canada
My Country
The Dionne Years
The Wild Frontier
The Invasion of Canada

PICTURE BOOKS
The New City (with Henri Rossier)
Remember Yesterday
The Great Railway

ANTHOLOGIES
Great Canadians
Pierre & Janet Berton's Canadian Food Guide
Historic Headlines

FOR YOUNGER READERS
The Golden Trail
The Secret World of Og

CONTENTS

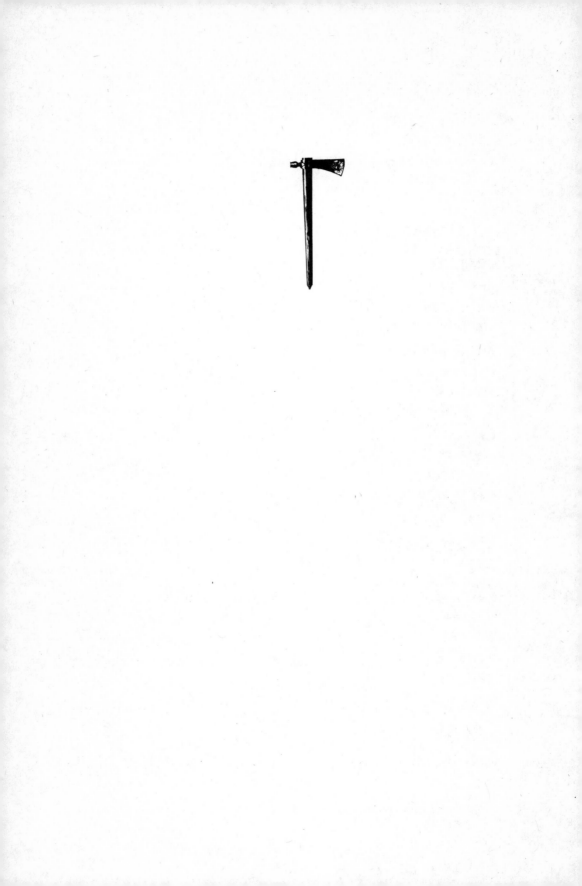

Maps

Maps by Geoffrey Matthews

Cast of Characters

PRELUDE TO INVASION

British and Canadians

Sir James Craig, Governor General of Canada, 1807–11.

Sir George Prevost, Governor General of the Canadas and commander of the forces, 1811–15.

Francis Gore, Lieutenant-Governor of Upper Canada, 1806–17. On leave in England, 1811–15.

Major-General Isaac Brock, Administrator of Upper Canada and commander of the forces in Upper Canada, 1810–12.

William Claus, Deputy Superintendent, Indian Department, Upper Canada, 1806–26.

Matthew Elliott, Superintendent of Indian Affairs at Amherstburg, 1796–97; 1808–14.

Robert Dickson (known as *Mascotapah*, the Red-Haired Man), fur trader. Led Menominee, Winnebago, and Sioux in attack on Michilimackinac.

Augustus Foster, British Minister Plenipotentiary to America, 1811–12.

Americans

Thomas Jefferson, President, 1801–9.

James Madison, President, 1809–17.

William Eustis, Secretary of War, 1809–12.

William Henry Harrison, Governor, Indiana Territory, 1800–1813. Commander of the Army of the Northwest from September, 1812.

William Hull, Governor, Michigan Territory, 1805–12. Commander of the Army of the Northwest, April–August, 1812.

Henry Dearborn, Secretary of War, 1801–9. Senior major-general, U.S. Army, 1812–13.

Henry Clay, Speaker of the House of Representatives, November, 1811. Leader of the War Hawks.

Indian Leaders
The Prophet. Born Laulewausika; later Tenskwatawa.
Tecumseh, the Prophet's older brother, leader of the Indian Confederacy.

THE DETROIT FRONTIER

Isaac Brock's Command: Summer, 1812
Thomas Bligh St. George, Lieutenant-Colonel; commanding officer, Fort Amherstburg.
Henry Procter, Lieutenant-Colonel; succeeded St. George as commanding officer, Fort Amherstburg.
J.B. Glegg, Major; Brock's military aide.
John Macdonell, Lieutenant-Colonel; Brock's provincial aide, Acting Attorney-General of Upper Canada.
Adam Muir, Major, 41st Regiment.

William Hull's Command: Summer, 1812
Duncan McArthur, Colonel, 1st Regiment, Ohio Volunteers.
James Findlay, Colonel, 2nd Regiment, Ohio Volunteers.
Lewis Cass, Colonel, 3rd Regiment, Ohio Volunteers.
James Miller, Lieutenant-Colonel, 4th U.S. Infantry (regular army).

Henry Procter's Command: Winter, 1812–13
Ebenezer Reynolds, Major, Essex Militia.
Roundhead, Wyandot chief.

William Henry Harrison's Command: Winter, 1812–13
James Winchester, Brigadier-General; commander, left wing, Army of the Northwest.
John Allen, Lieutenant-Colonel, 1st Kentucky Rifles.
William Lewis, Lieutenant-Colonel, 5th Regiment, Kentucky Volunteers.
Samuel Wells, Lieutenant-Colonel, 17th U.S. Infantry (regular army).

Isaac Brock's Command: Fall, 1812

Christopher Myers, Lieutenant-Colonel; commanding officer, Fort George.

Roger Hale Sheaffe, Major-General; second-in-command to Brock. Commanded British forces on Brock's death.

Thomas Evans, Brigade Major, Fort George.

John Dennis, Captain, 49th Regiment; commander of flank company defending Queenston.

John Williams, Captain, 49th Regiment.

James Crooks, Captain, 1st Lincoln Militia.

William Holcroft, Captain, Royal Artillery.

Frederic Rolette, Lieutenant, Provincial Marine.

Robert Irvine, Second-Lieutenant, Provincial Marine.

John Brant, Mohawk chief.

John Norton, Captain, Indian Department; leader of Mohawks.

Henry Dearborn's Command: Fall, 1812

Stephen Van Rensselaer, Major-General, New York state militia; senior commander on the Niagara frontier.

Solomon Van Rensselaer, Lieutenant-Colonel; cousin and aide-de-camp to Stephen Van Rensselaer.

John Lovett, Major; aide to Stephen and Solomon Van Rensselaer. In charge of artillery at Fort Grey at Battle of Queenston Heights.

William Wadsworth, Brigadier-General, Upper New York State militia.

Alexander Smyth, Brigadier-General, regular army, Niagara frontier. Replaced Stephen Van Rensselaer following Battle of Queenston Heights.

John Chrystie, Lieutenant-Colonel, 13th U.S. Infantry (regular army).

John Fenwick, Lieutenant-Colonel, U.S. Light Artillery.

John E. Wool, Captain, 13th U.S. Infantry.

Winfield Scott, Lieutenant-Colonel, 2nd U.S. Artillery.

Peter B. Porter, Quartermaster General, Upper New York State. Member of the War Hawk faction in Congress.

Jesse D. Elliott, Lieutenant, U.S. Navy.

The Strategic Significance of Michilimackinac

PREVIEW: *Porter Hanks's War*

*MICHILIMACKINAC ISLAND, MICHIGAN TERRITORY,
U.S.A. The small hours of a soft July morning in 1812.*

*The lake is silent, save for the whisper of waves lapping the shoreline.
In the starlight, the island's cliffs stand out darkly against the surrounding flatland. In the fort above the village at the southern tip the American
commander, Lieutenant Porter Hanks, lies asleep, ignorant of a war that
will tragically affect his future. Napoleon has entered Russia; Wellington
is pushing toward Madrid; and in Washington, the die has been cast for
invasion. But history has passed Hanks by. It is nine months since he has
heard from Washington; for all he knows of the civilized world he might
as well be on the moon.*

*The civilized world ends at the Detroit River, some 350 miles to the
southeast as the canoe travels. Mackinac Island is its outpost, a minor
Gibraltar lying in the narrows between Lakes Huron and Michigan.
Whoever controls it controls the routes to the fur country — the domain of
the Nor'Westers beyond Superior and the no man's land of the upper
Missouri and Mississippi. It is a prize worth fighting for.*

*Hanks slumbers on, oblivious of a quiet bustling in the village directly
below — of low knockings, whispers, small children's plaints quickly
hushed, rustlings, soft footsteps, the creak of cartwheels on grass — slumbers fitfully, his dreams troubled by a growing uneasiness, until the drum
roll of reveille wakes him. He suspects something is going to happen. He
has been seven years a soldier, knows trouble when he sees it, has watched
it paddling by him for a week. An extraordinary number of Indians have
been passing the fort, apparently on their way to the British garrison at
St. Joseph's Island, forty-five miles to the northeast, just beyond the
border. Why? The answers are strangely evasive. The Ottawa and
Chippewa chiefs, once so friendly, have turned suspiciously cool. On the
British side, it is said, the tribes have gathered by the hundreds from
distant frontiers: Sioux from the upper Mississippi, Winnebago from the
Wisconsin country, Menominee from the shores of Green Bay.*

*Hanks peers over the palisades of the fort and gazes down on the
village below, a crescent of whitewashed houses, following the curve of a
pebbled beach. He sees at once that something is wrong. For the village is
not sleeping; it is dead. No curl of smoke rises above the cedar-bark roofs;*

no human cry echoes across the waters of the lake; no movement ruffles the weeds that edge the roadway.

What is going on? Hanks dispatches his second-in-command, Lieutenant Archibald Darragh, to find out. But he does not need to wait for Darragh's report. Clambering up the slope comes his only other commissioned officer, the surgeon's mate, Sylvester Day, who prefers to live in the village. Dr. Day's breathless report is blunt: British redcoats and Indians have landed at the opposite end of the island. All the villagers have been collected quietly and, for their own safety, herded into an old distillery under the bluff at the west end of town. Three of the most prominent citizens are under guard as hostages.

Hanks reacts instantly to this news: musters his men, stocks his blockhouses with ammunition, charges his field pieces, follows the book. He must know that he is merely playing soldier, for he has fewer than sixty effective troops under his command — men rendered stale by their frontier exile. Presently he becomes aware of a British six-pounder on the forested bluff above, pointing directly into his bastion. Through the spring foliage he can see the flash of British scarlet and — the ultimate horror — the dark forms of their native allies. A single word forms in his mind, a truly terrible word for anyone with frontier experience: massacre — *visions of mutilated bodies, decapitated children, disembowelled housewives, scalps bloodying the pickets.*

Hanks can fight to the last man and become a posthumous hero. If it were merely the aging troops of Fort St. Joseph that faced him, he might be prepared to do just that. But to the last woman? To the last child? Against an enemy whose savagery is said to be without limits?

A white flag flutters before him. Under its protection a British truce party marches into the fort, accompanied by the three civilian hostages. The parley is brief and to the point. Hanks must surrender. The accompanying phrase "or else" hangs unspoken in the air. The hostages urge him to accept, but it is doubtful whether he needs their counsel. He agrees to everything; the fort and the island will become British. The Americans must take the oath of allegiance to the King or leave. His troops are to be paroled to their homes. Until exchanged they can take no further part in the war.

The war? What war? *The date is July 17. A full month has passed since the United States declared war on Great Britain, but this is the first Hanks has heard of it. An invasion force has already crossed the Detroit River into Canada and skirmished with the British, but nobody in Washington, it seems, has grasped the urgency of a speedy warning to*

14

the western flank of the American frontier. It is entirely characteristic of this senseless and tragic conflict that it should have its beginnings in this topsy-turvy fashion, with the invaders invaded in a trackless wilderness hundreds of miles from the nerve centres of command.

For its dereliction the American government will pay dear. This bloodless battle is also one of the most significant. The news of the capture of Michilimackinac Island will touch off a chain of events that will frustrate the Americans in their attempt to seize British North America, an enterprise that most of them believe to be, in Thomas Jefferson's much-quoted phrase, "a mere matter of marching."

OVERVIEW
The War of 1812

THE INVASION OF CANADA, which began in the early summer of 1812 and petered out in the late fall of 1814, was part of a larger conflict that has come to be known in North America as the War of 1812. That war was the by-product of a larger struggle, which saw Napoleonic France pitted for almost a decade against most of Europe. It is this complexity, a war within a war within a war, like a nest of Chinese boxes, that has caused so much confusion. The watershed date "1812" has different connotations for different people. And, as in Alice's famous caucus race, everybody seems to have won *something*, though there were no prizes. The Russians, for instance, began to win their own War of 1812 against Napoleon in the very week in which the British and Canadians were repulsing the invading Americans at Queenston Heights. The Americans won the last battle of their War of 1812 in the first week of 1815 – a victory diminished by the fact that peace had been negotiated fifteen days before. The British, who beat Napoleon, could also boast that they "won" the North American war because the Treaty of Ghent, which settled the matter, had nothing to say about the points at issue and merely maintained the *status quo*.

This work deals with the war that Canada won, or to put it more precisely *did not lose*, by successfully repulsing the armies that tried to invade and conquer British North America. The war was fought almost entirely in Upper Canada, whose settlers, most of them Americans, did not invite the war, did not care about the issues, and did not want to fight. They were the victims of a clash between two major powers who, by the accident of geography, found it convenient to settle their differences by doing violence to the body of another. The invasion of Canada was not the first time that two armies have bloodied neutral ground over issues that did not concern the inhabitants; nor has it been the last.

Of all the wars fought by the English-speaking peoples, this was one of the strangest – a war entered into blindly and fought (also blindly) by men out of touch not only with reality but also with their own forces. Washington was separated from the fighting frontier by hundreds of miles of forest, rock, and swamp. The ultimate British authority was an ocean away and the nominal authority a fortnight distant from the real command. Orders could take days, weeks, even months to reach the troops.

Like some other wars, this one began bloodlessly with expressions of civility on both sides and the conviction that it would be over by Christmas. It did not end that way, for horror breeds hatred, and no war (certainly not this one) can be free of atrocity. Nor was it free of bombast. As in most wars, the leaders on both sides were convinced that their cause was just and that the Deity was firmly in their camp, leading them to victory. Slogans about "freedom" and "slavery," "despotism" and "liberty" were batted back and forth across the border like shuttlecocks. Each side believed, or pretended to believe, that the other was held in thrall by a pernicious form of government.

At the outset, it was a gentlemen's war. Officers on opposing sides met for parleys under flags of truce, offered hospitality, exchanged cordialities, murmured the hope that hostilities would quickly end. Belligerents addressed one another in flowery terms. The same men who declared they would never be slaves of the enemy had "the honour to be y'r humble and obedient servant." When Isaac Brock fell at Queenston, the men responsible for his death joined in the general grief. Roger Sheaffe, his successor, expressed in writing his great regret for the wounds suffered by an opposing commander – wounds that put him out of action and helped Sheaffe win the day. "If there be anything at my command that your side of the river cannot furnish, which would be either useful or agreeable...I beg you will be so good as to have me apprised of it," he wrote to the enemy. When the first word of the declaration of war reached the British post at Fort George on the Niagara frontier, its officers were entertaining their American opposite numbers at dinner. They insisted that the meal continue as if hostilities had not commenced, then, with much handshaking and expressions of regret, accompanied their guests to their boats. Within a few weeks, the former dinner companions were ripping through one another's homes and fortifications with red-hot cannonballs.

For a war of thirty months' duration, the casualties were not heavy. In those same years many a European battle counted far more dead and wounded in a single day. But for those who did fall, it was a truly terrible war, fought under appalling conditions far from civilization and medical aid. Those victims who were torn to pieces by cannon-balls, their brains often spattering their comrades, might be considered lucky. The wounded endured agonies, banged about in open carts, exposed to blizzards or driving rain, hauled for miles over rutted tracks to the surgeon's table where, with a musket ball clamped between their teeth and when possible a tot of rum warming their bellies, they suffered the horrors of a hasty amputation.

As the war progressed, it grew more vicious. There was savagery on both sides by white frontiersmen as well as Indians, who scalped the fallen sometimes when they were still alive. Men were roasted in flaming buildings, chopped to pieces by tomahawks, sliced open by bayonets, drowned, frozen, or felled by sickness, which took more lives on both sides than all the battles combined. There were times when a third of an army was too ill to fight. The diseases were given vague names like "ague" and "swamp fever," which might mean influenza, pneumonia, malaria, typhus, dysentery, or simply that the combatants were too cold, too weary, or too dispirited to march or even stand. And no wonder: on both sides the armies, especially the citizen soldiers of the militia, were ill equipped for war. Men were forced to trudge through ankle-deep snow and to wade freezing rivers without shoes; to sleep in the open without blankets; to face the Canadian winter lacking mitts and greatcoats, their clothes in tatters, their hands and feet bound in rags, tormented by frostbite in January and insects in June. The military may have seen the war coming, but the politicians were not prepared to pay its price.

At the planning level, the war was marked by incredible bungling. As in so many wars, but especially in this one, the day was often won not by the most brilliant commander, for there were few brilliant commanders, but by the least incompetent. On the American side, where civilian leaders were mixed in with regular army officers, the commands were marked by petty jealousies, vicious infighting, bitter rivalries. On certain memorable occasions, high-ranking officers supposedly fighting the British preferred to fight each other with pistols at dawn. Old soldiers were chosen for command simply because they *were* old soldiers; they acted like sports heroes long past their prime, weary of the contest, sustained only by the glamour of the past, struggling as much against the ambitions of younger aspirants as against the enemy. Some were chosen capriciously. One general was given an important command solely for political reasons – to get him out of the way.

On the Canadian side, where "democracy" was a wicked word and the army was run autocratically by British professionals, there was little of this. Many of these men, however, were cast-offs from Europe. The officers gained their commissions through purchase, not competence. With certain exceptions, the cream of the British Army was with Wellington, fighting Napoleon's forces on the Iberian Peninsula. Aging veterans made up part of the garrison forces in Canada. Boys of fourteen and fifteen fought with the militia. Lacklustre leadership, incompetent planning, timidity and vacillation were too often the concomitants of command on both sides of the border.

The militia on both sides was a rabble. Hastily summoned and hastily trained when trained at all, they fought sometimes reluctantly, sometimes with gallantry. On the Canadian side these citizen soldiers were drilled about three days in a month. They were called up when needed, placed away from the centre of the line, on the flanks (when the line existed at all), and, after an engagement, sent back to their homes and farms until needed once more. The more patriotic signed up for the duration and became seasoned warriors. The American army was a confusion of regular soldiers, state militia, and federal volunteers recruited from the militia for terms of service that ranged from one month to a year or more.

On both sides men thought nothing of leaving the scene of battle to thresh their grain at harvest time. For most of the men who fought it, then, it was a part-time war. Some refused to fight. In spite of the harsh discipline, men on both sides mutinied. Soldiers were shot for desertion, forced to ride bent saplings, to stand barefoot on sharpened stakes, branded, or flogged almost to death. Neither threats nor pleas could stop thousands of American militiamen from refusing to fight on foreign soil. To the dismay of their commanders, these amateur soldiers took democracy at its face value, electing their own officers and, on occasion, dismissing them. In Upper Canada treason worked its slow poison, even invading the legislature. Farmers were hanged for abetting the enemy; tribunes of the people took refuge on foreign soil to raise squads of traitors; dark suspicions, often unfounded, seeped down the concession roads, causing neighbour to denounce neighbour.

The war, like other wars, brought disaster to thousands and prosperity to thousands more. Prices rose; profits boomed. The border might be in flames, its people at each other's throats, but that did not prevent merchants on both sides from crossing over in the interests of commerce. Americans on the eastern shore of Lake Champlain fed the British troops fighting on the western side. Montreal middlemen grew rich supplying the needs of New England. Pork, beef, and grain from Vermont and other states found their way into the commissariats of Upper Canada. Before the invasion came to an end, two out of every three soldiers fighting for the safety and honour of Canada were subsisting on beef brought in by enemy contractors.

In the Atlantic provinces and the neighbouring New England states, the war scarcely existed. On July 3, 1812, the Lieutenant-Governor of Nova Scotia issued a proclamation announcing that his province and New Brunswick would abstain from predatory warfare against their neighbours and that trade would continue "without Molestation." Between Maine and New Brunswick it was more than business as usual; it was frolic as usual. The border town of St. Stephen, realizing that its American neighbour, Calais, could not obtain fireworks for its Independence Day celebration, obligingly helped out with a gift of gun powder.

But on the fighting frontier it was civil war. There is a story that the man who fired the first cannonball across the river during the battle of Detroit killed his best friend on the American side – a legend, possibly, but perfectly plausible. Almost everyone had a friend or a relative on the other side of the border. Sheaffe, the British general, had a sister Margaret in Boston. William Hull, the defender of Detroit, had a brother Isaac living on the Thames. The border was irrelevant; people crossed it as they would a street. Many owned land or had business interests on the other side. One of these was John Askin of Sandwich, Upper Canada, the venerable fur trader and patriarch (various members of whose extensive family will appear from time to time in these pages). During the war, Askin continued to correspond with his friend and kinsman Elijah Brush, the militia commander at Detroit, who was married to Askin's daughter Adelaide. When the Americans invaded Sandwich and Askin was forced to flee, Brush obligingly detailed some of his men to harvest Askin's crops. When Detroit fell, Brush consigned his personal papers, money, and members of his family to Askin's care. None of this prevented Askin's sons, nephews, and grandsons from taking up arms and killing Americans.

They did so reluctantly, for this was a war that almost nobody wanted. The British, who had been embroiled with Napoleon for seven years, certainly did not want it, did not believe it would occur, and in a clumsy, last-minute effort tried to prevent it. The Canadian settlers, struggling to master a forbidding if fertile wilderness, did not want it either; at best it was an interruption, at worst a tragedy. The majority, whenever possible, did their best to stay out of it. Nor did the mass of the American people want to go to war; a great many, especially in the New England states, sat it out; others fought half-heartedly. Congress, in the words of a Kentucky editor, was "driven, goaded, dragged, forced, kicked" into the conflict by a small, eloquent group that Thomas Jefferson dubbed the War Hawks.

America went to war as a last resort because her leaders felt that the nation's honour had been besmirched to a point where any other action would be unthinkable. In their zeal to conquer Napoleon, the British pushed the Americans too far and dismissed their former colonists with an indifference that bordered on contempt, thus repeating the errors of 1776. In that sense, the War of 1812 was a continuation of the American Revolution.

It began with Napoleon, for without Napoleon there would have been no war. (The President, James Madison, remarked after the fact that had he known Napoleon would be defeated his country would have stayed out of it.) Great Britain, fighting for her life against France, was bent on all-out maritime warfare. If a neutral America, reaping the economic benefits, was bruised a little on the high seas, well, that was unfortunate but necessary. America, in British eyes, was a weak, inconsequential nation that could be pushed around with impunity. In the words of the London *Courier*, "two fifty gun ships would be able to burn, sink and destroy the whole American navy."

This attitude was expressed first in the British policy of boarding American ships and impressing American seamen for service in the Royal Navy on the grounds that they were deserters from British service. At least three thousand and perhaps as many as seven thousand fell victim to this practice, which infuriated the country and was one of the two chief causes of the war.

The other was the equally galling Orders in Council, the last enacted in November, 1807, as an act of reprisal against the French. With cool disdain for the rights of neutrals as well as for American sea power, the British warned that they would seize on the open ocean any ship that dared sail directly for a Napoleonic port. By 1812 they had captured almost four hundred American vessels, some within sight of the U.S. coast, and played havoc with the American export trade.

There were other irritants, especially in the more volatile southern and western states, where a serious economic depression was blamed, not without reason, on the British blockade. The slump hit the Mississippi Valley in 1808, shortly after Britain proclaimed the Orders in Council. Prices collapsed. Cotton and tobacco could no longer be exported. This, combined with the growing Indian threat to the frontier settlements, was used to bolster the arguments of those seeking an excuse for war. In Kentucky especially – the most hawkish of states – and in Ohio and the territories, it was widely believed that British agents were goading the various tribes to revolt. There was talk of teaching the Indians a lesson, even driving the British out of North America, thereby breaking the fur monopoly, opening the land to settlement, and strengthening the Union. Certain western expansionists also saw the coming war as one of liberation. It was widely believed that most Canadians wanted to become Americans. If they did not, well, that was their destiny.

In the summer of 1812, with three American armies threatening the border strongpoints – Amherstburg, Queenston, Montreal, and Kingston – the early fall of Upper Canada and the subsequent collapse of Quebec seemed certain. In British North America there were some three hundred thousand souls, in the Union to the south, almost eight million. In Upper Canada, three out of five settlers were newly arrived Americans, people of uncertain loyalties, lured from New York, Pennsylvania, and Connecticut by the promise of cheap land. They

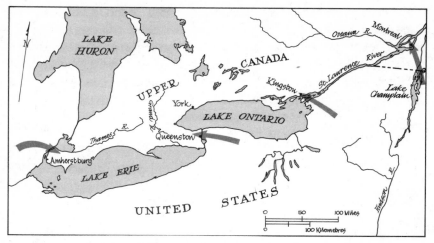

American Invasion Strategy, Summer, 1812

scarcely thought of themselves as British, though they were forced into a token oath of allegiance, and they certainly did not call themselves Canadian. (That word was reserved for their French-speaking neighbours, many of whom lived on American soil in the vicinity of Detroit.) Surely these people would not oppose an invasion by their compatriots!

Nor, on the face of it, would they. There is little evidence of any surge of national pride rippling across the grain fields, swamps, and forests of Upper Canada in the early days of the war; quite the opposite. The main emotion was not patriotism but fear: fear of the invaders who could and did loot the farms to feed themselves; fear of the British regulars, whose task it was to stiffen the backbones of the reluctant citizen soldiers; fear of the Indians; fear of losing a harvest, a homestead, and above all a life. Many of the militia had to be goaded into fighting, while large numbers of settlers expressed pro-American sympathies, sometimes openly, more often privately. It is possible, even probable, that without the war the province would eventually have become another state in the Union. The Americans could have had it by osmosis. But the war intervened.

How was it that a tiny population, badly divided, with little claim to any national sentiment, was able to ward off continued attack by a powerful neighbour with vastly greater resources? There are at least three considerations.

First, the British presence. The regulars were few in number but well disciplined. Raw troops were no match for them. And, thanks to Isaac Brock's prescience, the country was better prepared for war than its enemy.

Second, American ineptness, especially in the war's first, crucial year. The United States was not a military nation. Her leaders were antiquated or inexperienced, her soldiers untrained, her government unready for conflict, her state militia reluctant to fight on foreign soil.

Third, and by no means least, the alliance between the Indians and the British, which led to decisive victories in the campaigns of 1812.

History has tended to gloss over the contributions made by the various tribes – and especially by the polyglot army under the leadership of the Shawnee war chief Tecumseh – in the first year of the war. Yet without the presence of the Indians at crucial turning points in the conflict, much of Upper Canada would surely have been in the hands of the Americans by the spring of 1813, if not sooner. British regulars alone could not have stemmed the tide. To shore up the thinly held garrisons the Indians were essential.

They were often a nuisance. Mercurial and unreliable, indifferent to the so-called civilized rules of warfare, difficult, even impossible to control, they came and went as they pleased, consuming vast quantities of scarce provisions. But as guerrillas they were superb. Their very presence was enough to terrify the Americans into submission.

For this, the United States had itself to blame. Jeffersonian policy, stripped of its honeyed verbiage, was to cheat the Indians out of their hunting-grounds. This thinly disguised thievery alienated the tribes in the Northwest, produced the phenomenon of the Shawnee Prophet, led to the inspired leadership of Tecumseh, and eventually drove thousands of native Americans into the arms of the British, leaving America's left flank dangerously exposed in the war that followed.

The only group of Americans who truly thirsted for war, apart from the handful of congressmen known as War Hawks, were Tecumseh's followers. In revenging themselves on the hated Long Knives they hoped to regain the lands from which they had been driven. It was a wistful fantasy, doomed to failure. One of the several ironies of this foolish and unnecessary war is that the warriors who helped save Canada gained nothing except a few American scalps.

The role of the Indians and that of the British regulars was played down in the years following the war. For more than a century it was common cant that the diverse population of Upper Canada – immigrants, settlers, ex-Americans, Loyalists, Britons, Scots, and Irish – closed ranks to defeat the enemy. This belief still lingers, though there is little evidence to support it. Certainly the old Loyalists and their sons rushed to the colours, and in the capital of York the British aristocracy (whose leading ornament was the Reverend Doctor John Strachan) glowed with patriotic fervour. But the mass of the people were at best apathetic and at worst disaffected. Some five hundred of the latter have been officially identified – men and women who either fled to the other side or supported the enemy by word or deed. Who can guess how many more kept prudently silent or worked in secret for the invaders? The reluctance of the militia to do battle when the war went badly suggests that the number was not small.

Traditionally, a common enemy unites a people in a common cause, especially when family farms are overrun, crops despoiled, homesteads gutted, livestock dispersed. But again there is little evidence of a united front against the enemy on the part of the people who suffered these disasters; it is doubtful if they were any angrier at the Americans than at the British and Indians, who actually caused a third of the devastation. The total bill for war losses came to almost a million dollars at a time when a private soldier's daily pay was twenty-five cents. Compensation was not paid until 1824 and never paid in full. None of that helped make the cause universally popular.

Yet, in an odd way, the war did help to change Upper Canada from a loose aggregation of village states into something approaching a political entity. The war, or more properly the *myth* of the war, gave the rootless new settlers a sense of community. In the end, the myth became the reality. In the long run it did not matter who fought or who did not, who supported the cause or who disdained it. As the years went by and memories dimmed, as old scars healed and old grudges evaporated, as aging veterans reminisced and new leaders hyperbolized, the settlers began to believe that they had repelled the invader almost single-handed. For the first time, Upper Canadians shared a common tradition.

It was a tradition founded to a considerable extent on a rejection of American values – a rejection encouraged and enforced by the same pro-British ruling elite who fed the myth of the people's war and who made sure that the province (and eventually all of Canada) would embark on a course markedly different from that of the people to the south. They were, after all, "the enemy," and to be pro-American in post-war Upper Canada was to be considered vaguely traitorous. This attitude affected everything – politics, education, civil liberties, folkways, architecture. It affects us to this day, even those who do not think of themselves as Upper Canadian.

Thus the war that was supposed to attach the British North American colonies to the United States accomplished exactly the opposite. It ensured that Canada would never become a part of the Union to the south. Because of it, an alternative form of democracy grew out of the British colonial oligarchy in the northern half of the continent. The Canadian "way" – so difficult to define except in terms of negatives – has its roots in the invasion of 1812–14, the last American invasion of Canada. There can never be another.

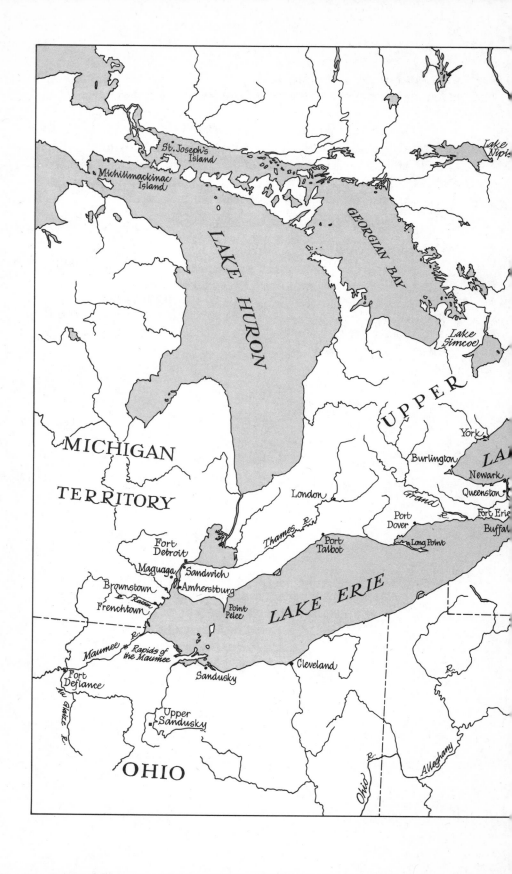

Lake Nipi[...]

St. Joseph's Island

Michilimackinac Island

GEORGIAN BAY

LAKE HURON

Lake Simcoe

UPPER

York

Burlington

LA[...]

Newark

MICHIGAN

Queenston

Fort Erie

TERRITORY

London

Grand

Buffa[...]

Port Dover

Fort Detroit

Thames R.

Port Talbot

Long Point

Maguaga

Sandwich

Brownstown

Amherstburg

LAKE ERIE

Frenchtown

Raisin R.

Point Pelee

Maumee R.

Rapids of the Maumee

Cleveland

R.

Sandusky

Fort Defiance

Au Glaize R.

Upper Sandusky

OHIO

Ohio R.

Alleghany R.

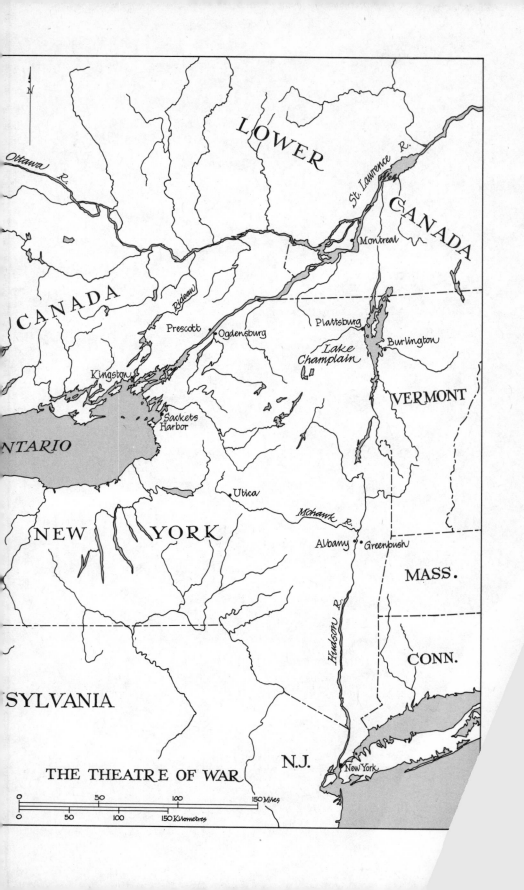

N

Ottawa R.

LOWER

St. Lawrence R.

CANADA

Montreal

CANADA

Rideau

Prescott

Ogdensburg

Plattsburg

Burlington

Lake
Champlain

Kingston

VERMONT

Sackets
Harbor

NTARIO

Utica

Mohawk R.

NEW   YORK

Albany   Greenbush

MASS.

Hudson R.

CONN.

SYLVANIA

N.J.

New York

THE THEATRE OF WAR

0   50   100   150 Miles

0   50   100   150 Kilometres

I

PRELUDE TO INVASION:
1807–1811
The Road to Tippecanoe

See our western brothers bleed!
British gold has done the deed.
Child and Mother, Son and Sire,
Beneath the tomahawk expire.

– On the Battle of Tippecanoe,
National Intelligencer, *July 11, 1812.*

ABOARD THE BRITISH FRIGATE *Melampus*, lying off Hampton Roads, Chesapeake Bay, Virginia, February, 1807.

The decks are clear of officers, for an entertainment is in progress. Music. Laughter. The tinkling of glass and silver. Leaning over the rail is an oddly assorted trio of impressed American seamen. One, William Ware, is an Indian from Pipe Creek, Maryland, a one-time wagoner who had served aboard the U.S. frigate *Chesapeake* until he was impressed, fifteen months ago, by a British boarding party in the Bay of Biscay. Another, Daniel Martin, is a Negro from Westport, Massachusetts, impressed at the same time as Ware. The third is a white man, John Strachan, also from Maryland, pressed on board *Melampus* off Cape Finisterre in 1805.

For two years Strachan has been waiting for a chance to escape, and now it has come. Because of the festivities, every boat except the captain's gig has been hoisted in. There is no chance of pursuit. Strachan and his companions leap into the gig and cast off. Somebody hails them: where do they think they're going? They shout back that they are going ashore, and as they pull for land, a hail of musket balls rains upon them. Unharmed, they reach Lowell's Point, haul the boat onto the beach, carefully place the oars on the seats, give three hearty cheers, and dash away to freedom.

It is short lived. At Hampton Roads, the three sign up for service in the American navy aboard *Chesapeake* and soon find themselves at the centre of the "*Chesapeake* incident," which brings America to the very brink of war with Britain.

35

The date is June 22, 1807. The American frigate is a few hours out of Hampton Roads, bound for the Mediterranean. As she passes a British squadron anchored in American waters, a fifty-gun man-of-war, *Leopard*, the flagship of Vice-Admiral George Berkeley, detaches itself and slips off in pursuit. James Barron, *Chesapeake*'s captain, knows exactly what is happening: the British dander is up; the captain of *Melampus* wants his men back. On the streets and quays of Hampton Roads, where British and American sailors and officers mingle, the presence of known deserters has not gone unnoticed. The Royal Navy has been especially infuriated by one Jenkin Ratford, a British deserter intemperate enough to shout gibes and insults at his former officers. In vain the British have asked for Ratford; the Americans have refused to give him up. Nor will they return the three men who stole the captain's gig from *Melampus*. Now, all four men have thumbed their noses at the British and are safely aboard *Chesapeake*, which is heading out to sea, its lower decks apparently crowded with other British deserters, all well known to the captain but concealed under assumed names. This is too much for Vice-Admiral Berkeley. Off goes an order to every British vessel to stop *Chesapeake* at sea and take the deserters by force. As it happens, Berkeley's own flagship is the one that will essay the task.

Stopped by *Leopard*, Captain Barron cannot believe the British will attack and so makes no attempt to clear *Chesapeake*'s decks for action. A young lieutenant comes aboard, demands the return of the four men – the only ones he can identify since the *Melampus* deserters have not taken false names and Ratford, who is now called Wilson, is easily recognizable from his earlier intemperate encounters. Barron, who has all four hidden below, feigns ignorance. After some fruitless talk, the Englishman leaves. *Leopard*'s captain continues the discussion through a loud hailer. When Barron refuses his demands, *Leopard* fires a shot across *Chesapeake*'s bow. No reply.

It is too late now for the British to back down. *Leopard* opens fire with her port guns, and a ten-minute cannonade follows. Twenty-one cannonballs tear into *Chesapeake*'s starboard hull. Another shatters her mizzen-mast. Her mainmast topples, her sails are shredded, shrouds cut away, spars splintered. By the time Barron strikes his colours, three of his men are dead and eighteen, including himself, are wounded. The British board the battered frigate but refuse to accept it as a prize. All they want are the three deserters from *Melampus* and the wretched Ratford, whom they will proceed to hang at Halifax to their own great satisfaction and the fury of the American public.

The Americans are in a ferment. The man on the street finds it intolerable that British boarding parties can seize sailors from American ships on the pretext that they are Royal Navy deserters, then force them to serve in the hell hole of a British man-of-war. There is some doubt that the *Melampus* trio *were* impressed (the British insist they volunteered, and certainly two are thoroughgoing rogues), but that evidence is kept secret. To the Americans it is a flagrant attack on national sovereignty. In the words of John Quincy Adams, "No nation can be Independent which suffers her Citizens to be stolen from her at the discretion of the Naval or military officers of another."

But to Britain, impressment is a necessity. Her navy has trebled in size since the war with France began. She cannot man her ships with volunteers. Worse, thousands of British sailors are deserting to American merchantmen, lured by better conditions and better pay – four times as much. Who can blame the British for recapturing bona fide deserters in time of war? Certainly not the British public; they applaud it.

But who is a bona fide deserter? Americans and British speak the same language, look alike, dress alike. British boarding parties, hungry for men, do not always bother with the niceties. They grab whom they can. No one knows how many American seamen have been pressed into British service (the figures run between three and seven thousand), but it takes only a few publicized cases to enrage the American public. Even when a case of mistaken identity is proved and admitted, months elapse before the seaman is returned. Service in the British Navy is like a prison sentence or worse, for as Samuel Johnson once remarked, "no man will be a sailor who has contrivance enough to get himself into jail; for being in a ship is being in jail, with the chance of being drowned." Some American seamen have been known to cut off their hands to avoid impressment; some who refuse to serve are flogged unmercifully by the British; and a few, including the three escapees from *Melampus*, are prepared to risk death to get away.

Their recapture from *Chesapeake* touches off an international incident. Riots break out in New York, where a mob does its best to dismantle a British ship. The British consul is forced to seek police protection while an English diplomat on a tour of the Union finds it prudent to assume an incognito. Public meetings throughout the land denounce the perfidious British. In Quebec, Lieutenant-Colonel Isaac

37

Brock notes that "every American newspaper teems with violent and hostile resolutions against England, and associations are forming in every town for the ostensible purpose of attacking these Provinces."

The future general is right: the country is emotionally ready for war, more so, in fact, than it will be in 1812. But its leaders are not ready. The President, Thomas Jefferson, threatens war but does not mean it – a dangerous posture. "If the English do not give us the satisfaction we demand, we will take Canada which wants to enter the Union," he tells the French minister to Washington. The Frenchman takes these bellicose remarks languidly and reports to Paris that he does not believe that either Jefferson or his foreign secretary, James Madison, wants war. Jefferson bans British warships from American waters, enforces an embargo preventing all ships from sailing out of U.S. ports for foreign destinations, and hopes that these threats will force the British to abandon impressment. But the British do not yield and the embargo is a failure. The public's ardour for war cools quickly. The crisis passes.

But there is one group of Americans whose ardour does not cool. In the oak and hickory forests of Ohio, in the cornfields along the Maumee and the Wabash, on the banks of the Au Glaize and on the Tippecanoe in Indiana Territory, there is a quickening of the blood, a stirring of old and painful memories of the defeat at Fallen Timbers and the surrender of hunting grounds at Greenville. The war fever, filtering through to the tribes of the Old Northwest, revives the dying hopes of the native Americans for a new conflict in which they will fight side by side with the British against the Long Knives. The Northwest has been at peace since General Anthony Wayne's decisive victory in 1794. But the *Chesapeake* incident acts as a catalyst to animate the tribes and shatter the calm that has prevailed north of the Ohio for more than a decade.

Among the British, the incident produces two oddly contrary reactions. On the one hand it convinces them that America will continue to bluff rather than fight, a conclusion that will lead to calamitous results in 1812. On the other hand they are encouraged to strengthen their defences in Canada against possible invasion. This is Isaac Brock's doing. "It is impossible to view the late hostile measures of the American government towards England, without considering a rupture between the two countries as probable to happen," the young lieutenant-colonel writes, and as the crisis smoulders, he goes on to press for a better trained and expanded militia and for repairs to the

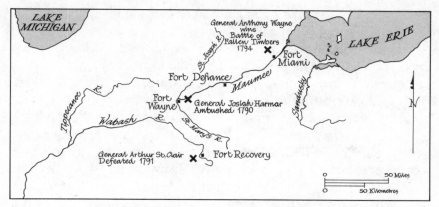

American-Indian Battles, 1790–1794

fortress of Quebec. He does not easily get his way, but from this time on the prospect of an American invasion is never far from that determined and agile mind. When and if the Americans come, Isaac Brock intends to be ready.

•

VINCENNES, INDIANA TERRITORY, August 17, 1807. William Henry Harrison is delivering his gubernatorial message to the legislature.

"The blood rises to my cheek," he cries, "when I reflect on the humiliating, the disgraceful scene, of the crew of an American ship of war mustered on its own deck by a British lieutenant for the purpose of selecting the innocent victims of their own tyranny!"

Harrison's cheeks are sallow, but the blood must rise to them with fair frequency. It rises again as he contemplates the malefactions of British Indian agents, who he is convinced are goading the Indians to violence and murder on the frontier, "for who does not know that the tomahawk and scalping knife of the savage are always employed as instruments of British vengeance. At this moment, fellow citizens, as I sincerely believe, their agents are organizing a combination amongst the Indians within our limits, for the purpose of assassination and murder...."

By British agents Harrison means certain members of the British Indian Department in Upper Canada, especially Thomas McKee, Simon Girty (the "White Indian"), and, worst of all, Matthew

Elliott, the Pennsylvania Irishman who defected to the British during the Revolutionary War and led Indian ambushes that wiped out American detachments. The American frontiersmen will not soon forget that Elliott and Girty watched while the Delaware slowly tortured and burned to death Colonel William Crawford, after wiping out most of his men. So great is the hatred of Elliott in Detroit, it is said, that he hesitates to cross the river from his palatial home in Amherstburg for fear of being tarred and feathered. He has been one of the key members of the British Indian Department; no white man has so much influence with the tribes, especially the Shawnee. At the moment he is under a cloud, dismissed for financial irregularities. Nonetheless he remains a force and will soon be back in the good graces of the British.

But the Governor of Indiana cannot get it into his head that it is not so much British conniving that has caused the Indians to rise up sporadically in defence of their lands as his own policies and those of his political superiors in Washington. Harrison is not a mean or wicked man. His sense of justice is outraged when white juries refuse to convict one of their own for killing a native. The Governor's problem is that he wants to turn the Indians into farmers in order to deprive them of their hunting-grounds. That is official government policy, laid down by Thomas Jefferson, who is not a mean or wicked man either but who, in a private letter to Harrison outlining that policy, sounds very much like a hypocrite:

"Our system is to live in perpetual peace with the Indians, to cultivate an affectionate attachment from them by everything just and liberal which we can do for them within the bounds of reason...."

So far so good, despite the qualification. But then:

"When they withdraw themselves to the culture of a small piece of land, they will perceive how useless to them are the extensive forests, and will be willing to pare them off...in exchange for necessaries for their farms and families. To promote this...we shall push our trading houses, and be glad to see the good and influential individuals among them in debt, because we observe that when these debts go beyond what the individuals can pay, they become willing to lop them off by a cession of lands...."

To this machiavellian scheme Jefferson appends a chilling warning. Should any tribe refuse the proffered hand and take up the hatchet, he says, it will be driven across the Mississippi and the whole of its lands confiscated.

It all fits neatly with Harrison's own ambitions, which include statehood for Indiana. To become a state the territory needs a population of at least sixty thousand, and there are fewer than half that number living in small settlements connected by trails cut through the jungle of the forest. To attract more people, Harrison requires the lure of cheap land. The Indians have the land. The Governor must secure it for the settlers, one way or another.

The blood rises to Harrison's cheek once more when he recalls how he has been bested by that one-eyed savage known as the Shawnee Prophet. The Prophet has sprung from nowhere and in two years has become more notorious than any other Indian. He seems to have invented a new religion, one tenet of which is the heresy, to the whites, that all Indian lands are held in common and cannot be divided, sold, or bartered away. The ritual includes much mumbo-jumbo – shaking, jerking, and dancing about (derived perhaps from the white sect known as the Shakers, who have helped spark a religious revival on the frontier). It is not confined to any particular tribe – indeed, it has split some tribes – but appears to attract the younger braves who are acting in defiance of their elders. To Harrison, this so-called Prophet is an imposter and a fool who "speaks not the words of the Great Spirit but those of the devil and of the British agents." Harrison sees British agents everywhere, in every wigwam, behind every bush, plotting and conniving.

Yet even Harrison must concede that the Prophet is not quite a fool, for on one memorable occasion he has fooled Harrison, who thought to discredit him by demanding that he produce a miracle.

"Who is this pretended prophet who dares to speak in the name of the Great Creator?" the Governor asked, in a message to the Delaware. "Examine him.... Demand of him some proof...some miracles.... If he is really a prophet, ask him to cause the sun to stand still, the moon to alter its course, the rivers to cease to flow.... No longer be imposed on by the arts of an imposter...."

To which the Prophet replied, blandly, that he would accept the challenge and cause the sun to darken. He even named the date and the time – 11:32 in the forenoon of June 16, 1806.

The story is told and retold. How the Prophet sent word to Indians for leagues around to assemble on June 16; how the day dawned clear; and how, an hour before the appointed time, the Prophet, gowned in flowing robes, stepped from his wigwam into the circle of onlookers and at exactly 11:32 pointed his finger at the sun.

Slowly the sky darkens; the dark shadow of the moon crosses the solar face; a murmur rises from the assembly. The Prophet waits, then calls out to the Great Spirit to remove his hand from the source of all light. The call is heeded. Pandemonium!

It is too much. Harrison, the soldier-scholar-statesman, outsmarted by an aborigine who managed to learn in advance the date of a solar eclipse! The long, moody features grow moodier. He will continue to call the Prophet a fool, but he knows that he is up against a force beyond his power to control. "This business must be stopped," he tells the head men of the Shawnee. "I will no longer suffer it." But he will have to suffer it, for the chiefs themselves cannot control the Prophet; he has put some of them in fear of their lives. When several of the older Delaware chiefs refused to go along with the new religion, the Prophet had them murdered. His messengers have carried his words to all tribes within a radius of six hundred miles, and the message is always the same: follow me; rid yourself of your old leaders; and (this is Harrison's real concern) don't give up the land.

The Prophet's land policy collides with Harrison's ambition. The tall slender governor with the sombre face and the brooding eyes is no frontier bumpkin or upstart party hack of limited vision. He looks like a scholar and is one. With his long nose and gaunt features he could, in different guise, be mistaken for a Roman priest or an Italian noble in a Renaissance painting. He is slightly out of place here in the wilderness, for he was reared in luxury on a Virginia plantation, trained in Greek and Latin, and has a passion for military history, whose lessons he hopes to absorb.

He has always been a little out of place. He might have made a good doctor, but his medical studies were cut short by a fall in the family fortunes. In the army, where young officers were drinking themselves into early graves, the temperate ensign buried himself in his books. He will not let himself be seen out of control, through drink or through any other vice, for he has the Harrison name to uphold: his father was one of the signers of the Declaration of Independence.

He was a good soldier – he might, someone once said, have been another Washington. He fought with the "mad general," Anthony Wayne, at the Battle of Fallen Timbers, the epic victory over the Indians that won twenty-five thousand square miles of territory for the white men. Now, a soldier no more but with a soldier's bearing and a soldier's outlook, he is, at thirty-nine, a rising politician, living like an aristocrat in the backwoods in his vast brick mansion – the first in the territory – on the outskirts of Vincennes. He calls it Grouseland; with its hand-carved mantels and doors, its four great chimneys, its thirteen rooms and its circular staircase, it has made him proud but property poor.

His problems are only beginning. He has heard from Billy Wells, the Indian commissioner and interpreter at Fort Wayne, that eighty Indians under the Prophet's leadership have gathered at Greenville. Wells, an old frontiersman married to the sister of Little Turtle, the Miami chief, sends a messenger to Greenville to deal with the Prophet and ask him and his supporters to come to Fort Wayne for a parley. The answer is given, not by the Prophet but by his elder brother, a handsome war chief with flashing hazel eyes. It is astonishingly blunt:

"Go back and tell Captain Wells that my fire is kindled on the spot appointed by the Great Spirit above, and if he has anything to communicate to me, *he* must come *here*; and I will expect him in six days from this time."

This is not the way Indians talk to white men. This is the way white men talk to Indians. For the first time an Indian has sent back a message that is stinging in its style and insulting in its content.

William Henry Harrison will hear from the Prophet's brother again and again in the years to come, for he is one of the most extraordinary native North Americans of whom history has record.

His name is Tecumseh, and six years later in the second year of the war, he and Harrison will meet face to face in mortal combat.

●

WASHINGTON, D.C., August, 1807. Augustus John Foster, aide to the British minister to the United States, has just dispatched a letter to his mother bewailing his "sad disappointment" over the *Chesapeake* affair. It is not the incident itself that disturbs him – like every upper-class Englishman, he is convinced that the Royal Navy acted correctly – but the cruel turn of fate that has forced him to remain in the United States, "a land of swamps and pawnbrokers," and especially in Washington, "a sink of imagination."

Foster, who has spent four years at the British legation, cannot wait to shake Washington's red gumbo from his boots, but the country is in such an uproar that he cannot leave while there is the slightest danger of a rupture between the two nations. Personally, he dismisses the

43

chance of war, cannot conceive that anyone in this ridiculous capital village would have the temerity to challenge the British lion. Still, as he has informed his mother, the Americans keep themselves in a constant ferment: "anything enflames them." He must remain at his post until tempers calm down.

He is an apple-cheeked young aristocrat of twenty-seven with the typical upper-class Englishman's view of Americans. To describe them, in his letters home, he beggars the lexicon of every defamatory epithet. Americans are "consummate rascals," "ragamuffins and adventurers," "the scum of every nation on earth."

"Corruption, Immorality, Irreligion, and, above all, self-interest, have corroded the very pillars on which their Liberty rests."

Clearly, Foster was not bred for America. His father was a Member of Parliament. His mother, an earl's daughter, lives with the Duke and Duchess of Devonshire in an amiable *ménage à trois*. His aunt is married to the Earl of Liverpool. After the London of Mrs. Siddons and Lord Byron, of Turner and Gainsborough, the tiny capital of seven thousand souls must indeed seem a sinkhole. Just seven years old, it has become the butt of jokes – a wretched community of bogs and gullies, broken tree stumps, piles of brushwood and refuse, ponds, potholes, and endless gluelike mud, which mires the carriages on Pennsylvania Avenue and makes sensible communication all but impossible. Paving is non-existent; the streets are mere ruts. Wells are the only source of water; there is no public supply. Petty thieves and burglars abound. Pigs and cattle wander the paths that pass for avenues. The climate is intolerable, the swamps malarial.

Above this morass, each on its separate hillock, rise, incongruously, two jerry-built Greek temples yet unfinished: the Capitol and the Executive Mansion. The columns in the former are so weak they crack under the weight of the visitors' gallery; the latter is still unplastered, its timber already rotting. The roofs of both are so badly constructed that they leak embarrassingly in every rainstorm. Even the politicians hate Washington. Some, if they had their way, would move the seat of government to Philadelphia.

Foster cannot stomach the politicians. Why, there are scarcely five congressmen who look like gentlemen! He treats them all with an amused disdain, which the more perceptive must find maddening. But then, one legislator has actually urinated in his fireplace! Foster relishes that tale. And then there was the business of the caviar that he had his *maitre d'* prepare from Potomac sturgeon. On serving it to his congressional guests, he found them spitting it out by the mouthful, having mistaken it for black raspberry jam. Is this what democracy has wrought? "The excess of democratic ferment in this people is conspicuously evinced by the dregs having got to the top," he reports to Whitehall. It is unthinkable that these grotesque politicians would dare declare war on his country!

Whitehall agrees. The outcry over the *Chesapeake* incident subsides, and by mid-October Foster feels able to escape from the country in which he believes he has sacrificed the four best years of his life. He would not return, he declares, were he to be paid ten thousand pounds a year. But return he will in 1811, a Yankeephobe, singularly blind to the impending war, the wrong man in the wrong place at the wrong time.

Foster's smug views are typical. He is scarcely back in London, reporting the state of affairs in Washington, when the British make a second move to enrage the Americans. Having called Jefferson's bluff, they proceed to tighten their blockade of the French ports. Spencer Perceval's government issues new Orders in Council forbidding neutral ships on pain of seizure to trade with Europe except through Britain. Any vessel that tries to enter any port controlled by Napoleon without first touching at Britain (and paying the required duties and taxes) will be treated as an enemy.

The British are clearly prepared to go beyond the accepted rules for dealing with non-belligerents. They will, if necessary, seize American shipping in the open seas as well as within territorial limits. In no other way can they hope to throttle the French.

In American eyes this is an intolerable return to colonial days. Using the excuse of war, the British are attempting to monopolize the commerce of the world – or so the Americans believe. The Orders represent a clear threat to the fledgling nation. Has the War of Independence been for nothing?

It is clear from Britain's maritime policy that she holds the new union in contempt. To Englishmen, Americans are all uncouth frontiersmen with little breeding and no culture, "less popular and less esteemed among us than the base and bigotted Portuguese, or the ferocious and ignorant Russians," in the words of the *Edinburgh Review*. The British ruling class believes, with Foster, that the Americans will not fight, and, believing that, thinks nothing of goading the former colonists to fury. "America," declares Lord Sidmouth, the Lord Privy Seal, "is no longer a bugbear; there is no terror in her threats."

For the moment, the policy works. In this yeasty winter of 1808 – the year of Goethe's *Faust* and Beethoven's Fifth Symphony – America will not go to war over the Orders in Council or the *Chesapeake* affair. The country is badly divided. The Federalist opposition centred largely in the New England states is staunchly opposed to any violent solution. Yet the country's honour has been slighted, her morale badly bruised, and there are some in the Congress who cannot forget the insult and will not let their colleagues forget. They are Republicans, mainly from the southwestern interior and the frontier states. Soon they will be known as the War Hawks, and the time is coming when they will prevail.

•

FORT AMHERSTBURG, UPPER CANADA, July 11, 1808. One thousand Indian warriors and one hundred chiefs are gathered on the Canadian side of the Detroit River to hear the Lieutenant-Governor of Upper Canada, Francis Gore, cautiously and delicately extend the hand of British friendship. A genial figure, he is in his fortieth year, the smooth face gone slightly to flesh, the cheeks pink from good living. He is careful to play down the possibility of war; that might excite his listeners to premature violence – the last thing the British want. But if war should come, the Indians will be needed.

"I am sure, my Children, that it is quite unnecessary for me to call to your remembrance the faithful assurance with which the King, your Father, has so uniformly complied with all his Engagements and Promises made to your Forefathers and yourselves in former times. . . .

"Nothing is required of you in return for your Great Father's benevolence and religious regard to his promises, but a renewal and faithful observance of the engagements made by your ancestors and yourselves. . . .

"I will not offend you by entertaining the smallest doubt of your readiness on all occasions, when called upon to prove your affectionate attachment to the King, your Great Father. . . .

"I came not to invite you to take up the Hatchet, but I wish to put you on your guard against any attempt that may be made by any enemy whatever to disturb the peace of your Country. . . ."

It is the *Chesapeake* affair that has brought the Lieutenant-Governor to Amherstburg – that and the whisper of a threat from Napoleon that the French may once again take an interest in North America. Since the end of the Revolution, the British have tended to neglect the Indians. Now it is time to mend fences. But the task is complicated: how to regain the affection of the natives, take advantage of their antagonism to the Americans, subtly include them in plans for the defence of Canada, yet at the same time give Washington no cause to believe that British agents are stirring up the tribes to attack? The council at Amherstburg, to which Gore comes late, has been going on for ten days. The public manifestations of friendship and goodwill are innocuous. But who knows what is said to the Indians in private?

Gore cannot even be sure that his listeners will be given an accurate account of what he is saying, for he speaks in English, his remarks interpreted by the superintendent-general of the British Indian Department, William Claus, and his deputy, Matthew Elliott. Elliott has just been reinstated in the key post of Amherstburg, and when the Lieutenant-Governor announces his restoration to favour there are grunts of approval from his audience. In their ritual reply, the Wyandot, senior to all the tribes, express pleasure: "We can place confidence in and rely on him as a man of experience."

It is through Elliott that the government's new Indian policy will be channelled. And he will interpret Whitehall's directives in his own way, according to his prejudices. These are well known: he is pro-Indian, especially pro-Shawnee, and violently anti-American. If war comes it is in Elliott's personal interest that the British win, and not merely for reasons of patriotism. Word has reached him that if the Yankees capture Fort Amherstburg, they intend to kill him and two of his colleagues.

On and off, he has been a member of the Indian Department since the days of the Revolution when he fought with the Shawnee against the Americans. (It remains a secret to the day of his death that he once acted as an emissary for the Americans to try to keep the Shawnee neutral before hostilities began.) Even while out of favour he has acted unofficially for the department, for he is part of that clique, like a band of brothers who follow their own conventions – men who have spent long years with the tribes, who speak the languages fluently, who have lived with Indian women, fathered Indian children, attended Indian councils, fought when necessary on the Indian side. It is a family compact: son often follows father in the service, and the sons are sometimes of mixed blood.

It is toward the Shawnee, especially, that the officers of the Indian Department lean – "that contemptible tribe...always more insolent and troublesome than any other," in the words of Elliott's nemesis, Captain Hector McLean. It was McLean's observation, in 1799, that "the whole of the Officers of the Department are indeed in some way connected with this tribe either by Marriage or Concubinage." That is certainly true of Elliott, who has fathered two sons by a Shawnee woman and often taken Shawnee chieftains as guests under his roof.

Captain McLean was the cause of Elliott's dismissal, under a cloud, in 1798. The scandal revolved around the traditional British practice of dispensing annual "presents" to the tribes – food, dry goods, tools, weapons. McLean, then in command at the fort, was convinced that Elliott was adding to his departmental pittance by diverting a generous portion of government largess to his own use. How else could he stock his extensive farm with cattle and feed and clothe some fifty servants and slaves? Trapping the slippery Elliott became a minor obsession with McLean. His chance came in the winter of 1797 when he was able to prove that the agent had requisitioned supplies for 534 Indians in a settlement whose total population was only 160. On this evidence Elliott was dismissed.

But now, in 1808, the government, set on a new and more aggressive course, finds it cannot do without him. Elliott's successor, Thomas McKee, son of his old comrade Alexander McKee, is a hopeless drunkard who cannot be depended upon to preside over delicate negotiations. Even before his official reappointment, Elliott has been working for the government without McKee's knowledge, dispatched on a secret mission to sound out the major chiefs in private: to impress upon them "with Delicacy and caution" that England expects their aid in the event of war and to remind them that the Americans are out to steal their lands. And who better than Elliott to invite the Prophet to attend the Amherstburg council? He, of all the Indian agents, knows the family most intimately; his chief clerk is married to the Prophet's sister. So here he is, back in charge again, his honour restored by Gore's convenient fiction that the charges against him were never proved.

A strange creature, this Elliott, Gore must feel – rather ugly and more than a little haughty, swarthy, with small features and a pug nose – a black Donegal Irishman transplanted early into the American wilderness, a rough diamond who has experienced everything, shrunk from nothing. There are Americans who believe that he and Alexander McKee took more scalps after General Arthur St. Clair's disastrous defeat by Little Turtle in 1791 than did the Indians. He cannot read or write; it is an effort for him to put his signature to a document; a clerk accompanies him everywhere to handle his extensive business. He has been a justice of the peace and is now a member of the legislature of Upper Canada, the richest farmer in the region. Though he is in his seventieth year, he will be quite prepared to lead his troops into battle in the war to come.

Elliott had expected the Prophet to travel to Amherstburg for the council, but the Prophet does not appear. In his stead comes his older brother, Tecumthe or Tecumseh, of whom the British have little if any knowledge. Of all the chieftains present at Amherstburg, only this tall catlike Shawnee is in favour of war with the Americans, as Gore, in his letter to his superior, Sir James Craig, the Governor General of the two Canadas, makes clear:

"The Prophet's brother, who is stated to me to be his principal support and who appears to be a very shrewd intelligent man, was at Amherstburg while I was there. He told Colonel Claus and Captain Elliott that they were endeavouring to collect the different Nations to form one settlement on the Wabash about 300 miles South West of Amherstburg in order to preserve their country from all encroachment. That their intention at present is not to take part in the quarrels of White People: that if the Americans encroach upon them they are resolved to strike – but he added that if their father the King should be in earnest and appear in sufficient force they would hold fast by him."

Tecumseh makes it clear that he does not fully trust the British. The Indians have long memories. They have not forgotten how, when Mad Anthony Wayne defeated them at Fallen Timbers in 1794, the British closed the gates of nearby Fort Miami, and he now reminds Elliott of the number of chiefs who fell as a result. Tecumseh is ready to fight beside the British, but on his own terms. If they are preparing to use him for their own ends (as they are) he is also planning to use them for his.

•

FORT WAYNE ON THE MAUMEE RIVER, September 22, 1809. William Henry Harrison has ridden deep into Indian territory to bargain for land. He is hungry for it. At Vincennes he has felt himself cramped, hemmed in, frustrated in his ambition. The country to the south of the capital is sunken and wet; the sere prairie to the northwest will not be fit for settlement for many years. But just

Harrison's Purchase

beyond the Indiana border, twenty-one miles to the north along the eastern bank of the Wabash, lie three million acres of farm land, the hunting-grounds of the tribes. Harrison means to have it all, has already secured the agreement of the President, James Madison, Jefferson's successor, who makes one stipulation only: get it as cheaply as possible.

The Governor has travelled on horseback for 350 miles on one of those tireless peregrinations for which he is so well fitted, temperamentally as well as physically. He has summoned the chiefs of the affected tribes – the Miami, Delaware, Eel, Potawatomi – to a great council here at Fort Wayne. But he has not summoned the Shawnee, for they are nomads and, in Harrison's view, have no claim to the land.

The council fire is lit. Eleven hundred tribesmen, squatting in a vast circle, listen as Harrison speaks against the murmur of the Maumee. Four sworn interpreters translate his message: the European war has ruined the price of furs, therefore the tribes must adopt a new way of life. The government will buy their lands, pay for them with a permanent annuity. With that income they can purchase domestic animals and become farmers. The Indians, says Harrison, wrongly blame their own poverty and the scarcity of game on the encroachment of white settlers – but that is not the true cause of their misfortunes. The British are to blame! It is they who have urged the wanton destruction of game animals for furs alone.

The chiefs listen, retire, drink Harrison's whiskey, wrangle among themselves. The Potawatomi, who are the poorest and most wretched of the tribes, want to sell; the Delaware waver. But the Miami are inflexible. The British have urged them to hold the lands until they are surveyed and can be sold at the going price of two dollars an acre. Harrison is offering a mere fraction of that sum. Why should they take less?

To counter this recalcitrance, Harrison summons all his histrionic abilities and at the next council fire on the twenty-fifth presents himself in the guise of a patient but much-injured father, betrayed by his own offspring:

"My Children: My Heart is oppressed. If I could have believed that I should have experienced half of the mortification and disappointment which I now feel, I would have entreated your Father the President to have chosen some other Representative to have made known his wishes to you. The proposition which I have made you, I fondly hoped would have been acceptable to all. . . . Is there some evil spirit amongst us?" This evil spirit, Harrison makes clear, is British.

The speech rolls on. Ironically, Harrison is urging tribal solidarity – Tecumseh's crusade – though for very different reasons. War with Great Britain is never far from his mind. The solidarity he proposes must include, also, the white Americans. ("The people upon the other side of the big water would desire nothing better than to set us once more to cut each other's throats.")

He ends with a remarkable pledge:

"This is the first request your new Father has ever made you. It will be the last, he wants no more of your land. Agree to the proposition which I now make you and send on some of your wise men to take him by the hand. He will set your Heart at ease. He will tell you that he will never make another proposition to you to sell your lands."

The palaver lasts for five more days, and in the end Harrison persuades the Miami to give up the idea that the land is worth two dollars an acre. "Their tenaciousness in adhering to this idea," he comments, "is quite astonishing and it required no little pains to get them to abandon it." And, he might have added, no little whiskey. A drunken frolic follows, in which one of the Miami braves is mortally wounded.

Harrison is jubilant. "The compensation given for this cession of lands. . .is as low as it could possibly be made," he writes to Washington. ". . .I think. . .upon the whole that the bargain is a better one for the United States than any that has been made by me for lands south of the Wabash." As soon as the treaty is ratified and a sales office opened "there will be several hundred families along this Tract."

Well may Harrison savour his triumph. The annuities paid the Indians for relinquishing the land are minuscule: the Miami, who get the most, will receive a total of only seven hundred dollars a year. To pay all the annuities forever the government will not have to set aside more than fifty thousand dollars. At two dollars an acre – the price the settlers will pay – the land is potentially worth six million dollars. Thanks to Harrison the government has made an enormous paper profit. No wonder, when his third term of office ends, a grateful legislature recommends him for a fourth, praising his "integrity, patriotism and firm attachment to the general government."

There remains one small cloud on the horizon: Harrison has ignored the Shawnee. By spring the cloud looms larger. The Prophet and his brother Tecumseh, furious with the old chieftains, refuse to concede that any land cession is valid unless approved by all the tribes. The Great Spirit, so the Prophet says, has directed him to collect all the Indians at the mouth of the Tippecanoe, where it joins the Wabash, whereupon one thousand tribesmen forsake their elders and flock to the new settlement, appropriately named Prophet's Town. With the Indians in ferment, Harrison does not dare put surveyors on the newly purchased land. Settlement comes to a standstill. Families flee the frontier. More will leave "unless the rascally prophet is driven from his present position or a fort built somewhere on the Wabash about the upper boundary of the late purchase."

It is not easy to cow the Prophet into submission. Some of the old chiefs have tried, but "this scoundrel does not appear however to be intimidated." In fact, the old chiefs are in fear of their lives. Harrison, determined to threaten his adversary with a show of force, sends for a detachment of regular troops. There is much bustling about with the local militia in Vincennes – constant musterings, parades and reviews – which serves only to increase the panic of the white settlers. Finally, Harrison dispatches his interpreter, James Barron, with a letter intended to convince the Prophet of the folly of taking up arms against the United States:

"Our bluecoats are more numerous than you can count, and our hunting shirts are like leaves of the forests or the grains of sand on the Wabash. Do not think that the red coats can protect you, they are not able to protect themselves, they do not think of going to war with us, if they did in a few moons you would see our flags wave on all the Forts of Canada."

Barron is lucky to escape with his life. The Prophet receives him, surrounded by Indians of different tribes, gazes upon him in silence and contempt for several minutes, then spits out his defiance:

"...You...are a spy. There is your grave. Look on it!" And points to the spot on which the interpreter is standing.

At this moment, there emerges from the Indian lodges a tall figure in fringed deerskin who takes the frightened Barron under his wing and asks him to state his business. Barron reads Harrison's message, which concludes with a canny invitation: if the Shawnee can prove title to the ceded lands then, of course, they will be returned to the tribe. It is a hollow promise, for there is no title as white men understand the term. But Harrison's message invites the Prophet to come to visit him: if his claim is just, the Governor will personally escort him to the President.

But it is not the Prophet who will lead the delegation to Vincennes. A new warrior is assuming leadership – the tall Indian who again that night saves Barron's life from a group of squaws sent to tomahawk him. Harrison has not yet met him, would not know him to see him, is only now becoming aware of his presence. Someone who has encountered him has described him to the governor "as a bold, active, sensible man, daring in the extreme and capable of any undertaking." He is the Prophet's brother, whom Harrison now sees as "the Moses of the family, really the efficient man" – Tecumseh, the Leaping Panther.

•

VINCENNES, INDIANA TERRITORY, August 16, 1810. Governor Harrison is seated in an armchair on his estate of Grouseland in the shade of a canopy on the southwest side of the great brick mansion that has all but beggared him. To pay the bills for its construction he has been forced to give up four hundred acres of prime land; but then, some might say, he wants the Shawnee (for whom he is waiting) to give up much more.

The Shawnee have kept him waiting for some days and the Governor is growing impatient. He has made much of this assembly, inviting the town's leading citizens and their ladies, territorial officers and supreme court justices, all arranged like chess pieces on the lawn, in the canopy's shade, guarded by a platoon of soldiers.

If Harrison is nervous, his long features do not reveal it. He operates under a strict maxim – never show fear in front of an

Indian. This particular Indian, however, has become uncommonly difficult. Harrison had asked him to come to Vincennes with a small escort, but Tecumseh, who does not take instructions from white men, arrived with more than three hundred armed and painted warriors. That was Saturday. Harrison wanted to start the council on Monday, but Tecumseh would not be hurried. Suspecting treachery, he sent his spies and informers to work through the community, warning of possible trouble. Now it is Thursday; he is coming at last, accompanied by thirty warriors, their faces smeared with vermilion war paint, all armed with tomahawks and clubs.

Tecumseh advances under the curious scrutiny of the dignitaries – a handsome figure, tall for his tribe (at least five foot ten), with an oval rather than an angular face, his complexion light copper, his nose handsome and straight, his mouth "beautifully formed like that of Napoleon." Everyone who has met him notices his eyes, which are a clear, bright hazel under dark brows, and his teeth, which are white and even. He is naked to the waist, his head shaved save for a scalp lock. He walks with a brisk elastic step in spite of a bent leg fractured and imperfectly set after a youthful fall from a pony. There are some who think him the finest specimen of a man they have ever seen, but no authentic likeness exists on paper or canvas, for Tecumseh refuses to have his portrait painted by a white man.

He halts, looks over the assemblage, sees the soldiers, feigns anger, pretends to suspect treachery. He will not go near the canopy, not because he fears the soldiers but because he wishes to place himself on an equal footing with his adversary. He intends to speak as in a council circle, which puts every man on the same level.

The game continues. Harrison's interpreter, Barron, explains that it will be a nuisance to rearrange the seats. Tecumseh disagrees; only the whites need seats, the Indians are accustomed to sitting on the ground: "Houses are made for white men to hold councils in. Indians hold theirs in the open air."

"Your father requests you sit by his side," says Barron, indicating the Governor.

Tecumseh raises an arm, points to the sky.

"*My* father! The Great Spirit is my father! The earth is my mother – and on her bosom I will recline." And so sits cross-legged on the ground, surrounded by his warriors.

The problem is that Tecumseh refuses to act like a Harrison Indian. Nor does he act like a white man. He is unique and knows it. On his endless missions to other tribes, in his dogged attempt to forge an Indian confederacy, it is necessary for him to say only "I am Tecumseh." That is enough to explain his purpose.

This attitude disconcerts Harrison. In his reports to Washington he tries to shrug off Tecumseh: his speeches here at the great council, he says, are "insolent and his pretensions arrogant." Yet he is forced to take him seriously. The talks drag on for days; but when the Shawnee war chief speaks, the Governor listens, for this half-naked man in the deerskin leggings is one of the greatest orators of his time.

His reputation has preceded him. He is known as a consummate performer who can rouse his audience to tears, laughter, fury, action. Even those who cannot understand his words are said to be held by the power of his voice. White men who have heard him speak at past councils have struggled to describe his style: in 1806 at a council at Springfield, Ohio, "the effect of his bitter, burning words...was so great on his companions that the whole three hundred warriors could hardly refrain from springing from their seats. Their eyes flashed, and even the most aged, many of whom were smoking, evinced the greatest excitement. The orator appeared in all the power of a fiery and impassioned speaker and actor. Each moment it seemed as though, under the influence of his overpowering eloquence, they would abruptly leave the council and defiantly return to their homes."

Like his physical presence, Tecumseh's oratory is, alas, filtered through the memories of eyewitnesses. Even the best interpreters cannot keep up with his flights of imagery, while the worst garble his eloquence. Occasionally, in the printed record – admittedly imperfect – one hears faintly the echoes of that clear, rich voice, calling across the decades:

"It is true I am Shawnee. My forefathers were warriors. Their son is a warrior. From them I take only my existence. From my tribe I take nothing. I am the maker of my own fortune. And oh! that I might make that of my red people, and of my country, as great as the conceptions of my mind, when I think of the Spirit that rules the universe....

"The way, and the only way, to check and stop this evil, is, for all the red men to unite in claiming a common and equal right in the land; as it was at first; and should be yet; for it never was divided, but belongs to all, for the use of each. That no part has a right to sell, even to each other, much less to strangers who want all and will not do with less....

"Sell a country! Why not sell the air, the clouds and the great sea, as well as the earth? Did not the Great Spirit make them all for the use of his children?"

In this three-hour speech at the great council of Vincennes, Tecumseh threatens to kill any chief who sells land to the white man:

"I now wish you to listen to me. If you do not it will appear as if you wished me to kill all the chiefs that sold you the land. I tell you so because I am authorized by all the tribes to do so. I am the head of them all. I am a Warrior and all the Warriors will meet together in two or three moons from this. Then I will call for those chiefs that sold you the land and shall know what to do with them. If you do not restore the land you will have a hand in killing them."

But from his opening words it is clear that Tecumseh feels that he is not getting through to Harrison:

"Brother, I wish you to listen to me well—I wish to reply to you more explicitly, as I think you do not clearly understand what I before said to you. I will explain again...."

He is like a patient parent, indulging a small unheeding child. But Harrison will never understand, cannot understand. Land is to him private property, circumscribed by fences and surveyors' pins, tied down by documents, deeds, titles. He wants to be fair, but he cannot comprehend this Indian. The land has been bought from its rightful owners and paid for. It is purely a business matter.

Now it is the Governor's turn to speak. He ridicules the idea of a single Indian nation, dismisses the Shawnee claim to ownership of the disputed lands (the Shawnee, he points out, come from farther south), praises the United States above all other nations for a long record of fair dealing.

The Indians listen patiently, waiting for the translations. Not far away on the grass lies the Potawatomi chief Winemac, in fear of his life at Tecumseh's hands, for he is one of those who has agreed to cede the land. He hides in his buckskins a brace of pistols, a gift from the Governor to guard him from assassination. A sergeant and twelve soldiers, originally detailed to guard the assembly, have moved off a distance to escape the searing sun.

The Shawnee translation of Harrison's remarks ends. The Potawatomi translation begins. Suddenly Tecumseh rises and, with violent gestures, starts to shout. Harrison notes, with concern, that Winemac is priming his pistols. John Gibson, the Indiana secretary, who understands the Shawnee tongue, whispers to Lieutenant Jesse Jennings of the 7th Infantry to bring up the guard quickly: "Those fellows mean mischief." Tecumseh's followers leap to their feet, brandishing tomahawks and war clubs. Harrison draws his sword. A Methodist minister runs to the house, seizes a rifle, and prepares to protect the Governor's family. Up runs the twelve-man guard, muskets ready. Harrison motions them to hold their fire, demands to know what Tecumseh is saying. The answer is blunt: the Governor is a liar; everything he has said is false; the United States has cheated the Indians. The angry Harrison banishes Tecumseh and his followers from Grouseland. They leave in a fury, but the following day, his anger spent, Tecumseh apologizes.

What is the meaning of this singular incident? Had Tecumseh planned a massacre, as some believe, only to be faced down by Harrison and his troops? That is unlikely. It is more probable that, hearing the translation of Harrison's words, he briefly lost his remarkable self-possession. It is also possible that it was a carefully staged part of a plan to convince Harrison of Tecumseh's strength and leadership.

Harrison, mollified by the apology, visits Tecumseh at his camp on the outskirts of Vincennes and finds the Shawnee in a totally different mood. The menacing savage has been transformed into a skittish adversary. The two sit together on a bench, Tecumseh talking all the while and edging closer to the governor, who is forced to move over. Tecumseh continues to talk, continues to crowd Harrison, who presently finds himself on the very end of the bench. Harrison at length protests. The Shawnee laughs: how would he like to be pushed right off, as the Indians have been pushed off their lands by white encroachment?

But beneath this burlesque Harrison recognizes a firmness of purpose that makes him apprehensive. As the council proceeds Tecumseh makes it clear that he intends to prevent, by force if necessary, the lands ceded at Fort Wayne from falling into the hands of the whites. His final words are unequivocal:

"I want the present boundary line to continue. Should you cross it I assure you it will be productive of bad consequences."

Harrison has no choice but to halt the surveys of the disputed territory. He will not get his two dollars an acre until the power of the Shawnee brothers is broken forever.

WHO ARE THESE SHAWNEE BROTHERS? Harrison may well ask himself. Where have they sprung from? What was it that produced from one Indian tribe and from the same parents the two most compelling native leaders of their time? What has made them rise above their own fellows, their own kin, so that their names are familiar to all the tribes from Michilimackinac to the borders of Florida?

The two do not even look like brothers. If Tecumseh is grudgingly admired, the Prophet is universally despised. To the white romantics one is a "good" Indian, the other "bad" – the noble savage and the rogue native, neat stereotypes in the bosom of a single family. Part of the contrast is physical. Tecumseh is almost too handsome to be true; his younger brother is ugly, awkward, and one-eyed, a handkerchief masking the empty socket, mutilated in childhood by a split arrow. One is a mystic, mercurial and unpredictable, the other a clear-eyed military genius. Yet the two are indivisible, their personalities and philosophies interlocking like pieces of an ivory puzzle.

In looking forward to a new future for the tribes, the brothers are gazing back upon an idyllic past when the vast hunting-grounds were open to all. The idea of land held in common springs directly from the Shawnee experience and must have been held by others before them. Always partially nomadic, the Shawnee were deprived of any share of the profits from lands sold to white men in Kentucky. The sedentary Iroquois pocketed the cash while the advancing pressure of settlement forced the Shawnee northward and westward always onto lands occupied by other tribes. For years now they have been hunting over the disputed territory east of the Wabash, but in Harrison's conventional view they do not "own" it because the Miami were there first. Tecumseh's own wanderings underline the Shawnee dilemma. He has no fixed home but has moved northward from settlement to settlement, from Kentucky to Indiana to Ohio to Prophet's Town on the Tippecanoe. Men with such a history must feel the land belongs to all.

Unlike the Prophet, Tecumseh is a warrior. The major influence in his life was his older brother, Cheeseekau, fourteen years his senior and clearly a replacement for his father, who died when Tecumseh was an infant. Cheeseekau taught him to hunt with bow and arrow (nurturing in him a contempt for firearms, which frighten away deer), to fight with a tomahawk, and to develop his scorn and hatred of the white man, especially white Americans. From the age of fifteen,

Lake of the Woods

LAKE SUPERIOR

INDIANA TERR.

Minnesota R.

Mississippi R.

Wisconsin R.

LAKE MICHIGAN

LAKE HURON

UPPER CANADA

ILLINOIS TERR.

MICHIGAN TERR.

Fort Detroit

Amherstburg

LAKE ERIE

Des Moines R.

Fort Dearborn

Illinois R.

Tippecanoe R.

Fort Wayne

Fort Miami

OHIO

Prophet's Town

Urbana

Springfield

INDIANA TERR.

Dayton

Old Chillicothe

Missouri R.

Chillicothe

Cincinnati

Wabash R.

Vincennes

Ohio R.

VIRGINIA

Lexington

KENTUCKY

Greenville Treaty Line, 1795

TENNESSEE

N.C.

Arkansas R.

Mississippi R.

100   200   300 Miles

100   200   300 Kilometres

Tecumseh's Frontier

when he survived his first skirmish at his brother's side against the Kentucky volunteers, he has done battle with American frontiersmen and American soldiers. He has fought in every major engagement, rising to band leader after Cheeseekau's death in the Cherokee war in 1792 and emerging unscathed two years later at the disastrous Battle of Fallen Timbers, when another brother fell to an American musket ball.

Yet his closest companion for fifteen years was a white youth, Stephen Ruddell, who has become a Methodist missionary to the Shawnee. Captured by the tribe during the Revolution and adopted into a Shawnee family, young Ruddell was present on the famous occasion when, at sixteen, Tecumseh impassively watching a white prisoner being consumed by the slow fire of the stake, rose up and in a speech that foreshadowed later eloquence swore he would never again allow such horror in his presence.

It is this mixture of savagery and compassion that baffles men like Harrison. In battle, stripped naked save for a breech cloth, his face daubed with ochre, his tomahawk stained with blood, Tecumseh is demonic. Yet Ruddell remembers that from his boyhood he was "remarkable...for the dignity and rectitude of his deportment." He does not like to take prisoners in battle, but when he does he treats them with humanity. Nor will he allow the killing of women and children.

Like his younger brother, he has managed to conquer alcohol, not as the result of the mystical experience that transformed the Prophet from an idler and a wastrel into a native messiah but as a simple act of will. Alcohol befuddled his ambition, interfered with the clarity of his vision.

For similar reasons he has managed to free himself from the tyranny of sex. To him, women are inferior creatures; he treats them with courtesy but will not hunt in their company. And like alcohol, they may divert him from his purpose. As a young man he realized his own attraction to the tribal beauties but was determined not to be ensnared. "The handsome are now anxious for me," he told a white acquaintance, "and I am determined to disappoint them."

His first wife, Manete, whom he married at twenty-eight, was a mixed blood, considerably older than he and certainly no beauty. From her as from all his other women he demanded affection and absolute obedience. The day of reckoning came when he asked her to make him a pouch to hold his war paint. She told him she did not know how and offered to find a friend who did. It was the end of the marriage. Tecumseh snatched back the materials, declared that he would save her the trouble, gave her some presents, and banished her forever.

Another wife – the Shawnee are allowed as many as they wish – received a similar rebuff. Tecumseh had killed a turkey and invited friends to dine; he was discomfited to find a few feathers clinging to the fowl when his wife served it. After his guests had gone, he handed her a bundle of clothing and ordered her to leave. Tears, entreaties, promises to do better next time all failed to move him. "I am ashamed of you," said Tecumseh. "We must separate." He did not see her again.

One woman, it is said, intrigued him above all others: Rebecca Galloway, a white girl of sixteen, the daughter of a literate frontiersman at Old Chillicothe, Ohio. She spoke his language, taught him English, introduced him to the Bible, Alexander the Great, Shakespeare's plays (his favourite was *Hamlet*). The passionate Shawnee fell in love; he brought her gifts (a silver comb, a birchbark canoe, furs, venison), called her Star of the Lake, asked for her hand in marriage offering thirty silver brooches as a lure. She was agreeable but made one condition: he must give up the Indian life, adopt white customs and dress. Tecumseh struggled with this dilemma, but his decision was foreordained. He could not bring himself to adopt a course that would cost him the respect of his people. Reluctantly they parted, never to meet again.

Now he is determinedly single. His last wife, White Wing, a Shawnee woman whom he married in 1802, parted from him in 1807. There would be no more women in Tecumseh's life. He is wedded irrevocably to an ideal.

He dreams Pontiac's ancient dream of an Indian confederacy stretching from Florida to Lake Erie – a confederacy strong enough to resist white pressure. To that end he is prepared to travel astonishing distances preaching to the tribes – to the Kickapoo, Wea, Creek, Wyandot, Sauk, Fox, Potawatomi, Miami, Choctaw, Osage and other Indian bands who, like Balkan communities, argue and squabble among themselves, to their own misfortune and the white man's benefit. The nucleus of this alliance already exists at the mouth of the Tippecanoe where the disaffected members of half a dozen tribes have flocked in response to the mystic summons of Tecumseh's younger brother.

The Prophet's background is as remarkable as Tecumseh's, though quite different. Born after his father's death, he was raised by a sister who clearly favoured his older brother. While Tecumseh was dazzling his fellow tribesmen with his skill as a hunter and, later, his prowess as a warrior, the future Prophet, born Laulewausika, was a layabout. He seemed to be a man with no future, no ambition. Then, with the suddenness of a rocket's flare, he changed, overcome by a sense of sin. There was talk of a trance, a visit to the Great Spirit, a vision in which he saw a forked road before him – misery in one direction, happiness in the other. What brought about this miraculous transformation that caused him to be as one reborn? There are only hints, but it is believed in Vincennes that the Shaker preachers, who were influential in the area (their new home only a few miles distant), had their effect. The new name that he adopted to symbolize his reform, Tenskwatawa, is translated as "I am the door," a phrase used by Jesus, and much of his preaching, which began in 1805, resembles fundamentalist Christianity. He urges his followers to give up strong liquor (as he himself did instantly), to stop beating their wives, to cease intertribal warfare, to renounce crimes of theft.

But there is something more, which suggests that the Prophet is in the mainstream of a mystical movement going back to the Delaware prophet who, in 1762, laid the basis for Pontiac's confederacy. The same movement will go forward to future prophets including the most influential of all, Wovoka of the Paiutes, who in the late eighties will spread the ritual of the Ghost Dance across the nation.

These native messiahs invariably appear during the death struggles of a threatened culture; their authority is supernatural, their message nostalgic: their people are to return to the old customs and rid themselves of the white man's ways. Tenskwatawa, the Open Door, preaches that his followers must revert to the clothing, the implements, the weapons, the foods that were in use before the Europeans reached North America. Implicit in this philosophy is a rejection of the white man. Harrison has been told, specifically, by two Indian messengers that the Prophet preaches that "the Great Spirit will in a few years destroy every white man in America."

Tecumseh has been fighting white Americans since 1783; how much has he contributed to the Prophet's thoughts? Harrison cannot know, but it is clear to him that at some time in the first decade of the century the two brothers, who like, respect, and listen to one another, have come together in their thinking. The Prophet's followers become

Tecumseh's followers; onto the Prophet's religion is grafted the politics of the older brother. It is a dangerous combination; Harrison cannot suffer it much longer, especially with the Indians leaning toward the British. The time is ripe for a preventive war.

•

FORT AMHERSTBURG, UPPER CANADA, November 15, 1810. Matthew Elliott sits in the council circle on the parade ground overlooking the wooded islands in the Detroit River and contemplates his dilemma. With him are the officers of the 100th Regiment, his clerk, George Ironsides (married to one of Tecumseh's sisters), James Girty, an Indian Department interpreter, and some two hundred Potawatomi, Ottawa, Winnebago, Sauk, and Fox. They have come to hear Tecumseh speak, and it is Tecumseh's words that illustrate Elliott's dilemma. The Indian Department has plainly done its work too well.

The Shawnee war chief has in his hands a great belt of wampum – thousands of small coloured shells sewn together – given to his predecessors by the British after the defeat of the French, a talisman, sacred in Indian eyes, symbolizing a treaty of friendship between the British and the natives.

"Father," says Tecumseh, "I have come here with the intention of informing you that we have not forgot (we can never forget) what passed between you English Men and our Ancestors – And also to let you know our present determination. . . .

"Father we have a belt to show you, which was given to our Kings when you laid the French on their back. Here it is, Father; on one end is your hand, on the other, that of the Red people. . .and in the middle the hearts of both. This belt, Father, our great Chiefs have been sitting upon ever since, keeping it concealed. . . . Now the Warriors have taken all the Chiefs and turned their faces toward you, never again to look towards the Americans; and we the Warriors now manage the affairs of our Nation; and we sit at or near the Borders where the Contest will begin.

"Father – It is only five Years ago that I discovered this Belt and took it from under our Kings. You Father have nourished us, and raised us up from Childhood we are now Men, and think ourselves capable of defending our Country, in which cause you have given us active assistance and always advice – We now are determined to

63

defend it ourselves, and after raising you on your feet leave you behind, but expecting you will push towards us what may be necessary to supply our Wants...."

The belt is passed around so that all may examine it. It shows two hands, dark against a white background (the Indian hand darker than the British) outstretched in friendship. As the belt moves round the circle, Tecumseh declares that his followers will never quit their father or let go his hand.

The translation is awkward, but the meaning is clear. The younger warriors who follow the Prophet and his brother have overridden the advice of their elders and are bent on war with the Americans; they want the British to help them. Elliott, it seems, has been too successful in implementing the government's Indian policy. His instructions were to win the tribes over to the British side. Well, he has done that. The difficulty is that in turning the Indians against the Americans and toward the British, he and his colleagues have brought the country to the brink of an Indian war.

Elliott is in a delicate position and knows it. If war should come, the Indians have been told, Elliott will be its messenger. The previous July he had told a Miami chief: "My son, keep your eyes fixed on me; my tomahawk is up now; be you ready but do not strike until I give the signal." The Indians are more than ready. Patience is not among their virtues; how does one keep them keyed up to fight, yet hold them back from action for months, perhaps years? For Elliott, it is an impossible task.

He is an old man, into his seventies, trying to act like a young man. This year he has taken his first legal wife, an Irish girl, Sarah Donovan, half a century his junior. No doubt she sees him as a father, for she married him shortly after the death of her own father, a schoolmaster. But it is no token relationship; she will bear him two sons.

He is wealthy enough to retire, has been for a generation. He is by far the richest farmer in the area, though farmer is scarcely the word for Elliott, who runs three thousand acres as a plantation with a staff of overseers, clerks, and several score slaves, both Indian and Negro. Some of the latter go back thirty years to his raids in Kentucky with Alexander McKee and the Girty brothers. The Indians have made Elliott a fortune. Some of the land on which his handsome home rests was bought directly from the Wyandot and Ottawa tribes in contravention of British government policy (but winked at by his superiors, who have so often winked at his activities).

64

His mansion, with its neat lawn, ornamented by tree clumps running down to the river, is furnished as few homes are. He has enough flatware and plate to serve one hundred people. His wife has at least fifty dresses and thirteen pairs of kid gloves. He himself owns eleven hats. There are no banks in the Canadas; one's wealth is stored in the attic. In one trunk, Elliott keeps nine hundred pounds' worth of silver plate.

It does not occur to the old man that he can retire. This is his life; he knows no other. He is close to exhaustion, but the job must be done. He dictates a note to his superior, Superintendent William Claus. Restraint is necessary, of course, he agrees, but – a little wistfully – would it not be proper to keep up "the present spirit of resistance"? Claus sends the note to Gore at York, who passes it on to the ailing governor general, Sir James Craig, at Quebec, who chews over it for months.

Craig is faced with the same dilemma; his own policy has brought about this problem. A distressing possibility confronts him: what if the Indians should attack prematurely and the British be blamed? His conscience tweaks him, and on November 25 he writes to the British chargé d'affaires in Washington asking him to warn the American secretary of state that he suspects the Indians are planning to attack the American frontier. That surreptitious message forms one of the strands in the skein of events that will lead to a bloody dénouement the following year at Prophet's Town on the Tippecanoe.

As the Governor General attempts to conciliate the Americans at the possible expense of the Indians, his underlings at Amherstburg have been attempting to conciliate the Indians at the possible expense of the Americans. For the traditional dispensation of presents includes a generous supply of hatchets, guns, and ammunition, ostensibly for hunting game but equally serviceable in the kind of frontier skirmish that is already arousing Yankee dander. Within a year the discovery of some of these weapons will fuel the growing American demand for war.

The ceremony follows a time-honoured ritual. Each chief hands Matthew Elliott a small bundle of cedar sticks to the number of his tribe, cut in three lengths to represent men, women, and children. With these, Elliott's clerks determine how the gifts are to be dispersed. Now the presents are brought from the storehouse and heaped around a series of stakes, each of which bears the name of a tribe. Elliott makes a brief speech, calls the chiefs forward, points to the mounds of gifts – bales of blankets and calico cloth, great rolls of tobacco, stacks of combs, scissors, mirrors, needles, copper pots, iron kettles – and weapons. On a signal the young men dart forward, carry the presents to the waiting canoes. Within three minutes the lawn is empty.

This lavish distribution disturbs the new commander of the British forces in Upper Canada, Brigadier-General Isaac Brock. How, he asks Governor General Craig, can the Indians be expected to believe the British are strictly neutral "after giving such manifest indications of a contrary sentiment by the liberal quantity of military stores with which they were dismissed"? Brock is critical of Elliott – "an exceedingly good man and highly respected by the Indians; but having in his youth lived a great deal with them, he has naturally imbibed their feelings and prejudices, and partaking in the wrongs they continually suffer, this sympathy made him neglect the considerations of prudence, which ought to have regulated his conduct." In short, Elliott can help to start an Indian war.

Sir James Craig agrees. He insists that Elliott and his colleagues "use all their influence to dissuade the Indians from their projected plan of hostility, giving them clearly to understand that they must not expect assistance from us."

Many months pass before Elliott is aware of this policy. Sir James is mortally ill with dropsy, his limbs horribly swollen, his energies sapped. Weeks go by before he is able to reply to Elliott's request to maintain "the present spirit of resistance." More weeks drag on before Elliott receives them. The regular mail service from Quebec extends no farther than Kingston and goes only once a fortnight. In the rest of Upper Canada post offices are almost unknown. Letters to York and Amherstburg often travel by way of the United States. It is March, 1811, before Elliott receives Craig's statement of neutrality and the Indians have long since gone to their hunting camps, out of Elliott's reach. He will not be in touch again for months. British policy has done an about-face on paper, but the Indians, goaded to the point of revolt by Harrison's land hunger, are not aware of it. Events are starting to assume a momentum of their own.

●

VINCENNES, INDIANA TERRITORY, July 30, 1811. Once again in the shade of an arbour on his estate of Grouseland, William Henry Harrison faces his Shawnee adversary in a great council. The stalemate continues over the disputed lands which, with Tecumseh's threat still hanging over the territory, remain unsurveyed. The Governor is convinced that Tecumseh has come to Vincennes to strike a blow for the Indian cause – that here on Harrison's home ground he intends to murder all the neutral chiefs and, if necessary, the Governor himself. He has ignored Harrison's request to come with a small party; three hundred warriors have arrived on the outskirts of Vincennes by land and water.

The town is in a panic; already in the back country some roving bands of Indians have been slaughtering white families encroaching on their territory. Harrison has responded with a show of force. On the day of Tecumseh's arrival, July 27, he pointedly reviews some seven hundred militiamen. He places three infantry companies on duty, moving them about in such a way that the Indians will believe there are five. He shifts his dragoons about the town at night on foot and horseback in order to place Tecumseh's followers in a state of "astonishment and Terror."

Tecumseh strides into the council with 170 warriors, all armed with knives, tomahawks, bows and arrows. Harrison meets him guarded by a force of seventy dragoons. Each man carries a sabre; each has two pistols stuck in his belt. In this warlike atmosphere the council begins, only to be interrupted by a violent downpour.

Harrison is impatient to end it. He is tired of palaver; a plan of action is forming in his mind. If the Indians want war he intends to give it to them, whether Washington condones it or not. He refuses to negotiate further over the new purchase; that, he tells Tecumseh, is up to the President. But if Tecumseh really wants peace, as he claims, then let him turn over to Harrison the Potawatomi braves in his camp who murdered four white men the previous fall.

Tecumseh speaks. His response, even Harrison admits, is artful. He affects to be surprised that the white men should be alarmed at his plans. All he wants to do is to follow the American example and unite the Indian tribes in the same way that the white men united the various states of the Union. The Indians did not complain of *that* union; why should the white men complain when the Indians want to accomplish the same thing? As for the murderers, they are not in his camp, and anyway, should they not be forgiven? He himself has set an example of forgiveness by refusing to take revenge on those who have murdered his people.

Again he makes it clear that he will not allow surveyors to split up the newly purchased territories for sale to white settlers. Harrison responds bluntly: the moon will fall to earth before the President will suffer his people to be murdered, and he would put his warriors in

67

petticoats before he would give up the land fairly acquired from its rightful owners.

There now occurs an oddly chilling incident that illustrates Tecumseh's remarkable self-possession as well as his power over his followers. A Potawatomi leader known as the Deaf Chief because of impaired hearing wishes to challenge Tecumseh's protestations of peace. A friend informs him that as a result Tecumseh has given orders that he is to be killed. The Deaf Chief, undismayed, puts on his war paint, seizes a rifle, tomahawk, war club, and scalping knife, and descends on Tecumseh's camp to find the Shawnee engaged in conversation with Barron, the interpreter. The Deaf Chief rails at him, calls him a coward and an assassin, and then cries out, "Here am I now. Come and kill me!" Tecumseh makes no answer, continues to talk with Barron. The Deaf Chief heaps more insults on him. "You dare not face a warrior!" he screams. Tecumseh, unmoved, keeps up his quiet conversation. The Deaf Chief raves on, calling Tecumseh a slave of the British redcoats. No response; it is as if the Deaf Chief did not exist. At last, exhausted and out of invective, he departs. But that is the last anyone in Vincennes sees of the Deaf Chief, alive or dead.

Tecumseh's zeal and his influence over his people win Harrison's admiration, even as the Governor plans to destroy him:

"The implicit obedience and respect which the followers of Tecumseh pay to him is really astonishing and more than any other circumstance bespeaks him one of those uncommon geniuses, which spring up occasionally to produce revolutions and overturn the established order of things. If it were not for the vicinity of the United States, he would perhaps be the founder of an Empire that would rival in glory that of Mexico or Peru. No difficulties deter him. His activity and industry supply the want of letters. For four years he has been in constant motion. You see him today on the Wabash and in a short time you hear of him on the shores of Lake Erie, or Michigan, or the banks of the Mississippi and wherever he goes he makes an impression favourable to his purpose."

These words are written on August 7, 1811. Harrison can afford to be generous in his estimation of his adversary, for Tecumseh has removed himself from the area. He is off on a six-month tour of the southern United States to try to persuade the tribes – Creek, Choctaw, Osage, and others – to join his confederacy. For the moment he poses no threat, and in his absence Harrison sees his chance. "I hope," he writes to Eustis, the Secretary of War, "...before his return that that part of the fabrick, which he considered complete will be demolished and even its foundations rooted up." Now that the brothers are separated it will be easier to tempt the Prophet into battle. As the Deaf Chief discovered, Tecumseh cannot be provoked unless he wishes to be. But "the Prophet is imprudent and audacious. . .deficient in talents and firmness."

The plan that has been forming in Harrison's mind has become a fixation. The confederacy is growing; the British are undoubtedly behind it. It must be smashed before Tecumseh returns, smashed on the enemy's home ground, at Prophet's Town on the banks of the Tippecanoe. Harrison cannot submit to further stalemate. He will march in September.

●

THE BATTLE OF TIPPECANOE is not the glorious victory that Harrison, down through the years, will proclaim. It is not even a battle, more a minor skirmish, and indecisive, for Harrison, in spite of his claims, loses far more men than the Indians. Overblown in the history books, this brief fracas has two significant results: it is the chief means by which Harrison will propel himself into the White House (his followers chanting the slogan "Tippecanoe and Tyler Too"); and, for the Indians, it will be the final incident that provokes them to follow Tecumseh to Canada, there to fight on the British side in the War of 1812.

Tippecanoe is unnecessary. It is fought only because Harrison needs it to further his own ambitions. For while the Governor is writing to Washington branding the Prophet as an aggressor ("I can assure you Sir that there is not an Indian. . .that does not know and acknowledge when asked that he is determined to attack us and wonder at our forbearance"), Tecumseh is warning his brother that he must on no account be goaded into battle.

Harrison means to goad him, but Washington, in the person of Dr. Eustis, the Secretary of War, equivocates. "I have been particularly instructed by the President," the Secretary writes, "to communicate to your excellency his earnest desire that peace may, if possible, be preserved among the Indians, and that to this end every proper measure be adopted. By this it is not intended. . .that the banditti under the prophet should not be attacked and vanquished, provided such a measure should be rendered absolutely necessary."

That is good enough for Harrison. He shores up his position with a series of letters making it clear that such measures *are* absolutely necessary. As soon as Tecumseh is safely out of the way, he informs Eustis that he intends in September to move up to the upper line of the New Purchase (the territory ceded at Fort Wayne) with two companies of regulars, fourteen or fifteen companies of militia, and two troops of dragoons, the latter consisting of about one hundred men. Harrison makes it seem that this is purely a precautionary measure. But "should circumstances render it necessary to break up the Prophet's establishment by force," well then, he adds – preparing Eustis for the inevitable – he can easily get more men to fight, as well as plenty of mounted volunteers from Kentucky, where Indian fighting is a glorious tradition.

The volunteers, in fact, flock to Vincennes. The best known is Joseph Daviess, one of Kentucky's most eloquent lawyers, a brilliant orator, a popular hero, and a mild eccentric, notorious both for his prosecution of Aaron Burr and for his addiction to colourful and often startling costumes. He has a habit of appearing in court wearing a coonskin cap and deerskin leggings and carrying a hunting rifle. In one memorable appearance before the Supreme Court in Washington (the first for any western lawyer) he turned up in ripped corduroy trousers, a threadbare overcoat, and a pair of dilapidated and muddy shoes, and proceeded to down a quantity of bread and cheese while his opponent tried to marshall his case. Now he is hot to do battle in any capacity under the leadership of his hero, Harrison.

"I make free to tell you," he declares, "that I have imagined there were two men in the west who had military talents: And you sir, were the first of the two.... I go as a volunteer, leaving to you sir, to dispose of me as you choose...." He arrives along with some sixty others from his state – former army men and Indian fighters – a commanding figure, thirty-seven years old, resplendent in the uniform of the Kentucky mounted volunteers, the plumes in his hat accentuating his six-foot stature. To one eyewitness, it seems "nothing could be more magnificent. He was the very model of a cavalry officer.... With his tall, muscular form and face of strong masculine beauty, he would have been the pride of any army, and the thunderbolt of a battlefield."

Harrison and the Indians are moving at cross purposes. On September 25, the Prophet sends off runners from his village on the Tippecanoe with a message of peace for Harrison. At ten o'clock the following morning, the Governor dispatches his troops on his "demon-

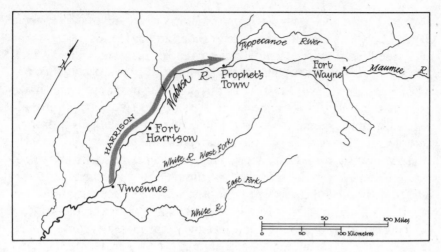

The Wabash

stration of force." They move up the Wabash in shallow flatboats, the regulars in brass-buttoned tailcoats and stove-pipe hats, the citizen soldiers of the militia in deerskin jackets and bearskin caps. When they reach the disputed territory, they build a blockhouse – Fort Harrison – the eloquent Daviess, now a major, chosen to smash a bottle over the new logs. There is much sickness, especially among the regulars, unused to frontier conditions, forced to wade up the Wabash in their skin-tight pantaloons. Shortly, however, the force is augmented by another two hundred and fifty regular soldiers of the 4th U.S. Infantry. On October 28 Harrison leaves the new fort and pushes on toward Prophet's Town at the head of one thousand men – a commanding figure in a fringed calico shirt and a beaver hat into which he has jauntily stuck an ostrich feather.

He moves cautiously, expecting Indians behind every tree, suspicious of ambush. Nothing. At two-thirty on the afternoon of November 6, some dozen miles from his objective, he reaches a small wood, halts, draws up his force in battle order, sends scouts forward. There are Indians just ahead, flitting through the trees, but they will not speak to the interpreters.

Back comes Major Daviess, eager for battle, urging an immediate attack against the insolent savages. Why is Harrison vacillating? Have the troops come this far for nothing? The Governor hesitates, mindful of Washington's order that he must try for a peaceful settlement; then, with his men murmuring their eagerness, moves on, yielding "to what appeared to be the general wish." It matters to no one that Prophet's Town is on land that has never been ceded to the United States.

Three Indians approach. Harrison recognizes one: Chief White Horse, principal counsellor to the Prophet. They are conciliatory. They have been trying to reach Harrison, but the messengers have been looking for him on the south side of the river; Harrison has taken the north bank. He assures them that all he seeks is a proper camping ground and they agree to parley on the morrow.

As the town comes into view, Harrison raises his field glass and through it observes the inhabitants running about in apparent terror and confusion behind a breastwork of logs. After some reconnoitring he camps his army about a mile to the northwest among the leafless oaks on a triangle of ground a few feet above the marshy prairie. Here, in the chill of the night, the men slumber, or try to (some have no blankets), in the warmth of huge fires, their loaded guns beside them, bayonets fixed, their coats covering the musket locks to keep them dry. Harrison has dug no trenches, erected no stakes because, he claims later, he has not enough axes.

What are the Indians thinking and planning? No one knows or will ever know, for most of the accounts of the battle come from white men. Those Indian accounts that do exist are second hand and contradictory, filtered through white reports.

Some things are fairly certain: the Indians, not trusting Harrison, expect him to attack and are determined to strike first; the battle, when it comes, is started accidentally when neither side is prepared; and of the several tribes represented at Prophet's Town it is the Winnebago and the Potawatomi and not the Shawnee who are the fiercest in wanting to disobey Tecumseh's orders not to fight.

It is four o'clock, the night still dark and overcast, a light rain rustling the bushes. On the left flank, directly in front of Captain Robert Barton's infantry company, a shivering picket, Private William Brigham, on his knees, his musket on charge, nervously tries to pierce the gloom. He cannot see farther than three feet. Suddenly – footsteps. Brigham raises his musket and almost shoots his fellow picket, William Brown, who has imprudently left his own post in a state of near terror, certain that Indians are lurking in the bushes ahead. His instinct is to flee at once.

"Brigham," he whispers, "let us fire and run. . ."

But Brigham fears a false alarm.

Suddenly something swishes past them. An arrow? Terrified, they turn and dash back toward the camp. Beside them a rifle barks.

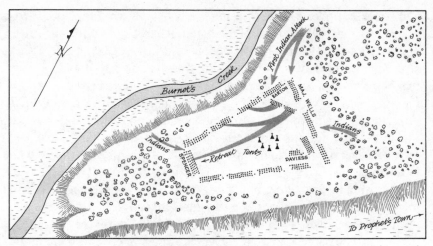

The Battle of Tippecanoe

Another sentry, Stephen Mars, has fired at something moving in the gloom and also dashed toward safety.

In Tent No. 1, Sergeant Montgomery Orr springs awake. Somebody has just rushed past, touching the corner of his tent. He jogs his corporal, David Thompson, awake. Something strikes the tent. Thompson leaps up, seizes his gun as four shots ring out accompanied by a high screaming and yelling. The corporal tumbles back upon the sergeant.

"Corporal Thompson, for God's sake don't give back!" cries Orr, then realizes he is talking to a dead man. He plunges out of the tent, gets a confused impression of a melee – soldiers and Indians firing at each other, Captain Barton trying vainly to form up his men.

Harrison is pulling on his boots when he hears a cacophony of yells and a burst of musketry. One of his officers and two of his men have already been tomahawked and scalped. He calls for his terrified black servant, George, to bring up his favourite mount – a pale grey mare. The boy cannot find her, so Harrison borrows another officer's horse – a black one – and rides into confusion. His men, perfect silhouettes in front of the fires, are falling about him. On the left, Barton's company is already badly mauled. Another has broken. When one of his colonels, mounted on a pale grey mare similar to his missing animal, tumbles to the ground, dead from an Indian musket ball, Harrison realizes that the Indians have mistaken the dead man for himself. An aide rides out on a similar horse; Harrison shoos him back for a black one.

Harrison moves swiftly to reinforce his shattered flank, rides from point to point trying to control the battle. After it is over he will write a careful account, describing the action as if it were a set piece, reconstructing all the movements, making them sound like parade-ground manoeuvres. But at this moment, with the blackened Indians shrieking, the musket fire deafening, the steam rising from fires quickly doused, the clouds of black gun smoke adding to the general overcast, it is impossible for anyone to tell exactly what is happening.

As in every battle, there are moments of horror and moments of heroism.

The Indians are acting in a most un-Indian-like fashion, responding with considerable discipline to signals made by the rattling of deer horns, firing a volley, retreating out of range to reload, advancing again. As Harrison approaches Captain Spier Spencer's company of Kentuckians, known as Yellow Jackets, on the right flank, he can hear the veteran Spencer crying, "Close up, men! Steady! Hold the line!" The Indians have mounted a third attack, so fierce that the balls are shredding the bark from the trees. One strikes Spencer in the head. He continues to shout. Another tears into his thigh, and then another. He calls out for help, and two men rush over, raise him up just as another ball penetrates his body, killing him.

Harrison rides up, sees young John Tipton sighting down a barrel.
"Where's your captain?"
"Dead, sir!"
"Your first-lieutenant?"
"Dead, sir!"
"Your second-lieutenant?"
"Dead, sir!"
"Your ensign?"
"Here, sir!"

Harrison searches about for reinforcements, sees Robb's militia company faltering, rallies them in support of the Yellow Jackets, braces the flank with a company of regulars. A close friend, Thomas Randolph, falls, mortally wounded. Harrison dismounts, bends over his friend, asks if there is anything he can do. Nothing, gasps Randolph, except to look after his child. Harrison keeps that promise.

The impetuous Major Daviess, in charge of the dragoons, is chafing at the rear. He wants to roar into action, but Harrison is holding him back:

"Tell Major Daviess to be patient, he will have an honourable station before the battle is over."

Daviess cannot stand the inaction; he presses Harrison again, gets the same reply, continues to nag. At last the Governor gives in:

"Tell Major Daviess he has heard my opinion twice; he may now use his own discretion."

Daviess has spotted Indians lurking behind some scattered logs seventy-five yards away. Gathering a force of twenty men, he prepares to charge the foe. He has dressed with his customary panache – an unmistakable target, six feet tall, in a white blanket coat that stands out starkly in the gloom. As he leads his men toward the enemy, three balls pierce his body. "I am a dead man," cries Jo Daviess. His followers carry him to the cover of a sycamore tree as the Indians vanish. He has not long to live. "Unfortunately, the Major's gallantry determined him to execute the order with a smaller force than was sufficient," Harrison comments, a little dryly, in his report of the action.

By the time Daviess falls, the entire line is engaged. Daybreak is at hand. As the Indians begin to falter, Harrison determines on a charge from the flanks. This is the climax of the battle. The level of sound is almost unbearable – an ear-splitting mixture of savage yells, shrieks of despair, roar of musketry, agonizing screams, victorious shouts, dying cries mingling in a continuous terrifying uproar that will ring in the ears of the survivors long after the last wound is healed.

Harrison's charge succeeds. The Indians, out of ammunition and arrows, retire across the marshy prairie where horses cannot follow. The Americans shout cries of triumph, utter prayers of thanks, bind up their wounds, scalp all the dead Indians, kill one who is wounded.

Two days later, they sweep through Prophet's Town, empty save for one aged squaw, on a mission of revenge and plunder. They destroy everything including all the beans and corn that they themselves cannot eat – some three thousand bushels stored up for the winter. In the houses they find British weapons, presents dispensed at Amherstburg the previous year; it confirms their suspicion that British agents have been provoking the Indians to attack (though American weapons distributed by the war department as part of the annuity payments to the tribes are also found). Then they burn all the houses and sheds and take their leave. Thus ends the Battle of Tippecanoe, which has often been called the first battle in the War of 1812.

Harrison has lost almost one-fifth of his force. Thirty-seven white corpses lie sprawled on the battlefield. One hundred and fifty men have been wounded of whom twenty-five will die of their injuries, including the luckless sentry Brigham. No one can be sure how many Indians took part in the skirmish. Nobody knows how many died. Harrison, like most military commanders, overestimates the enemy's losses, declares that the Prophet's casualties run into the hundreds. This is wishful thinking; only thirty-six Indian corpses are found.

The battered army limps back to Vincennes. As soon as Harrison is gone, the Indians, who have retreated across the Wabash, return to the ruins of their village. Although a Kickapoo chief reports to the British that "the Prophet and his people do not appear as a vanquished army," Harrison, intent on beating out some flames of dissent from Kentucky (where Daviess's death is mourned and Harrison's strategy and motives scrutinized), has already launched the long propaganda battle that will convince his countrymen that Tippecanoe was a glorious victory.

What has it accomplished? Its purpose was to teach the Indians a lesson they would never forget, to break Tecumseh's confederacy and the Prophet's power, and to stop the sporadic raids on frontier settlements. But the raids increase in fury. Settlers and soldiers are ambushed. Whole families are wiped out, scalped, mutilated. Farmers abandon their fields and cabins; neighbours club together to build blockhouses; some flee the territory. At Grouseland, Harrison constructs an underground escape tunnel, ships his wife and eight children off to safety in Kentucky, buffers the principal homes of Vincennes with log parapets. Instead of terrifying the Indians, Tippecanoe has stirred them to fury. In March, 1812, both Governor Howard of Missouri Territory and General William Clark, the explorer and superintendent of Indian Affairs, voice the opinion that a formidable combination of Indians are on the warpath, that a bloody war must ensue is almost certain, and that the Prophet is regaining his influence.

Tecumseh returns that same month to Prophet's Town. Later he speaks of his experience:

"I stood upon the ashes of my own home, where my own wigwam had sent up its fires to the Great Spirit, and there I summoned the spirits of the braves who had fallen in their vain attempts to protect their homes from the grasping invader, and as I snuffed up the smell of their blood from the ground I swore once more eternal hatred – the hatred of an avenger."

His mission to the south has failed. The Sauk and Osage tribesmen will not follow him. But his northern confederacy is not shattered as

Harrison keeps repeating (and repeating it, is believed). Tecumseh sends runners to the tribes; twelve respond, each sending two leading chiefs and two war chiefs. By May, Tecumseh has six hundred men under his command, making bows and arrows (for they no longer have guns). In Washington, war fever rises on the tales of frontier violence and the legend of Tippecanoe. Tecumseh waits, holds his men back for the right moment. For a while he will pretend neutrality, but when the moment comes, he will lead his confederacy across the border to fight beside the British against the common enemy.

2

PRELUDE TO INVASION:
1812
Marching As to War

We're abused and insulted, our country's degraded
Our rights are infringed both by land and by sea;
Let us rouse up indignant, when those rights are invaded,
And announce to the world, "We're united and free!"

— Anon., circa 1812.

LITTLE YORK, the muddy capital of Upper Canada, February 27, 1812; Brock, in his study, preparing a secret memorandum to that spectacular frontier creature whom the Dakota Sioux call *Mascotapah*, the Red-Haired Man.

His real name is Robert Dickson, and though born a Scot in Dumfriesshire, he is as close to being an Indian as any white can be. His wife is To-to-win, sister to Chief Red Thunder. His domain covers the watershed of the upper Mississippi, some of the finest fur country on the continent, a land of rolling plains, riven by trough-like valleys and speckled with blue lakes, the veinwork of streams teeming with beaver, marten, and otter, the prairie dark with buffalo. He is out there now, somewhere – nobody knows quite where – a white man living like an Indian, exercising all the power of a Sioux chieftain. Brock must find him before the war begins, for Brock is planning the defence of Upper Canada – carefully, meticulously – and the Red-Haired Man is essential to that plan.

Isaac Brock has been preparing for war for five years, ever since the *Chesapeake* affair when, as colonel in charge of the defences of Lower Canada, he forced a grudging administration into allowing him to repair and strengthen the crumbling fortress of Quebec. Now he has power. He is not only a major-general in charge of all the forces in Upper Canada, he is also, in the absence of Francis Gore, the province's administrator, which in colonial terms makes him close to being a dictator, though not close enough for Brock's peace of mind. His years in Canada have been a series of frustrations: frustrations with the civil authorities, whom he views as a nuisance and who prevent him from getting his own way; frustrations with his superior, the new governor general Sir George Prevost, who keeps him on a tight leash lest he do something precipitate and give the Americans cause for war; frustrations with the militia, who are untrained, untidy, undisciplined, and unwilling; frustrations with the civilian population, who seem blithely unaware of the imminence of war; frustrations over money, for he is in debt through no real fault of his own; frustrations, one suspects, over women, for he loves their company but has never been able to bring himself to marry; and finally, frustrations over his posting.

More than anything else, Brock yearns to be with Wellington on the Peninsula, where there is opportunity for active service and its concomitants, glory and promotion. He does not care for Canada, especially this wretched backwater of York with its tiny clique of pseudo-aristocrats, its haggling legislature, and its untutored rabble. In Quebec at least there was sophistication of a sort, and Brock is no rustic: a gourmet, a lover of fine wines, an omnivorous reader, a spirited dancer at society balls, he longs for a larger community.

For all his days in Canada he has been trying to escape his colonial prison. The irony is that this very month the Prince Regent, through Governor General Prevost, has given him leave to depart. Now he cannot go. Duty, with Brock, takes precedence over personal whim. The gentlemen who form the Prince Regent's government may not believe that war is coming, but General Isaac Brock believes it, and "being now placed in a high ostensible situation, and the state of public affairs with the American government indicating a strong presumption of an approaching rupture between the two countries, I beg leave to be allowed to remain in my present command." *Etc. Etc.* Or is it, possibly, more than a strict sense of duty that holds Brock in Canada? Expecting war, does he not also welcome it? May he not now hope to encounter in the colonies what he has longed for on the continent? Glory, honour, adventure all beckon; all these – even death.

His colleagues, friends, subordinates, and adversaries are scarcely aware of the General's inner turmoil. Though his features are not always expressionless – he was once seen to shed a tear at the execution of a soldier – he keeps his frustrations to himself. He is a remarkably handsome man with a fair complexion, a broad forehead, clear eyes of grey blue (one with a slight cast), and sparkling white teeth. His portraits tend to make him look a little feminine – the almond eyes, the sensitive nostrils, the girlish lips – but his bearing belies it; his is a massive figure, big-boned and powerful, almost six feet three in height. He has now, at forty-two, a slight tendency to portliness, and the flush of middle age is on his cheeks; but he is, in his own words, "hard as nails."

He is popular with almost everybody, especially the soldiers who serve him – a courteous, affable officer who makes friends easily and can charm with a smile. But there is also an aloofness about him, induced perhaps by the loneliness of command; on those rare occasions when he does take somebody into his confidence it is likely to be a junior officer of the volunteer army rather than one of his immediate subordinates.

He has no use for democracy. It is an American word, as treasonous in his lexicon as communism will be to a later generation of military authoritarians. Even the modest spoonful of self-determination allowed the settlers of Upper Canada annoys him. He has gone before the legislature this very month to ask that the civilians, who train part time in the militia, be forced to take an oath of allegiance. The militia in his view contains "many doubtful characters." In addition, he wants to suspend the age-old right of habeas corpus. The House of Assembly turns him down on both counts, a decision that, to Brock, smacks of disloyalty: "The great influence which the numerous settlers from the United States possess over the decisions of the lower house is truly alarming, and ought immediately, by every practical means, [to] be diminished." To Brock, the foundations of the colonial superstructure are threatened by treacherous foreign democrats, boring from within, but he cannot convince the Assembly of that.

So he turns to military matters and the secret message to the Red-Haired Man. As a good military commander, Brock has put himself in the boots of his opposite numbers. He is confident that he knows what the Americans will do.

Through their hunger for land they have managed to alienate almost all the tribes on their northwestern frontier. The Indians, then, are the key to American intentions. In other circumstances, it would make sense to hit Canada in the midriff, at Kingston and Montreal, cutting off the supply routes to the upper province, which then must surely fall. But Brock knows that this militarily attractive option is no option at all as long as America's left flank is in flames. The Indians must be subdued, and for that enterprise a very considerable force will be required, drawn principally, Brock believes, from Ohio, whose people are "an enterprising, hardy race, and uncommonly expert on horseback with the rifle." To meet this threat he has already dispatched two hundred regulars to reinforce the garrison at Fort Amherstburg, across from the American military base at Detroit. These will not be enough to counter any American thrust across the Detroit River, but Brock hopes that their presence will stiffen the resolve of the militia, and more important, convince the Indians that Britain means business. For it is on the Indians that the security of Upper Canada depends. If he can rouse the Indians, the United States will be forced to concentrate much of its limited military strength on the northwestern frontier, thereby weakening any proposed thrust along the traditional invasion routes toward Montreal and the St. Lawrence Valley.

Brock views the Indians as a means to an end. His attitude toward them changes with the context. They are "a much injured people" (a slap at American Indian policy), but they are also a "fickle race" (when some insist on remaining neutral). To Brock, as to most white men, Indians are Indians. (It is as if Wellington lumped Lapps with Magyars and Poles with Scots.) He makes little distinction between the tribes; Sioux and Shawnee, Wyandot and Kickapoo are all the same to him – savages, difficult to deal with, inconstant but damned useful to have on your side. Brock means to have as many oddly assorted Indians on his side as he can muster, and that is the substance of his secret communication with the Red-Haired Man.

The Indians, in Brock's assessment, will fight the Americans only if they are convinced the British are winning. If he can seize the island of Mackinac in the far west at the outset of the war, he believes the Indians will take heart. Some will undoubtedly help him attack Detroit (for Brock believes the best defence is offence), and if Detroit falls, more Indians will join the British – perhaps even the Mohawks of the Six Nations, who have been distressingly neutral. The main American invasion, Brock believes, will come at the Niagara border along the neck of land between Lake Ontario and Lake Erie. Anything else will be a diversion.

To put his domino theory into practice, at the outset Brock needs Indians to subdue by their presence, if not their arrows, the defenders of Michilimackinac. He expects the Red-Haired Man to supply them. The secret letter is deliberately couched in euphemisms, and even Brock's immediate superior, the cautious Governor General Prevost, is not aware of it:

CONFIDENTIAL COMMUNICATION TRANSMITTED TO MR. ROBERT DICKSON RESIDING WITH THE INDIANS NEAR THE MISSOURI

Sir,

As it is probable that war may result from the present *state of affairs*, it is very desirable to ascertain the degree of cooperation that you and *your friends* might be able to furnish, in case of such an Emergency taking place. You will be pleased to report with all practicable expedition upon the following matters.

1st. The number of your friends, that might be depended upon.

2. Their disposition toward us.

3. Would they assemble, and march under your orders.

4. State the succours you require, and the most eligible mode, for their conveyance.

5. Can *Equipment* be procured in your *Country*.

6. An immediate direct communication with you, is very much wished for.

7. Can you point out in what manner, that object may be accomplished.

8. Send without loss of time a few *faithful* and *Confidential* Agents – Selected from *your friends*.

9. Will you individually approach the Detroit frontier next spring.

If so, state time and place where *we* may meet. *Memo.* Avoid mentioning names, in your *written communications*.

Almost five months will pass before Brock receives an answer to this memorandum. And when on July 14, at Fort George at the mouth of the Niagara River, an Indian runner finally arrives with a reply from Robert Dickson, it will already be outdated by events. Long before that, the Red-Haired Man and his friends, anticipating Brock, will have departed for the British post at St. Joseph's to prepare for the invasion of the unsuspecting island of Mackinac.

•

WASHINGTON, D.C., March 20, 1812. Spring has come to the capital after an unseasonably cold winter. It is, as one newspaper points out, excellent weather for campaigning; the roads are no longer rivers of mud and slush. Why are the troops not moving north?

At the British legation on Pennsylvania Avenue this bright afternoon, a young officer arrives with dispatches from the British foreign secretary. They tell a familiar tale. In the face of French intransigence, the British government cannot – will not – repeal the Orders in Council that are at the heart of the dispute between the two nations. Lord Wellesley has felt that decision important enough to justify chartering a special ship to rush word of it across the Atlantic.

The Minister Plenipotentiary to America, who must now carry this news to the President, is the same Augustus John Foster who once swore he would not return to Washington for ten thousand pounds a year. Nevertheless, he is back, and no longer in a junior post. His absence from the London social scene since the spring of 1811 has lost him his intended – a priggish young woman named Annabella Milbanke, who will later conclude a loveless and disastrous marriage with Lord Byron. But how could any ambitious young diplomat refuse such a promotion?

How, for that matter, could His Majesty's government have selected Foster to be its eyes, ears, and tongue at this most critical of times? To the clear indications of approaching war Foster's eyes are uncommonly blind, his ears remarkably deaf, and, in his dispatches, his tongue lamentably silent. At thirty-three, with his round, boyish face, he is, to quote one politician, "a pretty young gentleman...better calculated for a ballroom or a drawing room, than for a foreign minister."

He spends a good deal of time in ballrooms, drawing rooms, and at dinner tables, entertains as many as two hundred guests at a time and lavishly overspends his expense account (perhaps to counteract the impression conveyed by his juvenile looks, for which, as he complains to his mother, the new Duchess of Devonshire, he is "greatly abused"). He seems to know everybody, rubs shoulders with all the major participants in the dangerous game being played out in the capital this spring, yet manages to miss the significance of what he sees and hears. He dines with the Speaker of the House, Henry Clay, whom he describes as "very warlike," John C. Calhoun, the fiery young congressman from South Carolina, Peter B. Porter, the bellicose leader of the House committee on foreign relations, and other members of the ginger group known as War Hawks, but he does not believe that war will come.

The War Hawks are only a handful, yet they effectively control Congress. Five of them room together in the same boarding house, predictably dubbed the War Mess. Clay is their leader, a brilliant, fervent orator who has been Speaker since the opening of the fall session. Poetically handsome, with fair, tousled hair and a quizzical smile, he is no disinterested chairman. He thinks nothing of leaving his neutral post and invading the floor of the House to speak, sometimes for hours. He has seen to it that his cronies chair the key committees, notably the naval committee and the foreign relations committee. The latter – Peter B. Porter's committee – is packed with Clay supporters. Its majority report, brought down in November, 1811, was unequivocal. Since Britain would not budge on the two major issues threatening peace – the Orders in Council and impressment – therefore "we must now tamely submit and quietly submit or we must resist by those means which God has placed within our reach." In short, a call to war.

At dinner with the President in the still unfinished Executive Mansion, Foster encounters another actor in the drama, the dashing Comte Edouard de Crillon, whose extraordinarily thick legs he cannot help remarking. The following day he invites the count to his own table where they discuss the count's estate in Chile. It is all bunkum, as Foster will presently learn: there is no Chilean estate and no Comte de Crillon, either – only a charlatan named Soubiron, a master at masquerade. This imposter has attached himself to a handsome Irish rascal named John Henry, and the two are in the process of palming off a series of letters that Henry has written while in the pay of Sir James Craig, the former governor general of Canada. It develops that Henry, at his own suggestion, was sent by Craig in 1808 as a spy to Federalist New England to see if anyone within the opposition party there might help force a separation from the Union – in short, to seek and make contact with traitors. Henry, being remarkably unsuccessful, was paid a pittance, but the cunning Soubiron believes that copies of the letters, now more than three years old, are worth a minor fortune.

And so, to James Madison, they appear to be. The President is persuaded to squander the entire secret service fund of $50,000 for documents he believes will discomfit the Federalists, lay some of their leaders open to the charge of treason, and embarrass the British.

Madison's coup backfires. Henry has named no names, mentioned no specifics. The President's enemies quickly discover that the Irishman is not the reformed patriot he pretends to be and that the chief executive has looted the treasury for a batch of worthless paper. But the Henry affair, revealing yet another instance of British perfidy, helps to arouse further public feeling already inflamed by Tippecanoe and its aftermath, by a depression in the southwest brought on by the Orders in Council, and by continuing British high-handedness on the seas – more sailors impressed, more ships seized. "If this event does not produce a war, nothing will do so," Augustus Foster comments after Madison tables the letters on March 9. But war does not come, and this helps shore up Federalist convictions (and Foster's) that for all the Republicans' warlike clamour, the government is bluffing, as it had been after the *Chesapeake* affair. Tragically, the congressional doves do not take the War Hawk movement seriously.

Nor does Foster. He is extraordinarily well informed, for he moves in the highest circles, dining regularly with congressmen, senators, and the President himself. He knows that William Hull, Governor of Michigan Territory, has come to town, hoping (Foster believes) to be made Secretary of War in place of the genial but ineffective incumbent, William Eustis. He knows that a former secretary of war, Henry Dearborn, is also in town, trying to decide whether or not to give up his sinecure as collector of customs in Boston and take over command of the expanding army. He must know that Hull, who is another of his dinner guests, is also pondering the offer of an army command in the northwest. The United States, in short, is acting like a nation preparing for war; the President himself, in Foster's words, is "very warlike," but there is no sense of urgency in the reports he sends to Whitehall. He prefers the company of the President's warm-hearted and unwarlike wife, Dolley, who could not attend his January ball marking the Queen's birthday for political reasons but was forced to gaze on the preparations at a distance, from her bedroom window.

Preparations for war are the responsibility of a trio of old hands – all sixtyish – from the Revolution – Hull, Eustis, and Dearborn. Unlike Clay and his Hawks, these ex-soldiers, none of whom has had experience with staff command, can scarcely be said to be champing at the bit. Hull and Dearborn cannot even make up their minds whether to shoulder the responsibility of leadership. Eustis, a one-time surgeon's assistant, is genial, courteous, and a staunch party man but generally held to be incompetent – an executive unable to divorce himself from detail. Congress has refused to create two assistant secretaries, and so the entire war department of the United States consists of Eustis and eight clerks.

Governor Hull has been invited to the capital to discuss the defence of the northwestern frontier. Brock's assessment has been dead on: the Indians have dictated Washington's strategy; with Tecumseh's followers causing chaos in Indiana and Michigan territories, the United States has no option but to secure its western flank.

Washington believes in Hull. He has a reputation for sound judgement, personal courage, decisive command. During the Revolution he fought with distinction, survived nine battles, received the official thanks of Congress. One gets a fleeting picture of a gallant young field officer in his mid-twenties, rallying his troops on horseback at Bemis Heights, stemming a retreat in the face of Gentleman Johnny Burgoyne's regulars, or helping Mad Anthony Wayne carry the Stony Point fort at bayonet point (a bullet creasing his hat, another clipping his boot).

The President and the Secretary of War listen carefully to Hull's advice. The Governor points out that the United States must secure Lake Erie by reinforcing the tiny fort at Detroit and building warships to command the water routes in order to allow the swift movement of men and supplies. Hull realizes that the Indians hold the key to defeat or victory. A formidable army at Detroit, denying the lake to British transport, can cut the Indians off from the British and perhaps prevent a general uprising of the tribes. And without the Indians, he is convinced, "the British cannot hold Upper Canada."

Eustis goes along with Hull's plan only to discover that no American captain can be found who will take command on Lake Erie. Besides, it costs money to build ships, and Congress is niggardly with naval funds. Hull and Eustis, caught up in the war fever, persuade themselves that it will be enough to march a considerable force north to strengthen Detroit, cow the Indians into neutrality, and convince the British across the river that the natives are under control. Should war come, Detroit will be the springboard for an invasion that will drive the British out of all the country west of Niagara.

Hull declines the command of the army that will reinforce Detroit; he does not wish to give up his post as governor of Michigan Territory. A substitute is found in Colonel Jacob Kingsbury, an old frontier campaigner, aged fifty-seven, who first accepts but then backs out as the result of an attack of gout – an episode that hints at the paucity of leadership material in the American military establishment. Hull is hurriedly called for and told he can keep the governorship if he will accept a commission as brigadier-general in command of the Army of the Northwest.

Finally, Hull agrees. He is to raise an army of twelve hundred volunteers from the Ohio militia (as Brock has predicted) to be augmented by some four hundred regular troops. With this force he is to cut a road through forest and swamp for two hundred miles from Urbana, Ohio, to Detroit and thus secure the frontier.

Henry Dearborn, after cautiously weighing the lifetime post of customs collector against the less secure appointment of Commander-in-Chief of the American Army, finally settles on the latter and is commissioned major-general. He, too, has a plan. If war comes, the main army will attack Montreal by the historic Champlain water route, thus cutting off all of Upper Canada from reinforcements and supplies. At the same time, three columns will strike at Canada from the border points of Detroit, Niagara, and Sackets Harbor. The attack from Detroit will take care of the Indians. The other two, from opposite ends of Lake Ontario, will serve to slice up the upper province, knocking out the major British fortresses at Niagara and Kingston. Dearborn's headquarters will be at Albany, the nerve centre from which roads veer off to the three eastern invasion points. (Detroit is so remote that Dearborn treats it as a separate command.)

On paper all of this makes sense, but it depends on inspired leadership, swift communications, careful timing, well-trained troops, an efficient war department, and a united, enthusiastic nation. None of these conditions exists.

Dearborn leaves the capital early in April for Boston, where he expects, with misplaced optimism, to raise his citizen army. Given the New England governors' violent opposition to war, it is a forlorn hope. Hull, who departs for the Ohio frontier, will have better luck.

In the capital, the war fever grows in the face of British stubbornness. On April 15, Augustus Foster attends a great dinner given by the New Orleans deputies to mark Louisiana's entry into the Union. He is in the best possible position to assess the temper of the Congress, for most of its members are present along with the cabinet. Foster finds himself sandwiched between – of all people – the two leading War Hawks. Henry Clay, on one side, is as militant as ever. The twenty-six-year-old John Calhoun, on the other, is "a man resolved," his tone cool and decided. It all seems very curious to Foster. He decides that a great many people are afraid of being laughed at if they don't fight and thus arrives, quite unconsciously, at the nub of the matter.

Far to the north, in Quebec City, the new governor general of Canada, Sir George Prevost, has no illusions about the future. He warns the British government that he shortly expects a declaration of war from Madison. Foster cannot yet see it. To him, it is merely "a curious state of things." The party grows too noisy for him, and presently he takes his leave, repairing to the Executive Mansion, there to enjoy the more peaceful company of the engaging Dolley Madison.

•

DAYTON, OHIO, April 6, 1812. Duncan McArthur, one of Wayne's old frontier scouts, now General of the Ohio militia, that "enterprising, hardy race" of which Brock has written, is haranguing his citizen soldiers.

"Fellow citizens and soldiers," cries McArthur, "the period has arrived when the country again calls its heroes to arms...!" Who, he asks, will not volunteer to fight against perfidious England – "that proud and tyrannical nation, whose injustice prior to 1776, aroused the indignation of our fathers to manly resistance?"

"Their souls could no longer endure slavery," says McArthur. "The HEAVEN protected patriots of Columbia obliged the mighty armies of the tyrant to surrender to American valor...."

He warms to his subject, sneers at Britain's "conquered and degraded troops," gibes at "the haughty spirit of that proud and unprincipled nation," calls for vengeance, justice, victory.

What is going on? Is the country in a state of war? The eager volunteers, harking to their leader's braggadocio, must surely believe that the United States and Britain are at each other's throats. Yet war has not been declared. Few Englishmen believe it likely nor does the majority of Americans. Nonetheless, the call has gone out from Washington for volunteers, and Ohio has been asked to fill its quota. For Duncan McArthur, the original war – the War of Independence – has never ended.

"Could the shades of the departed heroes of the revolution who purchased our freedom with their blood, descend from the valiant mansions of peace, would they not call aloud to arms?" he asks. "And where is that friend to his country who would not obey that call?"

Where indeed? McArthur is preaching to the converted. By May, Ohio's quota of twelve hundred volunteers will be over-subscribed. Sixteen hundred militiamen answer the call. These will form the undisciplined core of the Army of the Northwest, which Brigadier-General William Hull, Governor of Michigan, will lead to Detroit.

The new general joins his troops at Dayton, Ohio, after a journey that has left him weak from cold and fever. In spite of his reputation he is a flabby old soldier, tired of war, hesitant of command, suspicious of the militia who he knows are untrained and suspects are untrustworthy. He has asked for three thousand men; Washington finally allows him two thousand. He does not really want to be a general, but he is determined to save his people from the Indians. A Massachusetts man, he has been Governor of Michigan for seven years and now feels he knows it intimately – every trail, every settlement, every white man, woman, and child, and much of the Canadian border country. He is convinced that the Indians, goaded by the British, are particularly hostile to the Michigan settlers. He sees himself as their protector, their father-figure, and he looks like a stereotype father in a popular illustration, the features distinguished if fleshy, the shock of hair dead white. (He is only fifty-eight, but some of his men believe him closer to seventy.) He chews tobacco unceasingly, a habit that muddies the illusion, especially when he is nervous and his jaws work overtime. There is a soft streak in Hull, no asset in a frontier campaign. As a young man he studied for the ministry, only to give it up for the law, but something of the divinity student remains.

On May 25, Hull parades his troops in the company of Governor Meigs of Ohio, a capable politician with the singular Christian name "Return." The volunteers are an unruly lot, noisy, insubordinate, untrained. Hull is appalled. Their arms are unfit for use; the leather covering the cartridge boxes is rotten; many of the men have no blankets and clothing. No armourers have been provided to repair the weapons, no means have been adopted to furnish the missing clothing, no public stores of arms or supplies exist, and the powder in the magazines is useless. Since the triumph of the Revolution, America has not contemplated an offensive war, or even a defensive one.

For these men, dressed in homespun, armed when armed at all with tomahawks and hunting knives, Hull has prepared the same kind of ringing speech, with its echoes of Tippecanoe, that is being heard in the Twelfth Congress:

"On marching through a wilderness memorable for savage barbarity you will remember the causes by which that barbarity has been heretofore excited. In viewing the ground stained with the blood of your fellow citizens, it will be impossible to suppress the feelings of indignation. Passing by the ruins of a fortress erected in our territory by a foreign nation in times of profound peace, and for the express purpose of exciting the savages to hostility, and supplying them with the means of conducting a barbarous war, must remind you of that system of oppression and injustice which that nation has continually practised, and which the spirit of an indignant people can no longer endure."

Hull and his staff set off to review the troops, a fife and drum corps leading the way. The sound of the drums frightens the pony ridden by one of Hull's staff; it turns about, dashes off in the wrong direction. A second, ridden by Hull's son and aide, Abraham, follows. Soon the General finds his own mount out of control. It gallops after the others, tossing its rider about unmercifully. Encumbered by his ceremonial sword, Hull cannot control the horse; his feet slip out of the stirrups, he loses his balance, his hat flies off, and he is forced to cling to the animal's mane in a most unsoldierly fashion until it slows to a walk. At last the staff regroups, confers, decides not to pass down the ranks in review but rather to have the troops march past. It is not a propitious beginning.

The volunteers have been formed into three regiments. Jeffersonian democracy, which abhors anything resembling a caste system, decrees that they elect their own officers, an arrangement that reinforces Great Britain's contempt for America's amateur army. McArthur is voted colonel of the 1st Regiment of Ohio Volunteers, and it is remarked that he "looks more like a go-ahead soldier than any of his brother officers." A go-ahead soldier on the Ohio frontier, especially an elected one, differs markedly from a go-ahead soldier in Wellington's army. To a later English visitor, McArthur is "dirty and butcher-like, very unlike a soldier in appearance, seeming half-savage and dressed like a backwoodsman; generally considered being only fit for hard knocks and Indian warfare" (which is, of course, exactly the kind of contest that is facing him).

In the volunteer army, officers must act like politicians. More often than not they *are* politicians. McArthur has been a member of the Ohio legislature. The 2nd Regiment of Ohio Volunteers elects a former mayor of Cincinnati, James Findlay, as its colonel. The 3rd votes for Lewis Cass, a stocky, coarse-featured lawyer of flaming ambition who is U.S. marshal for the state. Almost from the outset Hull has his troubles with these three. Cass has little use for him. "Instead of having an able energetic commander, we have a weak old man," he writes to a friend. Hull, on his part, is contemptuous of the militia, whom he found unreliable during the Revolution. Imagine *electing* officers to command!

"Elected officers," he believes, "can never be calculated upon as great disciplinarians. In every station the elected will be unwilling to incur the displeasure of the electors; indeed he will often be found to court their favour by a familiarity and condescension which are totally incompatible with military discipline. The man that votes his officer his commission, instead of being implicitly obedient, as every soldier ought to be, will be disposed to question and consider the propriety of the officer's conduct before he acts...."

Another problem faces Hull. The three militia commanders are full colonels. But James Miller, who will lead the regulars, is only a half-colonel. When Miller protests the injustice of this – if anything, he should outrank the amateurs – Cass, Findlay, and McArthur threaten to quit and disband their regiments unless their rank is maintained. There is nothing that Hull or his superiors in Washington can do about this small-boy petulance. The militia colonels continue to out-rank Miller.

The army starts the march north on June 1. A few days later at the frontier community of Urbana, the last outpost of civilization, Hull's suspicions about the militia are reinforced. From this point to Detroit the troops face two hundred miles of wilderness with no pathway, not even an Indian trail to follow. The volunteers turn ugly. They had been promised an advance of fifty dollars each for a year's clothing but have received only sixteen. One unpopular officer is ridden out of camp on a rail, and when the orders come to march, scores refuse to move. Into camp, at this impasse, marches Miller's 4th Infantry Regiment of regulars. These veterans of Tippecanoe prod the wavering volunteers into action, and the troops move out, with McArthur's regiment in the lead, hacking a way through jungle and forest. The following day, three mutinous ringleaders are court-martialled and sentenced to have their heads half shaved and their hands tied and to be marched round the lines with the label "Tory" between their shoulders – a punishment the prisoners consider worse than the death-sentence.

Hull's force is as much a mob as an army. The volunteers mock the General's son Abraham, who, mounted upon a spirited horse, in full uniform and blind drunk, toppled into the Mad River in front of the entire assembly.

"Who got drunk and fell in the Mad River?" somebody calls from the ranks, to which a distant companion answers, "Captain Hull!" and a third echoes, "That's true!"

94

Hull's March to Detroit

The jests are needed, for the rain falls incessantly. The newly built road becomes a swamp; wagons are mired and have to be hoisted out by brute strength. The troops keep up their spirits on corn liquor supplied by friendly settlers.

Then, at the brand-new blockhouse on the Scioto named Fort McArthur, a bizarre episode dries up the supply of moonshine. A guard named Peter Vassar lies slumped under a tree, befuddled by drink. He hears a sudden noise, seizes his musket, makes sure it is charged, takes deliberate aim, and shoots another sentry, Joseph England, through the left breast, just missing his heart. Vassar is court-martialled and given a grotesque sentence: both ears are cropped and each cheek branded with the letter M. McArthur issues an order restraining settlers from selling liquor to his men without his written permission. The ban does not extend to his officers.

Thus dispirited, the troops plunge through the pelting rain into the no man's land of the Black Swamp, a labyrinth of deadfalls and ghostly trees behind whose trunks Tecumseh's unseen spies keep watch. A fog of insects clogs the soldiers' nostrils and bloats their faces; a gruel of mud and water rots their boots and swells their ankles. They cannot rest at day's end until they hack out a log breast-work against Indian attack. Strung out for two miles day after day, the human serpent finally wriggles to a halt, blocked by rising water and unbridgeable streams. Hull camps his men in ankle-deep mud, builds a blockhouse, names it Fort Necessity, and there, from necessity, the sodden army waits until the floods ebb. Yet Hull is not cast down. He has more than two thousand rank and file under his command and believes his force superior to any that may oppose it.

Finally the troops move on to the head of navigation on a branch of the Maumee River (also known as the Miami of the Lakes). And here a letter catches up with Hull. It is from Eustis, the Secretary of War, urging him to advance with all possible haste to Detroit, there to await further orders. The letter is dated June 18, but it must have been penned on the morning of that day because it fails to include the one piece of information that is essential to prevent a major blunder: in the afternoon of June 18, the United States has officially declared war on Great Britain.

•

IN WASHINGTON, while Hull's army trudges through the swamps of Ohio and Robert Dickson's Indians head for St. Joseph's Island, Henry Clay and his War Hawks are in full cry. In their eyes, Augustus Foster will write, long after the fact, war is "as necessary to America as a duel is to a young naval officer to prevent his being bullied and elbowed in society."

Spurred on by hawkish rhetoric, Washington has been playing a dangerous game of "I dare you" with Westminster. Most Republicans in the Twelfth Congress are opposed to war, but they do not balk at voting for increased military appropriations or an expanded militia. They are confident that Great Britain, faced with the threat of a nuisance war in North America and heavily committed to the struggle against Napoleonic France, will back down at the last moment, cancel the damaging Orders in Council, and abandon the maddening practice of impressment.

But the British do not back down, believing in their turn that the Americans are bluffing, a premise encouraged by Foster's myopia. By the time this fact sinks in, those who have gone along with the War Hawks in Congress cannot in honour vote against what John C. Calhoun calls "the second struggle for our liberty."

By midwinter, Clay and his followers had all but made up their minds that in the face of British intransigence, the only honourable course was war. Their strategy was to make retreat impossible, even for the most dovish Republicans. They will act as the catalyst that, in June, leads to declaration.

Unlike the aging veterans, pondering possible strategies for possible invasion, these are young, vigorous men between the ages of twenty-nine and thirty-six, lawyers all, with an eloquence exceeded only by verbosity. They have been raised on tales of the Revolution told by elders who have forgotten much of the horror but remember all of the glory. They are men of the old frontier, from Kentucky, Tennessee, South Carolina, and the outer edges of New Hampshire and New York – the kind of men who believe in the need to avenge any insult, imagined or real, who know what it means to fight for the land, and who are convinced that the only good Indian is a dead one.

Tippecanoe has given them new impetus. In speech after fiery speech they use every device to convince their colleagues and the country that war – or at least the threat of war – is both necessary and attractive: if Britain can be brought to her senses through an attack on Canada, America's export trade will again flourish, the depression will end, the Indians will be put forever in their place, and the troublesome Canadian border will be done away with. These are debating points. The essence of the Hawks' position is contained in the words of Felix Grundy, the young Tennessee criminal lawyer with the piercing blue eyes who cries that America must "by force redress the violated rights and honor of an injured and insulted people."

There is more than an echo here of Tecumseh and the young braves who have deserted their own elders to follow him down the path of revenge and glory. The leaders of the two war parties are not dissimilar. Both are handsome men, tall and lithe, with flashing eyes and vibrant personalities. Both dress stylishly and with purpose: Clay shows his patriotism by wearing Kentucky homespun instead of British broadcloth; Tecumseh dresses in unadorned deerskin for similar reasons. Each is courageous, quick to take offence; Clay bears the scar of a duel on his thigh, the result of an acrimonious debate in the Kentucky legislature. In an age of oratory, these two who have never met and never will meet are the most eloquent of all. One white witness who heard Tecumseh at the Springfield, Ohio, council in 1806 declares that it was not until he heard Henry Clay speak that he felt he was again in the presence of an orator of the Shawnee's rank. Each man is the acknowledged spokesman of his small group of followers, a group in each case whose influence is far out of proportion to its numbers. And both are convinced that war is the only solution to the slights and grievances which have angered and humiliated them. The British are to Clay what the Americans are to Tecumseh.

Like Tecumseh, Clay is a master of persuasion. In the fall, when the Congress met, few of its members had made up their minds. By June, the majority has become convinced that war is the only answer. John Smilie of Pennsylvania speaks for the formerly uncommitted when he declares: "If we now recede we shall be a reproach to all nations." Inch by inch Smilie has been nudged into a hawkish position, voting a little grudgingly for the various military proposals that have pushed the nation closer to war, but believing almost to the end that commercial retaliation is the answer. James Madison, too, is prepared by spring to go along with war, even though, like his predecessor Jefferson, he has struggled against the idea of involvement in a European conflict. He is a small man, benign of temperament, soft-voiced, distant in his relationships, a scholar, modest and moderate, who owns a single black suit and once lost an election for refusing to supply free whiskey to the voters. His outward composure is sometimes mistaken for weakness; the Federalists think him a pawn of Henry Clay. He is not. Though he dislikes the idea of war, he too comes to believe that his country has no other course. Apart from other considerations, submission would badly damage the Republican Party. Party politics and party unity are important considerations. He is prepared to accept the results of a vote in Congress.

Ironically, during these same weeks the British are preparing to back down. Reports from America are conflicting; Augustus Foster, who is supposed to man their listening post in the capital, continues to believe that the Americans are bluffing; but the oratory in the war congress and Sir George Prevost's warning from Quebec convinces many in Parliament that war is actually possible. Britain responds by dispatching three battalions of regulars to Canada and begins to consider the possibility of a repeal of the Orders in Council. By June, Foster too has changed his mind and reports that the Yankees mean what they say.

The British government, which has been bumbling along, holding a series of sedate hearings into the Orders in Council, now starts to move with uncharacteristic speed. Unfortunately, political affairs have been thrown into disarray by an unprecedented act, the assassination of the Prime Minister, Spencer Perceval, in the lobby of the House of Commons. It is June 16 before the formal motion to repeal the Orders is announced. The move comes too late. There is no Atlantic cable to alert the men of Washington. On June 18, the United States proclaims that a state of war exists between herself and Great Britain. When the news reaches the War Mess on New Jersey Avenue, Calhoun flings his arms about Clay's neck and the two, joined by their fellow Hawks, caper about the table in an approximation of a Shawnee war dance. But would Clay be so boisterous if he could foresee the tragedy that will be visited on his family in less than a year on the frozen banks of the River Raisin?

The news that America is at war brings a more mixed reaction across the nation. The tolling of church bells mingles with the firing of cannon and rockets; flags fly at half-mast while drums beat out the call for recruits; there are parades, cheers, hisses and boos, riots and illuminations depending on the mood of the people, which is divided on both regional and political lines. Five days later, the British motion to repeal the Orders becomes law and the chief reason for the conflict is removed.

At this point, General Hull's army of twenty-two hundred men is in sight of Detroit and within striking distance of the lightly held British fort across the river at Amherstburg. If Hull can capture the fort and disperse his enemies, the route lies open to the capital at York on Toronto Bay. The object is to seize Canada, not necessarily as a permanent prize (although that is in the minds of some) but to hold her hostage to force concessions from the British. Canada, after all, is the only portion of the empire that is open to American attack. Only later in the war, when American defeats are supplanted by American victories, will Madison and his foreign secretary, James Monroe, consider clinging to the conquered nation as part of the Union.

It is a long-held and almost universal belief that Canada is entirely vulnerable, an easy prey to American attack. The campaign, it is thought, will last a few weeks only. The freshman War Hawk, Calhoun, has already declared that "in four weeks from the time that a declaration of war is heard on our frontier the whole of Upper and a part of Lower Canada will be in our possession." Clay's words to the Senate in 1810 are recalled: "...the conquest of Canada is in our power...." Felix Grundy, Clay's fellow boarder at the War Mess, declares: "We shall drive the British from our continent," and adds, charitably, that he is "willing to receive the Canadians as adopted brethren."

The general optimism is reflected in the words of Jefferson himself, who writes to a friend at the outset of war that "upon the whole I have known no war entered into under more favourable circumstances... we...shall strip her [Great Britain] of all her possessions on this continent." The Hawk press reflects these sentiments. In the words of the Kentucky *Gazette*, "Upper and Lower Canada to the very gates of Quebec will fall into the possession of the Yankees the moment the war is started, without much bloodshed, for almost the whole of Upper Canada and a great part of the Lower Province is inhabited by Americans."

At first glance it *does* seem a mere matter of marching. The United States has ten times the military potential of Canada. Congress has authorized a regular force of thirty-five thousand men to serve for five years and undertaken a military call-up of one hundred thousand. But the country is so badly divided that by June only about four thousand regulars have been recruited, bringing the total force to ten thousand, almost half of them untrained recruits and only half available for service in the north. As for the militia, nobody can be sure how many are available or whether they can legally be forced to fight on foreign soil. Like the generals who lead them, few have experience of war.

Even at that, the American forces outnumber the British. In all of British North America there are only forty-five hundred troops, thinly distributed. In Upper Canada a mere fifteen hundred regulars are available to receive the main thrust of the American attack. But as in most wars, the events to follow will be determined not so much by the quality of the men as by the quality of the leadership. The Americans pin their hopes on Hull and Dearborn. Canada is more fortunate. She has Tecumseh, the Leaping Panther, and she also has that impulsive but consummate professional, Major-General Isaac Brock.

3

MICHILIMACKINAC
The Bloodless Victory

...unless Detroit and
Michilimackinac be both in
our possession at the
commencement of hostilities,
not only Amherstburg but
most probably the whole
country, must be evacuated
as far as Kingston.

— *Isaac Brock, February, 1812.*

THE WISCONSIN–FOX PORTAGE, ILLINOIS TERRI-
TORY, June 18, 1812.

On the very day that war is declared, Brock's courier catches up at
last with the Red-Haired Man, Robert Dickson. The courier's name
is Francis Rheaume; he and a companion have logged two thousand
miles scouring the plains and valleys seeking their man. At Fort
Dearborn (Chicago), their quest was almost aborted when the American military commander, Captain Nathan Heald, sniffing treachery,
had them arrested and searched. Heald found nothing; the two men
had hidden Brock's letters in the soles of their moccasins. So here they
are at last, after three months of travel, standing on the height of land
(and also on Brock's letters) where the water in the little streams
trickles in two directions – some toward the Gulf of Mexico, the rest
north to the Great Lakes.

Dickson reads Brock's message, scrawls an immediate reply. He
has, he writes, between two hundred and fifty and three hundred of
his "friends" available and would have more but for a hard winter
with "an unparalleled scarcity of provisions." His friends are ready to
march. He will lead them immediately to the British post at St.
Joseph's Island and expects to arrive on the thirtieth of the month.

With his report, Dickson encloses copies of speeches by three of
the chiefs who will accompany him. They leave no doubt about the
Indians' sympathies: "We live by our English Traders who have
always assisted us, and never more so, than this last year, at the risk of
their lives, and we are at all times ready to listen to them on account of
the friendship they have always shown us."

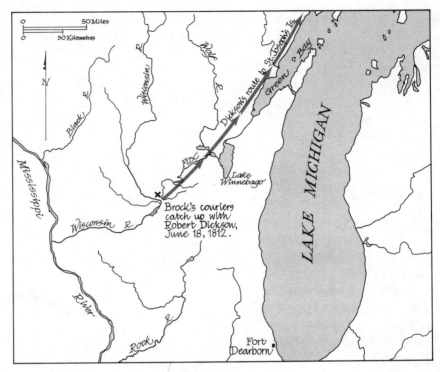

The Wisconsin-Fox Portage

The Prophet's message has also penetrated this lonely land: "We have always found our English father the protector of our women and children, but we have for some time past been amused by the songs of the bad Birds from the lower part of the River – they were not songs of truth, and this day we rejoice again in hearing the voice of our English Father, who never deceives us, and we are certain never will." So speaks Wabasha of the Sioux. The others echo his sentiments.

The Indians will follow Dickson anywhere. Here in this land of chiefs and sub-chiefs he is the real chief – their friend, their protector, and in this last harsh winter their saviour. When he arrived the previous August from St. Joseph's Island with his cargo of winter supplies, he found them starving. A disastrous drought had withered their crops and driven away the game. Dickson beggared himself to save his people, distributing all his provisions – ten thousand dollars' worth – among the tribes. He did this out of patriotism as well as humanity, for he knew that American agents were moving about the country, doing their best to influence the Indians. He assumes American hostility toward Britain, but fortunately, as he tells Brock, he is "possessed of the means of frustrating their intentions."

He is a man of commanding presence, a massive and genial six-footer with a flaming shock of red hair and a ruddy face to match. Everybody likes him, for there is an easy sociability about Dickson, a dignity, a sense of honour and principle. Men of every colour trust him. He is of a different breed from Elliott, McKee, and Girty. Highly literate, he is also humane. He has tried to teach the Indians not to kill and scalp when they can take prisoners; the greatest warriors, Dickson tells his people, are those who save their captives rather than destroy them. The infrequent explorers who cross the empty continent are attracted by Dickson. Zebulon Pike, the young army officer who has given his name to the famous peak, writes of his open, frank manner and his encyclopaedic knowledge of the country. Another, William Powell, reports that the Indians reverence and worship Dickson, who is "generous to a fault."

What is he doing out here in this lonely land? Living often in great squalor, existing for weeks on wild rice, corn, and pemmican or sometimes on nothing but melted snow, going for months without hearing his native tongue, trudging for miles on snowshoes or struggling over long portages with back-breaking loads, he is a man never at rest, like the Cut Head Yanktonais, the roving Sioux with whom he travels, knowing no real home but moving ceaselessly along his string of trading posts like a trapper tending a trapline.

His two brothers, who have also emigrated from Dumfriesshire, prefer the civilized life. One is a rising barrister and future politician at Niagara, the other a well-to-do merchant and militia colonel at Queenston. But Robert Dickson has spent twenty years in Indian country. Why? Certainly not for profit, for he has little money; the fur trade is a risky business. Nor for glory, for there is no glory. For power? He could have more in the white man's world. The answer seems to be that he is here, like so many of his countrymen, for the adventure of the frontier, the risks, the dangers, the excitement, and now, perhaps, because after two decades these are his people and this wild, untravelled country is his home. Who else but Dickson has trekked alone across that immense tract – larger than an American state – that lies west of the Mississippi between the Des Moines and the Missouri? He is a man of extraordinary energy and endurance; nowhere else, perhaps, can he feel fulfilled. In the Canadian Northwest, beyond the Great Lakes and the great bay, there are others like him, living among the Indians, exploring the land. Most are Scotsmen.

Dickson likes the Indians for themselves. He is faithful to his Indian wife, prides himself that he is educating his half-Indian children, is angered by the treatment his people receive from American frontiersmen who see the Indian as a dangerous animal to be exterminated. Added to these grievances against the Americans are the strictures enforced against British traders who still insist on flying the Union Jack over American territory. To evade the recent Non-Importation Act, by which the Americans have tried to prevent British traders from bringing goods into the United States, Dickson has been forced to become a smuggler. So incensed was he over this outrage that he knocked down the customs officer at Michilimackinac who tried to make him pay duty on his trade goods. His patriotism needs no fuelling. He is more than delighted to aid his countrymen.

He loses no time. This very day he dispatches a reply to Brock and sends it to Fort Amherstburg with thirty Menominee warriors. Then, with 130 Sioux, Winnebago, and Menominee, he sets off for St. Joseph's Island at the western entrance to Lake Huron, arriving as promised on the dot of June 30.

St. Joseph's Island, in the words of a young ensign exiled there for satirizing the lieutenant-governor, is "the military Siberia of Upper Canada." It is so remote that its garrison has trouble getting supplies and pay. Quarters are primitive. Rain, snow, and wind pour through the gaps between the blockhouse logs. The troops have shivered all winter for want of greatcoats. They turn out on parade wearing a short covering tailored from blankets intended for the Indians. These blanket coats are not named for St. Joseph's but acquire the phonetic name of the American fortress, forty miles away. As Mackinac or "Mackinaw" coats, created out of necessity, they are destined to become fashionable.

St. Joseph's unpopularity is understandable. Officers almost on arrival begin to think about requesting a transfer. For the troops, the only way out is through desertion. There have been several attempts: in April, 1805, twelve men took off in the garrison's boat; in March, 1810, two privates of the 100th Regiment attempted to escape on foot. Their pursuers found them, one half-dead of cold (he eventually lost both legs), the other a corpse. An investigation uncovered a plan for a mutiny involving a quarter of the garrison.

The fort's commander, Captain Charles Roberts, a twenty-year veteran of the British Army in India and Ceylon, has been in charge since September, 1811. He has, in effect, been pensioned off for garrison duty along with the newly formed 10th Royal Veteran Battalion, a new idea of Brock's for making use of men too old to fight. Brock has been too optimistic about the value of these veterans. In Roberts's words, they are "so debilitated and worn down by unconquerable drunkenness that neither fear of punishment, the love of fame or the honour of their Country can animate them to extraordinary exertions." There are only forty-four of them defending a crumbling blockhouse armed with four ancient and nearly useless six-pound cannon. Roberts himself is experienced, incisive, and eager for action, but he is also mortally ill with a "great debility of the stomach and the bowels."

It is the Indians, then, and the clerks and voyageurs of the North West Company who will form the spearhead of the attack on Michilimackinac. In addition to the members of Dickson's native force, already chafing for action, there are the neighbouring Ottawa and Chippewa tribesmen under John Askin, Jr., a member of the sprawling Askin family, whose patriarch, John, Sr., lives at Sandwich across the river from Detroit. Askin, whose mother is an Ottawa, is interpreter and keeper of the Indian stores at St. Joseph's. His people have blown hot and cold on the subject of war with the Americans. There was a time after the *Chesapeake* incident, when Tecumseh and the Prophet were rallying the tribes, when they were filled with ardour for the old way of life. Sixty, to Askin's astonishment, even refused a gift of rum. But now that ardour has cooled; no one can keep the Indians in a state of animation for long. That is Roberts's problem as the days move on without word from Brock. Dickson's men are becoming restless, but the attack on Mackinac cannot begin without a specific order. If there is going to be a war at all, Roberts wishes it would begin at once.

•

BALTIMORE, MARYLAND, June 18, 1812. John Jacob Astor is hurrying toward Washington, his ample rump rising and falling as he posts his horse. He has come in haste from New York to try to stop the damnfool war. No doubt he feels he has the clout to do just that, but here in Baltimore he learns that he is too late. The war is on – a war that Astor needs as much as he needs a case of smallpox.

He is not a pacifist, merely a businessman. His South West Company straddles the border, the first of the multinational corporations. He has a fortune in trade goods tied up at St. Joseph's on the Canadian side, another fortune in furs at Mackinac on the American side. What will become of these investments? It has apparently not occurred to Astor that the country might actually go to war. As late as February he wrote, in his semi-literate style: "We are happey in the hope of Peace and have not the Smalest Idia of a war with england." He is neither pro-British nor anti-British, merely pro-business, pro-profit. He has been in Canada the past winter, tendering successfully on government bills of specie to support the British army, too preoccupied to sense what is coming. Only at the last moment, as the debates in Congress grow shrill, does he become uneasy and so decides to put his personal prestige on the line and gallop out of New York to reason with the politicians. But now, with war declared, the best he can do is to try to mend his imperilled fortunes.

He determines to get the news as swiftly as possible to his Canadian partners in the South West Company. It does not occur to him that this may be seen as an act approaching treason any more than it occurs to him that his news will travel faster than the official dispatches. The South West Company is owned jointly by Astor and a group of Montreal fur "pedlars," which includes the powerful North West Company. Astor engages in a flurry of letter writing to his agents and partners. Thus the British are apprised of the war before the Americans on the frontier, including General Hull en route to Detroit and Lieutenant Hanks at Michilimackinac, realize it. Brock gets the news on June 26 and immediately dispatches a letter to Roberts at St. Joseph's Island. But a South West Company agent, Toussaint Pothier, based at Amherstburg, has already had a direct communication from Astor. Pothier alerts the garrison, leaps into a canoe, and paddles off at top speed. He beaches his canoe at St. Joseph's on July 3.

Roberts puts his men and Indians on the alert. Lewis Crawford, another South West employee, organizes 140 volunteer voyageurs. A twelve-day interval of frustration follows. Brock's message, which arrives by canoe on July 8, simply advises that the war is on and that Roberts should act accordingly. Roberts requisitions stores and ammunition from the South West Company (the very stores that concern John Jacob Astor, who will, of course, be paid for them), takes over the North West Company's gunboat *Caledonia*, impresses her crew, and sends off a message by express canoe to the North West Company's post at Fort William, asking for reinforcements.

Just as he is preparing to attack Mackinac, a second express message arrives from Brock on July 12. The impetuous general has had his enthusiasm curbed by his more cautious superior, Sir George Prevost. The Governor General is hoping against hope that the reports of war are premature, that the Americans have come to their senses, that a change of heart, a weakness in resolve, an armistice – anything – is possible. He will not prejudice the slightest chance of peace. Brock orders Roberts to hold still, wait for further orders. The perplexed captain knows he cannot hold the Indians for long – cannot, in fact, afford to. By night they chant war songs, by day they devour his dwindling stock of provisions.

Then, on July 15, to Roberts's immense relief, another dispatch arrives from Brock which, though equivocal, allows him to act. The Major-General, with an ear tuned to Sir George's cautionary instructions and an eye fastened on the deteriorating situation on the border, tells Roberts to "adopt the most prudent measures either of offense or defense which circumstances might point out." Roberts resolves to make the most of these ambiguous instructions. The following morning at ten, to the skirl of fife and the roll of drum – banners waving, Indians whooping – his polyglot army embarks upon the glassy waters of the lake.

Off sails *Caledonia* loaded with two brass cannon, her decks bright with the red tunics of the regulars. Behind her follow ten bateaux or "Mackinac boats" crammed with one hundred and eighty voyageurs, brilliant in their sashes, silk kerchiefs, and capotes. Slipping in and out of the flotilla are seventy painted birchbark canoes containing close to three hundred tribesmen – Dickson, in Indian dress, with his fifty feathered Sioux; their one-time enemies, the Chippewa, with coal-black faces, shaved heads, and bodies daubed with pipe clay; two dozen Winnebago, including the celebrated one-eyed chief, Big Canoe; forty Menominee under their head chief, Tomah; and thirty Ottawa led by Amable Chevalier, the half-white trader whom they recognize as leader.

Ahead lies Mackinac Island, shaped like an aboriginal arrowhead, almost entirely surrounded by 150-foot cliffs of soft grey limestone. The British abandoned it grudgingly following the Revolution, realizing its strategic importance, which is far more significant than that of St. Joseph's. Control of Mackinac means control of the western fur trade. No wonder Roberts has no trouble conscripting the Canadian voyageurs!

They are pulling on their oars like madmen, for they must reach their objective well before dawn. Around midnight, about fifteen miles from the island a birchbark canoe is spotted. Its passenger is an old crony from Mackinac, a Pennsylvania fur trader named Michael Dousman. He has been sent by Hanks, the American commander, to try to find out what is taking place north of the border. Dousman, in spite of the fact that he is an American militia commander, is first and foremost a fur trader, an agent of the South West Company, and an old colleague and occasional partner of the leaders of the voyageurs and Indians. He greets Dickson, Pothier, Askin, and Crawford as old friends and cheerfully tells Roberts everything he needs to know: the strength of the American garrison, its armament (or lack of it), and – most important of all – the fact that no one on the island has been told that America is at war.

Dousman's and Roberts's concerns are identical. In the event of a struggle, they want to protect the civilians on the island from the wrath of the Indians. Dousman agrees to wake the village quietly and to herd everybody into the old distillery at the end of town where they can be guarded by a detachment of regulars. He promises not to warn the garrison.

At three that morning, the British land at a small beach facing the only break in the escarpment at the north end of the island. With the help of Dousman's ox team the voyageurs manage to drag the two six-pounders over boulders and through thickets up to the 300-foot crest that overlooks the fort at the southern tip. Meanwhile, Dousman tiptoes from door to door wakening the inhabitants. He silently herds them to safety, then confronts the bewildered Lieutenant Hanks, who has no course but surrender. The first objective in Brock's carefully programmed campaign to frustrate invasion has been taken without firing a shot.

"It is a circumstance I believe without precedent," Roberts reports to Brock. For the Indians' white leaders he has special praise: their influence with the tribes is such that "as soon as they heard the Capitulation was signed they all returned to their Canoes, and not one drop either of Man's or Animal's blood was Spilt...."

Askin is convinced that Hanks's bloodless surrender has prevented an Indian massacre: "It was a fortunate circumstance that the Fort Capitulated without firing a Single Gun, for had they done so, I firmly believe not a Soul of them would have been Saved.... I never saw so determined a Set of people as the Chippawas & Ottawas were. Since

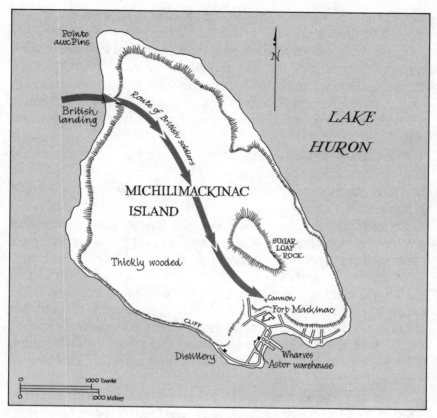

Michilimackinac Island

the Capitulation they have not drunk a single drop of Liquor, nor even killed a fowl belonging to any person (a thing never known before) for they generally destroy every thing they meet with."

Dickson's Indians feel cheated out of a fight and complain to the Red-Haired Man, who keeps them firmly under control, explaining that the Americans cannot be killed once they have surrendered. To mollify them, he turns loose a number of cattle, which the Sacs and Foxes chase about the island until the bellowing animals, their flanks bristling with arrows, hurl themselves into the water.

They are further mollified by a distribution of blankets, provisions, and guns taken from the American commissariat, which also contains tons of pork and flour, a vast quantity of vinegar, soap, candles, and – to the delight of everybody – 357 gallons of high wines and 253 gallons of whiskey, enough to get every man, white and red, so drunk that had an enemy force appeared on the lake, it might easily have recaptured the island.

These spoils are augmented by a trove of government-owned furs, bringing the total value of captured goods to £10,000, all of it to be distributed, according to custom, among the regulars and volunteers who captured the fort. Every private soldier will eventually receive ten pounds sterling as his share of the prize money, officers considerably more.

The message to the Indians is clear: America is a weak nation and there are rewards to be gained in fighting for the British. The fall of Mackinac gives the British the entire control of the tribes of the Old Northwest.

Porter Hanks and his men are sent off to Detroit under parole: they give their word not to take any further part in the war until they are exchanged for British or Canadian soldiers of equivalent rank captured by the Americans – a device used throughout the conflict to obviate the need for large camps of prisoners fed and clothed at the enemy's expense. The Americans who remain on the island are obliged to take an oath of allegiance to the Crown; otherwise they must return to American territory. Most find it easy to switch sides. They have done it before; a good many were originally British until the island changed hands in 1796.

Curiously, one man is allowed to remain without taking the oath. This is Michael Dousman, Hanks's spy and Roberts's prisoner. Dousman is given surprising leeway for an enemy, being permitted to make business trips to Montreal on the promise that he will not travel through U.S. territory. He is required to post a bond for this purpose but has no trouble raising the money from two prominent Montreal merchants.

Dousman's business in Montreal is almost certainly John Jacob Astor's business. All of Astor's furs are now in enemy territory. But the South West Company is still a multinational enterprise, and Astor has friends in high positions in both countries. Through his Montreal partners he manages to get a passport into Canada. In July he is in Montreal making arrangements for his furs to be forwarded from Mackinac Island (which has not yet fallen). These furs are protected in the articles of capitulation; over the next several months, bales of them arrive in Montreal from Mackinac. Astor's political friends in Washington have alerted the customs inspectors at the border points to pass the furs through, war or no war. Over the next year and a half, the bullet-headed fur magnate manages to get his agents into Canada and to bring shipment after shipment of furs out to the New York market. A single consignment is worth $50,000, and there are many such consignments. For John Jacob Astor and the South West Company, the border has little meaning, and the war is not much more than a nuisance.

4

DETROIT
The Disintegration of William Hull

Those Yankee hearts began to ache,
Their blood it did run cold,
To see us marching forward
So courageous and so bold.
Their general sent a flag to us,
For quarter he did call,
Saying, "Stay your hand, brave British boys,
I fear you'll slay us all."

— From "Come All Ye Bold Canadians,"
a campfire ballad of the War of 1812.

ABOARD THE SCHOONER *Cuyahoga Packet*, entering Lake Erie, July 2, 1812. William K. Beall, assistant quartermaster general in William Hull's Army of the Northwest, stretches out on deck, admiring the view, ignorant of the fact that his country has been at war for a fortnight and the vessel will shortly be entering enemy waters.

Beall counts himself lucky. He reclines at his ease while the rest of Hull's tattered army trudges doggedly toward Detroit, spurred on by Eustis's order to move "with all possible speed." Thanks to the *Cuyahoga*'s fortuitous presence at the foot of the Maumee rapids, Hull has been able to relieve his exhausted teams. The schooner is loaded with excess military stores – uniforms, band instruments, entrenching tools, personal luggage – and some thirty sick officers and men, together with three women who have somehow managed to keep up with their husbands on the long trek north.

It is a foolhardy undertaking. War is clearly imminent, even though Eustis, the bumbling secretary, gave no hint of it in his instructions to the General. Hull's own officers have pointed out that the *Cuyahoga* must pass under the British guns at Fort Amherstburg, guarding the narrow river boundary, before she can reach Detroit; but their commander, sublimely unaware of his country's declaration, remains confident that she will get there before the army.

The schooner rolls in Erie's swell. The passengers grow queasy, but not William K. Beall. He is enchanted by the vastness of the lake, has never seen anything like it before. He is a prosperous Kentucky plantation owner whose estate on the Ohio River, not far from

Newport, is thirty-six miles square. But this lake! It is hard to conceive of so much fresh water, stretching on beyond the horizon. The only water he has seen since leaving home has flowed sluggishly in the saffron streams veining the dreadful swamps through which the army has just toiled. Beall puts all that out of his mind, basks in the novelty of the heaving deck, opens an appropriate book of poetry – Scott's *Lady of the Lake* – commits three verses to memory, then catnaps as the *Cuyahoga* sails toward the mouth of the Detroit River.

He wakes as the schooner approaches the village of Amherstburg, nestled outside the British fort (which the Americans call Fort Malden). Again he is charmed by what he sees. The little town seems indifferently built, but the countryside is quite lovely – green meadows and sunny wheat fields rippling in the breeze. This southern fringe of orchards is the garden of Upper Canada, but most of the province beyond remains a wilderness, its great forests of pine and oak, maple and basswood broken here and there by small patches of pioneer civilization, like worn spots on a rug. Vast swamps, dark and terrifying, smother the land. Roads are few and in some seasons impassable, being little more than rivers of rutted mud. Sensible travellers move by water, and it is along the margins of the lakes and the banks of the larger rivers that the main communities such as Amherstburg have sprung up. Between these villages lie smaller settlements. Plots of winter wheat, oats, and rye, fields of corn and root vegetables blur the edges of the forest. Here, along the Detroit River, the fruit trees have been bearing for a decade, and cider has become a staple drink. Beall notes that everything appears to wear "the cheering smiles of peace and plenty."

In the distance an Indian canoe contributes to the picturesqueness of the scene. But as the canoe comes closer it is transformed into a Canadian longboat commanded by an officer of the Provincial Marine, Lieutenant Frederic Rolette, with six seamen, armed with cutlasses and pistols, pulling on the oars.

Rolette calls to the *Cuyahoga*'s captain, Luther Chapin, to lower his mainsails. Chapin is open mouthed. He had expected a friendly hail; now he sees six muskets raised against him. Before he can act, Rolette fires his pistol in the air. Chapin struggles with the sail. Beall and his fellow passengers are in confusion. What is happening? Beall orders the captain to hoist the sail again and press on, but Chapin replies that this is not possible.

Rolette now points his pistol directly at young George Gooding, a second-lieutenant in charge of the soldiers and baggage of the U.S. 4th Infantry Regiment. "Dowse your mainsails!" Rolette orders.

Gooding equivocates. "I have no command here, sir," he shouts. Rolette fires directly at the schooner, the ball whistling past Beall's head. The captain pleads for instructions. "Do as you please," answers the rattled Gooding, whose wife is also on deck. As the mainsails tumble, Frederic Rolette boards the packet.

He is astonished to find the decks jammed with American soldiers. They are not aware that the war has started, but Rolette cannot be sure of that. Nor does he know that all but three are ill and that the muskets and ammunition are out of reach in the hold. All he knows is that he is outnumbered five to one.

This does not dismay him, for he is a seasoned seaman, accustomed to act with boldness and decision. At the age of twenty-nine, this French-speaking Quebecker has a naval record any officer might envy. He has fought in the two greatest sea battles of the era – the Nile and Trafalgar – under the finest commander of his time, Horatio Nelson. He has been wounded five times and, before this newest contest is over, will be wounded again. Now, as William Beall approaches to demand his authority for boarding the schooner, Rolette informs him curtly that an express reached Amherstburg the previous night announcing the commencement of hostilities. Then, losing no time, he orders everybody below decks, posts sentries at the hatches and arms chests with orders to shoot any man who approaches them, orders the helmsman to steer the ship under the water battery at Amherstburg and the band to play "God Save the King."

As the schooner docks at the naval yard, the passengers are released under guard to the open deck and all the baggage is removed. Now the British realize the magnitude of their prize. For here are discovered two trunks belonging to General Hull containing documents of extraordinary value. Hull's aide-de-camp – his son Abraham – has foolishly packed the General's personal papers with his baggage. The astonished British discover that they now possess all the details of the army that opposes them: field states, complete returns of the troops, the names and strengths of the regiments, an incomplete draft of Hull's own memorial of March 6 outlining his strategy, and all his correspondence to and from the Secretary of War. It is a find equal to the breaking of an enemy code. The entire package is dispatched to

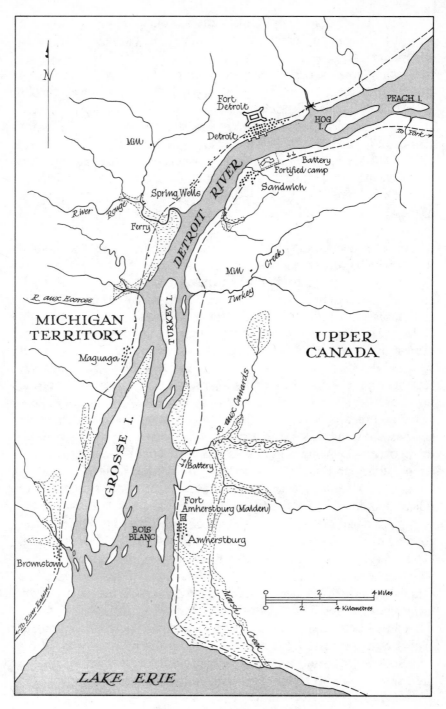

The Detroit Frontier

Brock at York, who immediately grasps its significance and lays his plans.

No one on either side, meanwhile, is quite certain how to behave. Has war actually come? Even the British are reluctant to believe it. William Beall, now a prisoner, doubts it. He is certain that his captors have been wrongly informed, that when Hull demands his return he and his companions will be permitted to go on to Detroit.

The British are polite, even hospitable. Lieutenant Edward Dewar, Beall's opposite number in the quartermaster's department at Fort Amherstburg, urges the Americans not to consider themselves prisoners but merely detainees. It is all very unpleasant, Dewar murmurs; he hopes the report of the war may prove incorrect; he hopes the Americans will be able to spend their time in detention as agreeably as possible; if there is any service he and his fellow officers can render to that end, they will be only too pleased to do so; he only wishes the packet could have passed by without interruption; if authentic information arrives that war has not been declared, they will be released at once. And so on.

George Gooding declares he would like to dine ashore and put up at an inn. Dewar gets permission from his commanding officer, Lieutenant-Colonel Thomas Bligh St. George, but points out the C.O.'s fear that the Indians are much enraged at the Americans and advises them to be on guard against attack. The detainees agree to accept billets aboard another ship, *Thames*, where a guard can be stationed. Meanwhile they must be very careful. At this stage of the war, the British are worried at the horrors their native allies may commit on their new enemies. Dewar tells Beall that he fears that the Indians, in a drunken rage, might enter a tavern and murder all the Americans. To underline the danger he tells how an infuriated Indian had recently stepped up behind a man walking with a British officer and tomahawked him. Don't go out into the streets alone, Dewar warns.

Now, having accepted the parole of Beall and his companions that they will not try to escape, Dewar invites them to his home until their accommodation is prepared. On the wharf, a crowd of Indians look them over. In Beall's eyes some appear to rejoice at their capture, while others terrify him with ferocious frowns. Gooding, who fought at Tippecanoe, recognizes some of his former adversaries. Harrison's bitter seed, broadcast on the banks of the Wabash, is already beginning to sprout.

At Dewar's home there is wine, cider, biscuits. It would be improper, says the Lieutenant, to invite the Americans to dine with him, but he accompanies them to Boyle's Inn and Public House, apologizing in his diffident British fashion for its poor quality but explaining that it is the best in town. Following dinner, the men leave the inn and, accompanied by a British officer, stroll through the streets through crowds of Indians who the nervous Beall feels are glaring directly at him. Every white man, however, bows politely to the strangers and one even invites them into his house and pours them several glasses of wine.

Many of these are Americans, lured to Upper Canada by the prospect of free land and low taxes. They have little interest in politics, less in war. In a province of some sixty thousand, they form a clear but powerless majority, having been shut out of all public office by the elite group of British and Loyalist administrators who control the government. This does not unduly concern them, for they are prospering on their free acreage. Democracy may be virtually non-existent in Upper Canada, but so are taxes, since the province is financed by the British treasury. Beall is intrigued to discover that the master of his floating prison, Captain Martin of the *Thames*, owns a well-stocked farm of three hundred acres but pays an annual levy of exactly $1.06¼.

As for the prospect of war, they dismiss it. During their walk through the village, Lieutenant Dewar remarks to Beall that he will be sorry if the two countries cannot adjust their difficulties without violence. Everyone to whom the American speaks echoes that sentiment.

The women, being non-combatants, are sent to the American side; the men remain aboard the *Thames*. Beall estimates that there are at least five hundred Indians in town. On July 4, as the sounds of Independence Day cannonades echo across the water from Detroit, two hundred Sauk warriors arrive, the largest and best-formed men Beall has ever seen, though in his eyes they are as savage and uncultivated as any other natives.

On the following day, the sound of Hull's bugler blowing reveille reveals that the Army of the Northwest has reached the village of Brownstown, directly across the river, less than a day's march from Detroit. By nightfall, Amherstburg is in a panic. Women and children run crying toward the vessels at the dockside, loading the decks with trunks of valuables. Indians dash about the streets shouting. Consternation and dismay prevail as the call to arms is sounded. The enemy, in short, is within striking distance of the thinly guarded fort, the sole British bastion on the Detroit frontier. If Hull can seize it in one lightning move, his army can sweep up the valley of the Thames and capture most if not all of Upper Canada.

Beall views it all with mixed feelings. A sensitive and compassionate man who is already starting to pine for his wife Melinda, back in Kentucky, he feels "sensibly for those on both sides who might loose [sic] their lives." Certainly his British hosts have been decent to the point of chivalry; it is difficult to think of them as the enemy. (Could Beall actually shoot at Dewar if he met him on the field?) On the other hand, he is convinced that his day of deliverance is at hand. Surely General Hull will cross the river, crush all resistance at Amherstburg, free him for further service, and, if the campaign is as decisive as everyone expects, return him swiftly to Melinda's arms!

•

THE CRUCIAL DISPATCH to General Hull, announcing the war, is hidden somewhere in the Cleveland mail. Frustration! Walworth, the postmaster, has written orders to forward it at once by express. But where is it? He can guess what it contains, for the news has already reached Cleveland. A young lawyer, Charles Shaler, stands ready to gallop through swamp and forest to the Rapids of the Maumee and on to Detroit, if need be, once the missing document is found. Nobody, apparently, thinks to send him off at once with a verbal message while others rummage for the official one. Hours pass. Shaler chafes. Then somebody suggests the dispatch might be in the Detroit mail. Reluctantly, the postmaster breaks the law, opens the bags, finds the missing paper.

Off goes Shaler, swimming the unbridged rivers, plunging through the wilderness, vainly seeking a relay steed to replace his gasping horse. Some eighty hours later, on the evening of July 1 (the *Cuyahoga* has already been dispatched) he reaches the rapids, discovers the army has decamped, gallops after it. He reached Hull's force at two the following morning. The General, half-dressed, reads the dispatch, registers alarm, orders Shaler to keep quiet in the presence of others, calls a council of his officers, orders a boat to take after the *Cuyahoga*. It is too late; she cannot be caught. At dawn the army moves on, Shaler riding with the troops. On reaching Detroit, his much-abused horse drops dead of exhaustion.

The army arrives on July 5, after thirty-five days of struggle through Ohio's swampy wilderness. The soldiers find a primitive settlement of twelve hundred straggling on the outskirts of a log fort. Like their neighbours on both sides of the river, most of the people are French speaking, descendants of families that settled the land a century before and whose strip farms with their narrow river frontage betray their Québécois background. In Hull's view they are "miserable farmers," being descended from voyageurs, traders, soldiers, and artisans – people with no agricultural tradition. They raise apples for cider and gigantic pears for pickling but pay little attention to other forms of agriculture, depending principally on hunting, fishing, and trading with the Indians. In short, they cannot provision his troops – and this is Hull's dilemma: his supply line is two hundred miles long, stretching south along the makeshift trace his men have hacked out of the forests. To secure his position, Hull must have two months' provisions. In Chillicothe, the capital, Ohio's energetic governor, Return Meigs, receives the General's plea, raises a company of ninety-five citizen volunteers, and sends them north through Urbana as escort for a brigade of pack horses, loaded with flour and provisions, and a drove of beef cattle. But to reach Hull, this supply train must eventually follow the road that hugs the southwestern shore of Lake Erie and the Detroit River. That will be dangerous because the British control the water.

Hull's more immediate concern is the fate of the baggage captured aboard the *Cuyahoga*. Have the British actually rifled his personal possessions, discovered his official correspondence? He pens a note to Lieutenant-Colonel St. George, the commander at Fort Amherstburg. Dripping with politeness and studiedly casual, it reads more like an interoffice memorandum than a communication between enemies:

Sir,
    Since the arrival of my army at this Encampment...I have been informed that a number of discharges of Artillery and of small arms have been made by some of the Militia of the Territory, from this Shore into Sandwich.
    I regret to have received such information, the proceeding was [un]authorized by me. I am not disposed to make War on Private Property, or to authorise a wanton attack upon unoffending individuals, I would be happy to learn whether you consider private Property a proper objective of seizure and detention, I allude to the Baggage of Officers particularly....

St. George, in his reply to Hull, outdoes the General in verbal niceties:

Sir,
    I am honoured with your letter of this days date; I perfectly coincide with you in opinion respecting private property, and any wanton attack upon unoffending individuals, and am happy to find, what I was certain would be the case, that the aggression in question was unauthorized by you.
    In respect to the property of officers not on board a vessel at the time of capture I must be judged by the customs of war in like cases, in justice to the captors, and shall always be ready to meet your wishes...when I receive orders...from my government....

Which, translated, simply means: go to hell.

The bearer of Hull's letter, under a flag of truce, is Colonel Cass, whose instructions are to spy out the situation at the British fort. Cass takes a good look, reports that rumour has exaggerated the garrison's strength and also the number of Indians. He believes, and will continue to believe, that Fort Amherstburg can be easily taken.

In spite of the suavity of his correspondence, Thomas Bligh St. George is a badly rattled commander. He is an old campaigner, with forty years of service in the British Army, much of it spent in active warfare on the Mediterranean. But he has been a staff officer for the past decade and clearly has difficulty coping with the present crisis. He commands a lightly garrisoned fort, in need of repair and reinforcement. Across the river an army of two thousand sits poised for invasion. Scrambling about in a fever of preparation he is "so harassed for these five days and nights, I can scarcely write." Brock, who receives this communication, is dismayed to discover that Lieutenant-Colonel St. George has let three days slip by before bothering to inform him that Hull's force has reached Detroit.

Fort Amherstburg is in chaos. Indians are coming and going, eating up the supplies; no one can guess their strength from day to day. The same is true of the militia: St. George has no real idea of how many men he commands or whether he has the resources to supply them. The accounts are in disarray, the returns non-existent. He has not enough officers to organize the militia – many of whom are leaving for home or attempting to leave – or enough arms to supply them. Nor does he know how he can pay them.

The little village of Sandwich lies directly across the river from

Detroit, upriver from Amherstburg. This, St. George knows, will be Hull's invasion point. He stations some militia units at Sandwich but has little hope that they will be effective. To "encourage" them, in St. George's euphemism, he sends along a detachment of regulars. To supply the wants of his confused and amateur army, St. George is obliged to make use of everything that falls in his way. This includes a brigade of eleven bateaux loaded with supplies that the North West Company has dispatched from Montreal to its post at Fort William at the lakehead. St. George seizes the supplies, impresses the seventy voyageurs.

On the docks and in the streets the Indians are engaged in war dances, leaping and capering before the doors of the inhabitants, who give them presents of whiskey. "I have seen the great Tecumseh," William Beall, still captive aboard the *Thames*, writes in his diary. "He is a very plane man, rather above middle-size, stout built, a noble set of features and an admirable eye. He is always accompanied by Six great chiefs, who never go before him. The women and men all fear that in the event of Genl. Hull's crossing and proving successfull, that the Indians being naturally treacherous will turn against them to murder and destroy them."

Tecumseh's followers have shadowed Hull's army all the way through Michigan Territory, warned by their leader to take no overt action until war is declared and he can bring his federation into alliance with Great Britain. Hull has done his best to neutralize him, sending messengers to a council at Fort Wayne, promising protection and friendship if the Indians stay out of the white man's war.

"Neutral indeed!" cries Tecumseh to the assembled tribes. "Who will protect you while the Long Knives are fighting the British and are away from you? Who will protect you from the attack of your ancient enemies, the western tribes, who may become allies of the British?"

Will a policy of neutrality lead to a restoration of the Indian lands, Tecumseh asks, and as he speaks, takes the emissary's peace pipe and breaks it between his fingers. And later:

"Here is a chance presented to us – yes, a chance such as will never occur again – for us Indians of North America to form ourselves into one great combination and cast our lot with the British in this war. . . ."

Tecumseh leaves Fort Wayne with a large party of Shawnee, Kickapoo, Potawatomi, and Delaware to meet Matthew Elliott at Amherstburg. Hull sends another emissary, urges another council at Brownstown, the Wyandot village directly opposite the British fort. Tecumseh refuses:

"I have taken sides with the King, my father, and I will suffer my bones to bleach upon this shore before I will recross that stream to join in any council of neutrality."

Like the Americans, the Wyandot are split into camps of hawks and doves. They are important to Tecumseh's cause because they are the senior tribe, looked up to by all the others. They are Huron, the remnants of the mighty nation destroyed during the French regime. At a great council held on the parade ground at Fort Amherstburg on July 7, one chief, Roundhead, supports Tecumseh. Another, Walk-in-the-Water, advocates neutrality and crosses back into U.S. territory. But Tecumseh has no intention of letting the Wyandot straddle the fence.

Upriver at Detroit, Hull prepares to invade Canada by landing his army at Sandwich. He attempts to move on July 10 but, to his dismay, discovers that hundreds of militiamen, urged on in some cases by their officers, decline to cross the river. They have not committed themselves to fight on foreign soil.

The next day Hull tries again. Two militia companies refuse to enter the boats. One finally gives in to persuasion; the other stands firm. When Hull demands a list of those who refuse to go, the company commander, a Captain Rupes, hands over the names of his entire command. Hull's adjutant harangues the men. Words like "coward" and "traitor" are thrown at them to no avail. Again the crossing is aborted.

The war has yet to develop beyond the comic opera stage. Across the river at Sandwich an equally reluctant body of citizen soldiers – the militia of Kent and Essex counties, only recently called to service – sits and waits. These young farmers have had little if any training, militia service being mainly an excuse for social carousing. They are not eager to fight, especially in midsummer with the winter wheat ripening in the fields. Patriotism has no meaning for most of them; that is the exclusive property of the Loyalists. The majority are passively pro-American, having moved up from New Jersey, New York, and Pennsylvania. Isolated on the scattered farms and absorbed in the wearisome if profitable task of clearing the land and working the soil, they have as yet no sense of a larger community. Few have ever seen a newspaper; they learn of the war tardily, through handbills. Whether or not Upper Canada becomes another American state they do not really care.

Lieutenant-Colonel St. George, who is convinced that these unwilling soldiers – most are not even uniformed – will flee to their homes at the first shot, decides to get them out of the way before the attack is launched. Otherwise, their certain rout would throw his entire force into a state of confusion. The only way he can prevent them from melting away to their farms is to march the lot back to the fort and make the most of them; perhaps their backs can be stiffened by the example of the regulars. Even that is doubtful: from his vantage point in the town of Amherstburg William Beall discovers that many of these former Americans express a desire to join Hull as soon as he crosses into Canada.

At last, on July 12, a bright and lovely Sunday, Hull resolves to make the crossing, even though two hundred of his men continue to stand on their constitutional rights. He fears further mutinies if he keeps his troops inactive, and it is also his fancy that the Canadian settlers will feel themselves liberated from the British yoke once he lands and that they and the Indians will stay out of the war.

Hull's landing is unopposed. Colonel Cass is the first to leap from the lead boat, and thus the first American to set foot on Canadian soil. He immediately unfurls the Stars and Stripes while Hull's staff searches about for a headquarters.

Sandwich is a placid little garden village, almost every house set in a small orchard where peaches, grapes, and apples flourish. The conquering general seizes the most imposing residence – a new brick home, built in the Georgian style the year before, its interior still unfinished, belonging to Lieutenant-Colonel François Bâby, a member of a distinguished pioneer fur-trading family. The Bâbys and the Hulls have been on intimate terms, but when James Bâby, a brother and also a militia colonel, protests (his own home not far away is quickly pillaged), all Hull can say is that *circumstances are changed now*, a phrase which Lieutenant-Colonel Bâby will throw back at him a month later.

Hull has scarcely landed when he insists on issuing a proclamation intended to disperse the militia and cow the inhabitants, many of whom are either terrified of his troops or secretly disposed to his cause. Most have fled, but those who remain welcome the invaders as friends, waving white handkerchiefs and flags from the windows and crying out such phrases as "We like the Americans." At Amherstburg, Beall encounters similar sentiments and confides to his journal that many solicit secret interviews with him, and when these are refused "occasionally and slily say 'Success to the Americans and General Hull', 'Let us alone and we will take Malden [Amherstburg] ourselves', et cetera, and many expressions showing their warmth for us and the Americans and their detestation of the British."

Yet Hull cannot resist issuing a bombastic proclamation that seems designed to set the Canadians on edge. He has it printed, rather imperfectly, in Detroit, borrowing the press of a Roman Catholic priest. It is soon the talk of the countryside:

A PROCLAMATION

INHABITANTS OF CANADA! After thirty years of Peace and prosperity, the United States have been driven to Arms. The injuries and aggressions, the insults and indignities of Great Britain have *once more* left them no alternative but manly resistance or unconditional submission. The army under my Command has invaded your Country and the standard of the United States waves on the territory of Canada. To the peaceful, unoffending inhabitant, It brings neither danger nor difficulty I come to *find* enemies not to *make* them, I come to *protect* you not to *injure* you.

Separated by an immense ocean and an extensive Wilderness from Great Britain you have no participation in her counsels no interest in her conduct. You have felt her Tyranny, you have seen her injustice, but I do not ask *you* to avenge the one or to redress the other. The United States are sufficiently powerful to afford you every security consistent with their rights & your expectations. I tender you the invaluable blessings of Civil, Political, & Religious Liberty, and their necessary result, individual, and general, prosperity: That liberty which gave decision to our counsels and energy to our conduct in our struggle for INDEPENDENCE and which conducted us safely and triumphantly thro' the stormy period of the Revolution....

In the name of my *Country* and by the authority of my Government I promise you protection to your *persons, property, and rights*, Remain at your homes, Pursue your peaceful and customary avocations. Raise not your hands against your brethren, many of your fathers fought for the freedom & *Indepennce* we now enjoy Being children therefore of the same family with us, and heirs to the same Heritage, the arrival of an army of Friends must be hailed by you with a cordial welcome, You will be emancipated from Tyranny and oppression and restored to the dignified status of freemen.... If contrary to your own interest & the just expectation of my country, you should take part in the approaching contest, you will be considered and treated as enemies and the horrors, and calamities of war will Stalk before you.

If the barbarous and Savage policy of Great Britain be pursued, and the savages are let loose to murder our Citizens and butcher our women and children, this war, will be a war of extermination.

The first stroke with the Tomahawk the first attempt with the Scalping Knife will be the Signal for one indiscriminate scene of desolation, *No white man found fighting by the Side of an Indian will be taken prisoner* Instant destruction will be his Lot....

I doubt not your courage and firmness; I will not doubt your attachment to Liberty. If you tender your services voluntarily they will be accepted readily.

The United State offers you *Peace*, *Liberty*, and *Security* your choice lies between these, & *War, Slavery, and destruction*, Choose then, but choose wisely; and may he who knows the justice of our cause, and who holds in his hand the fate of Nations, guide you to a result the most compatible, with your rights and interests, your peace and prosperity.

WM. HULL

The General, who is afraid of the Indians, hopes that this document will force his opposite number at Fort Amherstburg to follow the lead of the United States and adopt a policy of native neutrality, at least temporarily. At the very minimum it ought to frighten the settlers and militia into refusing to bear arms. That is its immediate effect. In Brock's phrase, "the disaffected became more audacious, and the wavering more intimidated." The proclamation terrifies the militia. Within three days the force of newly recruited soldiers has been reduced by half as the farm boys desert to their homes.

Yet Hull has overstated his case. These are farmers he is addressing, not revolutionaries. The colonial authoritarianism touches very few. They do not feel like slaves; they already have enough peace, liberty, and security to satisfy them. This tax-free province is not America at the time of the Boston Tea Party. Why is Hull asking them to free themselves from tyranny? In the words of one, if they had been under real tyranny, "they could at any time have crossed the line to the United States."

Hull has made another error. He threatens that anyone found fighting beside the Indians can expect no quarter. That rankles. *Everybody* will be fighting with the Indians; it will not be a matter of choice. Some of the militiamen who secretly hoped to go over to Hull in the confusion of battle have a change of heart. What is the point of deserting if the Americans intend to kill them on capture?

Precipitate action does not fit the Upper Canadian mood. This is a pioneer society, not a frontier society. No Daniel Boones stalk the Canadian forests, ready to knock off an Injun with a Kentucky rifle or do battle over an imagined slight. The Methodist circuit riders keep the people law abiding and temperate; prosperity keeps them content. The Sabbath is looked on with reverence; card playing and horse racing are considered sinful diversions; the demon rum has yet to become a problem. There is little theft, less violence. Simple pastimes tied to the land – barn raisings, corn huskings, threshing bees – serve as an outlet for the spirited. The new settlers will not volunteer to fight. But most are prepared, if forced, to bear arms for their new country and to march when ordered. In the years that follow some will even come to believe that they were the real saviours of Upper Canada.

•

MONTREAL, LOWER CANADA, July 4, 1812. Sir George Prevost has moved up from his capital at Quebec to be closer to the scene of action. An American army is gathering at Albany, New York, poised to attack Montreal by the traditional invasion route of the Lake Champlain water corridor. If it succeeds, Sir George is perfectly prepared to abandon all of Upper Canada and withdraw to the fortress of Quebec.

At this moment, however, the Captain-General, Governor-in-Chief, Vice-Admiral, Lieutenant-General and Commanding Officer of His Majesty's Forces in Upper Canada, Lower Canada, Nova Scotia, New Brunswick, Cape Breton, Newfoundland and the Bermudas is faced with a crisis on his own doorstep. A riot has broken out at Lachine over the Militia Law, which provides for the drafting of two thousand bachelors for three months' training. Some of the men from the parish at Pointe Claire have refused to go, believing – or pretending to believe – that the act has not been properly passed and the government is simply seizing an excuse to turn young French Canadians into soldiers.

When the army tries force, a mob resists and marches off to Lachine to seize a flotilla of boats in which the draftees hope to escape. The Riot Act is read; shots whistle over the insurgents' heads and are returned; two civilians are killed. Four hundred and fifty soldiers invade the community and begin taking prisoners – so many, indeed, that they are finally released on the promise that they will "implore the pardon of His Excellency the Governor."

His Excellency is a suave diplomat whose forte is conciliation. He has learned that delicate art as governor of St. Lucia and later of Dominica, French-speaking islands in the Caribbean wrested from the mother country by the British but soothed into passivity by a man who has none of the hauteur of a British colonial bureaucrat. Born of a Swiss father and perfectly at home in the French language, Prevost has the exact qualifications needed to win over a race who also consider themselves a conquered people.

Now, before some three hundred insurgents, the Great Conciliator appears and turns on his considerable charm.

"His Excellency expostulated with them as a Father and pointed out to them the danger of their situation in a style truly honourable to his own feelings, assuring them of his forgiveness on delivering up those who had been promoters of the insurrection...which they cheerfully agreed to do...."

Thus with the crisis defused and the approving comment of the Montreal *Herald* putting the seal on his actions, the Governor General can turn to graver matters. He is resolved to fight a defensive war only; he does not have the resources to go on the attack, even if he wished to. But he does not wish to. His own natural caution has been sustained by specific instructions from Lord Liverpool, the Secretary of State for War and the Colonies, to do nothing rash.

Rashness is not Sir George's style. He finds it difficult to countenance it in others. Surely the United States will do nothing rash! He is half convinced that the Americans do not actually mean to fight; that some accommodation can be made with them; that the war is not a real war; and that, in any event, it cannot possibly last for more than a few weeks. "Prudent" is a word that slips comfortably into his correspondence. He considers it "prudent and politic to avoid any measure which can in its effect have a tendency to unite the people in the American States," for "whilst disunion prevails among them, their attempts on these provinces will be feeble." Therefore it is important not to anger the enemy. Brock, specifically, is enjoined from "committing any act which may even by construction tend to unite the Eastern and Southern states."

Brock, with his reputation for dash and daring, worries Prevost. The impetuous subordinate is more than a week away by express courier and a month away by post. His audacity is legendary. Prevost has certainly heard the stories. One goes all the way back to Brock's early days, when his regiment, the 49th, was stationed at Bridgetown in Barbados. There was in that company a confirmed braggart and duellist whose practice was to insult fellow officers and finish them off at twelve paces. Brock, when accosted, accepted the challenge but refused to fire at the regulation distance. Instead, he produced a handkerchief and demanded that both men fire across it at point-blank range, thus equalling the odds and making the death of at least one of them a virtual certainty. His adversary panicked, refused to fire, and thus shamed was forced to leave the regiment.

There are other tales: Brock in the saddle, insisting on riding to the very pinnacle of Mount Hillaby, twelve hundred feet above the Caribbean – a feat most horsemen consider impossible; or, in 1803, personally leading an eight-hour chase in an open boat across Lake Ontario to apprehend six deserters, a venture that brought him a reprimand.

To a prudent commander, Brock's presence can be disquieting, even alarming. He is known as a man who believes that "nothing should be impossible to a soldier; the word impossible should not be found in a soldier's dictionary!" Will Brock attempt the impossible in Upper Canada? Prevost is determined that he shall not.

The contrast between the two commanders can be seen in their official portraits. At forty-four, Prevost is a handsome man, his lean face framed by dark sideburns; yet even in his painted likeness there is a furtiveness. The eyes swivel back as if to watch the artist; little furrows crease the brow. There is a slackness of mouth, a hesitancy of stance, none of the knife-edge sharpness that distinguishes the features of his subordinate who, in his portraits, looks off resolutely and serenely into the middle distance.

If Prevost is more diplomat than soldier, Brock is more soldier than diplomat. He remains disdainful of civilians, though he has learned to curb in public the tactlessness that once marked his dealings with the administration in Quebec. Prevost on the other hand has, in less than a year, worked a miracle in Lower Canada by managing to conciliate the French Canadians whose loyalty to the Crown had been placed in jeopardy by the racial arrogance of his predecessor. Under Sir James Craig, the Québécois found themselves shut out of all important government posts.

In contrast to Craig, who believed the French Canadians disloyal, Prevost is convinced they will fight to retain their land. The bombast in Washington prophesying the easy conquest of the Canadas will, he believes, help swell the ranks of the militia. Nonetheless, diplomacy will be needed: "The Canadians in general are grossly ignorant, it will therefore require vigilance and circumspection to prevent the proposed changes from being attended by any circumstance prejudicial to the tranquillity of the colony."

Circumspection Prevost has in quantity; but circumspection does not win wars. In material supplies he is hopelessly deficient. He has no coin with which to pay his troops and will have to persuade the legislature to issue paper money. He is embarrassed that he cannot supply the militia with enough rifles, let alone other equipment. A ship has set out from Bermuda to Halifax with six thousand stands of arms; apparently it has foundered in a storm. The mother country's priorities are Wellington's; she can supply Prevost with little to repel invasion – neither money, nor arms, nor men. He is short of officers; there are only two generals in Lower Canada, himself and Baron Francis de Rottenburg, and in Upper Canada two more: Roger Sheaffe and Isaac Brock.

Brock! In many ways he is worth five generals; Prevost admires and likes him. But – one can see the pursed lips, the furrowed brow – how to keep him in check? Overall British strategy does not envisage the seizure of American territory. Prevost does not wish to provoke the enemy. There is only one way to contain Brock, dictated as much by circumstance as by design, and that is to keep his regular force to a minimum. Upper Canada will get five hundred reinforcements, no more. And Brock must be convinced that these numbers will not "justify offensive operations being undertaken, *unless they were solely calculated to strengthen a defensive attitude.*"

The italics are not Prevost's. But the phrase is one that undoubtedly burns its way into the mind of the military commander of Upper Canada. When the moment comes, he will place the broadest possible interpretation on Sir George Prevost's cautious instructions.

SANDWICH, UPPER CANADA, July 23, 1812; with General Hull's Army of the Northwest.

"Why does the army dally?" Robert Lucas asks rhetorically, as he scratches away in his diary. "Why do they not make the Stroke on Maldon [Amherstburg] at once, had proper energy been used, we might have been in Maldon now, we are tampering with them untill they will be able to drive us back across the river...."

Why indeed? Hull's troops are eager to maintain some momentum, have been since the day of the landing when it was expected Hull would sweep down the river to attack the British fort at Amherstburg – a place name that has a sinister connotation for western Americans who have suffered at the hands of the Indians. For this has been the head-quarters of Elliott, McKee and Girty, whom the frontiersmen believe were behind the raids on white settlements in the Northwest.

Like his fellow volunteers, Lucas wants to get on with it. Once Fort Amherstburg's guns are silenced, the way to Upper Canada lies wide open. The only other British forts on the western frontier are at the other end of Lake Erie and along the Niagara River. A second American army has been dispatched to attack these strong points. Its task is to cause a diversion, pin down the defending British and prevent reinforcements from reaching Fort Amherstburg.

To Lucas, speed is essential. Amherstburg must be attacked and taken before Brock can divert more men to its defence. Lucas is used to swift, flexible movements, for he has been acting as a scout for Hull. In the General's mixed bag of raw recruits, untrained civilians, professional commanders, and elected leaders, he is a hybrid – general, captain, and private soldier rolled into one. The anomaly springs out of his country's awkward military philosophy, which disdains the idea of a standing army and relies on volunteers for the nation's defence. Lucas had been for some time a brigadier-general in the Ohio state militia. Eager to serve in the regular army, he applied in April for a captain's commission. A few days later, before it came through, McArthur ordered him to transmit from his brigade a proportion of the twelve hundred men required from the state in the coming war. What to do? Lucas, thirsty for action, set an example to his men by enrolling as a private in a volunteer company. To add to the confusion, the men elected his younger brother John as their captain.

Now, at Sandwich, Lucas vents his disgust in his diary: *Why does the army dally?* Hull is not short of supplies, for he has sent McArthur foraging up the Thames, raiding the farms, the barns, and the fields for food and equipment. McArthur and his men, moving without blankets or provisions, living off the land, penetrate sixty miles into the heart of Upper Canada: a land of stump and snake fences; of cabins and shanties of basswood and cedar; of Dutch lofts and clay ovens; of grist mills, fanning mills, and windmills; of chicken hutches, corn cribs, hog pens, and cattle sheds; of pickled pork and pigeon pie and fresh milk kept cool in underground sheds; of oxen hitched in tandem, furrowing the glistening fields, and raw-boned men in homespun linsey-woolsey scything the tawny harvest of midsummer. The raiding party leaves a trail of devastation in its wake, returning in five days with two hundred barrels of flour, four hundred blankets, and wagons loaded with whiskey, salt, cloth, guns, ammunition, household goods, tools – even boats. Grain fields are destroyed, homes ransacked, orchards levelled, corn trampled, fences burned or shattered – actions that enrage the settlers and help to turn them against their former compatriots.

John McGregor, a trader and merchant who has removed his goods to Matthew Dolsen's house and mill on the Thames for safety, loses everything – flour, merchandise, grain, livestock, and boats – and almost loses his life. He and Dolsen are forced to flee when it is learned that McArthur intends to shoot them on sight in the belief that they are rousing the Indians and militia to resistance.

Farmers and townspeople are beggared by the raiders. Jean-Baptiste Beniteau's orchard of sixty fruit trees is destroyed, his fences and pickets reduced to ashes. His neighbour, Jean-Baptiste Ginac, is looted of all his livestock, pork, flour, oats, and corn. Another Jean-Baptiste – Fourneaux – loses 480 bushels of grain, all his cider, as well as his winter's wood supply and furniture. A fourth, Jean-Baptiste Boismier, a fur trader, sees his entire fortune of 620 skins together with his livestock, tools, utensils, and harvested corn go to the enemy.

Hull's men make no allowance for old friends. Lieutenant-Colonel François Bâby, whose house has become Hull's headquarters, has tried to save some of his chattels by hauling them off to Jean-Baptiste Goyeau's home, three miles distant. But Hull dispatches a party of dragoons with six wagons who remove everything at gunpoint, then, emboldened by conquest, slice up one of Bâby's finest coats with their sabres. Bâby's loss is staggering; he reckons it at 2,678 pounds sterling.

Another raiding party ransacks the estate of the Earl of Selkirk at Baldoon on Lake St. Clair, seizing a thousand pounds' worth of booty, from pewter plates to pitchforks, including the greatest prize of all, more than nine hundred prize Merino sheep, which are ferried across the river to Fort Detroit along with the aged Scot who is their shepherd.

McArthur brushes all complaints aside with the promise that everything will eventually be paid for because, he says, Hull has such a footing in Canada that the British will never be able to drive him out.

And so it appears. At Fort Amherstburg the situation is deteriorating. Militia service works real hardship on those families who depend upon the able-bodied for their livelihood. Hundreds desert. Those who remain loyal—men like Robert Pike of Port Dover or John Williams on the Thames—have no one to harvest their wheat and so lose it all to rot. St. George, the commander at the fort, feels himself obliged to release the oldest and least efficient to return to their farms. Others slip away. On July 8, St. George counts 850 militiamen under his command. A week later the number has dropped to 471. "I expect that in two or three days we shall have very few of them at the post," Matthew Elliott informs his superior, adding that there is no ammunition left in the Indian stores "and, if more Indians come, I really do not know how to act." St. George expects an attack almost hourly, but it does not come. In Robert Lucas's rueful belief, Hull's dallying has given the British hope. "Our conduct has at least incouraged them much," he notes.

One of the keenest soldiers in Hull's army, Lucas has managed to see more action than most of his followers. As a ranger and scout he has always been in the vanguard of the main army, often in danger. He is one of those natural soldiers, found in every army, who thrive on action. When Hull's boats crossed over to Sandwich, Lucas arranged to switch companies temporarily in order to be one of the first to set foot on Canadian soil because he "could not endure to be behind."

On July 16, Lucas volunteers again: Colonels Cass and Miller are ordered to reconnoitre enemy country up to the River aux Canards, a deep but sluggish stream that winds through the marshes three miles above Amherstburg. Lucas immediately offers to go along. This war will help to make his reputation; one day he will be governor of Ohio and later of Iowa Territory.

Colonel Cass is as eager for glory and for action as Lucas. The bridge at the Canard is held by a detachment of British regulars and Indians – the same Menominee dispatched to Amherstburg from the Wisconsin country the previous month by Robert Dickson. Cass resolves to ford the river upstream and attack in a flanking movement while Miller pins down the sentries. Again Lucas and the rangers are in the vanguard.

Faced with an attack on their rear, the British retire. Cass cannot pursue, for a tributary stream blocks the way. But the British sentries – John Dean and James Hancock of the 41st – stubbornly hold their ground and become the first soldiers to shed their blood on Canadian soil in the War of 1812. Dean, one arm broken by a musket ball, fights on with his bayonet until he is knocked to the ground and disarmed. Hancock, bleeding from at least two wounds, unable to support himself, continues to fight on his knees until he is captured. He dies that night and is scalped by one of the Indians, who sells the trophy to the British – "a good trick for an Indian to make the British Gov. pay for their own Soldiers Scalps," comments Robert Lucas.

This is the first time the Americans have come up against British regulars, that tough, stubborn, hard-drinking, somewhat unimaginative breed whom Wellington has called, not without affection, "the scum of the earth." America, nurtured on the ideal of a free-wheeling grassroots democracy, scorns the British professional as a semi-robot and mercenary, wedded to no political ideal. It is true, certainly, that many a British working man joins for the money: the handsome bounties offered those who transfer from the militia, the prospect of a substantial prize after a successful engagement. But there are other reasons. Wellington believes, not without considerable evidence, that "they have all enlisted for drink." Yet drink is only a symptom; like enlistment, it is a form of escape from the appallingly drab conditions of the British lower classes. The army is composed of men fleeing from a variety of bedevilments – brutal taskmasters, nagging wives, pregnant girl friends, intolerable parents, constables and judges, or simple boredom. Black-sheep sons of well-born families ("gentlemen rankers") rub shoulders with footpads, pickpockets, roustabouts, poachers, smugglers, or plain, resolute English labouring men hungry for adventure in a far-off land, even if that be nothing more glamorous than garrison duty with the 41st in the backwater of Amherstburg.

Wellington's scum are actually in a minority. It is estimated that in a battalion of some three or four hundred men, perhaps fifty are rogues – drunkards, stragglers, potential deserters. A harsh system of discipline keeps them in line. In the summer of 1812, for instance, the 103rd Regiment in Quebec holds thirty-seven courts martial and sentences thirty-one men to a total of 5,725 lashes, of which at least 1,589 are actually laid on the bare back, the others being remitted. (One unfortunate is lashed three hundred times.) But it is the parade-ground drill, hammered into the rankers' subconscious, that trains the men to act automatically – to stand fast as the enemy advances, to hold their fire until ordered, to discharge their muskets in a single shattering volley without flinching, even as the cavalry sweeps down upon the square or hostile bayonets attempt to break the scarlet line. The wounded Dean, now a prisoner of war, and the dying Hancock are products of this system. It simply does not occur to them to desert their posts.

The Americans now hold the bridge that can lead the army to Amherstburg. It appears to Cass and Miller that the entire force should immediately move up to within striking distance of its objective. But Hull dithers. He is going by the book, planning a careful set-piece siege of the British fort. That he will not undertake until his heavy artillery is ready. The fort might be taken by an infantry assault, but the slaughter would be appalling; and that the former divinity student cannot abide. The bridge is abandoned.

He has other concerns. What is happening on the Niagara frontier? It is essential that an American army be in place along that river. Otherwise there is nothing to stop the British from deploying all their resources against him. Eustis and Dearborn have promised a diversion on the Niagara to support his invasion, but communications are such that the General has no way of knowing whether this has been done.

A closer problem torments him. He is certain that Colonel Cass is trying to pressure him for reasons of personal ambition. He feels his authority slipping away; his officers' complaints are beginning to destroy his influence. He calls council after council to try to quell their impatience; it only erodes his command. "They seem to have thought," he will later argue, "that when a council of war was called, it was to be governed by the laws of a town meeting."

He is determined not to advance until there is "an absolute certainty of success." How long will it take to prepare the cannon? Two days? Two weeks? After each meeting, the time stretches. Hull fears defeat. Defeat will mean starvation for the troops and, worse, devastation by the Indians. The militia fear the Indians. At the bridge over the Canard and also at Turkey Creek and Petite Coté, where desultory skirmishing continues almost daily, Dickson's Menominee and Tecumseh's followers terrify the raw recruits. One regular officer writes to the New York *Gazette*:

"Had it not been for the dastardly conduct of the drafted Ohio militia who composed one half of the party and who took to their heels when they evidently had the advantage, the whole of the Indians would have been killed or taken. The officers endeavoured to rally them and said they would be fired at by their own party if they did not stand. They replied that they would rather be killed by them than by the damned Indians."

There is savagery on both sides. The first Indian scalp is taken by Captain William McCullough of the Rangers, who describes in a letter to his wife how he tore it from the corpse's head with his teeth.

Word of these skirmishes reaches William K. Beall and his fellow prisoners aboard the *Thames*, docked at Amherstburg. It fuels their hope for speedy deliverance. On the night of the encounter at the Canard bridge, Beall learns that Hull's army is camped within reach. Glorious news! But instead of seeing American soldiers marching into town he is greeted by a more macabre spectacle: Thomas McKee of the Indian Department (the perennial drunkard whom Elliott has replaced) arrives at the head of about fifty Indians, all naked except for their breech cloths. McKee, who is also dressed as a native, halts opposite the gaping prisoners and hoists a fresh scalp, fastened to a long pole, which he shakes exultantly, all the time taunting the prisoners with savage cries.

For this spectacle, "which would have chilled the frigid blood of a Laplander or...crimsoned the tawny cheek of an unrelenting Turk," Beall abuses everything British, from the King on down. His fury is misplaced, for the scalp is undoubtedly that of the unfortunate British sentry Hancock.

Beall and his fellow prisoners have other concerns. Where is Hull? What can be keeping him? Gone now is the optimism, the good humour, the gallantry of those first days in captivity. Beall no longer sees the British as gentlemen but as monsters. And he is desperately homesick. His nights are troubled by visions of his young wife, far away on their estate of Beallmont in Kentucky. "In my sleep the air drawn figure of my Melinda often rises to my view: beautious as an Angel, gentle as the spring, smiling on me with enchanted tenderness and yealding to my fond embrace. In dreams, with rapturous fondness, I have pressed her to my bosom, felt her soft touch, heard the sweet accents of her voice, and gazed upon her lovely countenance till every sense was lost in extacy and love."

These visions are rendered more poignant by Beall's disillusionment with his general: "The British officers and soldiers begin to laugh at Hull.... He is now the object of their jest and ridicule instead of being as he was formerly their terror and greatest fear."

Even as Beall is committing these thoughts to paper, on July 26, Hull, at Sandwich, is shaken by an alarming piece of intelligence. A ship, the *Salina*, flying British colours, is brought about by a shot from the shore. Aboard is a group of American citizens and soldiers, led by Lieutenant Porter Hanks, the former commander at Michilimackinac, paroled by his adversary, Roberts. Now, for the first time, Hull learns of Mackinac's fall. It is a major disaster. "I can scarcely conceive of the impression made by the fall of Mackanac," Colonel Cass writes to a relative. For the western anchor on the American frontier has come unstuck, releasing, in Hull's phrase, "the northern hive of Indians," who will shortly come "swarming down in every direction."

Hull feels himself surrounded by Indians. He reasons that there must be two or three thousand Ottawa, Chippewa, and Sioux at his rear, advancing from Mackinac. On his left are the Iroquois of the Grand Valley. They are still neutral, as far as he knows, but he also has news that Brock has sent a detachment to try to bring them into the fight – a task rendered less difficult by the news of Mackinac's fall. In front of him, at Amherstburg, lies another potent force: hundreds more Indians led by the great Tecumseh. Hull fears these more than he does the handful of British regulars.

Within the fort, by the end of the month William Beall and the other American officers have lost all hope of rescue. "I can scarcely think that Genl. H. will be defeated," Beall writes, "but appearances justify such a belief. I am confident that he will not take Malden, though 300 men could do it.... Why does he not, by taking Malden, silence and drive the Indians away who infest the Country and secure a safe communication with the States, and safety to our Frontiers. Heaven only knows. I for a Harrison, a Daviess or a Wells."

●

YORK, UPPER CANADA, July 28, 1812. Isaac Brock, administrator of Upper Canada, resplendent in military crimson and gold, is opening the legislature and managing to mask the emotions of contempt, frustration, and even despair that boil up within him.

...when invaded by an Enemy whose avowed object is the entire Conquest of this Province, the voice of Loyalty as well as of interest calls aloud to every Person in the Sphere in which he is placed, to defend his Country.

Our Militia have heard that voice and have obeyed it, they have evinced by the promptitude and Loyalty of their Conduct, that they are worthy of the King whom they serve, and of the Constitution which they enjoy...

This is hokum, and Brock knows it. He has already written a private note to Prevost declaring his belief that it seems impossible "to animate the militia to a proper sense of duty" and that he almost despairs of doing anything with them. Worse, at Long Point on Lake Erie, where he has attempted to muster five hundred men to march to the relief of Fort Amherstburg, there has been open mutiny. The men have refused to march under Lieutenant-Colonel Thomas Talbot, the eccentric and domineering Irish aristocrat who controls some sixty thousand acres of land in the area. One reason for the mutiny has been the wives' fear of being left alone to the mercy of the neutral Iroquois at the Grand River. Another has been the inflammatory speeches made to them by pro-American civilian dissidents. A third, one suspects, has been Talbot himself, a curious specimen, tyrannical in his control over the settlers – a man who once lived in luxury but who now dresses in homespun, bakes his own bread, labours like a peasant, drinks like a toper, and affects a harsh mode of life which, in the words of a former lieutenant-governor, "might suit a Republic but is not fitted to a Monarchical Government."

In spite of this disaffection, Brock continues the charade:

...it affords me particular satisfaction, that while I address You as Legislators, I speak to men who in the day of danger, will be ready to assist, not only with their Counsel, but with their Arms...

He does not believe it, and his private correspondence reflects his dismay and cynicism. The people and their leaders appear convinced that the war is lost: "...a full belief possesses them that this Province must inevitably succumb.... Legislators, magistrates, militia officers, all have imbibed the idea, and are so sluggish and indifferent in their respective offices that the artful and active scoundrel is allowed to parade the country without interruption and commit all imaginable mischief."

The artful and active scoundrels include a big, ginger-haired blacksmith named Andrew Westbrook and a land surveyor from Montreal named Simon Z. Watson. Westbrook, a recent arrival from the United States, has enthusiastically espoused Hull's cause, helped distribute his proclamation, and volunteered to fight with the Detroit militia. Watson, "a desperate character" in Brock's view, is a bitter enemy of Thomas Talbot, and thus of the government, because of a long-standing rivalry over land fees and speculation. Created a temporary colonel by Hull, he has "vowed the most bitter vengeance against the first characters of the Province." There are other dissidents, such as John Beamer, a justice of the peace, who has chaired a meeting in Norfolk County urging the militia not to fight.

But Brock plays all this down:

A few Traitors have already joined the Enemy.... Yet the General Spirit of Loyalty which appears to pervade the Inhabitants of this Province, is such as to authorize a just expectation that their efforts to mislead and deceive, will be unavailing...

In private he reports:

"A petition has already been carried to Genl. Hull signed by many inhabitants about Westminster inviting him to advance with a promise to join him – What in the name of heaven can be done with such a vile population?"

Yet who can blame the mass of the people? The nature of the colonial aristocracy denies them a say in their own destiny, even though they are required to swear allegiance to the King, George III, who being certifiably insane is king in name only, the real monarch being his son, the Prince Regent, known to the irreverent masses as Prinny. The province is administered by the Prince Regent's appointee, Francis Gore, and in his absence by Isaac Brock, who also commands the army and the militia and is thus a near dictator. He sits at the head of a seven-man council, which, being appointed for life, can be said to be almost as conservative as the mad king himself, and a fourteen-man assembly, elected by freeholders, whose members serve for four years – or less, at the governor's pleasure. Anyone who dares speak disrespectfully of the King, the government, or its officers is treading perilously close to sedition.

The Church of England clergy, the military, and the leading

officeholders form a ruling elite, the legacy of the first lieutenant-governor, John Graves Simcoe, who was convinced that a landed aristocracy, conservative in its attitudes and British in its antecedents, was the only way to combat the twin viruses of democracy and republicanism creeping across the border. The tight little group that forms the apex of the social triangle in Upper Canada, entrenched by nepotism and by an educational system that ignores the masses, will shortly become known as the Family Compact. It does not tolerate opposition.

The "vile population" wants to be left alone. Militia service deprives the farms of their greatest asset, able-bodied men. Loyalists and the sons of the Loyalists – men like John Beverley Robinson, or the Ryersons of Norfolk County – will flock to the colours because their whole heritage represents a rejection of American values. And there are others who see in war a chance for adventure or escape. But these are in a minority. Brock is determined to rally the rest by Draconian methods, if need be. He wants to suspend habeas corpus and establish martial law but finds that in spite of his impressive authority he has little hope of either. The legislature will not vote for the first, and if he attempts the second "I am told the instant the law is promulgated the Militia will disperse...."

He is convinced that the legislators, expecting an American victory, are fearful of taking any overt action that might displease the conquerors. "I really believe it is with some cause that they dread the vengeance of the democratic party, they are such a set of unrelenting villains."

Pinned down at York by his civilian duties, he has taken what action he can to stiffen the defence at Fort Amherstburg, dispatching a younger and more energetic officer, Lieutenant-Colonel Henry Procter, to take over from the confused and harassed St. George.

Amherstburg is vital. If Hull seizes it – as he seems likely to do – he can sweep up the Thames or turn eastward to attack the British rear at Fort George on the Niagara and link up with the second American army already forming along that gorge. Brock *must* maintain a strong defence on the Niagara, yet his force at Amherstburg is distressingly thin. His only immediate solution is to move some men from Fort George to Fort Erie, a mid-point between the two bastions. From there they can be dispatched swiftly in either direction, depending upon the threat. Fortunately, he commands the Lakes.

He has also sent detachments down the valley of the Thames, recalling the militia from the harvest fields, attempting to waken the countryside to action, and distributing a proclamation of his own designed to counter Hull's. In this paper battle with the enemy, Brock, conjuring up the spectre of Napoleon, shows that he is no stranger to the art of magniloquence:

...it is but too obvious that once estranged from the powerful protection of the United Kingdom you must be reannexed to the dominion of France, from which the Provinces of Canada were wrested by the Arms of Great Britain, at a vast expense of blood and treasure, from no other motive than to *relieve* her ungrateful children from the oppression of a cruel neighbor: this restitution of Canada to the Empire of France was the stipulated reward for the aid offered to the revolted Colonies, now the United States; The debt is still due, and there can be no doubt but that the pledge has been renewed.... Are you prepared Inhabitants of Upper Canada to becoming willing subjects or rather slaves to the Despot who rules the nations of Europe with a rod of Iron? If not, arise in a Body, exert your energies, co-operate cordially with the King's regular Forces to repel the invader, and do not give cause to your children when groaning under the oppression of a foreign Master to reproach you with having too easily parted with the richest Inheritance on Earth – a participation in the name, character and freedom of Britons...

In his proclamation, Brock praises "the brave bands of Natives who inhabit this Colony," but the ink is scarcely dry on the paper when he learns that one brave band – the Iroquois of the Grand Valley – remains totally uninterested in fighting the Americans. Brock is infuriated. Their conduct is "ungrateful and infamous...mortifying." He would like to see them all expelled from their land. By refusing to take sides, the Iroquois "afford the Militia a plausible pretext for staying at home – They do not like leaving their families within the power of the Indians...."

Honourable Gentlemen of the Legislative Council and Gentlemen of the House of Assembly.
We are engaged in an awful and eventful Contest. By unanimity and despatch in our Councils, and by vigour in our Operations, we may teach the Enemy this lesson – that a Country defended by Free men, enthusiastically devoted to the cause of their King and Constitution, can never be Conquered.

Brock's closing words have a hollow ring. According to inviolable ritual, they will be parroted back to him twice: first by the Speaker of the Council and on the following day by the Speaker of the House, while Brock frets. He yearns to be at Amherstburg in the thick of things, away from the stuffy corridors of York and in sight of the enemy. Words are not his long suit, though in his loneliness he has become a voracious reader, devouring Plutarch's *Lives*, Hume's *Essays*, Pope's *Homer*, and dozens of military volumes. It is even said that much of his proclamation is the work of his friend Mr. Justice William Dummer Powell. Action is his forte, and it is action he craves. On the Iberian peninsula, Wellington has just won the battle of Salamanca and is basking in the approbation of Francisco Goya, the irascible Spanish court painter who has somehow got through the lines to commence an equestrian portrait of the victor. But it is thirteen years since Brock has seen real action (setting aside the naval attack on Copenhagen when he was sequestered aboard one of Nelson's ships, *Ganges*). He is not likely to forget that October afternoon at Egmont-op-Zee when death whispered to him as a musket ball, happily near spent, buried itself in his silk cravat, knocking him insensible from his horse. He was a lieutenant-colonel of the 49th then, a regiment that he had thoroughly shaken up, transforming it (in the Duke of York's opinion) from one of the worst to one of the best in the service. Now a whole country needs shaking up. Defeatism, timidity, irresolution, and treason stalk the land. It is Brock's task to achieve another miracle, and he cannot accomplish that in the dust and gumbo of provincial York. Duty calls. Immortality beckons. A new October awaits.

•

AUGUST 5, 1812. At the River aux Ecorces, on the American side of the Detroit, Robert Lucas the scout lies hidden in the bushes, waiting for the dawn, watched by unseen eyes. Two fellow rangers lie beside him along with the ranger captain McCullough, who has the dubious distinction of being the only American thus far to take an Indian scalp.

The four men lie on the left flank of an armed body sent across the river by Hull to make contact with the wagon train of supplies, which he desperately needs to feed his army. The supply train, under the command of a young Chillicothe lawyer, Captain Henry Brush, has reached the Rapids of the Maumee and is moving on to the River Raisin after a gruelling march through dense thickets and treacherous mires. But Brush does not dare continue to Detroit without an escort, for his cattle train and pack animals must pass within cannon shot of Fort Amherstburg. Hull has answered his plea by dispatching two hundred Ohio volunteers under Major Thomas Van Horne. Some of these are the same men who refused to cross the river in July; Van Horne has picked them up at Detroit along with their company commander, the recalcitrant Captain Rupes, who, astonishingly, is still in charge, having been re-elected by democratic vote after a court martial ordered him cashiered.

Dawn breaks. McCullough and his scouts rise and mount their horses, making a wide reconnaissance sweep around the detachment. They scent trouble, noting tracks on the road and trails in the grass – evidence that a party of Indians has been watching them during the night. Out on the river, a faint splish-splash penetrates the shroud of mist that hangs over the water. Oars! Hull's army cannot remain long on Canadian soil unless its supply lines are secured. The British, who control the river, intend that this shall not be.

The detachment moves, McCullough, Robert Lucas, and Van Horne's black servant riding out in front. Lucas continues to eye the river. Is a British force crossing over from Fort Amherstburg? The mist frustrates his view.

They ride through the Wyandot village of Maguaga. It is deserted, the houses empty. Tecumseh and Matthew Elliott have preceded them and persuaded the wavering Walk-in-the-Water to cross to British territory with his followers. Brock's assessment has been correct: news of the victory at Michilimackinac has tipped the scales, and the tribe wants to be on the winning side.

The road forks around a corn field. Lucas and a companion take the right fork; McCullough takes the left and rides into an ambush. Lucas hears a volley of shots, but before he can reach him, the scalper is himself scalped, tomahawked, riddled with musket balls. The rear guard is in a panic, but the Indians have already vanished into the tall corn.

Shaken, the detachment moves on, leaving three corpses under a cover of bark and ignoring a Frenchman's warning that a large force of Indians is waiting for them at Brownstown. The Americans do not trust the French settlers, some of whom are pro-British and seek to confuse them with false reports.

The war party moves in double file. Between the files, mounted men escort the mail – a packet of personal letters written by Hull's soldiers to their families and friends, many of them critical of their general, and, more significantly, Hull's official dispatches to Washington, revealing both his plans and his pessimism.

Brownstown village lies ahead, but Brownstown Creek must first be crossed. The only practical ford lies in a narrow defile with thick bushes on the right and fields of tall corn on the opposite bank and on the left. It is the perfect spot for an ambush; Lucas recognizes the danger and rides along the right column warning the men to see that their muskets are freshly primed. Tecumseh has recognized it, too. He and his followers are flat on their bellies directly ahead – twenty-four Shawnee and Ottawa and one white man, Matthew Elliott's son Alexander.

As Tecumseh silently waits, the American files close up to cross the creek. Then, at a range of no more than twenty-five yards, the Indians rise out of the corn, their high-pitched war cries mingling with the explosion of their weapons. Lucas's horse is shot, topples sideways against another wounded animal, pitches its rider onto the ground, his musket flying from his hand. Weaponless, Lucas tries with little success to rally the men. The odds are twenty to one in favour of the Americans, but the Indians are shouting so wildly that Van Horne believes himself outnumbered. It is scarcely necessary to order a retreat; his men fling down their weapons, scatter the mail, and plunge headlong back the way they came, actually outrunning their pursuers, who follow them for three miles before giving up the chase. Robert Lucas, covering the retreat as best he can, is the last man to escape.

The Battle of Brownstown, as it will be called, represents a serious setback for Hull. Van Horne has lost eighteen men killed and twenty wounded. Some seventy are missing, many hiding in the bushes; the following day, most straggle back. Worse than the loss of seven officers is the abandoning of the mail. This will raise Brock's spirits, for here, in letters home, is strong evidence of the discontent and illness in the ranks, of a lack of confidence in the leadership, and, even more important, Hull's letter of August 4 to the Secretary of War, outlining the critical situation of his army, pleading for another two thousand men, and expressing his deep-seated fear of the Indians who he believes will shortly be swarming down from Mackinac Island.

At Brownstown, meanwhile, a strong detachment of the British 41st accompanied by militia and civilian volunteers under Major Adam Muir has crossed the river, too late to take part in the skirmish but prepared to frustrate any further attempt by Hull to open the supply line. The men have waited all night, unable to light a fire, shivering in the damp, without blankets or provisions. Now they are exposed to a spectacle calculated to make them shudder further.

The Indians hold a young American captive and are intent on killing him. Muir does his best to intervene, offers a barrel of rum and articles of clothing if the prisoner's life is spared. But then a series of piercing cries issues from the forest – the funeral convoy of a young chief, Blue Jacket, the only casualty among Tecumseh's followers. Four tribesmen carry in the body. Thomas Verchères de Boucherville, a citizen volunteer and experienced fur trader from Amherstburg, realizes there is no hope for the American, for the Indians are intent on avenging their chief. They place his corpse at the captive's feet and he, too, seems to understand his fate.

The American turns pale, looks about him, asks in a low voice if it is possible that the English allow such acts of barbarity. The cries of the Indians drown out the response.

The oldest Potawatomi chief raises his hatchet over the prisoner; a group of Indian women draw near. At the chief's signal, one plunges a butcher knife into the victim's head; a second stabs him in the side while the chief dispatches him with a tomahawk. Tecumseh, who would surely have prevented the execution, is not present.

The white witnesses including Alexander Elliott (himself in Indian dress) are stunned. They feel impotent, knowing that these dark allies hold the keys to British success. Young Thomas de Boucherville, the fur trader, who will never shake the incident from his memory, puts their dilemma into words:

"We all stood around overcome by an acute sense of shame. We felt implicated in some way in this murder...and yet, under the circumstances what could we do? The life of that man undoubtedly belonged to the inhuman chief. The government had desperate need of these Indian allies. Our garrison was weak and these warriors were numerous enough to impose their will upon us. If we were to rebuke them in this crisis...they would withdraw from the conflict, and retire to their own country on the Missouri whence they had come to join us."

De Boucherville is coming to realize what others will soon grasp – that the British are, in a subtle way, as much prisoners of the Indians as the young American whose tomahawked corpse lies stretched out before them.

•

SANDWICH, UPPER CANADA, August 6, 1812. In his head-quarters in François Bâby's half-finished mansion, General Hull continues to vacillate. He has promised his impatient officers that he will attack the fort whether the artillery is ready or not. Now he has second thoughts. In Washington he allowed himself to be talked out of his original proposal: that America take steps to control the water routes. Now he himself is paying the price for that negligence. He cannot float his artillery downriver in the teeth of British gunboats. But his enemies can cross the river at will to harass his supply lines and herd Walk-in-the-Water's Wyandot followers into Canada to reinforce Fort Amherstburg.

He seriously considers retreat but backs off after a stormy meeting with Colonel McArthur. He broods, changes his mind, calls a council of his commanders, finally agrees to adopt their plan of attacking Fort Amherstburg. He will move against it at the head of his troops "and in whatever manner the affair may terminate, I will never reflect on you, gentlemen."

Dazzling news! Robert Lucas, back from the debacle at Browns-town, is exultant: the long faces of his comrades have been replaced by smiles. A wave of good cheer surges over the camp. The sick rise from their beds and seize their muskets; the wounded urge the sur-geons to pronounce them fit for duty. Orders are issued for five days' rations, three to be cooked – pork the staple fare. Ammunition and whiskey (twelve barrels) are loaded into wagons, axes, picks, and spades requisitioned, cannon placed on floating batteries. All unneces-sary tents, baggage, and boats are sent back to Detroit.

Then, on the afternoon of August 7, hard on the heels of the news from Brownstown, comes an express rider with dispatches for Hull from two American commanders on the Niagara frontier. Boats loaded with British troops have been seen crossing Lake Erie and heading for Amherstburg; more British regulars accompanied by Canadian militia and Indians are en route from Niagara by boat to the fort. Since the British control the lakes, there is nothing the Americans can do to stop them.

Hull is badly rattled. What is happening? Washington's over-all strategy was to pin down the British forces on the Niagara frontier by a series of attacks that would leave Fort Amherstburg lightly held. Now the British are taking troops from Fort George and Fort Erie, leaving that frontier exposed to attack. That may be of some comfort to his colleagues on the Niagara River, but it is disastrous for Hull; it is impossible for him "to express the disappointment which this information occasioned." What he does not know is that Prevost has sent an emissary to discuss an immediate armistice with General Henry Dearborn, the American commander-in-chief. Brock does not know this, either, but things are so quiet on the Niagara frontier that he feels justified in taking a gamble; he will reduce his forces there to a minimum in order to bolster his defence at Amherstburg and frustrate any attack by General Hull.

Both commanders – Hull at Sandwich, Brock at York – are suffering from bouts of gloom and frustration. Half blinded by the myopia of war, each believes his own position to be untenable, his adversary's superior. Brock, thwarted by timid civilians and a lukewarm militia, expects Hull to attack his weak garrison at Fort Amherstburg at any moment. He is desperate to reinforce it but despairs of holding it against greater numbers. Hull, isolated on Canadian soil, is convinced that Brock's combined force is not only stronger but also growing at an alarming rate.

Unlike Brock, Hull is no gambler. He feels doomed by bad fortune: the supposedly friendly Indians turning their coats and crowding into Amherstburg; the blocking of his supply train; now a fresh onslaught of fighting men. The General sees himself and his troops suddenly trapped in an unfriendly country, their backs to the river, their food running out, surrounded by Indians, facing Brock's regulars and Tecumseh's braves. Irresolution at last gives way to decision, but a decision tainted with panic. He must get his army back onto American soil, with the barrier of the river between him and his enemies – to Detroit at the very least, and perhaps all the way to the Maumee.

He sends again for his officers and breaks the news. It is his responsibility, and his alone, he declares, to decide the ultimate fate of the army. "Well, General," says the swarthy McArthur, "if it is your opinion, it must be so, but I must beg leave to decline giving any further opinion as to the movements of the army."

Hull suggests, hesitantly, that the army might be well advised to withdraw as far as the Maumee. Cass retorts that if he does that, every man in the Ohio militia will leave him. That puts an end to it: the army will withdraw across the river to Detroit, but no farther.

Lewis Cass is beside himself. In his eyes, Hull's decision is both fatal and unaccountable; he cannot fathom it. Coming after a series of timid, irresolute, and indecisive measures, this final about-face has dispirited the troops and destroyed the last vestige of confidence they may have had in their commander. Cass is undoubtedly right; far better if Hull had never crossed the river in the first place – at least until his supply lines were secure. A sense of astonishment, mingled with a feeling of disgrace, ripples through the camp. Robert Lucas feels it: the orders to cross the river under cover of darkness are, he thinks, especially dastardly. But cross the army must, and when night falls the men slink into their boats. By the following morning there is scarcely an American soldier left on Canadian soil.

●

WHILE BROCK is advancing toward the Detroit frontier, intent on attack, his superior, Sir George Prevost, is doing his best to wind down the war. He informs Lord Liverpool that although his policy of conciliation has not prevented hostilities, he is determined to do nothing to exacerbate the situation by aggressive action:

"...Your Lordship may rest assured that unless the safety of the Provinces entrusted to my charge should require them, no measures shall be adopted by me to impede a speedy return to those accustomed relations of amity and goodwill which it is the mutual interest of both countries to cherish and preserve."

Sir George, who has never believed in the reality of the war, is now convinced it will reach a swift conclusion. Augustus Foster has written from Halifax, en route home from Washington, with the news that Britain has revoked the hated Orders in Council. American ships may now trade with continental Europe without fear of seizure. Madison in June made it clear that the Orders were America's chief reason for going to war. Surely, then, with Britain backing off, he will come to his senses and halt the invasion.

Sir George sees no reason to wait for the President. Why not suspend hostilities at once – at least temporarily? Why spill blood senselessly if the war is, in effect, over?

On August 2, he dispatches his aide, Lieutenant-Colonel Edward Baynes, with a flag of truce to treat with Major-General Henry Dearborn, the U.S. commander, at his headquarters at Greenbush, across the river from Albany, New York.

The American in charge of the overall prosecution of the war in the north has not seen military service for two decades. A ponderous, flabby figure, weighing two hundred and fifty pounds, with a face to match, Dearborn does not look like a general, nor does he act like one. He is a tired sixty-one. His soldiers call him Granny.

His reputation, like Hull's, rests on the memory of another time. As a Revolutionary major he fought at Bunker Hill, then struggled, feverish and half-starved, with Arnold through the wintry forests of Maine to attack Quebec, was captured and exchanged to fight again – against Burgoyne at Saratoga, at Monmouth Court House in '78, with General John Sullivan against the Indians in '79, at Yorktown in '81. A successful and influential Massachusetts politician in the post-war era, Secretary of War for eight years in Jefferson's cabinet, he is now an old soldier who was slowly fading away in his political sinecure until the call to arms restored him to command.

The American strategy, to attack Canada simultaneously at Detroit, Niagara, Kingston, and Montreal, is faltering. Given the lack of men and supplies it is hardly likely that these thrusts can occur together. It is assumed, without anybody quite saying so, that Dearborn will co-ordinate them, but General Dearborn does not appear to understand.

Strategically, the major attack ought to be made upon Montreal. A lightning thrust would sever the water connection between the Canadas, deprive the upper province of supplies and reinforcements, and, in the end, cause it to wither away and surrender without a fight. The problem is that the New Englanders, whose co-operation is essential, do not want to fight, while the southerners and westerners in Kentucky, Tennessee, South Carolina, and Ohio are eager for battle. There is also the necessity of securing America's western flank from the menace of the Indians. Thus, the American command pins its initial hopes on Hull's army while the forces on Lake Champlain remain stagnant.

To describe Dearborn's prosecution of the war as leisurely is to understate that officer's proclivity for sluggish movement. He has spent three months in New England, attempting in his bumbling fashion to stir the people to belligerence with scarcely any success. The governors of Massachusetts and Connecticut are particularly obdurate. When Dearborn asks Caleb Strong to call out fourteen companies of artillery and twenty-seven of infantry for the defence of his Massachusetts ports and harbours, Governor Strong declares that the seacoast does not need defending since the government of Nova Scotia has "by proclamation, forbid[den] any incursions or depredations upon our territories." Governor John Cotton Smith of Connecticut points out that the Constitution "has ordained that Congress may provide for calling forth the militia *to execute the laws of the Union, suppress insurrections, and repel invasions.*" Since there has been neither insurrection nor invasion, he argues, no such emergency exists. Of course, Governor Smith adds, the militia stands ready to repel any invasion should one take place. Clearly, he believes that will never happen.

Dearborn dawdles. Eustis tries to prod him into returning to his base at Albany to get on with the invasion of Canada, but Eustis is not much of a prodder. "Being possessed of a full view of the intentions of government," he starts out – then adds a phrase scarcely calculated to propel a man of Dearborn's temperament into action; "take your time," he finishes, and Dearborn does just that.

It is an odd coincidence that the Secretary of War and his predecessor, Dearborn, are both medical men, former physicians trained to caution, sceptical of haste, wary of precipitate moves that might cause a patient's death. One of Dearborn's tasks is to create diversions at Kingston and at Niagara to take the pressure off Hull; but when Hull crosses the Detroit River, Dearborn is still in Boston. "I begin to feel that I may be censured for not moving," he remarks in what must be the understatement of the war, but he doubts the wisdom of leaving. To which Eustis responds: "Go to Albany or the Lake. The troops shall come to you as fast as the season will admit, and the blow must be struck. Congress must not meet without a victory to announce to them." Dearborn ponders this for a week before making up his mind, then finally sets off, reaching Greenbush on July 26, where some twelve hundred unorganized troops await him.

His letters to Washington betray his indecision ("I have been in a very unpleasant situation, being at a loss to determine whether or not I ought to leave the seacoast"). He is woefully out of touch with his command, has no idea who runs his commissary and ordnance departments, is not even sure how far his authority extends, although this has been spelled out for him. In a remarkable letter he asks Eustis: "Who is to have command of the operations in Upper Canada? I take it for granted that my command does not extend to that distant quarter." These are the words of a man trying to wriggle out of responsibility, a man for whom the only secure action is no action at all. He has been ordered to keep the British occupied while Hull advances. But he does nothing.

This, then, is the character of the commander who is to receive an offer of truce brought to his headquarters by the personable Lieutenant-Colonel Baynes.

It takes Baynes six days to reach Albany from Montreal. An experienced officer with thirty years' service behind him, he keeps his eyes open, recording, in the pigeon-holes of his mind, troop dispositions, the state of preparedness of soldiers, the morale of the countryside. At Plattsburg he is greeted cordially by the ranking major-general, a farmer named Moore, who gets him a room at the inn. Baynes notes that the militia have no uniforms, the only distinguishing badge being a cockade in their hats, and that they do not appear to have made any progress in the first rudiments of military drill. All the officers at Plattsburg express approval of Baynes's mission and one of them, a Major Clarke, is ordered to accompany him by boat to Burlington near the southern end of Lake Champlain. From this point on Baynes proceeds with more difficulty; the commander at Burlington is not enchanted by the spectacle of an enemy officer coolly looking over his force. But Baynes finally persuades him to let him proceed to Albany, 150 miles to the south.

For Lieutenant-Colonel Baynes the journey is salutary. He fails to see any military preparation but forms a strong opinion of the mood of the people, which he reports to Prevost:

"My appearance travelling thro' the country in uniform excited very great curiosity and anxiety. The Inns where the coach stopt were instantly crowded with the curious and inquisitive. I did not hear a single individual express a wish but for the speedy accommodation of existing differences and deprecating the war, in several instances these statements were expressed in strong and violent language and on Major Clarke endeavouring to check it, it produced a contrary effect. The universal sentiment of this part of the country appears decidedly adverse to war. I experienced everywhere respect and attention."

On the evening of August 8, Baynes reaches Albany and goes immediately to Dearborn's headquarters at nearby Greenbush. The American commander receives him with great affability, says he personally wants an armistice on honourable terms, and admits that "the burden of command at his time of life was not a desirable charge." Baynes finds him in good health but shrewdly concludes that he "does not appear to possess the energy of mind or activity of body requisite for the important station he fills."

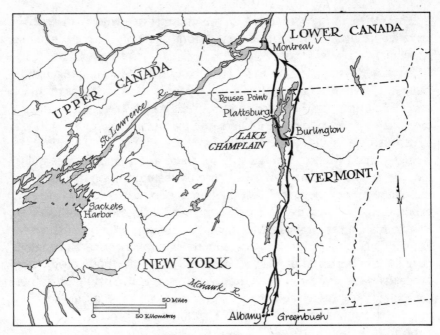

Baynes's Journey to Albany

An agreement of sorts is quickly concluded. Dearborn explains that his instructions do not allow him to sign an armistice, but he can issue orders for a temporary cessation of hostilities. The two men agree that should Washington countermand this order, four days' notice will be given before hostilities are resumed. Under this arrangement, the troops will act only on the defensive until a final decision is reached. To Dearborn, the procrastinator, this agreement has the great advantage of allowing him to recruit his forces and build up his supplies without fear of attack. "It is mutually understood that. . .no obstructions are to be attempted, on either side, to the passage of stores, to the frontier posts."

And Hull, who is desperate for both supplies and men? Hull is not included, specifically at Dearborn's request: "I could not include General Hull. . .he having received his orders directly from the department of war."

Thus is concluded a kind of truce, in which both sides are allowed to prepare for battle without actually engaging in one.

These arrangements completed, Lieutenant-Colonel Baynes prepares to take his leave. There is a brief altercation over the use of

156

Indians in the war. Dearborn, in strong language, attacks the British for using native warriors, implying that the Americans are free from reproach in this area. Baynes retorts that Hull's captured dispatches make it clear that he has been doing his best to persuade the Indians to fight for the Americans. That ends the argument. But Baynes has misread Hull's intentions. At Madison's insistence, the Americans use the Indians as scouts only. Hull's efforts have been designed only to keep the Indians neutral.

With great difficulty, Baynes convinces Dearborn to allow him to return to Montreal by a different route along the eastern shores of Lake Champlain; it allows him to size up American strength and assess the mood of the New Englanders.

The little coach clip-clops its way through Vermont's beguiling scenery, rattling down crooked clay roads and over rustic bridges, past stone mills perched above gurgling rivers, through neat, shaded villages hugging the sloping shoreline – a peaceful, pastoral land of farms, wayside inns, and the occasional classical courthouse, as yet untouched by battle. The war seems very far away and, Baynes notes, the people almost totally unprepared. The militia do not impress him.

"The men are independent in their habits and principles, their officers ignorant and totally uninformed in every thing relating to the possession of arms and possess no influence over the militia but in proportion as they court it by popular and familiar intercourse." A few, he notes, are prepared to march on Montreal; the rest just want to go home. More than half of them are absent with or without leave, and nobody seems able to control them.

Recruiting for the regular army, he reports to Prevost, is proceeding very slowly, even though the term of service is only five years and the bounty pay for signing up very liberal:

"There appears to exist in the United States the greatest contempt and repugnance to the restraint and discipline of a military life and few gentlemen of respectability are willing to become officers but prefer the militia where they obtain high rank without serving."

As the coach moves on along the maple-shaded roads, Baynes is subjected to a series of minor astonishments. He learns that one militia general is a farmer, another a sawmill keeper, a third a millwright. The coach pulls up at a tavern. Out comes the innkeeper to take the reins and water the horses. Baynes's sense of military decorum is severely shaken when he discovers that this servitor is a colonel and second-in-command of the entire Vermont militia. The gap between the British and the American attitudes toward their military is obviously wider than Baynes suspected, and he has more than a little trouble absorbing it. He concludes that of all the officers he has observed there is only one with any real military talent – the same commander at Burlington who vigorously opposed his presence in the United States.

As for the American people, they "have a very high and overrated opinion of their military prowess, conceiving it to be in their power to pillage Montreal and to march to Quebec whenever they think proper. The siege of the fortress alone they consider as a task of difficulty. From the actual state of the American forces assembled on Lake Champlain, I do not think there exists any intention of invading this part of the province."

As Baynes moves back to Canada, Dearborn dispatches a note to Hull, dated August 9, explaining what has happened and suggesting that the General of the Army of the Northwest make his own decision as to whether he should join in the truce. (Hull has just withdrawn from his beachhead at Sandwich, but Dearborn has no knowledge of that.) Reinforcements are, of course, out of the question. "The removal of any troops from Niagara to Detroit, while the present agreement continues, would be improper and incompatible with the true interest of the agreement."

Thus does Dearborn relieve himself of the responsibility of reinforcing Hull or of creating the promised diversion along the Niagara frontier that might prevent Brock from reinforcing Amherstburg. Communications being what they are, Hull cannot know this. And by the time Dearborn's letter reaches him, it will not matter.

•

BROWNSTOWN, MICHIGAN TERRITORY, August 9, 1812. Thomas Verchères de Boucherville, the fur trader and Amherstburg storekeeper, is weary of waiting. On and off for four days he and his comrades have been on the alert on the American side of the river, expecting to surprise another of Hull's armed escorts seeking to bring in the wagon train of supplies held up at the River Raisin. But the Americans do not come and finally Major Muir gives the order to embark for the Canadian shore.

The men are clambering into the boats when from the woods there issues a series of piercing cries. In a few minutes Tecumseh's scouts come bounding out of the thickets to report that a detachment of Long Knives has been spotted upriver "like the mosquitoes of the swamp in number." This is no minor force of the kind that was routed a few days before; Hull has sent six hundred men including two hundred regulars, supported by cavalry and cannon. He is determined that this time the supply train will get through.

Muir puts into action a plan proposed by Tecumseh: his troops will march to a ravine near the Indian village of Maguaga, three miles upriver from Brownstown, and there lie in wait. Their orders are to charge with the bayonet as soon as the first volley of musket balls is fired. The Indians will conceal themselves in the corn fields on the right and the left, securing the flanks.

De Boucherville and his companions, having no uniforms, stick sprigs of basswood into their caps for identification and set out along the muddy track for Maguaga. Soon an odour, sickly sweet, assails their nostrils, and a horrifying spectacle comes into view at the turn of the trail – the battlefield of the previous week. De Boucherville shudders and is seized with revulsion as he sees displayed before him the corpses of the cavalrymen, already decomposed and impaled on stakes by Tecumseh's men, who have left the cadavers in full view to terrify the Americans. Gnawed and mangled by crows and animals, the rotting bodies give off an indescribable stench.

At almost the same moment, James Dalliba, a young American artillery officer in Lieutenant-Colonel Miller's advancing force, sees the bloated and scalped carcass of the luckless ranger captain, McCullough, lying beside the road under its covering of bark.

Marching with the British is an Amherstburg acquaintance of de Boucherville, young John Richardson, a member of the widespread Askin family (John, Senior, is his grandfather). Richardson, not yet turned sixteen, is a gentleman volunteer in the 41st and a future novelist – one of Canada's first. He will never forget this silent march to Maguaga; thirty years later it remains vividly in his mind:

"No other sound than the measured step of the troops interrupted the solitude of the scene, rendered more imposing by the wild appearance of the warriors, whose bodies, stained and painted in the most frightful manner for the occasion, glided by us with almost noiseless velocity...some painted white, some black, others half black, half red; half black, half white; all with their hair plastered in such a way as to resemble the bristling quills of the porcupine, with no other covering than a cloth around their loins, yet armed to the teeth with rifles, tomahawks, war-clubs, spears, bows, arrows and scalping knives. Uttering no sound, intent only on reaching the enemy unperceived, they might have passed for the spectres of those wilds, the ruthless demons which War had unchained for the punishment and oppression of man."

Screened by the forest, the two forces move blindly towards one another, neither side knowing when or where the clash will take place but all sensing that within minutes men will fall and some will die. Most have had no experience of battle; many have had no military training; save for Miller's Tippecanoe veterans, few have fired a musket at a living human.

At Maguaga, the British and Canadians take up their position behind a low rise, each man hugging the ground as he would a friend. De Boucherville finds himself next to another acquaintance, Jean-Baptiste Bâby, whose family home at Sandwich has been seized by Hull. Nervous, he asks Bâby for a pinch of snuff "to keep me in countenance a little." A moment later comes the sound of an enemy drum, the stroke wavering slightly as if the drummer, too, fears whatever lies ahead.

The British remain concealed, waiting for the signal. Suddenly an American officer, brilliant in blue and gold, riding a superb horse, his hat covered by a three-foot plume, appears on an eminence. A shot rings out; the American falls dead at his horse's feet, and the battle is joined.

Confusion! A melee of painted bodies, scarlet tunics, snorting horses, flying tomahawks, splintered foliage, black musket smoke. On the left, Tecumseh leads his men forward in an attempt to turn the American flank. Five hundred yards to the right, another group of Indians, trying a similar manoeuvre, is forced back. To the British volunteers all Indians look alike; they believe the retreating natives to be part of the advancing enemy and fire on them. Ally battles ally as the skirmish grows hotter.

"Take care, de Boucherville!" cries an officer on the left. "The Kentuckians are aiming at you." Even as he speaks a ball strikes him in the head, and he falls into de Boucherville's arms. "Well, old fellow," thinks the volunteer to himself, "you came out of that all right." But a moment later he is hit in the thigh by a musket ball.

Muir, the British commander, seeing an American taking deliberate aim at him, hastily raises his short rifle and lays it across the shoulders of a fellow officer, Lieutenant Charles Sutherland. Both adversaries fire at the same time. The American drops dead; his rifle ball enters Sutherland's cheek, comes out the back of his neck and passes through Muir's shoulder. (Sutherland's wound is not mortal, but he will shortly die of loss of blood as a result of brushing his teeth before it is properly healed.)

Now occurs one of those maddening misunderstandings that frustrate the best-laid plans. Brock's reinforcements from the Niagara frontier, hustled across the river by Procter, arrive on the scene, sixty strong, just as Muir's bugler, by pre-arrangement, sounds the bayonet charge.

The new troops, confused, take this as a signal to retreat, and the British centre begins to break. Muir receives a second wound in the leg but carries on.

By now the American six-pounder is in action spraying grape-shot, its initial discharge so terrifying Lieutenant-Colonel Miller's horse that it throws the American commander to the ground. Tecumseh's warriors rush forward to take his scalp but are forced back. Miller remounts, cries for a cavalry charge. But the cavalry fails to respond, and the main advance is made by foot soldiers. The smoke is now so dense that no one can see for more than twenty paces.

Tecumseh is making a strategic withdrawal toward the west, drawing the American fire away from the retiring British and forcing Miller to divide his forces. The manoeuvre slows down the American advance, allows the British to reach the boats they have concealed on the beach and make their escape out of range of the American muskets.

Miller draws his men up in line and utters the obligatory words of commendation:

"My brave fellows! You have done well! Every man has done his duty. I give you my hearty thanks for your conduct this day; you have gained my highest esteem; you have gained fresh honor to yourselves and to the American Arms; your fellow soldiers will love you and your country will reward you...."

With this accolade ringing in their ears, the Americans move through the woods, seeking the dead and the wounded. Hidden in a cedar swamp under a gigantic deadfall lie three men—Thomas Verchères de Boucherville, his friend Jean-Baptiste Berthe (another member of the Askin family and a civilian volunteer), and a regular soldier. Caught in the crossfire between the British rear and the advancing Americans, they have run into the woods to escape the shower of musket balls. It is now four in the afternoon, but they cannot leave their soggy retreat for the enemy is only a few feet away. Finally, at ten, under cover of a violent thunderstorm, they crawl out of the water onto a drier knoll, guided by lightning flashes, and here they crouch, soaked through, for the rest of the night, while the rain beats down on them and a violent gale, wrenching the branches from the trees, puts them in as much danger as the battle itself.

De Boucherville's wound is bleeding but painless. He cakes earth over it as he has seen the Indians do, binding it with a towel brought along for just such a misfortune, and considers his plight. Only a few days before he was at dinner with some guests when he heard a drummer parading the streets of Amherstburg, beating the call to arms. With his friend Berthe and several others he answered the summons for volunteers, not pausing to finish his meal but taking care to bury all his money, secretly, in his backyard. Now here he is, wounded, wet, and miserable, waiting for the dawn.

At first light, he and his two companions set out for the river, watching all the time for the enemy. They reach it at four o'clock, gather some planks and strands of basswood from a deserted Indian village, construct a crude raft, and cross to an island in midstream. Here they do their utmost to attract attention, wiping their muskets dry and firing them off, making flags of their shirts and waving them on long poles. Eventually a boat rescues them. On the dockside are friends, officers, natives, civilians, all cheering. They had given de Boucherville and Berthe up for dead.

De Boucherville stumbles home, flops onto a sofa, falls into a dead sleep. When he wakes he is astonished to find an Indian by his bedside. It is Tecumseh himself, who has been sitting silently for hours waiting for him to wake.

A surgeon removes the ball from de Boucherville's thigh but cannot extract a quantity of shot. Tecumseh fetches a Shawnee healer, who prescribes a herbal remedy. In ten days the wound is healed, de Boucherville is back behind the counter of his store, and the Battle of Maguaga is a memory to be savoured in the retelling for the remainder of his days.

Hull, in his message to Washington, treats the battle as a stunning victory. It is scarcely that, for it has failed in its purpose of opening his line of supply. Captain Brush's wagon train still cannot get through, and Lieutenant-Colonel Miller, even in victory, cannot help. In the heat of the battle his troops have thrown away their knapsacks and are without rations, forced to lie all night in the open in the same driving thunderstorm that poured down on de Boucherville. Miller himself is tottering with fatigue, ague, and two wounds; he has been on and off the sick list for weeks. He sends to Hull for reinforcements and provisions in order to move on. Colonel McArthur arrives with a fleet of bateaux bringing two barrels of flour, one of pork, and considerable whiskey, all of which the troops devour in a single breakfast. The wounded are loaded into bateaux for the return voyage. But the British, who have control of the river, seize twelve boats, capture some fifty Americans, and recapture two of their own men held as prisoners.

At sunset an express arrives from Hull: because he cannot spare further reinforcements, Miller and his men are ordered to return to Detroit without completing their mission. They make their way to the river in the driving rain, soaking wet, shoeless, sleeping that night as best they can in dripping blankets. They reach Detroit at noon on August 11. Brush and the supply train remain pinned down at the River Raisin.

Miller has lost eighteen men killed and some sixty wounded. The British casualties are fewer: six killed, twenty-one wounded. But Hull writes to Eustis that "the victory was complete in every part of the line," and that is the way the history books will record it.

•

ISAAC BROCK has no time for democratic chatter. He prorogues the legislature on August 5 and, with the consent of his appointed council, declares martial law. He has decided on a mighty gamble: he will gather what troops he can, speed post-haste to Amherstburg at their head, and, if that fort has not fallen, provoke Hull into a fight, then try to get back to the Niagara frontier before the Americans attack. He is taking a long chance, but he has little choice. Off he goes, moving swiftly southwest through the province, calling for volunteers to accompany him to Amherstburg. Five hundred rush to apply, "principally the sons of Veterans, whom His Majesty's munificence settled in this country." He can take only half that number. The York Volunteers will become Brock's favourite militia unit, including among its officers such names as Ridout, Jarvis, and Robinson, all of them scions of the tight Upper Canada aristocracy, trained at the Reverend John Strachan's famous school at Cornwall. The war will entrench them in the Family Compact.

Brock reaches Port Dover on the north shore of Lake Erie on August 8, where he hopes enough boats have been commandeered to move his entire force to Amherstburg. The British have the immense advantage of being able to move troops swiftly by water in contrast to the Americans' slow drive through the wilderness. But at Dover, Brock finds that not nearly enough boats have been provided, while those available are leaky, uncaulked, dilapidated. A day is required to make ten of them ready, and these are in such bad shape that the men grow exhausted from constant bailing.

The flotilla can move no faster than the slowest vessel, the hundred-ton schooner *Nancy*, which must be manhandled over the narrow neck of the Long Point peninsula – a backbreaking task that requires the energy of all the boat crews – and later dragged by ropes onto the beach at Port Talbot. Here the troops take refuge from the same thunderstorm that is drenching the Americans after the battle of Maguaga.

All that day the men, joined by sixty volunteers from the village of Queenston on the Niagara, lie in the boats or on the sand as the rain pelts down.

Yet they remain in good spirits. Brock notes it: "In no instance have I witnessed greater cheerfulness and constancy than were displayed by these Troops under the fatigue of a long journey in Boats and during extremely bad Weather...their conduct throughout excited my admiration."

The admiration is mutual. At one point Brock's own boat strikes a sunken rock. His boat crew goes to work with oars and poles. When they fail to push her free, the General, in full uniform, leaps over the side, waist deep in water. In an instant the others follow and soon have the boat afloat. Brock climbs aboard, opens his liquor case, gives every man a glass of spirits. The news of this act, spreading from boat to boat, animates the force.

On August 11, the weather again turns capricious. The wind drops. The men, wet and exhausted from lack of sleep, are forced to row in relays for hours. Then a sudden squall forces the flotilla once more in to shore. That night the weather clears, and the impatient general makes another attempt to get underway, this time in the dark, his boat leading with a lantern in the stern. They sail all night, the boats too crowded for the men to lie down. The following day they hear that Hull has re-crossed the river to Detroit and that there has been a skirmish (Maguaga) on the American side. At Point Pelee that after-

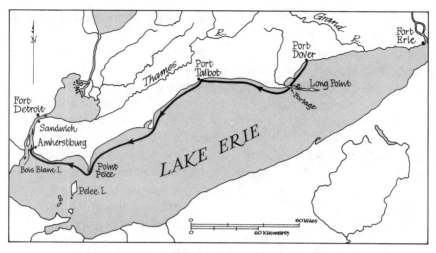

Brock's Passage to Amherstburg

noon, some of the men boil their pork; others drop exhausted onto the beach. Early next morning they set off again and at eight in the forenoon straggle into Amherstburg, exhausted from rowing, their faces peeling from sunburn.

Brock has preceded them. Unable to rest, the General and a vanguard of troops have departed the previous afternoon and reached their objective shortly before midnight on August 13. Lieutenant-Colonel Procter and Matthew Elliott are waiting on the quayside. Across the water from Bois Blanc Island comes the rattle of musketry. It startles Brock. When Elliott explains that the Indians, bivouacked on the island, are expressing their joy at the arrival of reinforcements, the General expresses concern over the waste of ammunition: "Do, pray, Elliott, fully explain my wishes and motives, and tell the Indians that I will speak to them to-morrow on this subject."

Midnight has passed. But before Brock can sleep he must read the dispatches and mail captured at Brownstown. He sits in Elliott's study with his aide, Major J.B. Glegg, the yellow light from tallow candles flickering across a desk strewn with maps and papers. Suddenly the door opens and Elliott stands before him accompanied by a tall Indian dressed in a plain suit of tanned deerskin, fringed at the seams, and wearing leather moccasins heavily ornamented with porcupine quills. This is clearly a leader of stature. In his nose he wears three silver ornaments in the shape of coronets, and from his neck is hung, on a string of coloured wampum, a large silver medallion of George III.

The Indian is beaming. Glegg gets an instant impression of energy and decision. This must be Tecumseh.

Brock rises, hand outstretched to his ally. The contrast is striking: the British general—fair, large-limbed, blue-eyed, impeccable in his scarlet jacket, blue-and-white riding trousers, and Hessian boots—towers over the lithe figure of the Shawnee. Brief salutations follow. Brock explains about the waste of ammunition. Tecumseh agrees. Each man has taken the other's measure and both are impressed. Brock will write to Lord Liverpool that "a more sagacious and gallant Warrior does not I believe exist. He was the admiration of every one who conversed with him...." Tecumseh's comment, delivered to his followers, is blunter. "This," says Tecumseh, "is a *man*!"

Brock calls a council of his officers, asks for a military appreciation. Tecumseh urges an immediate attack on Detroit, unrolls a strip of elm bark, pulls his scalping knife from his belt, and proceeds to scratch out an accurate map of the fort and its surroundings.

Brock points out that the British and Indians will be outnumbered by the Americans: "We are committed to a war in which the enemy will always surpass us in numbers, equipment and resources." One by one his officers are polled. One by one they opt for caution: a crossing is too dangerous to attempt. Lieutenant-Colonel Henry Procter, who will one day clash with Tecumseh over tactics, is particularly cautious. Only one man, Colonel Robert Nichol, the diminutive ex-storekeeper who has just been named quartermaster general of the militia, supports Brock. Nichol has lived in Detroit, knows every cranny of town and fort, boasts that he can lead the troops to any point that Brock wants to attack. He and the commander are old friends, their acquaintance going back to 1804 when Brock commanded at Fort Erie and Nichol ran a general store. Nichol's sudden appointment to field rank has offended some of the political higher-ups, but Brock knows his man. It is said that Nichol would follow his general into Vesuvius if need be.

At this midnight council the contrast between Brock and Hull is starkly clear. Brock listens carefully to his subordinates' reservations, then speaks: nothing, he says, can be gained by delay. "I have decided on crossing, and now, gentlemen, instead of any further advice, I entreat of you to give me your cordial and hearty support."

The following morning, standing beneath a great oak on the outskirts of the fort, he addresses several hundred Indians representing more than a dozen tribes on both sides of the border. (Even the recalcitrant Iroquois are here, though only thirty in number.) He has come, says Brock, to battle the Long Knives who have invaded the country of the King, their father. The Long Knives are trying to force both the British and the Indians from their lands. If the Indians will make common cause with the British, the combined forces will soon drive the enemy back to the boundaries of Indian territory.

Tecumseh rises to reply. This polyglot assembly is of his making – the closest he will ever get to achieving the confederacy of which he dreams. The hazel eyes flash, the oval face darkens as he conjures up the memory of Tippecanoe:

"They suddenly came against us with a great force while I was absent, and destroyed our village and slew our warriors."

All the bitterness against the land-hunger of the frontier settlers is revived:

"They came to us hungry and cut off the hands of our brothers who gave them corn. We gave them rivers of fish and they poisoned our fountains. We gave them forest-clad mountains and valleys full of game and in return what did they give our warriors and our women? Rum and trinkets and a grave!"

Brock does not intend to reveal the details of his attack plan to such a large assembly. The oratory finished, he invites Tecumseh and a few older chiefs to meet at Elliott's house. Here, through interpreters, he explains his strategy as the chiefs nod approval. The General is concerned, however, about alcohol: can Tecumseh prevent his followers from drinking to excess? The Shawnee replies that before his people left the Wabash they promised to abstain from all spirits until they had humbled the Long Knives. Brock responds with satisfaction: "If this resolution be persevered in, you must conquer."

He has one further act of diplomacy before he leaves for Sandwich. He issues a general order intended to heal the wounds caused by Hull's divisive proclamation:

"The major-general cannot avoid expressing his surprise at the numerous desertions which have occurred from the ranks of the militia, to which circumstance the long stay of the enemy on this side of the river must in great measure be ascribed. He is willing to believe that their conduct proceeded from an anxiety to get in their harvest, and not from any predilection for the principles or government of the United States."

This pretty fiction serves its purpose of uniting the people behind him. Hull has deserted them: Brock, by implication, has promised an amnesty. As he rides that same afternoon past the ripening apple trees to Sandwich he knows he is passing through friendly country.

●

DETROIT, MICHIGAN TERRITORY, August 12, 1812. Colonel Lewis Cass is seething with frustration over what he conceives to be the inadequacies and follies of his commander. He can contain himself no longer and finds a temporary outlet for his anger in a letter to his brother-in-law:

"Our situation is become critical. If things get worse, you will have a letter from me giving you a particular statement of this business. As bad as you may think of our situation it is still worse than you believe. I cannot descend into particulars for fear this should fall into the hands of the enemy."

From the outset he has thought of Hull as a weak old man. Now other, more sinister epithets begin to form in his mind. Cass is contemplating something very close to treason, a word he will shortly apply to his commanding officer.

His style is as blunt as his body. He has powerful arms and legs and a trunk like an ox. Nobody would call him handsome. Long, unruly hair dominates a coarse face. A later official portrait shows him scowling blackly at the artist, one hand thrust into his tunic, Napoleon-fashion. At thirty, he has the resonant voice of a frontier lawyer, toughened on the court circuit, his endurance tested by years spent on horseback on old Indian trails or on pitching flatboats in wilderness rivers, arguing and pleading in primitive courthouses where the judge, on occasion, has been known to descend from the bench to wrestle a pugnacious spectator into submission.

He is an ambitious man, Cass. He has been a member of the Ohio House, a state marshal, a brigadier-general in the militia. He loves the military life, likes to wear splendid uniforms (his officer's plume is the highest of any), insists on parading his men whenever the opportunity allows, believes in regular, arduous drilling. For all that he is popular, for his is the easy camaraderie of the circuit court. He mixes freely with his men, who respect him in spite of a certain humourlessness. Unlike Hull, Cass conveys an air of absolute conviction; he *knows* he is right; and the fact that Hull, in Cass's view, is wrong drives him to distraction. In spite of his ponderous appearance he has all the nervous energy of a tomcat—not the kind of man to sit quietly by and watch the enemy preparing for an assault.

Cass's disillusionment with Hull is shared by his fellow officers and has filtered down through the ranks. On this same day (the very day on which Wellington's forces enter Madrid), the scout Robert Lucas is writing to a friend in Portsmouth, Ohio, in much the same vein:

"Never was there a more Patriotic army...neither was there ever an army that had it more completely in their power to have accomplished every object of their Desire than the Present, And must now be sunk into Disgrace for want of a General at their head—

"Never was there officers...more united than our Patriotic Colonels...to promote the Public good neither was there ever men of talents as they are so shamefully opposed by an imbesile or Treacherous Commander as they have been.... Would to God Either of our Colonels had the command, if they had, we might yet wipe off the foul stain that has been brought upon us...."

The army is close to mutiny. A round robin is circulating among the troops urging that Hull be replaced by McArthur. Cass, Findlay, and McArthur meet with Miller and offer to depose Hull if he will take command. Miller refuses but agrees to unite with the others to oppose Hull and give the command to McArthur. McArthur, who has already said privately that Hull will not do, also refuses—nobody wants to bell the cat. All three turn to Cass, who agrees to write secretly to Governor Meigs of Ohio, urging him to march at once with two thousand men. The assumption is that Meigs will depose Hull.

"From causes not fit to be put on paper but which I trust I shall live to communicate to you, this army has been reduced to a critical and alarming situation," Cass writes. When he finishes the letter, he, McArthur, Gaylor (the Quartermaster General), and Elijah Brush of the Michigan state militia all affix their signatures to a cryptic postscript:

"Since the other side of this letter was written, new circumstances have arisen. The British force is opposite, and our situation has nearly reached its crisis. Believe all the bearer will tell you. Believe it, however it may astonish you; as much as if told by one of us. Even a c—— is talked of by the ———! The bearer will supply the vacancy. On you we depend."

The missing words are "capitulation" and "commanding officer." The signature of Lieutenant-Colonel Miller, the career officer, is conspicuously absent.

Hull by this time knows of the incipient plot against him but hesitates to arrest the ringleaders, fearing perhaps a general uprising. He has, however, the perfect excuse for ridding himself temporarily of the leading malcontents. Captain Henry Brush, still pinned down at the

River Raisin, has discovered a back-door route to Detroit; it is twice as long as the river road but hidden from Fort Amherstburg. When he asks again for an escort for his supply train, Hull is only too pleased to dispatch both Cass and McArthur with 350 men for this task. They leave Detroit at noon on August 14.

The General has, of course, weakened his own garrison in spite of strong evidence that the British, now directly across the river at Sandwich, are planning an attack. What is in Hull's mind? Has he already given up? He has in his possession a letter, intercepted from a British courier, written by Lieutenant-Colonel Procter to Captain Roberts at Michilimackinac, informing him that the British force facing Detroit is so strong that he need send no more than five thousand Indians to support it!

It is a sobering revelation. Brock and Tecumseh face Hull across the river; now at his rear he sees another horde of painted savages.

He cannot know that the letter is a fake, purposely planted by Brock and Procter, who already have an insight into his troubled state of mind through captured documents. There are only a few hundred Indians at Mackinac, and on August 12 they are in no condition to go anywhere, being "as drunk as Ten Thousand Devils" in the words of John Askin, Jr. But Brock well knows that the threat of the Indians is as valuable as their presence and a good deal less expensive.

Many months later, when his peers sit in judgement upon him, Hull will swear to his firm belief that the British had no intention of attacking Detroit. He believes their conduct of the war will be entirely defensive. He has put himself in Prevost's shoes but certainly not in those of Isaac Brock who, contrary to all instructions, is preparing to invade the United States.

Brock is completing the secret construction of a battery directly across from Detroit – one long eighteen-pound gun, two long twelve-pounders, and a couple of mortars – hidden for the moment behind a building and a screen of oak. Lieutenant James Dalliba of Hull's ordnance department suspects what is going on. Dalliba, who has twenty-eight heavy guns and has constructed his own battery in the centre of town, asks Hull if he may open fire.

"Sir, if you will give permission, I will clear the enemy on the opposite shore from the lower batteries."

Dalliba will not soon forget Hull's reply:

"Mr. Dalliba, I will make an agreement with the enemy that if they will never fire on me I will never fire on them," and rides off, remarking that "those who live in glass houses must take care how they throw stones."

The following morning, to the army's astonishment, Hull has a large marquee, striped red and blue, pitched in the centre of camp, just south of the walls of the fort. It is a measure of the army's low morale and lack of confidence in their general that many believe Hull is in league with the British and that the coloured tent is intended as a signal.

In a barrack room, a court of inquiry under the ailing Lieutenant-Colonel Miller is investigating Porter Hanks's surrender of Mackinac. Hanks has asked for a hearing to clear his name. But part way through the testimony an officer looking out onto the river spies a boat crossing from the opposite shore under a white flag. Miller adjourns the hearing. It will never be reopened.

Up the bank come Brock's two aides, Major J.B. Glegg and Lieutenant-Colonel John Macdonell, with a message for Hull. They are blindfolded and confined to a house in the town near the fort while Hull ponders Brock's ultimatum:

"The force at my disposal authorizes me to require of you the immediate surrender of Fort Detroit...."

The force at his disposal! Brock has at most thirteen hundred men; Hull has more than two thousand. Brock is proposing to attack a fortified position with an inferior force, an adventure that Hull, in declining Amherstburg, has said would require odds of two to one.

But Brock has studied his man, knows his vulnerable spot:

"It is far from my intention to join in a war of extermination; but you must be aware that the numerous body of Indians who have attached themselves to my troops will be beyond my control the moment the contest commences.... Lieutenant-Colonel M'Donnell and major Glegg are fully authorised to conclude any arrangement that may lead to prevent the unnecessary effusion of blood."

What Brock is threatening *is* a war of extermination – a bloody battle in which, if necessary, he is quite prepared to accept the slaughter of prisoners and of innocent civilians, including women and children. He is, in short, contemplating total war more than a century before the phrase comes into common use. The war is starting to escalate as all wars must; a zeal for victory clouds compassion; the end begins to justify the means.

Like other commanders, Brock salves his conscience with the excuse that he cannot control his native allies; nonetheless he is quite happy, in fact eager, to use them. It is sophistry to say they have "attached themselves" to his troops; he and his colleagues have actively and consistently enlisted their support. The Americans are equally hypocritical; they pompously upbraid the British for waging uncivilized warfare, but their own men take scalps indiscriminately. The conflict, which began so softly and civilly, is beginning to brutalize both sides. The same men who censure the Indians for dismembering non-combatants with tomahawks are quite prepared to blow the limbs off soldiers and civilians alike with twenty-four-pound cannonballs. Though it may offer some comfort to the attacker, the range of the weapon makes little difference to its victim.

Hull mulls over Brock's extraordinary document for more than three hours while the General's two aides fidget behind their blindfolds. At last he summons up an answer:

"...I have no other reply than to inform you, that I am prepared to meet any force which may be at your disposal, and any consequences which may result from any exertion of it you may think proper to make."

At about three that afternoon, Major Josiah Snelling of Miller's 4th Infantry steps out onto the street to see the General's son and aide, Captain Abraham Hull, heading off with his father's reply in his pocket. The little village is alive with people running toward the fort carrying their family possessions or burying their valuables. Snelling picks up his glass and sees that the British across the river are chopping down the oaks and removing the building that masks their battery. He forms up his men, marches them through the gates of the fort, and, on Hull's orders, mans the ramparts.

Hull's back seems to have stiffened.

"The British have demanded the place," he says. "If they want it they must fight for it."

He sends a messenger to recall the party under Cass and McArthur, who have become entangled in a swamp some twenty-five miles away. The troops in Detroit, knowing their force to be superior, are astonished at what they consider the insolence of the British.

The boat carrying Brock's aides has no sooner reached the Canadian shore than the cannonade commences. Hundreds of pounds of cast iron hurtle across the mile-wide river, tearing into walls and trees and plunging through rooftops but doing little damage. James Dalliba with his battery of seven twenty-four-pounders replies immediately to the first British volley. He stands on the ramparts until he sees the smoke and flash of the British cannon, then shouts "Down!" allowing his men to drop behind the parapet before the shot strikes. The British are aiming directly at his battery, attempting to put it out of action.

A large pear tree near Dalliba's battery is blocking the guns and giving the British a point to aim at. Dalliba orders a young Michigan volunteer, John Miller, to cut it down. As he is hacking away, a cannonball finishes the job for him. Miller turns and shouts across the water: "Send us another, John Bull; you can cut faster than I can!"

The artillery duel continues until well after dark. The people scramble after every burst, ducking behind doors, clinging to walls, until they become used to the flash and roar. In the doorway of a house by the river a *Canadien* stands unconcerned, puffing on his pipe, as the hot metal screams by him until a shell fragment tears the stem from his mouth. Infuriated, he seizes his musket, wades out into the river, and fires back at the British battery until his ammunition is exhausted.

A mortar shell, its fuse burning brightly, falls upon the house of Augustus Langdon on Woodward Avenue. It tears its way through the roof, continues through the upper storey and into the dining room, dropping directly upon the table around which Langdon and his family are sitting. It rips through the table, continues through the floor and into the cellar as the family dashes for safety. They are no sooner clear than the shell explodes with such power that it tears the roof away.

Hull's brigade major, Thomas Jesup, reports that two British warships are anchored in midstream just opposite Spring Wells, two miles from the fort, and that the British appear to be collecting boats for an invasion. At sundown, Hull sends Major Snelling to Spring Wells to report on the British movements. Snelling reports that the *Queen Charlotte* is anchored in the river but can be dislodged by one of the fort's twenty-four-pounders. Hull shakes his head, finds reasons why the gun can't be moved. Something odd is happening to the commander. To Jesup he seems pale and very much confused.

At ten that evening the cannonade ceases. Quiet descends upon the American camp. The night is clear, the sky tinselled with stars, the river glittering in the moonlight. At eleven, General Hull, fully clothed, his boots still laced, slumps down in the piazza of the barracks and tries to sleep. Even as he slumbers, Tecumseh and his Indians are slipping into their canoes and silently crossing to the American side.

SANDWICH, UPPER CANADA, August 16, 1812. Dawn.

The moment is at hand. Brock's couriers have scoured the country-side, roused the militia from the farms, emptied the mills and harvest fields. Now these raw troops gather on the shore at McKee's Point, four hundred strong, waiting their turn to enter the boats and cross to the enemy side. Three hundred have been issued the cast-off crimson tunics of the 41st to deceive Hull into believing that Brock's force of regular soldiers is double its actual strength.

The Indians are already across, lurking in the forest, ready to attack Hull's flank and rear should he resist the crossing. Thomas Verchères de Boucherville has watched their war dance the night before; he finds it an extraordinary spectacle – six hundred figures, leaping in the firelight, naked except for their breech cloths, some daubed in vermilion, others in blue clay, and still others tattooed with black and white from head to foot. Even to de Boucherville, with his years of experience in the fur trade, the scene is macabre – frightful and horrifying beyond expression. It occurs to him that a stranger from Europe witnessing it for the first time would believe he was standing at the very entrance to Hell "with the gates thrown open to let the damned out for an hour's recreation on earth!"

But on this calm and beautiful Sunday morning, a different spec-tacle presents itself. A soft August sun is just rising as the troops climb into the boats and push out into the river, their crimson jackets almost perfectly reflected in the glassy waters. Behind them, the green meadows and ripening orchards are tinted with the dawn light; ahead, in the lead boat, stands the glittering figure of their general. Charles Askin thinks it the handsomest sight he has ever seen, even though in a few hours he may well be fighting his own brother-in-law. Already cannonballs and mortar bombs are screaming overhead.

On the far bank, pocked and riven by springs (hence the name Spring Wells), the figure of Tecumseh can be discerned, astride a white mustang, surrounded by his chiefs. The enemy is not in sight and the troops land without incident or opposition.

Brock's plan is to outwait Hull, draw him out of his fort, and do battle in the open where, he believes, his regulars can devastate the wavering American militia. But now an Indian scout rides in with word that enemy horsemen have been spotted three miles to the rear. This is the detachment, 350 strong, that Hull has sent to the River

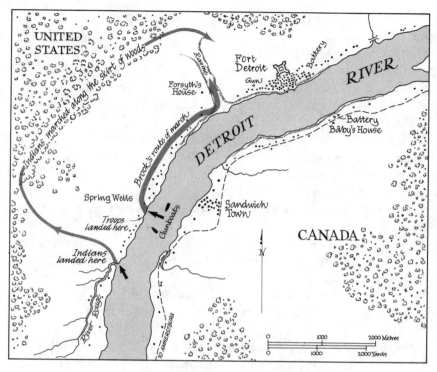

The Capture of Detroit

Raisin and recalled to reinforce Detroit. Brock's position suddenly becomes precarious. His men are caught between a strong fortification and an advancing column in their rear. Without hesitation Brock changes his plans and decides to attack immediately.

He draws up his troops in column, doubling the distance between the sections to make his diminutive force seem larger. His route to Detroit hugs the river bank at his right, protected by the guns of the *Queen Charlotte* and the *Hunter* (Frederic Rolette's command) and by the battery at Sandwich. On his left, slipping through the corn fields and the woods, are Tecumseh's Indians. To many of the militia this is familiar territory. Charles Askin, marching with the 2nd Brigade, greets and waves to old friends along the road, many of whom seem happy to see him.

At the town gate, the forward troops can spot two long guns – twenty-four-pounders – positioned so that they can enfilade the road. A single round shot, properly placed, is capable of knocking down a file of twenty-five men like dominoes. American gunners stand beside

175

their weapons with matches burning. William McCay, who has come up from Queenston as a volunteer and is marching with Captain Hatt's company just behind the British 41st, screws up his courage, expecting to be fired upon at any moment. Young John Richardson, the future novelist, cannot help a sinking feeling in the pit of his stomach that he and his comrades are marching directly into the jaws of death, for the road "is as bad as any cul-de-sac."

Brock, at the head of the line, rides impassively forward, a brilliant target in his cocked hat and gold epaulettes. His old friend, little Colonel Nichol, trots up to remonstrate with his commander:

"Pardon me, General, but I cannot forbear entreating you not to expose yourself thus. If we lose you, we lose all; let me pray you to allow the troops to pass on, led by their own officers."

To which Brock replies: "Master Nichol, I duly appreciate the advice you give me, but I feel that in addition to their sense of loyalty and duty, many here follow me from a feeling of personal regard, and I will never ask them to go where I do not lead them."

Why have the guns not fired? There is a host of explanations after the fact. One is that Hull refuses to give the order for reasons of cowardice or treason. Another, more plausible, is that the British are still out of effective range and the American artillery commander is waiting until they draw closer so that his grape-shot – a large number of musket balls packed in canvas bags – can mow down the column.

If so, Brock outwits him, for suddenly, the British wheel to the left through an orchard and into a ravine protected from the enemy guns. John Richardson, for one, breathes more freely. Brock, meanwhile, commandeers William Forsyth's farmhouse as a headquarters, then climbs up the bank to reconnoitre his position.

The town of Detroit, a huddle of some three hundred houses, lies before him. Its population, three-quarters French-speaking, is inured to siege and plunder. It has been transferred three times by treaty, twice besieged by Indians, burned to the ground only a few years previously. It is enclosed on three sides by a wooden stockade of fourteen-foot pickets. Entrance can be gained only by three massive gates. On the high ground to the northeast, covering three acres, sprawls the fort, built originally by the British, repaired by the Americans. The parapet is eleven feet high, twelve feet thick. A ditch, six feet deep and twelve feet across, together with a double row of pickets, each twice the height of a man, surrounds the whole. It is heavily armed with long guns, howitzers, and mortars. Most of the troops are quartered outside the walls.

The American position seems impregnable, but Brock has a secret weapon – psychology. Hull has already been led to believe that three hundred militiamen are regulars. Now Tecumseh and his Indians are ordered to march in single file across an open space, out of range but in full view of the garrison. The spectacle has some of the quality of a vaudeville turn. The Indians lope across the meadow, vanish into the forest, circle back and repeat the manoeuvre three times. Hull's officers, who cannot tell one Indian from another, count fifteen hundred painted savages, screeching and waving tomahawks. Hull is convinced he is outnumbered.

Brock is still scrutinizing his objective, all alone, some fifty yards in front of his own troops, when an American officer suddenly appears, waving a white flag and bearing a note from his general. The American commander, it seems, is on the verge of giving up without a fight.

●

INSIDE THE PALISADE, William Hull appears on the edge of nervous collapse. Except for Colonel Findlay, he has no battalion commanders to fall back on. Cass and McArthur have not yet returned. Miller is too ill to stand up. Hull's son and aide, Abraham, is not only drunk but has picked a fight with a senior officer, in his father's presence, and challenged him to a duel. A dozen Michigan volunteers on picket duty at the rear of the fort have allowed themselves to be captured by Tecumseh's Indians. Elijah Brush, in charge of the Michigan militia, believes that if attack comes his men will flee. The fort itself is so jammed with soldiers, civilians, and cattle, all seeking refuge from the bombardment, that it is difficult to manoeuvre.

The cannonade has unnerved Hull. He saw blood enough in his Revolutionary days, but now he is transfixed by a spectacle so horrifying that it reduces him to jelly. Lieutenant Porter Hanks, relieved for the moment of appearing at his court of inquiry, has come into the fort to visit an old friend and is standing in the doorway of the officers' mess with several others when a sixteen-pound cannonball comes bouncing over the parapet and skipping across the open space. It strikes Hanks in the midriff, cutting him in two, then tears both legs off Cass's surgeon's mate, Dr. James Reynolds, instantly killing him and mangling a second man with the appropriately grisly name of Blood.

A second cannonball dispatches two more soldiers. Blood and

brains spatter the walls and the gowns of some women who have sought refuge nearby. One drops senseless to the ground; others begin to scream. Hull cannot be sure from a distance who is dead, but a frightful thought crosses his mind: can it be his own buxom daughter, Betsey? It is more than possible. She and her child have taken refuge in the fort with most of the civilians, all of whom Hull knows as well as his own family.

Something very odd is happening to Hull: he is becoming cata- tonic; his brain, overloaded by too much information, refuses to func- tion. It has happened before to better commanders when events crowded in too quickly, to Washington at the Battle of Brandywine, for one, and it will happen again – to Napoleon at Waterloo, to Stonewall Jackson at White Oak Swamp, to Douglas MacArthur at Manila.

Hull's brigade major, Jesup, finds his commander half-seated, half-crouched on an old tent that is lying on the ground, his back to the ramparts under the curtain of the fort that faces the enemy. Save for the movement of his jaws he seems comatose. He is chewing tobacco at a furious rate, filling his mouth with it, absently adding quid after quid, sometimes removing a piece, rolling it between his fingers and then replacing it, so that his hands run with spittle while the brown juice dribbles from the corners of his mouth, staining his neckcloth, his beard, his cravat, his vest. He chews as if the fate of the army depended upon the movement of his jaws, rubbing the lower half of his face from time to time until it, too, is stained dark brown. Jesup, who has reconnoitred the British position, asks for permission to move up some artillery and attack their flank with dragoons. Hull nods, but he is clearly not in control. All he can say, as much to himself as to Jesup, is that a cannonball has killed four men.

It is the future as much as the present that renders him numb. A procession of ghastly possibilities crowds his mind; his troops desert- ing pell-mell to the enemy; the women and children starving through a long siege; cannon fire dismembering more innocent bystanders; and finally – the ultimate horror – the Indians released by Brock and Tecumseh, bent on revenge for Tippecanoe and all that came before it, ravaging, raping, burning, killing. He sees his daughter scalped, his grandchild mutilated, his friends and neighbours butchered. He believes himself outnumbered and outmanoeuvred, his plea for rein- forcements unheeded. Sooner or later, he is convinced, defeat is inevitable. If he postpones it, the blood of innocent people will be on his hands. If he accepts it now, before the battle is joined, he can save hundreds of lives. He can, of course, fight on to the last man and go into the history books as a hero. But can he live with himself, however briefly, if he takes the hero's course?

There is another thought, too, a guilty thought, lurking like a vagrant in the darker recesses of that agitated mind. The memory of the notorious proclamation has returned to haunt him. He himself has threatened no quarter to any of the enemy who fight beside the Indians. Can he or his charges, then, expect mercy in a prolonged struggle? Might the enemy not use his own words to justify their allies' revenge?

The shells continue to scream above his head and explode. Six men are now dead, several more wounded, the fort in a turmoil. Hull determines to ask for a cease-fire and a parley with Brock, scrawls a note, hands it to his son, asks him to have Major Snelling take it across the river. (Incredibly, it does not occur to him that Brock may be with his troops outside the palisade.) At the same time he orders a white tablecloth hung out of a window where Dixon, the British artillery commander on the Canadian shore, can see it. He will not fight to the last man; in the future metropolis of Detroit there will be no Hull Boulevard, no Avenue of the Martyrs.

Abraham Hull ties a handkerchief to a pike and gives it to Snelling, who declares he'll be damned if he'll disgrace his country by taking it out of the fort. Young Hull takes it himself and crosses the river, only to discover that Brock is on the American side. When he returns, Snelling is persuaded to seek out the British general.

Outside the fort, Jesup, seeking to take command of the dragoons to meet Brock's expected attack, finds the whole line breaking up, the men marching back toward the fort by platoons. Baffled, he asks what on earth is going on. An officer riding by tells him: "Look to the fort!" Jesup for the first time sees the white flag.

He rides back, accosts Hull, demands to know if surrender is being considered. Hull's reply is unintelligible. Jesup urges Hull to hold out at least until McArthur and Cass return. But all Hull can exclaim is, "My God, what shall I do with these women and children?"

Hull has ordered the Ohio volunteers to retreat into the fort. Their commander, Colonel Findlay, now rides up in a rage and asks, "What the hell am I ordered here for?" Hull replies, in a trembling voice, that several men have been killed and that he believes he can obtain better terms from Brock if he capitulates now than if he waits for a storm or a siege.

"Terms!" shouts Findlay. "Damnation! We can beat them on the plain. I did not come here to capitulate; I came here to fight!"

He seeks out the ailing Miller.

"The General talks of surrender," says Findlay. "Let us put him under arrest."

But Lieutenant-Colonel Miller, a regular officer, is no mutineer:

"Colonel Findlay, I am a soldier; I shall obey my superior officer."

By now the shelling has ceased. Hidden in the ravine, Brock's men are enjoying breakfast provided by William Forsyth, one of 120 British males who refused to change their allegiance when Detroit became an American community in 1796. Forsyth's house lies in the ravine, and its owner, who has been plundered by Hull, is glad to open his doors to Brock's officers and the contents of pantry and cellar to his troops, who manage in this brief period to consume twenty-four gallons of brandy, fifteen gallons of madeira and nine of port.

In the midst of this unexpected revel, some of the men spot Brock's two aides, Glegg and Macdonell, moving toward the fort with a flag of truce. A buzz of excitement: is it all to be over so quickly? Some – especially the younger officers – hope against hope that Hull will not give in. They thirst for glory and for promotion, which can only be gained in the smoke of battle and (a thought swiftly banished) the death or incapacity of their superiors. In this they resemble Tecumseh's young men, who have flocked to his side also seeking glory and hoping, some of them, to gain precedence over the older chiefs who try to dissuade them from rashness. But most of Brock's followers breathe a little more freely. Charles Askin, a seasoned son of the frontier, wishes for a cease-fire for the sake of the women and children who, he believes, will be massacred by the Indians once the action commences.

Hull wants a truce, has asked for three days. Brock gives him three hours: after that he will attack.

After this no-nonsense ultimatum it becomes clear that Hull is prepared for a full surrender. He will give up everything – the fort, its contents, all the ordnance, all supplies, all the troops, even those commanded by the absent Cass and McArthur and by Captain Henry Brush at the River Raisin. *Everything.* When Hull tries tentatively to make some provision for those Canadian deserters who have come over to his side, Macdonell replies with a curt "Totally inadmissible." Hull makes no further remonstrance. The surrender details he leaves to Elijah Brush and Miller, actually to Brush alone, since Miller, trembling with ague, is now prostrate on the ground. But sick or not, he is in no mood to sign any surrender document and does so only reluctantly.

Two more signatures are required – those of Hull and Brock. The British general now rides into the fort accompanied by a fife and drum corps playing "The British Grenadiers" and by his advance guard, which includes John Beverley Robinson, the future chief justice of Upper Canada, Samuel Peters Jarvis, whose family will give its name to one of Toronto's best-known streets, and two members of the Askin family, Charles and his fifteen-year-old nephew, John Richardson. Askin, for one, has never felt so proud as at this moment.

The advance guard, however, has advanced a little too quickly. The articles of surrender stipulate that the Americans must leave the fort before the British enter. A confused melee follows. The American soldiers are in a turmoil, some crying openly, a few of the officers breaking their swords and some of the soldiers their muskets rather than surrender them. Others cry "Treason!" and "Treachery!" and heap curses and imprecations on their general's head. One of the Ohio volunteers tries to stab Macdonell before the advance guard moves back across the drawbridge.

Within the fort, Abraham Hull wakens in his quarters from a sound sleep, doubtless brought on by his earlier inebriation, to discover enemy soldiers entering the fort. He breaks through a window and, hatless, rushes up to a British officer to demand his business there with his "redcoat rascals." The officer raises his sword and is about to run him through when an American runs up to explain that the General's son is temporarily deranged.

Finally the tangle is straightened out. The Americans stack their arms and move out of the fort. The 4th Regiment of regulars, its members in despair and in tears, gives up its colours, sewn by a group of Boston ladies and carried through the Battle of Tippecanoe. Charles Askin, watching them shamble past, wonders at the legend of their invincibility. To him they look like the poorest set of soldiers he has seen in a long time, their situation and their ragged clothing making them appear as sick men.

Now the British and Canadians officially enter the fort, the regulars in the lead, followed first by the uniformed militia, then by those not in uniform and, bringing up the rear, Tecumseh's followers led by the chiefs and the officers of the British Indian Department, themselves dressed and painted as Indians.

Down comes the Stars and Stripes. A bluejacket from one of the gunboats has tied a Union Jack around his body in preparation for this moment. It is hoisted high to the cheers of the troops. John Richardson, whose musket is taller than himself, is one of those chosen to mount the first guard at the flagstaff. He struts up and down his post, peacock proud, casting his eyes down at the vanquished Americans on the esplanade below the fort. Almost at this moment, in Kentucky, Henry Clay is predicting the fall of Fort Amherstburg and the speedy conquest of Upper Canada.

As the flag goes up, the Indians pour through the town, cheering, yelling, firing off their guns and seizing American horses. There is looting but no savagery; Tecumseh keeps his promise to Brock that his people will not molest the prisoners. As the two ride together through the fort, the general seems larger than life in his black cocked hat – his crimson uniform and gilt epaulettes contrasting sharply with the fringed buckskin of his lither Shawnee ally. It is a moment for legend: a story will soon spring up that Brock has torn off his military sash and presented it to Tecumseh. If so, Tecumseh is not seen to wear it. Perhaps, as some say, he has turned it over to Roundhead, who as senior member of the senior tribe of Wyandot is held by the Shawnee to be more deserving. Perhaps Tecumseh feels the gaudy silk is too much out of character for the plain deerskin garb that, in a kind of reverse vanity, he has made his trademark. Perhaps. The incident becomes part of the myth of Tecumseh, the myth of Brock.

Brock has one more symbolic act to perform. He goes directly to the guardroom to release John Dean, the British regular who struggled to hold the bridge during the first engagement at the River aux Canards. He releases him personally, shakes his hand, and in the presence of his men, his voice breaking a little with emotion, tells Dean he is an honour to his military calling.

These and other formalities observed, he turns the command of the captured territory over to Lieutenant-Colonel Procter and prepares to leave for York, where he will be hailed as the saviour of the province. In just nineteen days he has met the legislature, arranged the public affairs of Upper Canada, travelled three hundred miles to invade the invader, captured an entire army and a territory as large as the one he governs. Now he must hurry back to the capital and return the bulk of his troops as swiftly as possible to the sensitive Niagara frontier, under threat of imminent attack.

On this triumphant journey across the lake he makes a remark to a captain of the York Volunteers, Peter Robinson, that is both self-revealing and prophetic.

"If this war lasts, I am afraid I shall do some foolish thing," says General Brock, "for I know myself, there is no want of courage in my nature – I hope I shall not get into a scrape."

•

ONCE THE SURRENDER is accomplished, Hull emerges from his catatonic state like a man coming out of an anaesthetic. Scarcely able to speak or act that morning, he is now both lucid and serene. "I have done what my conscience directed," he declares. "I have saved Detroit and the Territory from the horrors of an Indian massacre." He knows that his country will censure him (though he cannot yet comprehend the magnitude of that censure), knows that he has "sacrificed a reputation dearer to me than life," but he is by no means downcast. A prisoner of the British, he no longer carries on his shoulders the crushing burden of command. As his former friend Lieutenant-Colonel Bâby remarks to him in his captivity – echoing Hull's own brittle comment of the previous month – *"Well, General, circumstances are changed now indeed."*

Of his surrender, Hull says, "My heart approves the act." His colleagues are of a different mind. McArthur and Cass, trotting to the relief of Detroit, their exhausted and famished troops riding two to a horse after a forced march of twenty-four miles, have heard the cannonade cease at 10 A.M. and are convinced that Hull has repulsed the British. The astonishing sight of the Union Jack flying over the fort changes their minds, and they move back several miles. Their men have had nothing to eat for forty-eight hours except green pumpkins and unripe corn garnered in the fields. Now they spy an ox by the roadside, slaughter and roast it. In the midst of this feast they are accosted by two British officers bearing a flag of truce who inform them that by the terms of their commander's surrender they are all prisoners.

"Traitor!" cries Cass. "He has disgraced his country," and seizing his sword from its sheath proceeds to break it in two.

It does not, apparently, occur to either of these commanders, so eager now to have at the enemy, that they might make their way back to Urbana without much fear of pursuit. Tired and dispirited, they meekly lay down their weapons and are marched into captivity.

Captain Henry Brush, at the River Raisin, is an officer of different mettle. When Matthew Elliott's son William, a militia captain, arrives to inform him of the surrender, Brush denounces the document of capitulation as a forgery, calls Elliott an imposter and spy, places him under arrest, and with all of his men except the sick decamps to the Rapids of the Maumee and thence through the Black Swamp to Urbana, where his followers disperse in small groups to their homes in Chillicothe. Tecumseh gives chase with three hundred mounted Indians, but Brush's men are too far in the lead to be captured. It makes little difference: the war still has rules of a sort, and under the terms of the surrender document, the United States officially recognizes Brush's men as prisoners. They cannot fight again until they are exchanged for an equal number of captured British.

Hull, who is worth thirty privates in a prisoner exchange, is shipped off to Quebec with his officers and the regular troops of Miller's 4th Infantry. Some of these men, hungry and emaciated, do not survive the journey. One regular, the enterprising Robert Lucas, has no intention of making it. The instant the British flag replaces the Stars and Stripes over the fort, he slips out of his uniform, hides his sword in his brother's trunk, and disguised as a civilian volunteer boards the vessel that is taking the Ohio militia on parole to Cleveland. Twenty years from now the Democratic party of Ohio will nominate him for governor over his only rival – Colonel James Findlay, his fellow prisoner.

Tecumseh knows many of the American prisoners by sight and greets them in Detroit without apparent rancour. This is his supreme moment. One of the militia engineers, Lieutenant George Ryerson (older brother of the great educator, Egerton) sees the buckskin-clad Shawnee chief shortly after the surrender, sitting with his brother, the Prophet, smoking his pipe "with his face perfectly calm, but with the greatest satisfaction beaming in his eye."

Now, in the aftermath of the bloodless victory, a number of tales are added to the legend of Tecumseh.

There is, for instance, the story of Father Gabriel Richard, the priest of Ste Anne's parish, who refuses to take the oath of allegiance to the British Crown because, he says, he has already sworn an oath to support the American Constitution. Procter, whom Brock has left in charge, imprisons the priest at Sandwich. When Tecumseh insists upon his release, Procter snubs him. Tecumseh swiftly assembles his followers, warns Procter that he will return to the Wabash if the priest is not freed. The Colonel gives in. It is the first but not the last time that he will clash with the Shawnee.

There are other tales: Tecumseh is speaking to his followers at the River Raisin when he feels a tug at his jacket, looks down, sees a small white girl. When he continues to speak, she tugs again: "Come to our house, there are bad Indians there."

He stops at once, follows her, seizes his tomahawk, drops the leader with one blow and, as the others move to attack, shouts out: "Dogs! I am Tecumseh!" The Indians retreat. Tecumseh, entering the house, finds British officers present. "You are worse than dogs to break faith with your prisoners!" he cries, and the British apologize for not having restrained the Indians. They offer to place a guard on the house, but that is not necessary, the child's mother tells them. So long as Tecumseh is near she feels safe.

Another incident occurs about the same time. Tecumseh's followers are ravenous. The game has fled; the settlers are short of supplies. Near the River Raisin, Tecumseh approaches a boy working with two oxen.

"My friend," says Tecumseh, "I must have these oxen. My young men are very hungry. They have nothing to eat."

The youth remonstrates. His father is ill. The oxen are their only farm animals. Without them they will die.

"We are the conquerors," Tecumseh says, "and everything we want is ours. I *must* have the oxen, but I will not be so mean as to rob you of them. I will pay you one hundred dollars for them, and that is more than they are worth."

He has his interpreter write out an order on Matthew Elliott for that sum, then takes the beasts, which his men roast and eat. But Elliott will not pay: Hull, after all, has stolen quantities of Canadian cattle, not to mention a herd of fine Merino sheep. When Tecumseh hears this he drops everything, takes the boy to Elliott, insists on payment. The Shawnee's anger rises when Elliott remains stubborn:

"You can do what you please, but before Tecumseh and his warriors came to fight the battles of the great King they had enough to eat, for which they only had to thank the Master of Life and their good rifles. Their hunting grounds supply them with enough food, and to them they can return."

"Well," Elliott responds, "if I *must* pay, I will."

"Give me hard money," says Tecumseh, "not rag money."

Elliott counts out one hundred dollars in coin. Tecumseh gives it to the boy, then turns to Elliott.

"Give me one dollar more," he says.

Elliott grudgingly hands him an extra coin.

"Here," says Tecumseh to the boy, "take that. It will pay you for the time you have lost getting your money."

There are many such tales growing out of the victory at Detroit. The Americans believe Tecumseh to be a brigadier-general in the British Army. He is not, but he dines with the officers at the victory dinner in Amherstburg, ignoring the wine in which the toasts are drunk yet displaying excellent table manners while his less temperate followers whoop it up in the streets of Detroit.

When news of Prevost's armistice reaches him, he is enraged. The action confirms his suspicions that the British are not interested in prosecuting the war to its fullest. If they will not fight, then the Indians will. Already the tribes are investing the American wilderness block-houses – Fort Harrison, Fort Wayne, Fort Madison. Tecumseh leaves them to it and heads south on a new journey, attempting once again to rally new tribes to his banner.

For the British, if not for the Indians, the results of Detroit's sur-render are staggering. Upper Canada, badly supplied and even worse armed, now has an additional cache of 2,500 captured muskets, thirty-nine pieces of heavy ordnance, forty barrels of gunpowder, a sixteen-gun brig, *Adams* (immediately renamed *Detroit*), a great many smaller craft, and Henry Brush's baggage train of one hundred pack animals and three hundred cattle, provisions and stores. The prize money to be distributed among the troops is reckoned at $200,000, an enormous sum considering that a private's net pay amounts to about four shillings, or one dollar, a week.

As a result of the victory at Detroit, every private soldier receives prize money of more than four pounds – at least twenty weeks' net pay. The amount increases according to rank and unit. Sergeants of the 41st Foot receive about eight pounds, captains, such as Adam Muir, forty pounds. General Brock is due two hundred and sixteen pounds. One luckless private bearing the Biblical name of Shadrach Byfield is left off the list by mistake and does not receive his share until May of 1843.

More significant is the fact that Brock has rolled back the American frontier to the Ohio River, the line that the Indians themselves hold to be the border between white territories and their own lands. Most of Michigan Territory is, for practical purposes, in British hands. A council of tribal leaders called by the U.S. government at Piqua, Ohio, for the express purpose of maintaining native neutrality collapses with the news of Hull's surrender. Many Indians, such as the Mohawk of the Grand Valley, who have been reluctant to fight on either side, are now firmly and enthusiastically committed to the British. The same can be said for all the population of Upper Canada, once so lukewarm and defeatist, now fired to enthusiasm by Brock's stunning victory. In Montreal and Quebec, the spectacle of Hull's tattered and ravaged followers provokes a wave of patriotic ardour.

The General, who has to this point treated the militia with great delicacy, reveals an iron fist. Now he has the power and the prestige to enforce the oath of allegiance among the citizen soldiers and to prosecute anybody, militiaman or civilian, for sedition, treason, or desertion.

In Canada Brock is the man of the hour, but in America the very word "Hull" is used as a derogatory epithet. In their shame and despair, Americans of all political stripes – civilians, soldiers, politicians – lash out blindly at the General, who is almost universally considered to be a traitor and a coward. On his drooping shoulders will be laid all the guilt for his country's singular lack of foresight and for its military naïveté. Forgotten now are Hull's own words of advice about the need for controlling the Lakes before attempting to invade Canada. Ignored is Major-General Dearborn's dereliction in refusing to supply Hull with the reinforcements for which he pleaded or launching the diversionary attacks at Niagara and Kingston, which were key elements in American strategy.

Hull is to be made the scapegoat for Dearborn's paralysis and Washington's bumbling. When he is at last exchanged (and Prevost is anxious to release him because he believes Hull's return will cause dissension in America), he faces a court martial that is a travesty of a trial. Here he comes up against his old adversaries, McArthur, Cass, Findlay, Miller. But his lawyer is not permitted to cross-examine these officers or to examine other witnesses; the old general, unschooled in law, must perform that task himself.

Though his papers were burned on their way from Detroit to Buffalo after the surrender, he is not allowed to examine copies at Washington. The court is packed against him: Henry Dearborn is the presiding judge. He is unlikely to be sympathetic, for if the court acquits Hull of the twin charges of cowardice and treason, Dearborn himself and his superiors in Washington must be held culpable for the scandal at Detroit.

The charge of treason is withdrawn on the grounds that it is beyond the court's jurisdiction. Three months later, when the weary process is at last completed and Hull is found guilty of cowardice, the court adds a rider saying that it does not believe him to be guilty of treason. There is more to this than simple justice, for the charge is based entirely on the loss of the *Cuyahoga* and all Hull's baggage before he knew war was declared. That misfortune cannot be laid at the ill-starred general's door but at that of Dr. Eustis, the Secretary of War, who was scandalously remiss in informing his outposts of the outbreak of hostilities.

Hull, officially branded as a coward, is sentenced to be shot. The President, taking into account the General's Revolutionary gallantry and perhaps also pricked by a guilty conscience, pardons him. Hull spends the rest of his life attempting to vindicate his actions. It is an irony of war that had he refused to surrender, had he gone down to defeat, his fort and town shattered by cannon fire, his friends and neighbours ravaged by the misfortunes of battle, his soldiers dead to the last man, the civilians burned out, bombed out, and inevitably scalped, the tired old general would have swept into the history books as a gallant martyr, his name enshrined on bridges, schools, main streets, and public buildings. (There is also the possibility that he might have beaten Brock, though somehow one doubts it.) But for the rest of their lives the very soldiers who, because of him, can go back whole to the comfort of their homesteads, and the civilians who are now able to pick up the strings of their existence, only briefly tangled, will loathe and curse the name of William Hull who, on his deathbed at the age of seventy-two, will continue to insist that he took the only proper, decent, and courageous course on that bright August Sunday in 1812.

5

CHICAGO
Horror on Lake Michigan

The wretchedness of that night who can tell! the despondency that filled the hearts of all, not so much in regard to the present as from apprehension for the future, who...can comprehend?... Alas, where were their comrades – friends, nay, brothers of yesterday? Where was the brave, the noble-hearted Wells...the manly Sergeant Nixon...the faithful Corporal Green – and nearly two-thirds of the privates of the detachment?

– From Wau-nan-gee, *by John Richardson.*

FORT DEARBORN, ILLINOIS TERRITORY, August 15, 1812. Billy Wells has blackened his face in the fashion of a Miami warrior. It is a sign that he expects to be killed before sundown.

He has come to escort the garrison and the people of Chicago from the protection of the fort to the dubious security of Fort Wayne on the Maumee. It is not his doing; the move has been explicitly ordered by General Hull, who is himself only a day away from defeat and disgrace. Billy Wells has greater reason than Hull for pessimism; his blackened face betrays it.

Billy Wells is that curious frontier creature, a white man who thinks like an Indian – citizen of a shadow world, half civilized, half savage, claimed by two races, not wholly accepted by either. His story is not unusual. Captured by the Miami as a child, raised as a young warrior, he grew to manhood as an Indian, took the name of Black Snake, married the sister of the great war chief Little Turtle, became a leader of his adoptive people. As the years drifted by, the memories of his childhood – he is a descendant of a prominent Kentucky family – began to blur. Did he dream them? Was he really white? In the successful attacks on the Maumee against Harmar in 1790 and St. Clair in 1791 he fought with tomahawk and war club by the side of his brother-in-law. In that last battle – the greatest defeat inflicted on any American force by Indians in pre-Custer days – he butchered several white soldiers. But when the grisly work was done, old memories returned, and Billy Wells was haunted by a nagging guilt. Was it possible that he had actually killed some of his own kinsmen? Guilt became obsession. The call of blood defeated the bonds of friendship. Wells could no longer remain an Indian: he must leave his wife, his children, his old crony Little Turtle and return to his own people. There was a legendary leave-taking: "We have long been friends [to Little Turtle]; we are friends yet, until the sun stands so high [pointing to the sky] in the heavens; from that time we are enemies and may kill one another."

Billy Wells joined General Anthony Wayne, advancing down the Maumee, became chief of Wayne's scouts, fought on the white side in the Battle of Fallen Timbers. The battle over, his wife and family rejoined him. Billy Wells was appointed government agent and interpreter at Fort Wayne; Little Turtle, rendered docile by defeat, continued as his friend and confidant.

Yet no one can be quite sure of Billy Wells, who, like Matthew Elliott, prospers from his government and Indian connections. William Henry Harrison does not trust him, believes him to be secretly conniving with his former people. Tecumseh despises him and Little Turtle as turncoats. Billy Wells is history's captive, and today he will become history's victim.

As the heavy stockade gate swings open, he leads a forlorn group down the road that will become Michigan Avenue in the Chicago of the future. He has brought along an escort of thirty Miami warriors to lead to safety the entire population of the fort and the adjacent village of Chicago – some hundred soldiers and civilians. Half of his Miami escort rides beside him. Directly behind is Captain Nathan Heald, commander of the fort (the same man who, the previous spring, intercepted Brock's couriers to Robert Dickson), with his wife Rebekah, who is Billy Wells's niece, and his garrison of regular soldiers. A wagon train follows with the women and children of the settlement, the younger children riding in one of the covered carts. The Chicago militia and the remainder of Wells's Miami bring up the rear.

Why are these people leaving the sturdy protection of an armed stockade and venturing into hostile Indian territory? Simply because General Hull, dismayed by the loss of Michilimackinac, has decided to evacuate the area. He has instructed Heald to destroy all arms and distribute the supplies, provisions, food, and blankets among the neighbouring Indians. The gesture, designed to placate the natives, has the opposite effect, especially as Heald decides to destroy all the garrison's liquor as well as its arms. Since whiskey and guns are what the Indians desire most, the deliberate destruction of these prizes has put them in an ugly mood. Moreover, one of Tecumseh's runners has arrived with news of Hull's crumbling position at Detroit. The momentum of British success and American failure has got their blood up. Just ahead, concealed behind a ridge of sand dunes, lurks a war party of six hundred Potawatomi, the tribe so prominent at the Battle of Tippecanoe.

Billy Wells's trained eye spots the ambush. He gallops back to warn Heald, swings his hat in a circle to indicate that the force is surrounded, then leads a bayonet charge up the bank.

It is a tragic error of judgement, bold but foolhardy, for it leaves the wagon train unprotected. Heald's two junior officers, together with twelve newly recruited militiamen and a handful of regulars, fight furiously with bayonet and musket butt but are quickly subdued by the superior force of Indians. Only one white civilian, John Kinzie, the Chicago trader, survives, spared, perhaps, by the same Indians with whom he is accustomed to do business. At the wagon train, the soldiers' wives, armed with their husbands' swords, fight as fiercely as the men. Two are hacked to pieces: a Mrs. Corbin, wife of a private, who has vowed never to be taken prisoner, and Mrs. Heald's black slave, Cicely, who is cut down with her infant son.

Within the wagons, where the younger children are huddled, there is greater horror. One young Indian slips in and slaughters twelve single-handed, slicing their heads from their bodies in a fury of blood lust.

Billy Wells, a musket ball in his breast, his horse wounded and faltering, hears the clamour at the wagons and attempts to turn back in a last effort to save the women and children. As he does so, the horse stumbles, and he is hurled to the ground, one leg caught under the animal's body. The Indians are bearing down, and Billy Wells knows that his hour has come. He continues to fire, killing at least one man. As he does so, he calls out to his niece Rebekah, bidding her goodbye. An Indian takes deliberate aim. Billy Wells looks him square in the eye, signals him to shoot.

A short distance away, Heald's sergeant, Hayes, is engaged in a death struggle with a Potawatomi warrior. Their muskets have been discharged; there is no time to reload. The Indian rushes at Hayes, brandishing his tomahawk. As the blow falls, the sergeant drives his bayonet up to the socket into his enemy's breast. They die together.

Walter Jordan, one of Wells's men, has a miraculous escape. One ball takes the feather off his cap, another the epaulette from his shoulder, a third the handle from his sword. He surrenders to the Indians and is recognized by a chief:

"Jordan, I know you. You gave me tobacco at Fort Wayne. We won't kill you, but come and see what we will do to your captain." He leads him to where Wells's body lies, cuts off the head, and places it on a long pole. Another cuts out the heart and divides it among the chiefs, who eat it raw, hoping thereby to absorb some of Wells's courage.

Heald, wounded in arm and thigh, abandoned by Wells's escort of Miami, half his force of regulars dead, all his officers casualties, decides to surrender. He approaches the Potawatomi chief, Black Bird, promises a ransom of one hundred dollars for everyone left alive if the Indians will agree not to kill the prisoners. Black Bird accepts; the soldiers lay down their arms and are marched back past the naked and headless bodies of the women and children. Heald, thinking he recognizes the torso of his wife, briefly repents the surrender, then is overjoyed to find that she is alive at the fort, weeping among a group of Indian women, saved apparently by the intervention of a friendly chief, Black Partridge.

Black Bird does not keep his promise. One of the wounded soldiers, Sergeant Thomas Burns of the militia, is killed almost immediately by the squaws. His is a more fortunate fate than that of five of his comrades who are tortured to death that night, their cries breaking the silence over the great lake and sending shivers through the survivors.

More than half the band that left the fort in the morning are dead by the following day. The remainder, twenty-nine soldiers, seven women, and six children, are captives of the Indians, destined to be distributed among the various villages in the area. Thus begins their long travail.

The Healds' captivity is short-lived. After a few days, with Michigan now in British hands, most of the Indians take off to attack Fort Wayne, and Heald is able to buy his way to St. Joseph's Island in British territory, where Captain Roberts sends them home under parole. At Detroit, Mrs. Heald's "inimitable grace and fulness of contour" together with her "magnificence of person and brilliancy of character" make a lasting impression on the fifteen-year-old John Richardson, who, at the end of his life, gives her a certain immortality by making her the heroine of his novel *Wau-nan-gee*.

Others are less fortunate. That winter one captive freezes to death on the trail; two more, who cannot keep up, are tomahawked; nine exist as slaves for almost a year before they are ransomed through the efforts of the red-headed trader, Robert Dickson.

The family of John Needs, one of Heald's regular soldiers, manages to survive the massacre only to die in captivity. The Needs's only child, crying with hunger, so annoys the Indians that they tie it to a tree to perish from starvation. Needs also dies of cold and hunger. His wife expires the following January.

The family of the murdered Sergeant Burns is shattered. One grown son is killed in the fighting; two small children are victims of the wagon massacre. A nine-year-old daughter, though scalped, succeeds in freeing herself. She, her mother, and an infant in arms survive for two years among the Indians before being ransomed by a white trader. For the rest of her life the scalped girl is marked by a small bald spot on the top of her head.

In the fate of the Lee family are all the ingredients of a nineteenth-century frontier novel. All its members except the mother and an infant daughter are killed in the fighting. The two survivors are taken by Black Partridge to his camp. Here the baby falls ill and Black Partridge falls in love — with Mrs. Lee. In order to win her hand he determines to save the infant's life. He takes her back to Chicago where a newly arrived French trader named Du Pin prescribes for her and cures her. Learning of Black Partridge's romantic intentions, Du Pin ransoms Mrs. Lee, then marries her himself.

These stories pale before the long odyssey of Mrs. John Simmons, whose husband also perishes during the defence of the wagons. Believing that the Indians delight in tormenting prisoners who show any emotion, this remarkable woman resolves to preserve the life of her six-month-old child by suppressing all outward manifestations of grief, even when she is led past a row of small, mutilated corpses which includes that of her two-year-old boy, David. Faced with this grisly spectacle, she neither blinks an eye nor sheds a tear, nor will she during the long months of her captivity.

Her Indian owners set out for Green Bay on the western shore of Lake Michigan. Mrs. Simmons, carrying her baby, trudges the entire distance, working as a servant in the evenings, gathering wood and building fires. When the village is at last reached, she is insulted, kicked, and abused. The following day she is forced to run the gauntlet between a double line of men and women wielding sticks and clubs. Wrapping the infant in a blanket and shielding it in her arms, she races down the long line, emerging bruised and bleeding but with her child unharmed.

She is given over to an Indian "mother," who feeds her, bathes her

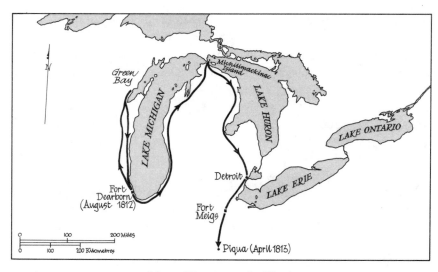

Mrs. Simmons's Trek

wounds, allows her to rest. She needs such sustenance, for a worse ordeal faces her – a long tribal peregrination back around the lake. Somehow Mrs. Simmons, lightly clad, suffering from cold, fatigue, and malnutrition, manages to carry her child for the entire six hundred miles and survive. She has walked with the Indians from Green Bay back to Chicago, then around the entire eastern shore of the lake to Michilimackinac. But a second, even more terrible trek faces her – a three-hundred-mile journey through the snow to Detroit, where the Indians intend to ransom her. Ragged and starving, she exists on roots and acorns found beneath the snows. Her child, now a year old, has grown much heavier. Her own strength is waning. Only the prospect of release sustains her.

Yet even after her successful ransom her ordeal is not over. The route to her home near Piqua, Ohio, is long and hard. By March of 1813 she reaches Fort Meigs on the Maumee. Here she manages to secure passage in a government wagon, part of a supply train that winds its way through swampy roads, depositing her, in mid-April, four miles from her father's farm.

Mother and child walk the remaining distance to find that the family, which has long since given her up for dead, has taken refuge in a blockhouse against Indian marauders. Here, safe at last, she breaks down and for several months cannot contain her tears. In August, she has further reason to weep. Her sister and brother-in-law, working in a nearby flax field, are surprised by Indians, shot, toma-hawked, and scalped in front of their four horrified children. Such, in part, is the legacy of Tippecanoe and all that preceded it.

To these tales of horror and heroism must be added a bizarre coda:

It is October, 1816; the war has been over for two years. Two workmen helping to rebuild Fort Dearborn are travelling by skiff up the north branch of the Illinois, searching out suitable timber, probing deep into the wilderness, far from human habitation. Suddenly they hear the cries of Indian women and, above that gabble, the sound of English words. They spy, half-hidden in the underbrush, an Indian hut and then a white man, standing on the bank, who pleads with them to stop and talk, for he has heard no English for four years. This is the tale he tells:

He is one of Heald's force of soldiers, badly wounded in the battle with the Potawatomi and saved by an aging Indian woman, to whom he has previously been kind. She prevents her people from scalping him and, with the help of her three daughters, moves him across the river, hides him in the undergrowth, and tends his wounds until he is well enough to be moved.

The four women secure a piece of timber from the ruined fort, tie him to it, and tow the makeshift raft forty miles northward to the shores of a small lake. And here all five live together. He marries his benefactor, Indian fashion. When she dies he takes the two older daughters as his wives. Since that day they have been living here together in the wilderness.

The workmen return to Chicago to report their strange discovery. Next day, the army surgeon accompanies them upriver with a boat-load of presents for the quartet, only to discover that the women are on the point of spiriting their joint husband away, deeper into the wild. He, for his part, has made no objection; indeed, he has decided to take their younger sister as his third common-law wife.

The doctor examines his wounds. They have healed; but one leg is shorter than the other, and one arm is useless. Does he wish to return to his own kind? The old soldier shakes his head: not as long as his harem will live with him and care for him, he says. He is already preparing to move further from civilization, further into the unpopu-lated forest. Perhaps he will visit the fort some day, he remarks, but only if the soldiers solemnly promise not to make fun of his little teen-aged bride.

But he does not come. No white man ever sees or hears of him again. He and his little family melt away into the recesses of the coniferous jungle that clothes the territory. No pen records his odyssey; no stone marks his grave; nor can anyone recall his name. Like so many others he is the faceless victim of a war not of his making; and, again like so many others, he has managed to come to terms with his fate and in that process to survive and even prosper in his fashion, a creature of the wild, at once its prisoner and its conqueror, master and servant of all he surveys, monarch of an empty empire.

6

QUEENSTON HEIGHTS
The End of Isaac Brock

No tongue shall blazon forth their fame –
The cheers that stir that sacred hill
Are but the promptings of the will
That conquered then, that conquers still
And generations shall thrill
At Brock's remembered name.

– Anon.

LEWISTON, NEW YORK, August 15, 1812; with the United States Army of the Centre.

Major John Lovett, who is more poet than soldier, leaps out of his quarters to the roar of musket fire on the heights above the Niagara River, flings himself onto his horse, and dashes off. The cries of his commanding officer, Major-General Stephen Van Rensselaer, echo behind him: *Come back! Come back!* But Lovett gallops on. Later, the General will tell him that he fully expected he was about to run away, never to be seen again; but this is mere badinage, for the two are old friends. Lovett serves the American commander officially as military aide and secretary; he is also confidant, political ally, and something of a court jester – an antidote against the loneliness and burden of command. To Lovett, soldiering is a new experience, war is something of a lark, the sound of musketry exciting.

As the Major gallops for the cliffs, he realizes that two other riders are close behind him. Both are high-ranking officers. Lieutenant-Colonel Solomon Van Rensselaer is the General's aide-de-camp, kinsman, and friend. Brigadier-General William Wadsworth of the Upper New York State militia has been in charge of recruiting for the coming thrust against Queenston – a difficult and thankless task, given the mood of the region.

As they run their horses up the broken rock of the precipice (the worst terrain Lovett has ever known), the musket fire increases. They burst out of a copse into open land; a soldier runs up crying, "General, do ride into that hollow, for the balls fly dreadfully here!" but they gallop in, seeking to discover the cause of the gunfire. One of the guards posted on the cliff starts to explain just as a ball fans his face. He leaps behind a great oak, pulling his arms close in to his body to make himself invisible, and then, seeing the ludicrousness of his position, grins ruefully, causing Lovett to burst out laughing. General Wadsworth maintains a straight face and is careful to present his breast to the enemy at all times, for he does not intend, he says, "that a Wadsworth should be shot through the back." A few minutes later the skirmish ends inconclusively. It has been caused, significantly, by the attempts of two Americans to desert to the Canadian side of the Niagara River by boat.

That evening, Lovett takes pains to write his friend and confidant, John Alexander of Albany, a breathless account of the incident "principally for the purpose of enabling you to meet the *lye* should any fool or scoundrel manufacture one, out of what little did actually take place." He does not want it "conjured up as to another *Sackett's Harbor Battle*." Lies there have been and rumours aplenty, including one monstrous falsehood, heard during the army's march north through Utica, that the American post at Sackets Harbor had been attacked and blockaded by the British – a piece of fiction that caused the General to abandon his route to the Niagara River and march to the relief of the town, only to find that nothing untoward had taken place.

Now, Stephen Van Rensselaer has set up his headquarters at Lewiston, concentrating his forces here, directly across from the Canadian village of Queenston. This very day, Dr. Eustis, the Secretary of War, has sent an order to Van Rensselaer's superior, General Dearborn, at Albany: "Considering the urgency of a diversion in favour of General Hull under the circumstances attending his situation, the President thinks it proper that not a moment should be lost in gaining possession of the British posts at Niagara and Kingston, or at least the former, and proceeding in co-operation with General Hull in securing Upper Canada." Both Eustis and Dearborn cling to the fancy that Hull has been victorious in Upper Canada and that Fort Amherstburg has already fallen.

In Lewiston, General Van Rensselaer is under no such illusion, though he will not learn of Hull's situation for several days. There is not much he can do to aid Hull. It is all very well for Eustis to talk of an attack on the Niagara frontier; it is quite a different matter to put his strategy into practice. The British control not only the far shore but also the Niagara River and the two lakes. Van Rensselaer has less than a thousand men to guard a front of thirty-six miles. One-third of his force is too ill to fight. None has been paid. His men lie in the open without tents or covering. Ammunition is low; there are scarcely ten rounds per soldier. There are no heavy ordnance, no gunners, no engineers, scarcely any medical supplies.

And even if, through some miracle of logistics, these deficiencies were rectified, it is questionable whether the state militia will agree to fight on foreign soil. On July 22, a humiliating incident at Ogdensburg made the General wary of his civilian soldiers. Across the St. Lawrence at Prescott lay a British gunboat. The General's aide and cousin, Solomon, had planned a daring raid to capture her; he and 120 men would row silently upriver at three in the morning, cross to the Canadian shore, seize the wharf buildings, and attack the ship simultaneously from land and water. At two, everything was in readiness; four hundred men were paraded and volunteers called for, but when only sixty-six agreed to go, the expedition had to be aborted.

If the troops are reluctant, their militia leaders, with the exception of Solomon Van Rensselaer, are inexperienced. Wadsworth, the militia general, knows so little of war that he has pleaded to be released from his assignment of assembling volunteers: "I confess myself ignorant of even the minor details of the duty you have assigned to me, and I am apprehensive that I may not only expose myself but my Government," he tells the Governor of New York.

Stephen Van Rensselaer is himself a militiaman without campaign experience. When the crunch comes, colleagues in the regular forces will refuse to co-operate with him. The irony is that the General is totally and unequivocally opposed to a war that he now intends, as a matter of honour, to prosecute to the fullest – even at the risk of his own reputation. He is a leading Federalist politician, a candidate for governor with a strong following in New York State, and that is precisely why he is here at the head of a thousand men, very much against his will.

For his appointment he has his political rival to thank – the iron-jawed incumbent, Governor Daniel D. Tompkins, an able administrator and machine politician who is up for re-election the coming spring. As the Republican standard-bearer, Tompkins is as interested in getting his Federalist opponent out of the way as he is in prosecuting the war, and there is little doubt that Stephen Van Rensselaer will be a formidable rival.

He is the head of one of the first families in New York, and in his name one hears the ring of history. He is the eighth and last patroon of the feudal estate of Rensselaerwyck on the outskirts of Albany, a vast domain close to twelve hundred square miles in size and after almost two centuries still in the hands of the original family. A relic of the early Dutch immigration to America, the General is a Harvard graduate, a farmer, a millionaire, a philanthropist, and, more from a sense of duty than from ambition, a politician. He has served in the state assembly, in the state senate, and as lieutenant-governor of New York. Though he is entitled to feudal tithes, he does not collect them. He is liberal enough to vote against his own class in favour of extending the suffrage. His military training and experience as a militia general are all but non-existent, but that does not bother Governor Tompkins. By appointing his rival to the command of the army on the state's northern frontier he has everything to gain and nothing to lose – except, possibly, the war.

Politically, it is a masterstroke. Stephen Van Rensselaer can scarcely refuse the post; if he does he will be discredited in the eyes of the voters. If he accepts, he ends Federalist opposition to the war in New York State. If he blunders, he will undoubtedly be relieved of his command, and that will work against him in the political contest to come. If he performs brilliantly he will not be able to relinquish command and so will pose no political threat.

He accepts – but under one condition: he insists that his cousin Solomon be his aide-de-camp. For Solomon, in the words of his friend Lovett, "is all formed for war." Unlike the General, with his pert and amiable Dutch features, the Lieutenant-Colonel looks like a soldier – "the handsomest officer I ever beheld," in the words of a contemporary. The son of a Revolutionary general, ensign at seventeen, he fought with distinction under Wayne at Fallen Timbers. (Though seriously wounded, he took command of his shattered force and for his gallantry was promoted to major.) For most of the intervening years since leaving the regular army at the century's turn he has been adjutant-general for the state of New York. Now thirty-eight, he is ten years younger than his commanding officer.

The two cousins with Lovett form a close triumvirate – "our little family," Lovett calls it. They can rely on no other counsel than their own, for their politics render them suspect, especially to such fire-breathing War Hawks as Peter B. Porter, chairman of the House committee on foreign relations, who has been appointed quartermaster general for the state of New York. (Porter and his brother are themselves in the contracting and provisioning business and thus in a position to profit from supplying the army, but no one worries about that; the phrase "conflict of interest" has yet to enter the language.) In Albany, Governor Tompkins and General Dearborn show no great eagerness to assist the beleaguered force along the Niagara. Solomon, for one, is convinced that his political enemies are deliberately trying to sabotage him.

Lovett is determined to keep a careful record of everything that happens (or does not happen) – "the history of every occurrence that can possibly be tortured into a lie" – in the event of later distortions or misunderstandings. He does so in a series of breathless letters to his friend John Alexander, scribbling away at night, even though exhausted from his unaccustomed soldiering. He has neither stamina nor time to scrawl out a sentence to his wife, Nancy; that duty he leaves to his friend: "Tell my good wife, I have not another moment to write, that I am neither homesick, crop-sick, war sick, nor sick of my Wife," he writes. And again: "Don't let my wife get alarmed" and "Don't forget my Wife and Children, nor suffer them to be lonely. Keep their spirits up" and so on. It does not seem to occur to Lovett that the best way to keep up the family spirits might be to send off a letter in his own hand. But then Mrs. Lovett, herself a general's daughter, prefers to relay her own messages to her husband through their chosen intermediary, Alexander.

To Alexander, Lovett pours out his own pessimism and despair, which he shares with his two friends, the Van Rensselaer cousins. The war, to him, is foolish:

"If any man wants to see folly triumphant, let him come here, let him view friends by friends stretched for hundreds of miles on these two shores, all loving and beloved; all desirous of harmony; all wounded by being coerced, by a hand unseen, to cut throats. The People must awaken, they will wake from such destructive lethargy and stupor. . . .

"What might not the good spirit of this great People effect, if properly directed. History while recording our folly, will dress her pages in mourning, the showers of Posterity's tears will fall in vain; for the sponge of time can never wipe this blot from the American Name. . . ."

And yet, when the men under his friends' command refuse to leave the boundaries of the state to attack the British gunboat on the opposite shore, he is "mortified almost to death." For John Lovett is torn by conflicting emotions. He hates the idea of the war but badly wants to win it. He adjures his friend Alexander not to breathe a word about the defections of the militia lest the news cause further defections. He worries about Hull, hoping against hope that he can hold out, but expecting the worst. His despair over the outbreak of war is accompanied by a despair over his general's inability to strike a decisive blow against the enemy. To him, this war is "the Ominous Gathering of folly and madness," yet he deplores the lack of two thousand disciplined troops who, he has been told, are necessary for a successful attack on Fort George, the British post at the Niagara's mouth.

He is a lawyer by profession, a *bon vivant* by inclination, a satirical poet, a dinner wit, an amateur politician. He is good with juries, bad with law, for he cannot abide long hours spent with dusty tomes in murky libraries. He is restless, always seeking something new, changing employment frequently. It is doubtful, however, that he ever expected to become a soldier.

"I am not a soldier," he tells his friend the General when he seeks to employ him. To which Stephen Van Rensselaer replies, "It is not your *sword*, but your *pen* I want."

Now, in spite of himself, in spite of his hatred of war and bloodshed, in spite of his aching back and his head cold, in spite of long hours spent in the saddle and damp days on the hard ground, he discovers that he is actually enjoying the experience. It is for him a kind of testing, and his letters bubble with the novelty of it all.

"If flying through air, water, mud, brush, over hills, dales, meadows, swamps, on wheels or horseback, and getting a man's ears gnawed off with mosquitoes and gallinippers make a *Soldier*, then I have seen service for – one week," he boasts. And he revels in the tale of how he and his two friends, shipwrecked in a thunderstorm near Sackets Harbor, sought refuge in an abandoned house where he went to sleep in a large Dutch oven, aided by a sergeant of the guard who laid him on a large board and pushed him into its mouth "like a pig on a wooden shovel."

He worships the Van Rensselaer cousins (after all he is employed as a propagandist):

"One thing I can with great truth say; nothing but General Stephen Van Rensselaer's having the command of this campaign could have saved the service from confusion; the State from disgrace, and the cause from perdition; and nothing could have been more fortunate for the General than the man he has at his elbow, for Solomon in *fact* and *truth* does know everything which appertains to the economy of a camp – Stop: – Away we must all march, at beat of drum, and hear an old Irish clergyman preach to us, Amen. I have become a perfect machine; go just where I'm ordered."

•

LEWISTON, NEW YORK, August 16, 1812. Consternation in the American camp! Excitement – then relief. A red-coated British officer gallops through, carrying a flag of truce. Hull may be in trouble on the Detroit frontier. (He is, at this very moment, signing the articles of surrender.) But here on the Niagara the danger of a British attack, which all have feared, is over.

Major John Lovett cannot contain his delight at this unexpected reprieve. "Huzza! Huzza!" he writes in his journal, "...an Express from the Governor General of Canada to Gen. Dearborn proposing an Armistice!!!!" The news is so astonishing, so cheering, that he slashes four exclamation marks against it.

The following night, at midnight, there is a further hullabaloo as more riders gallop in from Albany bearing letters from Dearborn "enclosing a sort of three legged armistice between some sort of an Adjutant General on behalf of the governor general of Canada and the said Gen. Dearborn." Now the camp is in a ferment as messages criss-cross the river: "There is nothing but flag after flag, letter after letter."

A truce, however brief, will allow the Americans to buy time, desperately needed, and to reinforce the Niagara frontier, desperately undermanned, that stretches thirty-six miles along the river that cuts through the neck of land separating Lake Erie from Lake Ontario. At the southern end, the British Fort Erie faces the two American towns of Buffalo, a lively village of five hundred, and its trading rival, Black Rock. At the northern end, Fort George on the British side and Fort Niagara on the American bristle at each other across the entrance into Lake Ontario. The great falls, whose thunder can be heard for miles, lie at midpoint. Below the gorge that cuts through the Niagara escarpment are the hamlet of Lewiston, on the American side, where Van Rensselaer's army is quartered, and the Canadian village

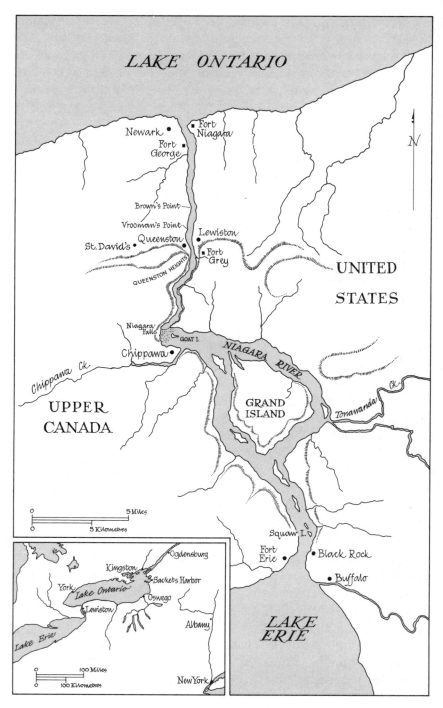

The Niagara Frontier

of Queenston, a partially fortified community, overshadowed physically by the heights to the south and economically by the village of Newark (later Niagara-on-the-Lake) on the outskirts of Fort George.

At Lewiston, the river can be crossed in ten minutes, and a musket ball fired from one village to the other still has the power to kill. For some time the Americans have been convinced that the British mean to attack across the river. It is widely believed that they have three thousand men in the field and another thousand on call. As is so often the case in war, both sides overestimate the forces opposite them; Brock has only four hundred regulars and eight hundred militia, most of the latter having returned to their harvest.

New York State is totally unprepared for war. The arms are of varying calibres; no single cartridge will suit them. Few bayonets are available. When Governor Tompkins tries to get supplies for the militia from the regular army, he is frustrated by red tape. From Bloomfield comes word from one general that "if Gen. Brock should attack...a single hour would expend all our ammunition." From Brownville, another general reports that the inhabitants of the St. Lawrence colony are fleeing south. From Buffalo, Peter B. Porter describes a state bordering on anarchy – alarm, panic, distrust of officers, military unpreparedness. If Hull is beaten at Detroit only a miracle can save Van Rensselaer's forces from ignoble defeat.

Now, when least expected, the miracle has happened and the army has been given breathing-space.

Lieutenant-Colonel Solomon Van Rensselaer, the old campaigner, immediately grasps the significance of the projected armistice, but he faces serious problems. All the heavy cannon and supplies he needs are far away at Oswego at the eastern end of Lake Ontario. The roads are mired; supplies can only be moved by water. At present the British control the lake, but perhaps the terms of the truce can be broadened to give the Americans an advantage.

The agreement with Dearborn is specific: the British will not allow any facility for moving men and supplies that did not exist before it was signed. In short, the Americans cannot use the lake as a common highway. Solomon is determined to force his enemies to give way; the security of the Army of the Centre depends upon it.

He goes straight to his cousin, the General.

"Our situation," he reminds him, "is critical and embarrassing, *something* must be done, we must have cannon and military stores from Oswego. I shall make a powerful effort to procure the use of the waters, and I shall take such ground as will make it impossible for me to recede. If I do not succeed, then Lovett must cross over and carry Gen. Dearborn's orders into effect."

"Van," says Lovett, "you may as well give that up, you will not succeed."

"If I do not," retorts his friend, "it will not be my fault."

He dons full military dress and crosses to the British fort. Three officers are there to meet him: Brock's deputy, Major-General Roger Sheaffe, Lieutenant-Colonel Christopher Myers, commanding the garrison, and the brigade major, Thomas Evans. Sheaffe agrees readily to the American's proposal that no further troops should move from the district to reinforce Brock at Amherstburg; the Americans do not know that most of the needed troops have already been dispatched. But when Van Rensselaer proposes the use of all navigable waters as a common highway, Sheaffe raps out a curt "Inadmissible!" The Colonel insists. Again the General refuses. Whereupon Solomon Van Rensselaer engages in Yankee bluff.

"There can be no armistice," he declares; "our negotiation is at an end. General Van Rensselaer will take the responsibility on himself to prevent your detaching troops from this district."

The British officers leap to their feet. Sheaffe grips the hilt of his sword.

"Sir," says he, "you take high ground!"

Solomon Van Rensselaer also rises to his feet, gripping his sword. "I do, sir, and will maintain it." Turns to Sheaffe and speaks directly: "You do not dare detach the troops."

Silence. The General paces the room. Finally: "Be seated and excuse me." Withdraws with his aides. Returns after a few minutes: "Sir, from amicable considerations, I grant you the use of the waters."

It is a prodigious miscalculation, but it is Prevost's as much as Sheaffe's. The British general has his orders from his cautious and over-optimistic superior. Brock, contemplating an all-out offensive across the Niagara River, is still in the dark at Detroit.

The truce, which officially begins on August 20, can be cancelled by either side on four days' notice. It ends on September 8 after President Madison informs Dearborn that the United States has no intention of ending the war unless the British also revoke their practice of impressing American sailors. By that time Van Rensselaer's army has been reinforced from Oswego with six regiments of regulars, five of militia, a battalion of riflemen, several batteries of heavy cannon and, in Brock's rueful words, "a prodigious quantity of Pork and Flower." As Lovett puts it, "we worked John Bull in the little Armistice treaty and got more than we expected." Not only has Lewiston been reinforced, but the balance of power on Lake Ontario has also been tilted. General Van Rensselaer, taking advantage of the truce, has shot off an express to Ogdensburg on the St. Lawrence to dispatch nine vessels to Sackets Harbor, a move that will aid the American naval commander, Captain Isaac Chauncey, in his attack on the Upper Canadian capital of York the following year.

In spite of his diplomatic coup, Solomon Van Rensselaer is not a happy man. Somehow, at the height of the negotiations with the British, he has managed to hold a secret and astonishing conversation with Sheaffe's brigade major, Evans, in which he has confided to his enemy his own disillusionment with the government at Washington, his hope that the war will speedily end, and his belief that the majority of Americans are opposed to any conflict. Solomon feels himself the plaything of remorseless fate – surrounded by political enemies, forced into a war he cannot condone, nudged towards a battle he feels he cannot win, separated from a loving wife whose protracted silence dismays him, and, worst of all, crushed by the memory of a family tragedy that he cannot wipe from his mind.

The vision of a sunlit clover lot near the family farm at Bethlehem, New York, is never far from his thoughts: his six-year-old son, Van Vechten, romps in the field with an older brother. Suddenly a musket shot rings out; the boy drops, shot through the ear, his brain a pulp. The senseless tragedy is the work of an escaped lunatic, and there is nothing anybody can do. Even revenge is futile, and Solomon Van Rensselaer is not a vengeful man. Again and again in his dreams and nightmares, he sees himself picking up the small bleeding corpse and struggling back across the field to his white-faced wife, Harriet.

It is she who worries him. The incident occurred on May 29, not long before he was forced to leave his family to take up arms. Why has she not written? Has the tragedy deranged her? Since leaving home he has sent her at least a dozen letters but has received no answer. "Why under the Heavens is the reason you do not write me?" he asks on August 21. Silence. A fortnight later he asks a political friend in Albany to tell him the truth: "The recollection of that late overwhelming event at home, I fear has been too much for her...." No doubt it has. But what he apparently does not know, and will not know until the affair at Queenston is over, is that Harriet is in the final stages of pregnancy and about to present him with a new son.

His unhappy state of mind is further agitated by his political opponents, "who even pursue me to this quarter of the Globe." The chief of these is Henry Clay's supporter Peter B. Porter, who, in Solomon's opinion, has with some Republican friends been causing "confusion and distrust among the Troops on this Frontier to answer party purposes against the Commander." The Lieutenant-Colonel blames Porter, as quartermaster general of the army, for "speculating and attending to mischief and his private affairs" when the army is in such want of supplies. The camp is short of surgical instruments, lint, bandages, hospital stores.

In Solomon's view, Porter is "an abominable scoundrel." He makes so little attempt to hide that opinion that Porter eventually challenges him to a duel. Solomon chooses Lovett as his second, but when his cousin, the General, hears of the affair he threatens to court-martial both antagonists. Their job, he points out, is to fight the British, not each other. Yet this quarrel reveals only the tip of an iceberg of dissension, which in the end will force the Van Rensselaers into rash action. For after the truce ends on September 8, Porter and his hawkish friends begin to whisper that the General is a coward and a traitor who does not really want to attack the heights of Queenston.

•

WITH ISAAC BROCK, aboard the schooner *Chippewa*, Lake Ontario, August 23, 1812.

Euphoric after his capture of Detroit, the General is hastening back to his capital at York when a provincial schooner, *Lady Prevost*, approaches and fires a seventeen-gun salute. The ceremony over, her commander comes aboard and presents Brock with a dispatch – his first intimation of the armistice that Prevost and Dearborn have concluded on the Niagara frontier.

The General's elation dissolves. He is stunned, mortified, disillusioned. He had planned to continue the relentless momentum of his victory, to roll up the entire New York frontier from Buffalo to Sackets Harbor, to hammer at the Americans while they were still off balance and poorly supplied. Now his hands are tied by Prevost, and he cannot conceal his bitterness. He does not share his superior's optimism that the armistice is the first step towards a permanent cessation of hostilities. He is convinced that the sharp Yankees are buying time to reinforce their own position, that John Bull has been gulled by Brother Jonathan.

What he desires most of all is a quick victory, one that will allow him to leave the stifling colonial atmosphere of the Canadas and return to Europe to serve under Wellington and to visit with his several brothers, to whom he writes regularly. Indeed, on the very day of Detroit's fall, while plagued by a score of problems, he has managed to send them a brief dispatch: "Rejoice at my good fortune, and join me in prayers to Heaven," adding, somewhat cryptically, "Let me hear that you are all *united* and happy."

For there has been a family falling out, which disturbs him mightily. It springs from the collapse of the banking firm of which his brother William was senior partner, a financial blow that has all but beggared the family, including the General himself. Years before, his brother advanced him three thousand pounds with which to purchase his commission in the 49th. William Brock, who has no close relatives except his brothers, had no intention that the money should be paid back; nonetheless, it remains on the books of the bankrupt firm as a debt, and the assignees are clamouring for it, even threatening legal action. Brock has pledged his entire civil salary as governor of Upper Canada – one thousand pounds a year – to pay off the debt ("Depend on my exercising the utmost economy.... Did it depend on myself, how willingly would I live on bread and water"). Typically, he is less concerned about this loss than about the estrangement between William Brock and his brother Irving, also connected with the firm.

On September 3, after stopping at York en route to Kingston (he is never still in these last days), he finds time aboard ship to write a longer letter, making use of the example of his recent victory to heal the family rift: "Let me know, my dearest brothers, that you are all again united. The want of union was nearly losing this province, without even a struggle, and be assured that it operates in the same degree in regard to families."

In spite of the depressing news of Prevost's armistice, he cannot conceal his ecstasy over the bloodless victory at Detroit. He knows he has taken a desperate gamble, but "the state of the province admitted of nothing but desperate remedies." He is irked that his enemies should attribute his success to blind luck. He believes in careful preparation, not luck. His victory has proceeded from "a cool calculation of *pours* and *contres*" and it is his alone, for he crossed the river against the advice of the more conservative Procter, who now commands at Detroit, and other advisers. "I have," he exults, "exceeded beyond expectation."

The best news is that as general he will receive the largest share of the Detroit prize money. The value of captured articles is now reckoned at between thirty and forty thousand pounds and may go higher. He does not want it for himself, but if it will enable him to contribute to the comfort and happiness of his nearly destitute family, he will "esteem it my highest reward." At the moment of victory, "when I returned Heaven thanks for my amazing success, I thought of you all; you appeared to me happy – your late sorrows forgotten; and I felt as if you acknowledged that the many benefits, which for a series of years I received from you, were not unworthily bestowed."

His brothers will, he believes, be able to see the colours of the U.S. 4th Regiment, which he expects his aide, Major Glegg, will bring to England. He doubts, however, that his fellow countrymen will hold the trophy in much esteem. "Nothing is prized," he writes acidly, "that is not acquired with blood."

In Canada he is a national hero, and he knows it. The plaudits pour in. The Chief Justice of Lower Canada hastens to send his congratulations "in common with every other subject of his majesty in British North America." General Alexander Maitland, the honorary colonel of the 49th, dispatches a gushing note from across the Atlantic, which Brock never receives. His old friend Justice William Dummer Powell cannot contain himself: "There is something so fabulous in the report of a handful of troops supported by a few raw militia leaving their strong post to invade an enemy of double numbers in his own fortress, and making them all prisoners without the loss of a man, that...it seems to me the people of England will be incredulous...." He can hardly wait to get the news in person from Brock when he reaches Kingston.

Brock himself is a little stunned by the adulation. He has received so many letters hailing his victory that he begins "to attach to it more importance than I was at first inclined." If the English take the same view as the Canadians, then "I cannot fail of meeting reward, and escaping the horror of being placed high on a shelf, never to be taken down."

He reaches Kingston on September 4, to be greeted by an artillery salute and a formal address of congratulation from the populace. As he has done at York a few days before, he replies with tact, praising the

York and Lincoln regiments of militia, now at Queenston, whose presence, he declares (stretching the truth more than a little), induced him to undertake the expedition that brought about the fall of Detroit.

He praises everybody – citizens, soldiers, magistrates, officers, militia – for he intends to squeeze every possible advantage out of his victory, uniting Canadians against the invader. The change in attitude is startling; he notes privately that "the militia have been inspired... the disaffected are silenced." People are calling him the Saviour of Upper Canada. It is an accurate title, and in more ways than one, for he has saved the province not only from the Americans but also from itself.

He cannot rest. Back he goes across the lake to Fort George on the Niagara to study the situation along the frontier. Lieutenant-Colonel Baynes has already written to him of his meeting with Dearborn, describing the mood at Albany where the Americans are convinced that the British are weak and their own resources superior, exaggerations that are both "absurd and extravagant." But Baynes has urged Prevost to send more reinforcements to Niagara, so that if matters come to a head the British force will be superior.

Brock reaches Fort George on September 6, chagrined to discover how heavily the Americans have been reinforced during the armistice, due to end in two days. He expects an immediate attack. "The enemy will either turn my left flank which he may easily accomplish during a calm night or attempt to force his way across under cover of his Artillery." He sends at once to Procter at Amherstburg and Lieutenant-Colonel John Vincent at Kingston asking for more troops.

There is one bright spot, the result again of the victory at Detroit: three hundred Mohawk Indians are on the ground and another two hundred on their way under the controversial John Norton of the Indian Department. Born a Scotsman, now an adopted Mohawk chief, Norton sees himself the successor of the great Joseph Brant and the arch-rival of William Claus, his superior in the service.

Brock has mixed feelings about Norton's followers, who have cast aside their neutrality only as a result of British victories. Any form of neutrality is, to Brock, little short of treason. He cannot forgive the Mohawk, cannot understand why they would not wish to fight for the British, cannot grasp the truth – that the quarrel is not really theirs, that its outcome cannot help them. Now, he notes, "they appear ashamed of themselves, and promise to whipe [sic] away the disgrace into which they have fallen by their late conduct." It is doubtful whether the Indians feel any sense of disgrace; they have simply been following a foreign policy of their own, which is to reap the benefits of fighting on the winning side.

Brock is a little dubious of their value: "They may serve to intimidate; otherwise expect no essential service from this degenerate race." Has he forgotten so quickly that the great value of the Indians at Michilimackinac and Detroit was not to fight but to terrify? In his account to Prevost of the capture of Detroit, he has mentioned both Elliott and McKee by name but not Tecumseh, without whose presence the state of affairs on the Canadian frontier might easily have been reversed. For Tecumseh and the Indians are also the Saviours of Upper Canada.

But Brock urgently needs to bolster the loyalty of the Indians on the western frontier in Michigan Territory, which the British hold. That loyalty has been badly shaken by Sir George Prevost's armistice; the natives, who have been suspicious of British intentions since the gates of the fort were closed to them after the Battle of Fallen Timbers, are growing uneasy again. Brock has ordered Procter to dispatch a force to invest Fort Wayne on the Maumee – the kind of aggressive move that is totally opposed to Prevost's wishes and intentions. He explains to Prevost that he has done this with the hope of preserving the lives of the garrison from an Indian massacre. This humanitarian motive is overshadowed by a more realistic if cynical objective. Brock wants to preserve the Indians' allegiance, to keep the native warriors active and at the same time demonstrate an aggressive policy on the part of the British against the Long Knives. If Tecumseh's followers desert him "the consequences must be fatal," and to preserve their loyalty he has pledged his word that England will enter into no negotiation with the United States in which the interest of the Indians is not consulted. He reminds Prevost of this and Prevost reminds Whitehall. The Governor General, who seems to believe that peace is just around the corner, revives the old British dream of an Indian buffer state – a kind of native no man's-land – separating British North America from the Union to the south.

But Prevost still believes that the path to peace lies in being as inoffensive as possible with the enemy. He wants to evacuate Detroit and indeed all of Michigan Territory – a possibility that appalls Brock, for he knows that it would cause the Indians to desert the British cause and make terms with the Americans. "I cannot conceive of a connexion so likely to lead to more awful consequences," he tells Prevost.

The Governor General backs down, but relations between the two men are becoming increasingly strained. Brock is prepared to attack across the Niagara River, is, in fact, eager to attack, convinced that he can sweep the Americans from the frontier and make himself master of Upper New York State, even though "my success would be transient." But Prevost has him shackled. Even after the armistice ends on September 8 Sir George clings to the wistful fancy that the Americans will come to terms if only the British do nothing to annoy them. This is fatuous. American honour has been sullied, and nothing will satisfy it but blood. It is psychologically impossible for the Americans to break off the war after the ignominy of Detroit. Thus far the only bright spot in America's abysmal war effort has been the defeat and destruction of the British frigate *Guerrière* by the *Constitution* off the Grand Banks on August 19. This naval encounter by two isolated ships will have little effect on the outcome of the war, but it does buoy up America's flagging spirits and makes a national hero of the *Constitution*'s commander, Isaac Hull, at the very moment when his uncle William has become a national scapegoat.

Sir George makes one telling point in his instructions to his frustrated general: since the British are not interested in waging a campaign of conquest against the United States but only in containing the war with as little fuss as possible while battling their real enemy, Napoleon, it surely makes sense to let the enemy take the offensive "having ascertained by experience, our ability in the Canadas to resist the attack of a tumultuary force."

There is a growing testiness in Prevost's correspondence with Brock – more than a hint that he is prepared, if necessary, to write off the Niagara frontier. Sir George berates Brock obliquely for weakening the line of communication along the St. Lawrence between Cornwall and Kingston: by moving troops from those points to Niagara he has encouraged predatory raids by the enemy. Between the lines can be seen Prevost's fear of giving his impetuous subordinate too many troops lest he make an overt move that will upset the fine balance with which Prevost still hopes to conciliate the Americans.

But Brock has not been a soldier for the best part of three decades without learning to obey orders: "I have implicitly followed Your Excellency's instructions, and abstained, under great temptation and provocation, from every act of hostility." To his brother Savery he pours out his frustrations: "I am really placed in a most awkward predicament.... My instructions oblige me to adopt defensive measures, and I have evinced greater forbearance than was ever practised on any former occasion. It is thought that, without the aid of the sword, the American people may be brought to a full sense of their own interests. I firmly believe that I could at this moment sweep everything before me from Fort Niagara to Buffalo...."

At last he has some officers he can trust. These come not from the 41st, which he finds wretchedly officered, but from his old regiment, the 49th, six companies of which he has brought to Fort George from Kingston: "Although the regiment has been ten years in this country drinking rum without bounds, it is still respectable...."

Many U.S. regulars, tired of service, are deserting to him; more, he believes, would do so if the opportunity offered. Those deserters who do not drown in the swirling river report a state of poor morale on the opposite side. They complain of bad food, scanty pay, continual sickness, and they are jealous of the militia, which they believe to be better fed and better treated. Brock disdains the American militia. He sees them as an undisciplined rabble of "enraged democrats...who... die very fast."

His enemies cannot help but admire him. Years later, Winfield Scott will recall how the Canadian commander of a small provincial vessel made a landing on the Erie shore and plundered several farm families of their table silver, beds, and other possessions. The indignant Brock seized the vessel, sent her back under a flag of truce with all the property that had not been destroyed and the money for the remainder. "Such conduct could not fail to win all noble hearts on both sides of the line."

But Brock has not the temperament for the kind of bloodless warfare that has been his lot since hostilities began. He is impatient for action and, since he cannot initiate it, hopes and expects the Americans will. He is convinced (correctly) that the Americans will have to make a move soon to keep their restless and undisciplined militia in line. To warn of attack he has ordered a line of beacon signals along the frontier. Now he can only sit and wait. His sword has yet to be raised in combat, and this clearly irks as much as it puzzles him:

"It is certainly something singular that we should be upwards of two months in a state of warfare, and that along this widely extended frontier not a single death, either natural or by the sword, should have occurred among the troops under my command, and we have not been altogether idle, nor has a single desertion taken place."

218

Who, in Europe, can take this bloodless colonial fracas seriously? On September 9, the day after Prevost's armistice ends, Napoleon launches and, at great cost, wins the Battle of Borodino, thus opening the way to Moscow. The casualties on that day exceed eighty thousand – a figure greater than the entire population of Upper Canada. On the Niagara frontier, two tiny, untrained armies face each other across the boiling river, each afraid to make the first move, each expecting the other to launch an attack.

Brock is certain that something decisive will happen before the month's end. "I say decisive, because if I should be beaten, the province is inevitably gone; and should I be victorious, I do not imagine the gentry from the other side will be anxious to return to the charge."

In short, he will either be confirmed as the Saviour of Upper Canada or there will be no Upper Canada. And whatever happens, Brock is convinced, this brief and not very bloody war will come to a swift conclusion. There are, of course, other possibilities, both glorious and at the same time tragic, but these he does not consider.

•

IN LEWISTON, during these same weeks, General Stephen Van Rensselaer finds himself pushed to the brink of a battle for which he is inadequately prepared by a series of circumstances over which he has little control. Events pile up, one upon another, like ocean breakers, driving him unwillingly towards a foreign shore.

On August 27 the camp is subjected to a dreadful spectacle: across the river for more than half a mile straggle the remnants of Hull's defeated army, ragged, shoeless, dispirited, the wounded groaning in open carts, the whole prodded onward by their British captors.

"The sensations this scene produced in our camp were inexpressible," Lovett writes his friend. "Mortification, indignation, fearful apprehension, suspicion, jealousy, dismay, rage, madness." The effect on Van Rensselaer's force is twofold: the militia is cowed by this demonstration of British invincibility while the Hawks among the officers salivate for action.

"Alarm pervades the country and distrust among the troops," the General writes to Governor Tompkins. Like Hull's beaten soldiers, many of his own are without shoes; all are clamouring for pay. "While we are thus growing daily weaker, our enemy is growing stronger." The British are reinforcing the high ground above Queenston, pouring in men and ordnance and fortifying every prominent point from Fort Erie to Fort George.

Governor Tompkins, who is thunderstruck by the disaster, receives another letter from his political ally, the belligerent quartermaster general, Peter B. Porter:

"Three days ago we witnessed a sight which made my heart sick within me, and the emotions it excited throughout the whole of our troops along the line...are not to be described. The heroes of Tippecanoe, with the garrisons of Detroit and Michilimackinac...were marched like cattle from Fort Erie to Fort George, guarded by General Brock's regular troops with all the parade and pomp of British insolence, and we were incapacitated by the armistice and our own weakness from giving them the relief which they seemed anxiously to expect, and could only look on and sicken at the sight....

"...This miserable and timid system of defense must be abandoned or the nation is ruined and disgraced. Make a bold push at any one point and you will find your enemy....

"The public mind in this quarter is wrought up almost to a state of madness. Jealousy and distrust begin to prevail toward the general officers, occasioned perhaps by the rash and imprudent expressions on politics of some of the persons attached to them, but principally to the surrender of Detroit, which among the common people is almost universally ascribed to treachery...."

On September 7, a day before the armistice ends, Major Lovett, the General's eloquent aide, comes to the conclusion that "we must either fight or run.... There are some pretty strong reasons to believe that Brock is attempting to *Hull* us...." Yet nobody on the American side can guess Brock's intentions or even estimate the true strength of his force because it is impossible to persuade a single man to risk his neck by acting as a spy on the Canadian shore. Van Rensselaer must resort to the timeworn artifice of sending officers across under flags of truce to treat with the enemy on various pretexts while peering about at the fortifications.

At Albany, General Dearborn's resolve is wavering. As late as mid-August he stated his belief that Montreal and all of Upper Canada would fall to the Americans before winter. Now Hull's defeat has shaken him. He still insists that he will attack Niagara, Kingston, and Montreal, but his purpose is circumscribed by a hedgerow of "ifs." *If* the governors of the neighbouring states will supply enough reinforcements quickly; *if* the Quartermaster General can get him sufficient supplies, ammunition, and guns, then "I am persuaded we may act with effect." *If* he can muster some five thousand regulars and additional militia, he will push on to Montreal to support Van Rensselaer's offensive on the Niagara, hoping to cut communications between the two Canadas, "but whether I shall be able to effect anything or not depends on so many contingencies as to leave all in doubt."

He has dispatched some five thousand troops to Plattsburg on Lake Champlain and another two thousand (all militia) to Sackets Harbor and expects to have an army of seven thousand on the Niagara, including three thousand regulars. Unfortunately Brigadier-General Wadsworth, the New York militia commander, who has grossly over-estimated Brock's forces, has warned him that anything fewer than ten thousand will not do.

In his reports to Washington, Dearborn manages to be gloomy and optimistic in the space of a single sentence: "I fear...that we shall meet with additional misfortunes on the borders of Upper Canada... but if we redouble our exertions and inspire a due degree of firmness and spirit in the country, all will ultimately go well."

He is an old man, indecisive, inexperienced, out of his depth, querulous and uninformed ("Will the militia consent to go into Canada?"), the victim of his country's military myopia, the prisoner of its bureaucratic confusion. Hampered by lack of supplies, lack of men, lack of money, he tells Eustis: "I have never found official duties so unceasing, perplexing and fatiguing as at this place" and then adds a sympathetic postscript: "I presume you are not on a bed of roses."

At Lewiston, while Dearborn vacillates, Peter B. Porter chafes for action. He and his cronies mount a whispering campaign against Van Rensselaer's command. The General's aide, Solomon, is convinced that "they have so far succeeded in the Camp and the Country that in the former it is only whispered, but in the Latter it is openly said, that Gen. Van Rensselaer is a traitor to his Country and the Surrender of the Army when it crosses the River is the price of his Infamy." As a result, "he cannot enforce the Subordination which is so necessary to the safety and glory of the Troops he Commands."

Reluctantly, Solomon writes to Morgan Lewis, a former Republican governor of New York and now the state's quartermaster general, suggesting that another commander – somebody of the same politics as the government – replace his cousin on the frontier. Nothing comes of it.

The General expects a British attack imminently and prepares to defend against it. He decides to maintain Fort Niagara, opposite Fort George, decrepit though it is, removes the roof from a stone building, sets up a battery of two twelve-pound cannon in its upper storey, establishes a second battery of three eighteen-pounders a mile upriver across from a similar British emplacement, builds a new communications road back of the river and beyond enemy fire, and co-opts an additional five hundred men stationed at Buffalo to strengthen his own force.

The British are also active. Gazing across the narrow river, General Van Rensselaer can see the *Royal George* arrive with two hundred gunners. He has learned that one hundred smaller boats loaded with stores for the enemy fort have passed up the St. Lawrence together with two regiments of troops. The situation, he admits, is critical, but "a retrograde movement of this army upon the back of that disaster which has befallen the one at Detroit would stamp a stigma upon the national character which time could never wipe away." He will hold out against superior strength until he is reinforced. There is no evidence that he contemplates an attack. It is the British who will attack, or so the General believes.

But the British do not attack, and the promised reinforcements do not arrive. In Van Rensselaer's army of two thousand, on September 22, one hundred and forty-nine are too sick to fight, including his cousin Solomon. The weather is dreadful; raw winds and cold rains harass the troops, soaking such blankets and tents as are available.

After suffering for six days with fever, Solomon attempts to return to duty, suffers a relapse, is bled thrice and doctored with enough salts, jalap, castor oil, and calomel to render an ordinary man insensible. It takes him another week to recover from the doctors' ministrations. By contrast Lovett, the amateur soldier, is in splendid condition, "hardened almost to the hide, muscles and houghs of an ox" and clearly having the time of his life:

"We are every few days, deluged in water, such storms of rain and wind I think I never experienced, the cloth of my Tent is mere sieve stuff; every third night I get wet as a Muskrat. But in the worst of it I sing, in proper tune: 'No burning heats by day, Nor blasts of evening air, Shall take my health away, If God be with me there.' ...I feel safe; for I feel myself in duty. I am glad I came...."

In Albany, General Dearborn continues to promise that money, men, and provisions are on the way, albeit tardily ("a strange fatality seems to have pervaded the whole arrangement" is the way he puts it), and urges aggressive action. His letter to Stephen Van Rensselaer bubbles with enthusiasm: on the western frontier, General Harrison is marching to the relief of Detroit with a new Army of the Northwest, six or seven thousand strong; two thousand more troops are stationed at Sackets Harbor; the American navy is operating in Lake Ontario. "In fact we have nothing to fear and much to hope."

Everything, however, depends on what happens on the Niagara River: *"By putting on the best face that your situation admits, the enemy may be induced to delay an attack until you will be able to meet him and carry the war into Canada. At all events, we must calculate on possessing Upper Canada before winter sets in."* Dearborn underlines this passage as if, by a pen stroke, he can will his ragtag army into victory.

At the end of September, the longed-for reinforcements arrive, including seventeen hundred soldiers under the command of one of the more curious specimens of American generalship, Brigadier-General Alexander Smyth. Smyth is bombastic, egotistical, jealous of his prerogatives. A regular officer, he disdains the militia and has no intention of co-operating with his nominal commander, Stephen Van Rensselaer. Though he knows nothing of the country and has only just arrived, he takes it upon himself to advise the General that the best place for a crossing of the Niagara would be above the falls and not below them. He has therefore decided not to take his troops to Lewiston but to encamp them near Buffalo, thus splitting the American force. Nor does he report personally to Van Rensselaer. He says he is too busy.

By now, General Stephen Van Rensselaer has, in the words of his cousin Solomon, "resolved to gratify his own inclinations and those of his army" and commence operations. The British show no inclination to attack. Dearborn has demanded action. For better or for worse, Stephen is determined that he shall have it.

If numbers mean anything, his chances for success are excellent. He now has some eight thousand troops under his command, half of them regulars, of whom forty-two hundred are encamped at Lewiston. (The remainder are at Fort Niagara and either at Buffalo or, in the case of some two thousand Pennsylvania volunteers, en route to Buffalo.) To counter this force Brock has about one thousand regular troops, some six hundred militia, and a reserve of perhaps six hundred militia and Indians, strung out thinly from Fort Erie to Fort George. The bulk of his strength he must keep on his wings to prevent the Americans from turning one of his flanks and attacking his rear. Thus his centre at Queenston is comparatively weak.

Yet numbers do not tell the whole story. Morale, sickness, discipline, determination – all these Van Rensselaer must take into account. By his own count he has only seventeen hundred *effective* militia men at Lewiston. The state of his army is such that he knows he must act swiftly, if at all:

"Our best troops are raw, many of them dejected by the distress their families suffer by their absence, and many have not necessary clothing. We are in a cold country, the season is far advanced and unusually inclement; we are half deluged by rain. The blow must be struck soon or all the toil and expense of the campaign will go for nothing, and worse than nothing, for the whole will be tinged with dishonor."

The key word is "dishonor." It creeps like a fog through the sodden tents of the military, blinding all to reality. It hangs like a weight over the council chambers in Albany and Washington. Stephen Van Rensselaer feels its pressure spurring him to action, *any* action. No purpose now in disputing the war and its causes, no sense in further recriminations or I-told-you-so's. Detroit must be avenged! "The national character is degraded, and the disgrace will remain, corroding the public feeling and spirit until another campaign, unless it be instantly wiped away by a brilliant close of this." The words might have sprung from the lips of Porter, the War Hawk; they are actually those of Van Rensselaer, the Federalist and pacifist.

He knows that with his present force at Lewiston it would be rash to attempt an attack. But Smyth has arrived with an almost equal number and that is enough. He plans a two-pronged assault: Smyth's regulars will cross the river near Newark and storm Fort George from the rear while he leads the militia from Lewiston to carry the heights above Queenston. This will divide the thinly spread British forces, cut their line of communications, drive their shipping from the mouth of the Niagara River (which will become an American waterway), provide the troops with warm and extensive winter quarters, act as a springboard for the following season's campaign, and – certainly not least – "wipe away part of the score of our past disgrace."

The scheme is plausible, but it depends on the co-operation of Brigadier-General Smyth; and Smyth has no intention of co-operating. He acts almost as if Van Rensselaer did not exist. The Commander invites him to a council of officers to plan the attack. Smyth does not reply. The General writes again, more explicitly. Still no reply. Several days pass. Nothing. A fellow officer now informs Van Rensselaer that he has seen Smyth, who is unable to name the day when he can come to Lewiston for a council. The General thereupon sends a direct order to Smyth to bring his command "with all possible dispatch." Silence.

In no other army would such insubordination be tolerated, but America is not yet a military nation. The amiable Van Rensselaer does not court-martial his recalcitrant underling; he simply proceeds without him. He has already told Dearborn that it would be rash to attack Queenston with the militiamen under his command at Lewiston. Now, with Smyth's regulars apparently out of the picture, he determines to do just that.

He has very little choice for, at this juncture, an incident occurs near Black Rock that reduces his options.

●

BLACK ROCK, NEW YORK, October 8, 1812. Lieutenant Jesse Elliott of the U.S. Navy, a veteran of the 1807 attack on *Chesapeake* (and said to be a nephew of Matthew Elliott), supervising the construction of three ships of war for service in Lake Erie, finds himself tempted by the sight of two British ships, newly anchored under the guns of Fort Erie. One is the North West Company's two-gun schooner *Caledonia*, which Captain Roberts impressed into service during the successful attack on Michilimackinac. The other is a former American brig, *Adams*, mounting six guns, captured at Detroit and renamed for that city by the British. Elliott conceives a daring plan: if he can capture both vessels and add them to the fleet under construction, the balance of power will shift to the American side on Lake Erie.

He needs seamen. Fortunately some ninety American sailors are on the march from Albany. Elliott sends a hurry-up call, selects fifty for the job. Isaac Roach, a young artillery adjutant (and a future mayor of Philadelphia), offers fifty more men from his own regiment. There is a scramble to volunteer. The battalion commander, Winfield Scott, then on the threshold of what will be a long and glorious career, warns his men that they can expect a hard fight, but this only excites them further. When Roach, a mere second-lieutenant, orders "Volunteers to the front: March!" the entire battalion steps forward. Officers senior to Roach attempt to resign their commissions in order to serve under him. Men are so eager for battle that Roach finds he must select ten more than his quota.

The attack is made in two longboats, each carrying about fifty armed men, who must track their craft against the rapid current of the Niagara to the mouth of Buffalo Creek – difficult work. Here the men are forced to wade into the freezing water to their shoulders to haul the empty longboats over the bar at the creek's mouth in order to enter Lake Erie. It is past midnight; the troops, soaking wet, with a chill sleet falling about them, must now row for three hours up the lake "and not allowed to even laugh to keep ourselves warm."

At three they come silently upon their unsuspecting quarry. A fire in the caboose of *Detroit* gives them a light to steer by. Roach and Elliott, in the lead boat, head straight for the vessel. Sailing Master George Watts and Captain Nathan Towson of Winfield Scott's regiment take their boat under the stern of *Caledonia*. It is not possible to achieve complete surprise for the sleet has ended, the night is calm, the lake glassy. Two volleys of musket fire pour into the lead boat from the deck of *Detroit*, whose captain is the same Lieutenant Frederic Rolette who captured *Cuyahoga* at the start of the war. Rolette and his crew are quickly overpowered as Elliott manages to loose the topsails in an attempt to get the ship underway. Suddenly a British cannon opens up; a heavy ball whizzes twenty feet above the heads of the boarding party ("John Bull always aims too high," says Roach), ricochets onto the opposite shore where half of Winfield Scott's men are lined up to watch the action and tears an arm off a Major Cuyler of the New York militia, knocking him from his horse, mortally wounded. Roach, with a bundle of lighted candles in his hand, touches off *Detroit*'s six-pound deck guns in reply.

Aboard *Caledonia*, the commander, a young Scot, Second-Lieutenant Robert Irvine, roused from his bed, has thrown himself down the gangway, calling on his inexperienced crew of a dozen men to follow him and discharging his blunderbuss into the attackers. He has time only for a second charge before he is felled by a cutlass stroke, but he has managed to kill or wound several of the boarding party. Watts and Towson get *Caledonia* underway – thus distracting the enemy fire from *Detroit*, whose attackers are axing through her cables – and sail her across the river, where she anchors under the protection of the American batteries at Black Rock. She is a considerable prize, being loaded with pork destined for Amherstburg, a rich cargo of furs, and a good many American prisoners captured at Michilimackinac and Detroit who now find themselves free men again.

Elliott and Roach, still facing a concentrated fire from Fort Erie, drift down the river, unable to manoeuvre *Detroit*. A half mile below Black Rock she grounds on the British side of Squaw Island. Exposed to enemy fire, the Americans abandon ship, taking the captured Lieutenant Rolette and his men and all but three American prisoners of war who had been held in the hold.

A seesaw battle ensues for the shattered *Detroit*. A British detachment crosses the river, seizes her, attempts to pull her off the shoal. This is too much for Winfield Scott, who dispatches another party to land on the northeast shore of Squaw Island and drive the British away. The Americans do their best to warp *Detroit* into open water, but she has lost her anchor and the British fire is so hot they are forced to abandon the attempt. They strip her of armament and supplies and burn her to the water line, thus denying her to the enemy.

It is a considerable blow to the British. The Americans have captured four cannon, two hundred muskets, and so much pork that Procter's men at Amherstburg will be forced on to half rations. But the real effect of the loss of one ship and the seizure of another will not be felt until the following year at the Battle of Lake Erie.

Brock, who gallops directly to the scene as soon as he receives the news, instantly sees the danger. The event, he tells Prevost, "may reduce us to incalculable distress. The enemy is making every effort to gain a naval superiority on both lakes, which, if they accomplish, I do not see how we can retain the country." Brock cannot resist a small gibe at Prevost's continuing policy of caution: "Three vessels are fitting out for war on the other side of Squaw Island, which I would have attempted to destroy but for Your Excellency's instructions to forbear. Now such a force is collected for their protection as would render any operation against them very hazardous."

Jesse Elliott's bold adventure has another equally far-reaching result. The only American victory on the frontier, its success will goad the Americans into premature attack. The newspapers seize upon it thirstily. The Buffalo *Gazette* headlines it as a GALLANT AND DARING EXPLOIT. Congress publicly thanks Elliott and presents him with a sword. A thrill runs through the nation. At Lewiston, General Van Rensselaer is presented with an ultimatum from his troops, who are now hot for action – or claim to be. The General is warned that if he does not take the offensive immediately, they will all go home. With Smyth sulking in his tent at Buffalo, Van Rensselaer decides to abandon his two-pronged attack and launch a single assault upon Queenston on October 11. What follows is high farce.

He has planned to cross the river at night in thirteen boats, each capable of carrying twenty-five men. Lieutenant-Colonel John Fenwick's artillery will come up from Niagara to support the attack, and it is hoped that Smyth will send further reinforcements. The crossing will be made from the old ferry landing directly opposite the heights of Queenston where the river is a tumult of eddies and whirlpools; thus experienced boatmen are mandatory. The best man for the job is one Lieutenant Sims, who is sent ahead in the darkness while the troops follow in wagons.

Now an extraordinary incident takes place which defies explanation. Sims, by accident or design, passes the embarkation point, lands his boat far upriver where it cannot be found, then, perhaps through panic at his error or perhaps from cowardice, abandons his boat and is not seen again. In the growing drizzle, the troops wait in vain for him to return. Solomon Van Rensselaer, roused from his sickbed to command the assault and shaking with fever, waits with them. Nothing can be done because, for reasons unexplained, the oars for all the boats are with the wretched Sims.

The troops wait all night as the storm rises in fury. (It will continue for twenty-eight hours, deluging the camp.) Finally, as daylight breaks, they are marched back to camp, the boats half-concealed in the rushes. Van Rensselaer calls a council, hoping that the incident will dampen the spirits of his eager officers. On the contrary, they are even keener to attack. Lieutenant-Colonel John Chrystie, newly arrived on the scene, has already reported that his officers and men are "full of ardor and anxious to give their country proof of their patriotism." Everybody, the General discovers, seems to "have gained new heat from the recent miscarriage." Events not of his making have him in their grasp. A friend in Albany, the Federalist congressman Abraham Van Vechten, realizes this and in a letter (delivered too late) warns Solomon that "the General's reputation forbids rashness. To shun the Enemy improperly would be censurable – but to seek him under manifest disadvantages would be madness." The time has long passed, however, when the General can accept such cool advice. The pressure on him is so great that he realizes that "my refusal to act might involve me in suspicion and the service in disgrace."

As his aide and friend John Lovett describes it, "the impetuosity of not only men but his first officers became such that he was absolutely compelled to go to battle or risk such consequences as no man could endure." It is not possible to wait, even though there is no proper plan of attack. He must strike the blow at once, this very night.

●

FORT GEORGE, UPPER CANADA, October 11, 1812. As Brock's brigade major, Thomas Evans, rises from his dinner at the officers' mess, his commander hands him an alarming note. It comes from Captain James Dennis, commanding one of the flank companies of the 49th at Queenston. Dennis's detachment is in a state of mutiny. The men have threatened to shoot their officers.

"Evans," says Brock, "you will proceed early in the morning and investigate this business, and march as prisoners in here half a dozen of the most culpable and I will make an example of them."

There can be little doubt what that example will be. Years before, Brock literally pounced on Fort George and in a few minutes seized and shackled a group of mutineers plotting to shoot their commander, Roger Sheaffe. The ringleaders were taken to Quebec, court-martialled, and shot by a firing squad in the presence of the entire company, a demonstration that shook everyone including Brock himself, who was seen to wipe the tears from his eyes as the order was executed.

Brock has a second instruction for Major Evans:

"You can also cross the river and tell Van Rensselaer I expect he will immediately exchange the prisoners taken in the *Detroit* and *Caledonia* for an equal number of Americans I released after the capture of Detroit."

Thus, on the very eve of the most famous battle on Canadian soil, a British officer will enter and reconnoitre the enemy camp.

Evans reaches Queenston the following morning to find the guardhouse gutted and Dennis in a state of alarm. The two repair to Dennis's quarters in the largest home in the village, a handsome stone edifice on the high bank above the river, built by the best-known trader on the frontier, the late Robert Hamilton. It is owned now by his son Alexander, sheriff of Queenston, member of the Legislative Council, and a lieutenant-colonel in the militia. Alexander is another of the many grandsons of John Askin of Amherstburg.

Just as Evans is about to leave the Hamilton house to arrest the ringleaders of the mutiny, he hears a scatter of musket fire from the opposite shore. A ball whizzes through the room, passing directly between the two officers. Evans is outraged and demands to know the meaning of "such unusual insolence." Dennis replies that sporadic firing has been going on for some days, making it hazardous to use the door on the river side of the building.

Evans decides to cross the river at once, musket balls or no, and orders Dennis to corral the prisoners for his return. Then, with the balls still hurtling past his ears, he walks over to the home of a militia captain, Thomas Dickson, the brother of Robert, the Red-Haired Man, and – such are the close-knit relationships of the frontier trade – a cousin of the late Robert Hamilton.

Evans asks Mrs. Dickson for a white kerchief to serve as a flag of truce and invites Dickson to join him in the river crossing. Mrs. Dickson expostulates. Others in the house join her: the venture is far too dangerous; the enemy is in a temper; they will no longer respect a white flag.

At this, Evans seizes Dickson by one hand, takes the flag in the other, descends the steep steps to a canoe at the water's edge, and starts off across the two-hundred-yard stream in an unceasing shower of musket balls. The canoe, battered by the eddies and filling with water, becomes unmanageable and seems about to founder when the American fire suddenly ceases and the two men are able to reach the far shore.

As Evans is about to leap to the ground, an American with a bayonet stops him. The Major asks to see the Adjutant-General, Solomon Van Rensselaer, but is told that Solomon is too ill to receive him. He replies that he carries an important message from Brock and is prepared to see either the General himself or somebody deputized by him. Eventually, Major Lovett appears, and Evans presents his request about the prisoner exchange. Lovett's reply is abrupt and curiously evasive. Nothing can be done, he says, "till the day after tomorrow."

Evans is instantly on the alert. What have the Americans planned for the morrow? When he presses his case, Lovett remains evasive. Evans urges him to consult the General. Lovett agrees and goes off.

It appears to Evans that Lovett is trying to delay his return to the Canadian side – it is already past midday. Lovett does not come back for two hours. He explains that the prisoners have been sent on to Albany and cannot quickly be brought back, but all will be settled "the day after tomorrow."

This constant harping on the morrow confirms Evans in his suspicions that the enemy is planning an immediate attack. Now he is anxious to get away and report to Brock. He has kept his eyes open and notices that the Americans' numbers have been "prodigiously swelled by a horde of half-savage troops from Kentucky, Ohio, and Tennessee." (The prevailing British opinion is that the American militia and volunteers consist of uncivilized wild men.) Even more significant, Evans spots more than a dozen boats half-hidden in fissures in the bank and partially covered with brush. This convinces him that "an attack on our shores could not be prudently delayed for a single day."

He and Dickson paddle swiftly to their own shore. Dickson's first task is to remove his family from their house on the river bank, clearly the site of any future battle. Evans, meanwhile, rushes to warn the 49th flank companies and the militia stationed at Queenston. It is now past three. Fort George is six miles away. Every man will be needed to defend the town, including the mutinous prisoners. On his own responsibility, Evans liberates them "on the specious plea of their offence proceeding from a too free indulgence in drink," appealing to their loyalty and courage, which he has no doubt will be tested by the following day.

Then, after making sure a fresh supply of ammunition has been distributed and "infusing all the spirit and animation in my power to impart," the harried brigade major sets off at a gallop for Fort George, alerting the various posts along the route to the coming danger. He reaches the fort at six, having been exposed for thirteen hours "to wet feet and extreme heat without refreshment of any kind." He is so exhausted he cannot speak. He takes some food, recovers his breath, and is ushered into the dining room before Brock and his senior officers.

At first they do not believe him, charge him with overreaction, offer to place bets against his predictions of an attack on the following day. Brock himself appears doubtful, then changes his mind as Evans talks on. With a grave face he asks Evans to follow him into his office where he questions him carefully on the day's occurrences. At last he is convinced. The two men return to the dining room where the General issues orders calling in all the militia in the neighbourhood that very evening; others in outlying districts are told to report as swiftly as possible. He thanks Evans, who is ordered to make all necessary preparations at headquarters to meet the coming assault. Brock then returns to his office to work late into the night. Evans toils until eleven, then slumps onto a mattress. A few hours later, his slumber is disturbed by the rumble of distant guns.

●

LEWISTON, NEW YORK, October 13, 1812. At 3 A.M. General Stephen Van Rensselaer opens the attack on Queenston, after some unfortunate skirmishing between his regular and militia officers on the touchy subject of seniority. Lieutenant-Colonel Winfield Scott refuses to serve under Solomon Van Rensselaer, who has been deputed to lead the first wave. Lieutenant-Colonel John Chrystie, another regular, also demurs. A solution is worked out that gives Chrystie a command equal to but separate from Solomon's. Chrystie will command the three hundred regular troops during the crossing; Solomon will be in charge of an equal number of militia – men picked carefully from the best-drilled battalions. Not all of the regulars are as touchy as Scott and Chrystie. Lieutenant-Colonel John Fenwick is so anxious to get into the battle that he drops his rank and puts himself under the command of the militia.

Stephen Van Rensselaer's attack plan and his preparations for the assault are both faulty. He has already lost the advantage of surprise; now he proposes to make the first crossing with only a handful of bateaux: two large boats, each holding eighty men, and a dozen smaller ones, each holding twenty-five. His initial attack force, which will cross in two waves, consists of some six hundred men, half of them militia. A few miles upriver are more boats, which could easily be floated down, but the General does not take advantage of these, believing that once the boats are emptied on the opposite shore they can quickly return for reinforcements. Half a dozen trips may serve to ferry the entire force across the river. It is a serious miscalculation.

Nor does Stephen Van Rensselaer think to make use of Jesse Elliott's bluejackets at Black Rock, men who might be considered experienced boatmen. His own militia, of course, know this part of the river well; they have been staring across it, sometimes navigating it under flags of truce, for some six weeks. But those who have just joined his force from Buffalo, Black Rock, and Fort Niagara are strangers to the area.

There are other problems. Van Rensselaer has failed to distribute enough ammunition. He has not insisted strongly enough on making use of Smyth's regular forces at Buffalo. Nobody has thought to find boats large enough to transport heavy field pieces across the river; the bateaux cannot handle cannon or caissons. Nor have the various commands been assigned to specific objectives. The orders are general: get across, seize the village, gain the heights.

It is still dark when the first boats push off in the teeth of a chill, sleety drizzle. To oppose the landing, the British have fewer than three hundred men in and about Queenston. But the defenders are on the alert. John Lovett, who has been placed in charge of the American battery at Fort Grey on the heights above Lewiston, notes that the Canadian shore is an incessant blaze of musketry and that his friend Solomon lands in what seems to be a sheet of fire. His own guns – eighteen-pounders – open up to cover the attack, aided by two six-pounders and a mortar on the Lewiston shore, the cannonballs and shells whistling over the heads of the troops in the bateaux.

At the same moment, the British open fire. Half-way up the heights, in an arrow-shaped emplacement known as a redan, a single cannon begins to lob eighteen-pound balls down on the boats. Darkness is banished as bombs burst and muskets flash. At Brown's Point, half-way between Queenston and Fort George, young Lieutenant John Beverley Robinson of the York Volunteers (the future chief justice) sees all of the village lit by gun fire.

In one of the boats approaching the shore sits the oldest volunteer in the American army, an extraordinary Kentucky frontiersman named Samuel Stubbs, sixty-two years old and scarcely five feet in height, gripping the rifle with which, in just three months, he has killed forty-five deer. Peering into the gloom illuminated now by the flash of cannon, Stubbs sees the opposite shore lined with redcoats "as thick as bees upon a sugar maple." In a few minutes he is ashore under heavy fire, "the damned redcoats cutting us up like slain venison," his companions dropping "like wild pigeons" while the musket balls whistle around him "like a northwest wind through a dry cane break."

Colonel Van Rensselaer's attack force has dwindled. Three of the boats, including the two largest containing almost two hundred men, have drifted downriver and turned back. On the bank above, Captain Dennis with forty-six British regulars and a handful of militia is keeping up a withering fire. Solomon Van Rensselaer is no sooner out of his boat than a ball strikes him in the right thigh. As he thrusts forward, waving his men on, a second ball enters his thigh – the British are purposely firing low to inflict maximum damage. As the Colonel continues to stumble forward, a third shot penetrates his calf and a fourth mangles his heel, but he does not stop. Two more strike him in the leg and thigh. Weak from loss of blood, his men pinned down by the killing fire, he totters back with the remnant of his force to the shelter of the steep bank above the river and looks around weakly for his fellow commander. Where is Chrystie? He is supposed to be in charge of the regulars. But Chrystie is nowhere to be seen.

Chrystie's boat has lost an oarlock and is drifting helplessly downstream while one of his officers attempts to hold an oar in place. None of these regulars is familiar with the river; all are dependent upon a pilot to guide them. But as they come under musket fire from the Canadian bank the pilot, groaning in terror, turns about and makes for the American side. Chrystie, wounded in the hand by grape-shot, struggles with him to no avail. The boat lands several hundred yards below the embarkation point, to which Chrystie and the others must return on foot.

In Solomon Van Rensselaer's later opinion, this is the turning point of the battle. Chrystie's return and the heavy fire from the opposite shore "damped the hitherto irrepressible ardor of the militia." The very men who the previous day were so eager to do battle – hoping, perhaps, that a quick victory would allow them to return to their homes – now remember that they are not required to fight on foreign soil. One militia major suddenly loses his zest for combat and discovers that he is too ill to lead his detachment across the river.

At the embarkation point, Chrystie finds chaos. No one, apparently, has been put in charge of directing the boats or the boatmen, most of whom have forsaken their duty. Some are already returning without orders or permission, landing wherever convenient, leaving the boats where they touch the shore. Others are leaping into bateaux on their own, crossing over, then abandoning the craft to drift downriver. Many are swiftly taken prisoner by the British. Charles Askin, lying abed in the Hamilton house suffering from boils, hears that some of the militia have cheerfully given themselves up in the belief that they will be allowed to go home as the militia captured at Detroit were. When told they will be taken to Quebec, they are distressed. Askin believes that had they known of this very few would have put a foot on the Canadian shore.

As Chrystie struggles to collect the missing bateaux, his fellow commander, Lieutenant-Colonel Fenwick, in charge of the second assault wave, arrives only to learn that he cannot cross for lack of boats. Exposed to a spray of grape- and canister-shot, Fenwick herds his men back into the shelter of the ravine until he manages to secure enough craft to move the second wave out onto the river. The crossing is a disaster. Lieutenant John Ball of the 49th directs the fire of one of his little three-pounders, known as "grasshoppers," against the bateaux. One is knocked out of the water with a loss of fifteen men. Three others, holding some eighty men, drift into a hollow just below the Hamilton house. All are slaughtered or taken prisoner, Fenwick among them. Terribly wounded in the eye, the right side, and the thigh, he counts nine additional bullet holes in his cloak.

None of the regular commanders has yet been able to cross the narrow Niagara. On the opposite shore under the sheltering bank, Solomon Van Rensselaer, growing weaker from his wounds, is attempting to rally his followers, still pinned down by the cannon fire from the gun in the redan and the muskets of Captain Dennis's small force on the bank above. Captain John E. Wool, a young officer of the 13th Infantry, approaches with a plan. Unless something is done, and done quickly, he says, all will be prisoners. The key to victory or defeat is the gun in the redan. It must be seized. Its capture could signal a turning point in the battle that would relieve the attackers while the fire could be redirected, with dreadful effect, among the defenders. But how can it be silenced? A frontal attack is out of the question, a flanking attack impossible, for the heights are known to be unscalable from the river side. Or are they? Young Captain Wool has heard of a fisherman's path upriver leading to the heights above the gun emplacement. He believes he can bring an attacking force up the slopes and now asks Solomon Van Rensselaer's permission to attempt the feat.

Wool is twenty-three, a lithe, light youth of little experience but considerable ambition. One day he will be a general. The fact that he has been shot through the buttocks does not dampen his enthusiasm. With his bleeding commander's permission, he sets off with sixty men and officers, moving undetected through a screen of bushes below the river bank. Solomon Van Rensselaer's last order to him is to shoot the first man in the company who tries to turn tail. Then, as Wool departs, the Colonel slumps to the ground among a pile of dead and wounded, a borrowed greatcoat concealing the seriousness of his injuries from his wet and shivering force. Shortly afterwards he is evacuated.

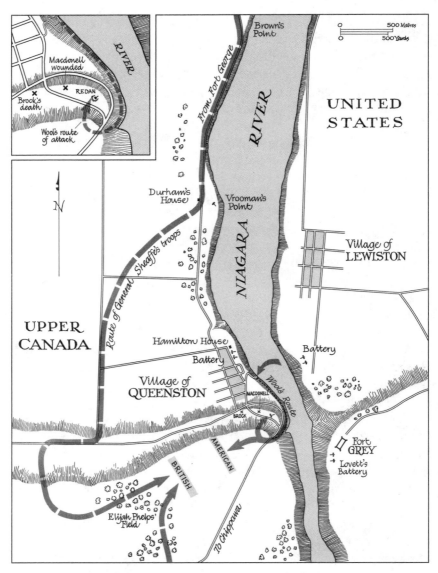

The Battle of Queenston Heights

Captain Wool, meanwhile, finds the path and gazes up at the heights rising almost vertically more than three hundred feet above him. Creased by gullies, blocked by projecting ledges of shale and sandstone, tangled with shrubs, vines, trees and roots clinging to the clefts, they look forbidding, but the Americans manage to claw their way to the crest.

236

Wool, buttocks smarting from his embarrassing wound, looks about. An empty plateau, bordered by maples and basswood, stretches before him. But where are the British? Their shelters are deserted. Below, to his right, half-hidden by a screen of yellowing foliage, he sees a flash of scarlet, realizes that the gun in the redan is guarded by the merest handful of regulars. Brock, who is a great reader of military history, must surely have studied Wolfe's famous secret ascent to the Plains of Abraham, yet, like the vanquished Montcalm, he has been assured that the heights are safe. He has brought his men down to reinforce the village, an error that will cost him dear. Wool's men, gazing down at the red-coated figures manning the big gun, cannot fail to see the tall officer with the cocked hat in their midst. It is the General himself. A few minutes later, when all are assembled, their young commander gives the order to charge.

●

AT FORT GEORGE, Brock has awakened in the dark to the distant booming of cannon. What is happening? Is it a feint near Queenston or a major attack? He is inclined to the former possibility, for he has anticipated Van Rensselaer's original strategy and does not know of Smyth's obstinacy. Brock is up in an instant, dressed, and on his grey horse Alfred, dashing out the main gate, waiting for no one, not even his two aides, who are themselves hurriedly pulling on their boots. Later someone will spread a story about Brock stopping for a stirrup cup of coffee from the hands of Sophia Shaw, a general's daughter, said to be his fiancée. It is not convincing. On this dark morning, with the wind gusting sleet into his face and the southern sky lit by flashes of cannon, he will stop for nobody.

As he hurries through the mud toward Queenston, he encounters young Samuel Jarvis, a subaltern in his favourite militia unit, the York Volunteers. Jarvis, galloping so fast in the opposite direction that he cannot stop in time, finally reins his horse, wheels about, tells his general that the enemy has landed in force at the main Queenston dock. Jarvis's mission ought not to be necessary because of Brock's system of signal fires, but in the heat of battle nobody has remembered to light them.

Brock gallops on in the pre-dawn murk, past harvested grain fields, soft meadows, luxuriant orchards, the trees still heavy with fruit. The York Volunteers, stationed at Brown's Point, are already moving toward Queenston. Brock dashes past, waving them on. A few minutes later his two aides also gallop by. John Beverley Robinson, marching with his company, recognizes John Macdonell, Brock's provincial aide and his own senior in the York legal firm to which the young volunteer is articled. Brock has reason to be proud of the York militia, who answered his call to arms with alacrity, accompanied him on the embarkation to Amherstburg, were present at Detroit's downfall, and are now here on the Niagara frontier after six hundred miles of travel by boat and on foot.

A few minutes after Brock passes, Robinson and his comrades encounter groups of American prisoners staggering toward Fort George under guard. The road is lined with groaning men suffering from wounds of all descriptions, some, unable to walk, crawling toward nearby farmhouses, seeking shelter. It is the first time that these volunteers have actually witnessed the grisly by-products of battle, and the sight sickens them. But it also convinces them, wrongly, that the engagement is all but over.

Dawn is breaking, a few red streaks tinting the sullen storm clouds, a fog rising from the hissing river as Brock, spattered with mud from boots to collar, gallops through Queenston to the cheers of the men of his old regiment, the 49th. The village consists of about twenty scattered houses separated by orchards, small gardens, stone walls, snake fences. Above hangs the brooding escarpment, the margin of a prehistoric glacial lake. Brock does not slacken his pace but spurs Alfred up the incline to the redan, where eight gunners are sweating over their eighteen-pounder.

From this vantage point the General has an overview of the engagement. The panorama of Niagara stretches out below him – one of the world's natural wonders now half-obscured by black musket and cannon smoke. Directly below he can see Captain Dennis's small force pinning down the Americans crouching under the riverbank at the landing dock. Enemy shells are pouring into the village from John Lovett's battery on the Lewiston heights, but Dennis is holding. A company of light infantry occupies the crest directly above the redan. Unable to see Wool's men scaling the cliffs, Brock orders it down to reinforce Dennis. Across the swirling river, at the rear of the village of Lewiston, the General glimpses battalion upon battalion of American troops in reserve. On the American shore several regiments are preparing to embark. At last Brock realizes that this is no feint.

He instantly dispatches messages to Fort George and to Chippawa to the south asking for reinforcements. Some of the shells from the eighteen-pounder in the redan are exploding short of their target, and Brock tells one of the gunners to use a longer fuse. As he does so, the General hears a ragged cheer from the unguarded crest above and, looking up, sees Wool's men charging down upon him, bayonets glittering in the wan light of dawn. He and the gunners have time for one swift action: they hammer a ramrod into the touchhole of the eighteen-pounder and break it off, thus effectively spiking it. Then, leading Alfred by the neck reins, for he has no time to remount, the Commander-in-Chief and Administrator of Upper Canada scuttles ingloriously down the hillside with his men.

In an instant the odds have changed. Until Wool's surprise attack, the British were in charge of the battle. Dennis had taken one hundred and fifty prisoners; the gun in the redan was playing havoc with the enemy; Brock's forces controlled the heights. Now Dennis is retreating through the village and Wool's band is being reinforced by a steady stream of Americans.

Brock takes shelter at the far end of the town in the garden of the Hamilton house. It would be prudent, perhaps, to wait for the reinforcements, but Brock is not prudent, not used to waiting. As he conceives it, hesitation will lose him the battle: once the Americans consolidate their position in the village and on the heights they will be almost impossible to dislodge.

It is this that spurs him to renewed action – the conviction that he must counterattack while the enemy is still off balance, before more Americans can cross the river and scale the heights. For Brock believes that whoever controls the heights controls Upper Canada: they dominate the river, could turn it into an American waterway; they cover the road to Fort Erie; possession of the high ground and the village will slice the thin British forces in two, give the Americans warm winter quarters, allow them to build up their invading army for the spring campaign. If the heights are lost the province is lost.

He has managed to rally some two hundred men from the 49th and the militia. "Follow me, boys," he cries, as he wheels his horse back toward the foot of the ridge. He reaches a stone wall, takes cover behind it, dismounts. "Take a breath, boys," he says; "you will need it in a few moments." They give him a cheer for that.

He has stripped the village of its defenders, including Captain Dennis, bleeding from several wounds but still on his feet. He sends some men under Captain John Williams in a flanking movement to attack Wool's left. Then he vaults the stone fence and, leading Alfred by the bridle, heads up the slope at a fast pace, intent on re-taking the gun in the redan.

His men, struggling to keep up, slide and stumble on a slippery footing of wet leaves. Above him, through the trees, Wool's men can be seen reinforcing the gun emplacement. There is a confused skirmish; the battle seesaws; the Americans are driven almost to the lip of the precipice. Someone starts to wave a white handkerchief. Wool tears it away, orders a charge. The British are beaten back, and later some will remember Brock's cry, "This is the first time I have ever seen the 49th turn their backs!"

The sun, emerging briefly from the clouds, glistens on the crimson maples, on the Persian carpet of yellow leaves, on the epaulettes of the tall general, sword in hand, rallying his men for a final charge. It makes a gallant spectacle: the Saviour of Upper Canada, brilliant in his scarlet coat, buttons gleaming, plumed hat marking him unmistakably as a leader, a gap opening up between him and his gasping followers.

Does he realize that he is a target? No doubt he does – he has already been shot in the hand – but that is a matter of indifference. Leaders in Brock's army are supposed to lead. The spectacle of England's greatest hero, Horatio Nelson, standing boldly on deck in full dress uniform, is still green in British memory. The parallels are worthy of notice. The two heroes share similar strengths and flaws: disdain for the enemy, courage, vanity, ambition, tactical brilliance, innovative minds, impetuosity. Both have the common touch, are loved by their men, whom they, in turn, admire, and are idealized by the citizens of the countries they are called upon to protect. And both, by their actions, are marked for spectacular death. They seem, indeed, to court it. Brock's nemesis steps out from behind a clump of bushes and when the General is thirty paces from him draws a bead with his long border rifle and buries a bullet in his chest, the hole equidistant from the two rows of gilt buttons on the crimson tunic. George Jarvis, a fifteen-year-old gentleman volunteer in the 49th, rushes over. "Are you much hurt, sir?" he asks. There is no answer, for Brock is dead. A grisly spectacle follows as a cannonball slices another soldier in two and the severed corpse falls upon the stricken commander.

The gallant charge has been futile. Brock's men retreat down the hill, carrying their general's body, finding shelter at last under the stone wall of the Hamilton garden at the far end of the village. Here they are joined by the two companies of York Volunteers, whom Brock passed on his gallop to Queenston. These men, arriving on the dead run, catch their breath as American cannon fire pours down upon them from the artillery post on the opposite heights. A cannon-ball slices off one man's leg, skips on, cripples another in the calf. Then, led by young John Macdonell, the dead general's aide, the augmented force makes one more attempt to recapture the heights.

Impulsively, Macdonell decides to follow Brock's example. Possessed of a brilliant legal mind – he was prosecuting criminal cases at sixteen and has been acting attorney-general of the province for a year – he has little experience in soldiering. Quick of temper and a little arrogant, he reveres his dead commander and, in the words of his fellow aide Major Glegg, determines "to accompany him to the regions of eternal bliss." Macdonell calls for a second frontal attack on the redan. Seventy volunteers follow him up the heights to join the remainder of the 49th under Captain John Williams taking cover in the woods. Together, Williams and Macdonell form up their men and prepare to attack.

"Charge them home and they cannot stand you!" cries Williams. The men of the 49th, shouting "Revenge the General!" (for he was *their* general), sweep forward. Wool, reinforced by several hundred more men, is waiting for them, his followers concealed behind logs and bushes.

As Macdonell on horseback waves his men on, his steed, struck by a musket ball, rears and wheels about. Another ball strikes Macdonell in the back, and he tumbles to the ground, fatally wounded. Williams, on the right flank, also falls, half scalped by a bullet. As Captain Cameron rushes forward to assist his fallen colonel, a ball strikes him in the elbow and he too drops. Macdonell, in terrible pain, crawls toward his closest friend, Lieutenant Archibald McLean of the York Volunteers, crying, "Help me!" McLean attempts to lead him away and is hit by a ball in the thigh. Dismayed by these losses, the men fall back, bringing their wounded with them. Dennis is bleeding from five wounds. Williams, horribly mangled, survives, but Macdonell is doomed.

Everything that Brock feared has happened. The Americans occupy both the village and the heights and are sending over reinforcements, now that they have unopposed possession of the river. The British have retreated again to the outskirts of the village. All of their big guns, except for one at Vrooman's Point, have been silenced.

At ten o'clock on this dark October morning, Upper Canada lies in peril.

●

AT THIS POINT, all General Van Rensselaer's forces should be across the river, but so many of his boats have been destroyed or abandoned that he is hard put to reinforce his bridgehead. He has no more than a thousand men on the Canadian side, and of these two hundred are useless. Stunned by their first experience of warfare, the militiamen cower beneath the bank; no power, it seems, no exhortation to glory or country, no threat of punishment can move them.

The General crosses at noon with his captain of engineers, whose job it is to help the troops on the heights. Unfortunately all the entrenching tools have been left at Lewiston; conditions are such that they will never arrive. The General sends the touchy Winfield Scott to the top of the ridge to take over from the wounded Wool, then prepares to return to the American shore. As he does so, a rabble of militiamen leaps into the boat with him.

During this lull, Winfield Scott works furiously with the engineers to prepare a defence of the high ground. The Americans know that British reinforcements are on their way from both Chippawa and Fort George; an American-born militiaman has deserted with that information. Scott would like to attack the Chippawa force, cutting it off from the main army, but has not enough men for the job; nor can he get more. His little force is diminishing. Whole squads of militia slink away into the woods or the brush above the bluffs. Scott posts his remaining men along the ridge with their backs to the village, his left flank resting on the edge of the bluff, his right in a copse of trees and bushes.

He realizes his danger. Ammunition is running out. He has managed to get a six-pound gun across the river in a larger boat, but there are only a few rounds available for it. In the distance he can see a long column of red-coated regulars marching up the road from Fort George under Brock's successor, Major-General Roger Sheaffe.

Now Scott becomes aware of an odd spectacle. Dashing back and forth along the ragged line of the militia is a man in civilian clothes, waving a naked sword, swearing profusely, and exhorting the men to form and fight to the death. This is Brigadier-General William Wadsworth of the New York militia, who has the reputation of being the most eloquently profane officer in the army. He has come across the river on his own, without orders, to try to instil some fighting spirit into his citizen soldiers.

Scott is nonplussed. Wadsworth outranks him, but he is not a regular. Scott cannot – *will* not – serve under him.

"General Wadsworth," he says, "since you are in command I propose to confine my orders strictly to the regular troops here!"

To which the militia general replies, quite sensibly and amiably:

"That's all damned nonsense, sir! You are a regular officer, you know professionally what should be done! Continue your command, sir, I am here simply for the honor of my country and that of the New York Militia!"

And off he rushes to raise some volunteers for the firing line.

Scott desperately needs to get the eighteen-pound cannon at the redan into action to protect his rear and cover the landing of the reinforcements that his general has promised him. But Brock has spiked it well: Scott's men cannot drive or drill the ramrod out. The Lieutenant-Colonel scrambles down the hillside to help, but as he does so a terrifying sound pierces the air. It is the screaming war-whoop of the Mohawk Indians, led by John Norton and his Indian friend, the young chief John Brant. They come swooping out of the woods and hurtling across the fields, brandishing their tomahawks, driving in Scott's pickets and forcing the trembling troops back. Only Scott's own presence and voice prevent a general rout. The Indians retire into the woods at the first volley, then work their way around toward the American left. No American soldier has fallen during this brief attack, but the damage is done, for the cries of the Indians have carried across the river and sent a chill through the militiamen on the far side.

Almost at the same time, two British guns have opened up in the garden of the Hamilton house, effectively barring passage across the river. Scott knows that his chances of getting reinforcements before the final battle are slim. He can see the men he needs – hundreds of them, even thousands, lined up on the far bank like spectators at a prizefight. For all the good they can do him, they might as well be back at their farms, where at this moment most of them fervently wish they were.

General Van Rensselaer is helpless. He has promised reinforcements and ammunition to the defenders on the heights but can supply neither. He has sent to Brigadier-General Smyth asking for more men, but Smyth again declines. And he cannot budge the troops at the embarkation point. They have been milling about for some hours in the drizzle, watching the boats return with terribly wounded men (and sometimes with deserters), watching other boats founder in the frothing stream, and now, with the screams of the Indians echoing down from the heights, they have no stomach for battle.

The General, riding a borrowed horse, with Major Lovett at his side, moves through the sulking soldiers, urging them to enter the boats. No one budges. One of their commanders, a Lieutenant-Colonel Bloom, returns from the heights wounded, mounts his horse and, still bleeding, exhorts, swears, prays. The troops refuse to advance. A local judge, Peck by name, appears from somewhere, a large cocked hat on his head, a long sword dangling from his broad belt, preaching and praying to no avail. The troops have broken ranks and assumed the role of witnesses to the coming battle, and there is nothing, under the Constitution, that their officers can do.

Frustrated to fury and despair, Van Rensselaer starts to compose a note to General Wadsworth:

"I have passed through my camp; not a regiment, not a company is willing to join you. Save yourselves by a retreat if you can. Boats will be sent to receive you."

The promise is hollow. The terrified boatmen refuse to recross the river.

●

AT NEWARK, early that morning, Captain James Crooks of the 1st Lincoln Militia, a Canadian unit, notes the inclement weather and decides against turning out. All that summer at daybreak the militiamen have paraded on one of the village streets, protected by intervening buildings from the eyes of the enemy in order to conceal their paucity. The wind and the sleet convince Captain Crooks that for once his subordinates can handle the parade. He turns over in his blankets, is starting to doze off again when a knock comes at his window and a guard reports that the Yankees have crossed the river at Queenston. Crooks is startled; this is the first he has heard of it. Even now he cannot hear the sound of the guns because of the gale blowing off the lake.

The orders are to rendezvous at the fort. Crooks leaps from his bed, pulls on his uniform, orders his men to form up, noting with pleasure the enthusiasm with which each unit outdoes the others to see which can reach the bastion first. Once there, the men stack their arms and wait. No one knows exactly what is happening, but the word is out that General Brock has already left for Queenston.

At the fort's gate, Crooks runs into the artillery commander, Captain William Holcroft, who tells him he is about to open fire on Fort Niagara across the river but is short of men. Crooks supplies him with several including Solomon Vrooman, who is sent to man the twenty-four-pounder on a point a mile away. Vrooman's big gun, which is never out of action, does incalculable damage and is one reason for the American militia's refusal to cross the river. From this day on, the emplacement will be known as Vrooman's Point.

At the naval yards, Crooks encounters Captain James Richardson, who is thunderstruck at the news of the attack. His ship, at dock loaded with gunpowder, is within point-blank range of the American battery, nine hundred yards across the water. He makes haste to unload his explosive cargo and send it to the fort. This proves fortunate; the powder in the fort's magazine, which has not seen use since the Revolutionary War, is so old it cannot propel shot more than half-way across the river.

A deafening artillery battle follows. The Americans heat their cannonballs until they glow red, then fire them into the village and the fort, burning the courthouse, the jail, and fifteen other buildings until, at last, their batteries are reduced by British cannon.

In the meantime Brock's express has arrived from Queenston with orders for 130 militiamen to march immediately to the relief of the heights. Captain Crooks is anxious to lead his men, but an older brother in the same company is the senior of the two. Crooks manages to talk him into staying behind, assembles men from five flank companies, forms them into a reinforcement detachment, and marches them off toward the scene of battle. A mile out of Newark he is told of Brock's death, tries to keep the news from his men, fails, is surprised to find it has little immediate effect. At Brown's Point, he passes one of the York Volunteers, who asks him where he is going. When he answers, "To Queenston," the officer tells him he is mad: if he goes any farther all his people will be taken prisoner; the General is dead; his force is completely routed; his aide is mortally wounded; four hundred Yankees are on his flank, moving through the woods to attack Newark. Crooks replies that he has his orders and will keep going. He tells his men to load their muskets and marches on. Shortly afterward he encounters a second officer who repeats almost word for word what he has heard a few minutes before. Crooks ignores him.

About a mile from town he halts his men at a house owned by a farmer named Durham. It is filled with American and British wounded, including the dying Macdonell. The troops are hungry, having missed their breakfast. He sends them foraging in a nearby garden to dig potatoes. Soon every pot and kettle in the house is bubbling on the fire, but before the potatoes can be eaten General Sheaffe arrives with the remainder of the 41st Regiment and orders the militia to fall in. Off they march to battle, still hungry.

Sheaffe, a cautious commander, has no intention of repeating Brock's frontal assault, has planned instead a wide flanking movement to reach the plateau above the village, where Wool's Americans are preparing for battle. His force will veer off to the right before entering the village, make a half circle around the heights, and ascend under cover of the forest by way of an old road two miles west of Queenston. Here Sheaffe expects to be joined by the second detachment that Brock ordered from Chippawa. In this way he can keep his line of march out of range of the American battery on the heights above Lewiston while the Indians, who have preceded him, act as a screen to prevent the enemy patrols from intercepting him as he forms up for battle.

Meanwhile, Captain Holcroft of the Royal Artillery has, at great risk, managed to trundle two light guns through the village, across a ravine, and into the garden of the Hamilton house, guided by Captain Alexander Hamilton, who knows every corner of the ground. It is these guns that Winfield Scott hears, effectively blocking the river passage, as Norton and his Mohawks harass his forward positions.

The Indians, screening Sheaffe's force, continue to harry the Americans. They pour out of the woods, whooping and firing their muskets, then vanish into the trees, preventing Scott from consolidating his position, driving in the pickets and flank patrols to inhibit contact with the advancing British, and forcing the Americans into a tighter position on the heights. Their nominal chief is John Brant, the eighteen-year-old son of the late Joseph Brant, the greatest of the Mohawk chieftains, whose portrait by Romney will later grace every Canadian school book. But the real leader is the theatrical Norton, a strapping six-foot Scot who thinks of himself as an Indian and aspires to the mantle of his late mentor. He is more Indian than most Indians, has indeed convinced many British leaders (including the English parliamentarian and abolitionist William Wilberforce) that he is a Cherokee. He wears his black hair in a long tail held in place by a scarlet handkerchief into which he has stuck an ostrich feather. Now, brandishing a tomahawk, his face painted for battle, he whoops his way through the woods, terrifying the American militia and confusing the regulars.

Directly behind the woods on the brow of the heights, hidden by the scarlet foliage and protected by the Mohawks, Roger Sheaffe forms up his troops on Elijah Phelps's ploughed field. He is in no hurry. He controls the road to Chippawa and is waiting for Captain Richard Bullock to join him with another 150 men from the south. Captain Dennis of the 49th has already joined his company, his body caked with blood. Exhausted and wounded as a result of the battle at the river's edge, he refuses to leave the field until the day is won. Now he stands with the others, waiting for the order to advance, while the American gunners pour down fire from across the river. For the unblooded militia the next hour is the longest they have known, as a rain of eighteen-pound balls and smaller shot drops about them.

At about four o'clock, just as Bullock comes up on the right flank, Sheaffe orders his men to advance in line. He has close to one thousand troops in all. The enemy has almost that number – or *had* almost that number, but now many of the American militia, with the war cries of the Indians echoing in their ears, have fled into the woods or down the cliff toward the river. When Scott counts his dwindling band he is shocked to discover that it numbers fewer than three hundred. In the distance he sees the scarlet line of British regulars, marching in perfect order, the Indians on one flank, the militia slightly behind, two three-pound grasshopper guns firing.

Van Rensselaer's despairing note has just reached Wadsworth: reinforcement is not possible. The Americans call a hurried council and agree to a strategic withdrawal.

Now the battle is joined. James Crooks, advancing with his militia detachment, has been in many hailstorms but none, he thinks wryly, where the stones fly thick as the bullets on this October afternoon. Little scenes illuminate the battle and remain with him for the rest of his days: the sight of an Indian tomahawking a York militiaman in the belief that he is one of the enemy. The sight of the Americans' lone six-pounder, abandoned, with the slow match still burning (he turns it about and some of his men fire several rounds across the river). The bizarre spectacle of Captain Robert Runchey's platoon of black troops – escaped slaves who have volunteered at Newark – advancing on the flank of the Indians. The sight of a companion, his knuckles disabled by a musket ball at the very moment of pulling the trigger. Crooks seizes the weapon and fires off all its spare ammunition, saving the final round for a man in a small skiff in the river whom he takes to be an American fleeing the battle. Fortunately he misses; it is one of his own officers crossing over with a flag of truce to demand General Van Rensselaer's surrender.

Scott's regulars are attempting to cover the American withdrawal. The Colonel himself leaps up on a fallen tree and literally makes a stump speech, calling on his men to die with their muskets in their hands to redeem the shame of Hull's surrender. They cheer him and face the British, but the advance continues with all the precision of a parade-ground manoeuvre, which, of course, it is. The Americans are trapped between the cliff edge on their left and the cannon fire from Holcroft's guns in the village below them on their right.

As the Indians whoop forward once more – the British and Canadian militia advancing behind with fixed bayonets – the American line wavers, then breaks. The troops rush toward the cliffs, some tumbling down the hill, clinging to bushes and outcroppings, others, crazed with fear, leaping to their deaths on the rocks below. Scores crowd the beach under the shoulder of the mountain, waiting for boats that will never come. Others, badly mangled, drown in the roaring river.

The three ranking Americans, Scott, Wadsworth, and Chrystie, carried downward by the rush of escaping men, now decide that only a quick surrender will save the entire force from being butchered by the Indians. The problem is how to get a truce party across to the British lines. Two couriers, each carrying a white flag, have tried. The Indians have killed both.

At last Winfield Scott determines to go himself.

There are no white handkerchiefs left among the company, but Totten, the engineering officer, has a white cravat, which Scott ties to his sword point. He will rely on his formidable height and his splendid uniform to suggest authority. These attributes, however, are of little value, for Scott is almost immediately attacked and seized by young Brant and another Indian, who spring from a covert and struggle with him. The American's life is saved by the timely appearance of

John Beverley Robinson and his friend Samuel Jarvis of the York Volunteers, who free him and escort him to Sheaffe.

The British general accepts Scott's surrender and calls for his bugler to sound the cease-fire. The Mohawk pay no attention. Enraged at the death of two of their chiefs, they are intent on exterminating all the Americans huddled under the bluff. Scott, seeing his men's predicament, hotly demands to be returned to share their fate. Sheaffe persuades the future conqueror of Mexico to have patience. He himself is appalled at the carnage, and after the battle is over some of his men will remember their general flinging off his hat, plunging his sword into the ground in a fury, and demanding that his men halt the slaughter or he, Sheaffe, will immediately give up his command and go home. A few minutes later the firing ceases and the battle is over. It is half-past four. The struggle has raged for more than twelve hours.

Now, to Scott's mortification and despair, some five hundred militiamen appear from hiding places in the crevices along the cliffs and raise their hands in surrender.

The British have taken 925 prisoners including a brigadier-general, five lieutenant-colonels, and sixty-seven other officers. One prisoner is allowed to go free – the diminutive sextuagenarian Samuel Stubbs of Boonsboro, Kentucky. Stubbs, expecting to be killed and scalped, discovers that the British look on him as an oddity, as if he had been born with two heads. A British officer takes one look at Stubbs and lets him go. "Old daddy," he says, "your age and odd appearance induce me now to set you at liberty, return home to your family and think no more of invading us!" Stubbs promises cheerfully to give up fighting, but "I didn't mean so for I was determined I wouldn't give up the chase so, but at 'um again." And so he will be – all the way from the attack on Fort York to the final bloody battle of New Orleans, where in his sixty-sixth year, he is responsible for the deaths of several British officers.

In addition, the Americans suffer some 250 casualties. These include the badly mangled Solomon Van Rensselaer, who will eventually recover, and John Lovett, who, though not hit by ball or shrapnel, is incapacitated for life. What began as a lark has for him ended as tragedy. For Lovett, the conversationalist and wit, the world has gone silent. Placed in charge of the big guns on the heights above Lewiston, he has been rendered permanently deaf.

British casualties, by contrast, are light.

"God, man," says the staff surgeon, Dr. Thorne, to James Crooks as the battle ends, "there does not seem to be any of you killed."

"Well, Doctor," replies the Captain, "it is well it is so but go into that guard house and you'll find plenty to do for your saws...."

The British have lost only fourteen killed and seventy-seven wounded, but there is one loss that cannot be measured and by its nature evens the score at the Battle of Queenston Heights. Isaac Brock is gone. There is no one to fill his shoes.

•

ALL OF CANADA is stunned by Brock's loss. His own soldiers, the men of the 49th who were with him in Holland and at Copenhagen, are prostrated by the news. Of all the scenes of sorrow and despair that day, the most affecting is the one reported by Lieutenant Driscoll of the 100th Regiment, who had come up from Fort Erie to help direct artillery fire against the American battery at Black Rock. At two that afternoon Driscoll looks up to see a provincial dragoon gallop up, dishevelled, without sword or helmet, his horse bathed in foam, his own body spattered with mud.

One of Brock's veterans, a man named Clibborn, speaks up:

"Horse and man jaded, sir; depend upon it, he brings bad news."

Driscoll sends the veteran across to discover what message the dragoon has brought. The soldier doubles over to the rider but returns at a funereal pace, and Driscoll realizes that something dreadful has occurred. He calls out:

"What news, Clibborn? What news, man? Speak out."

Clibborn walks slowly toward the battery, which is still maintaining a brisk fire at the Americans across the river. Musket balls plough into the ground around him; he does not seem to see them. He cannot speak, can only shake his head. At last he slumps down on the gun platform, his features dead white, his face a mask of sorrow.

Driscoll cannot stand the silence, shakes Clibborn by the shoulder:

"For heaven's sake, tell us what you know."

Clibborn answers at last, almost choking:

"The General is killed; the enemy has possession of Queenston Heights."

At those words, every man in the battery becomes paralysed. The guns cease firing. These are men of the 49th, all of whom have served under Brock in Europe; they are shattered by the news. Some weep openly. Others mourn in silence. Several begin to curse in frustration. The sound of enemy cheers, drifting across the river, rouses them to their duty. In a helpless rage over the death of their general, they become demonic, loading, traversing, and firing the heavy guns as if they were light field pieces, flinging round after round across the river in an attempt to avenge their former chief.

All over the province, similar expressions of grief are manifest. Glegg, Brock's military aide, calls it "a public calamity." Young George Ridout of the York Volunteers writes to his brother that "were it not for the death of General Brock and Macdonell our victory would have been glorious...but in losing our man...is an irreparable loss." Like many others, Ridout is convinced that Brock was the only man capable of leading the divided province. Samuel Jarvis crosses the lake to bring the news of the tragedy to York where "the thrill of dismay... was something indescribable."

In Quebec, an old friend, Anne Ilbert, who once volunteered to embroider some handkerchiefs for the bachelor general so the laundresses wouldn't steal them, writes to an acquaintance that "the conquest of half the United States would not repay us for his loss...by the faces of the people here you would judge that we had lost everything, so general is the regret everyone feels for this brave man, the victory is completely swallowed up in it." She fears for the future, wonders what the troops will do under another commander, suspects that Upper Canada will fall to the Americans before winter's end. "This is the first real horror of war we have experienced. God send it may not lead to a train of others."

Prevost, when he learns of his general's death, is so badly shaken that he can scarcely hold the pen with which to report the tragedy to Sir John Sherbrooke in Halifax. Yet he mentions the matter only briefly in that letter. And later, when a dispatch reaches him quoting the Prince Regent at some length on Brock's heroism and ability, he publishes in the Quebec *Gazette* the first non-committal sentence only, omitting phrases about "an able and meritorious officer...who... displayed qualities admirably adapted to awe the disloyal, to reconcile the wavering, and animate the great mass of the inhabitants against successive attempts by the enemy to invade the province...."

Meanwhile, Sheaffe concludes an immediate armistice with the Americans, "the most ruinous policy that ever was or could have been adopted for the country," to quote a nineteen-year-old subaltern, William Hamilton Merritt, the future builder of the Welland Canal. Brock, who has been knighted for the capture of Detroit (posthumously, as it develops), would certainly have pursued Van Rensselaer's badly shaken force across the river to attack Fort Niagara and seize the northern half of New York state, but Sheaffe is a more cautious commander – Prevost's kind of general.

Brock's body, brought back to Newark, lies in state for three days. His funeral, in George Ridout's words, is "the grandest and most solemn that I have ever witnessed or that has been seen in Upper Canada." Brock's casket and Macdonell's are borne through a double line of Indians and militia – five thousand men resting on reversed arms. The twin coffins are buried in the York bastion of the fort. Guns boom every minute during the procession while across the river, at both Niagara and Lewiston, the Americans fire a salute to their old enemy. Sheaffe, on hearing the American guns, is overcome and says in a choked voice to one of his officers that "noble minded as General Brock was, he would have ordered the same had a like disaster befallen the Enemy."

Upper Canada is numb, its people drawn closer by a common tragedy that few outsiders can comprehend. In the United States, attention is quickly diverted by another naval skirmish in which the American frigate *Wasp*, having incapacitated and captured the British sloop of war *Frolic*, is herself taken by the enemy.

Europe is far more interested in the fate of Moscow, under attack by Napoleon, who at the very moment of the naval skirmish on October 18 is preparing to withdraw his army from the charred and deserted Russian capital. This bitter decision, still unknown to most of the world, marks the beginning of the end of the war with France. Had Madison foreseen it, the invasion of Canada, scarcely yet underway, would never have been attempted.

With Brock's burial, the myth takes over from the man. The following day, the Kingston *Gazette* reports "the last words of the dying Hero."

General Brock, watchful as he was brave, soon appeared in the midst of his faithful troops, ever obedient to his call, and whom [he] loved with the adoration of a father; but, alas! whilst collecting, arranging, forming, and cheering his brave followers, that great commander gloriously fell when preparing for victory – "*Push on brave York Volunteers*," being then near him, they were the last words of the dying Hero – Inhabitants of Upper Canada, in the day of battle *remember BROCK.*

If Brock ever uttered these words it could only have been when he passed the York Volunteers on the road to Queenston. It was the 49th, his old battalion, that surrounded him at the moment of his fall. Nor do dead men utter school-book slogans. Nonetheless, the gallant injunction passes into common parlance to become almost as well known as "Don't give up the ship," uttered in the same war by an American naval commander whose men, on his death, did give up the ship. The phrase will be used in future years to support a further myth – that the Canadian militia really won the war. In December, the York *Gazette* gushes that "it must afford infinite satisfaction to every Loyal Bosom that on every occasion, the Militia of the Province has distinguished itself with an alacrity & spirit worthy of Veteran Troops." It is not an assessment with which the dead general would have agreed, but it is a fancy that will not die. John Strachan, future bishop of Toronto, leader of the Family Compact and mentor of the young officers who formed the backbone of the York Volunteers, helps to keep it green. In Strachan's belief, the militia "without the assistance of men or arms except a handful of regular troops" repelled the invasion.

The picture of Brock storming the heights at Queenston, urging on the brave York Volunteers, and saving Canada in the process is the one that will remain with the fledgling nation. He is the first Canadian war hero, an Englishman who hated the provincial confines of the Canadas, who looked with disdain on the civilian leaders, who despised democracy, the militia, and the Indians, and who could hardly wait to shake the Canadian mud from his boots and bid good-bye forever to York, Fort George, Quebec, and all the stuffy garrison towns between. None of this matters.

His monument will be erected on the ridge, not far from where he fell, by the leaders of a colonial aristocracy intent on shoring up power against republican and democratic trends seeping across the border. This Tuscan pillar, 135 feet high, becomes the symbol of that power – of the British way of life: the Loyalist way as opposed to the Yankee way. In 1840, a disaffected Irish Canadian named Benjamin Lett, one of William Lyon Mackenzie's followers in his failed rebellion against an elitist autocracy, determines on one last act of defiance and chooses the obvious site: he blows up Brock's monument. The

Family Compact cannot do without its symbol, mounts a long public campaign, raises fifty thousand dollars, builds a more splendid monument, half as high again as its predecessor – taller, it is said, than any in the world save for Wren's pillar marking London's Great Fire. John Beverley Robinson, Strachan's protégé and the Compact's chief justice, is on hand, of course, at the dedication, and so is his successor and fellow subaltern in the Brave York Volunteers, Mr. Justice Archibald McLean. Robinson's spectacular career dates from Queenston Heights when, a mere law student of twenty-one, he is named acting attorney-general of the province to replace the mortally wounded Macdonell. ("I had as much thought of being made Bey of Tunis," he recalled.) By Confederation the field on which he and McLean did battle has become, in the words of the *Canadian Monthly*, "one of Canada's sacred places" and the battle, in the description of the Canadian nationalist George Denison, is "Canada's glorious Thermopylae."

So Brock in death is as valuable to the ruling class as Brock in life. He will not be remembered for his real contribution to the country: his military prescience, his careful preparation for war during the years of peace, his astonishing bloodless capture of an American stronghold. When Canadians hear his name, as they often will over the years, the picture that will form in their minds will be of that final impetuous dash, splendidly heroic but tragically foolish, up the slippery heights of Queenston on a gloomy October morning.

7

BLACK ROCK
Opéra Bouffe on the Niagara

Hearts of War! Tomorrow will
be memorable in the annals
of the United States.

– Brigadier-General Alexander Smyth,
November 29, 1812.

BUFFALO, NEW YORK, November 17, 1812. Brigadier-General Alexander Smyth is putting the finishing touches to a proclamation, which, like Hull's, will return to haunt him.

"*Soldiers!*" he writes, underlining the word. "You are amply prepared for war. You are superior in number to the enemy. Your personal strength and activity are greater. Your weapons are longer. The regular soldiers of the enemy are generally old men, whose best years have been spent in the sickly climate of the West Indies. They will not be able to stand before you when you charge with the bayonet.

"You have seen Indians, such as those hired by the British to murder women and children, and kill and scalp the wounded. You have seen their dances and grimaces, and heard their yells. Can you fear *them*? No. You hold them in the utmost contempt."

Smyth warms to his task. Having stiffened the backs of the regular troops he will now imbue the recalcitrant militia with a fighting spirit:

"VOLUNTEERS!" he prints in large, bold capitals. "I esteem your generous and patriotic motives. You have made sacrifices on the altar of your country. You will not suffer the enemies of your fame to mislead you from the path of duty and honor, and deprive you of the esteem of a grateful country. You will shun the *eternal infamy* that awaits the man, who having come within sight of the enemy, *basely* shrinks in the moment of trial.

"SOLDIERS OF EVERY CORPS! It is in your power to retrieve the honor of your country; and to cover yourselves with glory. Every man who performs a gallant action, shall have his name made known to the nation. Rewards and honors await the brave. Infamy and contempt are reserved for cowards. Companions in arms! You came to vanquish a valiant foe. I know the choice you will make. Come on my heroes! And when you attack the enemy's batteries, let your rallying word be *'The cannon lost at Detroit – or death.'*"

Out it goes among the troops and civilians, most of whom greet it with derision. To this Smyth is absolutely oblivious, for he is a prisoner of his ego. The word "vanity" hardly does justice to his own concept of himself. He is wholly self-centred. His actions and words, which others find bizarre and ridiculous, are to him the justifiable responses of a supreme commander who sees himself as the saviour of the nation. The newspapers scoff at him as "Alexander the Great" and "Napoleon II." Smyth is the kind of general who takes that satire as a compliment.

If words were bullets and exclamation points cannonballs, Smyth might cow the enemy through the force of his verbiage. A master of the purple passage, he bombards his own countrymen with high-flown phrases:

Men of New York: The present is the hour of renown. Have you not a wish for fame? Would you not choose to be one of those who, imitating the heroes whom Montgomery led, have in spite of the seasons, visited the tomb of the chief and conquered the country where he lies? Yes – You desire your share of fame. Then seize the present moment. If you do not, you will regret it....

Advance, then, to our aid. I will wait for you a few days. I cannot give you the day of my departure. But come on, come in companies, half companies, pairs or singly. I will organize you for a short tour. Ride to this place, if the distance is far, and send back your horses. But remember that every man who accompanies us places himself under my command, and shall submit to the salutary restraints of discipline.

Smyth is now in total charge of the Niagara campaign. Stephen Van Rensselaer has resigned in his favour. (He will run for governor in the spring, to be beaten by the craftier Tompkins.) His cousin Solomon is recovering from his wounds and dandling his new son on his lap; he will not fight again. Smyth, who never came face to face with either, reigns supreme.

On paper, the new commander's qualifications seem suitable

enough. He is an Irishman whose father, a parish rector, brought him to Virginia at the age of ten. A member of his state's bar, he has also been an elected representative in the lower house. As the colonel of a rifle regiment, he was ordered to Washington in 1811 "to prepare a system of discipline for the army." Within eighteen days of the declaration of war he was promoted to inspector general and ordered to the Niagara frontier.

"I must not be defeated," he declares on taking over from Van Rensselaer; and he enters into a flurry of boat building, for he intends, he says, to land more than four thousand men on the Canadian shore. This is bombast: more than half his force is in no condition to fight. The bulk of the regulars are raw recruits who have never fired a musket. The militia continue to desert – one hundred in a single night. Hundreds more clog the hospitals suffering from measles, dysentery, grippe. The cemetery behind the camp, where men are buried four to a grave, has expanded to two acres. The ill-clothed army has not yet been paid; two regular regiments and one militia company have already mutinied on this account; the captain of another volunteer company warns that his men will not cross the river until they receive pay and clothing allowances. The troops of Fort Niagara are starving for want of bread, and there is considerable doubt whether the eighteen hundred Pennsylvania volunteers due to arrive in mid-November will agree to fight on foreign soil.

Nonetheless, on November 9 the General announces that he will invade Canada in fifteen days. So loudly does he boast about his intentions that the British are well prepared for any attack; on November 17 they launch a heavy bombardment of Smyth's headquarters at Black Rock, burning the east barrack, exploding the magazine, and destroying a quantity of the furs captured from *Caledonia*. Just as the Quartermaster General, Peter B. Porter, is sitting down to dinner, a twenty-four-pound cannonball crashes through the roof of his home, a disaster not calculated to improve a digestion already thrown out of kilter by Smyth's bizarre and inconclusive orders. Another cannonade begins at dawn on the twenty-first opposite Fort Niagara. The British pour two thousand rounds of red-hot shot into the American fort, which replies in kind. Buildings burn; guns blow up; men die; nothing is settled.

On November 25, Smyth issues orders for the entire army to be ready to march "at a moment's warning." Two days later he musters forty-five hundred men at Black Rock for the impending invasion.

"Tell the brave men under your command not to be impatient," he writes to Porter, who is in charge of the New York volunteers. "See what harm impatience did at Queenston. Let them be firm, and they will succeed."

At three on the morning of the twenty-eighth, Smyth sends an advance force of some four hundred men across the river to destroy the bridge at Frenchman's Creek (thus cutting British communications between Fort Erie and Chippawa) and to silence the battery upstream. The British are waiting. Boats are lost, destroyed, driven off. In the darkness there is confusion on both sides, with men mistaking enemies for friends and friends for enemies. In spite of this the Americans seize the battery and spike its guns while a second force reaches the bridge, only to discover that they have left their axes in the boats and cannot destroy it before the British counterattack. In the end some of the advance party are captured for lack of boats in which to escape. The remainder cross to the safety of the American camp with little accomplished.

An incredible spectacle greets the British next morning. Lining their own shore in increasing numbers, they watch the American attempt at embarkation as if it were a sideshow. Smyth himself does not appear but leaves the arrangements to his subordinates. The operation moves so ponderously that the afternoon shadows are lengthening before all the troops are in the boats. Some have been forced to sit in their craft for hours, shivering in the late November weather – a light snow is falling and the river is running with ice.

The only logical explanation for an action that defies logic is that Smyth is attempting to terrify the British into surrendering through what General Sheaffe calls "an ostentatious display" of his force. If so, it does not work. When Smyth sends a message across to Lieutenant-Colonel Cecil Bisshopp, urging him to surrender to "spare the effusion of blood," Bisshopp curtly declines.

Late in the afternoon, with the entire force prepared at last to cross the river, the General finally makes an official appearance and issues an amazing order. "Disembark and dine!" he cries. At this point the troops are on the edge of rebellion. Several, reduced to impotent fury, pointedly break their muskets.

Smyth returns to his paper war:

Tomorrow at 8 o'clock, all the corps of Army will be at the Navy yards, ready to embark. Before 9 the embarkation will take place.

The General will be on board. Neither rain, snow, or frost will prevent the embarkation.

It will be made with more order and silence than yesterday; boats will be alloted to the brave volunteers....

The cavalry will scour the fields from Black Rock to the bridge & suffer no idle spectators.

While embarking the music will play martial airs. *Yankee Doodle* will be the signal to get underway....

When we pull for the opposite shore, every exertion will be made. The landing will be effected in despite of cannon, The whole army has seen that cannon is to be little dreaded.

The information brought by Captain Gibson assures us of victory....

Smyth's council of officers is aghast. Surely, with the British alerted, the General does not propose a daylight frontal assault from the identical embarkation point on a strongly fortified position! But Smyth declines to change his plans.

Next morning, however, the troops, who arrive at the navy yard promptly at eight, are sent into the nearby woods to build fires and keep warm. Smyth's staff has managed overnight to knock some sense into their commander. The departure time is changed to three the following morning. The troops will not cross directly but will slip quietly down the river, hoping to avoid the enemy cannon, and will land above Chippawa, attack its garrison and, if successful, march through Queenston to Fort George.

In the dark hours of the following morning, the wet and exhausted men are once more herded down to the boats. As before, the embarkation proceeds in fits and starts; when dawn arrives the boats are still not fully loaded. Now Smyth discovers that instead of three thousand men he has fewer than fifteen hundred in the boats, many of these so ill they cannot stand a day's march. The Pennsylvania volunteers have not even arrived on the ground; they are, it develops, perfectly prepared to fight on foreign soil but not under General Smyth. Other troops, lingering on the shore, sullenly refuse to embark.

Out in midstream, about a quarter of a mile from shore, Peter B. Porter has been waiting impatiently in a scout boat to lead the flotilla downriver to the invasion point. Hours pass. On the shore, the confusion grows. In his quarters, General Smyth is holding a council with his regular officers to which the militia commanders have not been invited. At last a message is sent out to Porter: the troops are to disembark. The invasion of Canada is to be abandoned for the present. Smyth does not intend to stir until he has three thousand men fit for action. The regulars will go into winter quarters; the volunteers are dismissed to their homes.

This intelligence provokes a scene of the wildest fury. Officers break their swords in rage; ordinary soldiers batter their muskets to pieces against tree trunks. The mass of the militia runs amok, firing off their weapons in all directions, some shouting aloud in frustration, others cheering in delight. Some of the volunteers offer to fight under Porter, promising to capture Fort Erie if Smyth will give them four cannon. The embattled commander turns the request aside.

Roused to a passion, the troops try to murder their general. Musket balls whiz through his tent, almost killing an aide who has his belt and cap shot off. Smyth doubles his guard, moves his headquarters repeatedly to protect his life.

Porter is outraged by Smyth's posturing. Some of the other officers are calling the General a traitor. Porter merely attacks him as a coward but puts that word into the public record in the Buffalo *Gazette* (which is forced, briefly, to cease publication, so great are the disturbances). A duel follows on Grand Island; shots are exchanged; both men's marksmanship is lamentable; unmarked, they shake hands, but the bitterness continues.

Smyth is the object of intense execration. Governor Tompkins's censure is blunt: "Believing that there was some courage and virtue left in the world, I did not, indeed could not, anticipate such a scene of gasconading and of subsequent imbecility and folly as Genl. Smith [*sic*] has exhibited. To compare the events of the recent campaign with those of the days of the Revolution, is almost enough to convince one, that the race of brave men and able commanders will before many years become extinct."

Smyth's career is finished. With his life in danger from both his officers and his men, he slips away to his home in Virginia where, within three months, the army drops him from its rolls.

Dearborn is aghast. He has sent four thousand troops to Niagara: how is it that not much more than a thousand were in a condition to cross the river? He himself has kept such a low profile that the firestorm of public disgust and fury with the losses of Hull, Van Rensselaer, and Smyth sweeps past him. Yet as the senior commander he is as culpable as any, and so is his fellow physician, the myopic secretary of war Dr. Eustis.

At Lake Champlain Dearborn has the largest force of all under arms, including seven regular army regiments with supporting artillery and dragoons. But these have been infected by the same virus as the others. Dearborn's overall strategy is to attack Montreal simultaneously with Smyth's invasion on the Niagara. On November 8, he informs Eustis that he is about to join the army under General Bloomfield at Plattsburg to march on Lower Canada. An attack of rheumatism delays him. On November 19, when he finally arrives, he finds Bloomfield too ill to lead his troops. Illness, indeed, has all but incapacitated his army, a third of which is unfit for duty. An epidemic of measles has raged through the camps. A neglect of proper sanitary measures has reduced one regiment from nine hundred to two hundred able-bodied men. Typhus, accompanied by pneumonia, has killed two hundred at Burlington. Fifteen per cent of Dearborn's entire force has died from one of these several afflictions.

Dearborn takes command of his depleted invasion force. Two separate and independent advance columns, numbering about 650 men, are dispatched north to surprise the British outposts at the border. They advance by different roads, run into one another in the dark, each mistaking the other for the enemy. A brisk skirmish follows until daylight, when, exhausted and dispirited by their error, they retreat with twenty casualties, a number that is shortly augmented by forty deaths from disease contracted during the expedition. Meanwhile Dearborn manages to get three thousand militia men as far as Rouse's Point at the northern end of Lake Champlain. When two-thirds refuse to cross the border, Dearborn gives up, slinks back to Plattsburg, and returns to Albany as quietly as possible. The news of Smyth's humiliation provides the final blow. Dearborn offers to surrender his command "to any gentleman whose talents and popularity will command the confidence of the Government and the country." But it will be another six months before his government, and a new and more aggressive secretary of war, get around to relieving him.

8

FRENCHTOWN
Massacre at the River Raisin

The Battle's o'er, the din is past!
Night's mantle on the field is cast,
The moon with Sad and pensive beam
Hangs sorrowing o'er the bloody Stream...
Oh! Pitying Moon! Withdraw thy light
And leave the world in murkiest night!
For I have seen too much of Death
Too much of this dark fatal heath...

– From "A Night View of the Battle of the Raisin,
January 22nd, 1813" (written on the field by
Ensign William O. Butler).

GEORGETOWN, KENTUCKY, August 16, 1812. Henry Clay is addressing two thousand eager Kentucky militiamen who have volunteered to march into Canada under the banner of William Henry Harrison to reinforce Hull's Army of the Northwest. The dark eyes flash, the sonorous voice rolls over the raw troops as he exhorts them to victory. More than most Americans, Clay is telling them, they have a twofold responsibility – to uphold the honour of their state as well as that of their country:

"Kentuckians are famed for their bravery – you have the double character of Americans and Kentuckians to support!"

This is more than posturing. Kentucky is a world unto itself, as different from Maine and New York as Scotland from Spain. No frustrated general will need to prod the Kentuckians across the Canadian border; they will, if necessary, swim the Detroit River to get at the British. When, the previous May, the Governor called for volunteers to fill Kentucky's quota of fifty-five hundred men, he found he had too many on his hands. Clay at the time wrote to the Secretary of State that he was almost alarmed at the enthusiasm displayed by his people.

Now, on the very day of Hull's defeat, Clay fires up the troops, who confidently believe that the American forces are already half-way across Canada. And why not? Kentucky has been told only what it wants to hear. The newspaper stories from the frontier have been highly optimistic. Editors and orators have bolstered the state's heroic image of itself. In these exhortations can be heard echoes of the Revolution. "Rise in the majesty of freedom," the Governor, Charles

Scott, has pleaded; "regard as enemies the enemies of your country. Remember the Spirit of '76."

The troops who are to march off through the wilderness of Michigan and into Canada expect the briefest of wars – a few weeks of adventure, a few moments of glory (swords glistening, bugles calling, drums beating, opponents fleeing), then home to the family farm with the plaudits of the nation and the cheers of their neighbours ringing in their ears.

Most have signed on for six months only, convinced that the war cannot last even that long. On this warm August day, standing in ragged, undisciplined lines, basking in Clay's oratory, they do not contemplate November. They wear light shoes and open shirts of linen and cotton: no coats, no blankets. Not one in twenty is prepared for winter. The war department has lists of goods needed for the campaign, but no one has paid much attention to that. The army is without a commissariat; private contractors, whose desire for profit often outweighs their patriotism, have been hired to handle all supplies. As for the Congress, it has not been able to screw up enough courage to adopt new taxes to finance the war; the unpopular resolution has been postponed, and Clay and his Hawks, eager to get on with the fighting, have gone along with the delay without a whimper.

Every able-bodied man in Kentucky, it seems, wants to fight. Six congressmen don uniforms. One, Samuel Hopkins, becomes a major-general; two are happy to serve as privates. Clay remains behind to fight the war in Congress, but his brother-in-law, Nathaniel Hart, goes as a captain, and so does John Allen, the second most eminent lawyer in the state. Thomas Smith, editor of the Kentucky *Gazette*, inflamed by the optimistic reports in his own newspaper, quits his desk and signs up to fight the British and the Indians. Dr. John M. Scott, a militia colonel and an old campaigner, insists on his right to command a regiment even though he is desperately ill; his friends expect (rightly) that he will not return alive. By the end of the year there will be more than eleven thousand Kentuckians in the army.

Most of these will be in the volunteer forces, for the people of Kentucky are confident that the war will be fought to a speedy conclusion by citizen soldiers enrolled for a single, decisive campaign. Regulars are sneered at as hired mercenaries who cannot compete for valour or initiative with a volunteer who has a direct interest in the outcome of the struggle.

268

The idea of individual initiative is deeply ingrained in the Kentucky character. They are a hardy, adventurous people, confident to the point of ebullience, optimistic to the point of naïveté – romantic, touchy, proud, often cruel. Not for them the effete pastimes of settled New England. Their main entertainments are shooting, fighting, drinking, duelling, horse racing. Every Kentucky boy is raised with a rifle. An old state law provides that every white male over sixteen must kill a certain number of crows and squirrels each year. Instead of raffles, Kentuckians hold shooting contests to pick winners. The very word "Kentuck" can cause a shiver of fear in the Mississippi River towns, where their reputation is more terrifying than that of the Indians. As scrappers they are as fearless as they are ferocious, gouging, biting, kicking, scratching. Kentuckians like to boast that they are "half horse and half alligator tipped with snapping turtle." A future congressman, Michael Taul, is elected captain of his militia company not because he has any military training – he has none – but because he has beaten his opponent, William Jones, in a particularly vicious encounter – a "hard fight," in Taul's words, "fist and skull, biting and gouging, etc."

Kentucky lies on the old Indian frontier, and though its Indian wars are history, bloody memories remain. Youths are raised on tales of British and Indian raiders killing, scalping, and ravaging during the Revolution. Tippecanoe has revived a legacy of fear and hatred. The reports of British weapons found at Prophet's Town confirm the people of the state in their belief that John Bull is again behind the Indian troubles.

Tippecanoe is seen as the real beginning of the war. "War we now have," the Kentucky *Gazette* exulted when news of the battle reached Lexington. The shedding of Kentucky blood on the banks of the Wabash fuelled the latent desire for revenge, so that when war was declared Kentucky indulged in a delirium of celebration. Towns were illuminated, cannon and muskets discharged in the villages. And in the larger towns, Senator John Pope, the one Kentucky member of the Twelfth Congress to vote against the war, was hanged in effigy.

On the Fourth of July, the state wallowed in patriotic oratory. At a public celebration in Lexington no fewer than eighteen toasts were drunk, the celebrants raising their glasses to "Our volunteers – Ready to avenge the wrongs and vindicate the right of their country – the spirit of Montgomery will lead them to victory on the Plains of

Abraham." Little wonder that a Boston merchant travelling through Kentucky a little later described its people as "the most patriotic...I have ever seen or heard of."

This yeasty nationalism springs out of Kentucky's burgeoning economy. It has become the most populous state west of the Alleghenies. In two decades its population has leaped from 73,000 to more than 406,000. Log cabins have given way to handsome brick houses. Frontier outposts have become cities. But all this prosperity depends on a sea-going trade – a trade now threatened by Great Britain's maritime strictures. The opposite side of the coin of nationalism is a consuming hatred of Great Britain. Henry Clay is its voice.

What Clay wants, Clay is determined to get; and Henry Clay wants William Henry Harrison to command the army going north to subdue the Indians and to reinforce General Hull at Detroit. The Hero of Tippecanoe is by all odds the most popular military leader in the state. Every Kentuckian, it seems, wants to serve under him; but the Secretary of War has long since chosen James Winchester of Tennessee to take command. Now an active campaign, spearheaded by Clay and orchestrated with all the cunning of a political *coup d'état*, is mounted to force the government's hand and replace Winchester with Harrison. In this enterprise, Clay has Harrison's willing co-operation. The Hero of Tippecanoe himself tours the state, rousing martial feeling, fuelling the clamour for his appointment.

Early in August a caucus of influential Kentucky politicians, including Scott, the retiring governor, Isaac Shelby, the governor-elect, and several of the War Hawks, agrees to appoint Harrison a brevet (honorary) major-general in the Kentucky militia. He accepts command of two regiments of infantry and one of mounted rifles (under Clay's young congressional colleague, Richard M. Johnson) which have already left to join General Winchester in Cincinnati. But Clay wants more. Harrison outranks Winchester, but Winchester is a regular army man. It is important that there be no ambiguity about who is in charge. Once more he puts pressure on James Monroe, the Secretary of State, rising to heights of hyperbole, which, even for Henry Clay, are more than a little florid:

"If you will carry your recollection back to the Age of the Crusades and of some of the most distinguished leaders of those expeditions, you will have a picture of the enthusiasm existing in this country for the expedition to Canada and for Harrison as the commander."

Up to this point, James Monroe has fancied himself for the post of commander-in-chief of the Army of the Northwest. The cabinet, in fact, has been seriously considering his appointment. But now, with Clay and his cronies in full cry, the Secretary's military ambitions are dashed. The pressure is too great. Harrison it will be.

●

AS THE CABINET vacillates over the choice of a commander for the new northwest army, Harrison marches to Cincinnati at the head of his troops. He is convinced that he can persuade Winchester to allow him to take command of all the forces for the relief of Detroit. On August 26, he receives the dreadful news of Hull's surrender. Two days later, he reaches Winchester's camp at Cincinnati and immediately assumes command of all the Kentucky militia, leaving Winchester in charge of the regulars. Stiff little notes pass between the generals' tents. Harrison insists that he, as a major-general, outranks Winchester. Winchester objects, points out that Harrison is only a political appointee, but when Harrison persists, Winchester at last gives in: Harrison can assume command under his own responsibility. Winchester returns to Lexington to continue recruiting.

The new commander has some twenty-one hundred men at Cincinnati; an equal number are on their way to join him. They inspire mixed feelings. The Kentuckians, in his opinion "are perhaps the best materials for forming an army the world has produced. But no equal number of men was ever collected who knew so little of military discipline." It is a shrewd assessment.

He has neither time nor personnel to instruct his raw recruits in the art of soldiering. He is, in fact, short of almost everything – of food, clothing, equipment, weapons, ammunition, flints, swords. His only ordnance piece is an ancient cast-iron four-pounder. Autumn is fast approaching with its chilling rain and sleet. He must hack new roads through forest and swamp, build blockhouses and magazines, all the time watched and harassed by the Indians on his flank.

And he must move immediately, for word has come that the British and the Indians are planning an attack on Fort Wayne, the forward outpost on the Maumee. Three hundred Indians are laying siege to the fort, a British column is moving south, houses have been burned, crops and livestock destroyed. The commander, James Rhea, has some eighty men with whom to withstand the siege but is himself nervous and frequently drunk. Harrison's first task is to relieve the fort.

That same day he dispatches all his available troops on that mission. He joins them at Dayton on September 1. Here are more cheers for Harrison and a salute of cannon, marred only by the tragic incompetence of the gunners. During the salute one man is seriously wounded, another has both hands blown off. And here Harrison receives a blow of a different kind: the government has officially confirmed his commission, but only as brigadier-general. Winchester now outranks him.

He does not give up. In another letter to Washington, he subtly advances his cause: "The backwoodsmen are a singular people.... From their affection and an attachment everything may be expected but I will venture to say that they never did nor never will perform anything brilliant under a stranger."

The message, though self-serving, is undoubtedly true. Winchester is unpopular largely because he *is* a stranger. Harrison is a known hero. All along his route of march, volunteers have flocked to his banner. At Piqua, en route to Fort Wayne, he makes from the tailboard of a camp wagon one of those tough little stump speeches for which he is famous. He is planning a forced march on half-rations, and some of the Ohio militia are hesitating. To them Harrison declares that "if there is any man under my command who lacks the patriotism to rush to the rescue, he, by paying back the money received from the government, shall receive a discharge. I do not wish to command such...." Only one man makes this choice. His comrades are given a permit to escort him part of the way home. They hoist him onto a rail and with a crowd following duck him several times in the river.

Harrison, at the head of three thousand men, reaches Fort Wayne on September 12. The fort is relieved without a shot being fired though not entirely bloodlessly, since during the march one man has been shot and killed in error by one of the guards. The bodies of two sentinels, killed by the Indians and buried within the palisade, are disinterred and brought out to be buried with full military honours. The troops, many of whom have never seen a dead man, stand by in awe. William Northcutt, a young dragoon in Captain William Garrard's company of "Bourbon Blues" (made up of men from Bourbon County, Kentucky, all uniformed in blue broadcloth), cannot help shedding tears as the corpses are brought out through the gate, even though the men are complete strangers. But before his term of service is over, Northcutt becomes so hardened that he could, if necessary, sleep on a corpse, and it occurs to him as the war grows nastier that "the man that thinks about dying in a Battle is not fit to be there and will do no good for his country...."

Harrison is determined to crush all Indian resistance. Columns of cavalry fan out to destroy all Indian villages within sixty miles. The ailing Colonel John Scott insists on leading the attack on the Elkhart River in Indiana Territory, though his officers urge him not to go. But he mounts his horse, crying out: "As long as I am able to mount you, none but myself shall lead my regiment...." It is the death of him. Exhausted, after a protracted march of three days and nights, he is scarcely able to return to camp. Shortly afterwards he is carried home in a litter where, the second day after arrival, he expires.

Harrison's policy of search and destroy makes no distinction between neutral and hostile tribes. His intention is to turn the frontier country into a wasteland, denying both food and shelter to the natives. Mounted columns, one led by Harrison himself, burn several hundred houses, ravage the corn fields, destroy crops of beans, pumpkins, potatoes, and melons, ransack the graves and scatter the bones. The Potawatomi and Miami flee to British protection at Brownstown and Amherstburg and wait for revenge.

On September 18, General Winchester arrives at Fort Wayne to take command of the Army of the Northwest. The troops are in an ugly mood. They do not wish to be commanded by a regular officer, fearing perhaps (without much evidence) that Winchester will be a greater disciplinarian than Harrison.

Winchester's ordeal has only begun. As he moves slowly north, the Kentuckians under his command refuse his orders, torment him with pranks and practical jokes, and are generally obstreperous. He cannot even visit the latrine without suffering some indignity. At one camp, they skin a porcupine and place the skin on a pole over the latrine pit; the General applies his buttocks to the hide with painful results. At another, they employ a trick that must go back to Caesar's army: sawing a pole partially through so that it fails to support the General's weight at a critical moment. The next morning, William Northcutt of the Bourbon Blues, passing Winchester's tent, notes with amusement the General's uniform, drying out, high on a pole.

What has Winchester done to deserve this? His only crime is to be less popular than Harrison. He does suffer by comparison, for Harrison at forty is vigorous, decisive, totally confident, while Winchester, at sixty, is inclined to fussiness, a little ponderous, and not entirely sure of himself. (He did not have to relinquish command to Harrison during that first encounter at Cincinnati.) Like Hull, he appears to the young recruits to be older than his years (Northcutt thinks him at least seventy) – a plump, greying figure who has to be helped to mount and dismount his horse. Worst of all, Winchester fears his own troops and places a bodyguard around his quarters day and night.

Like so many others, he is a leftover from another war, his reputation resting on the exploits of his youth – on those memorable years in the mid-seventies when America struggled for her independence and young James Winchester, at twenty-four, was promoted in the field for his gallantry, wounded in action, captured, exchanged, recaptured and exchanged again to fight as a captain at Yorktown. All that is long behind him, as are his years as an Indian fighter in North Carolina. Honours he has had: brigadier-general in the North Carolina militia; Speaker of the state senate of Tennessee; master of a vast Tennessee estate, surmounted by the great stone mansion known as Cragfont; father of fourteen children, four of them born out of wedlock but rendered legitimate by a tardy marriage. A kindly, sedentary man, fond of rich, easy living, known for his humanity. But no Harrison.

He lacks Harrison's style, has not Harrison's way with men, cannot bring himself to mingle with the troops in Harrison's easy, offhand manner. It is impossible to think of Winchester, dressed in a simple hunting shirt, making a stump speech to the Kentucky volunteers; it is equally impossible to believe that anyone would saw through a log in Harrison's latrine.

The murmurings against Winchester are not confined to the men. A group of officers, led by Henry Clay's congressional colleague Captain Sam McKee, is drawing up a petition, apparently with Harrison's blessing, urging that the command be taken from Winchester. The rebels get cold feet, temporize, delay, and are relieved at last of the charge of mutiny by a war department order authorizing Harrison to assume command of the Army of the Northwest.

•

OLD FORT DEFIANCE, OHIO, October 2, 1812. It is close to midnight when William Henry Harrison, accompanied by a strong escort, gallops into camp, summoned by a frantic note from General

Winchester warning that a combined force of British redcoats and Indians is marching south. Winchester's intelligence is accurate but out of date. The British, believing themselves outnumbered, have already withdrawn.

Now Harrison breaks the news that he is in full command of the new Army of the Northwest, charged with the task of subduing the Indians in his path, relieving Detroit, and invading Canada. Winchester is crestfallen. Convinced that Harrison has secretly connived against him, he seriously considers resigning, then thinks better of it and decides to hang on until Fort Amherstburg is captured. Harrison determines to mollify him by giving him command of the army's left flank and naming in his honour the new fort being built not far from the ruins of the old: Fort Winchester.

The troops are unaware of Harrison's presence. Half starved, inadequately clothed, they have lost the will to fight. A delegation of Kentucky officers wakes Harrison to warn him that one regiment intends to quit and go home. All attempts to dissuade them have been met with insults.

Early the next morning, Harrison acts. He orders Winchester to beat the alarm instead of the customary drum roll for reveille. The Kentuckians pour out of their tents, form a hollow square, and, as Winchester introduces them to their new commander, holler their enthusiasm.

Harrison knows exactly what to say. He tells them they can go home if they wish to, "but if my fellow soldiers from Kentucky, so famed for patriotism, refuse to bear the hardships incident to war... where shall I look for men who will go with me?"

Cheers and shouts greet these words and continue as the General reveals that two hundred wagons loaded with biscuit, flour, and bacon are on their way; some supplies, indeed, have already arrived. This kills all talk of desertion. One Kentuckian writes home that "Harrison, *with a look*, can awe and convince...where some would be refractory...All are afraid and unwilling to meet with his censure."

Harrison has been given authority to requisition funds and supplies, to protect the northwestern frontier, and after retaking Detroit to penetrate Upper Canada "as far as the force under your command will in your judgment justify." For this purpose he expects to have ten thousand troops.

His strategy is to move the army to the foot of the Rapids of the Maumee in three columns. Winchester, protecting his left flank, will

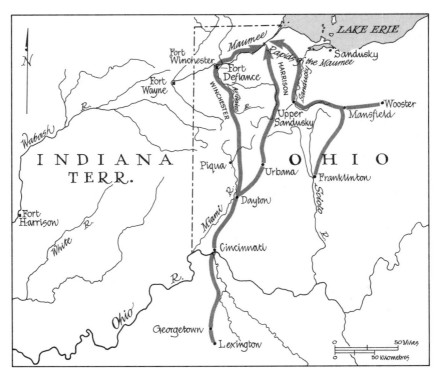

Harrison's Three-Column Drive to the Maumee Rapids

march from the new fort along the route of the Maumee. A central force of twelve hundred men will follow Hull's road to the same rendezvous. The right division, under Harrison himself, is proceeding from Wooster, Ohio, by way of the Upper Sandusky.

But Winchester is pinned down at the newly constructed fort that bears his name. He dare not move without supplies, and the promised supplies are not forthcoming. Harrison has ordered Brigadier-General Edward Tupper's mounted brigade to dash to the foot of the Rapids of the Maumee to harvest several hundred acres of corn for the famished troops. But the scalping of a ranger not two hundred yards from the camp has the men in such a panic that only a handful will follow. The mission is abandoned.

On October 8, the day after Tupper's fiasco, Frederick Jacob of the 17th Regiment is caught asleep at his post, and Winchester, faced with growing insubordination, decides to make an example of him. A court martial sentences Jacob to be shot. The following morning Winchester's entire force, reduced now to eighteen hundred, forms a

276

hollow square to witness the execution. Drums roll, the chaplain prays, the prisoner is led to the post, blindfolded, made to kneel. The troops fall silent, waiting for the volley. Then, at the last instant, a reprieve arrives. The General has judged the wretched guard "not to be of sound mind," a verdict which if unjustified at the outset may well be applicable in the days following the ordeal.

There are other punishments: "riding the wooden horse," in which the offender is placed astride a bent sapling and subjected to a series of tossings and joltings to the great amusement of the troops, or a dozen well-laid blows on the bare posterior with a wooden paddle bored full of holes to help break the skin. In spite of these salutary examples, the army is murmuring its discontent over the continued lack of supplies. Rations remain short, Harrison's promises to the contrary. There is little flour, almost no salt, and the beef—what there is of it—is deplorable.

Disdaining strict orders, men wander out of camp and waste their ammunition in search of game, many barefoot, their clothes in rags. They sleep on frozen ground, some without blankets. More than two hundred are sick at one time. By November, three or four die each day from typhus. Civilian contractors reap a harvest; the price of hogs goes sky high while clothing ordered for the troops comes in sizes so small it seems to have been designed for small boys. Materials are shoddy, delays calculated. One contractor's profit, it is said, amounts to $100,000.

Nothing seems to be going right. In late September, the new governor of Kentucky, Isaac Shelby, has ordered two thousand mounted thirty-day volunteers—"the most respectable citizens that perhaps were ever embodied from this or any other State in the Union"—to march under Major-General Samuel Hopkins, one of Clay's congressional War Hawks, against the Indians of Indiana and Illinois territories. Shelby does not wait for war department authorization or equipment. The men, whipped to a high pitch of enthusiasm, bring their own arms and blankets. The quota of volunteers is exceeded; twelve hundred disappointed Kentuckians have to be sent home.

The euphoria does not last. By October 14, after two hard weeks in the saddle, the volunteers are dispirited. They cannot find any Indians, their rations dwindle away, they become hopelessly lost. At this point, their unseen quarry fires the tall prairie grass, threatening all with a painful death.

Hopkins's choice is retreat or mutiny, a situation that leaves the

Governor aghast. What has happened to Kentucky's *élan*? "...the flower of Kentucky are now returning home deeply mortified by the disappointment." On mature consideration, Shelby decides to put the blame on "secret plotting."

There is worse to come. A note of uncertainty begins to creep into Harrison's dispatches to Washington: "If the fall should be very dry, I will retake Detroit before the winter sets in; but if we should have much rain, it will be necessary to wait at the Rapids until the Margin of the Lake is sufficiently frozen to bear the army and its baggage."

"The one bright ray amid the gloom of incompetency" (to quote John Gibson, acting governor of Illinois Territory) is the news of Captain Zachary Taylor's successful defence of Fort Harrison – a desperate struggle in which a handful of soldiers and civilians, many of them ill, withstood repeated attacks by Miami and Wea warriors until relief arrived. It is the first land victory for the United States, and it wins for Taylor the first brevet commission ever awarded by the U.S. government. Nor will the moment of glory be forgotten. One day, Brevet Major Taylor will become twelfth president of the United States.

The news from the Niagara frontier banishes this brief euphoria. Another army defeated! A third bogged down. By October 22, Harrison finds he can no longer set a firm date for the attack on Detroit. There are no supplies of any kind in Michigan Territory; the farms along the Raisin have been ravaged. He will require one million rations at the Rapids of the Maumee before he can start a campaign; but the fall rains have already begun and he cannot move his supplies, let alone his artillery. By early November, the roads are in desperate condition and horses, attempting to struggle through morass and swamp, are dying by the hundreds.

The army switches to flatboats, but just as these are launched the temperature falls and the boats are frozen fast along the Sandusky, Au Glaize, and St. Mary's rivers. By early December, Harrison despairs of reaching the rapids at all and makes plans to shelter his force in huts on the Au Glaize. He suggests that Shelby prepare the public for a postponement in the campaign by disbanding all the volunteer troops except those needed for guard and escort duty. But Washington will have none of it. The Union has suffered two mortifying failures at Detroit and Queenston; it will not accept a third.

The setbacks continue. Hopkins's failure has left Harrison's left flank open to Indian attack. He decides to forestall further Indian

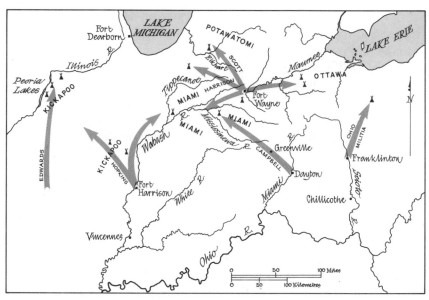

American Search and Destroy Missions against the Tribes, Autumn, 1812

raids on Winchester's line of communications by striking at the Miami villages along the Mississinewa, a tributary of the Wabash in Indiana Territory. On November 25, Lieutenant-Colonel John Campbell and six hundred cavalry and infantry set out to do the job. The result is disastrous.

In spite of Campbell's attempts at secrecy, the Miami are fore-warned. They leave their villages, wait until the troops are exhausted, then launch a night attack, destroying a hundred horses, killing eight men, wounding forty-eight. A false report is spread that the dreaded Tecumseh is on the way at the head of a large force. Campbell's dejected band beats a hasty retreat.

It is bitterly cold; provisions are almost gone; the wounded are dying from gangrene, the rest suffer from frostbite. A relief party finally brings them into Greenville, where it is found that three hundred men – half of Campbell's force – are disabled. One mounted regiment is so ravaged it is disbanded. Harrison has lost the core of his cavalry without any corresponding loss among the Indians. The General decides to put a bold front on the episode: he announces that the expedition has been a complete success. He has learned something from the experience of Tippecanoe.

By December 10, Harrison has managed to get his cannon to Upper Sandusky, but at appalling cost. He has one thousand horses, hauling and pulling; most are so exhausted they must be destroyed, at a cost of half a million dollars. Wagons are often abandoned, their contents lost or destroyed. The teamsters, scraped up from frontier settlements, are utterly irresponsible. "I did not make sufficient allowance for the imbecility and inexperience of public agents and the villainy of the contractors," Harrison writes ruefully to the acting secretary of war, James Monroe, who has replaced the discredited Dr. Eustis.

Winchester's left wing is still pinned down near the junction of the Maumee and the Au Glaize, waiting for supplies. It is impossible to get them through the Black Swamp that lies between the Sandusky and the Maumee. William Atherton, a diminutive twenty-one-year-old soldier in Winchester's army who is keeping an account of his adventures, writes that he now sees "nothing but hunger and cold and nakedness staring us in the face." The troops have been out of flour for a fortnight and are existing on bad beef, pork, and hickory nuts. Sickness and death have reduced Winchester's effective force to eleven hundred. Daily funerals cast a pall over the camps, ravaged by the effects of bad sanitation and drainage (Winchester is forced to move the site five times) and the growing realization that there is no chance of invading Canada this year.

On Christmas Eve, another soldier, Elias Darnell, confides to his journal that "obstacles had emerged in the path to victory, which must have appeared insurmountable to every person endowed with common sense. The distance to Canada, the unpreparedness of the army, the scarcity of provisions, and the badness of the weather, show that Malden cannot be taken in the remaining part of our time.... Our sufferings at this place have been greater than if we had been in a severe battle. More than one hundred lives...lost owing to our bad accommodations! The sufferings of about three hundred sick at a time, who are exposed to the cold ground, and deprived of every nourishment, are sufficient proofs of our wretched condition! The camp has become a loathsome place...."

On Christmas Day, Winchester receives an order from Harrison. He is to move to the Rapids of the Maumee as soon as he receives two days' rations. There he will be joined by the right wing of the army. Two days later, a supply of salt, flour, and clothing arrives.

Winchester, eager to be off, sets about building sleds, since his boats are useless. On December 29, he is ready. The troops are exuberant – anything to be rid of this pestilential camp! But Darnell realizes what they are facing:

"We are now about commencing one of the most serious marches ever performed by the Americans. Destitute, in a measure, of clothes, shoes and provisions, the most essential articles necessary for the existence and preservation of the human species in this world and more particularly in this cold climate. Three sleds are prepared for each company, each to be pulled by a packhorse, which has been without food for two weeks except brush, and will not be better fed while in our service. . . ."

The following day, the troops set off for the Maumee rapids. Few armies have presented such a ragtag appearance. In spite of the midwinter weather, scarcely one possesses a greatcoat or cloak. Only a lucky few have any woollen garments. They remain dressed in the clothes they wore when they left Kentucky, their cotton shirts torn, patched, and ragged, hanging to their knees, their trousers also of cotton. Their matted hair falls uncombed over their cheeks. Their slouch hats have long since been worn bare. Those who own blankets wrap them about their bodies as protection from the blizzards, holding them in place by broad belts of leather into which are thrust axes and knives. The officers are scarcely distinguishable from the men. They carry swords or rifles instead of long guns and a dagger – often an expensive one, hand-carved – in place of a knife.

Now these men must become beasts of burden, for the horses are not fit to pull the weight. Harnessed five to a sleigh, they haul their equipment through snow and water for the next eleven days. The sleighs, it develops, are badly made – too light to carry the loads, not large enough to cross the half-frozen streams. Provisions and men are soon soaked through. But if the days are bad, the nights are a horror. Knee-deep snow must be cleared away before a camp can be made. Fire must be struck from flint on steel. The wet wood, often enough, refuses to burn. So cold that they cannot always prepare a bed for themselves, the Kentuckians topple down on piles of brush before the smoky fires and sleep in their steaming garments.

Then, on the third day, a message arrives from Harrison: *turn back!* The General has picked up another rumour that the redoubtable Tecumseh and several hundred Indians are in the area. He advises –

does not order – Winchester not to proceed. With the Indians at his rear and no certainty of provisions at the rapids, any further movement toward Canada this winter would be foolhardy.

But James Winchester is in no mood to retreat. He is a man who has suddenly been released from three months of dreadful frustration – frustration over inactivity and boredom, frustration over insubordination, frustration over sickness and starvation, and, perhaps most significant, frustration over his own changing role as the leader of his men. Now at least he is on the move; it must seem to him some sort of progress; it is action of a sort, and at the end – who knows? More action, perhaps, even glory...vindication. He has no stomach to turn in his tracks and retreat to that "loathsome place," nor do his men. And so he moves on to tragedy.

•

AT FORT AMHERSTBURG, Lieutenant-Colonel Procter has concluded that the Americans have gone into winter quarters. His Indian spies have observed no movement around Winchester's camp for several weeks, and he is convinced that Harrison has decided to hold off any attempt to recapture Detroit until spring. It is just as well, for he has only a skeleton force of soldiers and a handful of Indians.

The Indians concern Procter. He cannot control them, cannot depend on them, does not like them. One moment they are hot for battle, the next they have vanished into the forest. Nor can he be sure where their loyalties lie. Matthew Elliott's eldest son, Alexander, has been killed and scalped by one group of Indians who pretended to be defecting to the British but who were actually acting as scouts for Winchester. Brock called them "a fickle race"; Procter would certainly agree with that. Neither has been able to understand that the Indians' loyalty is not to the British or to the Americans but to their own kind. They will support the British only as long as they believe it suits their own purpose. But the British, too, can be fickle; no tribesman, be he Potawatomi, Wyandot, Shawnee, or Miami, can ever quite trust the British after the betrayal at Fallen Timbers in 1794.

Nor do the British trust them – certainly not when it comes to observing the so-called rules of warfare, which are, of course, white European rules. Tecumseh is the only chief who can restrain his followers from killing and torturing prisoners and ravaging women and children. Angered by Prevost's armistice and ailing from a wound received at Brownstown, Tecumseh has headed south to try to draw the Creeks and Choctaws to his confederacy. His brother, the Prophet, has returned to the Wabash.

Procter needs to keep the Indians active, hence his attempt to capture Fort Wayne with a combined force of natives and regulars. The attempt failed, though it helped to slow Harrison's advance. Now he is under orders from Prevost to refrain from all such offensive warfare. His only task is defence against the invader.

He must tread a line delicately, for the Indians' loyalty depends on a show of British resolution. As Brock once said, "it is of primary importance that the confidence and goodwill of the Indians should be preserved and that whatsoever can tend to produce a contrary effect should be carefully avoided." That is the rub. The only way the confidence and goodwill of the Indians can be preserved is to attack the Americans, kill as many as possible, and let the braves have their way with the rest. Procter is not unmindful of how the news of the victory at Queenston has raised native morale – or of how the armistice has lowered it.

Prevost, as usual, believes that the British have overextended themselves on the Detroit frontier. Only Brock's sturdy opposition prevented the Governor General from ordering the evacuation of all captured American territory to allow the release of troops to the Niagara frontier. But Brock understood that such a show of weakness would cause the Indians to consider making terms with the enemy.

Brock's strategy, which Procter has inherited, has been to let the Americans keep the tribes in a state of ferment. The policy has succeeded. Harrison's attempt to subdue the Indians on the northwestern frontier has delayed his advance until midwinter and caused widespread indignation among the natives. Some six thousand have been displaced, nineteen villages ravaged, seven hundred lodges burned, thousands of bushels of corn destroyed. Savagery is not the exclusive trait of the red man. The Kentuckians take scalps whenever they can, nor are women and children safe from the army. Governor Meigs had no sooner called out the Ohio militia in the early fall than they launched an unprovoked attack on an Indian village near Mansfield, burning all the houses and shooting several of the inhabitants.

The worst attacks have been against the villages on the Peoria lakes, destroyed without opposition by a force of rangers and volunteers under Governor Ninian Edwards of Illinois Territory. One specific foray will not soon be forgotten: a mounted party under a captain named Judy came upon an Indian couple on the open prairie. When the man tried to surrender, Judy shot him through the body. Chanting his death song, the Indian killed one of Judy's men and was in turn riddled with bullets. A little later the same group captured and killed a starving Indian child.

In their rage and avarice, Edwards's followers scalp and mutilate the bodies of the fallen and ransack Indian graves for plunder. Small wonder that the Potawatomi chief Black Bird, in a later discussion with Claus, the Canadian Indian superintendent, cries out in fury, "The way they treat our killed and the remains of those that are in their graves to the west make our people mad when they meet the Big Knives. Whenever they get any of our people into their hands they cut them like meat into small pieces."

All that fall the Indians continue to concern Procter. They have been devouring his provisions at an alarming rate. The white leadership is shaky. At seventy, Matthew Elliott can scarcely sit a horse, and McKee is worn down by drink. Tecumseh's restraining hand is absent. Procter has some hope of reorganizing the tribes around Amherstburg into a raiding party under Colonel William Caldwell, a veteran of Butler's Rangers during the Revolution. Caldwell possesses enormous influence among the Wyandot, whom he has persuaded to adopt the British cause.

Meanwhile, Procter solves part of his supply problem by dispatching most of the Indians under Elliott to the Rapids of the Maumee, where several hundred acres of corn are waiting to be harvested – the same corn that Harrison has been trying vainly to seize. Elliott may be old and infirm, but he has lost none of his frontier cunning. He has sent Indian spies into Ohio who report that Winchester is again advancing. Elliott dispatches couriers to the villages of the Ottawa and the Potawatomi in Michigan Territory and to the Miami at the ravaged villages of the Mississinewa in Indiana. War parties begin to trickle into Amherstburg; within a month the native force has increased from three hundred to almost eight hundred braves, all stirred to a fever by the depredations of Harrison's army.

Winchester's army, meanwhile, is advancing toward the rapids. He arrives on January 11; Procter learns of this two days later. The British commander moves swiftly, calling out the militia, assembling the Indians. It is his intention to scorch the earth (whatever is not already scorched) along the Detroit frontier to deny the Americans provisions and shelter. The following day he dispatches Major Ebenezer Reynolds of the Essex militia with two flank companies and a band of Potawatomi to the little village of Frenchtown on the River Raisin. Reynolds's orders are to destroy the village and all its supplies and to remove the French-speaking settlers – forcibly, if necessary – to Canadian soil.

It is not a pleasant task. Who wants his home destroyed, his property removed, and his cattle driven off and killed by Indians? The settlers have worked hard to improve their farms, which lie on both sides of the narrow, low-banked river. Their town, a simple row of some twenty dwelling houses, squatting on the north bank three miles from the mouth, is not designed as a fort. Its only protection is a fence made of split pickets to secure the yards and gardens. The villagers are in a panic; as Reynolds and his men move in, a delegation slips away, heading for the Rapids of the Maumee to plead with Winchester for help. They carry with them a note for Harrison from Isaac Day, a long-time Detroit citizen, who writes that "five hundred true and brave Americans can secure the District of Erie – A timely approach of our armies will secure us from being forced to prison and the whole place from being burned by savage fury." Day has scarcely sent off this letter when he is seized and jailed. If Winchester is to act at all to save the settlement, he must act at once.

●

RAPIDS OF THE MAUMEE, January 17, 1813. Winchester and his senior officers sit in council. Should they go to the relief of Frenchtown? For almost four days word has been coming back of Indian outrages and British highhandedness. Everything is being removed from the village – cattle, carrioles, sleighs, grain, foodstuffs. Citizens such as Isaac Day, suspected of pro-American feelings, have been bundled off to confinement across the river. Winchester's information is that the British force is ridiculously small: between forty and fifty militia and perhaps a hundred Indians. It is, however, building rapidly. If the Americans move quickly, Day's note has told them, they can provision themselves at Frenchtown by securing three thousand barrels of flour and much grain. That possibility must seem as tempting as the succour of the villagers.

Lieutenant-Colonel John Allen rises – a graceful, commanding presence, perhaps the most popular man in Winchester's army, certainly the most distinguished, the most eloquent. A handsome Kentuckian, tall, sandy-haired, blue-eyed, close friend and boyhood companion of the lamented Jo Daviess (Tippecanoe's victim), next to Clay the state's greatest orator, leading lawyer, state senator, one-time candidate for governor. When he speaks all listen, for Allen commands as much respect as, if not more than, his general.

He is fed up with inactivity – weary of slow movements that get nowhere, as he complains in one of his letters to his wife, Jane, herself the daughter of a general. He hungers for action; now he sees his chance.

Winchester's forces, he points out, have three choices: they can withdraw – an ignominy which, piled upon other American setbacks, is unthinkable. They can wait here at the Maumee rapids for the rest of Harrison's force, but if they do that they will give the British time to build strength. Or they can go to the aid of the beleaguered inhabitants of Frenchtown, secure the desperately needed food at the settlement, strike a decisive blow against the British, open the road to Detroit, and – certainly not least – cover themselves with glory.

The council does not need much convincing, nor does Winchester. Why wait for Harrison, who is sixty-five miles away? A victory over the British – *any* victory – can make Winchester a national hero. His men, he knows, are as eager to move as he is. The term of the six-month volunteers will end in February; they have refused to re-enlist. All want one brief taste of glory before returning home. They have just received a welcome shipment of woollen underwear, and their morale, reduced by long weeks of inactivity and hunger, has risen again. And there is *food* at Frenchtown! Winchester, who has already written to General Perkins at Lower Sandusky asking for reinforcements for a proposed advance, now dispatches a second letter to Harrison announcing his intention to send a detachment to relieve Frenchtown and hold it.

One of Harrison's many frustrations during this exhausting fall and winter has been a collapse of communications. His letter to Winchester, urging him to abandon his march to the rapids, arrived too late. Winchester's reply, announcing his intention to move ahead to the rapids, does not reach him until the force is actually at its destination. It is carried by an eighteen-year-old Kentucky volunteer named Leslie Combs, who, with a single guide, crosses one hundred miles of trackless forest through snow so deep that the two men dare not lie down for fear of suffocation and are forced to sleep standing up. Exhausted, ill, and starving, the pair reach Fort McArthur on January 9. Harrison, at Upper Sandusky, gets Winchester's letter two days later.

Five days pass during which time Harrison has no idea of Winchester's position or intentions. Then on the night of the sixteenth he hears from Perkins at Lower Sandusky that Winchester has reached the rapids and wants reinforcements, apparently contemplating an attack.

The news alarms him – if it were in his power he would call Winchester off. He sets off at once for Lower Sandusky, travelling so swiftly that his aide's horse drops dead of exhaustion. There he immediately dispatches a detachment of artillery, guarded by three hundred infantrymen, to Winchester's aid. The camp at the rapids is only thirty-six miles away, but the roads are choked with drifting snow, and the party moves slowly.

Two days later, on January 18, he receives confirmation of Winchester's intention to send a detachment to relieve Frenchtown. Now Harrison is thoroughly alarmed. The proposed move is "opposed to a principle by which I have ever been governed in Indian warfare, i.e. never to make a detachment but under the most urgent circumstances." He orders two more regiments to march to the rapids and sets off himself, with General Perkins, in a sleigh. Its slowness annoys him. He seizes his servant's horse, rides on alone. Darkness falls; the horse stumbles into a frozen swamp; the ice gives way; Harrison manages to free himself and pushes on through the night on foot.

Winchester, meanwhile, has already ordered Lieutenant-Colonel William Lewis and 450 troops to attack the enemy at Frenchtown on the Raisin. Off goes Lewis, with three days' provisions, followed a few hours later by a second force of one hundred Kentuckians under the eager Lieutenant-Colonel Allen. They rendezvous at Presqu'Isle, a French-Canadian village on the south side of the Maumee, twenty miles from the rapids, eighteen from the Raisin. Elias Darnell is overwhelmed, as are his comrades, by this first contact with anything remotely resembling civilization:

"The sight of this village filled each heart with emotions of cheerfulness and joy; for we had been nearly five months in the wilderness, exposed to every inconvenience, and excluded from everything that had the appearance of a civilized country."

The inhabitants pour out of their homes, waving white flags, shouting greetings. The troops are in high spirits; they know that some will be corpses on the morrow, but with the eternal optimism of all soldiers, most hew to the conviction that they will survive. Nonetheless, those who can write have sent letters home to wives, parents, or friends. One such is Captain James Price, commander of the Jessamine Blues, who writes rather formally to his wife, Susan, at Nicholasville, Kentucky, that "on the event of battle I have believed it proper to address you these lines."

It is his two-year-old son that concerns Captain Price rather than his three daughters who, he feels, are his wife's responsibility: "Teach my boy to love truth," he writes, "to speak truth at all times.... He must be taught to bear in mind that 'an honest man is the noblest work of God'; he must be rigidly honest in his dealings.... Never allow him to run about on Sabbath days, fishing. Teach my son the habits of industry.... Industry leads to virtue.... Not a day must be lost in teaching him how to work.... It may be possible I may fall in battle and my only boy must know that his father, next to God, loves his country, and is now risking his life in defending that country against a barbarous and cruel enemy.... Pray for me that you may be with me once more."

The following morning, January 18, as the Kentucky soldiers march along the frozen lake toward their objective, they meet refugees from Frenchtown. What kind of artillery do the British have, the troops want to know. "Two pieces about large enough to kill a mouse," is the reply. From Frenchtown comes word that the British are waiting. Lewis forms up his troops on the ice, and as they come in sight of the settlement, the lone British howitzer opens up. "Fire away with your mouse cannon!" some of the men cry, and as the long drum roll sounds the charge, they cross the slippery Raisin, clamber up the bank, leap the village pickets, and drive the British back toward the forest.

Later, one of the French residents tells Elias Darnell that he has watched an old Wyandot – one of those who took part in the rout of Tupper's Ohio militia at the rapids – smoking his pipe as the Americans come into sight. "I suppose Ohio men come," he says. "We give them another chase." Then as the American line stampedes through the village he cries, "Kentuck, by God!" and joins in the general retreat.

The battle rages from 3 P.M. to dark. John Allen forces the British left wing back into the forest. The British make a stand behind a chain of enclosed lots and small clusters of houses, where piles of brush and deadfalls bar the way. The American centre under Major George Madison (a future governor of Kentucky) and the left under Major Benjamin Graves now go into action, and the British and Indians fall back, contesting every foot. When dusk falls they have been driven two miles from the village, and the Americans are in firm possession.

Lewis's triumphant account of the victory is sent immediately by express rider to Winchester, who receives it at dawn. The camp at the rapids is ecstatic. Harking back to Henry Clay's speech of August 16, Lewis reports that "both officers and soldiers supported the double character of Americans and Kentuckyans." The state's honour has been vindicated. The soldiers at both Frenchtown and the rapids now feel they are unbeatable, that they will roll right on to Detroit, cross the river, capture Amherstburg. General Simon Perkins, after the fact, will write dryly: "I fancy they were too much impressed with the opinion that Kentucky bravery could not fall before [such] a foe as Indians and Canadians."

The troops on the Raisin are dangerously exposed. Yet their eagerness for battle is such that Winchester would be hard put to withdraw them even if he wished to – even Harrison will admit that. But Winchester does not wish to. Caught up in the general intoxication of victory, seeing himself and his army as the saviours of his country's honour, he takes what troops he can spare – fewer than three hundred – and marches off to Frenchtown.

There is another force drawing him and his men toward the little village – an attraction quite as powerful as the prospect of fame and glory: Frenchtown, at this moment, is close to paradise. Here on the vine-clad banks of *la Rivière au Raisin* is luxury: fresh apples, cider by the barrel, sugar, butter, whiskey, and more – houses with roofs, warm beds, hearthsides with crackling fires, the soft presence of women. When Winchester arrives late on the twentieth, Lewis's men have already sampled these delights. Billeted in no particular order in the homes of the enthusiastic settlers, they are already drunk and quarrelsome, wandering about town late into the night. There is some vague talk of entrenching the position, but it is only talk. The men are weary from fighting, unruly from drink, and in no mood to take orders.

The village is surrounded on three sides by a palisade constructed of eight-foot logs, split and sharpened at the ends. These pickets, which do not come all the way down to the river bank, enclose a compact community of log and shingle houses, interspersed with orchards, gardens, barns, and outbuildings. The whole space forms a rectangle two hundred yards along the river and three hundred deep.

On the right of the village, downriver, lies an open meadow with a number of detached houses. Here Lieutenant-Colonel Samuel Wells, brother to the slain scout Billy Wells and a veteran of Tippecanoe, encamps his regulars. Winchester demurs: the regulars would be better placed within the palisade. But Wells insists on his prerogatives: military etiquette determines that the regular troops should *always* be on the right of the militia. Winchester does not argue. Wells's men are exposed, but he expects to find a better campground for them on the following day.

Leaving Wells in charge of the main camp, the General and his staff, including his teen-aged son, take up quarters on the south side of the river in the home of Colonel Francis Navarre, a local trader. It is a handsome building, the logs covered with clapboard, the whole shaded by pear trees originally brought from Normandy. Winchester is given a spacious guest-room at the front of the house, warmed by a fireplace. It is now Wells's turn to demur. He believes the General and his officers should be as close as possible to the troops on the far side of the river in case of sudden attack. The British fort is only eighteen miles away.

But James Winchester has made up his mind. For twenty years as a wealthy plantation owner he has enjoyed the creature comforts of a sedentary life. For five months without complaint he has slept out in the elements, enduring the privations with his troops, existing on dreadful food – when there was food at all – drinking, sometimes, stagnant water scooped out of wagon tracks. Later, he will argue that there was no house in Frenchtown; he would have had to move some of the wounded. But this is palpably false.

A strange lassitude has fallen over the General and his troops. The sudden euphoric victory, the almost magical appearance of food, drink, warmth, and shelter – the stuff of their dreams for these past weeks – has given them a dreamlike confidence. There is talk of moving the camp to a better position, and on the following day the General and some of his officers ride out to look over the ground. Nothing comes of it. It does not apparently occur to them that it might be a good idea to put the river between themselves and the British.

Wells leaves camp that morning claiming that he has baggage to collect at the rapids. Winchester, who believes that Wells has lost faith in him, sends a note with him to Harrison, detailing his situation. It reflects his sense of security: his patrols have detected no British in the vicinity; he does not believe any attack will take place for several days. His own intentions are far from clear. Later that night, Captain Nathaniel Hart, Harrison's emissary, rides in with the news that Harrison has arrived at the Maumee rapids and that reinforcements are on the way. This adds to the general complacency.

It is an axiom of war that from time to time even the best of generals suffer from a common failing – a refusal to believe their own intelligence reports. Psychological blinkers narrow their vision; they decline to accept any evidence that fails to support their own appreciation of the situation. Winchester seems deaf to all suggestions that the British are massing for an attack. On the morning of the twenty-first, he sends Navarre's son Peter and four of his brothers to scout toward the mouth of the Detroit River. En route, they intercept Joseph Bordeau, Peter's future father-in-law, crossing on the ice from the British side. Bordeau, who has escaped from Amherstburg, brings positive news that the British, with a large body of Indians, will be at the Raisin some time after dark. But "Jocko" La Salle, a voluble and genial French Canadian – and a possible British plant – convinces Winchester that this news must be in error. Winchester and his officers, "regaling themselves with whiskey and loaf sugar" as Elias Darnell believes, dismiss Peter Navarre with a laugh.

That afternoon, a second scout confirms the story, but again Winchester is deaf. Later in the evening, one of Lewis's ensigns learns from a tavern keeper that he has been talking to two British officers about an impending attack. But Lewis does not take the report seriously.

Some of Winchester's field officers expect that a council will be called that night, but no word comes from the General. Though Winchester has issued vague orders about strengthening the camp, little has been done. Nor does he issue the ammunition, stored at Navarre's house. Wells's detachment is down to ten rounds per man.

It is bitterly cold. The snow lies deep. Nobody has the heart to send pickets out onto the roads leading into the settlement. William Atherton notices that most of the men act as if they were perfectly secure, some wandering about town until late into the night. Atherton himself feels little anxiety, although he has reason to believe the situation is perilous. He sleeps soundly until awakened by the cry "To arms! to arms!" the thundering of cannon, the roar of muskets, and the discordant yells of attacking Indians.

AMHERSTBURG, UPPER CANADA, January 19, 1813. It is long past midnight. From the windows of Draper's tavern comes the sound of music and merriment, laughter and dancing. The young people of the town and the officers of the garrison have combined to hold a ball to celebrate the birthday of Queen Charlotte, the consort of the mad old king of England. Suddenly the music stops and in walks Procter's deputy, Lieutenant-Colonel St. George, equipped for the field. His voice, long accustomed to command, drowns the chatter.

"My boys," says the Colonel, "you must prepare to dance to a different tune; the enemy is upon us and we are going to surprise them. We shall take the route about four in the morning, so get ready at once."

Procter has just received word of the British defeat at the Raisin. The Americans, he knows, are in an exposed position and their numbers are not large. He determines to scrape up as many men as possible and attack at once. This swift and aggressive decision is not characteristic of Procter, a methodical, cautious officer who tends to follow the book. It was Procter, after all, who strongly opposed Brock's sally against Detroit. Now Brock's example – or perhaps Brock's ghost – impels him to precipitate action. The moves are Procter's, but the spirit behind them is that of his late commander.

He plans swiftly. He will send a detachment under Captain James Askin to garrison Detroit. He will leave Fort Amherstburg virtually defenceless, manned only by the sick and least effective members of the militia under Lieutenant-Colonel Jean-Baptiste Bâby. The remainder – every possible man who can be called into service, including provincial seamen from the gunboats – will be sent across the river. In all, he counts 597 able men and more than five hundred Indians – Potawatomi displaced from their homes by Harrison, with bitter memories of Tippecanoe; Miami, victims of the recent attacks at Mississinewa; and Chief Roundhead's Wyandot, formerly of Brownstown.

The first detachment leaves immediately, dragging three three-pound cannon and three small howitzers on sleighs. John Richardson, the future novelist, is young enough at fifteen to find the scene romantic – the troops moving in a thin line across the frozen river under cliffs of rugged ice, their weapons, polished to a high gloss, glittering in the winter sunlight.

Lieutenant Frederic Rolette, back in action again after the prisoner exchange that followed the battle of Queenston Heights and fresh from his losing struggle to regain the gunboat *Detroit* from the Americans, has charge of one of the guns. He is suffering from such a splitting headache that Major Reynolds urges him to go back. Rolette looks insulted, produces a heavy bandanna. "Look here," he says, "tie this tight around my head." Reynolds rolls it into a thick band and does so. "I am better already," says Rolette and pushes on.

The following day the rest of Procter's forces cross the river, rest that night at Brownstown, and prepare to move early next morning. As darkness falls, John Richardson's favourite brother, Robert, aged fourteen, a midshipman in the Provincial Marine, sneaks into camp. His father, an army surgeon, has given him strict orders to stay out of trouble on the Canadian side, but he is determined to see action and attaches himself to one of the gun crews.

In the morning, Procter moves his force of one thousand to Rocky River, twelve miles from Brownstown, six miles from the American camp. Two hours before dawn on the following day they rise, march the intervening distance, and silently descend upon the enemy.

The camp at Frenchtown is asleep, the drum roll just sounding reveille. This, surely, is the moment for attack, while the men are still in their blankets, drowsy, brushing the slumber from their eyes, without weapons in their hands. But the ghost of Isaac Brock has departed. Procter goes by the book, which insists that an infantry charge be supported by cannon. Precious moments slip by, and the army's momentum slows as he places his pieces. A sharp-eyed Kentucky guard spots the movement. A rifle explodes, and the leading grenadier of the 41st, a man named Gates, drops dead: a bullet has literally gone in one ear and out the other. Surprise is lost. The battle begins. Procter's caution will cost the lives of scores of good men.

It is still dark. The British and Canadians can see flashes of musketry several hundred yards to the front but nothing else. Slowly, in the pre-dawn murk, a blurred line of figures takes shape, standing out in front of the village. They fire a volley at this welcome target, but the line stands fast. They fire again without effect. Who are these supermen who do not fall when the muskets roar? Dawn provides the answer: they have been aiming, not at their enemies, but at a line of wooden pickets that protects them.

A second problem frustrates them. Procter has placed one of his three-pounders directly in front of his centre, so that the American

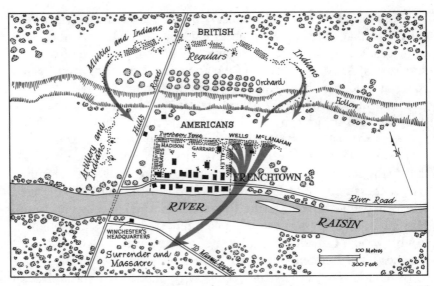

The Battle of Frenchtown

fire aimed at the gun plays upon the men behind it while the gunners themselves are in jeopardy from their own men in the rear.

A British musket ball strikes Frederic Rolette in the head. The tightly rolled silk bandanna saves his life. The ball is caught in the fold and flattens against his skull, increasing his headache and causing a goose egg but no further damage.

The fire grows hotter. Behind the palisades the Americans can easily pick out targets against the lightening sky. When the British abandon a three-pounder twenty yards from the fence, the Kentuckians leap over the puncheons to capture it. But Rolette's mate, Second-Lieutenant Robert Irvine, the same man who tried to beat off the attack on *Caledonia*, seizes the drag rope and hauls it back to the British line just as a musket ball shreds his heel.

Private Shadrach Byfield, whose name was left off the list for prize money after the fall of Detroit, is fighting in Adam Muir's company of the 41st when the man on his left falls dead. It is light enough now to see the enemy, and he spots a Kentuckian coming through the palisades. "There's a man!" cries Byfield to a friend. "I'll have a shot at him." As he pulls the trigger, a ball strikes him under the left ear and he topples to the ground, cutting his friend's leg with his bayonet in the process. He is only twenty-three, a Wiltshire man who joined the

British army at eighteen – the third in his family to enlist – an action that caused his poor mother to fall into a speechless fit from which she never recovered. Now he believes his last moment has come. "Byfield is dead!" his friend cries out, and Shadrach Byfield replies, in some wonder, "I believe I be." An age-old question flashes across his mind, a question that must occur to every soldier the instant he falls in battle. "Is this death?" he asks himself. *Is this how men die?*

But he is not dead. He raises his head and begins to creep off on his hands and knees. "Byfield," calls a sergeant, "shall I take you to the doctor?" But Shadrach Byfield at twenty-three is an old soldier. "Never mind me, go and help the men," he says, and makes his way to a barn to have his wound dressed. Here he encounters a spectacle so affecting that he can never forget it – a young midshipman, wounded in the knee, crying in pain for his mother, convinced he is going to die.

At the palisade, John Richardson feels as if he were sleep-walking. The early call and the six-mile march have exhausted him. Even as the balls begin to whistle about his head he continues to feel drowsy. He tries to fire his musket, finds it will not respond; someone the night before has stolen his flintlock and replaced it with a damaged part. The infantry manual lists twelve separate drill movements for firing a Brown Bess musket and Richardson goes through all of them without effect, but all he gets is a flash in the pan. He finds a bit of wire, tries to fix his weapon, fires again, gets another flash. He feels more frustration than fear at being fired upon by an unseen foe and not being able to fire back, even though he later comes to realize that if he had fired fifty rounds not one of them would have had any effect on the pickets (and probably not on the enemy, either, for the musket is a wretchedly inaccurate weapon).

To his horror, Richardson notes that the American sharpshooters are picking off the wounded British and Canadians as they try to crawl to safety and that some are making use of the tomahawk and scalping knife. He is still struggling vainly with his useless weapon when he hears his name called. Somebody shouts that his brother has been wounded – young Robert's right leg was shattered as he applied a match to a gun. Now, in great pain, Robert begs to be carried off, not to the staff section where his father is caring for the wounded, but to another part of the field so that he may escape his parent's wrath. And there Shadrach Byfield is witness to his suffering.

On the left of the British line, Richardson can hear the war-whoops of the Indians who, with the help of the Canadian militia, are driving directly through the open field in which Lieutenant-Colonel Wells insisted on placing the regulars of the 17th U.S. Infantry. Wells is still at the Maumee. His second-in-command, Major McClanahan, cannot hold his unprotected position. The troops fall back to the frozen Raisin, and the American right flank is turned.

The Americans are in full flight across the river with Caldwell and his Indians under Roundhead, Split Log, and Walk-in-the-Water in hot pursuit. One of the Wyandot overtakes an American officer and is about to tomahawk him when Caldwell intercedes, makes him prisoner, takes him to the rear. The Kentuckian, catching him off guard, draws his knife and slits Caldwell's throat from ear to ear, but the wound is shallow and Caldwell, who is as tough as his Indian followers, catches his assailant's arm, pulls the dagger from his throat, and plunges it again and again into his prisoner's body until he is dead. Caldwell survives.

But where, when all this is going on, is the General?

Winchester has awakened to the sound of musket fire and howitzer bombs exploding. He runs to the barn, borrows a horse from his host (who, fearing British retribution, is glad to be rid of him), dashes into action. His two battalion commanders, Lewis and Allen, join him, and the three attempt to rally the fleeing men under the bank of the Raisin. It is too late; the troops, pursued by the Indians, are in a panic. Lewis has sent two companies to the right flank to reinforce the regulars, but these too are in retreat.

The three officers withdraw across the river and attempt a second rally behind the fences on the south side. It is futile. The men dash past into a narrow lane leading to the main road. This is suicide, for the Indians are ahead of them and behind them, on both sides of the lane. One hundred men are shot, tomahawked, scalped. Winchester attempts a third rally in an orchard about a mile and a half from the village. It also fails.

The right flank is in full retreat, the men throwing away their weapons in panic. The Potawatomi are in no mood to offer quarter. Lieutenant Ashton Garrett tries to form up a group of fifteen men but finding some sixty Indians running along both sides and in front with their arms at the trail decides instead to surrender. The Indians order Garrett and his men to ground their arms; then, securing all the weapons, they coolly shoot and scalp every one except Garrett himself.

John Allen, shot in the thigh during his attempts to stem the retreat, limps on for two miles until he can go no farther. Exhausted and in pain, he slumps onto a log, resigned to his fate. One of the Potawatomi chiefs, seeing his officer's uniform, determines to capture and ransom him, but just as he signals that intention a second Indian moves in. Allen dispatches him with a swipe of his sword. The other shoots the Colonel dead and scalps him.

Winchester and Lewis are more fortunate. They fall into the hands of Roundhead, the principal chief of the Wyandot, who, after stripping the General of his cocked hat, coat, and epaulettes, takes the two officers and Winchester's seventeen-year-old son by a circuitous route back behind the British lines. The battle for the village is still raging, but Winchester, noting Procter's artillery, dazed by the rout and despairing of any reinforcements from Harrison, has given up hope. As the Indians return with as many as eight or nine scalps hanging from their belts, he asks to see Procter. The British commander is blunt:

"Some of your troops, sir, are defending themselves from the fort in a state of desperation – had you not better surrender them?"

"I have no authority to do so," replies Winchester, shivering in the cold in his silk shirt. "My command has devolved upon the senior officer in the fort, as you are pleased to call it."

Procter now makes the classic answer – Brock's threat at Detroit, Roberts's at Mackinac: if there is no surrender he will be forced to set the town on fire; if he is forced to attack, he cannot be responsible for the conduct of the Indians or the lives of the Americans; if Winchester will surrender, he will be responsible for both. Winchester repeats that he is no longer in command but will recommend surrender to his people.

The command of the American forces still fighting inside the palisade has devolved on Major George Madison, a forty-nine-year-old veteran of the Revolution and of St. Clair's defeat at the hands of the Indians in 1791 and for twenty years keeper of public accounts for the state of Kentucky. At this moment he is concerned about the possession of an empty barn 150 yards from the palisade. If the enemy seizes that building, they will hold a commanding position overlooking the defenders. Madison calls for a volunteer to fire the barn, and a young ensign, William O. Butler, steps forward, seizes a blazing stick of firewood, vaults the fence, and dashes toward the barn under direct fire from the British and Indians on both sides.

Butler reaches the barn, flings the burning brand into a pile of hay, races back through a hail of musket balls, has almost reached the safety of his own lines when he realizes that the hay has not caught. Back he goes, re-enters the barn, fans the hay into a roaring blaze, outstrips the Indians trying to head him off, and with his clothes ripped by passing musket balls tumbles across the pickets and comes to a full stop, standing upright, trying to catch his breath. It is then that a musket ball strikes him full in the chest. Fortunately, it is spent, and Butler survives. Like his commander, George Madison, he will one day run for governor of Kentucky.

Now comes a lull in the fighting. Of the sixteen British gunners, thirteen are casualties; the remainder are too numb with cold to fire their weapons. Moreover, their ammunition is low; a wagon bearing additional rounds has been shot up and its driver killed by Kentucky riflemen. Procter has withdrawn his forces into the woods, waiting for the Indians to return from the chase before resuming the attack. The defenders seize this interlude to devour some breakfast. This is the moment when Winchester agrees to attempt a surrender.

The Americans, seeing a flag of truce, believe that Procter is asking for a respite to bury his dead. It does not occur to any that surrender is being proposed. When he learns the truth, George Madison is mortified; yet he knows his position is hopeless, for he has only a third of a keg of cartridges left. The reserve supply remains at the Navarre house across the river. He insists, however, on conditions.

"It has been customary for the Indians to massacre the wounded and prisoners after a surrender," he tells Procter. "I shall therefore not agree to any capitulation which General Winchester may direct, unless the safety and protection of all the prisoners shall be stipulated."

Procter stamps his foot:

"Sir, do *you* mean to dictate for *me*?"

"I mean to dictate for myself," Madison coolly replies. "We prefer to sell our lives as dearly as possible rather than be massacred in cold blood."

Procter agrees, but not in writing. Private property, he promises, will be respected; sleighs will be sent the following morning for the American sick and wounded; the disabled will be protected by a proper guard.

Thus the battle ends. Some of the troops plead with their officers not to surrender, saying they would rather die in action. Many are reduced to tears. Others, in a rage, throw down their guns with such force as to shiver the stocks from the barrels. Some joke and laugh. One stands on a stile block and shouts to the English, "You have taken the greatest set of game cocks that ever came from Kentuck." But the general feeling is one of despair. Atherton notes that news of the surrender is "like a shock of lightning from one end of the lines to the other." To Thomas P. Dudley, another Lexington volunteer, "the mortification at the thought of surrender, the Spartan band who fought like heroes, the tears shed, the wringing of hands, the swelling of hearts, indeed, the scene beggars description."

Only thirty-three men have managed to escape. McClanahan, Wells's second-in-command is one. Private John J. Brice is another; he gets away by pulling off his shoes and running through the snow in his stocking feet in order to leave tracks resembling those of an Indian in moccasins and so becomes the first man to report the defeat and surrender to Harrison.

Winchester's loss is appalling. Two hundred Kentuckians are dead or wounded, another seven hundred are prisoners of the British, and the worst is yet to come. The blow to American morale, already bruised by the losses at Mackinac, Detroit, and Queenston, is overwhelming. As for Harrison, the Battle of Frenchtown has wrecked his plans. His left wing has been shattered, his advance on Detroit halted indefinitely. He must now withdraw up the Maumee, out of reach of the enemy. The idea of a swift victory over Canada is gone forever.

•

FRENCHTOWN, MICHIGAN TERRITORY, January 23, 1813. William Atherton wakes at dawn, the wound in his shoulder throbbing. He cannot escape a feeling of dread that has tormented his sleep. An ominous stillness hangs over the village where the American wounded are still hived. Procter, fearing an imminent attack from Harrison, has long since dragged his own wounded off on sleds, and since there are not enough of these for the Americans, he has promised to return early in the morning to take them all to Amherstburg.

No one points to the illogic of this. If Procter fears Harrison's early arrival, why would he return for the wounded? If he doesn't fear it, why has he departed, taking everybody with him except one officer, Major Reynolds, and three interpreters? Actually, Harrison, learning of the disaster, has withdrawn his relief force. In the chorus of recriminations that will follow, nobody apparently bothers to ask why. With Procter's forces off balance and Fort Amherstburg virtually defenceless, he might easily have snatched victory from defeat. But he contents himself with putting all the blame on Winchester.

The camp at Frenchtown is uneasy. Some time in the dark hours of the night, Reynolds and the interpreters have slipped away. Atherton's fears have been further aroused by an Indian, apparently a chief, who speaks fluent English and who came into his quarters the evening before, seemingly trying to gain information about Harrison's movements. Just as he left, the Indian made an oddly chilling remark: "I am afraid," he said, "some of the mischievous boys will do some mischief before morning."

The sun has been up for no more than an hour when Atherton's fears are realized. Without warning, the door of the house in which he and some of the wounded are being cared for is forced open, and an Indian, his face smeared with red and black paint, appears waving a tomahawk, followed by several others. Their purpose is loot: they begin to strip the clothing and blankets from the wounded, groaning on the floor. Atherton, near the door, manages to slip out of the room, only to come face to face with one of the most savage-looking natives he has ever seen. This creature's face is painted jet black. Half a bushel of feathers are fastened to his scalp lock, an immense tomahawk gleams in his right hand, a scalping knife hangs from his belt. He seizes Atherton by the collar, propels him out the front door, leads him through the gate and down the river for a hundred yards to the home of Jean-Baptiste Jerome, where several wounded officers have spent the night. The building has also done duty as a tavern, and the Indians are ransacking the cellars for whiskey.

In front of the house Atherton sees a scarecrow figure, bleeding, barefoot, clad only in a shirt and drawers. This is Captain Nathaniel Hart, commander of the Lexington Light Infantry, inspector of the North West Army, the emissary whom Harrison sent to Winchester the night before the battle. He is twenty-eight and wealthy, having made a fortune in hemp. Now he is pleading for his life. The previous night, Hart, badly wounded in the knee, was visited by an old friend, Matthew Elliott's son William, a militia captain who was once cared for in the Hart home in Lexington during a bout of illness. Hart has Elliott's assurance that he will send his personal sleigh for him in the morning and convey him to his home in Amherstburg. In fact, Elliott has assured all the wounded in Jerome's house that they are in no danger. The promise is hollow; they are all in deadly peril. Some are already dying under the tomahawk blows of the Indians.

Hart turns to an Indian he recognizes – the same English-speaking chief whom Atherton encountered the evening before – and reminds him of Elliott's promise.

"Elliott has deceived you," the Indian replies. "He does not intend to fulfill his promise."

"If you will agree to take me, I will give you a horse or a hundred dollars," Hart declares. "You shall have it on our arrival at Malden."

"I cannot take you."

"Why?"

"You are too badly wounded."

"Then," asks Captain Hart, "what do you intend to do with us?"

"Boys," says the Indian, "you are all to be killed."

Hart maintains his composure, utters a brief prayer. Atherton expects at any moment to feel the blow of a tomahawk. Now follows a scene of pure horror: Captain Paschal Hickman, General William Hull's son-in-law, emerges from Jerome's house, dragged by an Indian who throws him face down into the snow. Hickman, who has already been tomahawked, chokes to death in his own blood as Atherton watches in terror, then, taking advantage of the confusion, turns from the spectacle and begins to edge slowly away, hoping not to be seen.

Albert Ammerman, another unwilling witness to the butchery, crouches on a log, guarded by his Indian captor. A private in the 1st Regiment of Kentucky Volunteers, he has been wounded in the thigh but is doing his best to conceal his injury, for he knows it is the Indians' practice to kill all who cannot walk. Now he watches helplessly while the Indians loot the houses, strip the clothes from the wounded, tomahawk and scalp their prey, and set fire to the buildings. Some, still alive, force their heads out of the windows, half-enveloped in smoke and flames, seeking rescue. But there is no rescue.

Ammerman is marched off at last toward Brownstown with some other prisoners. After limping about half a mile, they are overtaken. One Indian has Captain Hart in custody and is engaged in a violent argument with another, apparently over the reward that Hart has offered for his safe conduct to Amherstburg. As Ammerman watches, the two take aim at each other as if to end the quarrel. But they do not fire. Instead they turn upon their prisoner, pull him from his horse, knock him down with a war-club, tomahawk him, scalp him, strip him of his remaining clothing, money, and effects. Ammerman (who will shortly be ransomed in Detroit) notes that Hart, during these final moments, refrains from making any pleas and appears, to the end, perfectly calm. The news of his death, when it finally filters through to Lexington three months later, will cause a particular shiver of despair and fury in Kentucky. For this mangled and naked corpse, thrown like carrion onto the side of the road, was once the brother-in-law of Speaker Henry Clay.

Back at Frenchtown, little William Atherton (he is only five foot five) is trying to reach a small log building some distance from the scene of horror. He edges toward it, is a few steps from it, when a Potawatomi seizes him and asks where he is wounded. Atherton places a hand on his shoulder. The Indian feels it, finds it is not serious, determines that Atherton shall be his prize, perhaps for later ransom. He wraps his new possession in a blanket, gives him a hat, takes him to the back door of one of the houses, and puts the wounded Kentuckian in charge of all his plunder.

Atherton is flabbergasted. For almost an hour he has expected certain death. Now he lives in the faint hope that his life may be spared. He experiences "one of those sudden transitions of mind impossible to be either conceived or expressed, except by those whose unhappy lot it has been, to be placed in like circumstances."

As the house blazes behind him, Atherton watches his fellow prisoners being dragged away to Brownstown. For the first time, perhaps, he has been made aware of the value a man places on his own life. He sees members of his own company, old acquaintances, so badly wounded they can scarcely be moved in their beds, suddenly leap up, hearing that the Indians will tomahawk all who cannot depart on foot. They hobble past him on sticks but, being unable to keep up, are soon butchered.

After two hours, Atherton's captor returns with an army pack horse and a great deal of plunder. The Potawatomi hands his prisoner the bridle, and the two set off on the road to Brownstown, bordered now by a ghastly hedgerow of mutilated corpses.

They halt for the night at Sandy Creek, where a number of Potawatomi are encamped. Here, around a roaring fire of fence rails, the Indians feed their captives gruel. And here another grisly scene takes place. An Indian walks up to Private Charles Searls and proposes to exchange his moccasins for the soldier's shoes. The exchange effected, a brief conversation follows, the Indian asking how many men Harrison has with him. The name of the Hero of Tippecanoe seems to drive him into a sudden rage. His anger rising, he calls Searls a "Madison," raises his tomahawk, strikes him a deep blow on the shoulder.

Searls, bleeding profusely, clutches the weapon embedded in his flesh and tries to resist, whereupon a surgeon's mate, Gustavus Bower, tells him his fate is inevitable. Searls closes his eyes, the blow falls again, and Bower is drenched with brains and blood. Not long after, three more men are indiscriminately dispatched.

When Atherton asks his captor if the Indians intend to kill all the prisoners, the Indian nods. Atherton tries to eat, has no stomach for it, even though he has had little nourishment for three days. Then he realizes his captor does not understand English and hope returns.

The march resumes with many alarms. Atherton is in daily fear of his life, sleeping with a kerchief tied around his head in the belief that the Indians will want to steal it before tomahawking him in his sleep, thus giving him some warning. But they do not kill him. His captor, whose brother has been killed at the River Raisin, has other plans. It is the custom of the Potawatomi, among others, to adopt healthy captives into the families of those who have lost sons in the same engagement. It is some time before Atherton realizes that his enemies do not intend to kill or ransom him. On the contrary, they are determined to turn him into an Indian. For the rest of his life, if they have their way, he will live as a savage in the forest.

From Frenchtown, Dr. John Todd, surgeon for the 5th Regiment of Kentucky Volunteers who has been left in charge of the wounded, is conveyed to the British camp where he again encounters Captain William Elliott. The two met the previous evening when Todd was a witness to the discussions between Elliott and Hart. Now Todd urges Elliott to send his sleigh back to the Raisin where some of the badly wounded, including his friend Hart, may yet be saved. But Elliott, who has lived all his life with the Indians and is half Shawnee, knows it is too late and says so. When Todd presses the case, Elliott remarks that charity begins at home, that the British and Canadian wounded must be cared for first, that when sleighs are available they will be sent to Frenchtown. He adds, in some exasperation, that it is impossible to restrain the Indians and tries to explain that they are simply seeking revenge for their own losses. Tippecanoe is only fourteen months in the past, Mississinewa less than two.

Along the frozen shores of the River Raisin a great stillness has fallen. The cold is numbing; nothing moves. Those few settlers who still remain in Frenchtown do not venture outside their doors.

In the little orchard across the river, along the narrow lane that leads from the Navarre home and beside the Detroit River road, the bodies of the Americans lie, unshriven and unburied. The Potawatomi have made it known that any white man who dares to touch the remains of any of the hated Harrison men will meet a similar fate.

The naked corpses lie strewn for miles along the roadside in the grotesque attitudes of men who, in a sudden flash, realize their last moment has come. In death they bear a gruesome similarity, for each skull is disfigured by a frozen smear of fleshy pulp where the scalp has been.

Here, contorted in death, lies the flower of Kentucky: Captain Hart and Captain Hickman; Lieutenant-Colonel John Allen; Captain John Woolfolk, Winchester's aide-de-camp, who offered one thousand dollars to anyone who would purchase him but was tomahawked in spite of it; Captain John Simpson, Henry Clay's fellow congressman and supporter; Ensign Levi Wells, the son of Lieutenant-Colonel Sam Wells of the 4th Infantry; Allen Darnell, whose brother looks helplessly on as he is shot and scalped because he cannot keep up with the others; and Ebenezer Blythe, a surgeon's mate, tomahawked in the act of offering ransom. And here, like a discarded doll, is the cadaver of young Captain Price of the Jessamine Blues whose last letter home gave instructions for the upbringing of his two-year-old son.

A few days after the battle, the French inhabitants, emerging at last from their homes, are treated to a ghastly spectacle. Trotting along the roadway come droves of hogs that have been feeding off the corpses and are now carrying off the remains – whole arms and legs, skulls, bits of torso and entrails clamped between their greedy jaws. The hogs, too, are victims of the war, for they seem now to be as demented as the men who fight it, "rendered mad," according to one opinion, "by so profuse a diet of Christian flesh."

The war, which began so gently, has turned ugly, as all wars must. The mannerly days are over. New emotions – hatred, fury, a thirst for revenge, a nagging sense of guilt – distort the tempers of the neighbours who live on both sides of the embattled border. And it is not over. Peace is still two years away. The blood has only begun to flow.

AFTERVIEW
The New War

WITH THE BATTLE OF FRENCHTOWN, the campaign of 1812 ended. It was too cold to fight. The war was postponed until spring, when it would become a new war with new leaders and new followers. The six-month volunteers from Kentucky, Ohio, Pennsylvania and other states went back to their farms, refusing to enlist for another term of service. Harrison withdrew up the Maumee to start work on a new outpost, Fort Meigs. Along the Niagara River the American regulars moved back ten miles while others went into winter quarters at Sackets Harbor, Burlington, and Greenville. The only American fighting men in Canada were the prisoners of war at Quebec.

It was as if both Canada and the United States were starting from scratch. America had a new secretary of war, John Armstrong. Most of the old commanders – Brock, Hull, Van Rensselaer, Smyth, Winchester – were gone. Dearborn's days were numbered as were Sheaffe's. Only two major leaders remained from the early days of 1812, Tecumseh and Harrison, old adversaries fated to meet face to face at the Thames in the autumn of 1813.

Now Canada had time to breathe. With Napoleon's army fleeing Russia, some of the pressure was off Great Britain. A detachment of reinforcements was dispatched to Bermuda, there to wait until the ice cleared in the St. Lawrence. The United States, too, had time to rethink its strategy – or lack of it – and to plan more carefully for the future.

It was not the war that the Americans, inspired and goaded by the eloquence of Henry Clay and his colleagues, had set out to fight and certainly not the glamorous adventure that Harrison's volunteers expected. The post-Revolutionary euphoria, which envisaged the citizen soldiers of a democratic nation marching off to sure victory over a handful of robot-like mercenaries and enslaved farmers, had dissipated. America had learned the lessons that most nations relearn at the start of every war – that valour is ephemeral, that the heroes of one war are the scapegoats of the next, that command is for the young, the vigorous, the imaginative, the professional. Nor does enthusiasm and patriotism alone win battles: untrained volunteers, no matter how fervent, cannot stand up to seasoned regulars, drilled to stand fast in moments of panic and to follow orders without question. It was time for the United States to drop its amateur standing now that it intended to do what its founding fathers had not prepared for – aggressive warfare.

It was clear that possession of the water held the key to victory. Britain, by seizing Michilimackinac and Detroit, both commanding narrow channels, effectively controlled all easy transit to the northwest and thus to the fur trade. Two other strong points, Kingston and Montreal, commanded the entrance to Lake Ontario and the St. Lawrence lifeline to the sea. And so, as winter gave way to spring, the ring of hammers on the Lakes announced a different kind of contest as both sides engaged in a shipbuilding race.

Immediately after Hull's defeat, Madison and Eustis had awoken to the fact that the disgraced commander's original proposals had been right. And so to Sackets Harbor that winter – the only available harbour at the eastern end of Lake Ontario – a new commander, Captain Isaac Chauncey, quickly dubbed a commodore, was dispatched with 700 seamen and marines and 140 ships' carpenters to help construct two fighting ships, each of thirty-two guns. Jesse Elliott, hero of the previous summer's attack, had added the captured *Caledonia* to the vessels he was already building. Brock had rightly seen that event as a serious and significant loss. At Erie, Pennsylvania, two twenty-gun brigs and several gunboats were also under construction. With Elliott's warships these formed the backbone of the fleet with which Oliver Hazard Perry would in the summer of 1813 seize control of the lake from the British, thus opening up Amherstburg and the valley of the Thames to American attack.

The British were also building ships – one big vessel at the protected harbour of Kingston, another at York, wide open to attack, a split decision that proved costly when Chauncey's fleet appeared off the capital in April. At Amherstburg a smaller vessel was under construction. But the British suffered from a lack of supplies, of mechanics, and, most important, of trained seamen. Already, following some skirmishing outside Kingston Harbour in November, control of Lake Ontario was in doubt. Was it possible that the upstart Americans could outsail, outmanoeuvre, and outfight the greatest maritime power in the world? On the Atlantic, in single engagements – the *United States* versus the *Macedonian* in October, the *Constitution* versus the *Java* in December – the Americans were the winners. After a season of reverses on land, these victories, though not significant in military terms, gave the country hope.

British strategy remained the same: to stay on the defensive. An attempt would be made to dislodge Harrison from his threatening position at Fort Meigs on the Maumee, but with Brock gone there was no hint of offensive warfare. The Americans planned to open the campaign with attacks on both Kingston and York to destroy the new warships, then to seize Fort George at the mouth of the Niagara and march on Fort Erie. By spring Dearborn had watered down this plan, eliminating Kingston, which was held to be too strong for an attack.

The United States remained deeply divided over the war. Following Napoleon's disastrous retreat from Moscow, the Russian minister in Washington proposed to Madison (now serving his second term as the result of the November election) that his emperor, Alexander I, mediate between the two belligerents. After all, with the Orders in Council out of the way the only real impediment to peace was the matter of impressment, and with the war in Europe apparently winding down, that would soon be of academic interest. Madison agreed, but before the issue could be negotiated, Alexander, to England's fury, made a separate peace with Napoleon. Russia, the British felt, like America before her had stabbed them in the back. And so the war went on.

The New England states continued, in effect, to be at peace with their neighbours in Britain's Atlantic colonies. But across the nation a new and savage emotion, which since the beginning of history has acted as a unifying force among peoples, was beginning to be felt. The contempt and disdain once felt for the British had been transformed into rage. Procter was the villain; his officers were seen as monsters. Harrison's troops, especially, thirsted for revenge and would get it finally when autumn reddened the leaves in the valley of the Thames.

In Kentucky, the failure at the Raisin cut deep. When the news reached Lexington, Governor Shelby was attending a theatrical performance. He hurried out as whispers of the defeat rippled from row to row. People began to leave, some in tears, all distressed, until by the play's third act the house was empty. Scarcely a family in the state was not touched in some way by the tragedy at Frenchtown. The idea of a swift victory was shattered. For hundreds of families, weeping over lost sons and lost illusions, the war that at the outset seemed almost like a sporting event had become a horror. Some did not learn for months whether their men were alive, dead, or in prison. Some never knew.

Captain Paschal Hickman's mother did not recover from the blow. "Sorely distressed about the massacre," in the words of her husband, "...she pined away and died on June 9, 1813."

Captain Hart's widow, Anna, suffered a similar end. Prostrated over her husband's fate, she was sent by relatives to New Orleans and then to New York in the hope that a change of scene would lighten her grief. It failed. She set out again for Lexington but could go no farther than Philadelphia, where she died at twenty-seven.

Lieutenant-Colonel Allen's widow, Jane, hoped against hope that her husband was not dead but a captive of the Indians. For eight years she watched and waited at her home on the Lexington-Louisville road, keeping the shutters open each night that he might see the candle she kept burning there. At last, with all hope extinguished, she, too, wasted away from grief. In February, 1821, she died.

It was not only in Kentucky that the tragedy struck home. All of America was dumbfounded. In the town of Erie, Pennsylvania, the citizens at a public meeting resolved to wear black crêpe on their arms and in their hats for ninety days out of respect for those who "gloriously fell in the field defending the only free government on earth." In Kentucky, a new slogan arose and was used to stimulate recruiting: *Remember the Raisin!* Nine counties were named in honour of nine officers slain on its frozen banks. Now the government's war loan, only two-thirds subscribed, was taken up in a new wave of patriotic fervour, partly as a result of the efforts of John Jacob Astor, whose own patriotism had been called in question as the result of his actions of the previous summer.

Lieutenant-Colonel Procter, the subject of almost universal excoriation in America, brushed off the massacre at the Raisin as he would an annoying insect. In his dispatch to Sheaffe he simply wrote that "the zeal and courage of the Indian Department never were more conspicuous than on this occasion, the Indian warriors fought with their usual courage." In a later report he referred to the massacre briefly and with regret but stated that the Kentucky soldiers too killed the wounded and took scalps; all perfectly true. That, however, scarcely justified the General Order issued at Quebec on February 8, which was enough to make the American prisoners grind their teeth:

> On this occasion, the Gallantry of Colonel Procter was most nobly displayed in his humane and unwearied exertions in securing the vanquished from the revenge of the Indian warriors.

That was not the view of some of Procter's people. Dr. Robert Richardson, two of whose sons fought at the Raisin, was outraged by the massacre and wrote to his father-in-law, John Askin, "We have not heard the last of this shameful transaction. I wish to god it could be contradicted."

Crowded into a small wood yard at Amherstburg, without tents, blankets, or fires, unprotected from rain and snow, Procter's prisoners shivered in their thin clothing for almost two days before being moved to a chilly warehouse. Eventually, they were marched five hundred miles by a roundabout route through the back country to Fort George, where the regulars were sent to Quebec City and the volunteers paroled to their homes under the guarantee that they would not take up arms against Great Britain or her allies until exchanged in the regular way.

Allies? When one Kentuckian sarcastically asked a British officer who Great Britain's allies were, the reply was evasive and shamefaced: Britain's allies, said the officer, were well known; he did not wish to continue the discussion. Nor did Henry Procter want to talk about the massacre, half convincing himself that it had never happened. In Detroit, when a group of citizens asked for an inquiry into the killing of the prisoners, he flew into a rage and demanded firm evidence that any such atrocity had occurred. Like Brock before him, Procter was a virtual prisoner of the Indians, whose American captives languished that spring in the villages of the Potawatomi. His own force, badly mauled at Frenchtown, was smaller than Harrison's on the Maumee. Indian support was essential to even the odds, and he knew that he would not get it if he tried to interfere with time-honoured rituals. He refused to bow to demands that the Indians release all their captives to him, agreeing to ransom them but for no more than five dollars a head – an empty gesture when the going rate in Detroit started at ten dollars and ran as high as eighty.

The Indians scattered that spring to their hunting-grounds. Tecumseh was still in the south, pursuing his proposal to weld the tribes into a new confederacy. The British saw eye to eye with his plan for an Indian state north of the Ohio; it would act as a buffer between the two English-speaking nations on the North American continent and make future wars unattractive. The idea had long been at the core of British Indian policy.

But the Indians were soon ignored. In the official dispatches they got short shrift. The names of white officers who acted with conspicuous gallantry were invariably recorded, those of the Indian chieftains never. Even the name of Tecumseh, after Brock's initial report, vanishes from the record. Yet these painted tribesmen helped save Canada's hide in 1812:

At Michilimackinac and Detroit, their presence was decisive. In each case the threat of an Indian attack broke the morale of the defenders and brought about unconditional surrender.

At the River aux Canards and Turkey Creek, Tecumseh's warriors, acting as a screen, contributed to Hull's decision not to attack Fort Amherstburg. At Brownstown and Maguaga, the same mixed group of tribesmen was essential to the British success in preventing Captain Brush's supply train from getting through to Detroit.

At Queenston Heights, the Mohawk advance guard so terrified Scott's militiamen that hundreds fled to the woods before the battle was joined, while the forward American scouts were prevented from probing the strength and position of Sheaffe's forces. The war-whoops of

Norton's followers, echoing across the gorge, sent a chill through thousands more, confirming them in their refusal to cross the river.

And at Frenchtown, the Wyandot and Potawatomi turned Winchester's right flank and caused the surrender of his entire force.

Perhaps if Brock and Tecumseh had lived, the Indian claims might have received greater consideration. Brock's attitude to the tribes was ambivalent, but he believed in keeping his promises; his dispatches to Prevost underline his concern for the Indian position. But with Brock gone, Tecumseh's death at the Thames in the fall of 1813 (the Indians fighting on after Procter and the British fled) meant an end to Shawnee aspirations for a native confederacy.

It was among the white settlers in Upper Canada that a new confederacy was taking shape. There the war was no longer looked on with indifference. In the muddy capital of York a new leader was about to emerge in the person of the Reverend Dr. John Strachan, perhaps the most significant and influential Canadian of his time, a product of the War of 1812. In December of that first war year Strachan presided over the formation of the Loyal and Patriotic Society of Upper Canada, organized to provide winter clothing for the militia and, later, to help their families and others who had suffered from the war. The directors of the Loyal and Patriotic Society included Strachan's protégés and the elite of York – the tight ruling group that would soon be known as the Family Compact.

Thus the key words in Upper Canada were "loyalty" and "patriotism" – loyalty to the British way of life as opposed to American "radical" democracy and republicanism. Brock – the man who wanted to establish martial law and abandon habeas corpus – represented these virtues. Canonized by the same caste that organized the Loyal and Patriotic Society, he came to represent Canadian order as opposed to American anarchy – "peace, order and good government" rather than the more hedonistic "life, liberty and the pursuit of happiness." Had not Upper Canada been saved from the invader by appointed leaders who ruled autocratically? In America, the politicians became generals; in British North America, the opposite held true.

This attitude – that the British way is preferable to the American; that certain sensitive positions are better filled by appointment than by election; that order imposed from above has advantages over grass-roots democracy (for which read "licence" or "anarchy"); that a ruling elite often knows better than the body politic – flourished as a result of an invasion repelled. Out of it, shaped by an emerging nationalism and tempered by rebellion, grew that special form of state paternalism that makes the Canadian way of life significantly different from the more individualistic American way. Thus, in a psychological as well as in a political sense, we are Canadians and not Americans because of a foolish war that scarcely anyone wanted or needed, but which, once launched, none knew how to stop.

CODA: William Atherton's War

MICHIGAN TERRITORY, *April, 1813*. To William Atherton, captive of the Potawatomi, home seems to be on another planet. Adopted into a Potawatomi family to replace a son killed at Frenchtown, he now lives as an Indian, wears Indian buckskin, hews to Indian customs. He hunts with bow and arrow, engages in the corn dance, sleeps in a wigwam, exists on boiled corn and bristly hogmeat. He neither hears nor speaks English.

His one contact with civilization is a tattered Lexington newspaper, found among the Indians' effects. This is his sole comfort: he reads and re-reads it, clinging to the brittle pages as a reminder that somewhere beyond the brooding, snow-covered forests there really is another world — a world he once took for granted but which comes back to him now as if in a dream. Will he ever see it again? As winter gives way to spring, Atherton gives way to despair, stealing out of camp for moments of solitude when he can think of home and weep without being discovered.

In May, the Indians head for Detroit. On the way, they encounter another band which has just captured a young American surgeon in battle. What battle? Atherton has no way of knowing that an American fleet has captured York and that the British have badly mauled Harrison's army during the siege of Fort Meigs on the Maumee. The two men converse eagerly in the first English that Atherton has heard in three months; then the other departs, Atherton believes to his death.

They reach Amherstburg, but Atherton has no hope of escape. With his long swarthy face and his matted brown hair, uncut for months, he is just another Indian to the British, who fail to notice his blue eyes. When the band moves across to Spring Wells to draw rations at the British commissary, Atherton's Indian father learns, with delight, that his new son can write. He has him double the original number of family members on the chit, thus increasing the handout of provisions. Again, the British do not realize that Atherton is white.

He loses track of time. Crawling with vermin, half-starved, with no hope of escape from the family that nurtures but also guards him, he throws himself on their mercy and pleads to be ransomed. To his surprise, his Indian father agrees, albeit reluctantly. It is clear that Atherton has become part of the family, more a son than a captive. They cannot refuse him, even though it means losing him. Eventually, in Detroit, they find a

315

man who will give a pony for him. Atherton bids his Indian parents goodbye – not without sorrow, for they have, in their fashion, been kind – and becomes a prisoner of war. All that summer he is lodged in a British guardhouse, almost naked, sleeping on the floor with a log for a pillow, wondering about the course of the war.

Fort George is assaulted and taken by the Americans. At Stoney Creek, a British force captures two American generals who mistake them for friends in the darkness. The Caughnawagas trounce the Americans at Beaver Dams, the battle that makes a heroine of Laura Secord. Of these triumphs and defeats Atherton knows nothing. Only when his captors return from the unsuccessful British siege of Fort Stephenson at Lower Sandusky, their faces peppered with small shot, does he have an inkling that beyond the guardhouse walls, all along the border, men are still fighting and dying.

Summer gives way to fall. On September 10, Atherton and his fellow prisoners can hear the rumble of heavy guns reverberating across Lake Erie. Clearly, a naval battle is raging, but his captors refuse details. At last a private soldier whispers the truth: Oliver Hazard Perry has met the enemy and they are his. The British fleet is obliterated. Erie is an American lake.

The victory touches off a major retreat. The British pack up hastily in the face of Harrison's advancing army. Atherton can hardly wait for the Kentucky forces to arrive and free him, but that is not to be. The prisoners are hurried across to the Canadian shore and herded up the Thames Valley to Burlington, then on to York, Kingston, Montreal.

It seems as if the entire city has turned out to stare at them – verminous, shaggy, half-starved after a journey of nine hundred miles. As Atherton trudges down the cobbled streets he notices the doors and windows crammed with curious women. In the jail they are given a little "Yankee beef," taunted with the fact that it has been purchased by the British from Americans trading with the enemy.

Two weeks later they are sent to Quebec City. Here, for the first time, Atherton learns that Harrison has captured Fort Amherstburg, rolled up the Thames, won the Battle of Moravian Town, and presided over the death of his enemy, Tecumseh.

The Kentuckians' reputation has preceded them. The Quebeckers think of them as a species of wildman – savage forest creatures, half-human, half-beast. They crowd to the jail, peering at the captives as they would at animals in a zoo, astonished, even disappointed, to find they do not live up to their billing. One man gazes at them for some minutes, then delivers the general verdict: "Why, they look just like other people."

Beyond the prison, the war rages on. The two-pronged American attack designed to seize Montreal fizzles out at Châteauguay and Crysler's Farm, but Atherton is only dimly aware of it. Fall turns to winter, with both sides once again deadlocked along the border. As the spring campaign opens, a more cheerful piece of news reaches Quebec: there is to be a general prisoner exchange. Eventually Atherton is released and sent back across the border, only a few weeks before the war's bloodiest battle at Lundy's Lane. In Pittsburgh he encounters a group of vaguely familiar men – British prisoners of war. Who are they? Where has he seen them before? He remembers: these are the soldiers who were once his guards when he was a captive in Detroit. It all seems a long time ago.

Atherton reaches his home at Shelbyville, Kentucky, on June 20, 1814, almost two years to the day since war was first declared. The invasion goes on. The battles of Chippawa and Lundy's Lane, the long siege of Fort Erie, and the naval encounter on Lake Champlain all lie ahead. But Atherton is out of it. He has had enough, will not fight again.

His story is not unique. Eighty or ninety Kentuckians have been captured by the Potawatomi braves, and of these a good number have been adopted into Indian families. Timothy Mallory has all his hair shaved off except for a scalp lock, his face painted half black, half red, his ears pierced for rings. John Davenport is painted, adorned with earrings, bracelets, and a silver band wound round his shaved skull. "We make an Indian out of you," one of his captors promises, "and by'n by you have squaw, by'n by you have a gun and horse and go hunting."

Both these men live as Indians for several months and like Atherton, who prefers his treatment by the Indians to that of the British (he finds them "brave, generous, hospitable, kind and...honest"), are surprised to discover that their Indian families are genuinely fond of them, that the women go out of their way to protect them when the braves indulge in drinking bouts, and that when at last they are ransomed, the Indians are clearly reluctant to part with them.

No one knows exactly how many Kentucky volunteers are held captive by the natives, adopted into families that have lost sons in the battle. No one knows exactly how many have escaped or been ransomed. It is possible, even probable, that as the war rolls on there are some Kentuckians who have gone entirely native, taken Indian wives and removed themselves from white society.

There is irony in this; but then it has been a war of irony and paradox – a war fought over a grievance that was removed before the fighting began; a war that all claimed to have won except the real victors, who, being Indians, were really losers; a war designed to seize by force a nation that could have been attached by stealth. Are there in the forests of Michigan among the Potawatomi – those veterans of Tippecanoe – certain warriors of lighter skin and alien background? If so, that is the final irony. Ever since Jefferson's day it has been official American policy to try to turn the Indians into white men. Who can blame the Indians if, in their last, desperate, doomed resistance, they should manage in some measure to turn the tables?

Sources and Acknowledgements
Notes
Select Bibliography
Index

Sources and Acknowledgements

This work is based largely on primary sources – official documents and correspondence, military reports and records, public speeches, private letters, diaries, journals, memoirs, and contemporary newspaper accounts. I have as well made a reconnaissance of those battlefields whose sites have not been obliterated by the advance of civilization.

As every lawyer knows, witnesses to any event rarely agree; thus it has often been necessary to compare various conflicting reports to arrive at an approximation of the truth. Confused recollections of even minor skirmishes are not easy to untangle. Each participant sees the engagement from his own point of view. Opposing generals invariably underestimate their own strength and overestimate that of the enemy, seeking in a variety of ways to shape their reports to make themselves seem brilliant. The memories of junior officers and common soldiers are distorted by the heat of the moment and often clouded by the passage of time. Fortunately, in almost every case there is such a richness of material available on the events of 1812–13 (much of the human detail ignored by historians) that it is possible to arrive at a reasonably clear and accurate account of what occurred, not only tactically and politically but also in the hearts and minds of the participants.

For each incident I have had to ask myself these questions: was the narrator – diarist, officer, soldier, correspondent, memoirist – present at the event described? How soon after the event did he set down his account of what happened? How competent was he as a witness? Can some of his statements be cross-checked against those of others to assess his credibility? A memoir written thirty years after the events, obviously, cannot be considered as reliable as one scribbled down on the spot.

Students of the war may be surprised that I have set aside John Richardson's famous account of the death of the young American captive after the battle of Brownstown (page 149) in favour of a less well known description by Thomas Verchères de Boucherville. Richardson, after all, belongs to the pantheon of early Canadian novelists; de Boucherville was only a fur trader and storekeeper. The two versions were both set down many years after the event and differ considerably in detail, Richardson's being the more dramatic. But a close reading of his account reveals that the future novelist, who was only fifteen at the time, was not actually present at the scene he describes while de Boucherville was. De Boucherville was also twelve years older and experienced in Indian customs. There can be no doubt that his version is the more reliable.

For the leading British, American, and Canadian figures in the war, a wealth of easily authenticated biographical and background material is available. But for the Indians, with two exceptions, there is very little. This was really their war; for them the stakes were higher, the victories more significant, the defeats more devastating. One would have liked to know more about Roundhead, Walk-in-the-Water, Black Bird, Little Turtle, and all the other shadowy tribesmen who appear briefly and often violently on the stage. History, alas, ignores them. They have come down to us as faceless "savages," brandishing their tomahawks, shouting their war cries, scalping their victims, melting into the forests.

Only Tecumseh and to some degree his brother, the Prophet, stand out as individuals – flesh-and-blood figures with human strengths, human weaknesses, and human emotions. Here, nevertheless, one must tread cautiously, for so much of their story – especially that of their early years – is overlaid with legend. It was Charles Goltz who recently revealed in his superb doctoral dissertation on the Shawnee brothers that one widely accepted tale of Tecumseh's early years was pure myth.

Most of his biographers have tried to explain Tecumseh's hatred of the white man with an anecdote about his father's death. As the story goes, the father was killed by a group of white hunters when he refused to act as their guide and died in the arms of his son, denouncing the faithlessness of white men. There is much detail: the mother at the graveside urging the young Shawnee to seek eternal revenge; Tecumseh's yearly visits to the scene to renew his pledge; and so on. But, as Goltz discovered, this web of convincing evidence was the invention of an Indiana woman who, in 1823, entered it in a fiction contest sponsored by the *New York Mirror*. The following year a Canadian magazine reprinted the tale, and it became accepted as history.

In compiling and sifting all this mountain of material I have again depended upon the extraordinary energy and wise counsel of the indefatigable Barbara Sears, for whom the term "research assistant" is scarcely adequate. I cannot praise her labours too highly. She and I wish to thank a number of people and institutions who helped make this work possible.

First, the Metropolitan Library of Toronto, with special thanks to Edith Firth and her staff at the Canadian History Department, to Michael Pearson and the staff of the History Department, and to Norma Dainard, Keith Alcock, and the staff of the newspaper section. Thanks also to Robert Fraser of the editorial staff of the *Dictionary of Canadian Biography*.

Second, the Public Archives of Canada, with special thanks to the staff of the manuscript division, to Patricia Kennedy of the Pre-Confederation Archives, to Peter Bower, Gordon Dodds, Bruce Wilson, and Brian Driscoll of British Archives, and to Glenn T. Wright and Grace Campbell of the Public Records Division; the Ontario Archives; the Library of Congress Manuscript Division; the Filson Club of Kentucky; and Peter Burroughs of Dalhousie University.

Third, the U.S. National Archives, Washington; the Buffalo Historical Society (Art Detmers); the Chatham Kent Museum (Mary Creasey); the Historical Society of Pennsylvania; the Indiana State Library; the Kentucky Historical Society; the Wisconsin Historical Society; the Lundy's Lane Historical Society; the Niagara Historical Society; the Niagara Parks Commission's Fort Erie staff; Parks Canada's staff at Fort George and Fort Malden; Robert S. Allen and Elizabeth Vincent at Parks Canada, Ottawa; the Public Record Office, London, England; the Tennessee State Museum; Esther Summers; Bob Green; Paul Romney; and Professor H.N. Muller.

I am especially grateful for the useful comments and suggestions made by Janice Tyrwhitt, Charles Templeton, Roger Hall, Elsa Franklin, Janet Berton, and Leslie Hannon, who read the manuscript at various stages. The several versions were typed by Ennis Armstrong, Catherine Black, and Lynne McCartney. I was rescued from certain grammatical imbecilities by my wife, Janet, and from various textual inconsistencies by my editor Janet Craig, for whose unsparing eye and great common sense I am specially grateful. The errors that remain are mine.

Kleinburg, Ontario
March, 1980

Notes

Abbreviations used:
ASPFR   American State Papers, Foreign Relations
ASPIA   American State Papers, Indian Affairs
ASPMA   American State Papers, Military Affairs
LC   Library of Congress
MTPL   Metropolitan Toronto Public Library
PAC   Public Archives of Canada
PAO   Public Archives of Ontario
SN   Secretary of the Navy
SW   Secretary of War
USNA   United States National Archives

Preview: Porter Hanks's War

page line

13 31 Brannan, pp. 34–35, Hanks to SW, 4 Aug. 1812.

14 11 Ibid.; May, p. 14.

14 35 Brannan, pp. 34–35, Hanks to SW, 4 Aug. 1812.

14 38 Ibid.

15 10 Jefferson, VI: 75–76, Jefferson to Duane, 4 Aug. 1812.

Overview

20 36 Bonney, p. 269, Sheaffe to Stephen Van Rensselaer, 16 Oct. 1812.

21 3 Kirby, p. 157.

23 18 PAC, RG 8, vol. 1219, p. 274, Prevost to Bathurst, 27 Aug. 1814.

23 23 PAC, MG 24 A57, vol. 19, Sherbrooke proclamation, 3 July 1812.

24 9 Quaife, *Askin Papers*, p. 709, [Askin] to McGill, 17 July 1812; p. 729, Brush to Askin, 11 Aug. 1812; p. 729, Brush to Askin, 24 Aug. 1812.

24 20 Quoted in Perkins, *Prologue*, p. 415.

25 8 Perkins, *Prologue*, pp. 90–93.

28 12 PAO, Register of persons connected with high treason during the War of 1812 with the U.S.A.

page line

28 24 PAC, RG 19 E5(a), vol. 3739, file 2, n.d. General abstract, claims for damages; *Upper Canada Gazette*, supplement, 3 June 1824.

Prelude to Invasion: 1807–1811

35 21 U.S. Congress, ASPFR, III: 17, Barron to SN, 7 April 1807.

37 2 Ibid., 18, Barron to SN, 23 June 1807, and enclosures; p. 19, return of dead and wounded; p. 19, Hunt to Gordon, 23 June 1807; p. 19, Smith, Smith and Brooker to Gordon, 23 June 1807; p. 21, L.W. Tazewell, report of court of inquiry; Steel, pp. 245–49.

37 9 Steel, pp. 250–52.

37 12 Quoted in Perkins, *Prologue*, p. 428.

38 3 Cruikshank, "Some Unpublished Letters," p. 19, Brock to Dunn, 17 July 1807.

38 12 Quoted in Burt, p. 243.

38 30 Burt, pp. 242–46.

39 1 Tupper, p. 64, Brock to Gordon, 6 Sept. 1807.

39 11 Harrison, I: 235, Harrison speech, 17 Aug. 1807.

39 20 Ibid., p. 236.

page	line	
40	*19*	Ibid., p. 234.
40	*40*	Jefferson, IV: 472, Jefferson to Harrison, 27 Feb. 1803.
41	*12*	Harrison, I: 251, Harrison to the Shawanese, Aug. 1807.
41	*32*	Ibid., pp. 183–84, Harrison to the Delawares, early 1806.
42	*10*	Ibid., p. 251, Harrison to the Shawanese, Aug. 1807.
43	*17*	Randall, pp. 462–63.
43	*28*	LC, Foster MSS, Foster to his mother, 31 July 1807.
43	*32*	Ibid., Foster to his mother, 20 Sept. 1806.
43	*33*	Foster, *Two Duchesses*, p. 228, Foster to his mother, 30 June 1805.
44	*4*	LC, Foster MSS, Foster to his mother, 16 July 1807.
44	*9*	Foster, *Two Duchesses*, p. 233, Foster to his mother, 30 July 1805.
44	*10*	Ibid., p. 240, Foster to his mother, 22 Feb. 1805.
44	*10*	Ibid., p. 233, Foster to his mother, 30 July 1805.
44	*12*	Ibid., p. 247, Foster to his mother, Nov. 1805.
45	*2*	LC, Foster MSS, Journal.
45	*36*	Quoted in Perkins, *Prologue*, p. 7.
45	*40*	Quoted in Perkins, *Prologue*, p. 187.
46	*34*	PAC, RG 10, vol. 11, Gore's speech, 11 July 1808.
47	*18*	PAC, RG 10, vol. 11, Indian reply, 13 July 1808.
48	*1*	Horsman, *Expansion*, p. 146.
48	*4*	Ibid.
48	*17*	Allen, p. 63.
48	*28*	Horsman, "British Indian Policy," pp. 53, 56.
49	*23*	PAC, RG 10, vol. 11, Gore to Craig, 27 July 1808.
50	*13*	Goltz.
50	*24*	Harrison, I: 365, Journal, 4 Oct. 1809.
51	*18*	Ibid., p. 367.
51	*30*	Ibid., p. 368.
51	*35*	Ibid., p. 389, Harrison to SW, 3 Nov. 1809.
51	*36*	Ibid., p. 376, Journal, 22 Sept. 1809.
52	*2*	Ibid., p. 389, Harrison to SW, 3 Nov. 1809.
52	*12*	Cleaves, p. 68.
52	*25*	Harrison, I: 419, Harrison to SW, 25 April 1810.
52	*28*	Ibid., p. 450, Harrison to SW, 25 July 1810.
52	*41*	Ibid., p. 448, Harrison to the Prophet, 19 July 1810.
53	*4*	Ibid., pp. 448–49.
53	*22*	Ibid., p. 456, Harrison to SW, 6 Aug. 1810.
53	*23*	Ibid.
54	*10*	Tucker, *Tecumseh*, p. 159.
54	*15*	Hatch, p. 113.
54	*27*	Tucker, *Tecumseh*, p. 160; Drake, pp. 125–26.
54	*38*	Tucker, *Tecumseh*, pp. 161, 348.
55	*6*	Harrison, I: 460, Harrison to SW, 22 Aug. 1810.
55	*22*	Hatch, pp. 99–100.
55	*40*	Klinck, p. 73.
56	*3*	Tucker, *Tecumseh*, pp. 163, 348.
56	*12*	Harrison, I: 466, Tecumseh's speech, 20 Aug. 1810.
56	*17*	Ibid., p. 463.
56	*28*	Ibid., p. 459, Harrison to SW, 22 Aug. 1810.
57	*3*	Cleaves, p. 74.
57	*10*	Harrison, I: 461, Harrison to SW, 22 Aug. 1810.
57	*12*	Ibid., pp. 461, 468.
57	*29*	Tucker, *Tecumseh*, pp. 166, 349.
57	*36*	Harrison, I: 469, Tecumseh's speech, 21 Aug. 1810.
60	*20*	Draper MSS, Tecumseh Papers, 2YY, p. 120, Ruddell's account of Tecumseh.
60	*35*	Ibid., 12YY, 1821, Drake's notes on conversation with Anthony Shane.
61	*4*	Ibid.
61	*12*	Ibid.
61	*25*	Tucker, *Tecumseh*, pp. 77–80; Randall, p. 455.
61	*29*	Draper MSS, Tecumseh Papers, 12YY, 1821, Drake's notes on conversation with Anthony Shane.

62 35 Harrison, I: 239, Wells to Harrison, 20 Aug. 1807.

64 3 PAC, CO 42/351/42, Elliott to Claus, 16 Nov. 1810, encl. Tecumseh's speech, 15 Nov. 1810.

64 22 Harrison, I: 447, Harrison to SW, 18 June 1810.

65 13 PAC, CO 42/351/ Elliott to Claus, 16 Nov. 1810.

65 22 Quoted in Goltz, Craig to Moirier, 25 Nov. 1811.

66 3 Weld, pp. 192–96.

66 14 Tupper, pp. 94–96, Brock to Craig, 27 Feb. 1811.

66 19 "Collections of Papers," pp. 280–81, Craig to Gore, 2 Feb. 1811.

67 15 Harrison, I: 546, Harrison to SW, 6 Aug. 1811.

68 2 Dawson, p. 184.

68 19 Drake, pp. 142–43.

68 33 Harrison, I: 549, Harrison to SW, 7 Aug. 1811.

69 6 Ibid.

69 28 Harrison, I: 527, Harrison to SW, 2 July 1811.

69 37 Ibid., p. 536, SW to Harrison, 20 July 1811.

70 13 Ibid., p. 550, Harrison to SW, 7 Aug. 1811.

70 29 Ibid., p. 558, Daviess to Harrison, 24 Aug. 1811.

70 36 " Jo Daviess," p. 355.

72 1 Harrison, I: 620, Harrison to SW, 18 Nov. 1811.

73 2 Ibid., p. 703, statement of William Brigham.

73 10 Ibid., p. 702, statement of Sergeant Orr.

73 25 Ibid., pp. 691–92, Harrison to Dr. John Scott, Dec. 1811.

74 21 Cleaves, pp. 100–101.

74 30 Ibid., p. 101.

74 36 Ibid.

75 4 Lossing, *Field-book*, p. 205.

75 10 Harrison, I: 703, statement of William Brigham.

75 15 Ibid., p. 624, Harrison to SW, 18 Nov. 1811.

75 22 Ibid., p. 702; Walker, pp. 24–25.

76 10 Cruikshank, *Documents Relating to the Invasion*, p. 6, Elliott to Brock, 12 Jan. 1812.

76 30 U.S. Congress, ASPIA, I: 808, opinions of Gov. Howard and Gen. Clark, 3 March 1812.

76 38 Tucker, *Tecumseh*, p. 230.

Prelude to Invasion: 1812

82 29 Tupper, p. 151, Brock to Prevost, 12 Feb. 1812.

83 5 Nursey, p. 82.

83 19 Tupper, p. 153, Brock to Prevost, Feb. 1812.

83 25 Ibid., p. 153.

84 2 Ibid., p. 125, Brock to Prevost, 2 Dec. 1811.

84 15 Ibid., p. 95, Brock to Craig, 27 Feb. 1811.

84 16 Ibid., p. 195, Brock to Prevost, 3 July 1812.

84 34 Ibid., pp. 123–30, Brock to Prevost, 2 Dec. 1811.

85 24 Wood, I: 423, ? to Dickson, 27 Feb. 1812.

85 35 Caffrey, p. 142.

86 6 Ibid.

86 23 Quoted in Perkins, *Prologue*, p. 275.

86 29 LC, Foster MSS, Foster to his mother, 2 Jan. 1812.

86 33 Ibid., Journal, 15 April 1812.

87 13 Quoted in Brown, p. 55.

87 17 LC, Foster MSS, Journal, 29 and 30 Jan. 1812.

87 18 Ibid., Journal, 31 Jan. 1812.

87 28 U.S. Congress, ASPFR, III: 546–47, Craig to Henry, 6 Feb. 1809.

87 34 Morison, pp. 271–72.

88 4 Quoted in Cruikshank, *Political Adventures*, p. 126.

88 15 LC, Foster MSS, Journal, 19 Feb. 1812.

88 22 Ibid.

88 26 Ibid., Journal, 20 Jan. 1812, 5 Feb. 1812.

89 20 Cruikshank, *Documents Relating to the Invasion*, p. 22, Hull to SW, 6 March 1812.

90 3 Mahon, p. 44.

page	line	
		1816, proceedings of inquiry; Cook, p. 29.
112	*36*	Porter, p. 263.
112	*40*	Ibid., p. 262.
113	*4*	Ibid., pp. 263–71.

Detroit

page	line	
118	*8*	Beall, p. 786.
118	*27*	Ibid., p. 787.
119	*8*	Ibid.
121	*32*	Ibid., p. 788.
121	*37*	Ibid., p. 789.
122	*33*	Ibid., pp. 789–90.
123	*8*	Ibid., p. 791.
123	*29*	Lossing, *Field-book*, p. 258.
124	*8*	Hull, *Memoirs*, p. 76.
124	*16*	Williams, p. 12, Hull to Meigs, 11 July 1812.
124	*20*	Ibid., pp. 13–14.
124	*40*	Cruikshank, *Documents Relating to the Invasion*, pp. 40–41, Hull to St. George, 6 July 1812.
125	*13*	Ibid., p. 41, St. George to Hull, 6 July 1812.
125	*28*	Ibid., p. 47, St. George to Brock, 8 July 1812.
125	*31*	Ibid., p. 74, Brock to Prevost, 20 July 1812.
126	*4*	Ibid., p. 45, St. George to Brock, 8 July 1812.
126	*10*	Ibid., p. 46.
126	*20*	Beall, p. 793.
126	*36*	Tucker, *Tecumseh*, p. 243.
127	*3*	Drake, p. 163.
127	*11*	Tucker, *Tecumseh*, p. 245.
127	*24*	Lucas, *Journal*, p. 27.
128	*6*	Cruikshank, *Documents Relating to the Invasion*, p. 51, St. George to Brock, 10 July 1812; p. 61, St. George to Brock, 15 July 1812.
128	*9*	Beall, p. 795.
128	*19*	Lossing, *Field-book*, p. 262; Woodford, p. 59.
128	*30*	Cruikshank, *Documents Relating to the Invasion*, p. 214, Cochran to his mother, 13 Sept. 1812.
128	*36*	Hatch, p. 28.
129	*2*	Beall, p. 795.
130	*20*	Cruikshank, *Documents Relating to the Invasion*, pp. 58–60.
130	*27*	Ibid., p. 157, Brock to Prevost, 17 Aug. 1812.

page	line	
130	*29*	Ibid., pp. 62–63, Elliott to Claus, 15 July 1812.
130	*37*	Smith, p. 83.
132	*9*	*Montreal Herald*, 4 July 1812.
132	*24*	Ibid.
133	*1*	Tupper, p. 201, Prevost to Brock, 10 July 1812.
133	*4*	Ibid., p. 201.
133	*17*	Ibid., pp. 5–6.
133	*21*	Nursey, p. 30.
133	*23*	Tupper, pp. 25–26.
133	*27*	Ibid., p. 258.
134	*7*	PAC, CO 42/146/42, Prevost to Liverpool, 3 March 1812.
134	*13*	Ibid.
134	*20*	PAC, CO 42/147/18, Prevost to Liverpool, 25 July 1812.
134	*35*	Tupper, pp. 200–201, Prevost to Brock, 10 July 1812.
135	*7*	Lucas, *Journal*, p. 174.
135	*37*	Ibid., pp. v and vi.
136	*25*	PAC, RG 19, E5(a), vol. 3746, no. 423.
136	*28*	PAC, RG 19, E5(a), vol. 3728, no. 147.
136	*29*	Ibid., no. 156.
136	*31*	Ibid., no. 137.
136	*34*	Ibid., no. 171.
137	*2*	PAC, RG 19, E5(a), vol. 3752, no. 1196.
137	*8*	PAC, RG 19, E5(a), vol. 3751, no. 1072; Hull, *Report*, p. 152.
137	*11*	PAC, RG 19, E5(a), vol. 3746, no. 423.
137	*17*	PAC, RG 19, E5(a), vol. 3728, nos. 44 and 51.
137	*20*	Cruikshank, *Documents Relating to the Invasion*, p. 49, Dixon to Bruyères, 8 July 1812; p. 61, St. George to Brock, 15 July 1812.
137	*24*	Ibid., p. 63, Elliott to Claus, 15 July 1812.
137	*27*	Lucas, *Journal*, p. 42.
137	*34*	Ibid., p. 28.
138	*18*	Ibid., p. 36.
138	*29*	Quoted in Oman, p. 42.
139	*6*	PAC, RG 8, vol. 165, return of regimental courts martial, 103rd Regt., 22 April to 10 Oct. 1812.
139	*22*	Hull, *Report*, Hull's defence, pp. 44–45.
139	*36*	Ibid., p. 57.

page	line	
139	38	Ibid., p. 45.
140	12	Cruikshank, *Documents Relating to the Invasion*, p. 76.
140	15	Richardson, *Richardson's War*, p. 32.
140	30	Beall, p. 799.
141	3	Ibid., p. 800.
141	7	Ibid., p. 802.
141	16	Hull, *Report*, p. 135.
141	18	Cruikshank, *Documents Relating to the Invasion*, pp. 185–86, Hull to SW, 26 Aug. 1812.
141	36	Beall, p. 805.
142	10	Cruikshank, *Documents Relating to the Invasion*, pp. 195–96, Brock, speech on opening legislature.
142	13	Ibid., p. 75, Brock to Prevost, 20 July 1812.
142	21	Ibid., p. 93, Talbot to Brock, 27 July 1812.
142	28	Quoted in Hamil, p. 46.
142	32	Cruikshank, *Documents Relating to the Invasion*, p. 196, Brock, speech on opening the legislature.
143	2	Cruikshank, *Documentary History*, III: 152, Brock to Baynes, 29 July 1812.
143	8	Ibid., p. 146, Brock to Prevost, 26 July 1812.
143	12	Ibid.
143	19	Cruikshank, *Documents Relating to the Invasion*, p. 196, Brock, speech on opening the legislature.
143	24	Ibid., pp. 119–20, Brock to Baynes, 4 Aug. 1812.
144	20	Ibid., p. 119.
144	25	Cruikshank, *Documentary History*, III: 152, Brock to Baynes, 29 July 1812.
145	21	Cruikshank, *Documents Relating to the Invasion*, p. 82, Brock, proclamation, 22 July 1812.
145	30	Ibid., p. 120, Brock to Baynes, 4 Aug. 1812.
145	37	Ibid., p. 197, Brock, speech on opening the legislature.
148	25	Lucas, *Journal*, pp. 46–51.
149	34	Quaife, *War*, pp. 92–93.
150	17	Hull, *Report*, p. 57.
150	20	Lucas, *Journal*, p. 52.
150	22	Quaife, *War*, p. 277.
150	26	Ibid.
151	2	Hull, *Memoirs*, p. 61.
151	33	Hull, *Report*, p. 58.
151	36	Hull, *Memoirs*, p. 64.
152	2	Cruikshank, *Documents Relating to the Invasion*, p. 219, Cass to SW, 10 Sept. 1812.
152	5	Hatch, p. 35.
152	7	Lucas, *Journal*, p. 105.
152	19	PAC, CO 42/147/80, Prevost to Liverpool, 5 Aug. 1812.
152	23	Ibid.
152	34	Ibid.
153	40	U.S. Congress, ASPMA, I: 323, Strong to Eustis, 5 Aug. 1812.
154	7	Ibid., pp. 325–26, Smith to Eustis, 2 July 1812.
154	13	Cruikshank, *Documents Relating to the Invasion*, p. 40, SW to Dearborn, 26 June 1812.
154	21	USNA, M221/43, Dearborn to SW, 13 July 1812.
154	25	Quoted in Adams, VI: 308, Eustis to Dearborn, 9 July 1812.
154	30	USNA, M221/43, Dearborn to SW, 13 July 1812.
154	36	Ibid., Dearborn to SW, 28 July 1812.
155	31	PAC, RG 8, vol. 677, pp. 31–32, Baynes to Prevost, 12 Aug. 1812, encl. report.
155	39	Ibid., p. 30.
156	11	Cruikshank, *Documents Relating to the Invasion*, p. 128, Dearborn to SW, 9 Aug. 1812.
156	15	Ibid., p. 127.
157	23	PAC, RG 8, vol. 677, pp. 33–34, Baynes to Prevost, 12 Aug. 1812, encl. report.
157	33	Ibid., p. 35.
158	13	Ibid., p. 37.
158	22	Cruikshank, *Documents Relating to the Invasion*, p. 129, Dearborn to Hull, 9 Aug. 1812.
159	3	Quaife, *War*, p. 94.
159	26	Quaife, "Brownstown," p. 74.
160	5	Richardson, *Richardson's War*, p. 34.
160	17	Quaife, *War*, p. 96.
160	19	Ibid.

page	line	
160	37	Ibid., p. 97.
161	3	Richardson, *Richardson's War*, p. 37.
161	5	Ibid.
161	12	Quaife, *War*, p. 97.
161	20	Ibid.; Quaife, "Brownstown," p. 75.
161	33	Quaife, "Brownstown," p. 77.
162	35	Quaife, *War*, pp. 103–5.
162	37	Cruikshank, *Documents Relating to the Invasion*, pp. 139–41, Hull to SW, 13 Aug. 1812.
163	8	Hull, *Report*, pp. 107–8.
163	10	Pearkes, p. 459.
163	21	Cruikshank, *Documents Relating to the Invasion*, p. 136, Procter to Brock, 11 Aug. 1812; p. 141, return of killed and wounded at Maguaga; p. 140, Hull to SW, 13 Aug. 1812.
163	24	Ibid., p. 195, Brock to Liverpool, 29 Aug. 1812, enclosure A.
163	32	Ibid., p. 192.
164	9	Ibid., pp. 130–31, Macdonald to Cameron, 10 Aug. 1812; Wood, I: 533, Askin Journal.
164	16	Wood, I: 535, Askin Journal; Pearkes, p. 459.
164	24	Cruikshank, *Documents Relating to the Invasion*, p. 193, Brock to Liverpool, 29 Aug. 1812.
164	31	Tupper, p. 259.
165	4	Wood, I: 534–35, Askin Journal; p. 548, McCay Diary.
165	14	Tupper, p. 243.
166	2	Ibid.
166	11	Cruikshank, *Documents Relating to the Invasion*, p. 192, Brock to Liverpool, 29 Aug. 1812.
166	12	Tupper, p. 262.
166	19	Tucker, *Tecumseh*, p. 264.
166	37	Tupper, pp. 260–61.
167	5	Nursey, p. 118; Tupper, p. 244.
167	18	Tucker, *Tecumseh*, p. 265; Nursey, pp. 118–19.
167	27	Tupper, p. 245.
167	37	Cruikshank, *Documents Relating to the Invasion*, p. 142, District General Order, 14 Aug. 1812.
168	10	Hull, *Report*, p. 135.
169	12	Lucas, *Journal*, pp. 59–60.
169	21	Cramer, p. 132; Van Deusen, p. 579.
169	33	Cruikshank, *Documents Relating to the Invasion*, p. 137, Cass to Meigs, 12 Aug. 1812; p. 219, Cass to SW, 10 Sept. 1812.
169	34	Ibid., p. 138.
170	18	Lossing, *Field-book*, p. 285.
170	21	Quaife, *Askin Papers*, p. 730, John Askin Jr. to John Askin Sr., 16 Sept. 1812.
170	25	Hull, *Report*, Hull's defence, p. 85.
171	2	Richardson, *Richardson's War*, pp. 49–51; Hull, *Report*, p. 82.
171	8	Lucas, *Journal*, p. 62.
171	31	Cruikshank, *Documents Relating to the Invasion*, p. 144, Brock to Hull, 15 Aug. 1812.
172	18	Ibid., pp. 144–45, Hull to Brock, 15 Aug. 1812.
172	27	Hull, *Report*, pp. 35–36.
172	30	Ibid., p. 150.
173	2	Lossing, *Field-book*, p. 287.
173	9	Ibid.
173	17	Witherell, p. 304.
173	24	Ibid., p. 303.
173	28	Hull, *Report*, p. 89.
173	32	Ibid., pp. 36–37.
173	33	Ibid., p. 89.
174	8	Lossing, *Field-book*, p. 285; Byfield, p. 65.
174	20	Quaife, *War*, p. 108.
174	28	Wood, I: 536.
175	4	Cruikshank, *Documents Relating to the Invasion*, p. 158, Brock to Prevost, 17 Aug. 1812; p. 187, Hull to SW, 26 Aug. 1812; pp. 219–20, Cass to SW, 10 Sept. 1812.
175	13	Wood, I: 536.
176	4	Ibid., p. 550, McCay Diary, 16 Aug. 1812.
176	7	Richardson, *Richardson's War*, p. 55.
176	17	Tupper, p. 260.
176	20	Clarke, p. 455.
176	23	Ibid., p. 456.
176	26	Richardson, *Richardson's War*, p. 55.
177	10	Cruikshank, "General Hull's Invasion," p. 281.
177	21	Hull, *Report*, pp. 90–91; Clarke, p. 450.

page	line	
215	*25*	Wood, I: 587, Brock to Prevost, 7 Sept. 1812.
215	*26*	Ibid., pp. 586–87.
215	*40*	Ibid., p. 587.
216	*5*	Ibid.
216	*22*	Cruikshank, *Documentary History*, III: 271–73, Brock to Procter, 17 Sept. 1812; Wood, I: 593, Brock to Prevost, 18 Sept. 1812.
216	*27*	Wood, I: 593, Brock to Prevost, 18 Sept. 1812.
216	*31*	Ibid., p. 593; Cruikshank, *Documentary History*, IV: 36–37, Prevost to Bathurst, 5 Oct. 1812.
216	*40*	Wood, I: 596, Brock to Prevost, 28 Sept. 1812.
217	*6*	Tupper, p. 316, Brock to Savery Brock, 18 Sept. 1812.
217	*25*	Ibid., p. 325, Prevost to Brock, 25 Sept. 1812.
217	*31*	Ibid.
217	*38*	Ibid., p. 314, Brock to Prevost, 18 Sept. 1812.
218	*5*	Ibid., pp. 315–16, Brock to Savery Brock, 18 Sept. 1812.
218	*10*	Ibid., p. 316.
218	*16*	Wood, I: 588–89, Brock to Prevost, 13 Sept. 1812.
218	*18*	Tupper, p. 316, Brock to Savery Brock, 18 Sept. 1812.
218	*26*	PAC, RG 8, vol. 677, p. 131, note signed "Winfield Scott," Nov. 1863.
218	*32*	Wood, I: 588–89, Brock to Prevost, 18 Sept. 1812.
218	*40*	Tupper, p. 317, Brock to Savery Brock, 18 Sept. 1812.
219	*12*	Ibid., pp. 316–17.
219	*29*	Bonney, p. 221, Lovett to Van Vechten, 28 Aug. 1812.
219	*36*	Cruikshank, *Documentary History*, III: 227, Stephen Van Rensselaer to Tompkins, 31 Aug. 1812.
220	*3*	Tompkins, III: 105, Tompkins to Porter, 9 Sept. 1812.
220	*23*	Cruikshank, *Documentary History*, III: 223–24, Porter to Tompkins, 30 Aug. 1812.
220	*27*	Bonney, p. 228, Lovett to Alexander, 6 Sept. 1812.
220	*30*	Ibid., p. 239, Lovett to Van Vechten, 8 Sept. 1812.
221	*2*	USNA, M221/43/D130, Dearborn to SW, 15 Aug. 1812.
221	*6*	USNA, M221/43/D154, Dearborn to SW, 22 Aug. 1812.
221	*10*	USNA, M221/43, Dearborn to SW, 14 Sept. 1812.
221	*13*	USNA, M221/43/D145, encl. Wadsworth, 26 Aug. 1812 (extract).
221	*18*	USNA, M221/43/D146, Dearborn to SW, 4 Sept. 1812.
221	*21*	USNA, M221/43/D158, Dearborn to SW, 8 Sept. 1812.
221	*26*	USNA, M221/43, Dearborn to SW, 14 Sept. 1812.
221	*35*	Bonney, p. 231, Solomon Van Rensselaer to Lewis, 11 Sept. 1812.
221	*39*	Ibid.
222	*9*	Cruikshank, *Documentary History*, III: 264–65, Stephen Van Rensselaer to Tompkins, 15 Sept. 1812.
222	*17*	Bonney, p. 233, Stephen Van Rensselaer to Dearborn, 17 Sept. 1812; p. 236, Stephen Van Rensselaer to Tompkins, 17 Sept. 1812.
222	*24*	Ibid., p. 237, Lovett to Alexander, 22 Sept. 1812; p. 242, Lovett to Alexander, 6 Oct. 1812.
222	*30*	Ibid., pp. 242–43, Lovett to Alexander, 6 Oct. 1812.
222	*32*	Ibid., p. 228, Lovett to Alexander, 6 Sept. 1812.
222	*38*	Ibid., p. 243, Lovett to Alexander, 6 Oct. 1812.
223	*1*	Cruikshank, *Documentary History*, III: 295–96, Dearborn to Stephen Van Rensselaer, 26 Sept. 1812.
223	*7*	Ibid., p. 296.
223	*12*	Ibid.
223	*26*	Ibid., p. 300, Smyth to Stephen Van Rensselaer, 29 Sept. 1812.
223	*29*	Van Rensselaer, p. 18.
224	*6*	Cruikshank, *Documentary History*, IV: 41, Stephen Van Rensselaer to Dearborn, 8 Oct. 1812.

334

page line

224   14   Ibid.
224   23   Ibid.
224   36   Ibid., p. 42.
224   40   Bonney, p. 242, Stephen Van
           Rensselaer to Smyth, 5 Oct.
           1812.
225   1   Ibid., p. 242, Stephen Van
           Rensselaer to Smyth, 6 Oct.
           1812.
225   4   Cruikshank, *Documentary His-
           tory*, IV: 79, Stephen Van
           Rensselaer to Eustis, 14 Oct.
           1812.
225   5   Severance, p. 218.
225   11   Cruikshank, *Documentary His-
           tory*, IV: 41, Stephen Van
           Rensselaer to Dearborn, 8 Oct.
           1812.
225   31   Cruikshank, *Documentary His-
           tory*, IV: 45, Elliott to SN, 9 Oct.
           1812.
225   37   Roach, p. 132.
226   3   Ibid., pp. 132–33.
226   11   Ibid., p. 134.
226   29   Ibid., pp. 134–35; Cruikshank,
           Documentary History, IV: 52,
           Hall to Stephen Van Rensselaer,
           10 Oct. 1812; p. 54, inquiry on
           loss of Detroit.
227   3   Richardson, *Richardson's War*,
           pp. 50–51.
227   9   Wood, I: 601–3, Brock to
           Prevost, 11 Oct. 1812; Cruik-
           shank, *Documentary History*, IV:
           60–62, quoting *Buffalo Gazette*,
           13 Oct. 1812.
227   17   Cruikshank, *Documentary His-
           tory*, IV: 60–62, quoting *Buffalo
           Gazette*, 13 Oct. 1812; pp. 45–
           47, Elliott to SN, 9 Oct. 1812, 10
           Oct. 1812; Elliott, pp. 51–53.
227   27   Wood, I: 601–3, Brock to
           Prevost, 11 Oct. 1812.
227   32   Ibid.
228   22   Cruikshank, *Documentary His-
           tory*, IV: 80–81, Stephen Van
           Rensselaer to Eustis, 14 Oct.
           1812; Van Rensselaer, pp. 21–23.
228   28   Bonney, p. 249
228   31   Cruikshank, *Documentary His-
           tory*, IV: 60, Fenwick to Stephen
           Van Rensselaer, undated.

page line

228   32   Ibid., p. 81, Stephen Van
           Rensselaer to Eustis, 14 Oct.
           1812.
228   38   Bonney, p. 251, Van Vechten to
           Solomon Van Rensselaer, 12 Oct.
           1812.
228   41   Cruikshank, *Documentary His-
           tory*, IV: 81, Stephen Van Rens-
           selaer to Eustis, 14 Oct. 1812.
229   4   Bonney, p. 271, Lovett to Van
           Vechten, 21 Oct. 1812.
229   14   PAC, MG 24 F70, Thomas
           Evans to ?, 15 Oct. 1812.
232   3   Ibid.
232   9   Scott, pp. 56–57.
232   10   Cruikshank, *Documentary His-
           tory*, IV: 96, Chrystie to
           Cushing, 22 Feb. 1813.
232   11   Ibid., p. 96; p. 81, Stephen Van
           Rensselaer to Eustis, 14 Oct.
           1812.
232   17   Scott, pp. 56–57; Elliott, p. 57;
           Cruikshank, *Documentary His-
           tory*, IV: 96, Chrystie to
           Cushing, 22 Feb. 1813.
232   27   Bonney, p. 279, Lovett to
           Alexander, 4 Nov. 1812; Cruik-
           shank, *Documentary History*, IV:
           93, Col. Meade's statement, 18
           Nov. 1812.
233   12   Bonney, p. 266, Lovett to
           Alexander, 14 Oct. 1812.
233   22   Cruikshank, *Documentary His-
           tory*, IV: 103, [J.B. Robinson] to
           ?, 14 Oct. 1812.
233   33   Stubbs, pp. 24–25.
234   7   Bonney, p. 266, Lovett to
           Alexander, 14 Oct. 1812.
234   17   Cruikshank, *Documentary His-
           tory*, IV: 96–97, Chrystie to
           Cushing, 22 Feb. 1813.
234   20   Van Rensselaer, pp. 28–29.
234   25   Ibid., p. 29.
234   32   Cruikshank, *Documentary His-
           tory*, IV: 98, Chrystie to
           Cushing, 22 Feb. 1813.
234   38   Cruikshank, "Letters of 1812,"
           pp. 45–47, C. Askin to J. Askin,
           14 Oct. 1812.
235   4   Cruikshank, *Documentary His-
           tory*, IV: 98, Chrystie to
           Cushing, 22 Feb. 1813.

page	line	
235	11	Bonney, pp. 275–76, Lovett to Alexander, 2 Nov. 1812.
235	29	Ibid., p. 272, Wool to Solomon Van Rensselaer, 23 Oct. 1812; pp. 267–68, Lovett to Alexander, 14 Oct. 1812; Crooks, p. 40.
237	14	Bonney, p. 272, Wool to Solomon Van Rensselaer, 23 Oct. 1812.
237	32	Nursey, pp. 158–59.
238	4	Robinson, p. 34, Robinson to ?, 14 Oct. 1812.
238	16	Ibid., p. 104.
238	40	Wood, I: 605–8, Sheaffe to Prevost, 13 Oct. 1812.
239	33	Cruikshank, *Documentary History*, IV: 116, Jarvis narrative.
239	36	Ibid.
240	8	Fortescue, p. 540.
240	10	Elliott, p. 61.
240	32	Canadian War Museum, Brock uniform; Elliott, p. 61; Kosche, pp. 33–56.
240	34	Cruikshank, *Documentary History*, IV: 116, Jarvis narrative.
240	37	Robinson, p. 35, Robinson to ?, 14 Oct. 1812.
241	5	Ibid., p. 36.
241	19	Cruikshank, *Documentary History*, IV: 105, [J.B. Robinson] to ?, 14 Oct. 1812.
241	20	Ibid., p. 116, Jarvis narrative.
241	26	Ibid., p. 115, McLean narrative, from *Quebec Mercury*, 27 Oct. 1812.
241	27	Robinson, pp. 36–37, Robinson to ?, 14 Oct. 1812.
241	29	Cruikshank, *Documentary History*, IV: 115, McLean narrative, from *Quebec Mercury*, 27 Oct. 1812.
241	31	Ibid., p. 115.
241	32	Ibid.
242	16	Cruikshank, *Documentary History*, IV: 101, Chrystie to Cushing, 22 Feb. 1813.
243	12	Elliott, pp. 63–64.
243	17	Scott, pp. 59–60.
243	24	Ibid., p. 60; Wood, III, part 2, p. 560, Merritt Journal.
243	35	Elliott, p. 65.
244	1	Fortescue, p. 54.
244	16	Bonney, p. 267, Lovett to Van Vechten, 14 Oct. 1812.
244	21	Scott, p. 60.
244	35	Crooks, pp. 32–33.
245	21	Ibid., pp. 33–34.
246	4	Ibid., p. 34.
246	30	Zaslow, pp. 39–40.
246	36	Norton, pp. 306–8.
247	3	Johnston, p. 101–2.
247	11	Wood, III, part 2, p. 561, Merritt Journal.
247	16	Crooks, p. 36.
247	20	Ibid.
247	27	Elliott, p. 65.
247	36	Crooks, p. 37.
248	10	Ibid.
248	14	Elliott, p. 66.
248	29	Cruikshank, *Documentary History*, IV: 102–3, Chrystie to Cushing, 22 Feb. 1813; Scott, pp. 60–61; Robinson, pp. 37–38, Robinson to ?, 14 Oct. 1812.
248	32	Scott, pp. 61–62.
249	2	Elliott, p. 67; Scott, p. 62.
249	8	Scott, pp. 62–63.
249	13	Zaslow, p. 43.
249	18	Elliott, p. 67.
249	20	Cruikshank, *Documentary History*, IV: 74, return, 15 Oct. 1812.
249	32	Stubbs, pp. 25–29.
249	39	Bonney, p. 268, Lovett to Alexander, 14 Oct. 1812; p. 274, Lovett to Alexander, 25 Oct. 1812; Van Rensselaer, p. 24.
250	5	Crooks, p. 37.
250	9	Cruikshank, *Documentary History*, IV: 74, return, 15 Oct. 1812.
250	18	Ryerson, pp. 368–71.
251	9	Cruikshank, *Documentary History*, IV: 83, Glegg to Brock, 14 Oct. 1812.
251	12	Ibid., p. 146, Ridout to his brother, 21 Oct. 1812.
251	16	Nursey, p. 213.
251	27	MTPL, S135, Sandham Col., Ilbert to Taylor, 22 Oct. 1812.
251	30	PAC, MG 24 B16, Cochran MSS, Cochran to Stewart, 25 Oct. 1812.

page line

251 31 Cruikshank, *Documentary History*, IV: 148, Prevost to Bathurst, 21 Oct. 1812.
251 37 Tupper, pp. 338–39; PAC, CO 42/147/233, 8 Dec. 1812, (Bathurst) to Prevost; Cruikshank, *Documentary History*, V, General Order, 10 March 1813.
251 40 Wood, III, part 2, p. 564, Merritt Journal.
252 10 Cruikshank, *Documentary History*, IV: 147.
252 18 Bonney, p. 274, Lovett to Alexander, 25 Oct. 1812.
253 2 *Kingston Gazette*, 24 Oct. 1812.
253 15 *York Gazette*, 12 Dec. 1812.
253 21 Loyal and Patriotic Society, *Report*, p. 365, Appendix no. 1, 22 Nov. 1812 (sermon).
254 12 PAO, Tupper MSS, Robinson to Tupper, 15 April 1846.
254 14 *Canadian Monthly*, July 1874.
254 16 Quoted in Berger, p. 97.

Black Rock
258 5 Severance, p. 228.
258 31 Cruikshank, *Documentary History*, IV: 194, Smyth's proclamation, 10 Nov. 1812.
259 8 Severance, p. 222, Smyth to Dearborn, 30 Oct. 1812.
259 10 Ibid.
259 16 Ibid., pp. 223–24, Smyth to Dearborn, 9 Nov. 1812; Cruikshank, *Documentary History*, IV: 249, statement of David Harvey.
259 23 Severance, p. 225, Smyth to Dearborn, 9 Nov. 1812.
259 25 Ibid., p. 225.
259 33 Lossing, *Field-book*, p. 426.
259 37 Cruikshank, *Documentary History*, IV: 227–28, Myers to Sheaffe, 22 [Nov.] 1812; pp. 233–35, McFeeley to Smyth, n.d.
259 39 Severance, p. 231.
260 4 Ibid., p. 232, Smyth to Porter [27 Nov. 1812].
260 17 Cruikshank, *Documentary History*, IV: 253–56, Bisshopp to Sheaffe, 1 Dec. 1812; pp. 260–63, Winder to Smyth, 7 Dec. 1812.

page line

260 25 Severance, p. 233.
260 28 Cruikshank, *Documentary History*, IV: 252, Sheaffe to Prevost, 30 Nov. 1812.
260 31 Ibid., p. 250, Smyth to Bisshopp, 28 Nov. 1812; p. 251, Bisshopp's reply, n.d.
260 34 Severance, p. 233.
261 13 Ibid., p. 234, Smyth to his "Hearts of War," 29 Nov. 1812.
261 25 Ibid., pp. 237–38, Smyth to McClure and others, 3 Dec. 1812.
261 33 Ibid., pp. 237–38; Lossing, *Field-book*, pp. 430–31.
262 12 Lossing, *Field-book*, p. 431.
262 16 *York Gazette*, 12 Dec. 1812, deposition of Bill Sherman, dated 3 Dec. 1812.
262 21 Severance, pp. 240–41, Porter to *Buffalo Gazette*, 8 Dec. 1812; *York Gazette*, 12 Dec. 1812, deposition of Bill Sherman.
262 23 *Buffalo Gazette*, 15 Dec. 1812.
262 31 Severance, p. 243, Tompkins to Fleming, 2 Jan. 1813.
263 7 USNA, M221/43/D227, Dearborn to SW, 8 Nov. 1812.
263 9 USNA, M221/43/D254, Dearborn to SW, 24 Nov. 1812.
263 13 Mann, p. 39; USNA, M221/43/D262, Dearborn to SW, 11 Dec. 1812.
263 27 USNA, M221/43/254, Dearborn to SW, 24 Nov. 1812.
263 30 USNA, M221/43/D262, Dearborn to SW, 11 Dec. 1812.

Frenchtown
267 10 Clay, p. 715, speech, 16 Aug. 1812.
267 18 Ibid., p. 697, Clay to Monroe, 29 July 1812.
268 2 Quoted in Mason, p. 84.
268 15 Ibid., p. 86.
269 14 Cruikshank, "Harrison and Procter," p. 151.
269 19 Hammack, p. 27.
269 29 Quoted in Hammack, p. 11.
270 1 Ibid., 7 July 1812.
270 3 Ibid., p. 21.

page	line		page	line	
270	7	*Niles Register*, 30 Nov. 1811; Mason, p. 79.			160–61, Harrison to Winchester, 4 Oct. 1812
270	27	Harrison, II: 91, Gibson to Hargrove, 20 Aug. 1812.	275	17	Cruikshank, "Harrison and Procter," p. 134.
270	39	Clay, p. 720, Clay to Monroe, 25 Aug. 1812.	275	27	Quoted in Cleaves, p. 126.
			275	33	Ibid.
271	2	Cruikshank, "Harrison and Procter," p. 130.	275	37	Harrison, II: 136–37, SW to Harrison, 17 Sept. 1812.
271	10	Harrison, II: 99, Harrison to SW, 28 Aug. 1812.	276	4	Ibid., pp. 156–57, Harrison to SW, 27 Sept. 1812.
271	13	Cleaves, p. 117; Harrison, II: 98–99, Harrison to SW, 28 Aug. 1812.	276	12	Ibid., pp. 167–72, Tupper to Harrison, 12 Oct. 1812.
			277	6	Darnell, pp. 27–28, 9 Oct. 1812.
271	15	Winchester, *Historical Details*, pp. 9–10; DeWitt, p. 90.	277	22	Lossing, *Field-book*, p. 348; Cleaves, p. 127.
271	16	Ibid.	277	24	Harrison, II: 184, Harrison to Eustis, 22 Oct. 1814.
271	17	Ibid.			
271	24	Harrison, II: 100, Harrison to SW, 28 Aug. 1812.	277	28	Ibid., pp. 153–54, Shelby to Harrison, 26 Sept. 1812.
271	28	Ibid.; ibid., pp. 103–4, Harrison to SW, 29 Aug. 1812.	277	39	Ibid., pp. 192–93, Shelby to Harrison, 1 Nov. 1812.
271	34	Ibid., pp. 103–4.	278	3	Ibid., p. 192.
272	8	Darnell, 1 Sept. 1812.	278	4	Ibid., p. 201, Shelby to Harrison, 7 Nov. 1812.
272	10	Harrison, II: 92, SW to Harrison, 22 Aug. 1812; DeWitt, p. 90.	278	9	Ibid., p. 177, Harrison to SW, 13 Oct. 1812.
272	16	Harrison, II: 110, Harrison to SW, 3 Sept. 1812.	278	10	Ibid., p. 133, Gibson to Hargrove, 12 Sept. 1812.
272	27	Cleaves, p. 119.	278	15	Ibid., pp. 124–28, Taylor to Harrison, 10 Sept. 1812.
272	29	Darnell, 5 Sept. 1812.			
273	5	Northcutt, p. 170.	278	25	Ibid., p. 242, Harrison to SW, 12 Dec. 1812; pp. 182–84, Harrison to SW, 22 Oct. 1812.
273	7	Harrison, II: 143–47, Harrison to SW, 21 Sept. 1812.			
273	11	Ibid., pp. 143–44.	278	29	Ibid., p. 241, Harrison to SW, 12 Dec. 1812.
273	20	Ibid., pp. 143–47.	278	32	Ibid., p. 238, Bodley to Harrison, 11 Dec. 1812; p. 241, Harrison to SW, 12 Dec. 1812.
273	27	DeWitt, p. 401.			
273	33	Northcutt, p. 176.			
273	38	Ibid.	278	36	Cruikshank, "Harrison and Procter," p. 134.
274	6	Ibid., p. 177.	279	9	Harrison, II: 228, Harrison to Campbell, 25 Nov. 1812; pp. 253–65, Campbell to Harrison, 25 Dec. 1812.
274	31	Winchester, *Historical Details*, pp. 71–72, Eve to Garrard, 22 Nov. 1814.			
274	34	Ibid.; Harrison, II: 136–37, SW to Harrison, 17 Sept. 1812.	279	15	Ibid., p. 261, Campbell to Harrison, 25 Dec. 1812.
275	2	Cruikshank, "Harrison and Procter," pp. 133–34.	279	19	Ibid., pp. 288–90, General Orders, 2 Jan. 1813.
275	4	Ibid.	280	8	Ibid., p. 243, Harrison to SW, 12 Dec. 1812.
275	10	Winchester, *Historical Details*, p. 13.			
275	13	Cruikshank, "Harrison and Procter," p. 134; Harrison, II:	280	17	Atherton, p. 19.

page line
280 35 Darnell, p. 40.
280 39 Winchester, *Historical Details*, p. 21.
281 12 Darnell, p. 41, 29 Dec. 1812.
281 25 Richardson, *Richardson's War*, p. 140.
281 28 Atherton, p. 27.
281 38 Winchester, *Historical Details*, p. 23.
282 18 Cruikshank, "Harrison and Procter," p. 152.
282 26 Cruikshank, "Harrison and Procter," p. 140.
283 13 Cruikshank, *Documentary History*, III: 272, Brock to Procter, 17 Sept. 1812.
283 32 Chalou, p. 163.
283 37 Cruikshank, "Harrison and Procter," p. 143.
284 6 Ibid., p. 141.
284 14 Cruikshank, *Documentary History*, VI: 242, Black Bird to Claus, 15 July 1813.
284 18 PAC, RG 8, vol. 677, pp. 163–65, Procter to Sheaffe, 30 Oct. 1812.
284 27 PAC, RG 8, vol. 677, pp. 176–77, Elliott to Claus, 28 Oct. 1812.
284 32 PAC, RG 8, vol. 677, p. 181, Elliott to St. George, 11 Nov. 1812; Chalou, pp. 207–8.
284 35 PAC, RG 8, vol. 677, p. 182, Ironside to Claus, 13 Nov. 1812; Chalou, pp. 207–8.
284 37 Wood, II: 5, Procter to Sheaffe, 13 Jan. 1813.
285 6 Cruikshank, "Harrison and Procter," p. 153.
285 20 Harrison, II: 308, Day to Harrison, 12 Jan. 1813.
285 21 Ibid., p. 314, Winchester to Harrison, 17 Jan. 1813.
286 10 Mason, p. 89.
286 29 DeWitt, p. 95; Harrison, II: 336, Harrison to SW, 26 Jan. 1813.
286 31 Harrison, II: 314, Winchester to Harrison, 17 Jan. 1813.
287 2 Lossing, *Field-book*, p. 350.
287 8 Harrison, II: 335, Harrison to SW, 26 Jan. 1813.
287 11 Ibid., p. 336; Cruikshank, "Harrison and Procter," p. 155.
287 13 Cruikshank, "Harrison and Procter," p. 155; Harrison, II: 331–32, Harrison to SW, 18 Jan. 1813.
287 17 Harrison, II: 314, Winchester to Harrison, 17 Jan. 1813; p. 336, Harrison to SW, 26 Jan. 1813.
287 21 Ibid., p. 337, Harrison to SW, 26 Jan. 1813.
287 25 Cleaves, p. 139.
287 28 Harrison, II: 314, Winchester to Harrison, 17 Jan. 1813.
287 38 Darnell, p. 46.
288 19 Quoted in Clift, p. 160, Price to his wife, 16 Jan. 1813.
288 27 Dudley, p. 1.
288 37 Darnell, p. 47.
289 7 Cruikshank, "Harrison and Procter," p. 154.
289 10 Harrison, II: 319, Lewis to Winchester, 20 Jan. 1813.
289 16 "Correspondence," Perkins to Meigs, 28 Jan. 1813.
289 19 Harrison, II: 330, Harrison to Meigs, 24 Jan. 1813.
289 33 Atherton, pp. 40, 42; Darnell, p. 50; Cruikshank, "Harrison and Procter," p. 156; "Correspondence," p. 102, Whittlesey to his wife, 25 Jan. 1813.
290 9 Lossing, *Field-book*, p. 353; DeWitt, p. 98.
290 20 Lossing, *Field-book*, pp. 353–54.
290 29 DeWitt, pp. 98–99.
290 35 Harrison, II: 339, McClanahan to Harrison, 26 Jan. 1813.
290 39 Winchester, *Historical Details*, pp. 32–33.
290 40 Ibid.
291 20 Lossing, *Field-book*, p. 354; Harrison, II: 340, McClanahan to Harrison, 26 Jan. 1813.
291 21 Darnell, pp. 50–51.
291 24 Ibid., p. 51; Lossing, *Field-book*, p. 354.
291 27 Darnell, pp. 51–52.
291 32 Harrison, II: 339, McClanahan to Harrison, 26 Jan. 1813.
291 40 Atherton, p. 42.

page _line_

_311_ _12_ PAC RG 8, vol. 678, pp. 61–
63, Procter to Sheaffe, 1 Feb.
1813.

_311_ _17_ PAC RG 8, vol. 1170, General
Order, 8 Feb. 1813.

_311_ _22_ Quaife, _Askin Papers_, p. 570,
Richardson to J. Askin, 7 Feb.
1813.

_311_ _26_ McAfee, p. 222; Witherell,

page _line_

p. 307; Winchester, _Historical
Details_, p. 45.

_311_ _35_ McAfee, p. 223.

_312_ _2_ Ibid., p. 225.

_312_ _10_ Beal, p. 338.

**Coda: William Atherton's
War**

_318_ _8_ Atherton, pp. 77–146, _passim_.

Select Bibliography

Unpublished manuscript material

Public Archives of Canada:
RG 8, "C" series *passim.*, British Military Records
RG 10, vol. 11, Indian Affairs
CO 42, vols. 143–149 (Lower Canada); vols. 351–354 (Upper Canada). Colonial
    Office, original correspondence, Secretary of State.
RG 19 E5(a), Department of Finance, War of 1812 Losses, vols. 3728–3768
    passim.
FO 5, vols. 84–86. Foreign Office, General Correspondence, United States of
    America, series II.
MG 24 A9 Prevost Papers
MG 24 A57 Sherbrooke Papers
MG 24 B15 Cochran Papers
MG 24 F70 Evans Papers

Library of Congress:
Harrison Papers
Augustus Foster Papers

U.S. National Archives:
RG 107 Records of the office of the Secretary of War
    M6, reel 5, Letters sent by the Secretary of War
    M221, reels 42–49, Letters received by the Secretary of War

Wisconsin Historical Society:
Draper MSS, Tecumseh Papers

Public Archives of Ontario:
Tupper Papers
Hiram Walker Museum Collection

Metropolitan Toronto Public Library:
Alfred Sandham Collection

Published primary sources

Armstrong, John. *Notices of the War of 1812*, 2 vols., vol. I. New York:
    G. Dearborn, 1836.

Atherton, William. *Narrative of the Suffering & Defeat of the North-western Army under General Winchester....* Frankfort, Ky., 1842.

Beall, William K. "Journal of William K. Beall," *American Historical Review*, vol. 17 (1912).

Bonney, Catharina V.R. *A Legacy of Historical Gleanings....* 2nd ed., vol. I. Albany, N.Y., 1875.

Boylen, J.C. (ed.). "Strategy of Brock Saved Upper Canada: Candid Comments of a U.S. Officer Who Crossed at Queenston," *Ontario History*, vol. 58 (1966).

Brannan, John (ed.). *Official Letters of the Military and Naval Officers of the United States, during the War with Great Britain in the Years 1812, 13, 14, & 15.* Washington: Way and Gideon, 1823.

[Brenton, E.B.] *Some Account of the Public Life of the Late Lieutenant-General Sir George Prevost, Bart., Particularly of His Services in the Canadas....* London: Cadell, 1823.

Byfield, Shadrach. "Narrative," *Magazine of History*, extra no. 11, 1910.

Claus, William. "Diary," *Michigan Pioneer and Historical Collections*, vol. 23, 1895.

"Collections of Papers on File in the Dominion Archives at Ottawa, Canada, Pertaining to Michigan As Found in the Colonial Office Records," *Michigan Pioneer and Historical Collections*, vol. 25, 1896.

"Correspondence Relating to the War of 1812," *Western Reserve Historical Society*, Tract no. 92.

[Clay, Henry.] *The Papers of Henry Clay*, vol. I, edited by James Hopkins. Lexington, Ky.: University of Kentucky Press, 1959.

Coyne, James H. (ed.). "The Talbot Papers," *Royal Society of Canada Transactions*, ser. 3, sect. 2, vols. I and III, 1909.

Crooks, James. "Recollections of the War of 1812," *Women's Canadian Historical Society of Toronto*, Transaction no. 13 (1913/14).

Cruikshank, E.A. (ed.). "Campaigns of 1812–14: Contemporary Narratives...," *Niagara Historical Society Publications*, no. 9 (1902).

——— (ed.). *The Documentary History of the Campaign upon the Niagara Frontier 1812–1814.* 9 vols. Welland: Lundy's Lane Historical Society, 1902–1908.

——— (ed.). *Documents Relating to the Invasion of Canada and the Surrender of Detroit*, Canadian Archives Publications, no. 7. Ottawa: Government Printing Bureau, 1912.

——— (ed.). "Letters of 1812 from the Dominion Archives," *Niagara Historical Society Publications*, no. 23 (n.d.).

——— (ed.). "Some Unpublished Letters of General Brock," *Ontario Historical Society Papers and Records*, vol. 13 (1915).

Darnell, Elias. *A Journal Containing an Accurate and Interesting Account of the Hardships...of...Kentucky Volunteers and Regulars Commanded by General Winchester in the Years 1812–1813....* Philadelphia: Lippincott, Grambo, 1854.

Dobbins, Daniel and Dobbins, William. "The Dobbins Papers," *Buffalo Historical Society Publications*, vol. 8 (1905).

Douglas, John. *Medical Topography of Upper Canada*. London: Burgess and Hill, 1819.

Dudley, Thomas. "Battle and Massacre at Frenchtown, Michigan, January 1813," *Western Reserve Historical Society*, Tract no. 1, 1870.

Edgar, Matilda. *Ten Years of Upper Canada in Peace and War, 1805–1815; Being the Ridout Letters....* Toronto: W. Briggs, 1890.

Foster, Vere (ed.). *The Two Duchesses*. London: Blackie, 1898.

[Harrison, William Henry.] *Messages and Letters*, 2 vols., edited by Logan Esarey. Indiana Historical Collections, vols. 8 and 9. Indianapolis: Indiana Historical Commission, 1922.

Grignon, Augustin. "Seventy-two Years' Recollections of Wisconsin," *State Historical Society of Wisconsin Collections*, vol. 3 (1856).

Hatch, William S. *A Chapter in the History of the War of 1812 in the Northwest....* Cincinnati: Miami Printing & Publishing, 1872.

Heriot, George. *Travels through the Canadas....* London: Richard Phillips, 1807; reprinted, Toronto: Coles, 1971.

Hull, William. *Memoirs of the Campaign of the North Western Army of the United States, A.D. 1812....* Boston: True and Greene, 1824.

[Hull, William.] *Report of the Trial of Brigadier-General William Hull....* New York: Eastburn, Kirk, 1814.

[Jefferson, Thomas.] *The Writings of Thomas Jefferson*, vols. IV and VI, edited by H.A. Washington. New York: Riker, Thorne, 1854.

Kingston Gazette, 1812.

[Kinzie, John.] "John Kinzie's Narrative of the Fort Dearborn Massacre," edited by Mentor L. Williams, *Journal of the Illinois State Historical Society*, vol. 46 (1953).

Klinck, Carl F. (ed.). *Tecumseh: Fact and Fiction in Early Records*. Englewood Cliffs, N.J.: Prentice-Hall, 1961.

Lajeunesse, Ernest J. (ed.). *The Windsor Border Region*. Toronto: University of Toronto Press, 1960.

[Larrabee, Charles.] "Lt. Charles Larrabee's Account of the Battle of Tippecanoe," edited by Florence G. Watts, *Indiana Magazine of History*, vol. 57 (1961).

Loyal and Patriotic Society of Upper Canada. *The Report of the...Society...with an Appendix, and a List of Subscribers and Benefactors*. Montreal: W. Gray, 1817.

[Lucas, Robert.] *The Robert Lucas Journal of the War of 1812 during the Campaign under General William Hull*, edited by John C. Parish. Iowa City: Iowa State Historical Society, 1906.

Mann, James. *Medical Sketches of the Campaigns of 1812, 13, 14*. Dedham, Mass., 1816.

Melish, John. *Travels through the United States of America....* Philadelphia: T. & G. Palmer, 1812.

Montreal Herald, 1812.

Niles Weekly Register, 1811–12.

[Northcutt, William B.] "War of 1812 Diary of William B. Northcutt," edited by G. Glenn Clift, *Register of the Kentucky Historical Society*, April, 1958.

[Norton, John.] *The Journal of Major John Norton*, edited by Carl Klinck and James J. Talman. Toronto: Champlain Society, 1970.

Palmer, T.H. (ed.). *The Historical Register of the United States*, 4 vols., vol. I. Philadelphia: G. Palmer, 1814.

[Pike, Zebulon.] *The Journals of Zebulon Montgomery Pike*, edited by Donald Jackson. Norman, Okla.: University of Oklahoma Press, 1966.

[Powell, William.] "William Powell's Recollections," intro. by Lyman C. Draper, *State Historical Society of Wisconsin Proceedings*, 1912.

Quaife, Milo M. *Chicago and the Old Northwest 1673–1835, A Study of the Evolution of the Northwestern Frontier together with a History of Fort Dearborn.* Chicago: University of Chicago Press, 1913.

———— (ed.). *The John Askin Papers, 1796–1820*, 2 vols., vol. II. Detroit: Detroit Library Commission, 1931.

———— (ed.). *War on the Detroit: The Chronicles of Thomas Verchères de Boucherville, and The Capitulation by an Ohio Volunteer.* Chicago: Lakeside Press, 1940.

Richardson, John. *Eight Years in Canada*. Montreal: H.H. Cunningham, 1847.

[Richardson, John.] *Richardson's War of 1812...*, edited by Alexander C. Casselman. Toronto: Historical Publishing, 1902.

[Richardson, John.] *The Letters Veritas....* Montreal: W. Gray, 1815.

Roach, Isaac. "Journal of Major Isaac Roach, 1812–1824," *Pennsylvania Magazine of History and Biography*, vol. 17 (1893).

Schultz, Christian. *Travels on an Inland Voyage through the States....* New York: I. Riley, 1810.

Scott, Winfield. *Memoirs of Lieut.-General Scott, Written by Himself*, 2 vols., vol. I. New York: Sheldon, 1864.

Severance, Frank H. "The Case of Brig.-Gen. Alexander Smyth, As Shown by His Own Writings...," *Buffalo Historical Society Publications*, vol. 18 (1914).

[Sheaffe, Roger Hale.] "Documents Relating to the War of 1812: the Letter-book of Gen. Sir Roger Hale Sheaffe," *Buffalo Historical Society Publications*, vol. 17 (1913).

Smith, Michael. *A Geographical View of the Province of Upper Canada...*, 3rd. ed. rev. Trenton, N.J.: Moore & Lake, 1813.

Stubbs, Samuel. *A Compendious Account of the Late War, to Which Is Added, The Curious Adventures of Corporal Samuel Stubbs....* Boston: 1817; reprinted, *Magazine of History*, extra no. 152, 1929.

[Tompkins, Daniel D.] *Public Papers of Daniel D. Tompkins...*, 3 vols., edited by Hugh Hastings. Albany: J.B. Lyon, 1898–1902.

Tupper, Ferdinand Brock. *The Life and Correspondence of Major-General Sir Isaac Brock, K.B....*, 2nd ed. rev. London: Simpkin, Marshall, 1847.

United States Congress. *American State Papers: Military Affairs*, vol. I. Washington: Gales and Seaton, 1832.

———— *American State Papers: Indian Affairs*, vol. I. Washington: Gales and Seaton, 1832.

———— *American State Papers: Foreign Relations*, vol. 3. Washington: Gales and Seaton, 1832.

United States Congress, House of Representatives. *Barbarities of the Enemy Exposed in a Report....* Troy, N.Y.: Francis Adancourt, 1813.

Van Horne, James. *Narrative of the Captivity and Sufferings of James Van Horne.* Middlebury, Conn.: 1817.

Van Rensselaer, Solomon. *A Narrative of the Affair of Queenstown, in the War of 1812.* New York: Leavitt, Lord, 1836.

Verchères de Boucherville, Thomas, *see* Quaife, Milo M., *War on the Detroit.*

Walker, Adam. *A Journal of Two Campaigns of the 4th Regiment of U.S. Infantry....* Keene, N.H.: Sentinal Press, 1816.

Weld, Isaac. *Travels through the States of North America and the Provinces of Upper and Lower Canada during the Years 1795, 1796 and 1797,* 3rd. ed. London: 1800.

Whickar, J. Wesley (ed.). "Shabonee's Account of Tippecanoe," *Indiana Magazine of History,* vol. 17 (1921).

Williams, Samuel. "Expedition of Captain Henry Brush with Supplies for General Hull 1812," *Ohio Valley Historical Series,* no. 2 (1870).

[Winchester, James.] *Historical Details Having Relation to the Campaign of the North-Western Army under Generals Harrison and Winchester....* Lexington, Ky.: Worsley and Smith, 1818.

Winchester, James. "Papers and Orderly Book of Brigadier General James Winchester," *Michigan Pioneer and Historical Society Collections,* vol. 31 (1902).

Witherell, B.F. "Reminiscences of the North-west," *State Historical Society of Wisconsin Collections,* vol. 3 (1856).

Wood, William C.H. (ed.). *Select British Documents of the Canadian War of 1812,* Champlain Society, vols. 13–15, 17. Toronto: The Society, 1920–28.

York [Upper Canada] *Gazette,* 1811–12.

Secondary sources

Adams, Henry. *A History of the United States of America during the Administrations of Thomas Jefferson and James Madison.* New York: Charles Scribner's Sons, 1889–91.

Allen, Robert S. "The British Indian Department and the Frontier in North America, 1755–1830," *Canadian Historic Sites: Occasional Papers in Archeology and History,* no. 14 (1975).

Babcock, Louis L. *The War of 1812 on the Niagara Frontier.* Buffalo: Buffalo Historical Society, 1927.

Bailey, John R. *Mackinac, Formerly Michilimackinac.* Lansing, Mich.: 1895.

Bayles, G.H. "Tecumseh and the Bayles Family Tradition," *Register of the Kentucky Historical Society,* October, 1948.

Bayliss, Joseph and Estelle. *Historic St. Joseph Island.* Cedar Rapids, Ia.: Torch Press, 1938.

Beal, Vernon L. "John McDonnell and the Ransoming of American Captives after the River Raisin Massacre, *Michigan History*, vol. 35 (1951).

Beard, Reed. *The Battle of Tippecanoe*, 4th ed. Chicago: Hammond Press, 1911.

Beasley, David R. *The Canadian Don Quixote: The Life and Works of Major John Richardson, Canada's First Novelist*. Erin, Ont.: Porcupine's Quill, 1977.

Beirne, Francis F. *The War of 1812*. New York: Dutton, 1949.

Berger, Carl. *The Sense of Power: Studies in the Ideas of Canadian Imperialism, 1867–1914*. Toronto: University of Toronto Press, 1970.

Bishop, Levi. "The Battle of Brownstown," *Michigan Pioneer and Historical Collections*, vol. 6 (1884).

————— "The Battle of Monguagon," *Michigan Pioneer and Historical Collections*, vol. 6 (1884).

Botsford, David P. "The History of Bois Blanc Island," *Ontario Historical Society Papers and Records*, vol. 47 (1955).

Brett-James, Anthony. *Life in Wellington's Army*. London: Allen and Unwin, 1972.

Brown, Roger Hamilton. *The Republic in Peril: 1812*. New York: Columbia University Press, 1964.

Burt, Alfred L. *The United States, Great Britain, and British North America from the Revolution to the Establishment of Peace after the War of 1812*. New Haven: Yale University Press, 1940.

Caffrey, Kate. *The Twilight's Last Gleaming: The British against America, 1812–1815*. New York: Stein and Day, 1977.

Calder-Marshall, Arthur. *The Two Duchesses*. London: Hutchinson, 1978.

Campbell, Maria. *Revolutionary Services and Civil Life of General William Hull....* New York: D. Appleton, 1848.

Carnochan, Janet. "Sir Isaac Brock," *Niagara Historical Society Publications*, no. 15 (1907).

Chalou, George C. "The Red Pawns Go to War: British-American Indian Relations, 1810–1815." Ph.D. dissertation, University of Indiana, 1971.

Clark, Jerry E. *The Shawnee*. Lexington, Ky.: University Press of Kentucky, 1978.

Clark, S.D. *The Social Development of Canada: An Introductory Study with Select Documents*. Toronto: University of Toronto Press, 1942.

Clarke, James F. "History of the Campaign of 1812, and Surrender of the Post of Detroit," in Maria Campbell, *Revolutionary Services and Civil Life of General William Hull....* New York: D. Appleton, 1848.

Cleary, Francis. "Defence of Essex during the War of 1812," *Ontario Historical Society Papers and Records*, vol. 10 (1913).

Cleaves, Freeman. *Old Tippecanoe: William Henry Harrison and His Time*. New York: Charles Scribner's Sons, 1939; reprinted, New York: Kennikat Press, 1969.

Clift, G. Glenn. *Remember the Raisin! Kentucky and Kentuckians in the Battles and Massacre at Frenchtown, Michigan Territory*. Frankfort, Ky.: Kentucky Historical Society, 1961.

Coffin, William F. *1812: The War, and Its Moral: A Canadian Chronicle*. Montreal: J. Lovell, 1864.

Coleman, Christopher. "The Ohio Valley in the Preliminaries of the War of 1812," *Mississippi Valley Historical Review*, vol. 7 (1920).

Coles, Harry L. *The War of 1812*. Chicago: University of Chicago Press, 1965.

Cook, Samuel F. *Mackinaw in History*. Lansing, Mich.: R. Smith, 1895.

Craick, W.A. "The Story of Brock's Monument," unpublished manuscript, Baldwin Room, Metropolitan Toronto Public Library.

Craig, G.M. *Upper Canada: The Formative Years, 1784–1841*. Toronto: McClelland and Stewart, 1963.

Cramer, C.H. "Duncan McArthur: The Military Phase," *Ohio State Archeological and Historical Quarterly*, vol. 46 (1937).

Cruikshank, E.A. *The Battle of Queenston Heights*, 3rd ed. rev. Welland: Tribune, 1904.

———— "The 'Chesapeake' Crisis As It Affected Upper Canada," *Ontario Historical Society Papers and Records*, vol. 24 (1927).

———— "The Contest for the Command of Lake Erie in 1812–13," *Royal Canadian Institute Transactions*, vol. 6 (1899).

———— "The Contest for the Command of Lake Ontario in 1812 and 1813," *Royal Society of Canada Transactions*, ser. 3, sect. 2, vol. 10 (1916).

———— "From Isle aux Noix to Chateauguay," *Royal Society of Canada Transactions*, ser. 3, sect. 2, vol. 7 (1913).

———— "Harrison and Procter: the River Raisin," *Royal Society of Canada Transactions*, ser. 3, sect. 2, vol. 4 (1910).

———— "General Hull's Invasion of Canada in 1812," *Royal Society of Canada Transactions*, ser. 3, sect. 2, vol. 1 (1907).

———— *The Political Adventures of John Henry*. Toronto: Macmillan, 1936.

———— "Robert Dickson, the Indian Trader," *State Historical Society of Wisconsin Collections*, vol. 12 (1892).

Currie, J.G. "The Battle of Queenston Heights," *Niagara Historical Society Publications*, no. 4 (1898).

Dawson, Moses. *A Historical Narrative of the Civil and Military Services of Major-General William H. Harrison....* Cincinnati, 1824.

Dewitt, John H. "General James Winchester, 1752–1826," *Tennessee Historical Magazine*, vol. 1 (1915).

Dictionary of American Biography, 22 vols. New York: Charles Scribner's Sons, 1928–58.

Dictionary of Canadian Biography, vol. IX: *1861–70*. Toronto: University of Toronto Press, 1976.

Dictionary of National Biography, 22 vols. Oxford: Oxford University Press, 1885–1900.

Douglas, R. Alan. "Weapons of the War of 1812," *Michigan History*, vol. 47 (1963).

Drake, Benjamin. *Life of Tecumseh, and of His Brother the Prophet, with a Historical Sketch of the Shawanoe Indians*. Cincinnati: E. Morgan, 1841.

Dunn, C. Frank. "Captain Nathaniel G.S. Hart," *Filson Club Quarterly*, vol. 24 (1950).

Eaton, Clement. *Henry Clay and the Art of American Politics*. Boston: Little, Brown, 1957.

Edgar, Matilda. *General Brock*. Toronto: Morang, 1904.

Egan, Clifford L. "The Origins of the War of 1812: Three Decades of Historical Writing," *Military Affairs*, vol. 38 (1974).

Elliott, Charles W. *Winfield Scott: The Soldier and the Man*. New York: Macmillan, 1937.

Ermatinger, Charles O. *The Talbot Regime, or, The First Half Century of the Talbot Settlement*. St. Thomas: Municipal World, 1904.

Erney, Richard A. "The Public Life of Henry Dearborn." Ph.D. dissertation, Columbia University, 1957.

Farmer, Silas. *The History of Detroit and Michigan....* Detroit: Silas Farmer, 1884.

Farr, Finis. *Chicago: A Personal History of America's Most American City*. New York: Arlington House, 1973.

Forester, C.S. *The Age of Fighting Sail: The Story of the Naval War of 1812*. Garden City, N.Y.: Doubleday, 1956.

Fortescue, Sir John W. *A History of the British Army*, 13 vols., vol. VIII. London: Macmillan, 1917.

Gilpin, Alec. *The War of 1812 in the Old Northwest*. Toronto: Ryerson Press; East Lansing, Mich.: Michigan State University Press, 1958.

Glover, Richard. *Peninsula Preparation: The Reform of the British Army, 1795–1809*. Cambridge: Cambridge University Press, 1963.

Goltz, Charles H. "Tecumseh and the Northwest Indian Confederacy." Ph.D. dissertation, University of Western Ontario, 1973.

Goodman, Warren H. "The Origins of the War of 1812: A Survey of Changing Interpretations," *Mississippi Valley Historical Review*, vol. 28 (1941).

Green, Constance McLaughlin. *Washington*, vol. I, *Village and Capital, 1800–1878*. Princeton: Princeton University Press, 1962.

Green, Thomas Marshall. *Historic Families of Kentucky....* Cincinnati: Robert Clarke, 1889.

Gurd, Norman S. *The Story of Tecumseh*. Toronto: W. Briggs, 1912.

Hacker, Louis M. "Western Land Hunger and the War of 1812...," *Mississippi Valley Historical Review*, vol. 10 (1924).

Hall, Ellery L. "Canadian Annexation Sentiment in Kentucky Prior to the War of 1812," *Register of the Kentucky Historical Society*, October, 1930.

Hamil, Fred Coyne. *Lake Erie Baron*. Toronto: Macmillan, 1955.

Hammack, James W., Jr. *Kentucky and the Second American Revolution: The War of 1812*. Lexington, Ky.: University of Kentucky Press, 1976.

Hare, John S. "Military Punishments in the War of 1812," *Journal of the American Military Institute*, vol. 4 (1940).

Hatzenbuehler, Ronald L. "The War Hawks and the Question of Congressional Leadership in 1812," *Pacific Historical Review*, vol. 45 (1976).

——— "Party Unity and the Decision for War in the House of Representatives, 1812," *William and Mary Quarterly*, 3rd ser., vol. 29 (1972).

Havighurst, Walter. *Three Flags at the Straits: The Forts of Mackinac*. Englewood Cliffs, N.J.: Prentice-Hall, 1966.

Heaton, Herbert. "Non-importation, 1806–1812," *Journal of Economic History*, vol. 1 (1941).

Higginson, T.B. (ed.). *Major Richardson's Major General Sir Isaac Brock and the 41st Regiment*. Burks Falls: Old Rectory Press, 1976.

History of Pike County, Missouri. Des Moines, Ia.: Mills & Co., 1883.

Hitsman, J. Mackay. *The Incredible War of 1812: A Military History*. Toronto: University of Toronto Press, 1965.

———— "Sir George Prevost's Conduct of the Canadian War of 1812," *Canadian Historical Association Report*, 1962.

———— "Spying at Sackets Harbor, 1813," *Inland Seas*, vol. 15 (1959).

Hodge, Frederick W. (ed.). *Handbook of American Indians North of Mexico*, 2 vols. Washington: Smithsonian Institution, Bureau of American Ethnology, Bulletin no. 30, 1906; reprinted, New York: Pageant Books, 1959.

Horsman, Reginald. "British Indian Policy in the Northwest, 1807–1812," *Mississippi Valley Historical Review*, vol. 45 (1958).

———— *The Causes of the War of 1812*. Philadelphia: University of Pennsylvania Press, 1962.

———— *Expansion and American Indian Policy, 1783–1812*. East Lansing, Mich.: Michigan State University Press, 1967.

———— *Matthew Elliott, British Indian Agent*. Detroit: Wayne State University Press, 1964.

———— *The War of 1812*. New York: Knopf, 1969.

———— "Western War Aims, 1811–12," *Indiana Magazine of History*, vol. 53 (1957).

Irving, L. Homfray. *Officers of the British Forces in Canada during the War of 1812–15*. Welland: Tribune Print. for Canadian Military Institute, 1908.

Irwin, Ray. *Daniel D. Tompkins: Governor of New York and Vice President of the United States*. New York: New York Historical Society, 1968.

Jacobs, James R. *The Beginning of the U.S. Army, 1783–1812*. Princeton: Princeton University Press, 1947.

James, William. *A Full and Correct Account of the Military Occurrences of the Late War between Great Britain and the United States of America*, vol. I, London, 1818.

"Jo Daviess of Kentucky," *Harper's New Monthly Magazine*, vol. 21, August, 1860.

Johnston, C.M. "William Claus and John Norton: A Struggle for Power in Old Ontario," *Ontario History*, vol. 57 (1965).

Jones, Robert Leslie. *A History of Agriculture in Ontario, 1613–1880*. Toronto: University of Toronto Press, 1946.

Keegan, John. *The Face of Battle*. London: Jonathan Cape, 1976.

Kellogg, Louise P. "The Capture of Mackinac in 1812," *State Historical Society of Wisconsin Proceedings*, 1912.

Kelton, Dwight H. *Annals of Fort Mackinac*. Detroit: Detroit Free Press, 1888.

Ketchum, William. *An Authentic and Comprehensive History of Buffalo...*, vol. II. Buffalo: Rockwell, Baker & Hill, 1864–65.

Kirby, William. *Annals of Niagara*. Welland: Lundy's Lane Historical Society Publications, 1896.

Kirkland, Joseph. *The Story of Chicago*. Chicago: Dibble, 1892.

Koke, Richard J. "The Britons Who Fought on the Canadian Frontier: Uniforms of the War of 1812," *New York Historical Society Quarterly*, vol. 45 (1961).

Kosche, Ludwig. "Relics of Brock: An Investigation," *Archivaria*, no. 9, Winter 1979–80.

Lamb, W. Kaye. *The Hero of Upper Canada*. Toronto: Rous and Mann, 1962.

Lossing, Benson J. *The Pictorial Field-book of the War of 1812....* New York: Harper and Brothers, 1868.

———— "Hull's Surrender of Detroit," *Potter's American Monthly*, August, 1875.

Lower, Arthur R.M. *Canadians in the Making: A Social History of Canada*. Toronto: Longmans, Green, 1958.

Lucas, Sir Charles P. *The Canadian War of 1812*. Oxford: Clarendon Press, 1906.

McAfee, Robert. *History of the Late War in the Western Country....* Lexington, Ky.: Worsley and Smith, 1816.

Macmillan Dictionary of Canadian Biography, 4th ed., edited by W. Stewart Wallace and W.A. McKay. Toronto: Macmillan, 1978.

Mahan, Alfred T. *Sea Power in Its Relations to the War of 1812*, 2 vols., vol. I. Boston: Little, Brown, 1905.

Mahon, John K. *The War of 1812*. Gainesville: University of Florida Press, 1972.

Marshall, Humphrey. *The History of Kentucky....* Frankfort, Ky.: G.S. Robinson, 1824.

Mason, Philip P. (ed.). *After Tippecanoe: Some Aspects of the War of 1812*. Toronto: Ryerson; East Lansing, Mich.: Michigan State University Press, 1963.

May, George S. *War 1812*. [Lansing?]: Mackinac Island State Park Commission, 1962.

Mayo, Bernard. *Henry Clay, Spokesman of the New West*. Boston: Houghton Mifflin, 1937.

Morgan, Henry J. *Sketches of Celebrated Canadians....* Quebec: Hunter, Rose, 1862.

Morison, Samuel Eliot. *By Land and Sea*. New York: Knopf, 1954.

Muller, H.N. "A 'Traitorous and Diabolic Traffic': The Commerce of the Champlain-Richelieu Corridor during the War of 1812," *Vermont History*, vol. 44 (1976).

———— "Smuggling into Canada: How the Champlain Valley Defied Jefferson's Embargo," *Vermont History*, vol. 38 (1970).

Murray, John M. "John Norton," *Ontario Historical Society Papers and Records*, vol. 37 (1945).

Naylor, Isaac. "The Battle of Tippecanoe," *Indiana Magazine of History*, vol. 2 (1906).

Nursey, Walter R. *The Story of Sir Isaac Brock*, 4th ed. rev. Toronto: McClelland and Stewart, 1923.

Oman, Sir Charles. *Wellington's Army, 1809–1814*. London: Edward and Arnold, 1913.

Pearkes, G.R. "Detroit and Miami," *Canadian Defence Quarterly*, vol. 11 (1934).

Perkins, Bradford. *Castlereagh and Adams: England and the United States, 1812–1823*. Berkeley: University of California Press, 1964.

———— *Prologue to War: England and the United States, 1805–1812.* Berkeley: University of California Press, 1961.

Petersen, Eugene T. *Mackinac Island: Its History in Pictures.* Mackinac Island, Mich.: Mackinac Island State Park Commission, 1973.

Pirtle, Alfred. *The Battle of Tippecanoe.* Louisville: J.P. Morton, 1900.

Porter, Kenneth W. *John Jacob Astor, Businessman.* Cambridge, Mass.: Harvard University Press, 1931.

Pratt, Julius. *Expansionists of 1812.* New York: Macmillan, 1925.

———— "Western Aims in the War of 1812," *Mississippi Valley Historical Review,* vol. 12 (1925).

Quaife, Milo M. "The Story of Brownstown," *Burton Historical Collection Leaflets,* vol. 4 (1926).

Randall, E.O. "Tecumseh the Shawnee Chief," *Ohio Archeological and Historical Society Publications,* vol. 15 (1906).

Read, David B. *Life and Times of Major-General Sir Isaac Brock, K.B.* Toronto: W. Briggs, 1894.

Redway, Jacques W. "General Van Rensselaer and the Niagara Frontier," *New York State Historical Association Proceedings,* vol. 8 (1909).

Richardson, John. *Wau-nan-gee, or the Massacre at Chicago.* New York: H. Long, 1852.

Risjord, Norman K. "1812: Conservatives, War Hawks and the Nation's Honor," *William and Mary Quarterly,* 3rd ser., vol. 18 (1961).

Robinson, Sir Charles W. *Life of Sir John Beverley Robinson, Bart., C.B., D.C.L....* Toronto: Morang, 1904.

Ryerson, Adolphus Egerton. *The Loyalists of America and Their Times, from 1620 to 1816,* 2 vols., 2nd ed. Toronto: W. Briggs, 1880.

Sapio, Victor A. *Pennsylvania and the War of 1812.* Lexington, Ky.: University Press of Kentucky, 1970.

Shortt, Adam. "The Economic Effect of the War of 1812 on Upper Canada," *Ontario Historical Society Papers and Records,* vol. 10 (1913).

———— "Life of the Settler in Western Canada before the War of 1812," Dept. of History and Political and Economic Science, Queen's University, *Bulletin,* no. 12 (1914).

Slocum, Charles E. "The Origin, Description and Service of Fort Winchester," *Ohio Archeological and Historical Society Publications,* vol. 9 (1901).

Smelser, Marshall. "Tecumseh, Harrison and the War of 1812," *Indiana Magazine of History,* vol. 65 (1969).

Stagg, J.C.A. "James Madison and the Malcontents: The Political Origins of the War of 1812," *William and Mary Quarterly,* 3rd ser., vol. 33 (1976).

Stanley, George F.G. "The Indians in the War of 1812," *Canadian Historical Review,* vol. 31 (1950).

———— "The Significance of the Six Nations Participation in the War of 1812," *Ontario History,* vol. 55 (1963).

Steel, Anthony. "More Light on the Chesapeake," *Mariner's Mirror,* vol. 39 (1953).

Taylor, George R. "Agrarian Discontent in the Mississippi Valley Preceding the War of 1812," *Journal of Political Economy,* vol. 39 (1931).

—— "Prices in the Mississippi Valley Preceding the War of 1812," *Journal of Economic and Business History*, vol. 3 (1930).

Tohill, Louis A. "Robert Dickson, Fur Trader on the Upper Mississippi," *North Dakota Historical Quarterly*, vol. 3 (1928).

Tucker, Glenn. *Poltroons and Patriots: A Popular Account of the War of 1812*, 2 vols., vol. I. Indianapolis: Bobbs-Merrill, 1954.

—— *Tecumseh: Vision of Glory*. Indianapolis: Bobbs-Merrill, 1956.

Turner, Wesley B. "The Career of Isaac Brock in Canada." Ph.D. dissertation, University of Toronto, 1961.

Upton, Emory. *The Military Policy of the United States*. Washington: Government Printing Office, 1907.

Van Deusen, John G. "Court Martial of General William Hull," *Michigan History Magazine*, vol. 12 (1928).

—— "Detroit Campaign of General William Hull," *Michigan History Magazine*, vol. 12 (1928).

Vincent, Elizabeth. "Fort St. Joseph: A History." Unpublished manuscript, Parks Canada, Ottawa.

Walden, Keith. "Isaac Brock: Man and Myth; A Study of the Militia of the War of 1812 in Upper Canada." M.A. thesis, Carleton University, Ottawa, 1972.

Widder, Keith R. *Reveille till Taps: Soldier Life at Fort Mackinac, 1780–1895*. N.p.: Mackinac Island State Park Commission, 1972.

Wilkinson-Latham, Robert. *British Artillery on Land and Sea, 1790–1820*. Newton Abott: David and Charles, 1973.

Wilson, Bruce. "The Enterprises of Robert Hamilton." Ph.D. dissertation, University of Toronto, 1978.

Wilson, Samuel M. "Kentucky's Part in the War of 1812," *Register of the Kentucky Historical Society*, vol. 29.

Wiltse, Charles. *John C. Calhoun, Nationalist*. Indianapolis: Bobbs-Merrill, 1944.

Wise, S.F. and Brown, R. Craig. *Canada Views the United States: Nineteenth Century Political Attitudes*. Toronto: Macmillan, 1967.

Woodford, Frank B. *Lewis Cass, the Last Jeffersonian*. 1950. Reprinted New York: Octagon Books, 1973.

Young, James S. *The Washington Community, 1800–1828*. New York: Columbia University Press, 1966.

Zaslow, Morris and Turner, Wesley B. (eds.). *The Defended Border: Upper Canada and the War of 1812*. Toronto: Macmillan, 1964.

Index

Fourneaux, Jean-Baptiste, 136
4th U.S. Infantry Regt., 71, 94, 181, 184, 214
Fox Indians, 63
Frenchman's Creek, attack at, 260
Frenchtown, Michigan Terr., 285, 286, 288–90; Battle of, 293–99, 313; massacre at, 300–302, 310–14
Frolic, 252

Galloway, Rebecca, 61
Garrett, Lt. Ashton, 296
Gates (grenadier), 293
Gaylor (quartermaster general), 169
Ghent, Treaty of, 19
Gibson, John, 56–57, 278
Ginac, Jean-Baptiste, 136
Girty, James, 64
Girty, Simon, 39, 40, 64
Glegg, Maj. J.B., 165, 166, 171, 180, 214, 251
Gooding, Lt. George, 119, 121
Gore, Francis, 46–49, 65, 143
Goya, Francisco, 146
Goyeau, Jean-Baptiste, 136
Graves, Maj. Benjamin, 289
Great Britain, American policy of, 45–46
Green Bay, 195
Greenville, O., 43, 307; treaty of, 38
Grouseland, 43, 53, 66, 76
Grundy, Felix, 97, 99–100
Guerrière, 217

Hamilton, Alexander, 229, 246
Hamilton, Robert, 229, 230
Hampton Roads, Va., 35, 36
Hancock, James, 138, 139
Hanks, Lt. Porter, 13–14, 110–11, 141, 171, 177
Harrison, William Henry, 62–63, 68–69, 192, 223, 286–87, 291, 299–300, 307, 316; speech to legislature of, 39, 41; described, 42; and land purchase, 49–53; at council, 1810, 53–57; at council, 1811, 66–68; and Tippecanoe, 69–77; and Win-

chester, 270–71; Indian policy of, 272–73, 278–79; appointed commander, Army of Northwest, 274; strategy of, 275–76; and relief of Detroit, 278, 280–82.
Harmar, Josiah, 191
Hart, Anna, 310
Hart, Captain Nathaniel, 268, 291, 300–302, 304
Hayes, Sgt., 193
Heald, Capt. Nathan, 103, 192, 194
Heald, Rebekah, 192, 193, 194
Henry, John, 87
Hickman, Mrs., 310
Hickman, Capt. Paschal, 301, 303
Holcroft, Capt. William, 245, 246
Hopkins, Maj.-Gen. Samuel, 268, 277–78
Howard, Gov., 76
Hull, Abraham, 93, 94, 119, 172, 177, 179, 181
Hull, Isaac, 217
Hull, William, 88–90, 91, 92–96, 117, 123, 124, 126, 136, 147, 156, 158, 159, 163, 167, 168, 170, 171, 184, 191, 192, 307; advice of, 89; described, 92; and invasion of Canada, 127, 128; proclamation of, 128–31, 179; at Sandwich, 139–41, 150–52; plot against, 169–70; and defence of Detroit, 172, 173, 175, 176; mental state of, 177–79; and surrender of Detroit, 179–80, 183; court martial of, 187–88
Hunter, 175

Ilbert, Anne, 251
Impressment, 25, 37–38, 87, 309
Indiana Territory, 41
Indian confederacy, 49, 56, 61, 67, 68–69, 76–77, 167, 283, 312, 313
Indians, 27–28, 38, 41–43, 72–76, 92, 103–5, 107, 111, 112, 121–22, 125, 126, 130–31, 140, 157, 165, 178, 182, 216, 271, 277, 300–303, 312–13; U.S. policy toward, 25, 27–28, 40, 83–84, 88–89, 97; British pol-

Maitland, Gen. Alexander, 214
Mallory, Timothy, 317
Manete, 60–61
Mars, Stephen, 73
Martin, Capt., 122
Martin, Daniel, 35
Mascotapah, see Dickson, Robert
Maumee River, 96; rapids of, 177, 276, 280–81, 284, 285–86, 287, 291
Meigs, Gov. Return, 92, 124, 169, 283
Melampus, 35
Menominee Indians, 13, 106, 109, 138, 140
Merritt, William Hamilton, 252
Miami Indians, 50, 51, 58, 192, 273, 278, 279, 284, 292
Michilimackinac, 84, 170, 196, 308; capture of, 13–15, 109–12, 141, 312
Milbanke, Annabella, 86
Militia, 21, 22–23, 93–94, 100, 124; Canadian, 22, 83, 125, 130, 131, 137, 142, 144, 145, 174, 187, 247, 253; Essex, 127–28; Kent, 127–28; Lincoln, 215; Michigan, 177; New York, 201; Ohio, 89, 91, 135, 140, 272; U.S., 22–23, 127, 155, 157, 203, 218, 231, 234, 242, 247, 259, 262; York, 215
Miller, Col. James, 94, 137–38, 161, 162–63, 169, 171, 177, 180–81, 187
Miller, John, 173
Mississinewa River, 279, 284
Mohawk Indians, 84, 187, 215–16, 246, 248–49, 312–13
Monroe, James, 270, 280
Montreal, 89, 131, 153, 187, 221, 308, 316
Moore, Maj.-Gen., 155
Moravian Town, Battle of, 316
Moscow, 252
Muir, Maj. Adam, 148–49, 158–59, 160–61, 186
Myers, Lt.-Col. Christopher, 210

Nancy, 164

Napoleon, 13, 24, 178, 219, 252, 309
Navarre, Col. Francis, 290
Navarre, Peter, 291
Needs, John, 195
Nelson, Horatio, 119, 240
Newark, 209, 244, 252
New England states, 23, 24, 153, 309
New York (city), 37
Niagara frontier, 163, 202, 207, 217, 218
Niagara River, 144, 203, 207, 224, 228, 307
Nichol, Col. Robert, 166, 176
Non-Importation Act, 106
Northcutt, William, 272–73
North West Company, 107, 108, 126
Norton, John, 215, 243, 246–47

Ogdensburg, N.Y., 203
Ohio, 25, 83; volunteers, 91–93, 94, 307
Ohio River, 186
100th Regiment (British), 63
103rd Regiment (British), 139
Orders in Council, 25, 45, 46, 86, 87, 96, 309; revoked, 98–99, 152
Orr, Sgt. Montgomery, 73
Osage Indians, 76
Oswego, N.Y., 209, 210
Ottawa Indians, 13, 63, 107, 109, 110–11, 141, 148, 284

Peck, Judge, 244
Pennsylvania volunteers, 223, 259, 261, 307
Perceval, Spencer, 99
Perkins, Gen. Simon, 286, 287, 289
Perry, Oliver Hazard, 308, 316
Petite Coté, 140
Pike, Robert, 137
Pike, Zebulon, 105
Piqua, O., 196, 272; council at, 186–87
Plattsburg, N.Y., 155, 221, 263
Pope, Sen. John, 269
Port Dover, 164

Van Rensselaer, Harriet, 211–12

Van Rensselaer, Lt.-Col. Solomon, 201, 203, 205, 207, 211–12, 221, 222, 228, 230, 249, 258; described, 204; and armistice, 209–11; and attack on Queenston, 232, 233–34, 235

Van Rensselaer, Gen. Stephen, 201, 206–7, 212, 220, 221, 222, 223, 258, 307; forces of, 203, 210–11, 219, 223–24; described, 203–4; attack plans of, 224–25, 228, 232–33; and attack on Queenston, 242, 243–44

Van Rensselaer, Van Vechten, 211

Van Vechten, Abraham, 228

Vassar, Peter, 95

Vincennes, Indiana Terr., 39, 52, 53; council at, 1810, 53–57; council at, 1811, 66–68

Vincent, Lt.-Col. John, 215

Vrooman, Solomon, 245

Vrooman's Point, 241, 245

Wabasha, 104

Wabash River, 52, 71

Wadsworth, Brig.-Gen. William, 201–2, 203, 221, 242–43, 244, 247, 248

Walk-in-the-Water, 127, 147, 296

Walworth (postmaster), 122

Ware, William, 35

War Hawks, 24, 27, 46, 86–87, 96, 270; strategy of, 96–97, 100

Washington, George, 178

Washington, D.C., 43–44

Wasp, 252

Watson, Simon Z., 143

Watts, George, 226

Wayne, Gen. Anthony, 42, 49, 192

Wea Indians, 278

Wellington, Duke of, 13, 138, 146

Wells, Billy, 43, 191–94

Wells, Ens. Levi, 304

Wells, Lt.-Col. Samuel, 290, 296

Wellesley, Lord, 86

Westbrook, Andrew, 143

White Horse, 72

White Wing, 61

Wilberforce, William, 247

Williams, John, 137

Williams, Capt. John, 239, 241

Winchester, James, 270, 271, 275, 276, 280, 282, 284, 290, 307; unpopularity of, 272, 273–74; described, 274; army of, 280–81; and relief of Frenchtown, 285–87, 289; and Battle of Frenchtown, 291, 296–98

Winemac, 56

Winnebago Indians, 13, 71, 106, 109

Wool, Capt. John, 235–37, 239, 240, 241

Woolfolk, Capt. John, 304

Wovoka, 62

Wyandot Indians, 47, 127, 150, 284, 292, 296, 313

Yellow Jackets, 74

York, 81–82, 144, 251, 309, 313, 315

York Volunteers, 163, 233, 237–38, 240, 245, 252–53

Stephen Van Rensselaer

Lewis Cass

James Winchester

Robert Lucas

William Henry Harrison

The Power of Entrepreneurs

The Power of Entrepreneurs

Politics and Economy in
Contemporary Spain

Mercedes Cabrera and Fernando del Rey

Translated by Robert Lavigna

Berghahn Books
New York • Oxford

First published in 2007 by
Berghahn Books
www.berghahnbooks.com

Library of Congress Cataloging-in-Publication Data

Cabrera, Mercedes.
    [Poder de los empresarios. English]
    The power of entrepreneurs : politics and economy in contemporary Spain / Mercedes
Cabrera and Fernando del Rey ; translated by Robert Lavigna.
        p. cm.
    Includes bibliographical references and index.
    ISBN-10: 1-84545-185-6 (hbk.) ISBN-13: 978-1-84545-185-1 (hbk.)
    1. Business enterprises--Spain--History--20th century. 2. Business and politics--Spain--
History--20th century. I. Rey Reguillo, Fernando del, 1960- II. Title.

HD2887.C3313 2006
330.946'08--dc22

                                                                            2006018117

British Library Cataloguing in Publication Data
A catalogue record for this book is available from the British Library
Printed in the United States on acid-free paper

ISBN-10: 1-84545-185-6   ISBN-13: 978-1-84545-185-1   hardback

Contents

Introduction

W hen this history begins at the turn of the twentieth century, Spain was a second-
rate power in Europe, in terms of economy as well as international politics.
Spain was a constitutional Monarchy whose origins date to 1875. The Constitution of
1876 gave Spain a stability it had not enjoyed all that century. The military, up to then
the protagonists of almost all the changes by means of their *pronunciamientos*
(uprisings), seemed to have disappeared from the forefront of the political scene. The
Crown retained an important capability to intervene in political life, limited by the
existence of two big parties, the conservative and the liberal. Both parties peacefully
took turns governing the country and enjoyed comfortable majorities in Parliament.
They were parties of 'elites', who controlled the electoral results thanks to their
networks of political *clientelismo* and *caciques* (local party bosses). Although as of 1890
there had been universal suffrage for men, political mobilisation was rare except in the
most important cities (Madrid, Barcelona, Bilbao, Valencia). The political forces of the
opposition (republicans, regionalists, socialists) struggled to establish themselves and
the effective democratisation of political life did not seem easy.

With the turn of the century and the atmosphere created by the loss of the last
colonies (Cuba, Puerto Rico and the Philippines) of what in its day had been an
enormous empire, there was increasing criticism of *caciquismo* (the political boss
system) on the part of conservatives and liberals, the lack of representation in
Parliament, the distortion of political life and the inefficiency of the State as factors
explaining Spain's backwardness. The value of stability lost importance to the demand
for political 'regeneration'. This coincided with the crowning of Alfonso XIII, a young
king who seemed willing to put all his effort towards achieving this 'regeneration'.

Spanish society was primarily rural. Inland, its agriculture was backwards and
protected. On the periphery, it was more specialised and productive, and capable of
exporting. Due to the unbalanced distribution of property, the problems of agriculture
were linked to the need for agrarian reform, especially in the southern half of the
peninsula, where the largest properties and day labourers accumulated and wages
were miserable. Industrial development was also concentrated in two peripheral
regions, Catalonia and the Basque Country, although there were other important
economic activities such as coal mining in Asturias. The industrialisation of Catalonia
had older roots. It started in the eighteenth century and was based on the expansion

of the textile industry and other consumer goods industries. In the Basque Country, industrialisation had come almost suddenly, as of 1875, and was based on iron and steel, metallurgy, shipbuilding and banking. Small businessmen, industrialists and traders were scattered in provincial towns and cities throughout the rest of the country. Foreign capital had gained a presence in important areas like banking, mining and railway companies. The financial system began to be structured on a small number of banks with headquarters in the capital, Madrid, and the Basque Country, which coexisted with other smaller, local or regional banks. The Bank of Spain, a private entity, was not a true central bank yet. The State, which was small and had a budget deficit and few resources, had maintained a protectionist policy since 1891 and began to intervene timidly in social and labour issues.

However, Spanish society was not immobile. In fact, in large part due to the political stability achieved, the country gained on its European neighbours. At the time our account begins, the growth fostered in some economic sectors by Spain's neutrality in the First World War, as well as the growing emigration from the country to the city, triggered important changes. The number of companies dedicated to mining, iron and steel, metallurgy, shipbuilding and textile manufacturing multiplied, and so did jobs. Entrepreneurs and employers accumulated unprecedented profits, while banks also made the most of the situation. The other side of the coin was the increase of prices and the scarcity of some products, the 'crisis of provisions', as it was called. In addition, despite Spain's neutrality in the war, there was a heated political debate between the supporters of each of the two sides in the conflict. The *aliadófilos* (groups that supported the Allies: liberals, republicans, Catalan regionalists and socialists) felt that France and Britain's victory provided a chance for Spain to introduce democratising political reforms, change the Constitution and restructure the party system. The *germanófilos* (groups that backed Germany: conservatives, traditionalists, the military and the Catholic Church) remained faithful to the established monarchist order. In the heat of the economic growth, workers' organisations also grew, dividing into a socialist trade union, the *Unión General de Trabajadores* (General Union of Workers, UGT), which was closely related to a slowly growing Socialist Party (PSOE), and the *Confederación Nacional del Trabajo* (National Confederation of Labour, CNT), consisting of anarchist, anarcho-syndicalist and strictly syndicalist currents. Economic lobbies also felt the urgency to organise, as much to pressure the State in defense of their interests or to prevent reforms as to deal with the workers' demands.

The monarchist, conservative and liberal parties continued to control the power, but they endured a profound crisis which mutated into internal divisions and a lack of clear leadership. The withdrawal of Antonio Maura, chief 'regenerationist' of the Conservative Party, and the death of Liberal Party leader José Canalejas by an anarchist attack, signified the end of a generation of leaders. The traditional alternation in the government became complicated as a result of these divisions, while other political forces believed the time had come to break from the traditional monopoly of the two parties. The *Lliga Regionalista* (Catalan Regionalist League), closely identified with Catalonia's bourgeoisie and working to achieve a statute of autonomy for Catalonia, was one of the forces involved under the leadership of Francisco Cambó. The Basque Nationalist Party, however, because of its pro-independence orthodoxy, did not obtain the same support from the Basque industrial bourgeoisie, which was mainly *españolista* (supporting Spanish nationalism), and had hardly any impact on the national political stage. Among the republicans, only Alejandro Lerroux's Radical Party, a populist, anti-clerical party, had found important support in Catalonia. In some other cities, there persisted a republican culture with enough support to put a handful of representatives in Parliament. The Socialist Party, with its long history that began in 1879, grew slowly in part because of the characteristics of Spanish society and politics, and in part because of its strategy of isolation until it decided to form an electoral coalition with the republicans in 1909. Thanks to this coalition, it earned one seat – its first in Parliament – a number it would not surpass until 1918, when it won six seats.

The battle for constitutional reform defended by the *aliadófilos* was lost and the Monarchy managed to overcome the serious crisis it endured in 1917. The economic depression of post war Europe and the radicalism of the social conflict made public order one of the most pressing problems. Furthermore, the enormous difficulties in maintaining a policy of peace in the protectorate that Spain had in North Africa, in Morocco, eventually strained relations between politicians and the military. The disaster suffered by the Spanish Army in Annual (Morocco) in 1921 triggered a campaign of indictment that implicated King Alfonso XIII himself. Moreover, the accumulation of problems occurred at a time when the two big monarchist parties and the opposition forces were enduring difficult moments. There was no political leadership capable of providing clear objectives. The changes that were taking place were interpreted as unmistakable symptoms of the regime's inability to survive. Some members of the military and King Alfonso XIII viewed the situation as such. Very few politicians and citizens were willing to defend the constitutional order. The atmosphere in Europe was not very favourable, either. The result was the military coup by General Primo de Rivera in September 1923.

Social and political historians have long insisted on the existence of an oligarchy of big landowners and important businessmen, big bankers and a few entrepreneurs, many of whom belonged to the nobility, a 'power block' that was formed in the final decades of the nineteenth century and which supposedly established the directives of Spanish politics since then. According to these historians, this 'block' saw its positions of privilege endangered in the years following the First World War and again in the 1930s. On both occasions, it managed to recover them thanks to military intervention. In September 1923, General Primo de Rivera overthrew constitutional normality with his coup d'état. King Alfonso XIII accepted it, and, because of the passivity of most of the country, there emerged a dictatorship which lasted until 1930. The Constitution and the functioning of political parties were suspended, and ambitious public works projects were undertaken. Although they were not the main cause, these projects helped spur important economic growth. However, when the dictator wanted to replace once and for all the constitutional order with a new corporate order and a single party, he lost the support of the King and important sectors of the military, and resigned. A year later, in April 1931, after a coalition of republican parties and the socialist party won local elections in the big cities, it was King Alfonso XIII who decided to go into exile, and the Second Republic was proclaimed.

The republican democratic experience transpired in a difficult context of international economic crisis and political tension in Europe, both of which affected Spain. Five years after the proclamation of the Second Republic, in July 1936, a new military uprising, initially unsuccessful, put an end to that experience and hurled the country into a bloody civil war won by the military insurgents and their leader, General Francisco Franco. The new dictatorship was much harsher, more repressive and more authoritarian than Primo de Rivera's, and also lasted much longer. The new State was based on the unconditional surrender of the defeated armies and erected a one-party State with absolute concentration of power in the hands of General Franco, although different political 'families' could be identified within the regime. The initial policy of autarky and international isolationism pushed the Spanish economy into a profound crisis that set it back to the situation prior to 1930. Only the relative liberalisation of the so-called Stabilisation Plan of 1959 enabled the beginning of an important growth, known as the Spanish 'economic miracle'. By the time Franco died in November 1975, Spanish society had changed radically. Thanks to this change, although not exclusively because of it, it was possible to make a transition to democracy. This transition had its problems and scares, but democracy was finally established and based on a policy of negotiation and consensus.

Spain was not free from the great political breakdowns of the first half of the twentieth century, although it did not participate in either of the two World Wars. The stability of the second half of the century was achieved at the cost of maintaining an authoritarian regime, while the countries around Spain settled into their democracies. This political abnormality left its mark on the transformation and modernisation of the Spanish economy and society that took place during the 1960s, but without these processes, it would be difficult to explain the success of the transition to democracy after Franco's death in 1975. Many of the factors that had made democracy impossible in the 1930s – the unequal distribution of farmland and the backwardness of agriculture, the radical social and regional inequalities, the weakness of the middle class, illiteracy and the weight of the most conservative Catholicism, the presence and power of the Catholic Church – disappeared in the 1970s. Also, the European and international contexts were different. However, the success was a consequence of the conviction that everything else had to be subordinate to the defense of democracy and loyalty to constitutional order. This conviction was held by politicians, different workers' and employers' organisations and public opinion in general. At the turn of the twentieth century, Spain was a primarily rural and relatively backwards country, isolated in its foreign policy and incipient in its political development. Today, with the new Constitution of 1978 having already celebrated its twenty-fifth anniversary, it is an important economic power, enjoys a stable democratic government and has been incorporated not only into Europe but also fully into the spectrum of international politics.

In this book, we intend to give an account of this long trajectory from the perspective of economic interests and their relation to politics and politicians. The main actors are entrepreneurs in the ample sense of the word: landowners, manufacturers, industrialists and traders, bankers, businessmen and company directors. The actors are individual entrepreneurs as well as those organised in pressure groups and employers' associations. Many economic historians have coincided in pointing out the shortage and low competitiveness of Spanish entrepreneurs, at least during the nineteenth century. The few big companies – in banking, railways and mining – were made possible by foreign initiative and investment. The reasons for this shortage perhaps reside in a past and cultural traditions that were not very favourable for the appearance of 'enterprising' entrepreneurs or big companies. However, the same historian that asserts this for the nineteenth century has spoken of the 'abundance of enterprising spirit, the capacity to organise, intelligence and, above all, the rational adaptation to complex historical circumstances' that can be deduced from the biographies of a hundred Spanish businessmen from the twentieth century. According to this view, these businessmen showed a 'surprising ability' to adapt to 'a very changeable and generally unfriendly institutional framework'. Other economic historians have also pointed out that the relative poverty of the Spanish economy until well into the twentieth century, the reduced size of the domestic market, the shortage of technical and educational resources and political and institutional factors imposed limits on the rise of a powerful business class. Resulting from this was the predominance of a network of small and medium businessmen on the one hand and the tendency to seek protection from the State against foreign and domestic competition on the other. Spanish businessmen systematically sought protectionist policies and situations of monopoly.[1]

This is not, however, a book about economic history, but rather a book about political history. Our objective is to consider the relations between economic power and political power in Spain over the course of the twentieth century. We want to show the complexity of these relations, their changes over time and the relative autonomy of the economic and political powers, or, in other words, their 'reciprocal instrumentation'.[2] We do not believe there was any 'oligarchic power block' capable of causing the serious political failures that occurred in 1923 and 1936. There were complex political reasons behind those crises, and although the economic factors played a part – perhaps an important one – they were not decisive. Although some entrepreneurs and businessmen profited from the dictatorships' economic policies, they also suffered their interventionism. In the years following the First World War as well as in the 1930s, there were different political attitudes and opinions among entrepreneurs, although it is logical that the defense of order and respect for private property were top priorities. The relation of businessmen to politics and politicians has also been conditioned by the growth of the State and the public sector, which began to achieve a certain significance under the Franco dictatorship and reached their maximum expression after the transition to democracy. During the last twenty-five years of the twentieth century, Spanish entrepreneurs adapted to the new political order and proved capable of responding to the serious economic crisis that accompanied the beginning of the transition, the challenge of the Spanish economy's gradual expansion into foreign markets and its incorporation into Europe.

The most schematic and clichéd explanations of the contemporary history of Spain were abandoned some time ago. Historiography has advanced appreciably over the last few decades and today we have enough research to offer new interpretations. This book is based in part on our own research, which covers the first decades of the twentieth century. It is further based on the abundant bibliography available. We owe much of what we say to the authors cited, although the responsibility is ours alone. In this book, there are assertions supported by sufficient and conclusive research, but there are also many expansions on interpretations that will have to be confirmed or refuted by future works that offer a broader perspective of more recent times.

Notes

1. Tortella (1996) and (2000a); Comín and Martín Aceña (1996a).
2. Pérez Díaz (1985).

Chapter 1
Capitalist Consolidation and the Crisis of Liberalism, 1914–1923

Catalans and Basques Defy Madrid

On 28 June 1916, in Madrid's Palace Hotel – a frequent meeting point located near the Chamber of Deputies – there was a mass assembly of *fuerzas vivas* (people with money and influence) representing the economic interests of practically all the regions of Spain. At the end of the speeches, Bilbao shipowner, Ramón de la Sota, read out some conclusions: given the attempts of the Government to tax the extraordinary profits the World War was producing for certain economic sectors, the assembly unanimously declared that the bill was 'totally unacceptable because if its injustice, its lack of equity, and the disastrous consequences that would result from its application'. Francesco Cambó, an MP for the Catalan League, defended the right to this protest amid high hopes, although others deemed it was selfish.

The congregation decided to appoint a committee that met with representatives of various political forces over the next two days, first in the Chamber of Deputies and then in the Senate, with the goal of raising support for the withdrawal of the bill. The function at the Palace Hotel, whose intense coverage by the press included long lists of the distinguished business elites in attendance, had been preceded by rallies in Bilbao and Barcelona and visits to councils, civil governors, representatives and other influential people, as well as a deluge of correspondence sent to Parliament in response to the public hearing opened by the Government. This correspondence reiterated that the bill was a veritable provocation capable of causing the 'withdrawal of capital'. There had even been announcements of dissolution on behalf of some shipping companies. The possibility of these dissolutions spreading as mere subterfuge to prevent the future tax had driven the Government to take a preventive measure in publishing a royal decree on 21 June, which put Article 3 of the bill into effect. This decree, published before any parliamentary debate could take place, and considered by the press and economic circles to be a true blow to law and justice, only intensified passions and precipitated the assembly at the Palace Hotel.[1]

The decree was the sign of what was to follow: a long parliamentary debate that would last until the end of the year. The debate was marked by an obstruction that flooded the chamber with amendments, interminable speeches, voting motions and incidental proposals, forcing Parliament to prolong the sessions and work on public holidays. All of this overthrew the bill affecting extraordinary profits, as well as much of the ambitious economic and financial programme that Santiago Alba had announced from the Treasury Department of the liberal government headed by the Count of Romanones. The result was deemed a great success for what *El Diluvio*, a Barcelona newspaper, called the 'absorbing and dominating plutocracy', proof of its enormous strength and organisational efficiency given the government's feeble political platform. Alternatively, it was construed by others as the triumph of industrial interests, embodied by Cambó and supposedly punished by the new tax, over agricultural interests, represented by Santiago Alba from his enclave in Valladolid. Horacio Echevarrieta, republican businessman from Bilbao, bluntly put it this way in another much-talked-about rally held at the Albia Colisseum in Bilbao just before Parliament resumed its sessions in January 1917. Santiago Alba's project accomplished only one thing: to divide Spaniards into two camps, one which sided with farmers, the other with industrialists. The guest of honour, Francesc Cambó, fêted by the multitudes since his arrival in Bilbao, had a few other things to add: the fight against the tax was the occasion for a happy meeting, a patriotic convergence of Basque and Catalan interests which had existed in the past and should continue in the future. The Basques could rest easy; the bill would not be approved. It was now merely the instrument the Government was saving for itself to die with gallantry. The day the debate was renewed in Parliament, the Government realised it had to step down from power or close the chambers.

Although there had been a large number and variety of speakers during the parliamentary battle inside and outside the chamber, it was the representatives of the Catalan League, with Cambó leading the way, who had neatly and efficiently taken charge of the obstruction. The defense of economic interests remained at the heart of their battle. Cambó believed it was time to break from the conservative and liberal politics of the moment in order to lay a new foundation for the State. This entailed the 'For Catalonia and Greater Spain' campaign, launched with great fanfare in March 1916 after the League's resounding electoral victory, which then Minister of Government Santiago Alba could not prevent despite his efforts. In the context created by the European war, the mobilisation of the industrialist bourgeoisie could be the ideal platform for the League's proposals. Cambó set to work with this objective in mind. There was not, however, such an unbreakable bond between the League and Catalan economic interests. The *Fomento del Trabajo Nacional*, an employers' lobby headed by the liberal Count of Caralt, had already been stung in 1915 when the League sought to capitalise the request for a free port for Barcelona, one of the lobby's old causes. Now, in the midst of the fight against Alba, the Catalan industrialists felt compelled to draw the line, nearly severing their ties. Cambó had to recognise that the League was not the *Fomento*, despite the considerable degree to which their members coincided. Embarking with nothing else in Cambó's political programme could have its risks.[2]

Cambó had discovered fertile ground for his plans also in Vizcaya (Basque Country), where the enormous increase in wealth resulting from Spain's neutrality in the First World War converged with the momentary triumph of the more moderate currents of Basque nationalism. One name embodied both processes: Ramón de la Sota. His family belonged to the rural nobility and also owned ironworks, and he was the schoolmate of Víctor Chávarri, who would become an important figure in Vizcaya's business and political circles. This background led Ramón de la Sota to form a business partnership with his cousin, Eduardo Aznar, in iron ore mining. The companies Minera de Setares (1886), Sierra Alhamilla in Almería (1893) and Sierra Menera in Teruel (1900) were among the first they established. In 1891, Sota took part in the founding of the Bank of Commerce, and shortly thereafter, undertook the venture of vertical merger, entering the business of sea transport and creating a different company for each of the ships he acquired. In 1906, he decided to merge all of them into Naviera Sota y Aznar. The Euskalduna shipyards began operations in 1901. On the eve of the First World War, the Sociedad Colectiva Sota y Aznar – the first producer/exporter of iron ore – was definitively consolidated. Although not all of his businesses had the same success, the shipping company amassed enormous profits during the war, and the services that Sota provided the English Admiralty even earned him a knighthood. The profits were so great that the company decided to invest in the construction of the Sagunto (Valencia) iron and steel mining complex. Due to numerous difficulties, the complex did not get off the ground until 1923, and would never reach the goals that had been projected for it. This experience converted Ramón de la Sota to protectionism, which until then he had loathed. Nonetheless, during the First World War, from the presidency of the Shipowners' Association and the Bilbao Public Port Authority, everything was rosy for the Vizcayan businessman.[3]

Sota had never belonged to that hegemonic group that was Vizcaya's powerful bourgeoisie, which was branded as 'españolista' (supporting Spanish nationalism). He had had a falling out with his old classmate, Víctor Chávarri, and La Piña (a group of Basque monarchist businessmen opposed to Basque nationalism). Sota's passion for the defense of Basque traditions and culture had moved him closer to Basque nationalism, although this was an attempt to erode its intransigence and emulate the model of the Catalan League. The opportunity presented itself in 1916, when he managed to gain control of the party. Some of Sota's profits ended up in the coffers of the Nationalist Communion and his success as a businessman broke the barrier that until then had always prevented Basque nationalism from becoming a real alternative for the well-to-do classes. The fight against Santiago Alba's tax bills opened the door for him to join the fray and consolidate his advances. Sota was aware of his debt to Cambó, and he acknowledged this the day after the rally at the Albia Colisseum, at a banquet he gave to honour the Catalan leader at the posh Club Marítimo del Abra, a place frequented by Bilbao's influential bourgeoisie, and also the scene of his many happy encounters with King Alfonso XIII. Sota recognised the great merit of the Catalan regionalist minority for putting economic interests ahead of political 'tournaments', and he offered them an alliance, 'a solidarity that unites

Catalonia and Vizcaya, those two hard-working and intelligent regions, with strong and lasting ties'. The following day, in the Champs Élysées Theater, Cambó openly advised the Basque nationalists to follow the moderate path of the Catalans in their struggle for the conquest of power in Madrid. One good example of the renown that the Vizcayan shipowner had earned was the offer of a cabinet post made by the former leader of the Conservative Party, Antonio Maura. Sota expressed pleasant surprise. He declined the offer, feeling it was not his proper place, but, still aware of the political distance that separated him from Maura, he offered himself to Maura as 'a good friend' in the private sphere.[4]

At the time, Sota was an MP. In the local and provincial elections of 1917, and for the first time in the general elections of 1918, Basque nationalism enjoyed unprecedented success. A number of individuals directly connected to Sota obtained certificates of election. It was known that Sota's money had flowed generously during the election campaign. Long-standing provincial representatives had to content themselves with seats in the surrounding districts. The only exception to the Basque nationalist triumph in Vizcaya was the seat won by socialist Indalecio Prieto in Bilbao. Prieto took over the post vacated by businessman Horacio Echevarrieta, who had decided to step down from the political leadership of Vizcayan republicanism that he had inherited from his father after being placed under house arrest for his supposed involvement in the general strike of 1917. After proclaiming his innocence before the military governor, Echevarrieta resigned from his public posts, the presidency of the Chamber of Commerce and his seat in Parliament to dedicate all his time to his businesses, and moved to Madrid. The dispute over the seats of the Basque nationalists in Parliament became a scandal, and some were revoked. In Vizcaya, the reaction was immediate. In January 1919, after a consolation banquet for the defeated candidates, the Monarchist Action League was born. The monarchists, or, what is essentially the same thing, Vizcaya's powerful industrial bourgeoisie, closed ranks against the nationalists and successfully garnered socialist backing to do so. In the elections of 1920, things returned to the status quo and the Basque nationalists disappeared from the Chamber of Deputies.[5]

Around that time, Francesc Cambó gave up trying to replace the party system. The serious political crisis of 1917 had led him from defiance of the Government to his participation in it. He was a minister for the first time in a coalition government presided by Maura in 1918, when he was awarded the important post of Minister of Public Works. When that experience ended, he continued to sponsor the battle for a statute of autonomy for Catalonia, but the grave conflicts in Barcelona convinced him to give up his efforts in the interest of social peace. There had also been a political reaction there to the Catalan movement. In February of 1918, a Monarchist National Union had been created under the leadership of Alfonso Sala, the first Catalan businessman to become a professional politician. After being active in dynastic liberalism, Sala broke from it in 1906, reappearing in politics some years later as an independent monarchist actively opposing the League. Along with him, José Caralt, former president of *Fomento de Trabajo Nacional*, his successor, Jaime Cussó, and other Catalan industrialists would form part of the Monarchist Union.

The more moderate monarchist elements, willing to meet halfway with regionalism, founded the Autonomist Monarchist Federation. Economic forces were also represented in this group. There were several political choices among the Catalan business classes, more even than in the Basque case. Cambó then was not only one of the most important politicians under the Monarchy of Alfonso XIII, but he was also becoming an important businessman. When he was a Barcelona city councilman in 1905, he had made very good contacts. One of them was Daniel Nusbaum Heineman, director of a Belgian financial firm that managed part of the investments of the German corporation AEG. In 1911, Cambó was one of the advisers for the establishment of Barcelona Traction, the electric company popularly known as *La Canadiense*, but his best opportunity came at the end of First World War. The fear of the confiscation of German firms abroad led the owner of AEG, Walter Rathenau, to promote the creation of a company in Spain which would pretend to take over its interests in Argentina. Rathenau put Heineman in charge of the matter, and Heineman turned to Cambó, who managed to attract the interest of several banks and personalities. That was how, on 22 June 1920, the Hispano-American Electric Company (CHADE) was born. CHADE became the third largest Spanish company in volume of capital, and was taken over by the leader of the Catalan movement. Cambó had received a substantial portion of the company shares as a reward for his efforts. He was 'suddenly wealthy', even very wealthy, and could freely dedicate his time to the cultivation of all his interests, which ranged from sailing and artistic patronage to politics. In 1921, Maura contacted him again, and Cambó accepted the post of Treasury Minister, which he used to promote laws with long-term effects, as we will see. But he did not come to power as a spokesman for economic interests, or even as a leader of Catalan regionalism – which, moreover, was undergoing a serious internal crisis – but rather thanks to his strictly personal attributes and the knowledge he had gained in the business and financial world.[6]

The Formation of a Capitalist Society

It was the battle against Santiago Alba's tax bills that wove the web of political interests, but who were the people he wanted to tax? Who was reaping the benefits of the war? Although Spain was neutral in the First World War, the impact of the conflict was felt in all spheres of economic, social and political life. The early stages of the war were marked by panic and uncertainty, with a strong contraction in the liquidity and circulation of money. In Barcelona, people flocked to banks, lining up to exchange their banknotes for silver, while shares plummeted in the Stock Market. The presidents of the most important Catalan financial institutions insisted that the Government should intervene fast to restore economic equilibrium and reconvene Parliament. The Bank of Spain tried to help the companies with the biggest problems, but even so, in Bilbao, the Mining Union Credit Bank was forced to suspend payments temporarily, while the Banks of Bilbao, Commerce and Vizcaya released a statement saying they had enough resources to promptly cover payment requests. Word spread that the bank directors backed this promise with their own personal fortunes, which reassured clients, as the press calculated these fortunes to be worth more than two hundred million pesetas. The situation was quickly resolved, but, as some people pointed out, it revealed the weaknesses of the financial system.

It did not take long for Spain's declaration of neutrality to produce beneficial effects. The increase in exports to cover the needs of the warring countries, and the need to substitute imports that had been cut off because the war caused the trade balance to change from surplus to deficit, began an expansive cycle that benefited important sectors of the national economy, although it hurt others, especially traditional exporters. The private sector accumulated profits and resources, the Bank of Spain built up its gold reserves, and new companies and jobs multiplied, but there were also serious problems of supply and a significant inflationary tension, as well as growing labour unrest. This was explicable in the context of the expansive cycle, but also as a consequence of the emergence of workers' organisations and management's response. As the profits rolled in, public opinion split between the Allies and the Germans, and at one point, between those who wanted to maintain neutrality at any cost and others who fought to break from it, seeking friends and alliances in the new international order that was to come. The different opinions reflected the clear options available with respect to the future of the Spanish Monarchy. The first mass party rallies were held in large public spaces like bullrings, and politics became complicated. In Spain, as in most European countries but for different reasons, the year 1917 was marked by profound political crisis. The government managed to weather the storm, but it had undergone serious changes along the way. The war had a lot to do with these changes, and would tear the whole of Europe far from that *Belle Époque* held in longing by some. The rise of corporate interests, increasing state intervention in new areas, protectionism and economic nationalism, proposals for new codes on public issues and, finally, the crisis of the liberal world before the war were also reflected in Spain.[7]

However, as of 1915, different economic circles enjoyed a climate of true euphoria. In Catalonia, the textile business began to accumulate orders from Italy, Serbia and many South American countries, but mainly from France. Many of the boots worn by French soldiers and the blankets they wrapped round themselves in the trenches came from Barcelona and other Catalan cities. There was growth in the chemical, pharmaceutical, mechanics, flour and food industries as well. Five hundred and forty-six companies were created in 1916 alone. That same year, the company Hispano Suiza began to manufacture airplane motors for the French government at the request of King Alfonso XIII. The iron and steel companies syndicated in the *Central Siderúrgica de Ventas*, an iron and steel cartel, benefited from price increases of more than 100 percent in 1916, while the exportation of iron and steel products rose in one year (1914 to 1915) from 39,177,605 kilograms to 125,838,834 kilograms, and although production fell in 1917, its value continued to increase. At a special shareholders' meeting in December of 1918, Altos Hornos de Vizcaya decided to increase its capital to one hundred million pesetas; its profits had risen from 9.5 million pesetas in 1914 to 18.7 million. In Asturias, the sharp drop in coal imports and the rise in exports triggered an era of prosperity. There were mergers and incorporations of coal and iron and steel companies, and the biggest mining companies doubled or tripled their profits. The number of jobs and the price of coal increased in similar proportions, with the consequent impact on the cost of many other activities. Before the War, *La Canadiense* had employed several thousand workers in the construction of large dams in the Pyrenees and in the laying of cables necessary for the transport of electricity to Barcelona. The scarcity and high price of coal led the company to extend the lighting to streets, establishments, hotels, theaters and private residences, as well as to many factories which would not have survived without linking up to its grids. A few years later, the Rotary Club of Barcelona would erect a monument in honour of *La Canadiense*'s founding engineer, Frank Pearson, who died on board the *Lusitania* in May 1915 when it was struck by a German torpedo. In 1918, the Sociedad Española de Construcciones Babcock and Wilcox was founded, merging the interests of the large steel and iron companies and banking, which diversified its investments by including the electricity sector. Furthermore, the difficulties of sea traffic for the warring countries and Germany's declaration of submarine warfare increased freight costs. Spanish shipping companies were among those who most benefited from the War. The Compañía Transatlántica and the shipping company Sota y Aznar were the two main firms in a sector consisting of primarily small companies before the start of the War. With the windfall of profits, new companies were established, some of them via mergers, as was the case of Transmediterránea in 1916. Also profiting from the War were the Ybarra brothers, whose shipping company in Sevilla expanded its routes. The company Echevarrieta y Larrinaga, one of the Basque Country's richest, doubled its social capital during the First World War, although after the Germans sank three of its ships, Horacio Echevarrieta sold his steamers and became a shipbuilder, purchasing the Cádiz shipyards. This seemed like a good move at the time, but it would cause him endless problems which led to his financial ruin many years later.[8]

The expansive cycle continued unabated until 1919, although around that time the first symptoms of crisis were appearing in some sectors. More new companies were established that year, 164 in Vizcaya, for example, worth a total of 96 million pesetas. But by then there were already signs of crisis in the iron and steel and metallurgical industries, as the *Liga Vizcaína de Productores* (Vizcayan Producers' Association) took it upon themselves to announce, while the *Fomento del Trabajo Nacional* spoke of 'notoriously ruinous decline' in the textiles industry. The volume of capital that moved in the stock market was still very large that year, as such bringing to a climax the speculative euphoria that accompanied the War. The biggest quantities of money ended up in banks. Banking profits had doubled between 1915 and 1917. Capital increased, but the increase of loans was even greater. Their value increased, and the most important banks decided to increase their capital. The growth was, in the beginning, disorganised. Local banks and small family businesses with little knowledge of bank loans multiplied, while the bigger banks set about opening new branches. Then came mergers, takeovers, and an associative process that would culminate in 1918. That same year, the Bank of Spain awarded private banks a kind of discount rate lower than the official rate, creating more opportunites to promote and finance industrial activities. Banks' securities portfolios rose from

564 million pesetas in 1915 to 1,071 million in 1918, and again to 2,344 million in 1921. This was how a small number of financial groups were consolidated around the biggest banks: the Hispano Colonial, the Spanish Credit Bank, the Bank of Bilbao, the Bank of Vizcaya, the Mining Union Credit Bank, and others. The chairmen of these banks also sat on the boards of another 264 companies which represented just over 7 percent of established businesses, but absorbed 49 percent of capital paid out. At the end of the war, two new banks came to join the bigger ones: the Central Bank and the Urquijo Bank. The Central Bank was created under the initiative of a series of regional and provincial banks which wanted to have a bank that would allow them to operate in Madrid. It was not the first time this project had arisen, but now the foundation was laid for what would be, decades later and after a series of tribulations, the biggest bank in the country.[9]

The Urquijo Bank was established in Madrid on 1 January 1918. Behind it was a long family line of financiers which began in the first decades of the nineteenth century and was related to the Rothschilds. One of the two Urquijo brothers, Estanislao, became involved in the different businesses the family had embarked on. Juan Manuel dedicated himself almost exclusively to banking. They founded the Urquijo Vascongado Bank in Bilbao, the Urquijo Guipuzcoano Bank, the Industrial Mining Bank in Asturias and the Catalán Urquijo Bank in Barcelona as independent companies which nonetheless had close personal ties. The increase of capital from 50 to 100 million pesetas in 1920 and the reform of the statutes the following year put two of Estanislao's brothers-in-law and two other trustworthy individuals unrelated to the family on the board. Another important element of the Urquijo Bank was the board secretary, Valentín Ruiz Senén, who became the brothers' right-hand man and sat on more boards of directors than the most renowned members of this business group. In the early 1920s, the Urquijo Bank was first among the top six banks with respect to the number of executives in big companies, and third in deposits. It was always poised for requests from the Government: a loan to France a few months before the end of the War earned the Marquis the title of Grandee, and Luis Urquijo was rewarded for his role in the signing of the trade agreement with the United States with the marquisate of Amurrio. The Urquijo brothers and the King had a very close relationship. 'Estanis', as Alfonso XIII called the oldest one of Urquijo brothers, very often acted as his personal adviser and represented him on various boards of directors. In the midst of that economic euphoria, the King, like some members of the most traditional aristocracy, seemed to become a 'businessman'.[10]

The postwar crisis that befell some of the economic sectors that had benefited most from the conflict also affected the banks. Speculations with foreign currency, the concession of loans with guarantees that lost their value when the War ended, the opening of too many branches, and the lack of preparation and knowledge among managers and directors were the causes put forward to explain it. In Madrid, the Bank of Castilla and the Matritense Bank went bankrupt, but the crisis affected Catalan banks in particular. The Bank of Terrasa, which had grown enormously during the previous years by embarking on risky and speculative activities, announced a suspension of payments on 15 November 1920. With the mediation of Cambó, all the bank directors in Barcelona held a meeting whose outcome was the creation of the *Compañía de Crédito Bancario*, the first fund of guarantees of deposit in Spain's history. Despite these attempts to control the situation, the distrust cultivated among the depositors also made one suspect the solidness of the Bank of Barcelona, directed at the time by the ex-president of *Fomento del Trabajo* and founder and president of the Catalan League, Luis Ferrer-Vidal. The Bank of Barcelona had enjoyed a history of rapid growth which culminated in the merger with the Mercantile Credit Bank in February 1920. As the alarm grew in Barcelona, so did the number of calls to Madrid, until the Treasury Ministry and the president of the Government, Eduardo Dato, announced their mediation before the Bank of Spain. But the guarantees of the Bank of Barcelona had dried up, and on 27 December 1920, the institution declared bankruptcy, shaking public opinion and sparking the mobilisation of the rich and powerful. The panic in the queues of people hoping to recover their money spread to other entities, but the situation gradually returned to normal. Depositors began to deposit their money again and the press proclaimed it had been a triumph of 'Catalan sensibility' and the coordination between the most important representatives of finance and government. The Catalan League, led by Cambó, made the defense of the Bank of Barcelona its own cause, accusing the press of creating unwarranted alarm and candidly blaming the Bank of Spain for its stinginess when it came time to help. Cambó managed to refute the rumour that had circulated during the moments of panic regarding the withdrawal of funds by the Bank's own board members, when in fact this was true. The procedures accompanying the liquidation of the entity and the insurmountable difficulties in determining exact figures further heightened distrust of the Catalan bank.[11]

Cambó was well aware of the Catalan banking crisis and the situation of all Spanish banks after the upheavals of the War when he came to the Treasury Ministry in 1921. He was convinced that the banking industry could not be 'absolutely free', because the losses of a bank affected not only its shareholders but the entire economy of the country, and the banking industry's imprudence had very dangerous repercussions. Cambó's banking regulation law in 1921 sought to alleviate these problems and create better discipline and coordination. Its objectives were twofold: to convert the Bank of Spain into a real central bank, eliminating the competition it posed to the others; and to put banks under the supervision of a Superior Banking Council in exchange for favourable discount rates. Cambó was a champion of 'strong banking concentration' to eliminate the dispersion and dysfunctions of Spanish banks, in order to make them a central element of overall economic development. But the crisis of the Catalan banks had certainly had political undertones that were aired out in the Chamber of Deputies, and which Cambó would take the blame for. Cambó was never indicted for damages caused by the bankruptcy of the Bank of Barcelona, and the Suspension of Payments law was viewed as tailor-made for him. As socialist Indalecio Prieto and Vizcayan monarchist Gregorio Balparda denounced in Parliament, it would have been impossible to clear the bank's executives from responsibility without this law. The lasting controversy over the bankruptcy of the Bank of Barcelona contributed to the deterioration of Cambó's political image. This, along with the eventual failure of his autonomist pretensions, led a large group to split from the Catalan League and form *Acció Catalanista* (Catalan Action Party). In June 1923, after a significant loss of votes, Cambó announced his retirement from politics. Catalan banks, for their part, were absent from the banking expansion that over the following years would continue in a more orderly fashion. It was the banks in Madrid and the Basque Country, obligated by the industrial crisis in Vizcaya to look beyond its provincial borders, that would lead this expansion. There emerged a new banking system which, in addition to its commercial activities, held large stock portfolios of companies in mining, metallurgy, electricity and chemicals. Perhaps without this important change in Spanish banking, the process of capitalisation would have been slower. But it is also true that this symbiosis could become an obstacle to the proper assignment of resources.[12]

The Incompetence of an Interventionist State

The War's biggest economic effect appeared to be the enrichment of a handful of individuals whose names crossed and were repeated on the boards of directors of banks and the leading companies. That 'plutocracy', that oligarchy, as many liked to call it, consisted of about a hundred individuals. Forming it, along with businessmen and bankers, were some renowned politicians. None of these individuals were among the *nouveaux riches* that made their fortunes in the shadier businesses the War had brought with it. Almost all of them were there before the War, although they certainly multiplied their wealth during those years. Now their presence was more evident, though they were jealous of their privacy and reluctant to undertake risky ventures. Many thought, then and afterwards, that it was Basque bankers and industrialists who earned the biggest profits and that, as of that moment, Basque capitalism had come to hold a 'hegemonic position' in Spanish society. The 'descent' of the Basques to Madrid, their ventures in capital, was revealed in very different ways. The main banks opened branches, the capital of Horacio Echevarrieta unblocked the stagnated project to develop the Gran Vía (one of Madrid's central avenues), and the Banco de Vizcaya contributed 50 percent of the capital necessary for the construction of the Compañía Metropolitana which, on 17 October 1919, inaugurated Madrid's first stretch of subway. They even ventured into the world of journalism, releasing the first number of *El Sol* on 1 December 1917. *El Sol* was touted as a modern, independent daily newspaper capable of becoming a business and teaching a lesson to the old and rickety political press. The president of *El Sol*, Nicolás María Urgoiti, was also the general manager of *La Papelera Española* (Spanish Paper Company). Urgoiti did not succeed in winning the support of the Basque and Catalan capitalists he interviewed for his project, but he was backed by the biggest paper manufacturer, which in those years was earning enormous profits thanks to the rise in the price of paper. The Madrid press immediately denounced *El Sol* as the mouthpiece of 'paper manufacturing capital, shipbuilding capital, iron and steel capital, export capital and Vizcayan capital', in other words, of all those millionaires fattened 'by the shady businesses of the war'.[13]

The communion of interests among bankers, entrepreneurs and politicians would have been the most effective result of the European war, because the real impact on the Spanish economy was not as great as it had seemed, and most importantly, because the profits gained were not so very useful. Economic historians have pointed out that, if inflation is taken into account, the growth of the gross national product would be considerably lower. The amassing of profits did not translate into gross capital formation, nor was the gold that accumulated in the Bank of Spain used to improve the country's industrial equipment or to arrange the incorporation of the peseta into the gold standard. This gold would disappear during the Spanish Civil War. The nationalisation of assets and companies until then under foreign control – one of the processes most generally pointed to as a positive outcome of that situation – was not as wide-sweeping as had been believed. Some cases in which more effort was made, such as the recovery of railway assets, were neither the most profitable nor involved the most internationally renowned companies among those operating in Spain. The elimination of the foreign debt undoubtedly had a greater impact. Many cash savings deposits disappeared as a result of postwar inflation. There was no consistent push for structural change, either. After all was said and done, nothing substantial or fundamental had changed. Economically speaking, Spain still lagged behind other European countries. There was no improvement in the competitiveness of the Spanish economy, which led to protectionist movements at the end of the War. In brief, the only positive effect of the conflict had been 'the greater enrichment of already privileged groups'.[14]

These privileged groups effectively defended themselves against the measures introduced by the governments during the War to confront problems of subsistence, the scarcity of certain export products, and price increases. The Subsistence Law was approved in 1916 to reinforce state intervention in the fixing of prices and freightage, the acquisition of raw materials and essential provisions, and the elaboration of plans for arranging the national food supply. The application of the law was entrusted to a Central Subsistence Council made up of numerous representatives from the Chambers of Commerce and Industry, farmers' associations and different economic interest groups, along with deputies, senators, subsecretaries and general managers. The measures proved to be inefficient. Exports continued, taxes were never paid and prices continued to rise until 1920. To finance the inflationary gap during the War, the Bank of Spain was authorised to increase fiduciary circulation, and financial entities were able to pawn bonds of the national debt in a system of indirect monetisation. The increase in public spending, combined with the rigidity of the tax system, obligated the government to resort to loans in 1917 and 1919, with great success. The banks in Madrid and Bilbao subcribed to the offer of titles, but the interests from the debt became a growing component of the budgetary deficit. The situation was all the more serious because, since 1914, Parliament had been unable to approve new budgets, repeatedly extending those from that year, although it took bigger political manoeuvers to do so each time. Tax reforms did not seem to be possible, either. This had been demonstrated not only by the failed tax on extraordinary profits, but also by many of the other proposals that

Santiago Alba had included in his economic programme. These proposals drove small industrialists, traders, viniculturists and urban proprietors to the streets in protest, and drew criticism from the Bank of Spain and from other big companies. Many deputies and senators, representing various interests, worked to respond to the affected sectors.[15]

The measures that hurt them were not approved, but those that could benefit them were. As such, a new law was passed in March 1917 as a result of another initiative by Treasury Minister Alba: the Protection of National Industry Law. The introduction stated that it was a good time for the State to award massive subsidies to Spanish industry, thus taking advantage of its growth. The law promised tax breaks and exemptions, aid via privileged loans, and guarantees for invested capital. There was also a *Comisión Protectora de la Producción Nacional* (Commission for the Protection of National Production) entrusted with applying the law. Forming the commission were representatives of the most important financial entities and the top figures of the industrial and financial bourgeoisie. Furthermore, an invitation to tender was organised by Royal Decree for the creation of an Industrial Credit Bank which would award loans granted by the State. The bid was won by a numerous group of bankers and industrialists. However, the assessment made in 1924 by the secretary of the Commission was hardly encouraging: total revenue that the State did not receive because of tax exemptions only came to 1.5 million pesetas; and of seventy-seven petitions to the Industrial Credit Bank, only forty-four had received a favourable response and fourteen had been resolved, for a total of thirty million pesetas in aid granted. The results of the government's measure to protect national industry were described as 'a mediocre performance in relation to the country's industrial development'.[16]

These frustrating results fuelled the discourse of those who clamoured for the defense of the national economy: 'For a long time, our economic nationalisation has seemed to be an impossible venture, not so much for the tremendous difficulty it presents in itself as for the lack of coherency in national policy, which is completely disoriented with respect to such a crucial problem. Today there is another aspect to the problem. The lessons learned from the War have clearly revealed to the public the great importance of an adequate national economic programme and have determined a collective will that is more or less conscious, but not at all favourable to the policy of emancipation and strengthening'. So stated the Second Conference of National Economy, which was held in Madrid from 3–10 June 1917. It was promoted by the Barcelona Society of Economic Studies, whose director was the secretary general of *Fomento del Trabajo Nacional,* and by the Centre for Administrative-Economic Studies of Madrid. The concerns they wanted to address in that forum had been growing for some time, and had found a channel of expression in publications like the *Revista Nacional de Economía,* which appeared in the spring of 1916. The journal stated that Spain lacked both a clear concept of national economy and organisations capable of creating one. This explained why the national resources were dispersed and, to a large degree, sterile, and why several sources of wealth remained inert while others were exploited by foreign capital under foreign management.[17]

These ideas were spread by business and economic circles, but they did not originate there. They were propagated by people interested and specialised in economic subjects – technicians, they would be called today – and politicians that made this organising and nationalising effort their personal rallying cry. On the Conference of National Economy's committee of honour, there were politicians, presidents of Chambers and financial entities, professors of economics and magazine directors, but among the speakers, there were not as many businessmen as there were lawyers, journalists, engineers, and some politicians. They wanted to create a collective opinion and a permanent forum of discussion about economic problems. Furthermore, the organisers of the Conference concluded it was necessary to promote new ties between society and the State, including channels for direct corporate representation in political institutions. At the Third Economic Conference, held at the end of May 1918, political power and financial oligarchy were highly criticised: 'Our front-line men, a mix of lawyers, journalists, adventurers and actors, are not up to the challenge of these problems. As such, we have problems without men and men without problems, and, in most cases, men who consider politics an art of realities, ignoring that it is also a science of possiblities', said Eloy Luis André in his speech about the need for a foreign policy with national objectives. The decadence of Spain, wrote Emilio Ríu shortly thereafter, was consistent with the idea that the constitutional government was mere appearance, the cause of the backwardness and gangrene that corroded the nation and prevented Spain from becoming a strong and independent country. It was that oligarchic regime that kept the country numbed under an illusion of well-being. 'Whoever thoroughly examines Spanish political life comes to the conclusion that the political oligarchy is the instrument of the financial oligarchy, and that both are, consciously or unconsciously, influenced by strong foreign imperialist organisations'.[18]

Governments in power during the First World War were harshly criticised for not taking advantge of the conflict to strengthen Spain's national economy. After the war, they had to confront the industrial crisis affecting the sectors that had most profited during the conflict and which now clamoured for the urgent adoption of measures that would alleviate the situation. The 'dismantling of customs tariffs' that had been promoted to take advantage of export opportunities, and the 'patriotic renunciations', like the subsidies that shipping companies sacrificed in October 1915, now came back to haunt them. More businessmen demanded greater protection, but, as always happened in battles over customs duties, interests collided and lobbies mobilised. The provisional tariff of May 1921 and the Royal Order in June that intended to halt the massive entry of imports from countries whose currency rapidly depreciated, as was Germany's case, were criticised as hasty and denounced for damaging certain sectors. When the definitive tariff was approved in 1922, it was said that it had been tailor-made to suit the 'artifical industries' created during the War so that they could keep their prices high. The composition of the *Junta de Aranceles y Valoraciones* (Council of Tariffs and Valuations) and the fact that Francesc Cambó was Treasury Minister at the time only confirmed the suspicions of those who believed the tariff had been copied from the project prepared by the

Catalan *Fomento del Trabajo Nacional*. Some Chambers of Commerce, including Madrid's, threatened to withdraw from the Council because they had not been consulted. On behalf of the *Asociación General de Agricultores* (General Farmers' Association), Jesús Cánovas del Castillo protested in the parliamentary debate because agriculture had not been conceded any members of free appointment on a Council whose representation obviously favoured industrial interests, and moreover, Catalans. However, the change in the relation of forces in favour of industrial interests, its 'irresistible push', must not have been so great, considering that one year later, in April of 1922, a law was approved to authorise the reduction of tariffs on certain products, and four trade treaties were negotiated – with Switzerland, France, Norway and, in October, Great Britain – applying that reduction. The visits to Madrid and the campaign organised by those who felt threatened – more so when the law was extended in the summer of 1923 – proved futile. *Fomento de Trabajo Nacional* declared that 'total disorientation' prevailed in Spain, and that all interests were in 'open conflict with each other'. The Barcelona Chamber of Industry complained that 'only the oligarchies that have taken control of this wretched country, void of any patriotic sentiment, concerned only with their own interests and parties, could carry out the demolition and national dissolution that we are witnessing'.[19]

That denunciation overshadowed the paradoxical reality that political institutions and Parliament especially were showing signs of greater vitality and legislative capacity. In the realm of economic policy, important laws like the Banking Ordination of 1921 and the new tariffs of 1922 were passed, as dubious and debated as they were. In 1919, the Government managed to devise new budgets for the first time in five years, just what the pluralist government presided by Manuel Allendesalazar needed. Other important new tax measures were passed as well. In April 1920, the profits tax was reformed to include regular companies, collectives and limited partnerships, to which the principle of progressivity in the tax on dividends and profits would be applied. In July 1922, the law was expanded to include large-volume, individually owned businesses. Furthermore, the industrial tax was increased by up to 50 percent. It was logical that such reforms would ignite a wave of criticism, not so much during the parliamentary debate, but rather when the time came to apply them. The tone of the denunciations was very radical among small-time industrialists and traders, who were affected most by the innovations. They felt abandoned by the political parties and criticised the 'dominant oligarchies' at length. The mobilisation against what was considered an 'exceptional arbitrariness' was massive, and reached its loudest expression in the spring of 1923, when the liberal government tried to apply the tax which the affected interests had managed to keep on ice since its approval the year before. The Superior Council of Chambers of Commerce vigorously protested against tax reform, which was considered unjustifiable and counterproductive in view of the administrative disorganisation and the disorder that characterised public spending. At the beginning of April, in Santander, there was a meeting attended by hundreds of representatives from Chambers of Commerce, commercial lobbies and other associations from those sectors. The assembly declared that 'Parliament did not represent the Spain that worked and toiled', and proposed to investigate the personal fortunes of its members. Facing 'dreadful Spanish politicians from all political parties', who moreover wanted to charge allowances for their work in Parliament, those present decided to send a message to the King, their only and final hope for a 'country of order' in the midst of the chaos. Perhaps they remembered what Alfonso XIII had said two years earlier in Córdoba, when he appealed to the 'provinces' to support their King and the projects they believed were beneficial. Perhaps then Parliament would remember the 'mandate of the people'.[20]

Conflict and Separation from the Regime

In the difficult postwar years, businessmen and employers also had to confront unprecedented social and labour disputes, whose foundations had been laid during the conflict, and which heightened the distrust of politicians. For the first time in their history, workers' organisations had become mass organisations, with nearly a million members. This growth was not reflected in the representation of workers' organisations in Parliament. The Socialist Party managed to break through with their first deputy, but they never had more than seven MPs in those years. The workers' presence in the street and in the workplace, tainted and complicated by disputes between the different unions and the preeminence of apoliticism, was not compensated by incorporation into political institutions. There were few reassuring signs for employers in the sudden erruption of the trade union movement. In the early years of the War, the fight against food shortages and the demand for pay raises met with a management open to concessions that would not hurt production. Strikes were becoming more frequent. The two biggest trade unions, UGT and CNT, were able to put aside their long-standing differences and, in the Zaragoza accord, make a pact which culminated in the general strike of 1916. It was not only the working class that was affected by the spread of the movement and the fight against inflation. A protest developing amongst infantry and cavalry officers was brought to the public eye by the manifesto from the *Juntas Militares de Defensa* (Military Defense Councils) in early June 1917. The awareness of the Army's technical and organisational backwardness, exposed by contrast in the deployment of European armies in combat, came to mesh with the unease caused by the rise in prices, the power of those promoted for war merits in Morocco and the fear of already announced military reforms. All this stirred a movement that was very critical of politicians and openly challenged civil authority. The opposition took this movement as an opportunity to advance towards a rupture with the regime.

Catalan MPs – republicans, regionalists and some liberals – took the initiative, and on 5 July 1917, demanded that the Government immediately reconvene Parliament, which had been suspended since the beginning of the year. Some requested a constituent assembly of Parliament to be able to debate Catalan autonomy, among other constitutional reforms. Not everyone agreed on this, but Cambó tried to reconcile the differing opinions. He declared that since the beginning of June, public powers had been suffering a grave crisis. The military had sounded the alarm, but the problem was not only within the armed forces; the entire country was growing tired of 'governmental, political and administrative disorder'. It was essential to reconvene Parliament in order to deal with the problems, because if the protest of the military councils was not followed up by political change, it would be interpreted as an act of insubordination and become a norm of conduct. If the government did not view it as such, the MPs would have to take it upon themselves to convene, but the government understood that the threat was of a rebellious nature and prohibited the meeting. However, an assembly of MPs was held in Barcelona on 19 July. It was broken up peacefully by the police, but not before the MPs approved a series of points which summarised their programme of political renovation. The Catalan League and Cambó were unable to add to their initiative the wide parliamentary range they had dreamed of. The backing political forces appeared dangerously tilted towards the left, especially when the movement of convergence among reformists, republicans and socialists was revealed in a dangerously revolutionary proposal: the call for a general strike in August, which combined trade union demands with political demands. The strike failed almost immediately in Madrid and Barcelona, while in the mines of Vizcaya and Asturias, the protests were more violent. Contrary to what many had thought possible, the military responded to the Government's call to repress the strike, although some months later, they would turn the tables and precipitate the fall of the conservative Government. The most unfortunate consequence of the crisis was the entrenchment of the military in the public stage; it was even worse when, in the years that followed, the country underwent a series of critical circumstances which were difficult to confront because of the undermining of the legitimacy of constitutional order.[21]

As we have seen, the end of the War brought with it the end of economic expansion and the crisis of the sectors that had grown the most during the conflict. There were salary reductions, job losses and even the definitive closure of factories and productive enterprises, while prices continued to rise at least until 1920. The fact that the crisis did not reach relevant levels in aggregate terms did not lessen the drama of certain situations; it certainly influenced the attitudes of trade unions and employers' organisations. In keeping with what was happening in other European countries, the Government appeased workers by approving an important number of social and labour laws, one of which was a landmark: the establishment of the eight-hour workday in April 1919. Another matter was the ability to implement it. There were also continued attempts to create mediating bodies that could serve as an instrument of prevention or negotiation of conflicts. However, as this entailed the recognition of trade unions, the attempts ran up against the resistance of some businessmen who, with a few exceptions, did not consider it the most opportune moment for such experiments. Furthermore, the most radical trade unions rejected any sort of state intervention. Old and new kinds of conflict; old suspicions but also confusion and uncertainty in the face of an opposition that was better organised and which would just as soon negotiate as walk out; delicate economic situations but also resistance to losing traditional privileges in labour negotiation; all this and more came together to ignite an uncontrollable situation.[22]

The disputes that began during the War continued their growing spiral at least until 1921, but in the last few years leading up to then, they were marked by unusual violence. The millenarian expectations bred among workers' organisations by the Russian Revolution in October 1917 and the terror of the well-to-do classes at the prospect of the revolution that appeared to threaten Europe at the end of the War were not unrelated to the intensification of the conflict. The 'proprietors' fear' was no longer fear of the workers as such, but rather of those minorities willing to organise workers and lead them down the path of insurrection. Manifestations of the disputes in rural areas were very different from those in industrial regions, and the effects on big and small businessmen differed as well. Apart from varying economic circumstances, the confrontations between different trade union movements had a lot to do with this. At the end of June 1918, the CNT culminated the process of organisational centralisation initiated some years earlier, and the *Sindicato Único* (singular syndicate) came to replace the old, almost guild-like methods of the trades that still survived in workers' circles. The threatening and coercion that marked the campaign to extend the *Sindicato Único* spread from Catalan cities to rural Andalusia a few months later. The socialists did not want to be left behind, and for the first time in the party conference of 1918, an agricultural programme was presented. The end of the War, economic pressures and the shrunken labour market turned the competition between both unions into an open battle for the control of hiring and the right to be the only legitimate intermediary. The radicalisation and violence defended by the *grupos de acción* (action groups) in the heart of the CNT spread to the more moderate elements of union management and sparked equally violent reactions in certain socialist sectors, which, moreover, were involved in the debate that gave birth to the Communist Party in 1921.[23]

From 1918 to 1920, Andalusia endured the so-called 'Bolshevik triennium', which later spread to Levante, Murcia and Zaragoza. The 'hunger for lands' was expressed in leaflets and posters, but the big novelty was the emergence of union and socialist groups that fought to enlist new members and were capable of calling long, difficult strikes and demanding collective contracts. The greatest unrest began in the spring of 1918, slowed during the summer, and picked up again in the autumn, lasting for several months afterwards. The sense of insecurity spread as farms were invaded, harvests were burned and houses were destroyed. The governments resorted to the military to repress the violence, and many landowners fled to the main cities, while others prepared to defend themselves. In the Andalusian province of Jaén, from March to August 1919, around twenty employers' organisations were created, enlisting nearly 7,000 members, an unbelievable figure bearing in mind that many of them were small and medium-size landowners – perhaps those who were most affected by the disputes and the demands of day labourers. The civil governor of Jaén wrote to the minister of Government that it had 'exposed to important individuals in the province the need to create a community of order-loving people that could have a group analogous and similar to the *Somatenes de Cataluña* (Catalan civil militia), which would be led by reserve and retired commanders and officers'. Automobile owners in the province had loaned their cars for the transfer of troops wherever they were needed. In the elections of 1920, all the conservative parties joined to form the Monarchic Union. In the province of Córdoba, the epicenter of the earthquake, landowners and employers seemed willing to talk and negotiate until the end of 1919. They were driven to do so by the civil governor when his intervention was required by the workers' organisations. During the general strike of 1919, the Government limited itself to maintaining public order, but during the trade union strikes at the end of May, it declared a state of war on the entire province. The army occupied villages, closed down workers' centres and arrested their leaders. Landowners and employers were not initially aware of what was on the horizon, or of the magnitude of the 'proletariat attack', but afterwards, they firmly believed, as did the trade union masses, that it would be something similar to the Russian Revolution. Even republican leaders worried that peasants might destroy estates, while in employers' centers, there was talk that workers were armed to the teeth and landowners were preparing to do the same. The number of registered associations increased, and a *Federación Agraria Patronal* (Federation of Agricultural Employers) was created in the province of Córdoba. Some associations opted for confrontation, but others tried to divide the workers' ranks, offering to negotiate collective contracts, which ended the strikes of 1919 and 1920. There were also cases like that of the Marquise of Valparaíso, daughter of the Count of Torres Cabrera, who worked to create social assistance institutions. By the time the worst phase of the conflict had passed, the conservative *Confederación Nacional Católico Agraria* (National Catholic Agricultural Confederation, CNCA) had had some successes among landowners. The CNCA was actively involved in a useful campaign of expansion across Castilla.[24]

In the extreme north, in the Basque Country, there had been considerable labour unrest during the War. The strike of August 1917 was general in the coal fields of Vizcaya and the factories of Bilbao. The army occupied strategic points and the battleship *Alfonso XIII* was sent in, but the tremor died down quickly. The greater influence of socialist organisations and the political convergence that took place between the Monarchist Action League and the socialist leader, Indalecio Prieto, against Basque nationalism had their correlate in the business world's conviction – at least among big companies like Altos Hornos in Vizcaya – that 'good harmony between capital and labour' had its advantages. This was helped by the growth of the most important socialist trade unions, especially the *Sindicato Metalúrgico* (Metallurgical Union), which at the time had 9,000 members, accounting for 80 percent of the workforce in that sector. Neither the attempts of a handful of unionists nor the provocations or dissenting attitudes of employers supportive of Basque nationalism, which at the time controlled the *Centro Industrial de Vizcaya* (Industrial Center of Vizcaya), could upset the move towards peace. Ramón de la Sota's business group had always promoted policies of high salaries and important improvements for its workers, obtaining their entry into the nationalist union *Solidaridad de Obreros Vascos* (Solidarity of Basque Workers) and refusing to negotiate with the 'revolutionary workers' movement'. However, in 1920, the split in the ranks of Vizcayan employers widened between the branch of construction and metalworkers, who wanted to confront the workers' organisations, and the big iron and steel businessmen, who opted for the policy of conciliation. In response to threats of a strike and the wish of the *cenetistas* (CNT unionists) to have only their members hired, there was a proposal to create a new *Asociación de Patronos del Gremio de Hierro y Metales* (Employers' Association of Iron and Metals Guild), which would centralise decisions in case of conflict. The refusal by Altos Hornos de Vizcaya and the Sociedad Española de la Construcción Naval to join this initiative led to its failure. Over the next several years, it was the big companies which set the norms, but a number of circumstances chilled employer-labour relations and produced serious conflicts: the assassination of the manager of Altos Hornos, the person who had designed the agreements with the trade unions; the deterioration of the industrial situation; and the weakening of the socialists after the founding of the Communist Party in 1921. In any case, while *cenetistas* and communists demanded a radical response, the socialists chose to support pressure by employers to obtain protective measures from the State. The attempts of the communists to radicalise attitudes crashed, not without provoking violent confrontations: on 9 April 1922, at the end of a meeting in Gallarta to protest the announcement by mining employers that salaries would be cut, a confrontation between socialists and communists left three dead and five injured.[25]

The Basque Country did not suffer the violence that affected other regions, Catalonia most notably among them. The strike by *La Canadiense*, which paralysed Barcelona for more than six weeks in the spring of 1919, submerging the city in darkness and panic, was a high water mark in the conflicts of those years. It was the acid test with which CNT wanted to show the force of its *sindicatos únicos* in their demands of employers and in their open challenge to authorities. The conquest of the trade union confederation leadership by the more radical elements displaced moderates like Salvador Seguí and Ángel Pestaña, who were willing to accept paths of negotiation and mixed commissions. The trade union movement became embroiled in the opportunistic and delinquent terrorism of action groups and gunslingers. But the same can be said of the reaction by the business community. The trade union movement faced a managing class that was prepared to respond in kind to its methods, using the same force and the same violence. Julio Amado, the civil governor of Barcelona, spoke in 1919 of the 'immense and definitive responsibility' of employers given the state of affairs at the time. The organisation of businessmen in entities specifically designed to defend their interests in labour issues had been on the rise for decades in the aftermath of the first strikes and the growing organisation of trade unions, but also in light of the increasingly evident will of the governments to legislate on labour matters. It was not merely a question of reducing the workday, but also of the regulation of collective contracts and what implicitly entailed the recognition of workers' trade unions. It was as of 1914, and out of the celebration of the first Conference of the *Confederación Patronal Española* (Congress of the Confederation of Spanish Employers), when this organisational process intensified, reaching its greatest activity at the end of the First World War as a result of the industrial crisis. Some of its federations played a larger role than others, especially the *Federación Patronal de Barcelona* (Employers' Federation of Barcelona). It was from the building sector that new leaders emerged, so different 'from the ancestral owners, the big manufacturers and industrialists of old stock, the long-established conservative classes'. And it was the second generation of directors of the Confederación Patronal which set the tone in the postwar years: Francisco Junoy, governing the Confederación with an iron hand, and, in Barcelona, Félix Graupera, a building contractor and good representative of that 'pure managing element, largely composed of socially-upward climbers, ambitious people and enriched workers, in whose hearts hatred towards their former colleagues often predominates above all other feeling'.[26]

It was Graupera who set the hardest line in the Second Conference of the Employers' Confederation, held in Barcelona in 1919 and convened with these words: 'the situation that the development of the trade union movement has created for national production is now morally and materially unbearable. It does not appear that the governments of Spain view it like this; concession by concession, they are subjecting the managing class to an impossible diet of humiliations and material burdens'. More than 3,000 people representing over 800 associations attended the Congress. Although they discussed presentations on labour contracts, industrial courts and salaries, many made a distinction between workers and their organisations, especially the *cenetista* movement. The most intransigent minority of employers capitalised on the Congress of 1919, and Graupera worked to convene the extremely difficult lockout that Barcelona endured for three months, from 23 November to 26 January 1920. The *managers' front* challenged the *sindicato único* with the same will to unify attitudes and prevent desertions in the ranks of the employers, and under those circumstances, they seemed to rise up in the name of the entire business class. In January of 1920, Graupera survived an assassination attempt. Just before that, unionist Salvador Seguí had been attacked. That year was even harder. The *Sindicatos Libres* (Non-Affiliated Unionists) then burst onto the scene. They were formed in 1919 as a reaction to the monopoly of the *cenetista* movement and eventually came to be regarded as management's trade union, the 'yellow trade union', although their formation and their trajectory responded to the contradictions and divisions of the trade union movement itself. Employers grew more critical of what it viewed as weakness, even condescension, on the part of the Government in Madrid, and decided to take matters into its own hands. Coercion was answered with coercion, and weapons with weapons. Obscure bands of hitmen emerged from employers' circles. The phenomenon of urban vigilantes spread, and the Catalan militia doubled its members, branching out into the main Spanish cities. In April 1919, Catalan employers had forced the resignations of Barcelona's chief of police and civil governor, who were sent back to Madrid for ignoring the orders of Field Marshal Milans del Bosch. Employers also enthusiastically implemented and sustained the repressive work of the new chief of police, General Arlegui, and did the same with another civil governor, General Severiano Martínez Anido, at the end of 1920. Martínez Anido always bragged about operating absolutely independently of central power. In February 1921, a Barcelona newspaper tallied the 197 attacks perpetrated in the two previous years: 103 dead and 173 injured. That pace increased afterwards: from

November 1921 to December 1922, there were 392 victims of crimes. It was easy to blame most of the violence on those in power, on management and their supposed bidders – non-affiliated unionists, soldiers and governments – but the chronology of events shows that the *cenetistas* were guilty first. The killings and attacks occurred mostly among those sectors opposed to anarchist unionism: employers, managers, policemen, and above all, non-revolutionary workers.[27]

The disputes in Barcelona put the governments in check, provoked crisis and the suspension of the constitutional guarantees. The peace that was finally imposed came at a very high price, and although the well-to-do classes strove to end the violence – at almost any cost – not everyone expressed the same enthusiasm about *terrorismo blanco* (employer-sponsored terrorism). In fact, among the ranks of the Catalan business community, attitudes were not homogeneous. The *Fomento del Trabajo Nacional* was an entity that had traditionally acted as a mediator between businessmen and government on the prestige it held as an institution and the prestige of its individual members. When social unrest exploded at the end of the First World War, *Fomento* and its executives hoped to maintain their dialogue and moderate attitude, and they were questioned in their traditional role by some businessmen who preferred to maintain their independence with respect to those issues. The most affected and most desperate employers found the protection of the *Federación Patronal* more adequate. The social upheaval not only provoked panic, but also created ruptures and differences among the business class.[28]

In October 1922, the conservative government dissolved the military councils, lifted the suspension of guarantees in Barcelona and dismissed Martínez Anido and Arlegui for fear that the tactics used by both men could intensify the violence. The assassination attempt against the unionist leader Ángel Pestaña was the straw that broke the camel's back. The reestablishment of constitutional guarantees, which caused the resignation of the Catalan Bertrán i Musitu from government in protest, allowed the anarchist 'affinity groups' to be revived. From December 1922 to May 1923, there were 34 killed and 76 wounded in attacks in Barcelona alone. Around March 1923, anarchist elements appeared to have regained control of the trade unions. On 10 March, Salvador Seguí, who had done so much to try to redirect the CNT along moderate lines, was killed, supposedly at the hands of the *Sindicatos Libres*. The transportation strike that began in May and paralysed Barcelona continued unresolved into July. Many felt it was dragged out intentionally by management in connivance with the Field Marshal of Barcelona, Miguel Primo de Rivera, while the government's stance tried to encourage an atmosphere of negotiation.

The Coup d'État

On the morning of 13 September 1923, García Prieto's liberal Government released a statement announcing that the Field Marshal of Catalonia had declared a state of war in his region, had seized communications and contacted the captains of other military regions to gain their support. 'To save the Fatherland', the Army had to press the King to remove the ministers and the politicians from the governing of the State. The Government, meeting in permanent council, kept its obligation to remain in its post, which it would only relinquish through force, and was awaiting the arrival of King Alfonso XIII in Madrid that day from San Sebastián, where he was vacationing. When the monarch arrived by train the morning of 14 September, the president of the Government went to receive him at the station. He requested the immediate detention of those involved in the coup and the immediate convening of Parliament. Alfonso XIII said he would need time to think about it. García Prieto, considering he had lost the trust of the Crown, presented his resignation. The King then informed him he was going to entrust General Primo de Rivera with the formation of a new government to be made up of politicians, technicians and soldiers. Parliament was dissolved, and it was said that it would be convened again within the legal time limit. In a communiqué, Alfonso XIII declared that an appointed governing board would assume power on an interim basis until the new president organised his cabinet. The board would provisionally consist of five generals. On the train from Barcelona to Madrid, Primo de Rivera changed his mind and decided to form a strictly military board, which he communicated to the generals when he arrived. That began a period of political exceptionality which, if initially believed to be temporary, resulted in a dictatorship whose long-term effects on the history of Spain would be difficult to overstate.[29]

'The Spanish dictatorship', Francesc Cambó later wrote, 'was born in Barcelona and created by the atmosphere of Barcelona, where trade union demagogy was intolerably intense and inveterate'. It is undeniable that the situation in Barcelona influenced the Catalan Field Marshal's decision, and not only because the violence that came with the social unrest had intensified. A gathering of the most radical Catalan, Galician and Basque nationalists culminated in an explosion of nationalism with cries of 'Long live a free Catalonia!', 'Death to Spain!', 'Death to the military!', and 'Long live the Catalan Republic!' This stirred passions among soldiers and sowed the seeds of fear among the regionalist bourgeoisie, whose political party, the Catalan League, had been showing symptoms of crisis for months. In the September 12th manifesto that Primo de Rivera read to publicise his intention to take down the government, he said that the moment had arrived to free the nation of 'professional politicians' and the 'dense network of the politics of lustfulness' that had sapped even the King's will. Rivera condemned the political parties to 'total removal' from government.[30]

Apparently, on the eve of the coup, Primo de Rivera had met with some important individuals in Barcelona. He read his manifesto, and those present promised him the support of the Catalan business classes in exchange for the protection of industries and the concession of autonomy to Catalonia. It was said that they put the promise in writing. In attendance were the Viscount of Cussó, ex-president of *Fomento del Trabajo Nacional*, and the Marquis of Comillas, among others. The Count of Güell and future third Marquis of Comillas had been a friend of Primo de Rivera's since 1911 when he volunteered for the war in Africa. He had known of the general's intentions since July. On the night of the coup, 12-13 September, he did not leave Primo de Rivera's side, nor did Alfonso Sala, another leading industrialist and monarchic politician, when the Ministry of War phoned to order them to cancel their plot. On 13 September, Primo de Rivera attended the inauguration of a furniture exhibition in Montjuïch, accompanied by the Marquis of Alella, mayor of the city, and by Puig and Cadafalch, president of the Catalan *Mancomunitat*. He received ovations on various occasions. At six o'clock that afternoon, the president of Fomento, Domingo Sert, urgently called a meeting of the High Council to announce that he had visited Primo de Rivera early that morning to express his support of the general's manifesto. He considered it to be a true plan of government which coincided with the view of businessmen. His support had been personal in nature, so he convened the Council in order to hear what the members thought. Opinions were divided. Some felt it would be prudent not to commit oneself in the future. The coup did not have the military's full support, and the Government of García Prieto was still functioning. However, the majority urged for a rapid declaration of support, an institutional visit to the general and an appeal to the other Catalan entities to subscribe to their position. In the document that was approved at the meeting, Fomento proclaimed its 'enthusiastic identification', its 'unshakable support', for a programme outlined with 'undeniable competence' that 'masterfully' condensed its corporate criteria: 'We, united in spirit and feelings with that brave army, so indignantly treated by the merchants of dying politics, extend and incorporate our action into that *gran Somatén español* which, united with the military element, will guarantee the protection of civil rights and security'.[31]

The reception of the coup by other economic and business circles was more cautious and slower. Among the national organisations, the most enthusiastic was the *Confederación Patronal Española*. As they communicated to Primo de Rivera from Madrid before the coup took place, they were already drawing up a manifesto of their support in an 'irresistible movement of sympathy towards the champions that hoisted the banner of regeneration'. Primo de Rivera's promises responded to the complaints and aspirations that had been expressed in many economic circles throughout the previous years: the exasperation before the disorderly and violent situations; the erratic and, according to some, completely erroneous economic policy; the abusive tax system and the waste in public spending; social legislation that was untimely and ill-conceived; and above all, the incompetence – if not lustfulness – of an incapable political class. In response to that political class and the insitutions of the regime, the proposals of a corporate representation had emerged from very diverse forums and with very different tones as an alternative to what the existing Consitution established. Primo de Rivera's coup suddenly gave a voice to these protests.[32]

However, the economic entities and business circles were aware that not everybody agreed and that their respective interests were at odds. What some circles demanded would come at the expense of the others. Not many businessmen believed Primo de Rivera's idea that there was only one, easy solution. As a result, the Chambers of Commerce and Industry, agricultural associations and also banking institutions spent the first several weeks drawing up statements that offered their own opinions and enumerated what they expected of the new situation. Moreover, the business classes and employers had mixed feelings about the political rupture. For as much as the politicians had been criticised and defamed, the links between economic and political interests were numerous and complex. In his manifesto, Primo de

Rivera had promised that all denunciations of malfeasance, bribery or 'duly proven' immorality would be welcomed. He had also announced the corresponding punitive processes for everyone who had commited an offense against the fatherland, 'corrupting and disgracing it'. These declarations were cause for concern, especially because those who reported the crimes would be treated in the strictest confidence. On 12 October 1923, a retroactive decree declared that high ministerial functions were incompatible with those of directors, advisers, lawyers or consultants of large companies, public service companies and state contractors. It intended to initiate, as Primo de Rivera liked to say, a period of 'Catonian severity and morality'. This not only engendered the fear of losing one's post – a fear which lifted almost immediately – but also cast uncertainty on the political horizon and bred distrust of a governing board consisting of generals possessed of their own sense of historical mission. And on that board, it was, for the moment, Primo de Rivera who had the final, incontestable word. Most of the Catalan business community welcomed the appointments of Martínez Anido as Undersecretary of Government and Arlegui as Director General of Security, as well as the institutionalisation of the Militia. But after the coup, civil governors were dismissed and replaced by military commanders. Municipal councils were dissolved, while 1,400 soldiers travelled around the country to purge civil servants in a genuine atmosphere of panic. This severed many of the ties between economic interests and political institutions.[33]

The *Fomento del Trabajo Nacional* persisted in its enthusiasm and affirmed that the Military Directorate had 'only one urgent mission to accomplish': to create a new political structure, a new parliamentary system that would prevent the return of the 'old elements', and take as much time as necessary to do so. The *Confederación Patronal* applauded the 'radical rectification and conduct in the State's governance to exlude all guilds', but understood it as the path to expressing the 'loyal and legitimate exercise of national sovereignty'. The *Confederación Gremial Española* (Confederation of Spanish Guilds), which united the merchant classes traditionally hostile to the oligarchies, was pleased the oligarchies had been erased from the political scene, but did not want to comment on the way it had been accomplished. It offered all its support in the 'destruction of the germs that debilitated national life', but also said that afterwards there should be 'an open path to a government founded on democratic principles'.[34]

The coup of 1923 had the feel of the previous century's military *pronunciamientos* (uprisings), but it was also the army's first corporate intervention as an institution, and the first time the military effectively held power, convinced of their legitimacy and ability to direct political life. Primos de Rivera's first declarations offered a glimpse of hope – however uncertain – for a new kind of regime, authoritarian but imbued with appeals to mobilisation and ambitious plans for regeneration.[35]

Notes

1. Roldán and García Delgado (1973, vol. I: 255–322).
2. For the differences between *Fomento* and the Catalan League in Rey Reguillo (1992: 748ff.); Martorell (2000: 184–1929); Sellès (2000: 131–142 and 348–349).
3. For the biography of Ramón de la Sota, see Torres Villanueva (1998).
4. Territorialism and nationalism, in Elorza (1978) and Corcuera (2001); Maura's offer to Sota, in Torres Villanueva (1998: 245–246).
5. Echevarrieta, in Díaz Morlán (1999). The elections of 1918 and the reactions afterwards, in Ybarra y Bergé (1947); Fusi (1975: 377–397); Arana (1982), Pablo et al. (1999: 109–148).
6. The political pluralism of Catalan businessmen, in Rey Reguillo (1992: 757–762). Alfonso Sala, in Puy (1983) and in Cabana (1997: 111–113). Cambó's businesses, in Pabón (1969: 215–231). A concise biography of Cambó, in Cabana (1997: 113–119) and in Riquer (2000a).
7. For the historical context of the War, see Meaker (1978: 53–91); Carr and Carr (1981); Seco Serrano (1995: 289–567).
8. The industrial situation, in Roldán and García Delgado (1973, vol. I); the growth of the merchant navy and coal mining in Roldán and García Delgado (1973, vol. II). Damián Mateu, in López Carrillo (2000); on Pearson, in Calvo (1994); for the Ybarras, Sierra (1992); Echevarrieta, in Díaz Morlán (1999).
9. The consolidation of private banking, in Roldán and García Delgado (1973, vol. II); the financial groups with their industrial interrelations in *ibid.*: Appendix IV. Also, Martín Aceña (1985). The biography of José Luis de Ussía, in Tortella (2000b); the Rodríguez Acosta brothers, in Titos (2000).
10. The Urquijos, in Díaz Hernández (1998) and (2000); Luis Sedó, in Moreno (2000); the King as a 'businessman', in Gortázar (1986).
11. The bankruptcy of the Bank of Tarrasa, in Cabana (1972) and Muñoz (1988: 60–77). The history of the bankruptcy of the Bank of Barcelona and its political implications, also in Muñoz (1988).
12. The suspension of payments law, in Muñoz (1998); the banking expansion from 1919, in Muñoz (1978); the consequences of the banking and industry conglomerates, in Tortella and Palafox (1983), and Tortella (1994: 337).
13. The list of the '100 big capitalists' and the posts they held, in Roldán y García Delgado (1973, vol. II: 386–415). Echevarrieta in Díaz Morlán (1999: 157–163); on the Compañía Metropolitana, in Gortázar (1986: 124–129); Urgoiti and *El Sol*, in Cabrera (1994).
14. The textual quote in Sudriá (1990: 390), and the general balance there and in Hoyo (2000: 48).
15. The provisions policy and the increase of prices, in Roldán and García Delgado (1973, vol. I); Santiago Alba's economic programme, in Cabrera, Comín and García Delgado (1989); tax reforms and the mobilisation, in Rey Reguillo (1992: 279–312) and Martorell (2000: 179–211).
16. Roldán and García Delgado (1973, vol. I: 367–379).
17. Quoted in Roldán and García Delgado (1973, vol. I: 328 and 331).
18. The conclusions of the Second Conference, in Roldán and García Delgado (1973, vol. I: Appendix IV). Eloy Luis André's quote, in the selection of texts by Muñoz, Roldán and Serrano (1978a: 306). Emilio Ríu's quotes in Roldán and García Delgado (1973, vol. I: 345).

19. Customs tariffs and quotes in Muñoz, Roldán y Serrano (1978a: 71–105); attitudes regarding the customs tariffs issue, Rey Reguillo (1992: 210–252). The quote from the Barcelona Chamber Industry in ibid.: 49.
20. Tax reforms, their parliamentary processing and the play of reciprocal interests, in Rey Reguillo (1992: 279–301) and Martorell (2000: 227–265). The quote from the King, his speech in Córdoba in May 1921, in González Calbet (1987: 45–46).
21. The words of Cambó and the Assembly of Members of Parliament, in Plá (1981: 445ff.); the crisis of 1917, in Lacomba (1970); the military, in Boyd (1990); a general interpretation of the period, in Arranz et al. (2000).
22. The policy of social reform and the employers' position, in Rey Reguillo (1992).
23. The changes and radicalisation in Spanish workers' organisations, in Meaker (1978), Arranz (1985) and Cruz (1997). The 'proprietors', in Rey Reguillo (1997).
24. The conflict in Jaén, in Tuñón de Lara (1978); the 'Bolshevik triennium', in Meaker (1978); the unrest in Córdoba, in Díaz del Moral (1979) and Barragán Moriana (1990); Catholic trade unionism, in Cuesta (1978) and Castillo (1979).
25. Fusi (1975: 383ff.) and Olábarri Gortázar (1978: 197-214 and 267–272).
26. The CNT and the *La Canadiense* strike, in Meaker (1978); The Confederación Patronal, in Rey Reguillo (1992: 106–154), and Bengoechea (1994) and (1998).
27. Employers' reaction to violence, in Rey Reguillo (1992); fear and employers' trade unionism, in Rey Reguillo (1997); the gunslinging years, in León-Ignacio (1981); the Militia, in González Calleja and Rey Reguillo (1995); the balance of the violence, in Cabrera and Rey Reguillo (2000). For the *Libres*, Winston (1989).
28. For differing opinions about the relations between *Fomento* and the *Federación Patronal*, Rey Reguillo (1992: 162–165); Bengoechea (1994: 313–319) and Sellés (2000: 356–357).
29. González Calbet (1987: 67–74); the note from the liberal government, in Tusell (1987: 85).
30. Cambó's quote is included in González Calbet (1987: 34). The nationalist chants, the civil governor's telegram to the Minister of Government and the text of the manifesto, in Casassas Ymbert (1983: 74–75 and 81–85).
31. García Venero recounts the meetings (1967, vol.II: 302–313), compiling the events from Perucho (1930:16–21); confirmed by Ben-Ami (1984: 43) and Rey Reguillo (1992: 849–850); the textual quotes, in Rey Reguillo (1983: 141–146) and Sellés (2000: 361–363). The adhesion, in Rey Reguillo (1992: 848–852).
32. The *Confederacion Patrinal*'s manifesto, in a letter to Primo de Rivera quoted by Tusell (1987: 191–192). The quotation, in Rey Reguillo (1992: 885). The proposals of corporativism, in Rey Reguillo (1992: 818–839).
33. The quote from the decree of 12 October, in Maura Gamazo (1930, vol.I: 66). For the atmosphere of panic, see Ben-Ami (1984: 71–75).
34. For a summary of the financial entities' responses, see Rey Reguillo (1992: 839–864); a shorter summary of the reactions, in González Calbet (1987: 81–84).
35. Ben-Ami (1984: 47–48) and Gómez Navarro (1991: 319).

Chapter 2
The Era of State Intervention and Confrontation, 1923-1936

The Regulated Economy

On 11 December 1923, in a circular addressed to the most important businessmen and financiers of the day, the Marquis of Urquijo, the Count of Zubiría, Ramón de la Sota and Luis M. Aznar, the Marquis of Arriluce de Ybarra, the Count of Gamazo and Juan Gandarias convened a meeting that was held on 14 December in the offices of the Industrial Credit Bank. The intentions of General Primo de Rivera to embark on a series of public works had caused some concern. The big banks had already collectively offered him their 'most disinterested and patriotic collaboration for the work of national reconstruction, consisting of the promotion of public works with Spanish capital', avoiding the potential dangers of resorting to 'that more or less imaginary foreign capital that people are talking about'. According to the Spanish banking community, requesting funds from abroad or accepting them implied a regrettable step backwards in the growth of the Spanish economy.[1]

The biggest industrial companies, closely linked to these financial institutions, decided to reinforce their own positions and convene a meeting to create a *Federación de Industrias Nacionales* (Federation of National Industrialists). Ramón Bergé y Salcedo, representing the Bilbao Chamber of Commerce, was in attendance at the meeting. From his father, Ramón Bergé y Guadarmino, he had inherited a comfortable economic position thanks to a series of flourishing businesses during Bilbao's economic, commercial and urbanistic boom, as well as noteworthy political status, born out of his close and faithful friendship with the Conservative leader, Antonio Maura, whom he served as economic advisor. The son played an active role in Basque conservatism and in the creation of the *Liga de Acción Monárquica* (Monarchic Action League) to counterbalance Basque nationalism. Bergé played a decisive role in the birth of the *Federación de Industrias Nacionales* and his presence in Madrid was a clear sign of the interest that the future entity awoke in the most industrialised regions.[2]

The companies represented at the meeting were the biggest companies in the iron and metal, metallurgical, electric and shipbuilding sectors. Other companies joined, and when the Federation was officially established, it represented capital worth 1.5 thousand million pesetas and the employment of 200,000 workers. It had a broad representation, composed of the most important industrialists and financiers, and it was essentially directed by a superior council presided by César de la Mora, with Ramón Bergé as chief executive. On 25 December 1923, Ramón Bergé wrote to Primo de Rivera, urging a meeting to dicuss the intentions of the *Federación de Industriales Nacionales.* 'Its counterparts abroad, The British Industries Federation and the Comité de Forges de France, have become invaluable collaborators of the English and French governments, and the same occurred in Italy with the Associazione fra Industriali Mettalurgici Italiani, and it is so logically obvious that the State would benefit enormously to have, in one entity at its disposal, direct contact with all the country's industries in close cooperation with the banks, and everything that this merger and cooperation entails in terms of efficiency and guaranteeing the development of public works is so clear in the case of our nation that I do not feel it is necessary to extend this letter with further details'.[3]

The 1920s were still happy years, years of 'considerable growth', unprecedented for national industry, which expanded at an annual rate of 5.5 percent over eight years from 1922 to 1930. This rate was, of course, much higher than it was during the Great War, and also higher than the more moderate 3 percent that represented overall economic growth. Economic historians have explained this growth as the consequence of a private investing cycle, which the great plans of the dictatorship had little to do with, although the dictator probably liked to believe that he deserved most of the credit. Miguel Primo de Rivera came to power in 1923 convinced of the uselessness of professional politicians, but also of the inability of private initiative to develop the economy and raise the country to the heights it merited. Both the bourgeoisie and the liberal state would have failed in this endeavor. It was up to the new State to take over and lead the country in a new direction. In March 1924, a *Consejo de Economía Nacional* (Council of National Economy) was created. It was headed by the dictator himself and was composed of eighty-two members, seventeen of which were official technicians, with the rest representing corporations and economic associations. A month later, a law was passed to help create new industries and develop existing ones, and fresh impetus was given to the Industrial Credit Bank. The *Estatuto Ferroviario* (Railway Statute) from the same year and the creation of a Railway Savings Bank initiated an important process of renovating infrastructures and railway equipment. In view of all this, the *Federación de Industrias Nacionales* encouraged the creation of a Public Works Construction Company Ltd., with the aim of assuring the State that it had enough resources to win any invitation to tender in the announced plans, and as of that moment it became a sort of watchdog organisation to assure the State adhered to its own laws.[4]

There was not much new in these regulations, except the will to reaffirm the State's role as a driving force. Primo de Rivera, thrilled about his triumphant pacification of Morocco after the landing at the Bay of Alhucemas at the end of

1925, decided to convert his Military Directorate into a Civil Directorate. The initial impression of the dictatorship's provisional status faded. Its first months had been a period of 'naïve political regenerationism'. The goal, highly praised by public opinion, had been to free institutions from the local political tyranny that dragged them down. The decree of 12 October 1923 concerning incompatibilities was issued in this context, as well as the will to persecute denunciations of corruption and fraud. The wave of accusations, many of them anonymous, had to be stopped by Primo de Rivera himself. This accusatory fever receded around the beginning of 1924. Primo de Rivera could not prove anything in the trials opened against some of the politicians of the Monarchy, as was the case of Santiago Alba, perhaps the most talked-about of all of them. This first stage was followed by another of 'socioeconomic regenerationism and political organisation'. It was then that the Unión Patriótica, a movement of spontaneous support for Primo de Rivera arisen from small and medium Castilian farmers, became an official party. Its expansion, under the direct sponsorship of the Government, caused quarrels and conflicts in many places. Although in some cases it was a refuge for old dignitaries and political bosses, in many places it represented the emergence of a new political class. This class was made up of members of the bourgeoisie, liberal professionals, civil servants, landowners, industrialists and traders, presidents of Chambers of Commerce and Industry, small banks and savings banks, Catholics and conservative Maurists. In July 1926, with its new statutes, the Unión Patriótica had Primo de Rivera as its national chief, and José Gavilán Díaz as president of the executive committee. Gavilán was a second-rate politician who was nonetheless well-connected with social Catholicism through his ties with agricultural organisations and employers' entities.[5]

This was the profile of the new political class promoted by the dictatorship. It was very different from the class that had held the power under the previous constitutional government. There was not much direct participation on the part of the high landowning aristocracy in the Unión Patriótica, although there was some provincial aristocracy. The relations between the Unión Patriótica and the Vizcayan royalists were not easy. In a visit to Bilbao after the approval of the Industry Protection Law, Primo de Rivera thought that the *Federación de Industrias Nacionales* would bestow a gesture of appreciation and support the new party, but the 'Basque plutocracy', perhaps encouraged by the King himself, who despised the Unión Patriótica, refused to bind their fate with it. The decree of incompatibilities had not been well received by Vizcayan businessmen and financiers, and the dismissal of civil servants from town halls, along with the renovation of the provincial councils, caused problems. In 1926, the familiar royalists were ousted from the Provincial Council of Vizcaya and new figures took over there as well as in the City Hall of Bilbao. Relations with the Catalan bourgeoisie had also been strained since 1924, when the *Lliga* endured a rupture and the regionalists felt that Primo de Rivera had betrayed the promises made before the September coup. With the regional councils dissolved, Puig I Cadafalch quit the presidency of the Mancomunitat. It was the *Unión Monárquica*, however, and not the *Unión Patriótica*, which took the political posts at the local and provincial levels in Catalonia. The lack of enthusiasm and institutional cooperation from Basques and

Catalans does not mean they did not benefit from the dictatorship's economic policy. Personal friendships and the proximity to or presence in corporate organisations like the *Consejo de Economía Nacional* could be very effective.[6]

At the end of 1926, the dictatorship entered a new stage of definitive rupture with liberal parliamentary ideology. Primo de Rivera wanted to create a new State with the creation of an *Asamblea Nacional Consultiva* (National Consultative Assembly), which intended to represent all national interests, functioning as a forum of debate and a source of information and advice – but not as a legislative institution. Its establishment was delayed by differences over its composition and, above all, by opposition from the King. Primo de Rivera launched a big, self-promoting propaganda campaign to put the initiative to a vote, a decision His Majesty took as a personal affront. Along with the three levels of administration (municipal, provincial and national) and the *Unión Patriótica*, there were 124 assembly members who represented the 'interests': fourteen from agriculture and ranching, twenty-one from industry, nine from banking and insurance, four from trade, five from employers' organisations and nine from unions. Among them were some of the biggest names from industry (the Count of Güell, the Marquis of Comillas, the Marquis of Cabanes, the Marquis of Alella, Carlos Prats and José Aresti, among others). Agriculture, proportionally underrepresented, as some complained, had Jesús Cánovas del Castillo and Francisco Marín y Beñtrán de Lis, the Marquis of la Frontera, among its representatives. But governmental control of the Assembly was absolute: 259 of its 383 members represented the Administration, and those who stood on behalf of the interests were appointed by the government. The Assembly deliberated by sections, and dedicated many of its sessions during the first year to debate 'The economic problem of Spain', but the speeches were reduced to defending sectorial interests. For its own part, the political debate showed that, beneath the apparent agreement on defending some type of corporate representation, the disagreements over important matters predominated. The project of the new Constitution that was finally born did not even have the Assembly's unanimous support. It also failed to win the King's approval.[7]

Although committed to their work, the business classes worried about the political future. Despite the relative relaxation of the dictatorship, it had become more interventionist in the economy and more inclined to corporatise labour relations. There was no way to control this, because the National Assembly had not been designed to this end. Three ministers on the Civil Directorate embodied the spirit of the new policy. Eduardo Aunós assumed the post of Minister of Labour and set up the *Organización Corporativa Nacional* (National Corporate Organisation), to which we will refer later; Rafael Benjumea, Count of Guadalhorce, took charge of the Ministry of Public Works, and José Calvo Sotelo was Treasury Minister. Rafael Benjumea was an engineer who belonged to a rich family of Sevillan cattle ranchers. He had been chief of the Militia in Málaga in 1923, councilman and creator of the *Unión Patriótica*, and also had close ties with industrial and financial business interests in the Basque Country and Madrid, which led him to participate in the creation of the *Federación de Industrias Nacionales*. His plans, which excited the dictator, were realised in the creation of the Department of Railways and Streetcars, the Network of Free Highways and the establishment of Valley Authorities. These projects, which many of the *Federación de Industrias Nacionales* members immediately benefited from, did not stop the organisation from declaring itself to be 'against a disproportionate development of public works', which could surpass the country's national industrial and financial capacity. Substituting the national capacity with foreign capacity would mean upsetting the balance of the national economy.[8]

Putting the public works in motion demanded an important economic effort. In 1926, José Calvo Sotelo, as Treasury Minister, elaborated an extraordinary budget. Calvo Sotelo had been a young, brilliant lawyer and supporter of Antonio Maura, who enthusiastically received the promises of 'regeneration' stated in the proclamation of the 1923 coup d'état. He was named Director General of Local Administration to put these matters in order, and he wrote the new Local and Provincial Laws, whose political points were never applied, but which provided town halls with more economic resources. When the dictator began to design the Civil Directorate, Calvo Sotelo expected to become Minister of Justice, but he was offered the post of Treasury Minister instead. His intention to undertake a sweeping, indispensable tax reform by personalising taxes as the first step towards a graduated income tax ran up against created interests. His fight against fraud and his attempt to speed up land registry raised the heated protest of the big landowners. Primo de Rivera himself forced him to abandon his project.[9]

Calvo Sotelo agreed with the dictator's wish to convert the State into an efficient instrument of economic growth and modernisation, and the reforms he introduced were designed along these lines. After overcoming resistance from certain private financial sectors, he created the Local Credit Bank in 1925 and the Foreign Investment Bank in 1929. He also reinforced intervention in the Mortgage Bank and amplified the operations of the Industrial Credit Bank, but Calvo Sotelo was not in favor of excessive State intervention or the uncontrolled increase in public spending. Primo de Rivera was only too happy to impose himself on the economic scene – a consequence of the 'fatal' propensity of dictators for interventionism – but the Treasury Minister was 'siempre verso suelto', always cool to this policy, as he later wrote. His alarm was immense when the dictator, 'suddenly and without much deliberation', prohibited the installation of two sugar refineries to head off the threat of overproduction. Until then, Calvo Sotelo had thought industrial freedom in Spain was unlimited. But, as a consequence of Rivera's decision, an Industry Regulating Committee was created by Royal Order on 4 November 1926. Any initiative to modify or create new industries had to be approved by this organisation. In Calvo Sotelo's opinion, it was a 'hindrance of destructive irradiation'. Smaller businessmen maintained that it hurt their chances to compete with big firms. However, the *Federación de Industrias Nacionales* was quick to say that official intervention in those matters was the 'most dangerous solution that could be adopted'; the problem of excess productive capacity had to be resolved by private initiative. Perhaps State intervention did not, for the moment, upset capitalists, who were 'not very keen on industrial risks and easily adaptable to seeking security under the protection of the

State', as the *Federación* recognised, but the excesses would be disastrous for industrial development, which could turn out to be 'one more sector dependent on the State'.[10]

Many of the important firms benefited, directly or indirectly, from the State's plans. Altos Hornos in Vizcaya, the Sociedad Española de Construcciones Navales, Duro-Felguera, the Siderúgica del Mediterráneo and the Maquinista Terrestre y Marítima increased their profits by 51 percent between 1925 and 1929. Unión Eléctrica Madrileña's profits increased by 90 percent between 1923 and 1928. *La Canadiense* doubled its profits in the first two years of the Civil Board. The 1920s were also important years for banking, which continued the process started at the end of the First World War: geographic expansion, concentration, agreements for the financing of industrial projects and the development of new banking techniques. All of this increased profits, especially for the six largest banks. After the crisis of the Mining Union Credit Bank was absorbed in 1925, and after the Central Bank avoided one of its own – not before the Marquis of Aldama and the Count of the Gaitanes were subpoenaed and spent a few days in jail – the big banks continued their specialisation while the banks in Madrid branched out nationally and became hegemonic within the country. Banking and private investors enthusiastically responded to the issuing of the public debt in November 1926, although most of the savings in those years were channelled to the stock markets, which echoed the general euphoria. The buying and selling of shares was the talk of the town; the Spanish were caught up in a genuine speculative mania. At the beginning of 1927, Calvo Sotelo consolidated the floating debt, reinforcing the image of financial soundness. However, the figures calculated by economic historians oblige us to qualify the impact of the Civil Dircetorate's public works plans: the growth of basic industries, which benefited the most from these plans, was less in those years than in the years 1922–1926, which reveals that this growth was due rather to the increase in demand prior to the plans. The rate of investment progressively diminished between 1925 and 1928; in this latter year there was no growth. Businessmen were aware of this, and kept insisting that the plans for public works that threatened to exceed the productive capacity of Spanish industry would have disastrous consequences. The diminishing investment rate and the 'corporate corset' created by the proliferation of auditing bodies were considered to be the causes of an increasingly perceptible exhaustion.[11]

On Monopolies, Larcenies and Responsibilities

Primo de Rivera was convinced of the wisdom to intervene and regulate in order to avoid the damaging consequences of what he considered 'ruinous competition' when market forces were left to run their own course. It was a simple matter. The dictator said that, when all was said and done, in the economic order of things, the Government, with all its advice and organs, was merely the 'nation's board of directors' that had to combat ravings, ambitions and selfishness. But that great board of directors embarked on a series of initiatives which fueled all types of rumours, and on occasion, genuine scandals. In many cases, these initiatives lacked transparency and, of course, any sort of public tax policy. The dictatorship's openly industrialist policy, favoring big firms and the creation of monopolies, could not but create conflicts which were often resolved according to one's proximity to power. Corruption, or simply favouritism, which the dictatorship had intended to fight at the outset, was threatening to become a disease. *Primistas* (supporters of Primo de Rivera), veritable brokers who obtained advantageous concessions for a private owner or firm thanks to the friendship of some minister, cropped up like mushrooms. There was no electoral benefit in exchange, because there were no elections or parliaments, and mediation was rewarded with money, paid-up stocks, or some sinecure. The dictatorship, as the socialist Indalecio Prieto would say after its collapse and in the middle of a campaign against the Crown, linked 'a series of larcenies which has no equal in the history of any civilised nation'. Some of those that Prieto cited certainly sounded humorous, like the monopoly of rodent control on ships, or mussel fishing on the crags of Barcelona's port – conceded, incidentally, to 'one of Mr. Martínez Anido's clients'. But there were other more talked-about deals. One of them was the strategic railway of Ontaneda-Calatayud (35 million pesetas of founding capital was issued in paid-up stocks for the payment of preliminary procedures). Another was the concession of the communications monopoly to the Compañía Telefónica Nacional, whose director was the Marquis of Urquijo. Many were scandalised by the fact that the U.S. firm IT&T was a major shareholder in this company.[12]

During the 1920s, the Urquijo Bank became the most important bank because of its presence on boards of directors. It competed for this ranking with the Bank of Bilbao. The Urquijo family had a history of initiative and presence in the biggest railway, iron and steel, and electric companies; now it was winning some of the most important State contracts. The Spanish Naval Construction Company, whose vice-president was Estanislao Urquijo, became the Navy's supplier. Urquijo had beaten out Horacio Echevarrieta, who, in alliance with the Germans, tried to win certain assignments in the hopes of bailing out his Cádiz shipyard. Echevarrieta had been Primo de Rivera's friend since leading the rescue of Spanish troops from Abd-el-Krim after the disaster of Annual, but it was not enough to emulate the power of the Urquijos. It was the beginning of the end for the great fortune of the old republican businessman. The Urquijo brothers also knew how to position themselves favourably for the leasing of State monopolies. They had been part of the creation of the Compañía Arrendataria de Tabacos in 1887. Luis de Urquijo y Ussía, Marquis of Amurrio, had been president of this company since 1923, and the brothers were its second most important shareholders behind the Bank of Spain. In 1924, they took part in the founding of the Compañía Telefónica Nacional, whose president was Juan Manuel de Urquijo y Ussía, Marquis of Urquijo. In addition, as we will see, they also headed the group of banks that won the leasing of the oil monopoly.[13]

Nationalism, the defense of national production and the nationalisation of those sectors considered to be strategic had been a central part of the dictator's speech, which Treasury Minister José Calvo Sotelo had fully agreed with. The most spectacular product of this agreement was the Royal Decree of 27 May 1927, which later became the law that established the oil monopoly. The Spanish oil market was merely a business of importation and distribution, given that Spain did not produce oil, and it was controlled by branches of big foreign firms: Standard, Shell and the Hispano-French Porto Pi. Despite his prejudices with regard to monopolies, the Treasury Minister was asked which was preferable: a State monopoly or a 'monopoly in fact foreign and governed by irresponsible powers' which could cause serious problems for consumers and the State itself. If monopoly was controlled by the State, he thought, the State would garner the profits that foreign companies had pocketed up to then. Moreover, it could be an 'instrument of nationalisation' of the refining industry, the transport industry and the petroleum industry itself. Fiscal arguments, important to Calvo Sotelo after the frustration of much of his tax reform, took a back seat to his goal of industrialising the nation.[14]

The gestation period was long. It was decided that the petroleum monopoly should remain under State control and only its administration would be leased to a private concessionary company. The idea was to avoid all criticism, and for that reason, the interest of the State was stressed – 'perhaps to excess', as Calvo Sotelo himself wrote. But 'arbitrary concession' would not be tolerated, as the interests in question were very powerful. The big oil companies, convinced of their strength, threatened to reduce supplies, while their branches in Spain denounced the existence of an 'official candidate' for winning contracts, prompting all sorts of rumours, debate and speculation. It is still a paradox that the *Revista Nacional de Economía*, a fervent defender of economic nationalism, affirmed that the monopoly would entail price increases for all petroleum products and that, from the doctrinal and scientific point of view, the State's monopolistic orientation in industries like petroleum was a big mistake. There was general opposition to the monopoly in both the economic and non-economic press because of the likely presence of the big oil companies behind the campaign and the battle among the different candidates to win the concession. For the newspaper *El Sol*, for example, the project implied a 'genuine bureaucratic socialisation of the industry' based on one of many 'false conceptions about economic policy' spread by the needs created during the First World War.[15]

Six entities presented proposals to the tender. Two were ruled out for not fitting in with the philosophy of the project. Two more were rejected because they entrusted the future supply of oil to only one country, which seemed very risky. Of the remaining two, the one headed by the Urquijo Bank seemed more solid from a legal and financial standpoint. The Urquijo Bank was joined by the Hispano-American Bank, the Spanish Credit Bank, the Herrero Bank, the Bank of Vizcaya, the Bank of Bilbao, the Hispano-Colonial Bank and the Bank of Catalonia; in other words, all the big ones. The Urquijo Bank could boast of a certain familiarity with the business because it was an important shareholder in, and had a major presence on the board of, the Sociedad Petrolífera Española, which until then had exclusive distribution of Dutch-Shell products. The proposals which Juan March and Horacio Echevarrieta participated in were rejected. On 24 October 1927, the constituent deed of the Compañía Arrendataria del Monopolio de Petróleos (Campsa, Petroleum Monopoly Leasing Company) was signed. Unlike what occurred with other State monopolies, such as the explosives monopoly, it was established that Campsa's profits would come only from a certain percentage of the revenue. The obsession with maximising State revenue and avoiding all manner of gossip led to fixing very strict conditions. On the other hand, the degree of State intervention and supervision by way of the Treasury Ministry was extreme, to the point that it hurt the functioning of the company. Lawsuits resulting from the expropriation of preexisting companies and supply problems owing to the opposition of the big oil companies made it a difficult start for the monopoly. It was even said the financial problems of the dictatorship in its final years were a direct consequence of the creation of the oil monopoly. Paradoxically for the dictatorship, it became necessary to resort to the Russian oil supply by way of the contract that the Soviet oil company, Nafta, had with the Porto-Pi Oil Company. When Porto-Pi was confiscated, so was the Russian contract. At the beginning of the 1940s, after the Spanish Civil War, the lawsuit that gave rise to the confiscation was still dragging on.

'While the general and I had endless arguments with the embassies regarding expropriations and valuations', wrote Calvo Sotelo, 'the Campsa bankers lived in the best of all worlds, happy and carefree, apparently with no other mission than that of mere and simple resale. But the monopoly was not simply an organisation of retail gasoline sales!' The Treasury Minister could not get the leasing company to address the tasks of industrialisation that he had set as goals. As a result, and because of other state interference considered unacceptable by the board members, there were serious confrontations with State representation. In January 1929, it was Calvo Sotelo himself who reminded them they had to construct a fleet, set up three refineries and acquire oilfields. The construction of the fleet got off the ground because it entailed jobs for shipbuilders. Attempts to acquire oilfields in the United States, Colombia, Venezuela and Mexico after visits there eventually failed. The refineries were a complicated matter for a leasing company like Campsa. As such, the Compañía Española de Petróleos (Cepsa) was created a few months later with the goal of exploring oilfields acquired in Venezuela. The company was an initiative of the Recasens brothers, founders of the Bank of Catalonia in 1920 and also members of Campsa's board of directors. Despite their links to nationalist republicanism, the brothers had won the friendship and trust of Calvo Sotelo. They proposed to him the creation of the Local Credit Bank, whose tender they won with no problem. Allied with the Hispano-Colonial Bank, the Arnús Bank and the March Bank – but this time pitted against the big banks of Madrid – they also won the tender for the Foreign Investment Bank of Spain. For the establishment of Cepsa, they had the participation of the Bank of Catalonia, the Hispano-Colonial Bank, the Central Bank and the Foreign Investment Bank. Relations between *petróleos* (big companies like Campsa) and *petrolillos* (small companies like Cepsa), as they were known back then, were often stormy, as Cepsa requested preferential treatment in the supply of oil for the monopoly, which the leasing company turned down. Despite the initial problems and the worst predictions, when the dictatorship fell, the petroleum monopoly had made big money for the State, although, as it has been written, greater revenue from import duties would have prevented the relative increase in the price of crude oil.[16]

In January 1930, Calvo Sotelo resigned, defeated by his failed attempts to stop the depreciation of the peseta, which was caused by high domestic prices, the excess of imports and the worsening of the public deficit, economic factors compounded by the political uncertainty. At the time, Spain was exploring the possibility of incorporating the gold standard. The report released by the commission charged to study the issue cited some protests from businessmen who lamented the 'abnormal containment of company spirit' and the 'loss of entrepreneurial initiative'. Spanish businessmen were discovering liberalism. One sign of the climate of growing distrust was the resounding failure of the debt bond issued by the Treasury Minister in December 1929. The Bank of Spain refused to let the Government use its gold reserves, which seemed like revenge by the Monarchy's 'old politicians' who had an important presence on the bank's board of directors. On 13 January 1930, the Catalan newspaper *La Vanguardia* published a manifesto signed by Catalonia's most important economic entities. The manifesto said that the only solution was for the dictatorship to give way to a national government. Francesc Cambó wrote that it no longer was what it had been and that it was asphyxiating private initiative. The waning trust on the part of the economic forces was a relatively important factor in the regime's final crisis, joining the growing opposition of important sectors of the middle classes, professionals, journalists, intellectuals and university students, but it was not the main cause. Primo de Rivera's coup de grace came when he realised the support he had won from the Army and King Alfonso XIII in 1923 was now lost. The general resigned and was exiled to Paris, where he died after a short time in the most wretched solitude.[17]

The new government, headed by another general, General Berenguer, began a slow recovery of constitutional normality that failed and led to the proclamation of the Second Republic on 14 April 1931. The new Treasury Minister, Manuel Argüelles, definitively eliminated the extraordinary budget and the public works programme, and reduced ordinary expenditures to try to balance the budget. The Comité Regulador de la Producción Nacional and other auditing and corporate organisations were also eliminated. Argüelles's declarations about the need to carry out an 'extremely thorough investigation' of the public accounts helped give rise to the controversy over the inheritance of the dictatorship and its possible excesses. The appointment of Calvo Sotelo as president of the Central Bank, a post from which he immediately resigned, contributed to poisoning the issue with accusations of corruption and favouritism. In the years that followed, the ex-minister would devote all of his efforts to dismantling these accusations. With regard to the petroleum monopoly, Calvo Sotelo denied all the rumours of generous compensations, shady supply contracts and appointments of friends before Campsa's general assembly. The press boasted about the decision to create Campsa, a manoeuver which aroused the envy of more than one powerful State.

The executives of the leasing company appointed during the dictatorship were sacked. The Marquis of Cortina assumed the post of company director while the Minister of Foreign Affairs, the Duke of Alba, stealthily interviewed with Sir Henry Deterding, director of Shell, because some people still believed that the continuing fall of the peseta was due to the posture of the big oil companies. However, they did not agree with Deterding's wish to dismantle the monopoly. The last governments of the Monarchy did not do it, nor would the socialist Indalecio Prieto, the first Treasury Minister of the Republic. Not even the 'truly tempting suggestions' of the powerful oil firms, which offered the millions of pounds necessary to erase the debt that Spain had abroad, were sufficient reasons to do so. The socialists, Prieto later said in Parliament, hopeful to reach a position of power in the near future, had had the luck of having past bourgeois governments that had monopolised branches of industry and trade. It was not going to be them who destroyed that work: 'Don't you understand that, in this case, you would have forged insurmountable instruments of socialisation for our social organisation? The petroleum monopoly is one of them'. As such, it was not dismantled, but the posts were renewed and the allocations of provincial agencies always suspected of favouritism were revised. Furthermore, the socialist minister even presented a project for a new contract between the State and the leasing company which would put State representation on the board of directors in the majority over shareholding financiers. It was a proposal along the lines of the new Ley de Ordenación Bancaria (Banking Regulation Law) approved at the end of 1931. This law, which tightened State control over the Bank of Spain, established the government appointment of three advisers and increased their role in the fixing of interest rates. Prieto could not stand the fact that the Bank of Spain, a private entity, earned substantial profits, even in times of economic depression; he wanted the State to receive a greater share of the profits. At no moment was the nationalisation of the central bank considered. In the case of Campsa, the new contract project, an 'arbitrary outrage', as the Marquis of Cortina described it, never got off the ground because the banks threatened to withdraw from the administration of the monopoly and take any legal action necessary to defend their interests.[18]

The effects of the regime change on Juan March, someone else who benefited from the dictator's politics, were very different. On 6 June 1931, then Treasury Minister Indalecio Prieto cancelled the concession of the tobacco monopoly in Spain's North African enclaves that José Calvo Sotelo had awarded Juan March by Royal Decree in August 1927. Juan March, a native of Majorca, 'of humble origin', as he described himself in his defense before the republican Parliament, had begun to make his fortune with the concession of the tobacco monopoly in Morocco that he had won from an international company in 1912. This monopoly had allowed him to extend a tobacco smuggling ring all over the Mediterranean that substantially cut in on the monopoly of the Compañía Arrendataria de Tabacos (Tobacco Leasing Company). In 1921, he had been denounced in the Parliament as a 'modern smuggling technician'. With skill, craftiness, an enormous capacity for work and the assumption that every man had a price, Juan March had amassed substantial profits during the First World War, diversifying his investments to include sea transport, electric companies, oil and banking. His political proximity to the liberal leader Santiago Alba at the end of the constitutional Monarchy and the campaign of purging at the start of the dictatorship drove him to leave the country temporarily. Meanwhile, a trial that was eventually dismissed was started against him. The Majorcan businessman decided to return to Spain, and in an interview with Primo de Rivera, convinced the dictator of the goodness of his intentions and of his intention to collaborate splendidly with his initiatives. It was the first step in persuading him that the best way to put an end to the tobacco smuggling and increase State revenues was to award him the monopoly in the North African enclaves as well, in exchange for the payment of a fixed levy. March also offered his collaboration in the work of colonising the region, one of the dictator's greatest aspirations. The concession of the monopoly was a very personal decision for the dictator, contrary to what some of his ministers thought. On at least two occasions, in 1927 and 1929, Primo de Rivera forestalled the rumours circulating about his relations with the Majorcan financier in unofficial statements: Mr March's huge fortune could have come from any source, but he had put it at the service of any 'patriotic or beneficial objective' that requested it.[19]

The reasons the republican Treasury Minister, Indalecio Prieto, gave in 1931 for cancelling the concession to Juan March were that March had been awarded it without a previous tender and without parliamentary approval. March did not leave Spain when the Republic was proclaimed, unlike he had done in 1923. He managed to be acquitted of charges from two lawsuits brought against him and he won a certificate of election for Majorca in the republican Constituent Parliament. But he eventually fell at the hands of the parliamentary commission created by the Republic to purge the political responsibilities of the dictatorship. With poorly defined powers and a clearly persecutory streak in some of its members, the commission aspired to purge not only political responsibilities, but also all those responsibilities of those who were suspected of having done big business with Primo de Rivera. Nearly all of these efforts proved useless. The most talked-about effort by some members of the commission was their accusing Juan March of bribery and malfeasance. They also wanted to implicate ex-minister Calvo Sotelo, who was living in exile at the time. A long and arduous battle to arrest and try March ended with his imprisonment in the Cárcel Modelo in Madrid on 15 June 1932. In Parliament the day before, in the middle of a tense debate, Indalecio Prieto said that the government of the Republic had to give the impression – within and outside of Spain – that the country was not controlled by Mr March. During the dictatorship's early drive for renewal and restructuring, March was viewed as a genuine threat to the State. As such, Primo de Rivera persecuted him more cruelly than the Republic, but gave in to him afterwards. This was a cycle that Prieto did not want to repeat. Prieto responded to the statements that Juan March had made in his own defense, recounting how, in 1930, the revolutionary committee that was looking for help to establish the Republic approached March to solicit financing. He refused, and perhaps that explains why they were persecuting him now. One had to be energetic in the face of such insinuations. The Republic, as President Niceto Alcalá Zamora had said, had been born free and independent. It had 'neither businessmen, nor bankers, nor capitalists' behind it.[20]

Juan March spent seventeen months in prison, waiting on a ruling from the *Comisión de Responsabilidades* (Responsibilities Commission), which was not presented until the Constituent Parliament was all but dissolved at the end of 1933. It did not seem easy to prove the charges of malfeasance and bribery, even treason, that rode against him and the former Treasury Minister. Irate, Calvo Sotelo had already given his declaration from exile when his arrest was solicited, describing it all as 'crude, clumsy, unprecedented conspiracy'. The long trial against March was stained with scandals that reached several members of the Partido Radical (Radical Party) headed by the Minister of Foreign Affairs, Alejandro Lerroux, and which contributed to the deterioration of the political situation during the Republic's first two years. Juan March bought some of the biggest newspapers that had supported the republican government, bailing out their owner, and in the spring of 1933, they joined in the criticism of the government. In a much-talked-about article, the trial against March was compared to the Dreyfus affair in the French Republic. To add to the scandal, on 3 September 1933, Juan March was elected to the Tribunal de Garantías Constitucionales (Constitutional Guarantees Council), although his election would be contested. Two months later, with the Constituent Parliament dissolved and his trial unfinished, the Majorcan financier escaped from prison and fled the country.[21]

The 'Sudden Socialisation' of the Spanish Economy

The case of Juan March was exceptional. There was no personal persecution on the part of republican authorities similar to his in the business and financial world. Entrepreneurs and employers had other problems to worry about in the 1930s and their response acquired the new forms required by the social mobilisation that the Republic brought with it. The names of big businessmen, industrialists and financiers disappeared from the public stage and were supplanted by leaders of new business and employers' organisations. The exasperation of owners, businessmen and employers grew over the first two years of the Republic.

Although in some circles there was no lack of suspicion about the proclamation of the new regime on 14 April 1931, attitudes were rather hopeful and even enthusiastic among many small and medium industrialists and traders. The Republic ended the impossible consolidation of the constitutional monarchy and was established peacefully amidst popular celebration after local election results in the most important cities favoured a republican-socialist coalition. The King, Alfonso XIII, decided to leave. However, as would soon be seen, there was no coherent and unanimous political project in the heterogeneous coalition of republicans and socialists; the hopes inspired among the different social classes by the proclamation of the new government were neither similar nor compatible. There was no doubt about the reforming will it had been born with. However, the economic situation was not the most favourable. The New York Stock Exchange's 'Black Thursday' and 'Black Tuesday' on 24 and 29 October 1929, put an end to the reigning optimism of the international economy in the mid-1920s. It was the start of a crisis that would soon affect Europe and grow into the Great Depression of the 1930s, already a universal phenomenon of an unusual depth and extension, with social and political consequences that would be difficult to overstate. In Spain, the impact of the international economic crisis in the sectors most open to the foreign market combined with the interruption of public works developed during the dictatorship of Primo de

Rivera to provoke the first worries just before the dawning of the Republic. The change of government caused an almost inevitable flight of capital and a decrease in bank deposits. However, there was not a financial crisis. Free from the ties that the gold standard entailed in other countries, the republican government was able to increase the quantity of money in circulation and the Bank of Spain was able to come to the aid of banks with the biggest problems to avoid having to sell their shares in industrial firms. The only notable crisis was endured by the Bank of Catalonia, which had an important but unappealing securities portfolio of industrial companies, as well as portfolios of foreign currency. Neither the Treasury nor the Bank of Spain discriminated against the Bank of Catalonia because of its loan policy, but the Treasury Minister, Indalecio Prieto, decided to withdraw the balance that Campsa had deposited there; the sum represented between 10 percent and 20 percent of deposits. This was the death blow, and the Bank of Catalonia suspended payments. Its founders, the Recasens brothers, had trusted their luck with the new government thanks to their republican past and the fact that another brother was a socialist, but they had also been friends of Calvo Sotelo's. They had no doubt that the bankruptcy was the result of Prieto's manoeuvers in connivance with the big financiers. The money withdrawn from the Bank of Catalonia, he said, went to the Bank of Vizcaya and the Bank of Bilbao, both of which Prieto had good relations with.[22]

Economic macrovariables reveal that the Spanish economic crisis was less severe than that of other European countries. In 1933, national income was 8 percent less than what it was in 1929. While prices in other countries dropped 20-30 percent, in Spain they remained stable until 1932, fell somewhat in 1933, then recovered afterwards. The relative isolation of the Spanish economy and the continuing influence of agriculture, which enjoyed excellent harvests in 1932 and 1934, could have compensated for the decline of the industrial sectors that had grown the most in the 1920s and whose production fell 15 percent between 1929 and 1933. This is why economic historians have said that what Spain experienced between 1930 and 1935 was a 'stagnation' or a 'superficial depression'. What is true is that the recovery in other countries after 1933 was hardly noticeable in Spain. Unemployment, one of the most dramatic manifestations of the economic crisis in the 1930s, reached 33 percent in the most industrialised countries. Despite the dubious nature of the figures, it can be said that there were significant levels of unemployment in Spain, 'a labour crisis', as it was also called, in sectors sensitive either to the importance of companies that suffered a major decline in activity, or to the conflictive potential of workers. Barcelona, Madrid, Valencia and Vizcaya were the provinces with the highest industrial unemployment. Construction was a sector with one of the highest rates of unemployment. In Madrid, unemployment in construction reached 57 percent in May of 1934. In the entire sector of metal, mainly in Vizcaya, there were layoffs, but almost more important than the real impact of unemployment was its threat when it came down to establishing labour conditions. In any case, the highest unemployment rates were in agriculture, around 60 percent at certain moments, although it is impossible to measure the effects of the traditional seasonal work in the fields or the effects of the economic crisis. The expectations awakened in the popular sectors by the change of government, the strength of the trade unions and the practical absence of a security net against job loss made unemployment one of the most serious problems the republican governments had to face.[23]

The depression coincided with the political change and entrepreneurs encountered an administration whose key posts, like the Treasury and Labour Ministries, were occupied by socialists: Indalecio Prieto, who would soon be replaced by Jaume Carner, and Largo Caballero, respectively. Prieto inherited the obsession with budgetary balance and the restriction in the depreciation of the national currency, both considered disastrous legacies of the dictatorship under Primo de Rivera. The depreciation of the peseta was not an easy problem to solve. It did not stop until the worldwide depression hit bottom, the international monetary system was completely dismantled and a strict control of foreign exchange could be implemented, as occurred in other countries. The obsession with budgetary balance led Prieto to maintain the cut in public spending initiated by the last government of the Monarchy. In doing so, he had to confront the demands of the businessmen most affected by the drop in public demand. Vizcayan businessmen, for example, managed to mobilise the local and provincial authorities and even the trade unions to pressure in favour of securing contracts for the iron and steel and naval construction industries. They felt that Prieto was still a friendly interlocutor. They obtained some concessions, but not nearly what they had hoped for. To the repeated demands made by numerous city halls and regional councils, the minister always replied that it was necessary to 'reduce the budget'. When, after the approval of the Constitution, he moved from the Treasury to the Ministry of Public Works, Prieto confessed before Parliament that he had spent his youth obsessed with industrial issues, but the more panoramic vision he had back then had given him the 'profound feeling' that the foundation of the economy, even at the expense of ruining industry, was agriculture. On several occasions, Prieto made the mistake of confessing his ignorance of the subjects he was in charge of, and also his will to resign, which did not help develop trust. He was deeply disturbed by an unemployment crisis for which he saw no easy solution without creating a budget deficit. He did not have time to come up with a budget, but it is difficult to place the blame on him, and on those who succeeded him in the post, for not stopping the crisis. It is said that the monetary and fiscal policies of Indalecio Prieto, and afterwards, Jaume Carner, actually helped to soothe the effects of the crisis. On the other hand, it is hard to imagine the Republic could have achieved what in many other countries had been impossible. Spanish governments, including those of the Republic, had shown a willingness to intervene in economic matters since the 1920s, but Spain did not have the resources necessary to regulate the economy. The evident mess that was the economic situation throughout the republican years is another matter. The profound political revolution that took place after 1931 caused instability and forced priorities to be placed on immediate political concerns so that there was hardly any time left for the economy.[24]

While Indalecio Prieto publicly expressed his doubts and concerns in the Treasury Ministry, his government colleague, Francisco Largo Caballero, had a much clearer picture of things. From the Labour Ministry he began an immediate task that culminated in the creation of the *Jurados Mixtos* (mixed labour juries). These *Jurados* were, in fact, the extension of the *Organización Corporativa Nacional* (National Corporate Organisation) created in 1926 by the Minister of Labour for the dictatorship. The *Organización Corporativa Nacional* was part of a labour policy that included the enactment of the first *Código del Trabajo* (Labour Code) and the first *Ley de Contrato de Trabajo* (Labour Contract Law), which recognised individual as well as collective contracts. The dictatorship had implemented regulatory projects in labour issues that had been presented in the final years of the constitutional monarchy, since the creation of the Labour Ministry in 1920. Primo de Rivera was able to do this thanks to the climate of economic prosperity, social pacification, the absence of parliamentary forums that could obstruct the projects and the cooperation of socialist trade unions. The establishment of the *Comités Paritarios* (Parity Committees) had the blessing of Francisco Largo Caballero, who had accepted the dictator's offer of a post in the *Consejo de Trabajo* (Labour Council), an advisory board for the ministry. The election of workers and employers as members of said committees gave all of the representation to the union or employers' organisation which obtained a majority of votes. With the anarchist trade unions dissolved, and with the limited and concentrated introduction of Catholic trade unionism, the organisations that benefited most were the *Sindicatos Libres* and, above all, socialists.[25]

The goal of the *Organización Corporativa* was to strengthen big employers' associations and professional, apolitical workers' groups within a harmonious conception of labour relations. At first, business and employers' organisations reacted cautiously. It was felt in some employers' circles that dialoguing with workers' organisations was necessary and advisable, but attitudes differed. *Estudios Sociales y Económicos* (Social and Economic Studies), an important entity created by big firms, dedicated itself almost exclusively to following the functioning of the Comités, which were considered to be an example of 'dangerous State interference' and a serious 'loss of freedom' for individual initiative. The *Confederación Patronal Española*, which united medium-sized industrialists and especially guilds from the building sector, was more receptive to the creation of the corporate organisation. In the end, however, it agreed with criticisms of its obligatory norms and the fact that the *Comités* could establish obligatory regulations. The attacks multiplied when the growing influence of the socialists was perceived and when the *Comités* were given the power to rule on all types of dismissals. Employers' organisations demanded changes in the method of electing members, the power to propose names for the presidency of the *Jurados*, whose appointment corresponded to the ministry, and limiting their powers with regards to dismissals and inspections.[26]

With the dictatorship over, businessmen nurtured the hope that the *Comités* would disappear. In February 1931, in a public hearing on the corporate organisation, its condemnation was nearly unanimous. The *Confederación Gremial* stood out among the critics for its radical opinions, although initially, it had welcomed the creation of the *Comités Paritarios*. Traders and small industrialists from Madrid had just agreed on a mass withdrawal from the committees and the condemnation of any employer that cooperated with them. But the employers' aspirations were frustrated. Furthermore, there was now a socialist in the ministry. Largo Caballero not only did not abolish the *Comités Paritarios*, but, by decree of 7 May 1931, also strengthened their powers and extended them to agriculture, giving them the name of *Jurados Mixtos*. The ministry issued many decrees in April and May of 1931. Their objective was to improve workers' bargaining positions in the negotiation of working conditions and respond to situations of unemployment, especially in rural areas. For the moment, this did not imply 'carrying out socialist reforms', he maintained, but rather taking positions that would afterwards permit the attainment of 'that supreme ideal'. Because of this stance, the business class warned that excessive, poorly conceived social legislation could mar the peace, and that party prejudices and the promises made to the masses in opposition campaigns could destabilise an already delicate economic situation. This warning was issued in the month of June, in a solemn act held in the Palacio del Senado before the president of the still-provisional government, Niceto Alcalá Zamora. The representatives of more than three hundred entities had gathered there to declare their adhesion to the republican government and celebrate its peaceful arrival. They wanted to wait for elections to be held and the assembly of a Parliament that would legislate with prudence. But if the other members of the government and the political forces representing it did not oppose the measures adopted by decree, the constituent Parliament summarily turned them into laws. Once more, businessmen addressed the authorities, this time by way of a letter to Parliament. Again they offered their 'most loyal and sincere cooperation', but now they spoke of the 'state of distrust' produced by disturbances of all sorts and the atmosphere of systematic strikes, on which they blamed the depreciation of the currency, the paralysation of the stock markets and the gradual disappearance of credit. Employers' representatives believed the economic crisis was essentially rooted in political problems.[27]

At the beginning of August, the *Federación de Industrias Nacionales* sent a document to Parliament that read: 'to all of us who make our living in trade, agriculture, industry, banking, and ground and sea transport, the concern about the national economy's difficult situation is increasingly pressing, and it has come about thanks to the growing effects of international and national circumstances'. It was not only the defense of individual interests that caused this grave worry, but also the perspective of a 'terribly serious crisis' that could ruin and destroy the national wealth, with 'terribly serious social disruption when hunger invades each and every Spanish household'. The apocalyptic document was also signed by members of the *Confederaciones Patronal y Gremial*, the *Federación de Círculos Mercantiles*, the *Asociación de Agricultores*, the *Asociación de Ganaderos*, the Chambers of Commerce and the Compañías de Ferrocarriles; in other words, the main organisations representing the different sectors of the national economy, all appealing to abandon 'any difference and partial contradiction of interests' in the interest of the common good.[28]

Ramón Bergé and the *Federación de Industrias Nacionales* played the leading role in this movement of convergence, sending letters, exchanging phone calls and making numerous visits. It was particularly difficult to incorporate the *Fomento*

Nacional de Trabajo. The Catalans felt that all that unifying effort was motivated only by the difficult circumstances of Vizcayan industry. When the Minister of Labour presented the so-called *worker control* project in October 1931, the hearing opened by the constituent Parliament received a flood of telegrams, letters and manifestos in response. The project revived an earlier one from 1923, which at the time provoked the withdrawal of employers' representation from the Institute for Social Reforms. To the Central Banking Association of Spain, it was inconceivable and without precedent anywhere that workers – even worse, unionised labourers – could have access to balances and accounting books, authorisation to attend board and shareholders' meetings, and information on administrative procedures, the constitution of capital and distributed profits, and the methods of all company departments save manufacturing secrets. In any case, it would require the existence of solid and responsible trade unionism, as the *Fomento del Trabajo Nacional* said. As this did not exist, it would result in genuine 'unionist tyranny'. According to the *Federación de Industrias Nacionales*, it was the most conclusive proof that the republican Government was treating the Spanish economy as a 'field of experimentation for socialist politics'.

The *worker control* project never got anywhere, but the reaction it provoked in business circles led to a multitudinous assembly held on 5 November 1931 in Madrid. Even the Catalan *Fomento* gave an 'unconditional yes'. Out of this meeting the *Unión Nacional Económica* (National Economic Union) was born. It was an alliance of different sectorial and regional organisations, 'separate from parties or groups', allowing its members freedom in this sense, but proclaiming the defence of the capitalist system, economic freedom, company spirit and free initiative. Respect of the rule of law and property, the defence of agriculture as a basic foundation of national wealth, the establishment of a moderate and stable plan of public works, a balanced budget and social improvement via harmony and legal processes were, in short, essential requisites for the reestablishment of economic activity and trust. To achieve this, all the elements that contributed to the production, circulation and distribution of the wealth were willing to join forces and cooperate with the governments that were inspired by those principles. This was the attitude regarding economic interests in the months prior to the proclamation of the Republic.[29]

Owners, businessmen and employers found themselves trapped in a difficult economic situation, with major increases in production costs and growing conflicts which caused the number of strikes to jump from the 368 declared in 1930 to 1,046 in 1933; strikers from 247,460 to 843,303; and workdays lost from 3,745,366 to 14,440,629. The measures imposed by Largo Caballero did not improve the situation, but rather exacerbated it. With the extension of the corporate network, the socialists increased their presence in regions and economic sectors in which they had been practically nonexistent until then, as shown by the spectacular growth of the *Federación Nacional de Trabajadores de la Tierra* (National Federation of Workers of the Land). The minister thought that this growth would corner the rival trade union, the anarchist CNT, and prevent the spread of more radical movements. This was hardly the case. The CNT reached a membership of 800,000 in the autumn of 1931 and confronted the Republic by openly rejecting parliamentarianism and corporatist methods of conflict prevention, confirming their recourse to *acción directa* (direct action). The policy of transparent 'favouritism' on the part of the Minister of Labour towards the socialist UGT contributed to the victory of the most radical postures in the direction of CNT unionism, which was also helped by the incapacity of the republican government to provide an efficient policy of public order. The result was the repeated call to uprising. The communists, although few in number and divided, contributed to sowing discord in the ranks of the workers with their calls to a 'single front of grass-roots members' against the management of socialist and CNT organisations.

'It is no secret', said the *Confederación Patronal* at the beginning of 1933, 'that the so-called social problem in Spain has two different sources: the *Jurados Mixtos*, which by mandate of law establish labour regulations; and syndicalist tactics, which by *direct action* try to impose union regulations, creating the outlandish circumstance whereby the *Jurado Mixto* approves the regulations and the *Síndicatos Únicos* immediately tighten the net and provoke crushing strikes to impose theirs. In this dangerous game of competition and supersedure between the two organisations with different tactics and ideas, the employers' class is the guinea pig on which all kinds of experiments are performed'. Whenever socialists, CNT members and communists joined in the attack, the conflict effectively became more radical, because they fought among themselves to control the labour market and increase their membership. This was the case in Sevilla, where people were fighting in the streets at the beginning of the Republic. It also occurred in traditionally socialist spheres, like Asturian miners' unionism, where *cenetistas* and communists, although among the minority, managed to channel the discouragement and the protest of their members against the leaders of the UGT and generalised the panic in a management accustomed to the policy of pacting with unionists to pressure the government.[30]

On 7 May 1933, 3,000 businessmen and employers arrived in Madrid, led by the *Federación Económica de Andalucía* (Economic Federation of Andalusia). This was a new association which united the Chambers of Commerce and Industry and agricultural, trade and industrial groups from the Andalusian capital, and whose secretary was Pedro Caravaca, a passionate monarchist. A few weeks earlier, they had sent the Government a letter which asserted they might well disappear as entrepreneurs if there was not a wise and strong intervention to solve all sorts of problems, from the grave situation of the domestic and foreign markets to the conduct of extremist workers' organisations: 'We are, your Excellency, punished with unfair strikes and boycotts, and insulted every day in fliers which describe us as beasts. Our lives and our interests are threatened. We feel our strength is exhausted, and we must confess to Your Excellency that we can hold out no longer'. The Andalusian businessmen held a mass assembly in Madrid to demand the immediate reestablishment of order and respect of the law. They visited the President of the Republic, the President of the Government and the President of Parliament, as well as leaders of parliamentary minorities. On their return to Sevilla, on 19 May, they held another meeting to take stock of their trip to Madrid. The following day, Pedro Caravaca was assassinated. The employers from Sevilla agreed to the indefinite cessation of trade, the paralysation of industry and banking and the reduction of tax payments. Fifteen thousand people attended Caravaca's burial, which turned into a massive demonstration of national mourning, obligating Interior Minister Casares Quiroga to transfer to Sevilla.[31]

Two months later, on 19 July 1933, a 'Magna Asamblea Nacional' (Grand National Assembly) was held in Madrid, convened by the most important business and employers' organisations: the *Confederación Gremial*, the *Confederación Patronal*, *Estudios Sociales y Económicos* and *Unión Económica*. The hundreds of employers in attendance were received by the organisers as 'that bourgeoisie that is so embattled now, and which, however, has been the foundation of modern civilization'. The essential objective of the meeting, product of a long process of conflict and unrest, was to protest the conduct of the *Jurados Mixtos*. The *Jurados* were created by the socialist Labour Minister Francisco Largo Caballero as negotiating bodies for labour regulations and the prevention and resolution of conflicts. The employers felt that these conflicts had become 'an instrument of heartless and cruel trade union struggles', and the main cause of the economic crisis that impoverished and exhausted sources of wealth. The debate among the assembly was intense. There was a radical sector that demanded the immediate suspension of the *Jurados*, or at least the resignation of employers from them. Others took a more moderate stance, requesting the reform of the *Jurados*. Some of the radicals defended the creation of a 'Unión General de Patronos' (General Union of Employers), with 'discipline and value', and a 'Frente Único Patronal' (United Employers' Front) with which to confront the workers' organisation on an even playing field. They also wanted the assembly to demand the immediate resignation of socialists from the government. The more moderate speakers, including Ramón Bergé, leader of the *Unión Económica*, tried to calm things down, affirming that the meeting was apolitical and that it was not appropriate to request the withdrawal of persons or parties. The more moderate positions apparently prevailed, but shortly thereafter, the Constituent Parliament received a document which requested the repeal of the Ley de Jurados Mixtos (Mixed Juries Law). According to the manuscript, the *Jurados* had become an instrument not of a social class but rather of a poltical party whose objective was to test a 'new economic organisation of production and trade with socialist influence'. Furthermore, given that socialist participation in the government had raised a 'unanimous clamour' across a nation which had not voted socialist in the 1931 general elections, the text demanded that a socialist presence in the government did not stamp a 'Socialist orientation' on the Republic'.[32]

A few weeks later, there was another meeting in Madrid which gathered 14,000 farmers from different Castilian provinces. The meeting was convened by the also newly created *Confederación Española Patronal Agraria* (Spanish Agrarian Employers' Confederation). In its founding manifesto, the Confederación had accused the Labour Ministry of artificially encouraging the 'hateful class struggle' in the country, a conflict that was destroying traditional 'agricultural democracy': 'Socialism is the enemy. Socialism and its allies. Socialism and its collaborators, under the political disguise of compound names. Farmers, war to those who waged war on us!' In the

Madrid assembly, which had to be held in two different places because of the huge attendance, a 'general employers' strike' was threatened. This was the only possible response to the situation in rural areas created by the biased conduct of the *Jurados Mixtos*, labour regulations that were impossible to uphold, the corrosive social doctrines that propagated the class struggle and the absolute lack of authority in the conduct of the Agriculture and Labour ministries. The farmers were willing to repeat, on an even bigger scale, the meeting of 18 September. The UGT threatened to stop the trains in order to prevent the meeting, but the farmers replied that they would get to the capital without worrying about the loss of that day's bread, because they were defending the bread of all Spaniards, who were 'threatened with losing it because of the ruinous and disastrous conduct of Marxism'.[33]

The increase of costs, the difficulties created by the corporativism of the *Jurados Mixtos*, and the strikes did not hurt big owners and businessmen more than the medium and small ones. It was this latter group that had more problems confronting the increase in their expenditures and especially assimilating limited workdays, collective negotiations of labour regulations or conflict prevention; in short, manners of conduct that had nothing to do with the more traditional and paternalistic methods still widespread among the trades of shopkeepers and small industrialists. In many cities, the owners of cafés and bars, textile and tailoring workshops and small shops also threatened by the appearance of department stores triggered conflicts which came to merge with building contractors and small construction companies. The exasperation grew in these social sectors, which, in many cases, had received the Republic with enthusiasm and nonetheless found themselves condemned to assume the premises of the 'class struggles'. Perhaps this is why these sectors would be the source of the most radical proposals to create a 'single employers' front' or an 'employers' block', and the cry of 'Employers of all Spain, unite!' In 1935, the multifaceted Ernesto Giménez Caballero, himself a small businessman in the graphic arts industry, tried to establish a new party: the PEPE, *Partido Económico de los Patronos Españoles* (Economic Party of Spanish Employers). Giménez Caballero was hoping to capitalise on the disappointment of many employers in light of the frustrating results of the political change at the end of 1933. The party was not very successful, even though it had the financial backing of Juan March. The speeches that accompanied its proposals in the press organs of the *Federación Patronal Madrileña* (Federation of Employers in Madrid), mainly from construction and the *Defensa Mercantil Madrileña* (Madrid Commercial Defense), revealed the confusion and split that had come to the ranks of these middle classes.[34]

In all its diversity, agricultural Spain was shaken by an unprecedented mobilisation. The *hambre de tierras* (hunger for land) in the regions of large estates, the wretched living conditions of the masses of day labourers, the habitual financial straits of *propietarios muy pobres* (very poor owners) and the fears of those who saw their large properties at risk created a breeding ground for the most explosive situations. The resistance of the owners was also greater. In some regions, they chose to let the land lie fallow, or tried to escape the legislation and labour norms approved by the Jurados. The explosion of conflicts and violence in the countryside was the result of the convergence of various factors: on one hand, the economic crisis that for different reasons affected export sectors and the traditional grain farming of Castile which, as a result of the excellent wheat harvests of 1932 and 1934, saw prices plummet; on the other, the premature announcement of agrarian reform, which the rapid organisation of the big owners managed to stop and refer to the constituent Parliament, where its approval was delayed in the midst of controversy, sowing uncertainties for the futures of both big and small owners. In an even more immediate way, the unrest was the result of the approval of measures which tried to solve unemployment. Two examples of such were the laws of *términos municipales* (municipal territories) and *laboreo forzoso* (forced farm work). These laws obliged owners to hire day labourers from their own municipality in labour markets controlled by trade unions. They also obligated many owners to allocate land among workers and feed the unemployed or cultivate land without using machinery to increase hiring. And of course, all of this came from the establishment of the *Jurados Mixtos*, which entailed the dizzying expansion of workers' organisations and forced owners to create entities under the name of employers' organisations. This broke from their traditional methods of organisation and turned the negotiation of labour regulations into 'genuine hell'. And these negotiations did not guarantee that the conflicts would be solved. In short, those owners accustomed to doing whatever they pleased suddenly found themselves restricted by a tangle of regulation that made it impossible for them to exploit their lands as they had done up to then. They lost control, and tried to avoid this wherever they were able to. It was said that there were places where the Republic was apparently not in place, places where things continued as usual and owners could turn a blind eye to the new norms. But in other places, the changes were radical and the conflicts were marked by violence. Labour regulations, within and outside the *Jurados Mixtos*, were often negotiated with pistols on the table. And although the big owners were the most threatened by the agrarian reform, there are sufficient examples of the damages caused among the smaller owners because of, as they themselves claimed, legislation conceived to benefit only the day labourers.[35]

It was in agriculture and land ownership where owners and businessmen felt the most immediately threatened by a law of agrarian reform that they took as a veritable attack on the principal of property and all that it entailed. The entities that united agricultural owners managed to arouse the attention of many other interests, which joined in the defence of agriculture as the foundation of national wealth. As the notification of a mass assembly held in April 1933 said, 'The agrarian reform is proposing a radical transformation of Spain's rural constitution, which has to be reflected in the entire national economy. But it also contains principles which affect the concept of property, modes of expropriation, and the role of the State in expropriation. All of this creates general concern for producers everywhere, and this concern should be transformed into a feeling of solidarity'. Many owners thought the agrarian reform debated in Parliament was not intended to solve the problems that Spanish agriculture suffered, but rather that, by way of expropriations and settlements, it implied 'a frank and clear attempt at nationalisation'.[36]

The intense political mobilisation that shook Spain in the 1930s, as well as the feeling of having lost political contacts and the power to pressure the decision makers, caused a great stir of activity: the reorganisation of large and small business and employers' entities and agricultural and industrial groups; the mailing of hundreds of letters to Parliament and different political institutions; the proliferation of magazines and publications; and the repeated calls for meetings, assemblies and street demonstrations. The old monarchic parties had been dismantled and the Republic began without the establishment of a right-wing party. When the right wing did emerge in the CEDA – *Confederación Española de Derechas Autónomas* (Spanish Confederation of Autonomous Conservatives) – it had little to do with the old parties. Although some old dignitaries and local political bosses managed to maintain their positions by joining the new political forces, they realised they had to act in a completely different institutional and political context. Some notable monarchists appealed to their followers to break up, and on several occasions, to join the ranks of the Partido Radical (Radical Party), which was headed by the veteran and now moderate Alejandro Lerroux. Many radicals brought to positions of power at the local and provincial levels came from the ranks of the *patronal* (employers' organisation). Some were already republicans; others tried to find a niche for themselves in the party, which in the end seemed to have a more extensive organisation and a greater chance of becoming a powerful political force. The general elections of June 1931 confirmed it, but the Partido Radical never became the party of management. The new radicals had to coexist with old republicans, who were faithful to their principles and reluctant to accept the upstarts. Some of the fluctuation and ambiguity of radical republicanism was due to this complicated mixture and Lerroux's efforts to incorporate the Catholic right into the republican order. It was the Republic's religious policy, added to the restlessness brought on by social reforms and public disorder, that spurred the recomposition of a right wing, CEDA, now converted into a heterogeneous party of masses, unstoppable although diverse in its composition and strategy. Castilian farmers and peasants accounted for a significant part of these masses, as well as certain sectors of the urban middle classes, although the more liberal ones were distrustful of the Catholics' corporate and interventionist proposals. In any case, CEDA's inability to mesh with the republican order ended up widening the internal rift of the middle classes in their view of the new government. It also paved the way for criticism of the Catholics' 'political accidentalism' by monarchic parties and other small, extreme right-wing groups. One of these groups was *Falange Española*, a fascist party that was founded by José Antonio Primo de Rivera, the dictator's son, and which had the support and financing of some eminent figures of the landowning nobility and Basque capitalism.[37]

The republican constituent Parliament introduced an entirely new makeup and an absolute break from the Parliaments of the Crown. The most numerous parliamentary group, and also the most disciplined and efficient, was the socialist contingent. They were followed by the radicals and radical socialists. Far behind these in representation were the Catalan Esquerra (Catalan left-wing party), which had replaced the *Lliga* as Catalonia's hegemonic party, then Azaña's Acción Republicana and the Agrarios. Of the 470 deputies, only sixty-four had been MPs under the

Monarchy. Not only the top figures, the dignitaries of the Monarchy's liberal parliament, had disappeared, but also second and third-rate politicians. In the Republic's first ordinary Parliament, elected at the end of 1933, the most numerous parliamentary groups were the Catholics and the radical republicans, but the old politicians did not return to Parliament, either: only ten of the 105 Catholic deputies had been MPs before. This proportion was even smaller in the Parliament of the Frente Popular in February 1936. By then the Partido Radical had disappeared, and for the first time, there were three parliamentary groups with similar weight: the socialists, the Catholics and the Izquierda Republicana (Republican Left). As such, and quite logically, the republican political mobilisation entailed the emergence of a new political class and a profound break from the past. There was also great discontinuity in parliamentary personnel during the Republic itself, and this had important political consequences: only 7 percent of the deputies remained during the three legislatures, which made the establishment of a parliamentary culture impossible. There were very few deputies who admitted to being businessmen: only eleven out of almost a thousand over those years. Twenty-seven professed to be traders or small businessmen; twenty-eight described themselves as farmers and fifteen as owners. Of all of these, only three held their seat for all three legislatures. It is reasonable to think that, of the more than a third of the total of deputies who declared themselves lawyers, a handful could have been included among these producing classes. But those republican Parliaments were above all composed of professional and cultivated middle classes: doctors, journalists, writers, engineers, architects, teachers, professors and civil servants. There were also skilled and unskilled workers and a few – very few – day labourers. Perhaps in this sense it would be accurate to describe that government as the 'Republic of intellectuals'. Many of them thought that the time had come to settle accounts with the past and bring the country up to date, as if reality could be molded at will without making trouble for others. This was because the Republic and the republican Parliament also had its agitators and revolutionaries, who had little respect for the rules of the democratic game. For owners, businessmen and employers, it was not merely a matter of having lost presence or influence in political institutions. They also had to deal with a rapid change in public life and the feeling that many of the decision makers thought, at the very least, that the capitalist economic system had to be regulated, directed, driven. This was not an easy situation. Eminent figures from the *Agrupación al Servicio de la República* (Association at the Service of the Republic), the political association of the best-known intellectuals led by the philosopher Ortega y Gasset, said that it was time to reduce political liberalism to a minimum and proceed with a 'progressive nationalisation' of the Spanish economy. That was not so original, however, as many people in other European countries thought the same thing. On the other hand, there were many on the left who felt the capitalist regime would soon be replaced by another which, after a necessary revolution, would eliminate inequalities and exploitation.[38]

In August 1932, there was an attempt of a coup d'état led by General Sanjurjo easily controlled by the Government. As a result of its failure, the republican Parliament, reinforced, passed the law of agrarian reform and the Catalan statute of autonomy. The coup had had the support of a handful of aristocrats and great landowners, but it was condemned by *Unión Económica*, that 'employer of employers' that was trying to consolidate itself. *Unión Económica* issued a press release that insisted on its loyal compliance with the Government. It confessed to repudiate many of its policies and measures, and announced that it would openly combat them with the legal means available, severely condemning all rebellion and all violence against legally established power. A few months later, in March 1933, in a note directed to the president of the Government, it affirmed that in April and June of 1931 the Spanish nation had voted in favour of the Republic, but at no time had it declared itself in favour of a policy of 'sudden socialisation', which was breeding distrust and artificially disseminating the class struggle. And, facing elections at the end of the year, it called upon all the economic forces to 'drive away the danger, inherent in the political game and the internal dyanmic of the parties, of entering a new period of socialist politics, overt or disguised, that repeat the mistakes and damages we are so dearly paying for'. Economic organisations repeatedly called for the removal of the socialists over the course of 1933, but the triumph of the radicals and the Catholics in the general elections held at the end of that year failed to stabilise the political situation. The revolution of October 1934 was the most explosive sign of the exasperation felt by some on the left who did not accept the results of the polls, and who took the victory of the 'right' – in which they openly and none too subtly included Lerroux's Partido Radical – as a threat to the survival of a Republic they considered their own. On the other hand, among the more radical sectors of Catholicism and in the ranks of the monarchists, there was no shortage of people who understood that the political turn of 1933 had to be the first step in the dismantling of what had been done during the first two years of the Republic.[39]

Many small and medium businessmen and employers who had trusted in the Radical Party became desperate in the face of the persisting conflicts, the continuation of the *Jurados Mixtos*, which still ruled in favour of workers, and the lack of sufficient measures that could ease their terrible economic situation. In the countryside, the repeal of the *términos municipales* (municipal territories) law opened the door for many owners to compensate themselves for damages previously suffered without waiting for legislative reforms. They lowered salaries and demanded an immediate paralysation of peasants' settlements on expropriated lands, which the *Instituto de Reforma Agraria* (Institute of Agrarian Reform) continued to carry out, in spite of everything. With the failure of the general strike called by the *Federación Nacional de Trabajadores de la Tierra* in June 1934, and especially after the revolution in October of the same year, many owners saw it was time for their final offensive. After the reformist Giménez Fernández was booted out of the Ministry of Agriculture by his own party, the CEDA, a law of 'reform of agrarian reform' was passed. It was then that cries of 'Eat Republic!' were heard. The 'suicidal selfishness' of owners, as CEDA leader Gil Robles himself said at one point, would end up causing the most serious radicalisation in the history of the Spanish peasantry. Many managers and industrial businessmen took advantage of the repression that followed the October revolution to purge staff from their factories and hire more trustworthy workers. Many workers' organisations were dissolved or suspended, but the new law from the *Jurados Mixtos* did not satisfy businessmen, who saw it as an attempt to promote Catholic trade unionism. The economic situation did not seem to have recovered significantly, and the 'labour crisis' continued to be a genuine obsession. There was no way to consolidate the political situation so that, for example, the economic reform plans of Joaquín Chapaprieta, Treasury Minister and later president of the Government, could come to fruition.[40]

Economic forces had little to do with the new political crisis at the end of 1935. The Partido Radical was sunk as a result of the political manipulation of the 'black market' scandal. The divisions within the CEDA were accentuated by the categorical refusal of the president of the Republic, Niceto Alcalá Zamora, to concede the presidency of the Government to its leader, Gil Robles. Meanwhile, from his privileged position, convinced of having the solution to the Republic's problems, he tried to establish a new centrist option. The monarchic and extreme right wingers denounced what in their opinion was the enormous failure of Gil Robles's moderate and legalistic tactics, a failure which cemented their conviction that the only solution was the overthrow of the government. The republic and proletariat left, united in a new electoral coalition, the Frente Popular (Popular Front), were very successful in their campaign for the amnesty of all those who suffered reprisals after the revolution of October 1934, and they pressured Alcalá Zamora to dissolve the Parliament. Throughout its history, the Republic had to confront many serious problems and structural strangulations of an economic and social nature. Furthermore, it came at a time when the international situation was hardly ripe for testing democratising processes. However, the inability of parties to gel as a system, along with other political factors, helped to discredit the Republic as a democratic regime and hinder its full consolidation.[41]

Notes

1. The note from the banks, in Muñoz (1978: 160–161).
2. Data on the Bergés, in Ybarra y Bergé (1947), Fusi (1975); for the economic relation of Bergé and Maura, see Rueda Laffond (1991).
3. Typewritten text of the letter, in the Archivo Histórico Nacional (National History Archive), Presidencia de Gobierno (Presidency of the Government), Dossier 457.
4. The 'considerable growth', in Comín (1987); the 5.5 percent, in Carreras (1990: 83–84). The Council of National Economy, in Martínez Mesa (1997: 30–31).
5. The Alba case, in García Venero (1963) and Cabrera et al. (1989). The stages of the dictatorship, in Gómez Navarro (1991: 337–351)
6. On the 'plutocracy' and the attitude of the King, in Calvo Sotelo (1974: 225), also included by Gómez Navarro (1991: 132–133). For the political reshufflings in Catalonia and Vizcaya, and in other regions, see Gómez Navarro, González Calvet and Portuondo (1979).
7. The Assembly, in Ben-Ami (1984: 142–156) and Gómez Navarro (1991: 261–304).
8. For the dictatorship's economic policy, see Velarde (1973); for the Count of Guadalhorce, see Martín Gaite (1977); the quotation from the *Federación de Industrias Nacionales*, in his Annual Report from 1926–1927, p. 8

9. Calvo Sotelo (1974); Rey Reguillo (2000).

10. The denunciations of small businessman, in Ben-Ami (1984: 163); the textual quotations of Calvo Sotelo, in Calvo Sotelo (1974: 174–177); those of the *Federación de Industrias Nacionales* in the Annual Reports from 1926–1927, 1927–1928 and 1929–1930.

11. The quotations of Primo de Rivera, in Ben-Ami (1984: 162); on the stock exchanges, the euphoria and the loans, in *ibid.*: 184; the references to company profits, in *ibid.*: 162–167. Banking, in Muñoz (1978) and Belford (1979).

12. On the *primistas* (supporters of Primo de Rivera), in Maura Gamazo (1930, vol. I: 267). Prieto's speech, from 25 April 1930 in the Ateneo de Madrid, reproduced in Prieto (1999).

13. The Urquijos, in Díaz Hernández (1998); Echevarrieta, in Díaz Morlán (1999: 179–226); the Compañía Arrendataria de Tabacos, in Comín and Martín Aceña (1999: 103–107 and 260).

14. The minister's arguments, in Calvo Sotelo (1974: 137ff.) The oil market and Campsa, in Tortella (1990) and Tortella et al. (2003).

15. The minister's quotations, in Calvo Sotelo (1974: 142). Those from the press, in Cabrera (1991). Also, Rey Reguillo (2000: 301–303). For the fiscal monopolies, Comín (1991).

16. The quotation, in Calvo Sotelo (1974). The Recasens brothers, Campsa and Cepsa, in Recasens (1956: 97–100) and Cabana (1972), (1997) and (2000b).

17. The resignation of Calvo Sotelo and the controversy, in Calvo Sotelo (1974); also, Rey Reguillo (2000). The opinions of the economic forces, in Ben-Ami (1984: 220–226) and Gómez Navarro (1991: 484–485).

18. Prieto's speech in Parliament on 18 May 1934, in Prieto (1975). Campsa's ups and downs, in Tortella et al. (2003). On Prieto and the Bank of Spain, in Juliá (2000a: 338).

19. The biography of Juan March, in Benavides (1976), Díaz Nosty (1977), Garriga (1976a), Dixon (1985), Ferrer Guasp (2000) and Torres Villanueva (2000b).

20. Prieto's speech, in Prieto (1975: 195–227).

21. In addition to the biographies of March cited above, for the conduct of the Comisión de Responsabilidades, Cabrera (2000a) and for March's relations with the radicals, Townson (2000: 83–86 and 124–126).

22. For Minister Prieto, Juliá (2000a); the financial crisis and the bankruptcy of the Bank of Catalonia, in Martín Aceña (1984: 225–232); also, in Tortella and Palafox (1983); on the persecution of Prieto, in Recasens (1956: 127 and 132-133); on the transfer of money, in Cabana (1972: 82).

23. The monetary and financial problems and the policy with respect to them, in Martín Aceña (1984) and (2000). The economic crisis, in Hernández Andreu (1986), and Comín (1987), who qualifies it as a 'superficial depression'. The unemployment figures, in Soto Carmona (1989: 345–356).

24. The crisis in heavy industry and the attitudes of the business entities, in Cabrera (1983: 83ff.) The mobilisation of the unions, in Olábarri Gortázar (1978: 330). The evolution in the attitudes of the Basque bourgeoisie, in Plata Parga (1991: 142–180); On Treasury Minister Prieto, Juliá (2000a). Differing opinions of economic historians about the impact of the supposed cut in public spending, in Comín and Martín Aceña (1984), Martín Aceña (1987) and Comín (1988), versus Palafox Gamir (1991a).

25. The dictatorship's social policy and the corporate organisation, in Ben-Ami (1984: 186–208) and Gómez Navarro (1991: 463–485).

26. The attitudes of the employers' organisations towards the corporativism of the dictatorship, in Gómez Navarro (1991: 463–485).

27. On the 'political objectives' of the socialist labour legislation, Juliá (1987) and (1997: 167–173). The writings of the employers' organisations, in Cabrera (1983: 253–255).
28. Cabrera (1983: 49–50).
29. Cabrera (1983: 46–60) and Calvo (1990).
30. The data on the strikes, from the *Boletín del Ministerio de Trabajo*, elaborated by Juliá (1999a: 93). The attitude of the CNT, in Casanova (1997). The communists, in Cruz (1987). The quotation from the Confederación Patronal, in Cabrera (1987: 69–70). Asturias, in Shubert (1984) and Castejón Rodríguez (2000).
31. Cabrera (1983: 42–43 and 209–211), Macarro Vera (1985: 186–195 and 324–325), and Álvarez Rey (1993).
32. Cabrera (1983: 215–218).
33. Cabrera (1983: 156–158).
34. The decline of profits, in Tafunell (1996: 32). On the radical change in the distribution of income, in Palafox Gamir (1991a). The evolution of small and medium employers by way of the Madrid case, in Juliá (1984). On Giménez Caballero, in Cabrera (1983: 245–246 and 261–263), and Selva (1999: 262–272).
35. On the villages the 'Republic did not come to', in Gil Andrés (2000: 203). On the pistols on the table, for Castilla-La Mancha, in Rodríguez Labandeira (1988). More weapons and violence, in Güerri Martín (1988). On the small owners affected, in the case of Jaén, in Cobo Moreno (2000).
36. The ups and downs of agrarian reform, in Malefakis (1972). The very poor owners, in Castillo (1979). The agrarian problem from the employers' point of view, in Cabrera (1983: 152–195).
37. For the Partido Radical, its role in the Republic and its relation with employers, see Townson (2000). The CEDA, in Montero Gibert (1977). The right, in Gil Pecharromán (1994), and González Cuevas (1998).
38. The data on the parliaments and the thesis of discontinuity, in Linz (1972). On the Republican Parliaments, Varela (1978) and Cabrera (1995). A recent reflection on the 'Republic of intellectuals', in Aubert (2000).
39. The press releases of *Unión Económica*, in Cabrera (1983: 269–274).
40. The reaction of the agricultural owners and their 'suicidal selfishness', in Malefakis (1972: 394–417 and 420–421). Management's reactions after October 1934, in Cabrera (1983: 240–250).
41. The decisive importance of political factors, in Payne (1993: 373–384). On the parties and the failure of the consolidation of a stable and legitimate system, Arranz (1995) and Juliá (1995a).

Chapter 3
Paths of Servitude, 1936-1950

Revolt and Conspiracy

'The elections have shown us that Spain is sensitively divided into two halves, and if no zone of compatibility is created between them, there will be no possible economy', the *Unión Económica* stated on 22 February 1936. The programme of the Popular Front, which won the first round of the third general elections, was 'intentionally moderate' compared to the doctrinal extremism of socialist, unionist and communist elements that endorsed it in conjunction with republicans. Another important employers' organisation, *Estudios Sociales y Económicos*, fervently hoped the republican parties were not subject to the hegemony of their 'circumstantial allies'. But several months later, the *Agrupación de Propietarios de Fincas Rústicas* lamented that, although there was not an overwhelming majority of left wingers in the government and the right had not been eliminated, the interregnum between elections and the opening of Parliament were being used to adopt measures 'inspired by the most acute sectarianism'. The situation was 'worse than in 1931'.[1]

The president of the Government, Manuel Portela Valladares, wasted no time in resigning when he read the writing on the wall. The results of the first round of the elections were discouraging. He realised his centrist alternative was a failure. People were demonstrating in the streets. And he was also pressured by Gil Robles to declare a state of war and prepare himself to govern by decree. Added to these pressures were the urgings received by the Minister of War, General Molero, and from the Chief of the General Military Staff, General Franco. The President of the Republic, Niceto Alcalá Zamora, warned Manuel Azaña, the leader of the Republican Left, that it was absolutely necessary to form a government that reflected the election results, and although he trusted there would be a reasonable amount of time for the transfer of power, on 19 February, a new, entirely republican Cabinet was announced: ten ministers were from the Republican Left, three were from the Republican Union, and one was an independent republican. Azaña's first public message as the new president of Government was a call for pacification and the reestablishment of justice and peace, which was applauded by economic journals. Two days later, he convened the Permanent Council of Parliament, which, with votes from the right, unanimously approved a general amnesty for all those condemned or jailed for political or social crimes after the elections of 1933. The new Government proceeded to dissolve city halls and provincial governments and replace them with *comisiones gestoras* (administrative commissions) in accordance with the new political situation.

On 1 March, 250,000 people celebrated the victory of the Popular Front in the streets of Madrid. Uniformed socialist and communist youths, marching separately, waved flags and chanted revolutionary proclamations. That same day, the Government issued a decree requiring managers and executives to rehire workers dismissed for political reasons after the beginning of 1934 and reimburse them for back wages. The second round of elections was held the next day in the few provinces where no party won 40 percent of the vote. After a heated argument over one of the certificates of election and a stormy preparatory session that concluded with the singing of The International, the socialists once again became the group with the most seats in Parliament, winning eighty-nine. The Catholics of the CEDA were close behind with eighty-eight. The Republican Left won eighty-seven, the Republican Union thirty-nine and the Catalan Left thirty-six. Portela's Centre Party held firm with sixteen seats, the Catalan Lliga won twelve, and the Basque nationalists ten. The monarchist National Block, led by Calvo Sotelo, had thirteen seats and the traditionalists nine. The communists emerged with sixteen deputies. Lerroux's Radical Party had disappeared. In April, Parliament's first act under constitutional legality was the debate over and dismissal of the Chief of State, Niceto Alcalá Zamora, who was accused of having improperly dissolved Parliament for the second time. The rise of Manuel Azaña to the President of the Republic and his quitting the presidency of the Government revealed how very weak the political situation was. The Popular Front had been an efficient electoral coalition, but at no time did it function well as a governing coalition. The proletarian left not only could not handle the responsibility of governing, but even seemed willing to let the situation slide into total disarray.[2]

The executive had to establish strict control over the export of gold, silver and currency, and especially over banknotes carried out of the country. Economic indices revealed an unsettling situation: industrial production, railway transport and sea transport were greatly diminishing; production costs increased while economic studies bureaus and specialised journals affirmed that Spanish production could achieve some degree of competitiveness only if it were drastically reduced. Unemployment continued to rise. Along with the freeing of political prisoners, the proclamation of the amnesty and the decree about rehiring, the *Jurados Mixtos* had been reestablished, although there were no new laws regarding mediating organisations until June. After the unions managed to impose the reinstatement of dismissed workers, they used their position of power to engage in tough negotiations over new labour regulations and the reduction of the workday. They ran up against resistance from some employers' organisations which not only considered the regulations unacceptable, but also felt that respect for the law and the principle of authority were shattered. The result was an unprecedented wave of strikes. There were more in May and June of 1936 than in all of 1934 and as many as in 1933.[3]

The political change had immediate effects on rural life. In March, 60,000 peasants from Badajoz mobilised and occupied 3,000 farms. The Government sent in troops, but they soon returned and measures were immediately adopted: eviction trials except those involving defaults were prohibited; ploughmen recovered their lands and peasant settlements were accelerated. More land was reallocated in five months than in the entire period of the Republic. The trade unions did not feel it was necessary to wait for the discussion and approval of corresponding laws; the new republican town halls were accused of being 'reactionary' and the technicians at the Instituto de Reforma Agraria (Institute of Agrarian Reform) were despised by the socialist *Federación Nacional de Trabajadores de la Tierra:* it was said 'they should be hanged'. Owners did not hold back in their criticisms, either, as they were forced to hire in strict turn, raise salaries and take in the unemployed. The negotiation of labour regulations became a living hell and strikes multiplied. In June, Parliament approved a new agrarian reform law that reduced the size of expropriable farms, as well as a new leasing law. A progressive surcharge on rural tax contributions was discussed. The complaints of the owners were taken as a clear attempt to sabotage the republican reforms, although it is doubtful that many of them were organised and wealthy enough to neglect their crops.[4]

There was no finished programme for revolution. The CNT was recovering from the failure of its insurrectional tactic, and the UGT was still too close to the experience of October 1934 to undertake new ventures. But people continued to talk about revolution. Owners from Madrid had their reasons when they appealed to the Government to ask clearly whether or not it intended to obliterate the managing classes. The voices of revolution echoed in the midst of a situation in which the conflict, and especially a political violence of new and threatening characteristics, spilled over into the streets and flooded the debates in parliamentary sessions, while the Government seemed unable to control it. José Calvo Sotelo, who, to the surprise of Catholics, was now a spokesman for the opposition, reeled off the number and cost of public disturbances before Parliament every day, and called directly for military intervention. The escalation of violence hit its peak when Calvo Sotelo was presented with a warrant for his arrest, taken from his home and assassinated. His body was dumped in a cemetery. The assassination of an opposition leader – moreover, an MP – made the deterioration of political life unbearable for many. For some, it was the invitation to act upon a decision they had plotted some time ago.[5]

What happened on those three days in 1936, from the night of 17 July to 20 July, was a military coup d'état devised within an army that was deeply divided. It was precisely that division, and the lack of state support for the coup, which first delayed the plan and then caused it to fail. It was supposed to be a repeat of Primo de Rivera's experience in 1923. General Mola, the mastermind of the plot, imagined a military dictatorship of four or five generals that could make the Republic a strong and disciplined state. In any case, there was no clear and common political design among the military commanders that had been discussing the matter. When the Government became aware of their intentions, it sent General Goded to the Balearic Islands, General Franco to the Canary Islands, and General Mola to Pamplona.

General Franco was hesitant until the last minute, unsure the operation would be successful. He was right, because the coup failed as such. It was a success in some regions, but not in those whose military commanders remained faithful to the Republic. The trade unions wanted the new Government to supply them with arms so they could defend themselves against the military. After an unsuccessful negotiation with the insurgents, the republican Government met the trade unions' request, unpardonably turning the failed coup into a civil war.

There had been civil conspirators against the Republic since the frustrated coup of General Sanjurjo in August 1932. At the time, a commission was formed to seek financing and promote the conspiracy. Support abroad for the plot was led by the Count of the Andes in connivance with the exiled monarchists, and at home by Fernando María de Ybarra y de la Revilla, Marquis of Arriluce de Ybarra, consultant for Altos Hornos de Vizcaya, founder of the Bank of Vizcaya, conservative and personal friend of Alfonso XIII. The list of contributors that both men managed to compile at the end of 1932 was topped by Juan March, and included important landowners and many big financiers and industrialists, several of them members of the nobility: the Marquises of Urquijo, Larios and Chávarri, the Duke of the Infantado, the Count of Aresti, the Count of Barbate, Juan Pedro Domecq and César de la Mora. The political solution represented first by Renovación Española and later the National Block did not mean the end of the conspiracy, which looked to fascist Italy and the Spanish military for support. Money was important in the uprising. Juan March financed the airplane that transferred General Franco from the Canary Islands to North Africa so he could take over the armed forces in Morocco. In the days immediately following the coup, Juan March and his financial support of the military received extensive coverage in both the national and international press. But at no time during the Republic, let alone at the decisive moment of the uprising, were civilians at the forefront of the events or the political future. 'I only hope to know the day and the hour when I am just one more following the orders of the Army', Calvo Sotelo had told General Mola. The discrepancies among the different extreme right-wing parties, Block and Carlist monarchists, Falangists and Catholics disillusioned with the 'accidentalist' strategy of Gil Robles had prevented the development of a consistent plot. They knew they depended on the military, so put themselves at its service beginning with the February 1936 elections. The Carlist and Falangist militias did as well, although at one point they appeared willing to carry out the uprising by themselves if the army could not make up its mind. But the generals who led the uprising, beginning with Mola, were certain of their protagonism. The politicians themselves had conceded them this role, and the objective was reached. Once more, but now with tragic, far-reaching consequences, the military and the insurgents acting on its behalf viewed themselves as saviors of the nation.[6]

War and Revolution

It was the beginning of the Spanish Civil War that shaped the map of the two opposing worlds and forced civilians to choose sides. In the case of owners, businessmen and employers, it was also the events that were taking place in republican territory. The most industrialised and wealthiest regions, the Basque Country, Catalonia and Valencia, remained faithful to the Republic. This gave an initial advantage to the Republic, but it would not last long. Moreover, the headquarters of the most important banks, companies and central financial institutions, beginning with the Bank of Spain and its gold reserves, were in Madrid. Other drawbacks for the Republic were territorial discontinuity and the fact that agricultural regions and zones producing other raw materials backed the insurgents, which would soon create supply problems and shortages. In any case, the beginning of the war entailed the rupture of a market which up to then had functioned as an integrated whole, and many companies lost contact with their suppliers, markets, debtors and creditors. Furthermore, in the territory faithful to the Republic, the handing over of weapons to the trade unions and the start of the war implied the disintegration of the State and the outbreak of a social revolution of enormous dimensions. At least during the intense summer months of 1936, both sides of the conflict were tainted with murderous violence.[7]

The military rebellion had not triumphed, but it had not been defeated, either. In the regions where it succeeded, the military took over the government, and this entailed the dismissal, imprisonment and very often the execution of republican authorities, along with prison or death for syndicate and leftist party leaders. Of course, strikes and meetings of any type were prohibited, regarded the same as armed resistance or sabotage and punished by immediate death. Generals Mola and Queipo de Llano had triumphed in Pamplona and Sevilla, and Franco had taken charge of the army in Morocco. Generals Fanjul and Goded could not capture Madrid and Barcelona, and they were executed. General Sanjurjo, flying back from Portugal to lead the rebellion, died when his plane crashed. Four days later, on 24 July 1936, the coup acquired a political arm with the creation of a National Defence Board that assumed all powers and representation in foreign affairs. The Board was formed in Burgos, and was headed by General Cabanellas and consisted of the generals and colonels involved in the uprising. The declaration of a state of war, which would have to remain in effect until 1948, was extended to include the entire territory. None of the political elements that had supported the uprising had the least objection to the absolute power of the military commanders. Two months later, on 30 September, after the Defence Board decided to elect General Franco as Commander-in-Chief of the Army, Navy and Air Force and President of the Government of Spain, conferring him 'all the powers of the New State', Franco created a Technical Board subject to his authority and organised in seven commissions – forerunners of future ministries – and converted his role as President of the Government into President of the country.[8]

On the other side of the conflict, the emerging revolution lacked leadership and objectives. The Republican government was not defeated, but it was powerless to control the outbreak of violence. Killing priests, owners, employers and rich people was an indispensable stage of the revolution. Over the first several weeks, the 'purifying torch' burned conservative politicians, soldiers, owners, members of the bourgeoisie, clerics – especially clerics – Catholics, factory and company technicians and personnel directors, and also workers singled out for their moderate ideas.

Militias and trade union committees became the bosses and performed a bloodletting on any symbol of economic, political or religious power, but they also targeted ordinary people. The revolution meshed inseparably with personal paybacks and old grudges. Those who could escape did; others tried to hide, or at least go unnoticed. In Madrid, the Government looked on astonished and powerless before the wave of unionism, the uncontrolled executions and kidnappings. The aspect of the city during the first moments of the war 'was incredible', as Clara Campoamor would write: 'members of the bourgeoisie saluting with a closed fist and giving the communist salute at every turn so as not to raise suspicions, men in overalls and espadrilles, copying the uniform adopted by the militias; women with heads bared, wearing old and worn dresses; a total invasion of ugliness and misery, more moral than real, in people who humbly begged for permission to go on living'.[9]

Railways, streetcars and buses; taxis and ships; energy, gas and water companies; engineering and automobile assembly factories; mines, cement and textile factories and paper mills; electric and chemical companies; glass and perfume bottling plants, food industries and breweries were confiscated or controlled by workers' committees, which also took over cinemas and theatres, newspapers and printers, warehouses and hotels, restaurants and bars, and occupied the headquarters of mercantile and professional associations. They also moved into the homes of the rich. The revolution also affected craftsmen, small industrialists and shopowners, shoemakers, cabinetmakers, hairdressers and barbers. Some of them settled in and continued with their businesses as workers, perhaps thinking that the revolution would soon end. The Madrid Chamber of Commerce, although controlled by the government, continued to operate until the end of the war, while other employers' venues were confiscated. Among other tasks that were carried out, the identity of traders and industrialists was verified by slips which replaced union or party I.D. cards. The workers' unions, although occupied mainly with their labour of purification and revolution, undertook the reorganisation of entire economic sectors, on occasion hiring former owners, who were promised a future of equality and happiness. On 11 August 1936, in Bujaraloz, anarchist leader Buenaventura Durruti issued an edict which abolished the property of big landowners and turned it over to the people, and established the control of the revolutionary committee over agricultural equipment, tractors and threshing machines, demanding of everyone their 'enthusiastic and unconditional support'. In some places, like Aragón, which was reconquered by columns of militiamen and overwhelmed by the brilliant rise of the CNT, and the regions of Andalusia and Castilla-La Mancha, dominated by the socialist Federación de Trabajadores de la Tierra, property deeds were destroyed and burned, and lands were occupied and collectivised, not always abandoned by their owners. They were mainly regions where small land ownership predominated, as the zones of large estates were soon under the control of the insurgents. The peasants, very often reluctantly, were pressed to become integrated in the collectivisations. Up to 70 percent of the lands in Aragón and Badajoz, 58 percent in Castilla-La Mancha and 49 percent in Andalusia were collectivised. In Valencia, however, where the collectivisations occupied few lands and did not last long, socialists and anarchists replaced the old exporting businesses and collectivised this activity, establishing the Consejo Levantino Unificado de Exportación de Agrios (Unified Levante Council of Citrus Fruit Exports).[10]

The republican Government in Madrid failed to impose order in the city, and had no say over the autonomous government of Catalonia, the recently established Basque Government, the Council of Aragón or the militia authorities spread throughout the country. These militia undermined the political power, and with it, economic and, more importantly, strictly military decisions. What sort of government was it if the revolution or the war turned out to be an issue that shattered what little unity was left in the Popular Front, sunk the State and severely weakened the Republic? On 30 August 1936, the Government ordered the intervention of the State in financial, production and distribution companies 'abandoned' by their owners or managers, focusing especially on public service companies, which would be taken over by the Treasury Ministry with the creation of a *Comité de Intervención de Industrias* (Industry Intervention Committee). A few days later, on 5 September, a new Government was formed with Francisco Largo Caballero as President. The Government incorporated workers' organisations and began the difficult process of reconstructing the State, which would culminate in the bloody crisis of the spring of 1937. The CNT and the little Workers' Party of Marxist Unification had a confrontation with the autonomous government of Catalonia and Catalan communists. Those who believed that winning the war was more important than leading the revolutionary process won the battle. The syndicates ended up being expelled from the republican Government and the role of the communists to impose order was gradually affirmed. The new government militarised the militias and tried to organise a regular army. It also wanted to reestablish the authority of the Government, centralise and coordinate economic activity, contain the revolution and guarantee public order and respect for small property. The socialist Juan Negrín, who had been Treasury Minister with Largo Caballero, became President of the Government on 17 May 1937. A General Department of Economy was created and placed under the control of the General Police Department. New executive committees were created to replace boards of directors of banks, and board members who had remained faithful to the Republic were allowed to participate in them. The *Consejo Levantino de Exportación de Agrios* was dissolved and a Department of Exports dependent on the ministry was created. With the transfer to Aragón of the Army's 11th Division under the command of Líster, the Council of Aragón came to a violent end in August 1937. Its leaders, accused of having seriously jeopardised the war effort, were jailed. Many collectives were destroyed and their lands returned to their owners. On 7 October 1937, the Minister of Agriculture, the communist Vicente Uribe, declared that only lands belonging to those who had directly or indirectly intervened in the uprising could be considered expropriable. His decision sparked confrontations and conflicts with the unions. The communists had banked on the defence of small land ownership, which had prompted the entry of several thousand small landowners and members of the urban middle class into their ranks. They organised the *Federación Catalana de Gremios y Entidades de Pequeños Comerciantes*

(Catalan Federation of Guilds and Entities of Small Traders), which was 'fiercely anti-union', according to the anarchist newspaper *Solidaridad Obrera*, and the *Federación Campesina* (Peasants' Federation) in Valencia, which was opposed to collectivisation.[11]

Many of the measures adopted in the second half of 1937 came too late, and were only partially effective. The fall of northern Spain was an irreparable loss for the Republic. There had not been any social revolution in the Basque Country. The uprising triumphed in Álava and Navarra, where it proved to be something more than a coup d'état or a 'reckless military adventure', turning into a 'massive armed mobilisation'. It failed in Vizcaya and Guipúzcoa, although in this latter province, there was intense fighting in the streets. The Basque Nationalist Party would have liked not to have had to choose sides in the conflict. On 19 July 1936, amidst deep internal divisions, it chose the Republic over fascism. Many did not like their fellow travellers, who were so far to the left, but it was the only way to achieve autonomy. On 1 October, the republican Parliament approved the Statute of Basque Autonomy and José Antonio Aguirre formed a Government of multi-party representation. Very few members of the Basque bourgeoisie were nationalists in the 1930s; the majority had remained faithful to the Monarchy. While older generations distanced themselves from politics, young people embarked on the creation of the *Juventud Monárquica-Renovación Española* (Spanish Monarchic Renovation Youth). These people were also well represented in the ranks of traditionalism. There were five Basques on the National Council of the Spanish Falangist Movement, among them José María de Areilza, who was very active in the mobilisation and the rapprochement between monarchists and Falangists. The Vizcayan bourgeoisie donated money to help finance the anti-republican conspiracy and maintain the Falangists, although it is difficult to guage the quantity or the impact it had. In the turbulent 1930s, they abandoned their former liberalism, more inclined to join forces with those they had previously considered incompatible. Many died at the beginning of the violent reprisal, often as a response to the bombings by the insurgents. José María de Urquijo e Ybarra, the influential owner of the Catholic newspaper *La Gaceta del Norte*, was arrested in Zarauz and, by order of the civil governor, sent to San Sebastián with Honourio Maura, son of the former Conservative Party leader and then-member of the monarchist *Renovación Española*. After being held incommunicado for several days, they were judged by a popular tribunal, condemned to death and executed on 5 September, the same day that Irún fell to the 'nationalists' and a few days before San Sebastián and then the entire province met the same fate. That same month, three sons of Tomás de Zubiría e Ybarra, Rafael, Pedro and Gabriel, were executed. Gabriel had been the president of the Monarchic Youth. Tomás de Zubiría y Somonte died on the prison ship Altuna Mendi. The fascists' offensive against Bilbao and the reaction to one of the bombings of the city led to the execution of Fernando María de Ybarra y de la Revilla and five members of his family on the prison ship Cabo-Quilates. The Marquis of Arriluce de Ybarra had been, as we have mentioned, an active fundraiser for the monarchist cause, as well as founder of *Renovación Española*. Juan Tomás Gandarias was arrested at his home in Portugalete on 19 July, released and arrested again a month later. Transferred to Guernica, he was forced to march in public with a militiaman pointing a rifle at his back, but he was eventually released. His money and perhaps also his friendship with Indalecio Prieto saved him.[12]

The Basque Government had inexorably promised to maintain public order and respect for small and medium property. The military insurgents sent messages to convince them only to 'guard buildings and persons' without taking up arms against the enemy. In exchange, they would be respected when the military took control of the region. There was no reply to the messages, but the Basque Government proceeded to guard buildings and persons, while mining and industrial production virtually ground to a halt. The shortage of coal and the tense social situation were the reasons businessmen used to justify the stoppage. The shortage or complete lack of raw materials, the 'ineffectiveness' of the Basque Government and the 'boycott', or, in the best of cases, the passivity of the business class, are the explanations that historians have given. The resistance on the part of the entrepreneurs obligated the Basque Government to order forced, uncompensated expropriations of the assets of some of the most important families, among them the Lezama Leguizamón family, the Counts of Heredia Spínola, the Marquises of Urquijo, José Luis de Oriol and Juan Tomás Gandarias. The *Ponencia Ordenadora del Trabajo Industrial* (Industrial Labour Regulation Board), designed to respond to the problem, was established on 9 June 1937, but its report came too late. Ten days later, Bilbao fell to the forces of General Mola. Incidentally, Mola had ardently championed the destruction of Vizcayan industry. In his opinion, Spain was dominated by its industrial centres, Barcelona and Bilbao, and if that did not change, the country would never recover. The general was a supporter of a genuine 're-ruralisation' of the Spanish economy.[13]

Mola's advice was ignored. The fall of Bilbao gave the insurgent army Vizcaya's industry intact. As occurred with all the industries of the 'liberated' territories, it was immediately militarised and used for the war effort, precisely what the Basque Government never did. The corresponding *Comisión Militar de Incorporación y Movilización Industrial* (Military Commission of Industrial Incorporation and Mobilisation) designed a reconversion plan, which had the consent and absolute support of the board of directors of Altos Hornos de Vizcaya. The reaction of industry was immediate: the production of iron recovered, in part thanks to the supply of coal from Germany and, shortly thereafter, from Asturias, but also because the big entrepreneurs, with whom the protocols of production were negotiated, quickly realised the opportunities for growth and future profits. In January 1938, the president of Altos Hornos, the Marquis of Triano, and the director, Eduardo Merello, journeyed to Burgos to reiterate to Franco the company's offer to 'contribute with maximum effort and interest to the supply of the necessities of war', for which they were even willing to expand their facilities. The Bilbao Stock Exchange, which during the war months had been converted by the Basque Government into Police Headquarters, was legalised as the only financial market in 'national' territory as of November 1938, and capital flowed there in large quantities.[14]

At the beginning of the year, in clear recognition of the importance of Basque industry, Bilbao was chosen as the seat of the Ministry of Industry and Commerce in Franco's first Government. The minister, Juan Antonio Suanzes, placed Areilza at the head of the *Servicio Nacional de Industria* (National Department of Industry), and decided to take up private residence in Las Arenas, at Elur-Maluta, one of the houses confiscated from the Sota family. Not all big industrialists were treated so well by Franco. There were those who paid dearly for the arrival of the 'liberating' Army. Ramón de la Sota had been, as we know, one of the few important Basque entrepreneurs closely linked to Basque nationalism. He gave financial support to the Republic, and his son, Ramón de la Sota y Aburto, played a leading role within that political current. In 1932, the Sota y Aznar partnership, founded in 1915, was dissolved because Ramón de la Sota no longer saw eye to eye with the heirs of his partner, Luis M. Aznar, who died in 1929. The securities portfolio was divided up and distributed according to the shares of the partners, and Sota took over the company business, which experienced hard times during the 1930s, culminating with the closure of the Sagunto iron and steel mine. Just after the war began, Ramón de la Sota died on 17 August 1936, after a long and terrible illness. When the 'nationalist' troops entered Bilbao, none of his sons or grandsons were in the city. His possessions were abandoned and plundered while his heirs tried to transfer the headquarters of the company to London. On 10 January 1937, the *Junta Técnica*, directed by Franco, began the process of confiscating all the assets of all *desafectos*, people 'indifferent' to the National Movement. Much of Ramón de la Sota's personal estate was never recovered by his heirs because it was seized by the State, as it was said, to compensate for damages his ideas had caused the homeland. The Sota family also lost control of the companies to the Aznar family. In 1940, Altos Hornos de Vizcaya bought the Sagunto iron and steel mine, created years earlier by Ramón de la Sota and Llano. It was necessary to fight against 'Basque nationalist capital and favour capital that supported the Franco regime', said the secretary of the confiscation commission. To do this, collaborators and informers were mobilised and 'good Vizcayans' were called upon to help. One of these 'good Vizcayans' was the new city mayor and later head of the National Department of Industry, José María de Areilza.[15]

After the fall of northern Spain, only Catalonia –with Madrid and Valencia– pertained to the Republic. There, the Commission of War Industries, under the direction of economic adviser Josep Tarradellas, controlled Hispano Suiza, Cros and Maquinista Terrestre y Marítima, among other companies. The central government's decision in June 1937 to place all companies capable of contributing to the war effort under its management was an endless source of friction. Now the Republic's largest industrial centre, Catalonia miraculously maintained many factories and companies unscathed, some of them even improving their facilities. Productive capacity recovered, but only until 1938, when the isolation and occupation of the power plants in Lérida by the insurgents began to cause unsolvable supply problems. At the end of October 1936, the autonomous government of Catalonia had ordered the collectivisation and control of all companies with more than one hundred employees and smaller firms that had been abandoned. These companies would be managed by councils of workers elected in assembly. In the preamble to the decree, it was said that 'the openly fascist bourgeoisie deserted their homes. Most have fled abroad; a minority have disappeared'. Indeed, the big entrepreneurs had fled, as well as many medium and small businessmen, because they feared for their lives. Whether or not they were 'openly fascist' is another matter. The Catalan bourgeoisie had not contributed significantly to the financing of the military conspiracy, but when the coup took place and the revolution broke out in the territory, they went along with the insurgents. Francesc Cambó, who on 18 July was on his yacht, the *Catalònia*, in the Adriatic Sea, did not hesitate to transfer a large portion of the funds he had abroad to Quiñones de León, former ambassador in Paris for the Crown and now a delegate there for the insurgents. At the end of September, he published two articles in the *Daily Telegraph*, wanting to reach public opinion in England. He thought the English were perhaps unaware of what had happened in Spain. Cambó said that the part of Spain controlled by the Popular Front – nothing beyond Catalonia – was not at the time controlled by a constitutional and parliamentary government, but rather 'below the boot of a barabaric and ruthless dictatorship'. The reign of 'red' terror in Catalonia was more cruel and savage than in other places in Spain. 'Churches have been burned, the majority of private residences have been looted, and all properties belonging to Spaniards and foreigners alike have been confiscated. Bank tills have been opened and the anarchist committees now have free access to all the bank funds and private accounts'. Cambó was not sure what type of government Franco would establish on winning the war, but in any case it would be one of a 'markedly national character', whose foreign policy would be dictated by patriotic considerations. If the 'nationalist' uprising in Spain failed, a Soviet Republic would be established and governed from Moscow.[16]

Cambó's diary revealed open contempt for the military insurgents, but he thought a politically weak and short-lived dictatorship would emerge from the situation and probably need the help of conservative Catalans to govern after the war. For the moment, one could only keep quiet and support it. On 22 October 1936, his was the first signature on a declaration that Catalans 'of different ideologies and origins' claiming their wish to remain part of Spain welcomed the thousands of 'brothers' that fought in the ranks of the 'liberating army'. The document was sent to Burgos but was never made public, perhaps for fear of reprisals. Of the nearly one hundred signatories, more than half were businessmen, industrialists and manufacturers, traders, company managers, owners and bankers; many of them, although not all, were members and directors of the regionalist League. Cambó offered the insurgents his network of international contacts, raised money from those who had fled Catalonia and settled in Belgium and Italy, channelled donations to Burgos and also set up the Press and Propaganda Office in Paris. He did not mind when Joan Ventosa I Calvell, head of the Catalan League's parliamentary minority in 1936 and now spokesman for Catalan interests in Burgos and one of Franco's economic advisers, expressed his doubts about taking a ministerial post in a future government. Cambó advised him to accept any such offer, provided there was a minimum of 'decorum and efficiency'. But after a few months, the military stopped consulting and listening to Ventosa. The Falangists were decisive in frustrating Ventosa's chances of obtaining a post. They were strengthened by the growing influence of Ramón Serrano Suñer, the *cuñadísimo* (a brother-in-law of Franco), former member of the Catholic CEDA and now leader of the Falangist Movement. It appears that Nicolás Franco and Juan March himself also had a hand in this. Ventosa faded from the picture. Cambó's pessimism grew, and as of April 1938, he began to consider the foreseeable victory of the insurgents a 'tragedy' for Catalonia. Unlike other party leaders who returned to Catalonia, Cambó died in exile.[17]

The Republic's economic situation was rapidly going downhill. The revolutionary experiments, the disorder, the impact of the war and the agreement of European powers not to intervene caused production to drop more than 70 percent. In addition, the insurgents waged an efficient 'monetary war'. On 12 November 1936, they froze the circulation of the peseta on ordering the stamping of banknotes as an essential requisite to legal circulation within their territory, and invalidated those circulating in the republican zone after 18 July. Around March 1937, new banknotes were issued, and the stamped notes had to be exchanged for the new ones. The republicans responded by prohibiting the 'nationalist' banknotes. There were other manifestations of this 'monetary war'. In the republican zone, different currencies and monetary systems coexisted in Catalonia and the Basque Country, and some collectivised factories even minted their own money for internal use. The news broadcasted by Radio Nacional about 'good currency' and 'bad currency' increased hoarding on the republican side, while the nationalists made the most of the currency they considered illegal and worthless: they purchased other currencies with it, sinking the value of the peseta abroad; they paid for foreign intelligence services and maintained the 'fifth column' in enemy territory by resending republican banknotes to the zones they had originated from. All of this contributed to the inflation that hit the republican side during the war, and helped contain it on the other.[18]

Banks were affected not only by the division of territory and the breakup of their branch networks, which made it impossible to keep accounts in order, but also by the monetary war and the measures that obligated citizens to declare and turn in gold, foreign currencies and assets, and afterwards, silver to the Bank of Spain. Both the republicans and the 'nationalists' did this. Against the resistance of many, the republican Government ordered banks to surrender the contents of their safe-deposit boxes after compensating their owners for the seizure. Many bank managers in republican territory retained their positions, but the big banks relocated their central headquarters to 'liberated' cities, in Burgos if possible. There, on 20 August 1936, the National Committee of Spanish Banking was created. Attending the meeting were the Count of Real Agrado, board member of Hispano Colonial Bank and president of the Bank of Gijón; Manuel Argüelles, board member of the Spanish Credit Bank, and José García Alía, director of the Burgos branch of the Bank of Spain. A short time later, they were joined by the Marquis of Aledo, president of Hispano and of the Herrero Bank, and Arturo López Argüello, director of the Castilian Bank. In mid-September, also in Burgos, the first meeting of the Bank of Spain was held, attended by a broad representation of the 'financial aristocracy': the Marquis of Amurrio, board member of the Bank of Spain, president of the Urquijo Guipuzcoano Bank and the Urquijo Vascongado Bank; Francisco Aritio Gómez, board member of the Bank of Spain and the Spanish Credit Bank; Alfonso Martos, Count of Heredia Spínola and board member of the Bank of Spain, the Industrial Credit Bank and the Bank of Bilbao. Valentín de Céspedes y Céspedes and Ramón Rivero Miranda, Count of Limpias, joined as shareholders' representatives. Orders were given to illegalise all decisions made by the republican Bank of Spain, and the entity's legitimate and authentic representation was restored. Although they were ardent defenders of the uprising against the Government of the republican Popular Front, those distinguished financiers were still not trusted by the more radical Falangists, whose programme included the nationalisation of banking. It was tempting to nationalise the banks, because Franco himself did not feel very comfortable among this sector. The banks were not nationalised, but they were subject to politico-military decisions while the hostilities lasted. In March 1938, former Maura supporter and leader of *Renovación Española*, Antonio Goicoechea, was appointed as Commissioner of the Official Bank, which entailed the management of the Bank of Spain, the Foreign Investment Bank and the Industrial Credit Bank. In case there were any doubts, the new governor was categorical at the Bank of Spain's first shareholders' meeting: 'we are the pillar to lean against, on the side of military victory, the victory that Spain longs for and needs, and has begun to realise'.[19]

At the beginning of the war, the republican Government had important gold reserves that were held at the Bank of Spain in Madrid. In September 1936, amidst fears of an imminent drop in capital, the President of the Republic, Manuel Azaña, signed a decree which authorised the Treasury Minister to transport the gold to a safer place. The gold was moved to the naval base in Cartagena. When the shareholders' representatives learned of the decision at a meeting at the Bank of Spain, they voted against the move. Franco's government was perfectly aware of the manoeuver. In October, when it qualified the export of gold as a crime of treason and contacted the major European banks to denounce the 'divestment', the republican Government decided to ship the gold to the Soviet Union. On 2 November, it arrived in the port of Odessa and was transported by train to Moscow under heavy security. A year and a half later, in September 1938, the gold supply had been drained, all of it used to purchase foreign currencies and pay back debts accumulated by the Republic in the war effort. From that point, there were as many interpretations of the story of 'the gold of Moscow' as there were opinions about the implications of France and Great Britain's policy not to intervene in the war and Italy and Germany's support of the insurgents. The 'gold of Moscow' was all spent and, in hindsight, not very efficiently. It was used to purchase war material that was often obsolete. Moreover, a large part of it was spent on bribes and commissions to ministers, Chiefs of Staff, officers, civil servants and harbour and stationmasters of different countries. However, all of this totalled much less than the sum accounted for by the Soviets' manipulation of exchange rates when fixing prices of the material they supplied.[20]

A New State

The end of the Spanish Civil War gave rise to a new State. It was not the restoration of an old power block, neither in its economic nor social character, and obviously not in its political character. In its tremendous brutality, the Spanish Civil War had been many other things in addition to a social war, and the military insurgents had won it demanding unconditional surrender of the losing side. Reconciliation was impossible. For everyone who had belonged to parties or trade unions, 'separatist' organisations or groups against the National Movement, the Political Responsibilities Act of 1939, the Repression of Freemasonry and Communism Act of 1940 and the condition of a state of war maintained until 1948 made the postwar period an era of persecution and political purging, especially in the regions where the fighting had lasted longer. Hundreds of thousands of Spaniards were jailed, and several thousand were sentenced to death or sent to prison or labour camps. Many more were fired from their jobs. Beyond the physical repression, there was an implacable will to 'purge' Spanish society of all that was considered degenerate excrescence in order to restore its impeccable and traditional purity. The root of all the evil had been the nineteenth-century liberalism that culminated in democracy, class struggle and economic disorder. Upon the firm will to change this course, and upon the legitimacy that total victory granted it, a new State was gradually established in the midst of a terrible economic situation. These were the years of autocracy and international isolation, of inflationary tensions and salary reductions, of the fall of farm and industrial production, of ration coupons, the black market and the triumph of black marketeers.

General Franco had emerged from the Spanish Civil War as *Caudillo*, the Leader, and with all the power in his hands. He had seen the death of generals who might have competed with him for this role, as well as the death of political leaders like José Antonio Primo de Rivera and Calvo Sotelo, who might have competed with him or tried to impose a specific political order. Historiography has shown there were two stages in the initial years of the regime. The first was marked by the predominance of the Falangists and the preeminence of fascist language, and coincided with trust in a German victory in the Second World War. The *Fuero de Trabajo* (Labour Law) was the first of the Franco regime's *Leyes Fundamentales* (Fundamental Laws) enacted in the middle of the War. It qualified the new State as 'national', insofar as it was a 'totalitarian instrument at the service of the integrity of the Homeland'. It also considered the State to be 'syndicalist', in that it represented 'an action against capitalism and Marxist materialism'. Lastly, the law spoke of a pending revolution which would restore 'the Homeland, Bread and Justice' to Spaniards once and for all. As of 1942–1943, the soaring sentiments died down when the tide turned on the Axis powers. Serrano Suñer's exit from the government and his loss of power marked the decline of Falangist hegemony, although not its disappearance. The monarchists, within and outside the country, saw an opportunity to pressure for the reestablishment of the Crown in the heat of the Allies' victory. Franco, however, while derailing their manoeuver, abandoned fascist discourse and appropiated the image of a traditional, Catholic monarchy. In July 1945, a few months after the Yalta Conference and the ultimatum by the heir to the throne from his exile in Lausanne, there was a change in the Government. Alberto Martín Artajo, president of the National Technical Board of Catholic Action, became Minister of Foreign Affairs. With the end of the Second World War, it was time for the regime to situate itself in the new international context. This move was a result of pressure by Catholics and a series of new laws which tried to cast the regime in a new light for foreign countries: the *Fuero de los Españoles* (another of the Fundamental Laws decreed by Franco), the Law of Referendum and the Law of Succession. The Law of Succession declared Spain a Kingdom, but assigned Franco the leadership of the country and the designation of his successor. In December 1946, the United Nations (U. N.) formally condemned the Spanish dictatorship, producing a general withdrawal of ambassadors, but the total isolation did not last very long. The French border, which had been closed two years earlier, opened again in February 1948, when contacts with the United States began. However, the U.N. resolution and the return of ambassadors would not take place until 1950.[21]

Franco's dictatorship was a one-party State, but that party was clearly subordinate to the State and its indisputable leader, Franco. The necessary unification in 1937 of the forces that had supported the uprising (monarchists, Catholics, Carlists and Falangists) into one party, the FET and the JONS (Traditionalist Spanish Falange and Councils of the National Syndicalist Offensive), was the first step in that subordination. It was the unions' turn in 1940, when they became a single and vertical trade union under the control of the Falangists. It was also the moment when the party expanded with the creation of the University Students' Union, the Youth Front and the Feminine Department, and an important presence in the regime's press and propaganda organs. The party seemed solid. It rhetorically condemned the old boss system and abuses of power, blaming these for a fraudulent liberal past. However, the apparent solidity hid a 'weak and chaotic' situation rife with intense confrontations between *camisas viejas* and *camisas nuevas*, old and new politicians who earned posts based on their politcal merits. The confrontations entailed a process of adaptation, which included criticism of the power and denunciations for abandoning the social principles some had started out with. By the end of the 1940s, most of this fight had ended. The criticism faded, although without disappearing completely, and the regime could rest assured that no threat would come from the Falangist ranks. The party had become a sort of great political boss which handed out privileges and multiplied positions of power.[22]

As for the Syndical Organisation, it never became an autonomous force capable of converting Spain into a 'gigantic syndicate of producers', as Article 9 of the Falangists' programme stated. After Gregorio Salvador Merino left the National Delegation of Trade Unions, the unions resigned themselves to their subordinate position. They had little or no say in the definition of economic policy, which was left to the Government, and the same impact on the negotiation of labour relations. With the *Jurados Mixtos* abolished, their judicial powers were transferred to *Magistraturas de Trabajo*, judges who were freely appointed by the Minister of Syndical Organisation and Action, while the Ministry of Labour was declared responsible for elaborating the corresponding regulations. The State reserved the power to establish labour conditions on national, regional and provincial levels in the different branches of production. Specific company norms, reflected in company codes of internal procedure, had to adapt to these conditions. The Syndical Organisation was limited to its function of controlling the working class, which would be compensated with a policy of individual worker protection. The biggest priorities were placed on guaranteeing job stability, subjecting layoffs to strict norms and requirements of administrative authorisation, and on developing what was called 'social work'. Many hundreds of supporters and civil servants of the new State were employed in their delegations, head offices and branch offices. In spite of everything, they never kept up their efforts to assert the presence of the syndicate.[23]

The new State was, above all, Franco's dictatorship, a personal dictatorship above the law and the different 'bureaucracies', not parties, with which a new political class was formed. This class was, above all, committed to Franco. The Army, the Falangist Movement and the Church were sources of recruitment to this new class. It helped to be a member of a well-known family from the industrial or financial bourgeoisie, or to own land. The greater the number of these characteristics one had, the greater the chance that person had of entering politics. 'Being well-connected' was decisive, and traditions and family names had some influence on these connections, but friendship with, or closeness to, those who mediated the selections was very often more efficient. The ones who made the selections were nearly always individuals who had come to prominence in the heat of the war and proven their allegiance to the new regime. The new politicians came from the middle classes. They were, with a few exceptions, relatively young, and this resulted in a large break from the political class prior to the war and even from previous regimes. Most of the new politicians were high-ranking civil servants of the Administration – engineers, state attorneys, diplomats and professors – and intended to become professional politicians. The conflicts between the different groups and the different bureaucracies were sometimes resolved by processes of fusion. On other occasions, especially those of a more personal nature, the decision rested with the word of the one who was always above everyone else: Franco. Whereas members of the military and Falangists predominated in politics during the first years of the regime, especially in ministerial posts, between 1945 and 1951, there was a certain balance between Falangists and Catholics which stabilised in the 1950s. Members of the military, bridging gaps between one group and another, increased their presence in the Ministries of Agriculture and Education, but especially in the new Ministries of Industry and Commerce. They had been actively involved in these tasks and also those related to the Presidency of the Government since the beginning of the new State. Some members of this new political class, who ended up forming a rather closed elite, got involved in the world of business, especially in businesses which arose after the war, taking advantage of their positions of power. Decades later, this overlap of politics and wealth gave rise to almost always scandalous stories about huge fortunes generated in the circles closest to the power and to Franco and his family. However, it would be ludicrous to narrow all of this down to a handful of cases.[24]

It would be ludicrous, because it was not only the old oligarchies or the most economically powerful who supported Franco during and after the war. The social bases of the Franco regime were much more complex, heterogeneous and extensive than people have often been willing to admit. The exhaustion of a bloody civil war made people long for peace and normality, even those who had fought against the insurgents. The conviction that Spaniards were too divided to live in peace, and therefore needed Franco, fuelled contempt for politics, which for many, not only the less cultivated, was the source of all the hardships, including the war. Franco had to be thanked even for that valiant gesture of keeping Spain out of the Second World War and for refusing Hitler's request. The consensus that the dictatorship would eventually be built on arose out of these convictions – and, of course, out of the repression.[25]

This consensus had a number of bases, but undoubtedly, some won a lot and others lost nearly everything. Despite the flightiness of the more radical Falangists and the reigning interventionism, the end of the war saw the reestablishment of the principle of property, well-protected by the recovery of order. Agrarian reform had been formally suspended on 28 August 1939. A few months earlier, the National Service of Social Reform of the Land had been created. One of its goals was to return properties to their former owners. Only half a million of the more than six million occupied hectares of land were returned by legal methods. In the territories which fell to the insurgents, the rest was taken by force, both during and after the war. Sharecropping contracts were nullified or revised, and the new leasing law, although restricting owners' freedom of action, paved the way for evictions. The dispossession and acts of injustice, especially in the areas where the rural conflict had been greatest during the 1930s and the war, were so rampant that even the Falangists complained. Promises of a true agrarian reform had been part of the Falangists' platform, which favoured rural areas. The Minister of Agriculture, the Falangist Raimundo Fernández Cuesta, claimed to be pursuing this programme, but the promises were never kept. The director of the National Institute of Colonisation later denounced the situation. Not only did the supposed reform go nowhere; the new State's entire agricultural policy turned out to be a complete failure and Spanish agriculture in the 1940s went through abysmal circumstances: the area of cultivated land diminished and production fell below pre-war levels, even though the number of available workers increased. The consequences were tremendous: shortages, hunger and ration coupons. And these were not effects of the destruction caused by the war, or of drought, or of the *maquis* (resistance fighters) – though these played some part – but rather of the enormous fiasco of interventionist policy and autarky. In some cases, official price fixing discouraged cultivation and, at the same time, caused the rise of a very profitable black market for those who could access it. Farm owners, freed from the pressure of workers' organisations, relieved by a drastic fall in wages and now able to speculate on the black market, made a killing: they could sell their products at up to three times the official prices. But there were also farmers who could not survive on official prices and who lacked the connections to access the black market with some degree of security. Many of these farmers decided to sell their lands, producing a whirlwind of real estate transactions. While previous owners added to their properties, a new kind of landowner emerged during the buying and selling spree: those who, thanks to their connections with the decision makers, such as the inspectors of the *Comisaría General de Abastecimientos y Transportes* (General Board of Supplies and Transport), could take advantage of the situation with total impunity. Both old and new landowners lacked incentives to take interest in the regime's policies of colonisation and irrigation, which were expensive and unclear in their aims. Until Rafael Cavestany became Minister of Agriculture in 1951, there were no signs of change or liberalisation, and the colonisation projects developed with greater momentum. The 1940s and 1950s were the last decades of what has been called 'traditional' agriculture. Afterwards, Spain would face the great crisis of readjustment and modernisation.[26]

In industry, the vast majority of businessmen and owners returned to their sites and recovered their properties and companies. The Committees of Industrial and Mercantile Incorporation were created to this end in May 1938. These committees were dependent on the Ministry of Industry and Commerce, and their function was to normalise industrial and mercantile activities in the areas that were being 'liberated', and to recreate 'an economic and social situation destroyed by the enemies of the Homeland'. Committee Number Two, for example, had jurisdiction over the four Catalan provinces. For the Catalan bourgeoisie, the Spanish Civil War had entailed an even bigger commitment than in 1923, but those who supported Franco – and there were many – knew exactly what they were doing. Those who escaped to 'national' territory had no problems on their return. They recovered their factories and businesses, which were even improved. This was the case of the Sedó i Guichard brothers, owners of one of the biggest textile manufacturers, and closely linked to the Catalan Urquijo Bank. Some of those who had left the country or hesitated to join the 'nationalist' side had more problems. One such person was Eusebi Bertrand y Serra, a textile businessman and president of Catalana de Gas. The Court of Political Responsibilities filed proceedings against him, but he was immediately absolved. The case of Josep Suñol, president of the Compañía de Industrias Agrícolas S.A., was worse. Suñol remained in Barcelona during the war. His son, a representative of the Catalan Republican Left and president of the Barcelona Football Club, was arrested by fascist soldiers during a journey and shot. An investigation was opened against Suñol and, by order of the civil governor, he was removed from his post as president of his company's board of directors in 1942. The old Catalan elite lost the political presence it had had, but the dictatorship was not imposed from outside of Catalonia. Some prominent names remained in important positions of the vertical syndicate and were eventually appointed ministers without portfolio in the Government of 1957. One example is Pere Gual Villalbí, perennial secretary of the Fomento del Trabajo Nacional, who travelled around Europe during the war to raise money for the insurgents, and later became president of the *Consejo de Economía Nacional* (Council of National Economy). Miquel Mateu, son of the founder of Hispano Suiza and nephew of Cardinal Enrique Pla y Deniel, was a good representative of the Catalan bourgeoisie, which now supported Franco. He had fled Catalonia in July 1936, and from Geneva went to Burgos. He entered the general staff, acted as unofficial representative of Franco in Paris and won his personal trust. Franco appointed him mayor of Barcelona immediately after the war. He had no objections to sanctioning the cleaning and purification of all the 'unworthy' civil servants, or to erasing all vestiges of Catalan nationalism from the city. After another stint in Paris, this time as ambassador of Spain, he retired from politics and dedicated himself to taking care of his important economic position. In 1952, he was elected president of the *Fomento del Trabajo Nacional*.[27]

Miquel Mateu was the mayor of Barcelona, just as many other Catalans were mayors of villages and towns in Catalonia. They were former members of monarchic or Catholic parties, perhaps with war merits, but among them were also some former regionalists. Many were middle-class owners, manufacturers, traders or professionals. It has been written that Franco was willing to put a sector of the Catalan bourgeoisie in municipal power, provided it did not harbour Catalan nationalist sympathies, but he excluded it from all direct participation in the upper echelons of government. It is also likely that many of these businessmen-turned-mayors accepted out of a sense of 'patriotism', although they would have preferred to dedicate themselves solely to their businesses. In the end, the Catalan bourgeoisie not only 'resigned itself' to the new political order, it settled comfortably into it for a long time, although deep down it was opposed to it. There were many 'Catalans of Franco'. The enthusiastic reception of the fascist army on their arrival in Barcelona was a clear sign that nobody wanted a return to 1935, and the industrial guilds never tired of recognising a debt of everlasting gratitude to the 'undefeated Leader' for putting an end to their captivity and recovering the industrial patrimony.[28]

Owners, businessmen and employers in the entire country could, moreover, purge their staff of *desafectos* or individuals opposed to the Movement, and they were assured of enjoying a climate of absolute social peace. The obligatory membership to the Syndical Organisation may have annoyed them, but, unlike workers' unions, some business and employers' entities like the centenarian *Fomento del Trabajo Nacional* were allowed to survive, even if that survival meant little more than hibernation. This was also true of the Chambers of Commerce. A few years later, the possibility of creating sections within the syndicate permitted businessmen to organise themselves autonomously. As such, it was easier for the business class to impose their interests, although they did so within a very different institutional framework, frequently subject to unforeseen arbitrariness. The new internal procedure guidelines drawn up by the companies were very strict in matters of discipline. Workdays grew longer and wages fell. Low salaries, the shortage of basic products, the implementation of ration coupons and exorbitant black market prices caused extreme situations of hunger, misery, and in some cases, even death. Local authorities, provincial inspectors from the Movement, some Falangists, the police, the Chambers of Commerce and even some economic organisations denounced the horrible living conditions of the lower classes. The High Council of the Chambers of Commerce explained in 1942 that the decline in labour performance and low productivity were a result of the 'physical debilitation of the worker owing to malnutrition'. This lamentable situation translated into an unease which, however, did not manifest itself in open protest. The extremely difficult living conditions, memories of the war and, of course, the repression prevented any collective act of protest. Affiliation with the syndicate, even before this was mandatory, might have been the only way to obtain the membership card required to get a job.[29]

The class struggle had been stamped out by law to promote disciplined harmony in each 'company community' of all 'producers', although merely considering the existence of 'labour relations' and a 'work contract' broke with that communal conception. The Syndical Unity Law anticipated the existence of syndical ties and also of the *Jurados de Empresa* (Company Juries) which were conceptually established in 1947. Although the expected workers' representation lacked specific powers and hardly entailed a threat to employers at the time, six years passed before the *Jurados* were actually functioning. In the opinion of many entrepreneurs, they represented a 'very dangerous innovation' reminiscent of the workers' committees of 'red' Spain. Businessmen did not forget which organisations workers had belonged to up until the civil war, and one had to be very careful with the resurrection of those experiments at a time – this was said in 1948 – when Communism was planning to 'assault the West'.[30]

In spite of everything, there were some conflicts. The first strike from those years, illegal as all of them were, took place in Barcelona in May 1945. It was still a political strike, encouraged by the defeat of fascism in the Second World War. The strikes that occurred six months later in Madrid, Barcelona again and Bilbao were a response to the increasingly difficult living and labour conditions. The most spectacular was, however, the one in Vizcaya in May of 1947: 20,000 workers from nearly 400 companies went on strike to protest the deterioration of the economy and the reduction of salaries. During the strike, the employers asked the government not to apply the harshest sanctions, and promised the workers they would not be punished. But once the conflict ended, they changed their minds, and the Industrial Centre of Vizcaya, in connivance with the authorities, fired workers, eliminated seniority rights and circulated blacklists, although many of the punishments were suspended to celebrate 18 July. It was the last strike organised by the former opposition, led by the illegal Basque Nationalist Party. The next big conflict, a boycott of the streetcars in Barcelona in 1951, was of a very different nature. It was by and large a spontaneous, massive boycott which turned into a general strike, unsettling for the authorities because it was not a political strike, and because, at least initially, radical Falangists and Catholics were involved. In Barcelona, as in other cities in the months that followed, it was poverty and desperation that drove people to the streets.[31]

Autarky and Industrial State

Juan Ventosa, former leader of the Catalan League and later frustrated candidate for a ministerial post in Franco's first Government, gave a conference at the Institute of Political Studies in Madrid on 19 February 1940. Ventosa said it was necessary to repair the damages caused by the civil war and alleviate the problems of essential foodstuffs and raw materials for industries, transportation and defence. To do so, Spain had to take advantage of her excellent geographic position and her neutrality in the Second World War. The policy of fanatical protectionism would only stymie the economy, more so if one was tricked into pursuing outlandish proposals such as converting water into gasoline. Censorship prohibited the publication of the conference, and Ventosa was almost severely punished for what was considered a serious affront to the Falangist Movement and to Franco himself. At the time, Franco was fascinated by projects like the one cited above, an idea proposed to him by an Austrian.[32]

In Spain there was a strong tradition of economic nationalism that had gained a lot of momentum, theoretically and practically, during the Primo de Rivera dictatorship. But what happened with this in the 1940s, as with many other matters, was not a mere continuation. The autarkic aim was influenced above all by the examples of Mussolini's Italy and Nazi Germany, the eagerness to produce everything in order to prove one's strength and guarantee maximum national independence. Franco himself said that the trade deficit had to be erased, otherwise the 'annual drain of hundreds of millions that leave [Spain] to invigorate the economies of exporting countries' would continue. According to the autarky's theoreticians, one had to discipline and exercise 'totalitarian' control over the economic world. The State had to be assured its authority would not be undermined, and that, once outlined, the plan would be followed 'inflexibly' by each productive sector.[33]

This is why Spain was unable to benefit from its neutrality – or non-belligerence – in the Second World War. The comparison with the evolution of other countries' economies reveals the extent of the opportunities lost. All of them suffered cuts in the supply of goods from abroad: fuel most of all, and some raw materials and semi-manufactured goods. In spite of this, the Second World War created export opportunities for Portugal, Turkey and Sweden, bringing positive changes to their industrial and manufacturing structure as well as a significant accumulation of reserves. In Spain, these opportunities were wasted. It was not because the country started out from a worse position or, as has been pointed out on occasion, because of the material destruction that occurred during the civil war. There was, however, an undeniable effect from the death, exile or postwar repression of many skilled workers, experts and technicians, whose absence was a major burden on the recovery of the Spanish economy. There were also driving forces for change and projects of adaptation to the new domestic and foreign demand, but these were overridden by the damaging effects of the economic policy deliberately adopted by Franco's governments. There were several factors that increased economic strangulation and created genuine 'speculative capitalism': the desire for independence, which translated into an erratic and often irrational policy of substituting imports; the shortage of means of payment together with the supreme contempt for offers of international loans, which did exist; the intervention by an inefficient State in the allocation of foreign currencies, quotas of raw materials and import and export licenses; and the directives that clearly gave priority to some sectors over others. In this 'speculative capitalism', huge fortunes – and these also existed – arose from the buying and selling of raw materials combined with the enormous differences between official and black market prices. With the end of the Second World War, the relative growth of production and foreign trade, which had occurred in spite of everything, collapsed. The second half of the decade was even more difficult.[34]

There were three keys to entrepreneurial success: be close to centres which had raw materials; obtain orders from military organisations and state companies; and establish privileged relations with members of the Administration. The clearest sign was the massive transfer of big company headquarters from all over the peninsula to Madrid, a trend which terminated in the early 1950s. Meanwhile, from very different points in Spain, like Bilbao or San Sebastián, Barcelona, Zaragoza or Valencia, the same surviving business entities and the Chambers of Commerce raised their voices in protest against privileged treatment, unfair allocations, and shortages suffered by those economies and businessmen that were not given priority by the new State. There were people who recognised in this a clear intention to penalise the provinces and regions considered to be *desafectas* (opposed to the Movement). In 1944, Catalan Pere Gual Villalbí spoke of the 'extraeconomic motives for exercising industrial dislocation' and the 'dispersion of (Catalan) industries', although he softened his criticism, affirming that when the Government believed it was in the country's best interests to put political motives before economic considerations, there was no choice but to give in to authority and obey. The same was suspected in the Republic's last outpost, Valencia, whose flourishing economy was clearly seen to be punished by the new economic policy until the 1950s.[35]

As then Director General of Industry and Falangist José María de Areilza put it so well at a conference held at the University of Barcelona in June 1940, the doctrine of the new State 'subordinates the economic to the political'. The spirit behind this message was influential in the creation of the new Council of National Economy. The Council intended to distance itself from interests and privileges, with a total break from corporate representations and 'single management', as its secretary general wrote. The Council gathered the best economists of the day and engineers as well, because the new State possessed the traits of modernity and technological dazzle, which would lead a few years later to the creation of the National Institute for the Rationalisation of Work. Also sitting on the board were some members of civil servants' corps. The president of the Institute was José María Zumalacárregui. He was Catholic, a professor of public finance, a mathematician, and a very influential figure in the academic world. Among the members were Demetrio Carceller, who we will speak about later; José María de Areilza, who, in addition to being an industrial engineer and having important ties with Basque economic interests, was also the most political; and the professor and ex-Secretary of the *Fomento del Trabajo Nacional* already mentioned, Pere Gual Villalbí. The Council's first report was about the urgent problem of the shortage of foreign currencies. It intended to harmonise the justification of interventionism with the harshest denouncements against the imbalances caused by the centralisation of currency concessions and the register of importers and exporters. Nothing else could be expected of an organisation that was supposedly technical, but subordinate to the priorities fixed by a policy whose principles, nonetheless, were held by many of its members. It would never manage to free itself from this subordination, or from the conflict of powers that arose in the red tape of ministries and institutions. These administrative bodies held poorly defined functions, but all of them could intervene. Contrary to the most popular opinions, far from reinforcing the development of the State, they helped to disintegrate it.[36]

Franco himself was convinced it was necessary to make a real effort to industrialise the Spanish economy and thereby give Spain the strength and independence it was due. In the best of military traditions, those who shared this objective – and many, though not all, were military men – believed it would not be difficult to achieve, as long as the government could discipline private initiative, make it work towards the state-defined goals and, if it did not respond quickly enough, replace it if necessary. Among those who followed this line of thought were individuals who had some prior experience in the world of economy and even business. Although they, too, were convinced of the need to industrialise the economy, they were also more sensitive to the complexities. There were others, like Franco, who were more ignorant; they believed that everything was possible and could fall for any inconceivable offer. Along with these differences, which caused serious conflicts when decisions had to be made, were the presence, pressure and influence of the economic interests involved. These interests were always more aware of the constraints set by the situation, the benefits that could be obtained, and the risks involved in the proposals that came from on high. They were also punished by and rather pessimistic because of the memory of difficulties experienced during the Republic, the shock of the civil war, the uncertainties after the end of the Second World War, and the perspectives of the new international order. However, whether or not private economic interests gained something from this experience, the big initiatives and the definition of the procedural framework came from the political power. The intervention of military agents in ministries and especially in public sector companies was decisive. Organisational innovations and a principle of 'national service', absent until then, were implemented in the public sector.[37]

The Protection and Development of National Industry Law had been passed on 24 October 1939. Its goal was to stimulate private initiative, offering certain benefits. The Administration reserved the right to declare as being 'of national interest' those industries which requested it, as well as the right to intervene in the functioning of the company through an auditor. A month later, another very similar law was passed. It seemed to be a continuation of the first, but was also intended to regulate and classify industrial activity, declaring all industries 'an integral part of the National Patrimony and subordinate to the supreme interest of the nation' in order to guarantee self-sufficiency and economic independence. Two years later, on 25 September 1941, a new law gave birth to the National Institute of Industry (INI), a public law entity whose goal was 'to promote and finance in the service of the Nation the creation and resurgence of our industries, especially those which set as their principal aim the resolution of the problems imposed by the demands of our country's defence, or which address the unravelling of our economic autarky, offering Spanish savings a secure and attractive investment'. In other words, in a span of two years, it had been decided that the amount of investments and effort were so great that they exceeded the capacities of companies and private banks. 'Only the State', it was written in the Institute's 1941–1942 annual report, 'can spur the industrial leap that the circumstances require'. Ten years later, in the early 1950s, the Institute participated in thirty-six companies. Half of them were created by the Institute; the others were pre-existing firms. The INI had complete ownership of ten of them, majority holdings in sixteen and minority holdings in eight. Nine were of a military or paramilitary nature (the Empresa Nacional de Construcciones Militares Bazán, for example), eight had autarkic objectives including the exploitation of natural resources (the Empresa Nacional Calvo Sotelo, Encaso; the Empresa Nacional de Electricidad, Endesa; the Refinería de Petróleos de Escombreras, Repsa, among others), seven were transport companies (the Empresa Nacional de Autocamiones, Enasa; the Empresa Nacional Elcano, and Iberia, incorporated in the INI), and two were iron and steel firms (the Empresa Nacional Siderúgica, Ensidesa, the more important of the two). They amounted to only 0.45 percent of all existing public companies in the country, but represented 13 percent of all authorised capital. Their average size was considerably bigger, as well: other companies had an average of 5.9 million pesetas in paid-up capital; in comparison, the companies in the INI group had an average of 95.6 million pesetas. In 1963, when the change of the INI's presidency clearly marked the end of an era, the total number of companies was sixty-one. The INI had complete ownership of eighteen of them, a majority share in twenty-nine and a minority share in fourteen. They represented 24 percent of all public companies and their average paid-up capital was 738 million pesetas, compared to the 15.7 million peseta average of the other companies. At that juncture, the INI's business group was very complex and diversified, although ten companies from priority sectors absorbed 75 percent of the funds. In 1960, only three of the ten biggest companies were private (Hidrola, Iberduero and Altos Hornos) and four belonged to the INI group: Ensidesa, Encaso, Bazán and Endesa. The most important firms were the railways that were generously nationalised in 1941, the RENFE; and the third in rank was the Compañía Telefónica Nacional, in which the state replaced IT&T as the main shareholder and awarded it the monopoly of telecommunication services. The importance of the public sector was unquestionable.[38]

It would be impossible to deny the importance of the rise of the INI and the public sector company after the Spanish Civil War or their role in the definitive industrialisation of the Spanish economy, although there were differences in opinion about their influence, including the most negative assesments of their initiatives and even their necessity. Nor can it be ignored that government intervention in the economy occurred in all European countries around the same time. However, in other countries, it happened in a clearly different political context and for different reasons. This did not prevent nationalisation in certain sectors and countries from being much greater than in Spain. In our case, this direct intervention changed and complicated relations among the State, politicians and private interests in a dictatorial context that should never be forgotten. This complication has also given rise to varying opinions, not about the wisdom of creating the INI or its economic protagonism, but about who had more influence, who set the guidelines, who really benefited, and whether the public sector worked more in the general interest or in private interests. In these often conflicting opinions, it is not always taken into account that the borders between both worlds were not so clear, and that many people moved from one to the other, which was an important novelty in the business world.[39]

When the law that created the INI was passed, the Minister of Industry and Trade was Demetrio Carceller. Carceller was a member in the early stages of the Falangist Movement, and considered by some to be its 'economic brain'. Others considered him pragmatic, even opportunistic, as the first businessman and first Catalan that entered the Franco Government. He replaced Luis Alarcón de Lastra, a Sevillian artillery captain whose only economic merit before the war was managing the Casa de Alba (one of the oldest and wealthiest noble families in Spain). Carceller was something different. Although he came from a family of peasants, he was an expert on petroleum. After an important career in this sector, which included a stint with Campsa, he became director of a private company – Cepsa – in the 1930s, and established the country's first refinery. By 18 July 1936, he had amassed a personal fortune. He arrived in Burgos, having crossed the Sierra de Guadarrama on foot, to offer his services to Franco. His mediation was crucial in convincing Standard Oil to supply the 'nationalists' during the Spanish Civil War. He was appointed Minister of Industry and Trade in Franco's first Government. He was expected to solve the problems of gasoline and chemical fertilisers. To do so, he travelled to Berlin with a commission headed by Serrano Suñer. Convinced of Germany's victory, he believed it was better to be generous with the Germans and not take advantage of their need of wolfram, which Spain was supplying them. But as of 1942, Carceller abandoned his subservience to Germany and began to act according to his business convictions, handling himself with greater ease in the international market and showing clear signs of having Anglo-American sympathies. Although fiercely anti-liberal in his politics, at that stage Carceller believed in private initiative and considered interventionism a necessary evil. He lost the battle against his enemies in the circles of power closest to Franco, and after his dismissal in 1945 until his death, he devoted his time to making his many businesses prosper.[40]

Carceller was replaced in the ministry by someone he had repeatedly clashed with: Juan Antonio Suanzes, at that moment president of the INI. Born in El Ferrol, Suanzes was an engineer for the Navy, although in 1922 he left the military and joined the Sociedad Española de Construcción Naval. In 1934, he was fired for energetically voicing his disagreement with the company's dependence on its English partner, Vickers. After the Spanish Civil War began, he immediately joined the Franco Administration, aided by his personal friendship with the Franco family, especially with Nicolás. Suanzes had been Minister of Trade and Industry from January 1938 to August 1939, during which time he expressed strong support for autarky and nationalisation: 'the totalitarian state', he wrote at the time, 'maintains the thesis of putting the economy, with all its integral components, at the strict orders of policy, or rather, the political aims of the state'. What he had in mind was a true project of industrial 'mobilisation' or 'planning', perhaps an heir of those commissions of military origin conceived during the First World War, and even a design of what the government of the new State should be. But in August 1939, he was dismissed from his ministry, and during the years when Serrano Suñer and the

Falangists were at the height of their power, he was completely removed from the decision-making process.

When the INI was created in 1941, Suanzes was promoted to the presidency, and he carried out the post with enthusiasm, but not without problems or conflicts, until 1963. From 1945 to 1951, the years of his greatest power, he was simultaneously president of the INI and Minister of Trade and Industry. The INI that was finally approved may not have been his creation, but it fit in with his ideas. In getting the project off the ground, he ran up against refusals to participate from those who wanted to be part of the management. He also sparked major conflicts at various moments with Carceller, Larraz and Joaquín Benjumea, successive ministers of the Treasury, with Foreign Affairs ministers Gómez Jordana and Lequerica, and as of 1945, with Carrero Blanco, the powerful Subsecretary of the Prime Minister Office. Suanzes was irritated by the interference in his plans, especially when he considered it unfair and damaging to his ambitious industrialisation project. He resigned on several occasions, doing so to pressure General Franco, who in the end ruled in his favour. Franco eventually dismissed him from the ministry in 1951, when Spain began to be more flexible in its negotiations with the United States. Suanzes had a lot of power, but it was never unlimited or unquestionable. The development of the Institute was, perhaps to his chagrin, necessarily pragmatic and opportunistic, and occasionally erratic. Ultimately, it was restricted by several factors: the regime's internal political struggles, in which Suanzes had no unconditional support; the needs imposed by the economic instability, which he perhaps helped to worsen; the evolution of the international context and the gradual search for support from the United States, which did not come at all easily for him; and the desires and pressures of private initiative. Sometimes he sought the backing of private enterprise, sometimes he subjected it to the will of the INI, and other times he acquiesced to its pressure. 'I am, and with great pride', he wrote in early 1944, in a long letter to Franco for one of his resignations, 'the enemy of several ministers, Big Banking and Big Industry, the pretender to the throne and a series of foreign representations'.[41]

When he took his ministerial post, Suanzes affirmed that the State did not have the least intention of becoming a government of industrialists while private initiative could satisfy the needs dictated by national interest. He appointed Eduardo Merello as Subsecretary of the Ministry of Industry. Merello had been the manager of Altos Hornos until then, and had had major confrontations with Suanzes. The iron and steel industry was the key element of his project, but private initiative did not live up to his expectations. Altos Hornos, after purchasing Siderúgica de Sagunto in 1940, accounted for two-thirds of all production in this sector. That same year, total production figures had approached the maximum reached in 1929, but afterwards, they levelled off. Difficulties in obtaining a sufficient supply of coal and scrap metal, the lack of skilled workers and the physical debilitation of workers were some of the many reasons put forward by Vizcayan businessmen, who, moreover, had a clash of interests with their Asturian counterparts. Production fell, but coal mine and iron and steel owners were compensated by the concession of subsidies, price increases, low wages and recourse to the black market, where much of their production ended up.

There is no other way to account for their significant profits, although these profits perhaps were not as great as some have indicated if inflation is taken into account.[42]

The conflicts between coal mine and iron and steel owners, between Asturian and Vizcayan businessmen, were probably resolved in private conversations. But this did not solve the problem that worried Suanzes so much. In that protected and oligopolistic market, it was difficult to get entrepreneurs to undertake more investments. In 1948, the Technical Council for the Iron and Steel Industry, one of the INI's advisory boards, spoke of the need for new coordination in this sector. Alarm spread, and the president of Altos Hornos, the Marquis of Triano, sought an audience with the minister. The big iron and steel owners met with the vice-president of the INI and seemed interested in the project. Time passed, and in May 1950, Suanzes wrote to them, encouraging them to participate in a new comprehensive plant which would be built in Asturias. The plan was for the INI to hold 40 percent of the shares and private companies 35 percent, with the remaining 25 percent allotted for foreign investment. The days of extreme nationalism were over. Once the development of the iron and steel industry was assured, the INI would be glad to turn over its shares to private companies. Around the same time Suanzes sent his letter, the ministry received another one signed by Altos Hornos, Duro-Felguera, Basconia, Nueva Montaña and Echevarría, which were all completely opposed to the project. They believed it was better to consolidate existing companies, which deserved all the public support, and that the government should not take measures which would hurt private companies. But Suanzes went ahead with it. At the Second National Congress of Engineering, Félix Aranguren, now president of the new company Ensidesa, presented some lengthy explanations that quickly reached the press. There was no response from the private sector until a few months later, and it was negative. The INI eventually subscribed 40 percent of the new company. The rest of the shares were deposited into a stock portfolio, but private initiative never subscribed them.[43]

Other interventions by the INI caused tensions between the public sector and private interests. Suanzes never lost his distrust of the private sector, despite occasionally moderating his language and insisting that public intervention was temporary. The INI never pulled out once it had made an investment. But it was also on many occasions a 'hospital for companies' and it lost battles. It failed to acquire Campsa (the petroleum monopoly leasing company) after renegotiating the contract with the State in 1947. This failure led it to initiate conversations with Cepsa and, again sacrificing its nationalism, with the U.S. firm Caltex. These conversations gave birth to Cepsa and the Escombreras refinery. Intervention in the electricity industry was also full of tensions. Here, as in other sectors, government intervention, erratic at the beginning, brought about the union of private companies. José María de Oriol y Urquijo was president of Hidroeléctrica Española and board member of the Spanish Credit Bank thanks to his excellent relations with the monarchists and with Franco himself. He had direct access to the *Caudillo* and convinced him that the best solution to the sector's problems was an intermediate position between absolute control of the market by private companies and the nationalisation that Suanzes wanted. He guaranteed him that, via an entity like the one they were going to create, the sector would be regulated and prepared to expand in a coordinated fashion. The result was that the fourteen biggest electric companies created Unidad Eléctrica, S.A. (Unesa). The electric industry, unlike what happened then in other European countries, was not nationalised in Spain. The two important public initiatives, Encaso and Endesa, coexisted with Unesa, which was responsible for regulating the sector and establishing the national network of interconnections. It is also true that there were private initiatives that were blocked and which the INI 'appropriated'. It occurred in negotiations between the Italian company Fiat and the Urquijo group for the creation of the Sociedad Ibérica de Automoviles de Turismo, which applied for the status of industry of national interest. That never got anywhere, and after much discussion, what was created in 1950 was Seat, not Siat: the INI had 51 percent of the shares, Fiat had 7 percent, and the remaining 42 percent went into a banking consortium comprised of the Spanish Credit Bank, the Hispano Americano Bank, the Bank of Vizcaya, the Bank of Bilbao and the Central Bank along with the Urquijo Bank.[44]

The creation of the INI was a shock for companies and banks, which were obligated to adapt to the new situation and respond to the challenges. The overwhelming power of public initiative, at times attributed to Suanzes and the INI, contrasts with the opinion of those who have maintained that those were the years when the traditional *financial aristocracy's* greater power was restored. From the big banks' boards of directors, the Bank of Spain itself and the reestablished High Council of Banking, this elite group would have dictated economic policy in its favour. However, these bankers were subject to new legislation that was more interventionist than ever before. The first tasks undertaken by the Franco regime were to restore the monetary system broken in 1936 and divest the public of excess money which threatened to trigger uncontrollable inflation. The author of the three laws which addressed this problem in 1939 was José Larraz, who was appointed Treasury Minister after he reorganised the Bank of Spain's Department of Studies. The sterilisation of more than twenty-five thousand million pesetas in banknotes and bank deposits unrecognised by the new State caused problems for citizens but was a success for Larranz. Nonetheless, Larraz resigned shortly after his tax reform project fizzled out. Around 1942, the majority of banks managed to balance their accounts. The balancing of the Bank of Spain's accounts was accomplished by law, but it did not occur without upsetting the representatives of private capital. They wanted recognition of all the money in circulation as well as the State's debt with the Bank of Spain, and they wanted to be compensated for the lost gold. This did not happen. The Bank of Spain continued to be a private bank for another twenty years. In September 1939, the Spanish Institute of Foreign Currency was created. It was dependent on the Ministry of Trade and Industry, and absorbed all powers related to the control and trade of currencies. Later, in 1946, the new Banking Regulation Law transferred the policy of loans and emissions to the Treasury Ministry. The aforementioned institute and law made the Bank of Spain irrelevant, a mere appendage of the Treasury Ministry. Practically speaking, its only function was to finance the Treasury.[45]

The Banking Regulation Law represented the greatest regulation and concentration in the financial sector up to this time. It required administrative authorisation for the opening of new banks, which moreover had to have a minimum of corporate capital. Already established banks were allowed to open new branches or expand their dimensions, but this was also strictly regulated. This status quo might have benefited existing banks and favoured takeovers. Reserves began to grow, paid-up capital accumulated and, at least for big banks, profits increased. Banking profitability grew until 1959, although, if inflation is taken into account, the 'extraordinary earnings' attributed to this sector in the postwar period were not so great. The possibility of pawning public funds in the Bank of Spain did allow the banks to acquire a liquidity that gave them gradual control of industrial activities. This control was also aided by the virtual absence of foreign investment and by a state interventionism that, despite its inflexibilities, encouraged – even obligated – banks to take on the industrial projects of the period. In the vast majority of companies designated as being of national interest, there was a joint presence of private banking and public capital.[46]

Many banks had to overcome the mistakes and disasters of the 1930s, first with the Republic and again during the war, then adapt to the new situation and respond to the commitments. On many occasions, these tasks fell on the shoulders of new figures who took over the reins and set clear directives: Pablo Garnica, the most veteran of them, in the Spanish Credit Bank; Andrés Moreno García, in the Hispano Americano Bank; Juan Lladó, in the Urquijo Bank; Ignasi Villalonga, in the Central Bank; and Emilio Botín-Sanz de Sautuola, in the Bank of Santander. Some became presidents; others held more technical or executive positions. Some had a political past. Garnica was liberal and had even been a minister for the Monarchy in 1919. At the outset of the Republic, he appointed Epifanio Ridruejo as managing director. Ridruejo got on well with Prieto. He lost two sons in the Spanish Civil War and was president of the National Banking Committee in Burgos, but he was one of the monarchists who wanted don Juan to occupy the throne at the end of the Second World War. As a result, he lost the presidencies of Campsa and Tabacalera. Villalonga founded the Unió Valencianista and later the Unió Valenciana Regional, which was part of the CEDA during the Republic. Faithful to his monarchist convictions, he was on the private council of don Juan de Borbón, which probably did not make him very popular in El Pardo, Franco's residence. Juan Lladó had joined the Urquijo Bank during the Republic, at the same time as Ramón Carande and Agustín Viñuales, replacing Valentín Ruiz Senén. He was tried and sentenced to twelve years in prison after the civil war for continuing to run the Urquijo Bank in Republican territory, moving from Madrid to Valencia and then to Barcelona. He served only one year of his sentence, but for the rest of his life, he tried to avoid any contact with Franco. Luis Usera, who was a close friend of Lladó's, a board member of the Urquijo Bank and top executive of the Hispano Americano Bank, said that everybody was liberal in the Urquijo Bank, but to do banking, it was necessary to go to El Pardo, and everybody went there except Lladó.[47]

All the bankers, or almost all of them, went to El Pardo to meet Franco, but they liked to call themselves liberals, at least economically speaking, and in the meantime, they did some business. The Spanish Credit Bank unveiled an important policy of expansion, especially in rural areas, opening branches in provinces where they had never had them before. It reached an agreement with the Pastor Bank and, as an industrial bank, obtained an important industrial stock portfolio. In 1943, Garnica told his shareholders that the banks had become public law entities whose functions went beyond merely private interests. In 1944, the Urquijo Bank and the Hispano Americano Bank signed the Las Jarillas pact and divided the work. Hispano Americano consolidated its commercial policy, reinforced by the transfer of its banks in Catalonia and Guipúzcoa to the Urquijo Bank, while the Urquijo Bank received a healthy injection of cash which allowed it to consolidate its industrial stock portfolio. It did not obtain Siat's automobile monopoly, but it participated in the founding of Seat. It played an important role in the laborious nationalisation process of the Río Tinto mines, and although it lost its initial protagonism, it formed part of the group of bankers that joined the new mining company. It entered the chemical industry with the creation of the Compañía Española de Penicilinas y Antibióticos in 1949, and after the acquisition of German companies at the end of the Second World War, it formed the Spanish Chemical Consortium with the Sociedad Anónima Cros, the Hispano Americano Bank, the Herrero Bank and the Unión Española de Explosivos. The Central Bank, for its part, found in Ignasi Villalonga the figure it needed to recompose its unity and overcome the awful situation it was in at the end of the war. Villalonga was appointed to the board of directors in 1940 and then president four years later, and created an industrial group with investments in the most important companies (Cepsa, Dragados y Construcciones, Minero-siderúgica de Ponferrada). Despite important takeovers like that of the International Bank of Trade and Industry, in 1943 it was still ranked fifth in deposits. Out of this came the idea to form a banking consortium, Bancor. The consortium would be geographically complemented, starting with the Hispano Colonial Bank, the Zaragoza Credit Bank and the Bank of Valencia, and would later be joined by the Popular Bank. The Popular Bank was still called the Previsores del Porvenir, the name it had been established with. Its president was Salvador Millet, a standout Catalan businessman dedicated to insurance and the defence of the Catalan language and culture. His cousins, the Valls Taberners, would join the business in the 1950s and lead the Popular Bank to the top of the Spanish banking system. The Santander Bank never joined the consortium, although it coincided with the Central Bank in several important industrial businesses.[48]

The Central Bank's takeover of the Hispano Colonial Bank in March 1950 was one of the last – and most surprising – takeovers from those years. It occurred in the midst of one of the most controversial economic events of the time, the bankruptcy of the electric company Barcelona Traction, called *La Canadiense*, which had national and international repercussions. This operation turned out to be very profitable but its development was very shady. It was also the end of a long personal confrontation between Juan March and Francesc Cambó which began when Cambó was Treasury Minister back in 1921 and March was accused of being the biggest smuggler in the country.[49] March had consolidated his commercial businesses during the Second World War, as he did in the First World War. His commitments to

Franco's insurgence and his role in the wolfram business with Germany did not stop him from keeping ties with Britain and helping the British secret service. Some people close to Franco, like Carceller and, initially, Suanzes himself, were wary of his immense power, despite his financial support of the military insurgents. Owing to this lack of trust, in 1941 he decided to settle in Portugal for a few years before going to Geneva, where he continued to manage his businesses and plan his great dream.

March had been interested in *La Canadiense* since 1940, when he got involved in the electric industry. After two failed attempts to purchase the company, he used all his influence to prevent the company from obtaining the currencies it needed to pay back old debts. He found invaluable support in the nationalism of Suanzes, who directed the Spanish Institute of Foreign Currency. To increase his pressure, he threatened the Belgian company Sofina, which owned *Barcelona Traction*, with laying siege to another of the group's companies. In particular, his target was the company CHADE (Compañía Hispano Americana de Electricidad), whose president was Francesc Cambó and whose headquarters were in Argentina. In a confidential message addressed to the head of state in 1946, March said that he was moved by 'only one objective, an objective of patriotic inspiration': to prevent a setback that was being prepared for Spain by 'the world's shadiest financial syndicates, whose claws are stuck in a part of Spain – the Catalan region – that is the richest and most interesting'. Alluding to CHADE, he said a Spanish entity, although 'poorly managed', with a group of Spaniards at the service of foreign capital, was aiding those 'anti-Spanish objectives', exhausting the Spanish State with its administration in favour of *Barcelona Traction*, and compromising the Spanish interests it oversaw. Behind everything, said March, was that 'politico-financial oligarchy' of Cambó, Bertrán y Musitu and Durán y Ventosa. The matter even made it to Parliament, where a union representative demagogically suggested that 'red leaders' were mixed up in the affair. Juan March's attack on CHADE was a surprise abroad, because its relations with the Spanish authorities had been excellent until then. It also irritated CHADE's Spanish shareholders, top banking executives among them. A 1947 decree that seemed to be aimed at this firm established that all Spanish companies had to base their headquarters in national territory and their transactions had to be properly authorised, requirements that CHADE – now CADE as a result of its preventative transfer to Luxembourg – did not meet. A commission was appointed to investigate its activities and it was concluded that its activities were illegal from the point of view of Spanish legislation.

At the beginning of 1948, *Sofina's* managing director, Heineman, still convinced that the big international interests it handled were a guarantee against the threats and suspicions in Spain, wanted to reach an agreement which entailed the dissolution of CHADE and the incorporation of its assets into an Argentine company, as well as the sale of the shares of *Barcelona Traction* to March. But March had other plans. He had purchased almost half the bonds of *Barcelona Traction* on the international market since the beginning of the decade, and he was CHADE's biggest shareholder at the time. In a surprising and unusual move, he got a court in Reus, a little Catalan village, to declare the bankruptcy of *Barcelona Traction* on 12 February 1948, at the behest of some previously briefed shareholders. While Heineman tried to get over his bewilderment, Madrid became a hotbed of foreign delegations and diplomatic pressures. At the time, Spain's first loans from the United States were being negotiated, and the treatment that *Barcelona Traction* and CHADE received might have been an insurmountable obstacle to success. But the Spanish government did not budge, saying it could not meddle in affairs that were up to the courts to resolve. In 1952, the assets of the bankruptcy were auctioned, awarded to the only bidder: Fuerzas Eléctricas de Cataluña, S.A. (Fecsa), just established by Juan March a few months earlier. It was said that March had earned between four and six thousand million pesetas with that operation, which mobilised international diplomacy and whose lawsuit would not be settled until 1970; March won the case. Thanks to his 'patriotic' effort, his success also enabled him to repair his image before the Spanish authorities. With part of the money he earned, March established one of the most prestigious institutions in the academic and scientific worlds today: the Juan March Foundation. In the hands of that Spanish Rothschild, as Giménez Caballero called him, that obscure, brilliant but inexplicable 'maverick of the Spanish economy', whose fortune was a 'monstrosity', Money transmuted into Spirit.[50]

At the beginning of the 1950s, the abandonment of autarkic doctrinairism and the increase in contacts with foreign countries made economic growth possible, though it was not free from strangulations and strong inflationary tensions. At this time one could begin to see the extent of the great changes that had taken place in the business world in the dark years of the postwar period, and the adaptation of business to the political order that emerged from the Spanish Civil War. That world had nothing to do with the world at the turn of the century.

Notes

1. The quotations, in Cabrera (1983: 286 and 189–190).
2. The demonstration and the decree, in Payne (1993: 283); on 'The International', Cabrera (1995: 42); the seats, in Varela (1978: 74). The Popular Front and ungovernability, in Juliá (1999a: 111).
3. The employers' attitude, in Cabrera (1983: 297–306); the unions and the wave of strikes, in Payne (1993: 337–344).
4. Malefakis (1972: 419–441); the owners' responses, in Cabrera (1983: 291–297).
5. The revolutionary language and the attitude of the CNT, in Casanova (1997: 150); the attitude of the unions, in (1999a: 115). The violence, in Payne (1993: 359–364).
6. The conspirators and the list of financial backers, in González Cuevas (1998: 172–174). The evolution of the right wing and its relations with the military, in Gil Pecharromán (1994), Rodríguez Jiménez (1997) and González Cuevas (2000). Mola's low opinion of the politicians, in Payne (1993: 365–366). The subordinate participation of civilians, also in Cruz (2001: 45).
7. The initial economic map of the war, in Bricall (1985: 365ff.) and Sánchez Asiaín (1999: 45ff.) On the deadly violence, its causes and manifestations, see Juliá (1999a: 117–118) and (1999b, coord.: 25–29)
8. Juliá (1999a: 119–121) and Moradiellos (2000: 37–44).

9. The 'purifying torch' in Casanova (1997: 158–163 and 172–173); the 'bloody summer' and the violence of the masses, in Casanova (1999: 57–80 and 117–158); Madrid, in Cervera (1998: 41–105); Clara Campoamor's text, cited by Bolloten (1989: 166).

10. Confiscations and seizures, in Bolloten (1989: 125–126 and 134–135); the Madrid Chamber of Commerce, in Bahamonde et al. (1988: 246–251); on Durruti, see Casanova (1997); the collectivisations, in Garrido González (1979), Casanova (1985) and (1988, comp.); on the percentages and Valencia, see Bosch (1983) and (2001: 245–250).

11. The political evolution of the Republic, in Juliá (1997: 139-281) and (1999a: 124–143); the Communists and the middle classes, in Bolloten (1989: 168-169), and the dissolution of the collectives, also in Bolloten (1989: 795–807); the dissolution of the Council of Aragón, in Casanova (1997: 200–204).

12. On the 'massive armed mobilisation', see Ugarte Tellería (1998). The biography of José María de Urquijo e Ybarra, in Robles (1997). The Zubirías, in Rojo Cagigal (2000: 100). Gandarias, in Echániz Ortúñez (2000: 190).

13. The evolution of Basque industry and the entrepreneurs' posture, in González Portilla (1987) and in González Portilla and Garmendia (1988); Mola's opinions taken from Viñas (1984: 102–104).

14. González Portilla and Garmendia (1988). On the Bilbao Stock Exchange becoming a detainee centre, see the *Guía del bolsista* (1940: 118–123).

15. Sota, in Torres Villanueva (1998).

16. The evolution of the republican economy, in Bricall (1985). The scarcity of economic elites, in Sánchez Asiaín (1999: 72); the quotation from the preamble to the decree and the fascist bourgeoisie, in Cabana (1997: 139); Cambó, his attitude and his articles, in Riquer Permanyer (1996: 287–294).

17. For all of this, Riquer Permanyer (1996).

18. The rupture and the 'monetary war', in Sánchez Asiaín (1999).

19. The bankers' movements, in Sánchez Asiaín (1999). The biography of Goicoechea, in González Cuevas (2001); also Moya (1984: 87).

20. The Bank of Spain and the gold, in Sardá Dexeus (1970) and Viñas (1984). On the manipulation of the exchange rates, see the conclusions of Howson (2000).

21. For the history of the Franco regime, see Payne (1987) and (1997), Juliá (1999a) and Moradiellos (2000).

22. The Falangist Movement until the unification, in Thomas (1999); the struggles for power and the 'weak and chaotic' party, in Cazorla Sánchez (2000); the party as a 'big political boss', in (1999a: 156).

23. Vertical unionism, in Aparicio (1980). The rupture of the idea of 'company community', in Montoya Melgar (1992: 330ff.)

24. On the bureaucracies, see Juliá (1999a: 159). The elites' sources of extraction, in Jeréz Mir (1982). An account of implications of politics and power, in Sánchez Soler (2001).

25. On the consensus, see Cazorla Sánchez (2000).

26. The owners and agricultural policy, in Barciela (1986). The repression in rural Spain, in Moreno Gómez (1989). Violence and dispossession in Aragón, in Cenarro (1997: 350–360).

27. On the commitment of the Catalan bourgeoisie, see Riquer Permanyer (2000b). An industry almost intact, in Cabana (2001: 24–28). The Sedó case, in Moreno Castaño (2000); Bertrand i Serra, in Cabana (2000d); Suñol, in Cabana (2000c). Mateu, in Cabana (1997: 176–184) and (2001: 32–34).

28. The 'resignation' of the Catalan bourgeoisie, in Riquer Permanyer (2000b); the power in the town halls, in Marín i Corbera (2000a) and (2000b). Also in Pinilla de las Heras (1996: 101). The recognition of the guilds, in Molinero and Ysàs (1991: 65–70).
29. The businessmen and trade union organisation, in Molinero and Ysàs (1991) and Moreno Fonseret (1999); the Chambers of Commerce, in Diez Cano (1992); the new state and the workers, in Molinero and Ysás (1998).
30. The resistance to the *Jurados*, in Molinero and Ysàs (1991).
31. The 1947 strike in Bilbao, in González Portilla and Garmendia (1988: 123–218); the hunger, restlessness and conflicts, in Cazorla Sánchez (2000).
32. The Ventosa conference, recounted by Garriga (1976b, vol. I: 141).
33. The example of the fascist countries, in Catalán (1995: 59–75), and the quote by Franco in Catalán (1995: 214–215). The last quotation is by Gay de Montellá (1940: 79).
34. On the lost opportunity and 'speculative capitalism', see Catalán (1989) and (1995). On the economy and the economic policy of this period, see also Clavera et al. (1973), and Carreras (1990).
35. The keys to entrepreneurial success, in Catalán (1995: 251–252). Complaints from the Barcelona Economic and Social Council, in Molinero and Ysás (1993: 174). The quote by Gual Villalbí, in Cabana (2001: 84). On Valencia, see Gómez Roda and Saz (2001).
36. For the Council of National Economy, see Martínez Mesa (1997).
37. On the military agents, see Moya (1984: 117–122).
38. For all of this, see Martín Aceña and Comín (1991: 134–144). The history of the INI, also in Schwartz and González (1978). On the ten largest companies, see Carreras and Tafunell (1996).
39. Differing opinions, in Martín Aceña and Comín (1991), San Román (1999) and Gómez Mendoza (ed.) (2000c).
40. On the importance and contradictions of the defence policy, see Martínez Ruiz (1994). On Carceller, see Cabana (1997) and (2001: 45–47), and Garriga (1976b, vol. I: 217–219). His role in the Falangist Movement, in Payne (1965: 28 and 169). Carceller as an influential businessman, in Sánchez Soler (2001: 150–154).
41. The biography of Suanzes, in Ballestero (1993). Criticism, in San Román (1999), Barrera and San Román (2000) and Gómez Mendoza (2000a).
42. The quote by Suanzes and the appointment of Merello, in Ballestero (1993: 219). The iron and steel sector and Basque industry in the postwar period, in González Portilla and Garmendia (1988); the conflict of interests in the Council of National Economy, in Martínez Mesa (1997: 195–240). The increase of profits, in Lorenzo Espinosa (1989).
43. The negotiations between the INI and private companies, in Ballestero (1993: 242–245). The performance of the INI in the sector, in Martín Aceña and Comín (1991: 170–181). The conflicts in the Council of National Economy, in Martínez Mesa (1997: 195–240). The structure of the sector and the 'capture' of the state, in Fraile Balbín (1992).
44. The INI as a 'hospital for companies', in Schwartz and González (1978). The history of Siat and Seat, in San Román (1999: 227–259). The electric companies, in Gómez Mendoza (2000b). José María de Oriol y Urquijo, in Cayón García and Muñoz Rubio (2000).
45. The Bank of Spain, in Sardá Dexeus (1970); also in Sánchez Asiaín (1999: 184–199). The irrelevance of the Bank of Spain, in Martín Aceña (2000: 112).
46. At the end of the 1960s and during the post-dictatorship transition, a lot was written about the power of banking: see Muñoz's classic book (1969); Tamames (1966) and (1978); Foessa Foundation (1976). Some similar conclusions, although qualified, in Moreno Fonseret (1999). On the opening-up of the financial aristocracy and the 'crude'

affirmation, in Moya (1984: 89). The presence of private banking and public capital in industries of national interest, in Braña et al. (1984: 170–174). The profitability of banking and the 1946 law as a 'zenithal moment', in Martín Aceñas and Pons (1996).

47. Biographies of those cited, in Rubio Gil (2000), García Ruiz (2000c), Tortella (2000c), Hoyo Aparicio (2000), and Torres Villanueva (2000c).
48. The banks, in Cabana (1972).
49. See Chapter V.
50. The history of the conflict, in the biographies of March by Garriga (1976a), Díaz Nosty (1977), Dixon (1985), Torres Villanueva (2000b), and in Ballestero's biography of Suanzes (1993). On Giménez Caballero, see Giménez Caballero (1965).

Chapter 4
Business in the 'State of Public Works', 1951–1977

The Accelerated Change of Spanish Companies

Entrepreneurs knew how to take advantage of the opportunities that opened up in Spain in the 1950s and came even faster in the early 1960s. These men emerged in a variety of productive industries, many of which had been limited by the disastrous autarkic and interventionist economic policy maintained by the Franco authorities since the end of the Spanish Civil War. They had all pursued different careers. Some took advantage of their families' longstanding business backgrounds, which either supplied them with resources and properties or a mercantile culture which helped them take on their own futures. Others were self-made men, climbing the social ladder from their humble origins through effort, ingenuity, a sense of opportunity or proximity to political power. Some had to consolidate their businesses and knew how to transfer them in solvent conditions to their heirs. There were also those who, after enjoying buoyant growth in the days of *desarrollismo* (the period of economic development in Spain in the 1960s), were then unable to endure the troubles of the 1970s' economic crisis or their long sequels afterwards.

On the list referred to above, there were, of course, the ever-present bankers, who were few in number but very powerful. One such man was Emilio Botín-Sanz de Sautuola, whose family roots in industry and finance dated to the nineteenth century. In addition to continuing the policy of takeovers that made so much money for his bank in the postwar period, the Bank of Santander, in the 1960s he increased the bank's industrial portfolio and stepped up investments in Latin America after the creation of Bankinter, his affiliate bank. The case of Ignasi Villalonga Villalba was different. When he joined the Central Bank as a board member in 1940, it was virtually bankrupt. Two decades later, it was among the five largest in Spain, thanks to his investments of the bank's shares in solvent industrial sectors (construction, services, electricity, transportation, etc.). At the beginning of the 1950s, the Valls-Taberner Arnó brothers took over the reins of the Popular Bank, a small family bank. They did not risk as much as Villalonga, but they made a good team. They modernised their bank's organisational structure and oversaw its steady growth until it took its place among the most traditonal, distinguished entities. However, this did not occur without their raising suspicions, given their close ties with the highest economic authorities of the period. These links were fostered by the brothers' religious affinities (read: connections by way of Opus Dei). Nonetheless, the banker who set the pace in the latter stages of the Franco regime was a man who did not come from the world of finance, but rather from the industrial sector itself: José María Aguirre Gonzalo, who in 1927 had founded the successful construction company Agromán. In addition to leading the Spanish Credit Bank (Banesto) to the top of Spanish banking, he maintained his leadership in construction, and used Japanese technology to launch Acerinox, another renowned company at the time. Aguirre was also president or board member of more than fifty other companies. He was one of the most recognised, most heeded businessmen of the day, and undoubtedly had the most political influence.[1]

Many other entrepreneurs took advantage of the construction boom of the 1960s. José Entrecanales Ibarra, José Banús Masdeu and Rafael del Pino Moreno were three of the leaders in this sector. Entrecanales and del Pino, although belonging to different generations, had many things in common. They were both civil engineers, and they prided themselves on technical excellence. They both took advantage of the public infrastructure boom through government contracts, did construction work for the private sector and had ventures abroad (South America, Portugal and Arab countries), something unusual for Spanish businessmen in those days. The construction company Entrecanales had been founded in 1931 and Ferrovial (del Pino's company) in 1952, but both grew as a result of the economic boom of the 1950s. José Banús, son and grandson of modest builders from Tarragona, did not begin his career with higher education, but he did not need it. Fortune knocked on his door when he managed to participate in the construction of the Valle de los Caídos (the monument to those killed on the nationalist side in the Spanish Civil War) in 1944, the springboard to a spectacular career which would qualify him as 'the builder of the regime'. At the end of the 1940s, his next step was to specialise in the construction of popular neighbourhoods in Madrid for the wave of rural migrants. His big business was the controversial, speculative promotion of thousands of small apartment buildings, constructed without the parallel development of services and infrastructures. It catapulted him to the construction of luxury developments, also in Madrid and on the Costa del Sol. His good relations with General Franco earned him the administrative authorisations that permitted him, unfettered by legal obstacles, to establish a construction empire on the coast of Malaga. The crowning jewel of this empire was the famous port named after him, Puerto Banus (Marbella). Very significantly, while Entrecanales and Ferrovial survived the crisis of the 1970s and afterwards continued to grow at a spectacular rate, the developer Banús plummeted at the beginning of the transition to democracy.[2]

Like the development of infrastructures and emigration for building contractors, the abandonment of autocratic policy was a stroke of good fortune for those productive sectors that had not been able to expand during the years of asphyxiating state interventionism. The economic liberalisation at the end of the 1950s opened the doors to exchanges with foreign countries, attracted capital, technology and new ways of business management, and increased the capacity and modernised the habits of consumption by Spaniards. The brightest native businessmen knew how to benefit from this new opportunity. In particular, those who had a vocation for wholesale commerce took advantage of the situation. One example was the Asturian José Fernández Rodríguez. After many years in Latin America, he revolutionised business techniques in Spain and became the leader in department stores with the founding of *Galerías Preciados*. This department store had great success in the 1960s. With a staff of over 10,000 workers, the sales volume of this store came to be twenty times greater than that of its closest rival, *El Corte Inglés*. El Corte Inglés was founded by the Asturian Ramón Areces. Areces also made his fortune in Latin America, and his store would eventually displace Galerías Preciados from the top spot. Increased contacts abroad and the establishment of greater levels of consumption also explain the rise of businessmen in the tourism sector. These entrepreneurs sprouted like mushrooms in a damp autumn, taking advantage of Spain's excellent natural geography. Tourism would become the most important Spanish industry in the 1960s, and the Valencian José Meliá Sinisterra was without doubt the pioneer of this industry. As early as 1947, he established a travel agency, *Viajes Meliá*. In 1955, he opened his first luxury hotel in Mallorca. It was the first in a chain that in a few years would become multinational, invoicing more than ninety million pesetas a year and employing approximately six thousand people.[3]

Thanks to the growth of demand and the entry of foreign capital and technology, the food industry also took off during these years. The boom in this sector was a far cry from the terrible times of hunger and endless rationing queues. During the autarkic period, industrialists in this sector had endured countless problems with maintaining stocks and selling them in great quantities at profitable prices. Everything was different now. Cantabrian Juan Gómez Cuétara was another businessman who had started out in Latin America. Exercising his technical knowledge and enterprising spirit, he revolutionised the Spanish biscuit market. His company became one of the top five on the continent. Allied with his foreign partners, the Catalán Lluís Carulla i Canals cornered the domestic market with his *Avecrem* bouillon cubes, produced in his company, *Gallina Blanca*. Later, Gallina Blanca diversified to include sweets, chewing gum and drinks and developed an export market for them. Valencian Luis Suñer Sanchis did not make it that far, but at the beginning of the 1970s, he held a quarter of the national ice cream market. His firm, *Avidesa*, was one of the model companies of *desarrollismo*. Later, it also raised and sold chickens. Eulogio Gómez Franqueira was another businessman who exploited this product. He was the architect of poultry farming cooperatives. These cooperatives expanded to include livestock, operating in the province of Orense. This initiative rescued hundreds of poor Gallegan farmers.[4]

On the list of examples, some manufacturers who worked outside the food industry deserve special mention. Among them was Antonio Beteré Salvador, who was from Aragón. In 1956, he launched the production of innovative spring mattresses after importing the idea from Belgium. Thanks to those mattresses, Spaniards no longer had to sleep on wool. His company, which adopted the brand name *Flex*, not only topped the Spanish market, but also consolidated itself as one of the top in the world in this sector. In the automobile sector, Eduardo Barreiros had 10 percent of the national production of cars and vans, thanks to his alliance with the U.S. firm Chrysler. He manufactured the dazzling Dodge luxury car and the more modest Simca. At the same time, his production of trucks put him on par with the state company Enasa. By the end of the 1960s, Barreiros accounted for nearly half of Spanish vehicle exports, including tractors for farm work. Given these results, it is clear that his relations with the INI under Suanzes would have been very bad. Suanzes refused to receive Barreiros in his office, all the more peculiar because they shared Gallegan ancestry. Barreriros's was an extraordinary case. In addition to working in a sector that had been monopolised by the State and creating nearly 10,000 jobs, his company was the only one in this sector that produced its own technological developments. It was a brilliant balance that was upset when Chrysler decided to take control of the company. This decision sparked a battle that Barreiros won. In the 1970s, Barreiros tried another venture in the food and agriculture sector. However, the circumstances were not as favourable then, nor was he very comfortable in this business sector, having spent his whole life in the motor trade.[5]

The phenomenon of *desarrollismo* in the 1960s showed that Spain did not lack good businessmen. Not all of them eagerly sought the protection of the State, although they did not scorn this way of earning revenue in principle. *Desarrollismo* made it clear that the subordination of the economy to politics, in accordance with the ideological dictates of the Falangists and the military, had been a disaster for the country in the previous decades. The abandonment of autarkic principles and the relaxation of interventionism occurred slowly, but the mere change of direction was an advance in itself after so much totalitarian-inspired, bureaucratic irrationality. The new circumstances in and outside Spain in the 1950s made this change possible. Military agreements with the United States and the economic aid they brought were the first step in breaking the economic isolation the country had lived in since 1939. Then came entry into the United Nations and international economic organisations (the Organisation for European Economic Cooperation and the International Monetary Fund), which also had important consequences in the evolution of the national economy. The rest was done by ministers who were more favourable to the market than their predecessors and the growing number of voices that demanded a change in economic policy.

The country soon began to feel the effects of the timid attempts to liberalise the economy in the 1950s. The GNP grew more than 4 percent a year from 1951 to 1958. Per-capita income nearly quadrupled. The industrial growth rate rose to an average of 6.6 percent per year from 1951–1955 and to 7.7 percent in the latter half of the decade. This made it possible for the INI to expand its basic industries (iron and steel, auto, refineries and petrochemicals). Private investments recovered and imports increased, with more emphasis on capital assets and a parallel decline in foodstuffs. Agricultural exports, productivity and production also increased (the latter two to an annual average of 3.9 percent and 5.7 percent, respectively), with the cereal sector enjoying a particularly favourable period. All the same, on the down side of the 1950s, the expansion was unbalanced. It was threatened by salaries rising faster than productivity, the budgetary deficit, the subsequent inflationary pressures, the inflexibility of supply, the proliferation of different exchange rates of the peseta abroad, the lack of foreign currency and an administrative bureaucracy that was still very prominent. Although their application was more relaxed, the autarkic laws were still very much in effect. The hurdles were so great that by the end of the decade, the Spanish economy was at the point of suspending foreign payments.[6]

In reality, the definitive rupture of the autarkic model occurred with the Decree of Economic Regulation, better known as the *Stabilisation Plan*. It was passed on 21 July 1959, although the effort began in 1957 when its architects, Navarro Rubio and Ullastres, became the Treasury and Trade Ministers, respectively. The creation of the Plan was a tacit admission that the previous economic policy had led the country down a dead end, although this was never officially acknowledged. With its collection of measures, the Plan intended to settle the Spanish economy on more flexible, rational bases and open it more to the foreign market. It put caps on loans and public spending; increased some taxes; made the Bank of Spain's discount and interest rates more flexible; froze salaries; eliminated the automatic pawning of the public debt; established a realistic exchange rate of sixty pesetas to the dollar (which meant a devaluation of 42 percent); liberalised foreign transactions and payments; created more opportunities for foreign capital; and lastly, liberalised prices and abolished a long list of interventionist organisations. Even with its limitations, the momentary ups and downs of 1967 and 1970, and the hesitancy of economic policy, the accelerated expansion that occurred was remarkable. Its positive effects would last nearly fifteen years. The industrial sector was the motor of the expansion, with the development of the service sector giving an additional push. The foreign sector played a crucial role too. Apart from foreign investment, remittances from emigrants and revenue from tourism, it provided technology, raw materials and cheap energy products. The results were spectacular. It took only a few months to feel the effects of the new measures and entrepreneurial expectations soared in a climate of euphoria.[7]

The threat of suspending payments disappeared. Prices stabilised. The GNP grew at an average annual rate of 6.7 percent from 1962 to 1972, which in per-capita terms meant a jump from 60.3 percent to 81.9 percent with respect to the European Common Market average. Industry increased production by 3.74 percent annually from 1960 to 1974, an unprecedented rate that has not been equalled since. Its annual growth rate averaged 11 percent until 1973. Per-capita income grew at an average annual rate of 5.6 percent. Exports of capital goods doubled, and manufactured exports increased by 50 percent. Foreign investment also practically doubled. The balance of payments recovered some of its deficit. With all of this, the structure of the economy altered drastically. The relative weight of agricultural production decreased notably (24 percent of the GNP in 1960, to around 10 percent in 1975) as did its active population (48.9 percent of the total in 1950 compared to only 21.7 percent in 1975). Industry (construction included) and services benefited from these declines

(40 percent and 50 percent of the GNP and 38 percent and 39.2 percent of the active population, respectively, in 1975). In light of this, agriculture continued a process of modernisation, adopting techniques which triggered a marked increase in production, productivity and greater production for the market. In short, in little more than a decade, the Spanish economy reached levels and a pace it had not nearly approached in the previous century and a half of Spanish capitalism.[8]

Inevitably, the process of growth deeply altered the structure of Spanish companies, in both their spatial distribution and their internal composition. For a start, it led to a greater geographic concentration of productive capacity, financial resources, wealth and human capital, in direct relation to the reduction of the active agricultural population and the amazing rural exodus that shook the country: between 1962 and 1975, 5.7 million Spaniards changed residence, moving to big cities and their suburbs. The tendencies shaped since the end of the nineteenth century were now definitive. Catalonia, Madrid, the Basque Country and the present-day region of Valencia strengthened their positions. Madrid grew especially fast, doubling its gross industrial product and becoming a great megalopolis. In 1940, the four regions accounted for 42 percent of the GNP; 47.56 percent in 1960, and nearly 52 percent in 1973. At the other end of the spectrum were Andalusia, Aragón, Castilla y León, Castilla-La Mancha, Extremadura, La Rioja and Galicia. This group, much larger in square kilometers than the four regions cited above, suffered a significant decline: 44.64 percent of the GNP in 1940 to 34.11 percent in 1973. Asturias and Cantabria, having achieved a certain level of industrialisation in the past, also began to decline appreciably. Two others, Murcia and Navarra, dropped off slightly. Lastly, the Balearic and Canary Islands, habitual stragglers, moved up the scale thanks to the lift provided by tourism. These trends towards the concentration of wealth and the imbalance in economic growth would be even clearer if we analysed the situation by province, which we will not do here. In general, it can be stated that the dizzying development of the 1960s benefited the provinces that were already at the top of the scale and did little for the stragglers, with the exceptions cited above. The primarily agricultural regions and provinces grew more slowly. Only the regions located within 100 kilometers of the most developed metropolitan areas achieved a certain growth from their industrial sector. If the main goal of the development plans was to reduce interterritorial economic inequalities, their actual results were decidedly limited. Only Valladolid, Huelva and Zaragoza, and, to a lesser extent, La Coruña, Sevilla, Vigo and some isolated points in the two Castillas reaped benefits from the policies inherent in the plans. But they continued to be industrial islets in the middle of overwhelmingly agricultural, backward environments. In 1973, only fourteen provinces had a per-capita income above the national average, while no less than thirty-one had a per-capita income below it.[9]

Industrialisation, the rural exodus, the growth of cities and the imbalanced spatial concentration of the wealth also explain the change in the sociological profile of Spanish businessmen in the context of *desarrollismo*. The businessman changed because the class structure of Spanish society itself changed. Underlying this process of modernisation was the hiring of agricultural workers. With respect to different types of businessmen, the generic trend cemented the drastic decrease of agricultural owners and farmworkers; the slight increase of managers and directors to the detriment of traditional businessmen in industry and services; and thirdly, the economic strengthening of a minority of businessmen tied to finance and big industry, parallel to the loss of influence held by landowners, who had been so important in the past. A 1964 census tallied 415,600 self-declared businessmen, managers and directors (it is understood this figure includes salaried workers from all productive sectors); 1,290,000 active businessmen without wage earners and independent workers in industry and services; and 2,662,900 farm owners without wage earners. In 1988, businessmen, managers and directors totalled 568,500 (38,500 of which were agro-businessmen with wage earners); independent workers and businessmen without wage earners in industry and services rose to 1,588,600; and farm owners and farmers – tenants and sharecroppers – without labourers had fallen to 987,800.

The most striking result was clearly that which affected this latter group. In 1964, they represented 22.7 percent of the active population; this figure was down to 13.8 percent in 1976. Emigration to the cities, which had radically reduced the number of day labourers in rural areas, also decimated the number of small business farmers. Modest beneficiaries of protection policies, these small businessmen partially disappeared as a social group due to decisive factors like the crisis of traditional agriculture, the concentration of plots and the mechanisation of the fields. Thousands were obligated to sell or lease their miserable properties, especially unirrigated plots. From 1962 to 1972, around half a million mini-plots vanished when the individual farming of small parcels became pointless under the new economic conditions. The average size of cultivated fields went from 14.9 to 17.9 hectares. The land registry recorded a significant increase only of farms consisting of fifty to 100 hectares. The survival of farmers who endured the tide of emigration – medium sharecroppers in general – had a lot to do with the development of cooperatives, the diversification of crops and the greater modernisation of the tasks. The spectacular increase in the number of tractors used in Spanish fields is a relevant fact in this respect: 12,800 in 1950 compared to 260,000 in 1975.[10]

In direct contrast to the evolution of farmers, the management of the general expansion fell on the shoulders of industrialists, who also changed. Basic industries and the consumer goods industry were at similar levels when the period of *desarrollismo* began. By the end of the period, the former was two and a half times greater than the latter, in terms of the total value of national production. With the exception of the shoe industry, which created a huge export market, traditional industrialists grew more slowly than the more modern branches of the chemical industry (fertilisers, pharmaceuticals, petrochemicals, plastics, etc.), basic metallurgy, and machinery construction. The star of the period was undoubtedly the automobile industry, dominated by the state company Seat, although foreign firms gradually made inroads after setting up factories in the country. Along with the automobile, another good indicator of the change in the industrial structure was the outstanding boom of the home appliance industry, a result of the increase in families' purchasing power and the official protection that made the incorporation of Spanish firms profitable (Werner, Inter, Balay, Bru). It is also worth noting activities linked to construction, where, along with the big building companies, the number of small businessmen grew considerably. The textile, food, wood and furniture industries also grew, as did the majority of industries, continuing a prolonged trend. This was possible because, beyond the demonstrable monopolies, many small businessmen in a variety of industrial activities managed to remain solvent, although the going was more difficult. Along with the splendid new factories in the metropolitan areas of big cities, thousands of workshops and small factories survived in the old workers' neighbourhoods. The oldest – those who employed few or no workers and preserved their traditional methods – knew their future was bleak and their days were numbered, but even under these conditions, they stubbornly persisted. Data from 1973 reveal that, in Madrid, where Franco's regime had favoured industrial concentration through investments by the INI, the big establishments accounted for 45 percent of employment in the sector with an average of more than 250 employees (1.5 percent), but there were still 25,500 small industrial companies – 90 percent of the total – holding out with fewer than twenty-six employees. In other urban areas, new and old activities underwent similar processes of rise and decline. In 1962, the big textile manufacturers accounted for more than 25 percent of all industrial activity in Catalonia. In 1977, this figure was down to just over 10 percent. In Barcelona alone, more than fifty companies shut down during this period, eliminating 7,000 of the more than 25,000 jobs in this sector. Following a similar pattern, the weight of mining activity, with coal the most important, diminished by 50 percent. As a result, regions like Asturias, León and Andalusia lost one of their traditional economic staples.[11]

Around 1969, the young economist Luis Ángel Rojo warned that the country's industrial scheme was still very deficient, typical of that 'small capitalism, shaky capitalism, capitalism of the old-time, petty bourgeois businessman', that had consolidated between 1939 and 1959. Rojo was right. However, this does not mean that big monopolistic companies sustained by national financial capital, foreign capital and, of course, the public sector itself were consolidated. Although the subject was of little interest after the transition to democracy, a lot was written in the 1970s about those 'two hundred big families' of the 'financial and industrial oligarchy' – consisting of approximately a thousand members – which, after overtaking landowners, achieved hegemony in Spanish economic power. That was one of the characteristic processes of the capitalist transformation during the Franco era, a consequence, among other factors, of the transfer of capital from agriculture to industry. That elite of financiers and industrialists, intimately related through family links or by sharing seats on numerous company boards and facing no competition thanks to state protection, were the big beneficiaries of the development plans and the accelerated growth, as they had been via other means during the autarkic period. Their economic resources were channelled through six big banking groups, in the following order: the Banesto group (which concentrated 13.5 percent of banking's debt capital); the group of the Hispano and Urquijo Banks (with 12.8 percent of the market share and the most important industrial shares portfolio); the group led by the Central Bank (12.4 percent); the Bilbao-Vizcaya group (10 percent and 7.6 percent); the banking group of Opus Dei (Popular Bank, Atlantic Bank and Rumasa Bank, with 6.65 percent, 3.44 percent and 2.8 percent, respectively); and the Bank of Santander group (with 7.23 percent). According to studies made then, these banks had the biggest profit margins in Western Europe, not only because of their commercial activities, but also due to their control of approximately 40 percent of national industry, which became heavily dependent on the banks. From this perspective, the banking reform undertaken by the Government in 1962 – although it nationalised state-owned banks and formally reduced the degree of monopoly in the sector – did not significantly alter the status quo established after the Spanish Civil War, because most of the new investment banks were closely linked to big, traditional, semi-private banks or had only a small share of the market. In 1971, Spanish private banking, having done nothing to improve its efficiency, was present in 1,491 firms with a volume of capital equivalent to 66 percent of the total paid up by companies. In 1973, it controlled at least two-thirds of the fifty largest industrial companies in the country. This is how private banks came to centralise the economic decisions in important industrial branches like electric and nuclear energy, chemicals and petrochemicals, iron and steel, automobiles, cement, paper, glass, sugar refinery and the public monopolies (Campsa, Telefónica, Tabacalera). Not even the INI escaped their sphere and influence at this stage, used by the financial elite for their own ends through a complex network of connections – by way of semi-private companies, the socialisation of losses or the privatisation of earnings – given the fact that private banking had shares in many of the INI's main companies. The figure of the big businessman in Spain came to be identified with the figure of the successful banker or financier, a consequence of that enormous power that is still true today.[12]

The creation of private monopolies and the establishment of big companies also had a lot to do with the internationalisation of the Spanish economy, a key factor in its modernisation in the final stages of the dictatorship. Foreign capital projected its financial, organisational and technological potential onto the most dynamic segments of national industry. It helped increase productivity. It proved to be crucial in the increase of exports. It had a big influence on the improvement of company management, and it spurred the rise of entrepreneurial initiatives. This capital came mostly from the United States, with the main countries of Western Europe making a smaller contribution. From 1959 to 1975, Spain received a total of nearly 800 thousand million pesetas in investments. In the automobile industry at the beginning of the 1970s, foreign capital accounted for more than half of all investments, 42 percent in the electronics industry and 37 percent in the chemistry industry. The investments were disproportionately directed towards the new industries in Madrid, Catalonia and, to a lesser extent, the Basque Country, especially Álava (30 percent, 26 percent and 10 percent for each of the three territories). Around 1971, a survey of three hundred big industrial firms showed foreign capital was present in seventy-one of them as a minority shareholder and directly controlled fifty-nine more. Burying its old prejudices, the INI accepted foreign capital, as it had previously accepted private domestic capital. This turned out to be one of the great paradoxes of the Franco regime, which for two decades had put the INI at the forefront of its economic nationalism and statist politics. In percentage terms, foreign capital reached high levels in some public sector companies, including several important ones. Firms in which the INI was an indirect shareholder had an even greater presence of foreign capital. Now that the patriotic rhetoric of autarkic times was a thing of the past, many of the regime's political figures – ex-ministers and high-ranking officials, including several members of the military and Falangists – had no qualms about sitting on boards of – and earning salaries from – companies backed by foreign capital.[13]

Naturally, not everyone was happy about the liberalisation of the Spanish market. In any case, this process was not absolute and even regressed after 1964. The circles which had been demanding it for years were very pleased, especially the Chambers of Commerce, whose directors were fully aware of the drain and anti-economic nature of the autarkic formulas. However, industrialists and agricultural businessmen, uncompetitive, scarcely involved in exports and dependent on favours from the Administration, were not so thrilled because they were used to living off the protection of the State. As of the mid-1960s, these entrepreneurs managed to slow down and in some cases stop the process of liberalisation and deregulation. The words and deeds of the most traditional Basque and Catalan businessmen, who had earned huge profits in the long postwar period, were very revealing in this respect. They rejected the Stabilisation Plan just after it was proposed, more so when they realised its consequences. In the Vizcayan economy, there was a general decline in domestic demand, which once more increased the requests for protection for industries like shipbuilding and iron mining. The same happened in Catalonia with the textile industry and the less technologically advanced food producers. These branches, like those in the Basque Country, were mired in uncertainty or were clearly regressing. When the development plans were presented, these sectors also claimed preferential treatment, urging the authorities not to squander resources on areas that had no connection to the traditional industrial centres. Up to a point, it was logical they would resurrect the rhetoric of victimisation, given the good results it had brought them long before the Franco regime. These same voices never acknowledged the privileges they had received for decades, just as they never admitted their territories were the wealthiest in the country. Clearly, the most traditional industrialists were not the only ones who benefited from the privileges. Extensive agriculture – cereal and olive growing – profited until the end of the regime from a protectionist policy that also sheltered it from the ups and downs of the market.[14]

As is logical, however, one of the most formidable critics of the new economic policy was the INI. It was no accident that the change in 1959 completely undermined its doctrinal and economic foundations. While military members were directing the INI under Suanzes' presidency, the change had virtually no effect on industrial legislation. After Suanzes was relieved from his post in 1963, the Government let the INI languish in the years that followed. The holding company lost its leading role in industrial development and was limited to functioning in second place behind private initiative. Its takeover of a growing number of bankrupt firms and its prominence in sectors hit hard by the economic crisis of 1973 only made matters worse, and its companies registered smaller profits or sunk into debt. As a result of the coal crisis, private mine owners were bought out and a public company, Hunosa, was established in 1967. With respect to the INI's troubles, this was a point of no return. Of the twenty-four thousand million pesetas in losses acknowledged by the INI in 1976, more than eight thousand million came from the mining industry. The practice of taking over bankrupt companies spread to other industrial branches. The opposite of this sequence – later maximised during the transition to democracy – was the gradual takeover by private groups of profitable public companies in which the INI was no longer a majority shareholder (Seat, Aeronáutica Industrial, Astilleros de Cádiz, Enasa, etc.). Despite all of this, the INI more or less maintained itself and even grew notably in some aspects like employment. This was not necessarily a sign of vitality, but rather of weakness. In 1970, it still accounted for 3 percent of the GNP, and in 1975 it totalled 10 percent of industrial production, 14.1 percent of exports and 5.7 percent of employment, also in the industrial sector – in total, 228,000 workers, more than two-thirds of whom were concentrated in ten of the group's companies. Although its labour cost per worker was ostensibly higher than the national average, one-fourth of the most important Spanish firms still belonged to the group. It was the country's biggest industrial conglomerate and was among the twenty biggest business corporations in Europe. As such, the liberalisation of 1959 did not manage to erase the long shadow of statist interventionism forged in the public sector during the postwar period. During the era of *desarrollismo*, the novelty was the public sector's seemingly magical change into a springboard for lucrative private profits or, depending on one's viewpoint, a safety net for some private interests. One way or another, most Spaniards paid the consequences, first with autarky, then with the so-called indicative planning in the technocratic phase of the regime.[15]

The Return of Class Struggle

Beyond its economic dimension, the development of the 1960s was influential in many other ways, having repercussions on political life, customs, the collective mentality and education. Without leaving the strictly productive and entrepreneurial framework, the partial economic liberalisation was inevitably reflected in the sphere of labour relations. After the passivity and virtual absence of conflict in the 1940s, the episodic outbreak of worker protest in 1951 had something to do with this. Workers were protesting the inflationary shocks that wreaked havoc on the popular stratum of society. Although low in intensity, this unrest was unsettling for the government because it appeared at a time when the Franco authorities were making a special effort to gain international acceptance. Foreign pressure was decisive, in particular the pressure from the International Labour Organisation, whose recognition the Spanish Vertical Syndicates painstakingly sought. Many business sectors were committed to the deregulation of the labour market. Although it contradicted the preexisting corporate structure, it was the only way to improve the productivity of their companies, make salaries more flexible and achieve a better distribution of the labour force in relation to the needs of the economy.[16]

The system of labour relations underwent a definitive change with the Law of Collective Agreements enacted on 24 April 1958. This law replaced the fascist structure of vertical unionism by promoting company tribunals and union links and determining that salaries and working conditions would be regulated via direct negotiation between company and worker reps. This open door to collective bargaining, although it did not recognise fundamental rights like the right to strike, signified a fundamental change in the sphere of labour. It made it possible for employees to improve labour conditions without the constraints of ministerial dictates, allowed for substantial increases in productivity for businessmen, and expressly recognised the existence of conflicting parties, thus shattering the myth of the fraternity among 'the producers' imposed by the Franco regime. From the point of view of entrepreneurs and wage earners, the 1958 law met their expectations, evidenced by the massive acceptance of the collective agreements over the following years. The seven agreements and 18,000 workers affected in 1958 rose to 1,538 agreements and 2.3 million workers in 1962. In 1969, more than four million wage earners benefited from collective bargaining, most of them from the industrial sector. Although the law stipulated that agreements had to be made within the institutional framework of the state syndicate, in practice, most of them were established via direct negotiation between the parties without the mediation of the verticalist functionaries. Whenever they were unable to reach an agreement, the Government held the power to dictate the 'regulations of obligatory fulfilment', which resolved the differences by law and forced businessmen and workers to assume them without complaint. However, these obligatory judgements were applied in only 9.5 percent of all negotiations between 1958 and 1975, affecting only 7.2 percent of workers with collective contracts. Such a result confirmed a certain decline in state interventionism. In many places, the Franco syndicates gradually became mere ornaments, a nuisance which, more than facilitate marred relations between employers and employees. All the same, the number of workers affected by the agreements, the number of agreements themselves and their duration varied greatly from province to province and according to productive sectors. Initially, the agreements were long-term accords, but at the end of the 1960s, they tended to be set for only one year. The most outstanding trait of the collective bargaining scheme was its fragmentation, because it dealt with a wide variety of situations, companies and territories on a year-to-year basis.[17]

The timid liberalisation of the labour relations system produced consequences that the dictatorship's legislators did not foresee and certainly did not desire. Two such consequences were the increase of strikes and the rise of illegal class unionism. This unionism was relatively ideologised, but to a large degree distinct from previous workers' traditions. Although functioning on a local level, it was poorly coordinated and had a very small membership. Nonetheless, its mere existence questioned the institutional foundations of verticalism. The nature of collective bargaining also pointed in this direction. The greater the number of agreements reached, the greater the chance that differences would arise and, as such, that conflicts would break out.

In the end, the class struggle, obsessively denied for two decades by national syndicalist discourse, became a reality. Strikes and other forms of protest continued to increase as of the beginning of the 1960s. Even though they were illegal, they were a key instrument of worker pressure in negotiations with businessmen. These protests were in part spontaneous and in part a product of that newly coined unionism – the *Comisiones Obreras* ('workers' commissions') – that was autonomously, quietly encouraged by a mix of people (communists, Catholics and socialists) from the lower levels of the Vertical Syndicates. The new trade unionism owed its success to the use of new legal avenues, especially union elections, which allowed the base of the verticalist structure to be partially occupied by workers who were not very faithful to the system. Despite the changes and new flexibility, the repressive nature of the existing legal framework was maintained until the end of the regime and even resulted in several states of emergency (1962, 1968 and 1969), but it did not prevent the erosion of the state syndicate. Although the workers' movement did not pose a threat, each labour conflict put a crack in the dictatorship's legality and questioned its order, repeatedly extolled by official propaganda with the argument of having established a period of peace unprecedented in the history of Spain.[18]

Labour unrest throughout the 1960s mainly affected the most industrialised regions with high worker and immigrant populations. It increased as of 1962 with strikes that rocked Asturian mining, the Basque Country and Catalonia, where between 200,000 and 400,000 workers participated in strikes. More than two-thirds of the conflicts took place in only five provinces: Barcelona, Madrid, Vizcaya, Guipúzcoa and Asturias, all quite different in their productive schemes and their union and political traditions. The presence of industrial branches most prone to conflict in these provinces explains this concentration of worker protest. The metals industry suffered much more than any other, registering over half the strikes. The mining, construction, textile and chemical industries were also affected. Although to a lesser degree, conflicts were also frequent in industrial areas established under *desarrollismo*, most of them new: Pamplona, Vitoria, El Ferrol, Vigo, Sevilla, Valencia, and Vallodolid. As such, the Franco regime had to face unforeseen sources of conflict created by its own industrial policy. At the beginning of the 1970s, serious conflicts arose in some branches of the tertiary sector, like banking, health and education. In terms of the volume and intensity of the conflict, 1970 signalled a point of no return. The workers' movement consolidated, political tension grew and violence increased (labour unrest resulted in some deaths in those years). Motivated up to that point mainly by the prospect of better wages, the movement became more radical and politicised. In response to a number of increasingly violent strikes, companies began to resort to lockouts, generalised dismissals, indiscriminate reprisals or the creation of blacklists to isolate the leaders of the movement. If a worker's name appeared on one of these blacklists, he was refused a job. In short, it was the authoritarian nature of the labour system and the political regime itself which contributed to exacerbating the unrest. The authorities viewed the labour protests as a political problem and a problem of public order, which made it very easy to call in the police to restore the peace.[19]

Most of the unrest occurred in medium and large companies. At least two-thirds of the strikes took place in companies with more than a hundred employees, in spite of the fact that these accounted for only 1.3 percent of all firms. However, companies with more than five hundred employees, and especially those with over thousand, avoided the worst of the conflicts. In many cases, these larger companies were supported by foreign capital, which perhaps made them more willing to negotiate and offer better wages. In the province of Barcelona, there were many conflicts in the industrial belt around the capital and in the county of Baix Llobregat. Important plants endured major strikes. The public firm Seat, for example, had been the Franco regime's prototype of industrial harmony. It was organised like the military and military figures had run the company since its founding in 1949. However, it became a model for trade union strategy, one example of which was the occupation of the factory by workers in October 1971. At that time, Seat had 28,000 employees in Barcelona. The factory was taken by mounted police after very violent confrontations that resulted in one death and more than two thousand million pesetas lost. There were also high-profile conflicts in the textile, chemical, graphic arts and contruction industries. In November 1970, 50,000 workers in the building sector went on strike, and employers responded with massive firings. Madrid's industrial belt and metropolitan area, which had attracted substantial foreign capital and investments by the INI, had enjoyed absolute calm in terms of labour disputes until the 1960s. However, this region was the scene of constant worker protest throughout the decade and until the end of the Franco regime. Here also, the conflicts took place mainly in large companies, especially metals firms. To limit ourselves to one more example, it is worth mentioning the strike of the company Bandas in Frío de Basauri, Vizcaya, perhaps the harshest confrontation endured by Basque workers during the dictatorship. Starting in November 1966, it lasted six months and resulted in the dismissal of the entire staff (more than five hundred employees). Faced with a strong solidarity movement in and outside the province, the Government decided to impose a state of emergency in April 1967.[20]

The importance of labour unrest during the Franco regime, particularly at the end of the dictatorship, cannot be overstated. To evaluate it properly, we must look beyond figures detailing the number of strikes, workers involved or days lost, and keep in mind that, within the dictatorial context, the fundamental right to go on strike was considered a crime, and unions not sanctioned by the government were illegal. However, the effects of that growing unrest on the regime itself and on businessmen must not be exaggerated. In the first place, the wave of worker protests did not affect the greater part of the national territory, the economy or Spanish society. No productive sector was ever completely paralysed by the strikes, either before or after the period in question. Important and vital sectors such as tourism, electricity and transportation were virtually unscathed. Not by chance, Spanish society was comfortable in the midst of the development, consumerism and relative prosperity of those years, which made it easy for much of the population to accept and become part of the system without complaints. Secondly, the massive emigration of workers to foreign countries – key to maintaining full employment in Spain – and, above all, the predominance of small firms with fewer than one hundred employees acted as safety valves that helped the Government contain the protests. In 1968, more than 80 percent of firms still employed fewer than ten workers. This dominance of industry by small businesses protected it from the trade union strategies tested in the big factories. Lastly, the fragmented nature of collective bargaining and labour protest created debilitating rifts in the working class by stimulating corporate attitudes in the battle for better wages. In this regard, it is illuminating that the new trade unionism of the 'workers' commissions' was able to mobilise only a small minority of workers in the entire country, doing so, moreover, in accord with local parameters. The majority of the conflicts never spread beyond the bounds of the factory, the city, or, at most, the productive sector in which they occurred.[21]

This does not negate that the trade union movement incurred great costs for many businessmen. The fact that a growing number of collective agreements were settled outside the framework of vertical syndicalism – which was, theoretically, more favourable to owners than to wage earners – surely had something to do with this. The corporatism of the State had accustomed the entrepreneur to a culture of aid and protection he was comfortably nestled in for two decades, until 1958. However, the relative liberalisation of labour relations created a new situation that was highly contradictory and no less complex. Even though a certain freedom of initiative was granted to the parties in collective bargaining, wide-ranging powers were reserved for state arbitration, which frequently gave rise to bothersome interference by verticalist functionaries. While small companies preferred to use the state syndicate in their dealings with employees, a growing number of big entrepreneurs – especially foreign companies – perceived the free negotiation with workers as a positive sum game for the development of productivity. These businessmen did not appreciate the anti-capitalist demagogy occasionally displayed by the state syndicate, even less when state intervention in disputes ruled against them. Government arbitrators, obsessed with preventing breakdowns in public order, tended to report wage increases higher than those that workers could have obtained in independent negotiations with companies. In fact, in the last fifteen years of the Franco regime, salaries increased more than productivity (6.5 percent compared to 5.5 percent a year, respectively), which increased their share of the national income (including Social Security payments, from 53 percent to 61 percent). Most of this differential evolution of salary costs and productivity occurred after 1973. State interventionism was also responsible for tremendous inflexibility in the hiring and firing of workers, so it is easy to understand why many businessmen were unhappy, convinced that the regime was becoming more costly for them. The flexibility they demanded was rejected by the Franco authorities, who always presented job stability as one of their great achievements. However, this did not entail a greater commitment from the public treasury in labour costs. In fact, in the financing of Social Security – which became universal under the Social Security Act of 1967 – Spanish company contributions were substantially higher than those of Common Market countries, except for Italy (63.4 percent of total expenditures compared to a Common Market average of 35.3 percent). In Spain, the contribution from the State and workers themselves was remarkably low, resulting in complaints by some employers' organisations about the public social security system, which they described as 'interventionist and socialist'.[22]

In any case, it would be wrong to conclude that the Franco dictatorship was inspired to redistribute the wealth. Prior to 1970, a small salary increase did not equate to any significant improvement of the very unequal distribution of Spanish income. The growth of productivity allowed for this increase without a decrease in profits or the accumulation of capital, which reached historic highs. The growth of the 1960s clearly favoured people in the highest income brackets. In addition to the hundreds of thousands of workers who were obliged to emigrate abroad, it is enlightening in this respect that in those years there was a significant increase in salaried employment. In 1955, 54 percent of the active population was engaged in this type of employment; in 1971, it accounted for 71 percent. This was directly linked to the significant decline in the number of small agricultural owners cited above. It was also related, although to a much lesser degree, to the fall in the number of self-employed workers and small businessmen with employees in the secondary and tertiary sectors. This decline took place in the final years of the dictatorship (although the numbers would recover in the 1980s). The increase in salaried employment varied greatly in the different branches of the economy. While it hardly fluctuated in agriculture, because the decline in the number of owners came with a decline in the number of day labourers, the rate of wage-earning workers grew notably in industry and, although somewhat less, in services as well. Such circumstances help explain how the gap in income distribution widened in the 1960s despite the expansion. This disparity was corrected only very slightly in the 1970s. If there were any doubt, the figures speak for themselves. Around 1974, the top 10 percent of Spanish households earned 40 percent of the wealth (after taxes), while the bottom 50 percent earned 20.9 percent. A decidedly regressive tax system could not compensate for this imbalance through public spending. There were three million people living below the poverty line during those years. Notwithstanding the demagogic rhetoric of the Falangists, one must conclude that workers were not exactly the main beneficiaries of Franco's economic policy. All of this coincides with the fact – also proven – that the numerous interventions on the part of the regime's syndical bureaucracy were a costly hindrance to business activity.[23]

Entrepreneurs on the Fringe of Power

The intricate and peculiar nature of political power in the Franco regime explains why businessmen did not have complete freedom of movement within the spheres of economy and employment. These areas were affected by interventionist practices which were often at odds with the business class. The dictatorship was much more than a return to old methods of social domination by an imagined oligarchy. It was a regime in which economic interests assumed a political role, but within the play of forces that had influence on a network of political power overseen by a dictator. Whether or not the phenomenon of *desarrollismo* increased this influence is a question to which there is no easy answer, or at least not only one answer. As a projection of the anti-republican coalition forged during the Spanish Civil War, the

Franco regime was propped on certain heterogeneous social and ideological supports whose political relevance changed over the years. It has been established that, in addition to the ever-present military figures, Falangists and clergymen sat at the top of this power structure during the autarkic period, high above monarchists and Carlists. As of the late 1950s, the regime relied mainly upon State civil servants to build its network – professors, diplomats, lawyers, engineers from various branches and lawyers from the council of state – without forsaking the usual sources of its elites (the Army, the Roman Catholic Church, trade unions, the single party, and local authorities).[24]

In reality, the presence of civil servants in top-level positions of authority fluctuated over the course of the dictatorship, as did the involvement of military figures. One-third of the *procuradores* (appointed representatives in Franco's Parliaments), half of the Movement's national advisers and 82 of the 113 ministers that made up the Franco governments were civil servants. In 1971, 53 percent of deputy secretaries and 24 percent of provincial governors also came from this group. All together, around 80 percent of the political posts were filled by civil servants. Added to these numbers were the thousands of appointments conferred upon regime supporters in public companies and middle and lower-level positions of all the institutions dependent on the State. This included the central Administration, of course, but also the Syndical Organisation; the party; the network of farmers' associations and guilds; ranchers and fishermen; the State media; and provincial town halls and councils. The dictatorial power structure was preserved by these circles and the networks of clients they generated. This prominence of civil servants, in quantitative and qualitative terms, can be traced to the growth of the State since the 1940s and the subsequent and spectacular increase in the number of government employees. It is logical that civil servants were recruited for government posts, not only because of their proximity to political authorities, but also because of the confusion of roles that existed among the Administration, the governments and top officials during the dictatorship. Another factor to keep in mind was the contempt for 'professional politicians' and 'policy' so characteristic of the period, in contrast to the parallel praise of 'technicians', who were all the rage back then. The end of the regime's institutionalising process was the work of the so-called 'technocrats', the highest professionals in public office. After approving a series of fundamental laws and fighting to oust other political families, these individuals took the reins of the State and modernised it along rational, efficient lines. The result was a higher quality, more orderly, functional and professionalised Administration, in keeping with the economic and social development of the period. The reform of the Administration was the other product of the relative economic liberalisation that was already in progress by the end of the 1950s. The authorities who carried out these intiatives did not, however, intend to alter the political foundations of Franco's State.[25]

Entrepreneurs played different roles in the clash of rivalries among the regime's political families and the rise and decline of their respective influence on the State. During the 1960s, there were very few who questioned the legitimacy of a regime in which they were comfortably settled. They had not done so during the long autarkic period, when they watched their influence on the State apparatus dwindle over time and bore the brunt of interventionism and certain economic curtailments that, for many of them, greatly restricted their freedom. They did not oppose the regime in the following period, either, because, in general, the new economic situation was much kinder to them and opened the doors to greater political influence. Fully aware of the benefits the dictatorship still brought and even increased for them, and mindful of the war that had threatened the foundations of social order, most business organisations reiterated their full support for the regime and the dictator in those years, jumping at any chance to demonstrate it. For example, until well into the 1970s, the *Fomento del Trabajo Nacional*, the most distinguished of the Catalan owners' entities, fully identified with the dictatorship and defended openly reactionary ideological positions, leading it to shamelessly defend the repressive policy and discredit the signs of democratisation and protest that were appearing more frequently in Spanish society. A small group of young Catalan businessmen, drawn together in the so-called *Círculo de Economía* (Circle of Economy) founded in Barcelona in 1958, did not share these political postures. But the vast majority were, by definition, addicted to the dictatorship until the end. Such was the case, even though, as some Catalan historians maintain but do not prove, there were fewer active supporters in Catalonia than in other Spanish regions. It was no coincidence that businessmen from this region fared especially well under the economic expansion of *desarrollismo*.[26]

The degrees of political vocation on the part of Spanish entrepreneurs ranged from those who had a clear calling to those who had none. Having fought in the Spanish Civil War or not may have determined the extent of one's political involvement, but this was not a fixed rule. In any case, regardless of political vocation, businessmen did not like being very far from the centre of power. By definition, they were fully aware of the advantages and disadvantages of being close to power. Andreu Ribera I Rovira, an important Catalan metallurgical industrialist who managed more than 1,700 employees, did not hesitate to enter politics in the 1960s, combining the job with his work as a corporate business executive. Starting out as a councilman in the Barcelona City Hall, he was later president of the *Consejo Económico y Sindical de Cataluña* (Catalonia Economic and Syndical Council), and headed the delegation of metal entrepreneurs in the Vertical Syndicate, first on the provincial level and then nationally. In 1965, he was elected president of the Chamber of Industry, which he directed to its reunification with the Chamber of Commerce and Shipping. He achieved a high level of authority among Catalan businessmen, explained in part by his tireless efforts to get the State to grant infrastructures to Catalonia. His good relations with some ministers helped him in this endeavour. Convinced that businessmen should always keep lines of dialogue open with the State, he was undoubtedly the most qualified representative of the Catalan economy over the last ten years of the dictatorship. With the arrival of democracy, he was awarded the post of senator by royal appointment. His career stands in direct contrast to that of Enque Masó y Vázquez. An engineer and businessman in the electronics industry, he became mayor of Barcelona in 1973 and quit the following year after a mandate full of tensions. Having never held positions of this sort before, he was, unlike Andreu Rivera, more of an administrator than a politician.[27]

Changing territories, it can be said that Basque industrialists and bankers enjoyed a proximity to power that was difficult to match during the dictatorship. One example of this is the figure of Isidoro Delclaux Aróstegui. A combatant for the Franco 'nationalists' during the Spanish Civil War and afterwards an important champion of the Vizcayan economy, his Carlist roots led him to the provincial council of Vizcaya. He was there from 1939 to 1947, helping to dismantle the administrative apparatus created by the abolished *Concierto Económico* (Economic Accord) between the Basque Country and the central political power. In the middle of the war, he had been appointed vice-president of the Bilbao Port Authority, a post he held until 1968. In 1964, to great acclaim and by unanimous choice, he rose to the presidency of the Chamber of Commerce. A good example of the close relation between banking and big industry, he was also a board member for the Bank of Bilbao from 1956 to 1981. Saying he was not especially fond of political posts – a common expression among businessmen who held them – he turned down the mayorship of Bilbao in 1959. However, that did not stop him from representing his region as a *procurador* in Parliament five years later. In this post, he acted as a spokesman for provincial economic interests for three terms, taking advantage of the position to claim protection for the most traditional Basque industries, which were then in obvious decline.

José María de Oriol y Urquijo, for his part, had a very similar career. He also came from a traditonalist background and also fought in the war. Likewise, he was an innovator in business and a defender of the electric industry, and later, of nuclear energy, in Spain. For a long time he held a post on the Council of National Economy. Lastly, he managed to keep politics his secondary interest, but certainly did not separate himself from it. In fact, he used it whenever he could to defend the industries he represented. He had been the mayor of Bilbao from 1939 to 1941, but turned down several public posts in later years, some as important as the Minister of Industry, which he was offered in 1945. However, in 1955, he returned to politics as a *procurador*, holding his seat for the following six legislatures. This return was relative, because in reality, he had never stopped practicing politics. A staunch monarchist, he became involved in attempts to fuse two dynastic branches, the *carlista* and the *alfonsina*, in the person of don Juan, the heir of Alfonso XIII. Moreover, his good relationship with Franco led him to mediate the famous interview between don Juan and the dictator on Franco's yacht, *Azor*, where they agreed that don Juan's son, Prince Juan Carlos, would be educated in Spain.[28]

However, the peerless archetype of the Basque entrepreneur who kept one foot in politics and the other foot out was, undoubtedly, José María Aguirre Gonzalo, the president of Banesto and Agromán. He always claimed his political passions were modest, not wanting to move beyond his status as an engineer, businessman and banker. Along these lines, he turned down Franco's offer to take over the Ministry of Housing, an opening created when another Basque, the Falangist Arrese, resigned. Even so, he held a seat in the *tercio sindical* (the third of Parliament representing the state union). Later, in the 1970s, Franco added him to the list of *procuradores* that he personally appointed. To his surprise, he was named vice-president of the Fundamental Laws commission, the most political in Franco's Parliament. He claimed to have little interest in politics, but this contradicted his propensity to act as a spokesman for bankers and entrepreneurs. José María Aguirre enjoyed giving opinions and especially having influence, so his conception of politics was circumstantial and instrumental. This was something very common among his counterparts, whether they were big, medium or small businessmen.

Another example was Félix Huarte Goñi, the famous builder from Navarra who made his fortune during the dicatorship with public works in the difficult 1940s. He entered politics in 1963 at the age of 67, when he felt compelled to promote the economic and social development of his region. He was retired, having turned over his businesses to his sons (around 1970, more than 17,000 workers were on his payrolls). An ardent Catholic, Huarte decided to follow the dictates of the encyclical *Pacem in terris* of Pope John XXIII. To do so, he announced his intention to seek public office and fully devoted himself to politics in the Autonomous Council of Navarra, where he was its highest representative a year after joining. Like so many others of his kind, he did not consider himself a politician, but rather a businessman from head to toe. However, this did not stop him from using his position on the Council to negotiate infrastructures for Navarra.

Eulogio Gómez Franqueira, the catalyst of poultry and ranching cooperativism in the province of Orense, shared the same utilitarian sense of politics. His long political career was sustained by the network of contacts he developed through the cooperatives, the provincial Rural Savings Bank and the local Chambers of Agriculture. He began as *procurador* in 1966 for the *tercio familiar* (the third of Parliament representing families). Later, during the transition to democracy, he was a representative of the UCD (Union of the Democratic Centre Party), and afterwards, of the Galician Coalition. In short, he was a true paradigm of political survival and adaptability thanks to the solid corporate framework he cemented over the years.[29]

Businessmen did not necessarily have to participate directly in politics to have political influence. Through personal contacts, flattery or favour, via generally subtle means, and above all through publicity, businessmen could gain access to the powerful people of the dictatorship. This political influence was exercised at various levels of government. The same strategy was used in local or provincial institutions to access a mayor or civil governor, a *procurador*, a minister, or in the case of a privileged few, the dictator himself. José Banús would have had a difficult time establishing his building empire in Marbella and his feverish speculative activity with popular housing in Madrid had he not exploited his personal friendship with Franco. José Fernández, the businessman of the department store Galerias Preciados, was a master of public relations. Without being a politician, he publicly supported the Franco regime. He never forgot to congratulate members of the government or important political figures in the most celebrated events, even taking out paid advertisements in the press to this end. He also personally saw to sending gifts to El Pardo, the dictator's residence, on a regular basis. These practices allowed him to establish close ties with the regime's political class and at the same time solve problems in his business via the *fast track*. In contrast, his competitor in the Corte Inglés, Ramón Areces, was never known to have political ideas, but at the time of Franco's death, his company was the Administration's main supplier. The fact is that if one wielded economic influence, it was not always necessary to resort to political influence. Emilio Botín-Sanz de Sautuola, as far as we know, was never explicitly engaged in politics, either, nor held a political post. He always led a discreet life outside of that realm, but his bank, the Bank of Santander, in addition to its commercial strategy, benefited from the lack of competition which protected the iron and steel sector, where the entity had invested a large part of its industrial portfolio. Lastly, the fact that Luis Suñer Sanchis, the owner of Avidesa, became an ideal businessman for the ideologues of national syndicalism surely had something to do with his cousin's holding a high-level post in Madrid in the hierarchy of the Movement. Franco and several ministers visited his factory on a number of occasions. The factory was awarded the honour of exemplary businesss, the Medal of Work and more than one substantial privilege, such as permits to import machinery in the 1950s, when it was very difficult to obtain them. In short, these entrepreneurs benefited from proximity to power but did not exercise it personally. As Luis Valls-Taberner Arnó pointed out, the ideal situation for businessmen (he was referring to big banking executives) was 'to be close to politics and not feel the need to intervene in them'. Valls-Taberner was vice-president of the Popular Bank in the 1960s, and never held a political post, although he did not lack political vocation and liked to be influential in other ways.[30]

If business elites had a rather passive role in decision making, including decisions about economic policy, in the first two decades of the regime, everything indicates that the influence of businessmen increased in the years of *desarrollismo*. This seems quite logical at a time when the dictatorship gave priority to economic growth as a path to political legitimacy over any other type of strategy. There is no research which covers the entire national territory, but partial studies give the impression that, at the local level, entrepreneurial presence in government grew. Of the thirty councilmen elected in 1963 for the *tercio sindical* (the third of Parliament representing the State syndicate) in the main cities in the province of Barcelona, including the capital, twenty-one were businessmen. Three years later, in 1966, important economic personages in the region took an active part in the campaign for the referendum on the *Ley Orgánica del Estado* (one of the fundamental laws established), participating in numerous public functions. The greater involvement of economic interests can also be observed in Parliament, where businessmen came to occupy more than a third of the seats over the course of the 1960s. In the 1968 Parliament, for example, from a sample of 146 *procuradores*, an estimated forty-two were businessmen, apart from other credentials they possessed. The 'technocrats' first appeared in the Government in 1957 and would occupy an increasing number of posts in subsequent years, facilitating this greater link of political power to the business world. It was then that the public firm took a back seat to private initiative, relegating the INI to a secondary role in industrial policy. In a trend that was maintained until the end of the dictatorship, a high percentage of ministers were directly related to big business and big banking. In more than a third of the cases, they came from the Madrid-Basque Country axis. Of the eighty-three ministers and ex-ministers that were still alive in 1974, sixty-four sat on the company board of some public or private firm in the last fifteen years of the dictatorship. Distinguished examples of these relations between governments and big companies, banking and even multinational firms were Gual Villalbí, Espinosa San Martín, Fontana Codina, Romeo Gorría, López Bravo, García Moncó, Allende y García-Baxter, García Ramal, Monreal Luque and López de Letona. The government formed in October 1969, a paradigmatic combination of experts in the Administration and executives of top companies, perhaps best typified this connection between political power and the economic world.[31]

The gradual overlap of high-ranking politicians with business and banking, in the public sector as well as in the private, did not necessarily imply that the business world as a whole played an important political role, let alone a decisive one, in the final phase of the dictatorship. With its economic features and a recognised collective identity, businessmen were practically absent from the big debates and strictly political processes of the period: the institutionalisation of the regime; the reform of the Administration; the tensions between those who believed in opening up and those who resisted change; the problems with a sector of the Church; foreign policy; the issue of succession; and the governmental crisis of 1969. The presence of businessmen in positions of political authority was the result of a process of individual recruitment in which, apart from the economic profile of the candidate, one's ideological curriculum mattered most. The more roles a person played, the better. One might be a businessman, but in the appointment to a post, a premium was put on the connections one had with any of the regime's political families. Enjoying many and good relations was an essential quality in a political order where it did not depend on the will of citizens to hold public office, but rather on the power of a reduced number of people. The more reduced it was, the higher one climbed the ladder. In the logic of selection, friends or colleagues were promoted first. To summarise, if one wanted to be politically influential in Franco's dictatorship, one had to demonstrate loyalty to the system and not their wealth or social status. The high-profile businessmen who achieved or preserved political influence did so insofar as they were also politicians, and to the degree that they guaranteed their ideological fidelity to the ruling system.[32]

Entrepreneurs did not have a recognised collective identity within the structures of the regime. This is why it is still a conceptual abstraction to speak of businessmen in political terms, because they did not act as they could have done in the transition to democracy. As members of associations, they did not integrate their interests and therefore did not have much political influence. Most businessmen did not trust pressure groups because, in fact, almost all of these groups lacked relevance in the period. Because of this, their specific influence as a group of power was weak.

Even big businessmen felt they really did not have much political influence. As a result, the image of the 'powerless business class' was coined about four decades ago in pioneer studies to conceptualise Spanish businessmen's restricted influence on politics at the time. Many Vizcayan industrialists, among others from other regions, could be excluded from this affirmation. In this period, the iron and steel, heavy machinery and shipbuilding industries, despite the fact they did not offer a promising future, still showed the capacity to pressure political authorities, which was unusual in most business circles. The same could be said of some big financiers, whose unquestionable economic power many authors have often extrapolated to politics. Their control of the industry and the fact that the status quo of banking was not altered, despite the reform of the financial system in 1962, would corroborate this idea. However, the territorial and sectorial exceptions do not tarnish the generic conclusion that economic interests had a marginal political impact on the Franco dictatorship. In 1939, the entreprenuer, in his sociological and economic sense, obtained full security after the previous shocks. However, he lost political power and paid the high price of having to confront powerful state interventionism. Looking at the political decisions of greatest impact during the period of *desarrollismo* – in particular, those regarding economic policy and the labour market – one finds that businessmen played a purely passive role. The Stabilisation Plan and the reform of the system of labour relations radically modified the country's economic structure and deeply conditioned the conduct of businessmen, leaving them exposed to foreign competition and worker pressure. These measures were implemented by politicians and designed behind the scenes by Administration technicians. Lawmakers found limited support as well as alarm and suspicion within the economic world, because many businessmen remained staunchly critical of economic liberalisation. In some cases, their criticism worked in their favour.[33]

Franco's imposed demobilisation of civil society damaged economic sectors from the moment their corporate organisation was limited. In fact, within the structure of the dictatorial regime, the real representation of interests was subordinate to the control of the bureaucracy and the political class. It is telling that the praises of corporatism sung by the state-owned media were never consummated with the creation of a national chamber representing economic and professional interests. The politics of interests did not disappear, but it remained subordinate to the ultimate power of the governments and the dictatorship's political class. The generally inefficient and hardly representative corporatism that the State imposed from above, through the Vertical Syndicates or in other ways, was the instrument of control it used to increase its own power. In global terms, this system did not grant freedom of action to the few independent business organisations that existed. This made it difficult for these organisations to fight against the arbitrary decisions and interventionism of the political class. Neither the Chambers of Commerce nor the few unofficial entities that survived the war, like the *Fomento del Trabajo* and the Vizcayan League, ever held more than a secondary role in the defence of business interests. Apart from always being in conflict with the Vertical Syndicates, which shamelessly absorbed and controlled them, they were hardly taken into account as consultative bodies of public power in the elaboration of economic policy. As mentioned above, many businessmen had privileged access to the network of influences and political favours, but only by virtue of arbitrariness and knowing the right people, which did not guarantee equal opportunity for everyone. The big industrialists tended to resort more to their personal contacts with political elites than to pressure by way of their specific interest groups. Those who best fit into the Syndical Organisation were small businessmen from less advanced regions, and also farmers, who were relatively comfortable in Franco's corporate institutions. Dependence on state protection, which applied to the better part of Spanish agriculture, was responsible for that comfortable integration. There are those who point out that, paradoxically, perhaps it was the business organisations that were most weakened by the dictatorship, which was supposedly conservative and pro-capitalist. As a result, the first legacy of the regime in the transition to democracy, no less paradoxically, was an economically and politically disorganised right wing. Businessmen left it to the State to look out for them and did not feel the need to – or were unable to – launch any organisations that articulated their interests from an independent platform.[34]

Nepotism, Corruption and Planned Economy

The preceding interpretation differs substantially from some of the more popular, well-known visions regarding the social roots of power in the dictatorship. Likewise, in the pages that follow, we intend to provide some nuances to the generalisations that are usually made in the bibliography on political corruption and business in the dictatorship. It is a bibliography of denunciation, generally of a journalistic nature, which successfully tries to impact the reader, but which unfortunately does not usually present empirical, conceptual evidence of the horrifying picture it paints. If this body of work is taken at face value, one reaches the inevitable conclusion that tremendous, unprecedented corruption reigned at all levels, from the highest spheres of political and economic circles to the lowest rungs of local government. As such, corruption, knowing the right people, and peddling influence and privileged information would have been the hallmarks of that era. From this standpoint, new fortunes would have accrued, old ones would have increased and even a new business class would have emerged.[35]

Independent of the accuracy of the assertions made, what appears evident is that speaking of corruption in a non-democratic system is probably redundant, because a system of that nature is by definition invalidated by the lack of effective mechanisms for controlling the actions of those in power. Furthermore, it is difficult to know whether this corruption, in terms of the estimated number of cases or the degree of fraud, was greater than at other periods in Spanish history. On the other hand, what does seem clear is that corruption depends above all on the size of the State, the opportunities that permit the practice of nepotism, the social acceptance or rejection of this practice and the degree to which the economy is politically regulated. The profile of the political regime (dictatorship or democracy) is not as great a determining factor as one might think. As we will see, the 1980s and 1990s, a period of greatly increased public spending, party system financing and political decentralisation, bore as many cases of corruption in Spanish democracy as in its European counterparts. Beyond the volume of corruption, the difference between a dictatorship and a regime of freedoms is, obviously, that the latter offers some counterweights that can at least partially nullify and publicise the vice and corruption inherent in politics. In dictatorships, corruption is a foregone conclusion and is usually institutionalised, but it does not usually cause social alarm, because without freedoms – especially freedom of the press – and parliamentary supervision, economic scandals involving political power generally go unnoticed.[36]

In the specific case of the Franco dictatorship, it can be added that the arbitrariness upon which economic policy was often based was perhaps more serious than the corruption itself. Essentially, this is because it broke the rules of the game in the market, giving privileges to that minority of businessmen who enjoyed strong ties with the power. Such a circumstance helps one understand why economic policy was often irrational after the liberalisation of 1959, especially with the beginning of the so-called 'development plans' as of 1964. These plans prompted a recurrence of State intervention, which in turn was responsible for cementing the structural defects of the Spanish productive system. Uncompetitive companies survived, especially in the oldest, most obsolete industries and least productive, unirrigated farming. The establishment of new companies in a wide range of sectors was limited. Government subsidies and tax incentives were approved for a small group without sufficient guarantees, subjecting the majority of businessmen to unequal treatment. Privileged circuits of financing that favoured both private and public companies were conserved. Against all logic, some tariffs were kept high, or prices of certain products were again fixed outside market parameters. These practices paved the way to arbitrariness in economic decisions, the consequent peddling of influences, and, on many occasions, the most searing corruption.[37]

The public sector was fertile ground for favouritism, privileges and arbitrary policies, either directly and personalised, or indirectly by way of aid to certain interest groups. On the one hand, public sector companies served as a refuge for many of the dictatorship's VIPs who lacked economic training. On the other hand, it was a shot in the arm for important private companies in difficulties. The INI, for example, maintained four thousand executive posts all over Spain, half of which were political sinecures. These positions were considered a prize for individuals who had had certain responsibilities in the regime, which explains why so many politicians were appointed to managerial positions in public firms, although they had no experience in the business world. However, the State also protected the most traditional, big private industry, many of whose companies were becoming obsolete just at that time. As we pointed out earlier in the chapter, the public sector fed off companies with this background, by way of 'pacted' nationalisations with their former owners. This increased the public deficit and significantly deteriorated the public sector itself. The small number of public companies created by the State is a relevant fact in this regard. Naturally, the transfer of failing companies to the public sector occurred as long as private interests wielded enough pressure on the political authorities. Without this pressure, the State could attack private companies. One famous example of the erratic, arbitrary criteria that still guided economic policy at the end of the dictatorship was the State's expropriation of the company Gas Natural and its supply contracts with Algeria. Gas Natural, established in 1970 under the presidency of Pere Duran Farrell, had helped bring natural gas to Spain for the first time. From the beginning, the INI had considered Gas Natural an intruder, arguing that control of the energy sector was the exclusive power of the State.[38]

Favouritism and arbitrariness were also revealed in the privileged circuits of financing established by the dictatorship, which provided risk-free loans to different public and private companies at interest rates lower than the market norm. From 1962 to 1972, no less than 35 to 45 percent of the resources channelled by the credit system were absorbed by these circuits. Around 1967, this accounted for one-fifth of private bank deposits and around half the deposits of *Cajas de Ahorro* (saving houses). In the end, the lack of a real fiscal policy hurt the effort to compensate for the imbalances caused by these discriminatory policies. It can be confidently asserted that, during the dictatorship, the Spanish public sector did not adequately perform any of the functions that justified its existence in a capitalist economy. It did not provide protection on equal terms, redistribute the wealth, or offer goods and services to the degree that the country's economy had developed. To the contrary, it applied a regulating, paternalistic policy that benefited only a few, and which soon proved incapable of continuing the process of growth.[39]

The lack of democratic control over the exercise of power was projected to many other fields in the business world, but few like the real estate business revealed the voracity of speculative interests acting in connivance with the authorities. The dictatorship allowed some enormous fortunes to amass in the sector, turning a blind eye to the gamut of abuses committed. Their breadth, the impunity shown and their consequences were unprecedented in earlier periods, and will possibly never be repeated: cities with their historic centres devastated; poorly constructed, incredibly ugly neighbourhoods of housing for the flood of rural emigrants; countless beaches and natural paradises wrecked by the expansion of tourism. Such chaotic growth – in which all kinds of small and middle businessmen took part as well – was possible only because the political authorities, especially municipal leaders, looked the other way. On many occasions, real estate owners and builders were among these authorities. Construction was poor and speculation unchecked with developable lands, even when it involved government-subsidised housing, constructed in 90 percent of the cases by private initiative during the 1960s. All the big, built-up urban areas of Spain, particularly new neighbourhoods and satellite towns around the main capitals, suffered this speculative plague, a product of a conspiracy by many unscrupulous businessmen – though there were also honourable exceptions – and politicians who avoided the very least rationality in urban development at the expense of hundreds of thousands of citizens. It can be asserted that in this particular business, by action or omission, local governments frequently worked in the service of shady private interests, to the detriment of the most basic public interests. The workers' neighbourhoods of Madrid, Bilbao, Valencia, Sevilla and Zaragoza, along with their bedroom suburbs and other built-up urban centres, exemplify ad nauseam what is affirmed here. One example among others was Barcelona, whose lucrative expansion is associated with the mayor that oversaw it from 1957 to 1973: Josep Maria de

Porcioles I Colomer, a notary born in the province of Gerona and a member of the Catalan League in his youth, who, like so many others of his ideological ilk, ended up fully supporting the dictatorship after the Spanish Civil War.[40]

As such, no one can dispute that the Franco regime represented a sort of paradise for doing good business outside the limits of the market and in the heat of political corruption. This corruption was, in fact, essentially political in origin. However, it needs to be qualified. Firstly, most businessmen were innocent of said corruption. Moreover, in reality, it is not always easy to distinguish corruption from nepotism, arbitrariness and political servitude. In fact, the regime's top officials undoubtedly used their power to obtain economic privileges. It was typical for them to sit on the boards of public and private companies, which almost never gave them control, but did earn them handsome profits, the same way it facilitated access to political power for economic interests that entered into such shady dealings. Ex-ministers, *procuradores* and, in general, persons of power thus found a solution in sitting on a board, a sort of reward for their political career and their relatively meager public salary. In particular, in the case of ministers, there was usually a relation between the ministry they occupied and the branch of business they would participate in afterwards.

It is not easy to determine where the political influence ended and the nepotism or corruption began. In reality, the rise to political posts by members of the corporate world was already an established practice which dates to the very origins of the liberal State and has continued up to the present day. Subsequently, it was not something the Franco regime invented. What was unique about the dictatorship was that the political market was not used for filling government posts, which later had its consequences in the economic sphere. In non-dictatorial periods, one tended to – and tends to – hire the services of politicians with a minimum of technical competence, proven and certainly profitable once put to use for companies. In the Franco dictatorship, there were countless personages who, without possessing any qualification, sat on a multitude of company boards merely because it was supposed they were influential. Certainly, the only economic merit that Nicolás Franco possessed was being the dictator's brother, which enabled him to hold key positions in a number of important firms. There were similar cases involving members of the military who had business ties without business qualifications but plenty of political influence thanks to their wealth.[41]

Opus Dei is worthy of special mention when talking about the slippery terrain of corruption, nepotism and political influence in the dictatorship, if only because of the harsh criticism this religious association has received. It was founded in 1928 by the Spanish priest José María Escrivá de Balaguer. It was criticised because of the power attributed to it, the controversial presence of some of its most important members in the Franco governments, and because these men were tarnished by what was undoubtedly the biggest scandal of the dictatorship, the Matesa affair. Beyond evaluations of other types, serious analysts credit the men of Opus Dei with promoting the Stabilisation Plan and administrative streamlining in the State. These men were identified as 'the technocrats', although not all technocrats were members of Opus Dei. They also implemented the so-called 'planned economy' launched in the mid-1960s, a very controversial economic policy that in fact put an end to previous liberalisation. From this perspective, Opus Dei would have contributed the sense of preeminence in economic matters and secular professionalism to Spanish society, two essential components in the modernisation of Spain. Despite their traditonal mentality (and that is in many senses of the word 'traditional'), the men of Opus Dei would have supported the capitalist spirit, in a kind of adaptation of the Protestant ethic to Spanish Catholicism. Starting from ideological precedents that can be traced to Ramiro de Maeztu and his 'reverential sense of money', or, above their intractable differences, to the Jesuits themselves with the founding of the University of Deusto, the ICAI-ICADE (a business school) and other institutes, Opus Dei made a valiant effort to provide intellectual elites with a solid bureaucratic and business education. It did so in their private schools, its own university (located in Pamplona) and its company management schools, preceding state initiative in its work. From this perspective, there was much more behind Opus Dei's rise to power than its link with the vice-president of the Government, Carrero Blanco, the 'thinking man of the regime'. These elites' rise to government office would be explained especially by their status as experts in matters that former civil servants were not specialised in. This specialisation proved to be miraculous in the years of *desarrollismo*.[42]

If the presence of Opus Dei members in the decision-making centres of power is unquestionable, it is more difficult to determine whether they constituted a political pressure group, an economic pressure group, both, or neither. The personal careers of Laureano López Rodó, Mariano Navarro Rubio, Alberto Ullastres, Gregorio López Bravo, Faustino García Moncó and Juan José Espinosa San Martín, all of them *ministers* belonging to Opus Dei, do not reflect the image of a tightly knit group subordinate to a well-defined political project, although they occupied important posts and had a dense network of contacts spread throughout the Administration. Specifically, these contacts were in key positions and organisations like the Council of National Economy, the Council of State, undersecretaryships, ministerial cabinets, the military hierarchy itself and even the syndical bureaucracy. They had less power in the syndical bureaucracy because of the Falange's open hostility towards them (despite the number of self-styled Falangists recruited by Opus). López Rodó himself joked about having appointed eighteen ministers in the Franco governments. Eleven of the nineteen members of the Government of October 1969 either belonged to or were supporters of Opus. However, data does not always reflect reality. In this respect, it is significant that, on more than one occasion, one could sense the lack of agreement between ministers and Opus Dei, even on fundamental issues. For example, in 1962, Navarro Rubio threatened to resign, but Franco prevented him from doing so, instead relieving him of his post as Treasury Minister by appointing López Rodó commissioner of the Development Plan. In addition, there is no clear evidence that these men put their faith in Escrivá de Balaguer above their faith in the regime while they were in government. Furthermore, their relative independence in political administration was supported by the fact that they knew how to surround themselves with prestigious technicians, many of whom had nothing to do with Opus Dei, and who worked as professionals to modernise the Spanish State and society above all other considerations. For example, the real architect of the all-important Stabilisation Plan in the Bank of Spain's Department of Studies was Juan Sardá Dexeus, the prestigious economist whose behind-the-scenes influence, second to that of the ministers Navarro Rubio and Ullastres, was crucial.[43]

Opus Dei's economic connections also gave birth to all sorts of suspicions and interpretations over the years. Given that it constituted a pool of elite managers who defended the interests of the Church and had access to positions of economic power, different authors have defined the organisation as an interest group, even though the technocrats were the only politicians in the dictatorship who were reluctant to be recognised as a group. Their close personal ties with the business world would refute that resistance. In this sense, it is argued that the expansion of companies and banks in which Opus had obvious personal and financial ties was related to the public role played by some of the ministers cited above. At the same time, these people's access to the financial world raises the interesting question of how much more political power could be transformed into economic power than vice versa, especially in an authoritarian regime where the order of the day is arbitrary reward for friends and punishment or ostracism for those not willing to cooperate. It has been asserted that Opus Dei, whose finances were always secret, received all kinds of investments which supposedly increased once their men landed in the Government in 1957. Along these lines, the interventionist criteria of the economic policy, once more emphasised as of 1964 after the period of liberalisation, would have continuously favoured their economic projects. Not in vain did its members come to occupy the central core of the financial system, both in the Bank of Spain – whose presidency was assumed by Navarro Rubio in 1965 – and other official lending institutions, saving houses and the Superior Banking Council itself. The pace of growth experienced by the Popular Bank, the Atlantic Bank, Bankunión and other financial entities – genuine upstarts compared to the status quo of previous banking – as well as the rise of Rumasa and the peak of other companies in different sectors (publishing, tourism, the press and construction) which purportedly had ties to Opus, would corroborate the political favouritism that supposedly benefited this organisation and its people.[44]

In reality, the verification of all these assertions should be supported by serious research which these days we lack. However, there is one issue which at least indirectly tarnishes Opus Dei, and which its critics used as ammunition for attacking the association: the so-called Matesa affair, a corruption scandal that understandably rocked Spain at the end of the 1960s. It was unusual because, along with other persons, three of the dictatorship's ex-ministers were tried by the Supreme Court; an investigative committee was formed; the press gave completely revealing coverage of the case; and it caused a remodelling of the government that was unprecedented in the history of the regime. The Matesa scandal erupted in August 1969 when it was known that the textile company, owned by businessman and Opus Dei member Juan Vilá Reyes, had gone into debt with the Industrial Credit Bank to the tune of around ten thousand million pesetas. The authorised loans, dating to 1964, amounted to half of all the loans it had granted and a quarter of all its funds. But the worst was not so much the suspected favouritism involved in the concession as the fact that it had been illegal. Matesa had specialised in the export of a recently invented mechanical loom. In accordance with the current laws, loans to export companies had to be conceded on the basis of demonstrable orders, something that Matesa could not produce. What was in fact proven was that it had inflated its orders to the point that fictitious exports accounted for two-thirds of the total. The idea that took root among public opinion was that an irregularity of this magnitude been had endorsed only because of political motives sheltered in Vilá Reyes's relations with the Opus ministers. This idea was supported by the rumour that the businessman had made donations of around 2.5 thousand million pesetas to the religious association. However, given the confusion of the facts, the truth about what had happened was never completely clarified.[45]

Beyond the corruption itself, the peculiarity of this scandal is that it quickly bore political consequences, causing a serious governmental crisis. It was every bit a novelty, because in the Franco dictatorship, there had been much shadier affairs that never saw the light of day and never put the authorities in serious binds. The seriousness of the crisis is understood only by keeping in mind that, although Matesa triggered it, in reality it was already brewing in the confrontations within the Council of Ministers for several years. These were confrontations over decisions of the highest importance for the political life of the country (the law of the press, the future syndical law, public order, foreign policy and the succession of Franco). The crisis of 1969 thus revealed itself to be a bloody struggle for power. The Matesa affair was the excuse taken advantage of by sectors opposed to Carrero Blanco and Opus Dei – the Falangists above all – to discredit the economic ministers identified with their postulates. The curious thing is that Carrero came out of it completely unscathed by his critics. On 29 October, Franco made the biggest governmental change that he had implemented to that moment: thirteen of the eighteen ministers were replaced. Of these, at least twelve could be considered faithful to Carrero. In addition to the imprisonment of Vilá Reyes, the ex-ministers of Finance and Commerce were dismissed and later tried. Another ex-minister, Navarro Rubio, was also tried, for having been president of the Bank of Spain and as such the highest official directing the lending strategy of public banking. With them, the figures that had led the opposition to the technocrats and Carrero Blanco were also dismissed from the cabinet. In light of the fear that the scandal and its ramifications could irreparably harm the regime, the trials of the defendants never produced convictions. With the exception of Vilá Reyes, who was sentenced with a hefty fine and spent several years in jail, Franco pardoned them in October 1971. Even so, this scandal seriously damaged the regime's prestige, not only because it brought to light the administrative irregularities, but also because it publicly revealed the disunity within the political class, something unusual in the dictatorship, although the divisions had occasionally been sensed since its beginning.[46]

Insofar as it was a typical outcome of the interventionist policy from the Franco regime's final phase, the Matesa scandal also had an unquestionable economic impact, reflecting the scandalous incompetence of the bureaucratic system that guided the developmental policy. This incompetence was much more serious than the corruption itself. It did not adhere to the logic of the market, it nurtured political favouritism, it maintained unprofitable industries in neglect of the most fundamental business practices, and, in short, it did not encourage the application of the best economic policies. The push towards liberalisation in the early 1960s did not a posteriori free economic development from the weight of the dictatorship's authoritarian system. The Development Plans started in 1964 in fact entailed a step backwards with respect to the reforms designed in 1959, upset the balance of growth and thwarted important opportunities for expansion in the second half of the 1960s. This regression was a result of the pressures by corporate interests opposed to liberalisation, but also and especially because of the political regime itself. The government was not willing to make serious changes in vital areas (the labour market, the tax system, the financial system and industrial policy), because it perceived such changes as a threat to its stability, its social support and its very survival. Economic change was tolerated only insofar as it was compatible with the continuity of the regime. As a result, monopolistic tendencies, interventionism and protectionism survived in the economic policy, although in different, more refined forms than in days gone by. The process of liberalisation was halted on all fronts when necessary to maximise political power. Likewise, the dense network of paternalistic interventions limited business activities to the benefit of those who for ages had been settled in the productive system and enjoyed preferential political treatment. As such, traditional corporate capitalism (iron and steel, metallurgy, coal, shipbuilding, grain farming) also restricted the great opportunities for economic development that arose in Spain in the 1960s. The growth could have been much greater, more efficient, and more equitable had the system openly committed itself to the market. It was as if the politicians of the 1960s, frightened by the reforms of 1959, went only halfway, fearful of the political and social consequences that liberalisation was inevitably leading to. Viewed in perspective, the truth is that their fears were not unfounded because, despite the obstacles that slowed it down, the economic liberalisation formed the basis for the cultural and social modernisation that undermined the political foundations of the dictatorship.[47]

In losing the opportunity for a greater, more rational growth, the system left a disastrous legacy that in the long run slowed down the modernisation of the Spanish economy: industrial specialisation in outmoded sectors that were very sensitive to the price of energy and imported raw materials; and a very rigid labour market, tightly controlled by the Administration, with inflated staffs, inflexible modes of hiring and elevated costs of firing that halted productivity. The distortions accumulated by the growth rate amplified the problems that arose with the oil crisis of 1973 (increased energy prices, inflation, unemployment and regional imbalances), revealing the fragililty of the productive structure established in previous years. A policy more aligned with market freedom would eventually have facilitated industrial reconversion and a better adaptation of the economy and the labour market to the new circumstances arisen from the international depression. The sustained inflationary trend probably would have been avoided and it would have been possible to overcome the crisis. Spanish industry was one of the worst prepared in

Europe to confront the new economic situation in 1973, due to its low competitivity, its extreme dependence on loans, its excessive propensity for import duty protection and its limited capacity to create jobs. From 1960 to 1970, despite the population increase that occurred in Spain, the total number of people with jobs remained practically the same because the intense economic growth and acclerated industrialisation were incapable of generating higher levels of employment. As a result, when the recession set in, foreign investment was withdrawn and Europe ceased to function as a safety valve for Spaniards looking for work. Unemployment grew rapidly and was worsened even more by the massive return of many of those emigrants who had left the country in the 1960s.[48]

Even big banking interests, habitually and deservedly regarded as the most favoured by the regime, paid for the economic mistakes of the dictatorial policy. In light of this, it is biased to consider banking a sector that was monolithically identified with the regime. For one thing, the same banking reform of April 1962, reflected in the so-called Loans and Banking Regulation Law, did not live up to its potential despite the complete nationalisation of the official banks. The reform, of course, angered the shareholders of the Bank of Spain – which saw its decision-making capacity curtailed – and private lending institutions, which feared the great power the State held in the financial system. From then on, the Government was authorised to set the guidelines that the Bank of Spain and the different lending institutions would have to follow in each stage. However, this step did not necessarily mean the preservation of the public interest, since the autonomy of the Bank of Spain did not exist. The central bank was not safeguarded against the intrusions of political power, an essential condition in order to achieve monetary stability, the containment of interest rates and limits on lending.

So then, the Bank of Spain was nationalised, but it hardly progressed in its conversion to a true central bank. Furthermore, there were also disputes between the State and some private banks. Relations with the Urquijo Bank, for example, were not always good. Back in the 1940s and 1950s, its liberal banking practice aroused suspicions among the Franco authorities. These suspicions grew because Suanzes and the INI were hostile towards it, viewing it as a competitor, given its industrial specialisation in sectors like the automobile and chemical industries, which the INI regarded as its own. The republican lineage of one of its most well-known executive directors, Juan Lladó y Sánchez-Blanco, who always tried to avoid all personal contact with Franco, did not help improve relations between between the bank and the State. Juan Villalonga Villalba, the president of the Central Bank, cannot have been liked very much in Franco's circle, either, not exactly because he was a republican, but because of his open monarchic inclination favourable to don Juan, the pretender to the throne. Be it for this reason or his opposition to the reform of 1962, the fact is that, three years later, when the merger of his bank, the Central Bank, with the Hispano-American Bank was nearly complete, Franco himself shot down the plan with his personal veto. The dictator, who was openly distrustful of Villalonga, justified his decision with the argument that the power of big banking was already excessive. He obligated the Treasury Minister to retract his initially favourable stance towards the merger and demanded such heavy taxes that the operation had to be cancelled. This is just one more example of how incompatible the free market was, even at this stage, with the political interests of the dictatorship, or, simply, with the administrative discretion and personal fears of its leaders.[49]

The Collapse of the Regime and Anti-capitalist Culture

The final years of the dictatorship and the first years of the transition to democracy, crucial for the whole of Spanish society, amounted to one of the most critical situations endured by Spanish businessmen in the course of contemporary history. Added to the problems stemming from the agony of the dictatorship, the political uncertainty and the intense social movement that accompanied it were the effects of the international economic crisis brought on by the sharp rise in oil prices as of 1973. The timid attempts at liberalisation in the previous decade went nowhere with the change of Government in 1969 and especially after the assassination of Carrero Blanco by the Basque separatist group ETA four years later. The political liberalisation promised in February 1974 by the Government did not improve the regime's situation, either. Much to the contrary, its loss of legitimacy and sclerosis were noticeable in proportion to Franco's failing health. Conflicts and social protest increased just then. This activity did not bring down the dictatorship, but it definitely contributed to its erosion. So did the economic crisis, which the dictatorship was especially vulnerable to after pinning all its popularity on the continued growth that had occurred since the early 1960s. The regime failed to come up with attractive alternatives to the deterioration of the economy. It was also unable to pacify the conflicts and build confidence that the system would carry on smoothly after Franco's death in November 1975. All of this unsettled many of the social groups that up to then had identified with the dictatorship, the majority of businessmen among them.[50]

In particular, economic policy from 1973 to 1977 was marked by a lack of political authority, the loss of the governments' legitimacy and the provisional nature of the economic teams responsible for applying it. These circumstances were tremendously negative for the national economy at a time when rising energy costs entailed a substantial shock, much worse than what other western European countries endured, given Spain's debilitating dependence in this area. The country grew poor very quickly because of the drastic decline of the economic situation. The crisis was reflected in the disequilibrium in the balance of payments, the growing foreign debt, the dramatic fall in the level of reserves, the reduction of exports, the stoppage of foreign and national investment, the decline in revenue from tourism, the general shrinking of business profits and the change in the direction of migratory movement, with the return of many of the emigrants who some years earlier had found opportunities to work and live on the other side of the border. Inflation, which had been 7.5 percent during the period 1960–1973, shot above the average of the OECD (Organisation for Economic Cooperation and Development) countries to 17 percent in 1974, compared to 5 percent in the countries cited, then increased to 26 percent in 1977. Its consequences were an alarming increase in unemployment and an abrupt halt to economic growth. The unemployment rate in Spain was soon the highest in

Europe. It had been insignificant in the 1960s, but rose sharply to 6 percent in 1977. That was only the start of what would become staggering figures. Economic growth plummeted in 1975 to 1.1 percent of the GNP, when the average yearly rate had been 7.2 percent in the period 1960–1973 (well above the European average of 4.7 percent in those years). Foreign debt rose to over 12 thousand million dollars. Numerous industrial sectors collapsed in a structural crisis, aggravated by the considerable parallel increase of labour costs. The crisis had a really critical impact on agriculture. First of all, the inflation thwarted the previous decade's model of growth, which was based on the availability of cheap oil and the emigration of huge contingents from rural areas; secondly, it seriously eroded agricultural income levels. In short, at the beginning of 1977, everything pointed to a climate of genuine depression prolonged and aggravated by the country's political situation. It was a period when all sorts of problems accumulated without an economic policy designed to contain them. The economic authorities, facing a climate of political uncertainty, did not feel capable of developing firm plans of action, refusing to offset high gas prices in Spain and failing to contain high wage increases. In manufacturing, for example, wages in 1977 grew by 30 percent in terms of gross salary per hour worked.[51]

The high salary costs were closely related to the increasingly more radical, politicised conflict that took hold of the labour market in the early 1970s. Strictly professional objectives went hand-in-hand with democratic demands. Figures on strikes and conflicts were truly astounding, especially in the latter years of this new wave of protest. The number of collective conflicts on record went from 616 in 1971 to 2,290 in 1974 and 3,156 in 1975. The number of workers involved jumped from 229,000 in 1971 to nearly 3 million in 1975. During the same period, the number of hours of work lost rose from 7 million to 156 million. In 1977, hours lost dropped to 110 million but the number of strikers increased from the previous year's total (3,265,000). The strikes and lockouts continued to be concentrated in the most traditionally combative productive branches (metal, mining, construction, chemicals and textiles), in big companies and in the most industrialised areas. But now they also affected sectors (banking, insurance, health, education, transportation, the postal service and the hotel and catering trade), cities (Vitoria, Pamplona, El Ferrol, Vigo, Valladolid, etc.), and people – white-collar workers who emulated manual labourers – previously asleep in their shoes. Only the figures from the province of Barcelona in 1976 were greater than the overall statistics for Spain in all the previous years. There, as in other big cities, labour unrest went hand-in-hand with other social movements (neighbours, students, anti-centralists, etc.). Nearly half of all workers figuring in the census took part in the conflicts. That same year in Madrid, strikes involved more than half a million people and accounted for about ten million hours of work lost. In public services (subways, trains and the postal service), the authorities ordered the militarisation of the workers. The unrest in Madrid was greatest in terms of number, intensity, politicisation, illegal strikes and sectorial diversity from 1975 to 1977. In 1976, a year marked by spectacular strikes, over two-thirds of salaried workers in the province took part in the labour conflicts. On 11 November 1974, a general strike in the Basque Country paralysed 80 percent of the active population. In the three years that followed, big Vizcayan companies endured long and crippling strikes. In only sixteen months, from January 1976 to May 1977, there were three general strikes in Basque provinces. Even in Álava and Navarra, whose industrialisation was very recent, their respective economies were often paralysed. This time almost nobody escaped the unrest where there were high concentrations of salaried workers, so the situation was very similar in other territories and industrial regions.[52]

The radicalism, severity and generalisation of the worker protest made many think that Spain was entering a prerevolutionary phase. Such a perception was exaggerated. There were no authentic signs of an anti-capitalist uprising, borne out by the 1977 general elections and the trade unions' propensity to pact and negotiate after the turbulent years. Nonetheless, the fear was obvious in business circles. A sense of vulnerability took hold of owners, leading them to increase their complaints to the authorities and demanding they toughen up repressive measures. 'Now we are obligated to dedicate most of our time to dealing with problems, to the detriment of our most important mission, which is creating wealth', it was said in a document sent by businessmen in the metal industry to the Barcelona Vertical Syndicate. Not in vain, the Catalan capital became the epicenter of Spanish social unrest and the point of reference for forces opposed to the dictatorship. More than anywhere else, the emergence of the unrest in Barcelona revealed the limitations of the official corporate framework for institutionalising the differences between entrepreneurs and workers. Via trade union elections, worker opposition won majority representation and the Falangist bureaucracy retained control only in the highest echelons of verticalism. When this bureaucracy no longer served their interests, many businessmen opted to negotiate directly with their employees, bypassing official mediation. The death of the dictator was also the coup de grâce for the Vertical Syndicates, but for a long time they had been incapable of containing worker unrest. In July 1974, a general strike was declared in Baix Llobregat, every bit a landmark in industrial Catalonia. From 1974 to 1976, businessmen unleashed a counteroffensive, responding to the strikes with lockouts and mass firings of union representatives. In the first two months of 1974 alone, a thousand workers were fired and more than 3,000 were temporarily suspended without pay. In November, Seat fired its entire staff in a span of ten days, and dozens of its workers were arrested. The employers' reaction was also very severe in Madrid. In 1976, there were 3,700 firings, 44,500 workers sanctioned and threatened with dismissal and several dozens of lockouts. But bad times were on the horizon for businessmen. In response to the workers' illegal activities, they resorted to existing legal channels in attempts to fire them, but very often, the judges threw out the cases, applying a softer version of the law in light of the circumstances.[53]

It should not be surprising that many employers considered the situation to be completely anarchistic, and they became demoralised. In the verticalist apparatus itself, the capitalist system was sometimes criticised. Opportunistically, this criticism coincided with the criticism levied by the illegal unions, purposely and simplistically associating businessmen with the regime. Of course, it cannot be affirmed that business circles distanced themselves from the dictatorship around this time, although there were a few exceptions which did. In any case, the equation 'businessman equals

Franco supporter' that spread through much of society was very disturbing for entrepreneurs in view of the circumstances they were facing. The figure of the businessman was also openly questioned outside the realm of labour: in much of the political spectrum, in academic circles, among university students, and even in the more progressive clergy (the so-called 'red priests', so typical of the era). Back then, most university students came from middle or upper-class backgrounds, but this hardly mattered to them. Some, despite being sons of medium or big businessmen, sold *Combate, Mundo Obrero* or *Bandera Roja* (Communist newspapers) on street corners, or even incited the workers of the family business to revolt.[54]

Historians in the 1960s held a view of Spanish history that blamed oligarchies for impeding the country's social progress and democratisation in the previous two centuries. This social perspective gave rise to generally negative impressions that later crystallised into historical assumptions, some of which are still in circulation today: the limitations of the 'bourgeois revolution'; 'the failure' of the industrial revolution; the squandering of national wealth in the nineteenth century (read: minerals, railways, etc.) by foreign capital; the centralisation imposed by a liberal State that fought cultural plurality, including regional languages; the infamous *caciquismo* (boss system) of the Restoration, which prevented most citizens from taking part in politics when they were supposedly eager to vote; the sufferings and tremendous exploitation of the working class; and, of course, among other countless unmentionable sins, the frustration of that great experience of democratisation that was the Second Republic. Beyond its many merits – which it also possessed – and its undeniably plural profile, the least that can be said of this historiography is that it encouraged a way of understanding the past that was very conditioned by the political situation in Spain at the time. The main objective was to present a negative image of the dictatorship, unveiling all of its horrors. This seemed to require condemning the long period from 1833 to 1923 that, for all its shortcomings, was essentially liberal and constitutional. But this was not so important; the times were not ripe for interpretative refinements. In the shadow of the spirit of 1968 and the prevalence of Marxism, 'the economy and business were contemptible activities' for the intellectual left (and also for more than one heir of Falangism or social Catholicism) and were projected onto the past as such. This negative image of the past did nothing more than reflect the widespread cultural demonisation by Spanish society of the entrepreneur and the market economy, in accordance with a 'premodern economic ethic'.[55]

So then, there was anti-capitalist sentiment everywhere, particularly in the big cities. The most striking feature of poor neighbourhoods was all the left-wing symbols and graffiti, whose unifying thread was the call to revolutionary strike and slogans that announced the imminent end of the *bourgeois order*. The symbols and aesthetic extended from the industrial outskirts and the universities to the city centres in streets and squares or subway stations. With this atmosphere and the uncertainty of the immediate political future, it is not surprising the majority of Spanish businessmen were feeling nervous, especially where the social movement was close at hand. However, this contrasts with the fact that most businessmen played no part in the transition to democracy, following it as mere spectators.

The businessmen's feeling of abandonment deepened as they watched labour costs grow much faster than productivity (from 1973 to 1979, around 40 percent) while the inflexibility of the job market inherited from the dictatorship stayed the same. Given the country's reigning political instability, the governors did not dare deregulate the market or make it more flexible. Along with rising salaries came the increasing costs of firing and the trend to shorten the workday. Under these circumstances, with the economic crisis and brutal inflation as a backdrop, entrepreneurs cut back on their investments. Confused, tense and feeling cornered, they went on the defensive in view of the agony of the regime and the social protest. Some businessmen who regarded the dictatorship with nostalgia felt the solution was to be found – as in other times – in the use of force. One person who held this view was Josep-Matias de España i Muntadas, an entrepreneur and textile engineer, and formerly a *procurador* in Franco's Parliaments, the mayor of Hospitalet and local boss and provincial councillor for the Movement. He decided to speak out. Perhaps he was thinking of the Catalan industrial elites who had repeatedly played a role in past manoeuvers of this sort: 'I believe there is no other solution than a mobilisation, by way of a coup d'état, which is what I am personally hoping for [...] I happened to like the former regime'. It is clear that reactionary postures like this spread in the rest of the country's economic circles. As late as September 1976, the president of the National Council of Businessmen – within the Vertical Syndicate – declared himself absolutely opposed to the concession of a labour amnesty. However, the more civilised and sensible employers (many of them Catalan as well), aware that the time had come to preserve their threatened interests, decided to intervene in the matter via peaceful channels. It is possible that the majority of them felt this way. This was how they came to appeal to the mobilisation, convinced that their future as entrepreneuers was at stake. They did not do so with aggressive intentions, but rather, realising their weakness, with enthusiasm, willing to dialogue and reach social pacts with the governments and union forces.[56]

Notes

1. Botín, in Hoyo Aparicio (2000); Villalonga, in Tortella (2000c); the Valls-Taberner, in Serrano Alcaide (2000); and Aguirre, in González Urbaneja (2000).
2. Entrecanales, in Moreno Castaño (2000b); del Pino, in Cabrera (2000b); Banús, in Gutiérrez Molina (2000).
3. Pepín Fernández y Areces, in Toboso Sánchez (2000a and 2000b); Meliá, in Galindo Vegas (2000).
4. Cuétara, in Moreno Lázaro (2000); Carulla, in Cabana (2000a); Suñer, in Reig Armero (2000); Gómez Franqueira, in Juana López (2000).
5. Beteré, in Germán Zubero (2000); Barreiros, in García Ruiz (2000a).
6. For the new economic situation, the fundamental study is still the one by González González (1979). See also Sardá Dexeus (1970: 461–466); Clavera et al. (1973: 9–151); Biescas and Tuñón de Lara (1980: 43–51); Tortella (1994: 273–280); Barciela et al. (1996: 86–88); Tedde (1996: 40–43); Fusi and Palafox (1997: 343–346); García Delgado and Jiménez (1999: 130–139).

7. Sardá Dexeus (1970: 467–469); Clavera et al. (1973: 155-284); Tamames (1978: 462–463 and 476–478); González González (1979: 134–296); Biescas and Tuñón de Lara (1980: 71–104); Alcaide Inchausti (1988: 648–649); Fuentes Quintana (1988: 4–24); Comín (1996); Tedde (1996: 45–48); Barciela et al. (1996: 89–94); García Delgado and Jiménez (1999: 139–143 and thereafter); Martín Aceña (2000: 151–163).
8. *Ibidem.*
9. Figures and percentages, in Tamames (1979: 417–422); Biescas and Tuñón de Lara (1980: 112–116); Payne (1987: 493–495); Cuadrado Roura (1988: 746–752); Martín Rodríguez (1988: 720–734); Llopis Agelán and Fernández (1997). Monographic studies on regional disparities in economic development can be found in Nadal and Carreras (dir.) (1990) and Germán et al. (2001).
10. Tamames (1979: 343–356 and 381–382); Payne (1987: 499); Flaquer et al. (1990: 44–45); Tezanos (1990: 124–126); Juliá (1991: 32–38).
11. Juliá (1991: 40–41); Martín Aceña and Comín (1991: 306–312); Martín Rodríguez (1988: 730); Balfour (1994: 57–60 and 186); Tortella (1994: 281–287); Babiano (1995: 37); Soto Carmona (1998: 213 and 215); Llopis Agelán and Fernández (1997: 82 and *passim*); Fusi and Palafox (1997: 353–354); Cabana (1997), who presents a list of seventy-four textile factories that closed in Catalonia between 1962 and 1977.
12. On Rojo, see Pániker (1969: 159–161). Tamames (1966), (1977) and (1978); Muñoz (1969); Muñoz et al. (1978b); and Moya (1975) and (1984) consolidated this interpretative model. In the following it is proven that the interpretation has stood the test of time: Biescas and Tuñón de Lara (1980: 131–141 and 153–158); Payne (1987: 495); Flaquer et al. (1990: 29–30 and 39–40); Pérez Ledesma (1990: 230–231); Tortella (1994: 278–280 and 336–348); García Delgado and Jiménez (1999: 155–156) and, from a more journalistic and methodologically weaker slant, Ynfante (1998). The identification of the banker-big businessman is intelligently explained by Torrero Mañas (1988: 596).
13. Tamames (1977: 212–217); Muñoz, Roldán and Serrano (1978b: 263–293) and appendices for the specific connections of companies and board members; Biescas and Tuñón de Lara (1980: 148–152); Payne (1987: 490); Balfour (1994: 62).
14. The Chambers, in Bahamonde et al. (1998), Díez Cano (1992) and Domínguez Jiménez (1994). The resistance of the autarkic entrepreneurs is pointed out by Martín Aceña and Comín (1991: 318). The Catalans, in Molinero and Ysàs (1991: 73–81, 89–91 and 114–118), and Pinilla de las Heras (1968: 205–207), who carried out a survey of 107 Barcelona businessmen. The Basques, by way of the biography of Isidoro Delclaux Aróstegui, their great corporate spokesman in the 1960s, in Alonso Olea (2000). The extensive agriculture, in Moyano Estrada (1984: 121–142).
15. Especially Martín Aceña and Comín (1990a) and (1991: 373–381 and 449–456). Also, Schwartz and González (1978); Tamames (1977: 212–216); Biescas and Tuñón de Lara (1980: 106 and 142–148); García Fernández (1990) and Myro (1988: 476–485). Baena del Alcázar (1999: 385–399) quantifies and explains the control of state companies by board members of private companies.
16. Balfour (1994: 82–85) and Molinero and Ysàs (1998: 26–43) explain the conflicts of the 1950s in detail. The International Labour Organisation and Spain, in Mateos (1997). The commitment by the businessmen, in Bahamonde et al. (1988: 304–308).
17. See Amsdem's classic study (1974). Also, Fusi (1986: 162–163); the contributions in D. Ruiz (dir.) (1994: 30–33 and 66–68); Balfour (1994: 82–85); Molinero and Ysàs (1998: 90–94); Soto Carmona (1998: 217–218) and Powell (2001: 51–57).

18. The celebration of the 'twenty-five years of peace', explained by Aguilar Fernández (1996: 164–183). The features of class unionism are mentioned by Pérez Díaz (1987: 100.) Ruiz (dir.) is essential reading (1994). Also Molinero e Ysàs (1998: 154–164 and 185–201, and 62–67 for the analysis of the repressive nature of the dictatorship's labour laws). The same in Babiano Mora (1995: 47–69).

19. The basic features of that conflict are pointed out by Maravall (1970). Caballero follows them faithfully (1972: 711–757). A more up-to-date account in Molinero and Ysás (1998: 95–258). A good brief vision in Pérez Ledesma (1990: 232–239). For the first conflicts of the cycle, see also Mateos (1997: 66–80). Some interesting points also in Flaquer et al. (1990: 30–32). The authoritarianism of the regime as the final cause is emphasised by Fusi (1986: 160–163).

20. Balfour (1994), *passim* for Barcelona; for Madrid, Babiano Mora (1995: 240–340); and for Vizcaya, Molinero and Ysás (1998: 165–166).

21. The first idea is mentioned by both Fusi (1986: 162 and 169) and Payne (1987: 580). The second, Flaquer et al. (1990: 31–32). The third is Balfour's (1994: 85 and 247).

22. The salary costs, in Pérez Díaz (1987: 75); Malo de Molina (1988: 938–941) and López Novo (1995: 133–140). The lack of flexibility and the expensive Social Security, in Molinero and Ysàs (1991: 94–97 and 119–123) and Soto Carmona (1998: 204–205).

23. The following completely coincide on the assessment: Biescas and Tuñón de Lara (1980: 106–111 and 120–124); Payne (1987: 509–510); Pérez Ledesma (1990: 231); Tezanos (1990: 122–130); Alcaide Inchausti (1988); Comín (1996), 170; Fusi and Palafox (1997: 352); Soto Carmona (1998: 209–213); García Delgado and Jiménez (1999: 159); Molinero and Ysàs (1999: 191 and 198–201); Sartorius and Alfaya (1999: 96–97 and 101–103); and Powell (2001: 37–39).

24. The restoration of the old methods of social domination are collected in Pérez Ledesma (1990) and Biescas and Tuñón de Lara (1980: 132–133 and thereafter). The latter, however, recognise a certain autonomy relative to the State under Franco, as does Moya (1975: 51 and *passim*). Miralles (1999) revives the interpretation with the oligarchic restoration. An impression of the heterogeneous social support of the dictatorship, in Tamames (1979: 331–360). The characterisation of *clientelismo* (the practice of obtaining votes with promises of government posts, etc.) in Franco's politics, in Robles Egea (1996: 240–244) and Jerez Mir (1996: *passim*). The biographic traits of the regime's ministers, in Equipo Mundo (1970) and Miguel (1975).

25. Thousands of civil servants in intermediate or low-level posts, in Robles Egea (1996); capillarity between public function and political power, in Miguel (1975: 63–139 and 223–229), who also offers an excellent sociological portrait of 'the technocrats'. The reform of the Administration, in Crespo Montes (2000). Also, Moya (1984: 123–124 and 142). Figures, in Beltrán Villalba (1990). Bañón Martínez (1978: 175), discovers 47 percent of the members of the last elected Parliament (in 1971) were civil servants. More figure and percentages, in Baena del Alcázar (1999). The exaltation of 'the technical', in Fernández de la Mora (1977), who came to be the regime's intellectual genius.

26. Cercle de Economía (1983), Molinero and Ysàs (1991: 65–70, 97–100, 159–161 and 167–168); Cabana (1997: 149–164 and 193–195), and Riera (1998: 159–161 and 167–174).

27. Ribera, in Cabana (1997: 227–230) and Riera (1998: 409–411). Masó, in Cabana (2001: 400–401).

28. Delclaux, in Alonso Olea (2000); Oriol y Urquijo, in Cayón García and Muñoz Rubio (2000).

29. Aguirre, in González Urbaneja (2000). Huarte, in Ortiz-Villajos and Dantart Pitarch (2000); see also Paredes (1997). Gómez Franqueira, in Juana López (2000).
30. Banús, in Gutiérrez Molina (2000); Pepín Fernández y Areces, in Toboso Sánchez (2000a and 2000b); Botín, in Hoyo Aparicio (2000); Suñer, in Reig Armero (2000); and Valls-Taberner, in Serrano Alcaide (2000).
31. On Catalonia, in Marín i Corbera (2000a: 257–265 and 487–493), and Molinero and Ysàs (1991: 98). The ministers and *procuradores*, in the excellent classic by Miguel (1975: 73–79, 93–94 and 117–127). The Government of 1969, in Biescas and Tuñón de Lara (1980: 409–412). See also Equipo Mundo (1970). The tracking of the ministers in any biographical dictionary is very useful.
32. On the principle of loyalty, we were inspired by Jerez Mir (1996: 255–264 and 274). The rest is ours.
33. The generic conclusions and the image of powerlessness, in Linz and Miguel (1966), *passim*, extracted from a survey of 460 businessmen around Spain in 1959 and 1960. They also comment on the Basques. The power of big banking, in Tamames (1966), (1977) and (1979: 345–349); Moya (1975) and (1984), and Biescas and Tuñón de Lara (1980: 131–132 and 153–158), among other authors. The high price of security, in Pinilla de las Heras (1968: 154–163 and 233). The marginal role in the big political decisions, in Pérez Díaz (1987: 131–134, 138 and 151).
34. The limitation of the coordination of interests and the absence of a corporate chamber, in Linz (1988: 99–100, 110 and 112). Also, Moyano Estrada (1984: 118–119 and *passim*), which, like Ortiz Heras (1992), studies the dictatorship's corporatism in the agricultural sector. The weakness of unofficial associations, also in Molinero e Ysàs (1991). The listless life of the Chambers of Commerce, in Bahamonde et al. (1988), Díez Cano (1992) and Domínguez Jiménez (1994). The final paradoxes, in Pérez Díaz (1987: 103).
35. Recent examples of the literature of denouncement, in Ynfante (1998) and Sánchez Soler (2001).
36. See the revealing work by Lamo de Espinosa (1997).
37. The following coincide on the assessment: González González (1979: 321–323); Biescas and Tuñón de Lara (1980: 116–119); Tortella (1994: 288), and Fusi and Palafox (1997: 325ff.)
38. The four thousand jobs, in Payne (1987: 491). The 'pacted' nationalisations, in García Fernández (1990); Tezanos (1990: 133–134) and Segura (1988: 840–841). On Gas Natural, see Cabana (1997: 211 and 230–236).
39. Privileged circles, in Fusi and Palafox (1997: 365–367). The rest, in Segura (1999).
40. Balfour (1994: 62); Riera (1998: 293–298 and *passim*); Molinero e Ysàs (1999: 204–205); Sartorius and Alfaya (1999: 370–372); Marín i Corbera (2000a: 489 and *passim*) and (2000b); Cabana (2001: 261–263).
41. Equipo Mundo (1970); de Miguel (1975) and Baena del Alcázar (1999). Tamames (1977: 218–228 and 235–259) compiles a list of about three hundred board members of public and private firms and specifies their official posts. It includes many former ministers, *procuradores*, members of the military, undersecretaries, mayors, civil governors. Another useful appendix with an account of political figures on boards of directors, in this case on companies with foreign capital, in Muñoz et al. (1978b: 361–374).
42. This interpretation is laid out in similar terms in Moya (1984: 134–142); Pérez Vilariño and Schoenherr (1990: 453–455); Tusell (1993: 232–234, 255–264, 269–274 and

281–282), and Powell (2001: 36). For Maeztu, see González Cuevas (1998: 65–77). Even the harshest critic of Opus Dei recognises that a basic goal of its followers was the modernisation of the State for the benefit of the economy: Ynfante (1996: 235 and *passim.*)

43. Biographical snippets of the Opus Dei ministers in Equipo Mundo (1970). For López Rodó, see his own works from (1979) and (1990) and Cabana (2001: 319–321). For Navarro Rubio, see Fernández Clemente (1997). Opus Dei's networks in the State apparatus, in Ynfante (1996: 229–250 and *passim*). The behind-the-scenes role of Sardá and the other technicians, in Martín Aceña (2000: 137–172).

44. Miguel (1975: 223) and Linz (1988: 101), who theorises about the interest group. For the rest, see Ynfante (1996: 255–299 and *passim.*)

45. The best analyses of the case, in Payne (1987: 566–570) and Jiménez (2000). The rumour, in Ynfante (1996: 415–416).

46. The political dimension of the crisis is highlighted in Tusell (1993: 344–364). The political perspective of one of those affected – Navarro Rubio – in Fernández Clemente (1997: 78–82).

47. The bureaucratic incompetence, in Tortella (1994: 287–289), who in his assessment of the end of *desarrollismo* and its causes coincides with González González (1979: 298–300 and 320–346) and Fuentes Quintana (1988: 1–24 and 61–62).

48. Biescas and Tuñón de Lara (1980: 105–106); Payne (1987: 507–509); Malo de Molina (1988: 927–929); Ruesga Benito (1995: 383–384); Tedde (1996: 48–49); Comín (1996b: 178–184); Fusi and Palafox (1997: 355 and 363); García Delgado and Jiménez (1999: 163–165).

49. The 1962 reform, in Pérez de Armiñán (1970) and Martín Aceña (2000: 164–172). On Urquijo and Lladó, see Torres Villanueva (2000c). On Villalonga, see Tortella (2000c), who, in (1994: 347–348), pointed out that banking could not be viewed as a united organisation in the dictatorship nor could its confrontations with the regime be ignored.

50. An excellent analysis of those turbulent years, up to 1977, in Powell (2001: 17–192); the conflicts and the erosion of the regime, in Fusi (1986: 161 and 169).

51. Tamames (1978: 473–479); Pérez Díaz (1987: 75 and 83); Rojo (1987); Fuentes Quintana (1988: 24–35); Comín (1996b: 179–186); Barciela et al. (1996: 94–95); Powell (2001: 26–27).

52. Villa and Palomeque (1977: 285–293); Pérez Ledesma (1990: 237 and 242–243); Babiano Mora (1995: 293–340); and Molinero and Ysás (1998: 251–258), who offers the most complete picture.

53. For Barcelona, Balfour (1994: 159–249).

54. The 'businessman-Franco supporter' equation, in Molinero and Ysàs (1991: 123–126 and 131). The rest is ours.

55. We already advanced some of these ideas in Cabrera and Rey Reguillo (1988) and (2001). The demonisation, also in Lamo de Espinosa (1997: 279–281), where the last quotation comes from.

56. The lack of political protagonism, in Linz (1988: 103 and 107), and Pérez Díaz (1987: 82–84 and 134–135), who also speaks about labour costs, restrictions and vulnerability. For the rest, we are inspired by Vidal-Folch (1990); Molinero and Ysàs (1991: 133–141 and 151–152); Riera (1998: 162–165), who quotes the businessman supporting the overthrow; and Sartorius and Alfaya (1999: 223–229), who cite the information on the National Council of Businessmen.

Chapter 5
The Powers of Democracy, 1977–2000

A Central Employers' Organisation

'My personal relationship with businessmen had not been good since 1976', Leopoldo Calvo Sotelo wrote in his memoirs. 'I undoubtedly share some of the blame because I forgot that nobody is a prophet in his own land, and my land had been private enterprise for a quarter of a century, from 1950 to 1975; and when the dialogue with those who had been my colleagues began to be a difficult dialogue between deaf people, I lost my patience more than once. The newly-formed CEOE (Spanish Confederation of Business Organisations) believed that it had to intervene against the Government of the UCD'. Leopoldo Calvo Sotelo was José Calvo Sotelo's nephew. José Calvo Sotelo was Treasury Minister with General Primo de Rivera in the 1920s and leader of the monarchists during the Republic. Forty years later, his nephew Leopoldo was a distinguished member of the *Unión de Centro Democrático* (Union of Democratic Centre), the party led by Adolfo Suárez and the winner of the first two elections in the democracy. He was an MP and the Minister of Trade first, then Minister of Public Works and Minister of Relations with the European Community. He was vice president for Economic Affairs in Suárez's last Government in 1980, and President of the Government after Suárez resigned in 1981. He was a civil engineer, had worked his whole life in private business, within the sphere of the Hispano Americano and Urquijo banks, and became CEO of Unión Explosivos Río Tinto. But he had reasons to believe what he said about businessmen: the president of the CEOE, Carlos Ferrer Salat, affirmed at the time that they did not feel represented by any political party, and that they felt 'politically orphaned'. In his opinion, Spain's problem was that everybody wanted to be a left winger, and those who were further to the right called themselves centrists. In a country where half of the people were Marxists and the other half Social Democrats, this could not work. From the point of view of what some called the 'economic right', the party in government, the UCD, was practicing left-wing politics with votes from the right.[1]

Relations between businessmen and politicians in the first democratic governments, UCD administrations, were not easy, because the circumstances in which they developed were not easy, either. The delicate process that was the transition to democracy began in a context of deep economic crisis and strong social and labour unrest accompanied by dramatic violence and terrorism that in some cases directly affected entrepreneurs. The political problems were so great that economic issues seemed to be relegated to second place, as had occurred in the final years of the dictatorship. The dismissal of Carlos Arias Navarro and the appointment of Adolfo Suárez as President of the Government unblocked the situation and allowed the approval – first by Franco's Parliaments and then in a referendum – of the Law for Political Reform. Only after the first general election in June 1977 and the formation of the second Government with Suárez as President did economic decisions become urgent. The newly appointed Minister of Economy and second vice-president of the Government, Enrique Fuentes Quintana, immediately proceeded to devaluate the peseta and announced an urgent economic plan to try to contain inflation through wage freezes – which achieved only partial success – and a restrictive monetary policy in exchange for the promise of tax reform and unemployment benefits. The project was not well received in trade union and business circles, which were then involved in complicated processes of reorganisation. As such, the commitment became political, and the parties ended up signing the Moncloa Accords on 8 October 1977. Thanks mostly to the monetary policy, they managed to reduce inflation, which had exceeded 25 percent, to 18 percent in February 1978. Business profits also recovered to some degree, but the biggest achievement of the Accords was the creation of a political climate favourable to discussion and consensus over the new Constitution, which was approved in a referendum by an overwhelming majority at the beginning of December.[2]

The vice-president Fuentes Quintana had resigned months before, in February. The programme of reforms that should have accompanied the economic plan's adjustment measures, or at least their effective implementation, stagnated in light of the second energy crisis, which occurred in 1979 when Spain was in a difficult situation. While the big industrial countries had reduced energy demand, in Spain it had increased 10 percent. The new increase in the price of oil sank all hopes of a recovery: the Spanish economy did not grow even 1 percent in 1979, something that had not happened in twenty years. The beginning of the 1980s was dramatic. Neither the inflation rate nor the foreign debt were reduced, while labour costs continued to grow and businessmen resorted to drastic staff readjustments, raising the unemployment rate to 16.6 percent. The increase in public spending precipitated the public deficit, although in part it mitigated the noticeable social effects of the crisis and permitted the Moncloa Accords to be fulfilled; in other words, it kept the lines of dialogue open. From a social and political standpoint, opting for a gradual digestion of increased energy prices was the right move, but it had serious economic consequences.[3]

The future was unpredictable for businessmen, who were dealing with the uncertainties of the political process, the economic crisis and social unrest, and who had no clearly designated interlocutors or consolidated organisations to rely on.

The resulting consolidation of democracy and the market economy seems nearly inevitable to us today, but it was not back then. The political class that would lead the way in the process hardly excelled, and the parties began to discover the limits of their influence on society. The inclination of the majority to vote towards the centre of the political spectrum was not a sufficient guarantee. The maturation and moderation of Spanish society, the surmounting of enormous inequalities, deeply entrenched backwardness and revolutionary proposals reminiscent of the 1930s were things that time and analysts would prove. But, for the moment, there were proposals to nationalise and socialise – or so it seemed to a lot of businessmen – in the programmes of the parties that won the most votes in the first elections: the Socialist Party (118 seats in 1977 and 121 in 1979), and the UCD (165 seats in 1977 and 168 in 1979). The right was represented first by the Popular Alliance and then by Fraga Iribarne's Democratic Coalition, which had more businessmen on their tickets than other parties. Conservative party seats dropped from a mere sixteen in 1977 to nine two years later. The politics of consensus disappeared with the second general elections in 1979. The Socialist Party had to convene an extraordinary session of Congress explicitly to renounce Marxism in the face of its most critical sectors, and in the spring of 1980, it promptly proposed a vote of no confidence against the Government of the UCD. There were still disputes over *reform* versus *rupture*. Incorporation into the North Atlantic Treaty Organisation (NATO) was the source of bitter confrontation, and nobody could guess how the so-called *factual powers* – undoubtedly the Army and the Catholic Church; for some it also meant the economic forces – would play out. The Constitution had given symbolic support to the market economy, but the horizon was not very comforting for those who had lived snugly under the protection of the dictatorship. Now it was not only a matter of confronting the economic crisis and social unrest, but also of getting used to new ways of dealing with political power, public opinion and trade unions. Many businessmen bore the stigma of their supposed connivance with the dictatorship, doubts about their honesty and morality, and a reputation for being exploiters, or hardly modern and competitive.[4]

It has been said that the political class of the transition was a class 'distant from businessmen', a class over which businessmen had no control. Entrepreneurs had serious doubts about, if not a horrible opinion of, its competence, and these doubts included civil servants. The economic ministers of the UCD were liberal professionals, in many cases civil servants in the upper echelons of the Administration, some of whom had been in international organisations and had the support of these organisations in a long battle to liberalise the Spanish economy. They had perhaps coincided in departments of studies in public entities like the Bank of Spain or the INI, or in private entities, or some had been advisers or board members of banks or companies, but they were not businessmen. They all agreed on the need to modernise and 'Europeanise' (translator's quotation marks) the Spanish economy, and they agreed on the assessment of the problems, but they did not always reach a consensus on proposals for specific solutions. This was because very different political tendencies had come to merge in the UCD, from liberals and Christian

Democrats to Social Democrats. The economic situation, the delicate balance of the transition process, and the urgency to make decisions about many other issues hindered them in reaching agreements and adopting measures, and the disintegrative factions within the party itself effectively contributed to weakening its positions. It is easy to understand why entrepreneurs viewed the UCD ministers with reluctance, as out-of-touch individuals who dictated economic policy and designed great reforms without taking into account the uncertainties or difficulties of the majority.[5]

Businessmen had different attitudes about the political process. There was a very numerous sector that was deeply 'disconcerted'. Other groups opted to anticipate the changes and decided to assume, in different projects, the task of providing the business class with an organisational and institutional framework in accordance with the new situation. In November 1976, a group of fifty important businessmen decided to create the *Circulo de Empresarios* (Entrepreneurs' Association), which had several goals: counterbalance the negative image of the business class; promote the role companies had to develop in a society based on a market economy as the primary mover of socio-economic progress; and make the public aware of the role of businessmen in a free and democratic society. They did not want to be just one more employers' organisation or pressure group. They were individuals dedicated to the defense of 'ideas' which they intended to pass on to decision-making bodies – governments, parties, the Administration – and to public opinion in general. The association's principal catalyst was José María López de Letona, who came from the construction industry. He had been Minister of Industry from 1969 to 1973. When Franco died, he was considered a possible candidate for President of the Government. He did not get that post, but he was appointed governor of the Bank of Spain in August 1976. His long business and political career had allowed him to make numerous contacts, professional as well as personal, that made it easy for him to promote the movement of the business class around him. The Círculo de Empresarios met with the presidents and directors of some of the most important firms in the country, and the studies, publications and debates held at its headquarters also involved government officials and ministers. Some of the ministers in Adolfo Suárez's government might have liked López de Letona to head the great 'central employers' organisation' that was being planned, but in the end, another group was established for this role.[6]

There was a rapid but difficult mobilisation and reorganisation of business associations that came from different origins. One of the first initiatives came from the vestiges of vertical unionism, from which a Spanish General Confederation of Businessmen emerged. There was also a Spanish Business Confederation led by Agustín Rodríguez Sahagún, who promoted the creation of the Spanish Confederation of Small and Medium Businesses (CEPYME). Traditional organisations like the Catalan *Fomento del Trabajo* were also revitalised. The directors of *Fomento* were joined in this association by others from the Barcelona Chamber of Commerce and Industry and the Vertical Syndicate. On 9 October 1976, at the Palace of Congresses in Barcelona, an act to assert the business movement was held. This function inaugurated a series of public events which ended with a mass assembly at the Blaugrana Palace a year later. There, Carlos Ferrer Salat, who was the leader of the Catalan movement and also of the incipient national organisation, synthesised the fears of the business class when he said, 'Spain, business and our individual futures are at stake'. It was a firebrand speech, easy to digest for businessmen in trouble and fearful of the future. On 22 September 1977, a first general assembly was held in Madrid. The Confederacion Española de Organizaciones Empresariales (CEOE) was born and Ferrer Salat was elected its first president.[7]

'Are you a politician or a businessman?' Ferrer Salat was asked in an interview five years later. 'I am above all a businessman', he replied. However, the presidency of the CEOE obliged him to spend a lot of his time dialoguing with the Government and with other institutional officials. As in 1931, he said, businessmen in 1975 had to confront a double crisis, economic and political, and all the uncertainty and distrust surrounding the prospects for business it implied. The previous regime had accustomed businessmen to paternalism, and now they had to start from scratch to consolidate their presence, build up influence and increase their representation. Indeed, the CEOE launched a mobilisation campaign with mass concentrations like the one which gathered 13,000 businessmen in the Sports Palace of Madrid on 5 February 1978, under the slogans of 'We react' and 'Unity, free enterprise and prosperity'. The CEOE worked very hard to establish itself as the 'central employers' organisation' and earn a virtual monopoly of employer representation. Unlike organisations in other European countries, it eventually incorporated everybody: farmers, industrialists, builders and service providers, banking employers (the Spanish Banking Association) and small and medium business owners (the CEPYME). The obstacles posed by the great mix of sectorial and regional interests along with the gradual adaptation to the development of the autonomous regions were overcome by an organisational structure that was not very bureaucratic, and by great flexibility in incorporating individuals or preexisting associations. However, the assembly of all these pieces and the disparity of attitudes among the associates still caused tensions, as the press revealed in its coverage of the CEOE's presidential elections in September 1978. Ferrer Salat was re-elected after laborious negotiations over the composition of a new management.[8]

In its initial years, the CEOE functioned more as an intermediary in trade union negotiations than as a lobby to pressure the government or as an entity capable of offering services to its members. The dismantling of Franco's Vertical Syndicate and its replacement with a new framework for labour negotiations would have been an important issue in any case, but it became a priority in the context of the economic crisis, worker protest and the reorganisational process of the trade unions themselves. The CEOE was just becoming established when the Moncloa Accords were signed. The Accords, as we know, were negotiated and approved by the political parties at the request of the Government. One of the main undertakings of the CEOE was to guarantee businessmen and workers the power to dialogue and make pacts without political interference. The business class was especially concerned about the *Comisiones Obreras* (Workers' Commissions, hereafter CCOO), which were considered a political instrument for a Communist Party that had not done as well as expected in the elections, but which made up for that shortcoming with the strength of its trade union. Businessmen ended up commiting to a policy of dialogue and at the same time tried to break the power of the Commissions in benefit of the socialist union, the General Union of Workers (UGT), taking advantage of and even stoking the competition between both organisations. The strategy was successful and, at the beginning of the 1980s, the UGT overtook CCOO in the union elections. Labour unrest, which had peaked in 1979, decreased drastically as of that moment. That year, employers and the UGT signed the *Acuerdo Marco Interconfederal* (a labour agreement) and renewed the pact the following year. In 1982, the CCOO decided to participate in the *Acuerdo Nacional de Empleo* (another labour agreement), although two years later, they refused to sign it. The policy of dialogue led to a degree of relative social peace, but had little effect on wage freezes, as wages were fixed for all those years according to past inflation and not future inflation. However, businessmen and workers were able to negotiate freely, relegating government intervention to an inferior role. On the other hand, the generalisation of some collective bargaining at such a high level prevented the rise or participation of any other employers' or workers' organisation. It also kept union membership at constantly low levels, with the two largest unions enjoying a much greater representation than what their actual membership reflected. The actions of subsequent governments helped strengthen the centralisation of business organisations. This was an issue that would later pose problems, because the negotiation of big agreements limited the role of simple companies and the flexibility of the labour market. Businessmen were pleased that social peace had been achieved, although they did not stop complaining about the inflexibilities of the labour market, a holdover mainly from the dictatorship, but reinforced by the success of corporate practices businessmen themselves supported.[9]

The CEOE concentrated its initial efforts on labour policy, functioning above all like an employers' organisation. The attention given to internal company problems was very little in comparison. The difficulties of businessmen seemed to come only from outside. The wage freeze was good news for businessmen, but it was also necessary to reduce Social Security costs and company taxes, and moderate interest rates. The competitivity of companies seemed to depend on these factors alone, as if entrepreneurs were not responsible for improving their businesses. As a result, the declarations of company directors were, in the opinion of the politicians, almost always 'catastrophic' and critical of Government decisions issued without specific plausible proposals or programmes. These were the same directors that in public demanded more economic freedom and limits on public spending, only to turn around and privately request intervention and protection from the State. And, of course, they never recognised the political difficulties posed by the transition to democracy or its social costs. The CEOE achieved genuine public recognition, but it could not influence decisions about economic policy. The result was its conversion into a political actor in competition with the party in government, the UCD, and the open resistance of Adolfo Suárez to accept its suggestions. However, in February 1978, Suárez called on Agustín Rodríguez Sahagún, one of the vice-presidents of the CEOE, to head the Ministry of Trade and Industry.[10]

The role of the CEOE owed much to the personality of its president. The image of Carlos Ferrer Salat was that of a young businessman who was dynamic, modern, athletic and worldy. He especially gave the impression that he had no ties to the Franco dictatorship, rather just the contrary. Ferrer Salat came from a Catalan family linked to the pharmaceutical industry since the nineteenth century. He earned a degree in Chemical Engineering from the Chemistry Institute of Sarriá. He also had degrees in Economics and Philosophy and Letters. At a very young age, he established Ferrer Labouratories in 1953. He worked hard to advance them and expand them into the international market. At the same time, he created the *Círculo de Economía* (Society of Economy) in Barcelona in 1958 with a group of friends – the 'four musketeers', they were called. The *Círculo de Economía* was an initiative they hoped would serve as a meeting point for businessmen, academics, economists and technicians from the Administration. It was tolerated by the regime although not legalised until 1968. The inaugural conference was given by the historian Jaume Vicens Vives, who convened the attendants to repeat the challenge of the 'nineteenth century captains of industry'. It was no accident that the beginning of the *Círculo* coincided with the atmosphere of liberalisation derived from the Stabilisation Plan in 1959. Although it had an important presence in companies, the *Círculo de Economía* was never an employers' organisation, but rather a space for debate. Carlos Ferrer Salat was its first president and one of its most active members afterwards. The concern he showed from so early on about the political action of businessmen later led him to posts of responsibility in the Barcelona Chamber of Industry, which merged with the Chamber of Commerce in the late 1970s. From there, he made the leap to the presidency of the *Fomento del Trabajo Nacional* in the mid-1970s and eventually to the presidency of the CEOE.[11]

Ferrer Salat participated in the creation of the *Centre Català*, a liberal reformist group whose members included important figures from the Catalan political and business circles, and which ran in the 1977 elections with Christian Democrats. They won two seats in Parliament. Although Ferrer Salat quit that political membership when he was appointed president of the CEOE, he did not quit his public calling. Before the general elections of 1979, he sent a letter to all businessmen, calling on them to join forces to demand of the Government an economic programme that defended 'the principle of free enterprise', and afterwards sent the new government a report on the economic situation. The UCD's new victory was, undoubtedly, an unhappy surprise for the CEOE. Perhaps their victory explains why the campaign of the *Fomento del Trabajo Nacional* was much more dynamic and clearly directed in Catalonia's first regional elections in 1980, because previous polls had predicted a 'Marxist majority' was likely. Catalan employers used all their resources, economic and human, to support an 'ideological rearmament' which would counterbalance Catalonia's image as a region of leftists with the image of Catalonia as a 'country of owners'. Their effort undoubtedly contributed to the victory of the conservative Catalan party *Convergencia i Unio* and its president, Jordi Pujol. In view of the success, a delegation of Catalan employers later transferred to Galicia to apply the same formula in the elections, which made the conservative candidate the first president of the *Xunta* (Galicia's regional government). The same was tried in the first Andalusian elections, in May 1982, although here the victory went to the socialists. The campaign for these elections was so intense that the Electoral Commission and later the Supreme Court had to intervene.[12]

The CEOE and Ferrer Salat himself played an important role in the UCD's definitive crisis after Suárez's unexpected resignation. His successor, Calvo Sotelo, thought that he had good relations with businessmen while he was the Government's vice-president of Economic Affairs with Suárez. However, on 18 February 1981, when he addressed the Chamber of Deputies at the session of investiture as President of the Government, the daily newspapers issued one of the most critical press releases in the history of the CEOE. Businessmen blamed politicians for not having been able to create a climate of trust necessary for good political and economic development and demanded them to stop hiding behind the problems of the transition, assuming the confusion that had accompanied it was over. Each political force had to play the role that corresponded to it: the new Government had to orient 'all' its actions to stimulating savings and private investment. If it did not reduce the deficit and taxes, facilitate loans, make hiring and firing more flexible, and diminish companies' social expenses, it could not continue to count on the cooperation of the CEOE, 'which [this body] had so generously and responsibly offered' up to then.[13]

It was not the best moment to assume the transition was over. In the second round of Calvo Sotelo's investiture as president of the government, there was an attempted military coup. Colonel Tejero entered the Parliament and tried unsuccessfully to take the MPs hostage and overthrow the government. On the morning of 24 February 1981, with the Parliament still held by the insurgents, Carlos Ferrer Salat made a declaration thanking the King for intervening. The same day, the CEOE published a statement proclaiming its support of the King and the Constitution, but Calvo Sotelo's new government was received by the *Fomento del Trabajo Nacional* with a manifesto titled, 'An Atypical Government for an Atypical Democracy', which collected the growing complaints about 'professional politicians'. In September, upon being re-elected president of the CEOE, Carlos Ferrer Salat declared that he would collaborate only with those political organisations that defended free enterprise within a system of peaceful coexistence. A few days later, the CEOE withdrew from the watchdog committee for the *Acuerdo Nacional de Empleo* signed some months earlier with the trade unions, denouncing the existence of a supposed secret pact between the Government and workers' organisations. The CEOE did not sink the UCD, but it intended to break the party in power and attract more moderates to the formation of a big right wing. Ferrer Salat was tempted to play a role in that alternative, which in the end did not work out in practice.[14]

In the general elections of 1982, with the UCD shattered, the CEOE did not support one particular party, but recommended 'coherence and reflection'. The right-wing party, Popular Alliance, multiplied its parliamentary representation by twelve and collected 46.5 percent of businessmen's votes, according to survey data. Twelve percent remained faithful to the centre, now divided between the remnants of the UCD and the Democratic Social Centre. Nationalists won a significant share of the business vote with 27 percent: 18 percent to Catalan Convergence and Union and 9 percent to the Basque Nationalist Party. The overwhelming victory in those elections went to the socialists: ten million votes with a very high participation in the elections, which enabled them to win twenty-six more seats than required for an absolute majority in the Chamber of Deputies. In the elections of 1979, 44 percent of the same businessmen polled had voted for the UCD and around 25 percent for the Popular Alliance; 20 percent voted for nationalist parties and 4.4 percent for the socialists. Businessmen had expected the centrist governments to perform better – to Calvo Sotelo's regret; they feared the worst from a socialist government but then gave it a passing mark. Although the socialists' grade was worse, the improvement with respect to what they had feared left businessmen with a feeling of gratitude towards the Partido Socialista Obrero Español (PSOE) and one of hostility towards the UCD. The end of the economic crisis and the subsequent euphoria did all the rest.[15]

Industrial Crisis and Reconversion

When the socialists came to power in 1982, the Spanish economy was still suffering the effects of the second energy crisis of 1979. Inflation had not been stopped, the public deficit had shot up, and the figures on and concentration of unemployment evidenced the depth of what was, evidently, an industrial crisis, or rather, a crisis of *deindustrialisation*. As a consequence of the destruction of many firms and the precarious situation they had endured, businessmen were convinced that this was not just a normal crisis and that the future would bring radical changes to the makeup of the Spanish business world. Some speculated that that future would favour small and medium businesses that could improve technological innovation and increase their productivity, adapting to new markets. It was more than a crisis; it was a mutation, as the president of the CEOE said, and when it was over – and nobody knew when that time would come – nothing would ever be like it had been. Many sectors, especially industrial sectors, could not be competitive again, but in public, businessmen attributed the crisis to the increase of costs, particularly labour costs, and to the priority given to political issues. Even when speaking of the resistance to technological innovation, Ferrer Salat put only part of the blame on businessmen and the rest on the Government and the trade unions. The last UCD governments had tried to confront the crisis. Calvo Sotelo's Government Economic Programme in 1981 and other sectorial measures were aimed at industrial reconversion and increased competitiveness, but these measures were insufficient, and it was not the best time politically to implement them.[16]

The crisis did not affect all industries the same, nor could all industries react the same. The so-called branches of weak demand (iron and steel, non-ferrous metals, shipbuilding, metallic products, non-metallic mineral products, wood, textiles, leather, etc.) and those of strong demand (aircraft, office machinery and electric material, precision instruments, etc.) were affected most by the shrinking of the domestic market. The branches of weak-demand had the most trouble adapting to the search for foreign markets as a safety valve. The crisis was concentrated in the regions with the most powerful industrial sectors: the Basque Country and Asturias, and, to a lesser degree because of their greater industrial diversification, Catalonia, Madrid and Valencia. Although the crisis affected all Spanish regions, its intensity varied and eventually changed the traditional map of industrial centres. The most dynamic regions now were the Mediterranean coast, the Ebro valley, Madrid and the two archipelagoes, while the entire Cantabrian coast, from El Ferrol to Irún, was clearly in decline. New industrial investments were still highly concentrated in Madrid and Barcelona, but bypassed areas of old industrialisation for new enclaves around the big capitals, and small and medium industries in smaller cities or rural areas. Asturias and Cantabria had been slipping in terms of family income and per capita income since before the crisis, but Vizcaya and Guipúzcoa held the two highest positions until 1975. In per capita terms, Vizcaya fell from second to sixteenth in production and from first to fourteenth in income from 1975 to 1985; over the same period, Guipúzcoa dropped from first to seventh and from third to eleventh, respectively. In disposable family income, Vizcaya fell from third to twenty-first place, and Guipúzcoa from first to fourteenth. From 1979 to 1985, annual growth rates fell to 1.1 percent, below the national average of 2.7 percent, while unemployment rose from 2.4 percent in 1975 to 23.5 percent in 1986. The disappearance of Altos Hornos de Vizcaya and the shipbuilding company Euskalduna, as well as the closing of other small shipyards and industrial companies from the region of the Nervión estuary, were the most telling signs of how bad the crisis in Vizcaya was. The oligopolised, protected structure in which the iron and steel industry had developed to that point had been reflected in the close ties between the leading private company in the sector, Altos Hornos de Vizcaya, and the INI. Just before the crisis, many were still dreaming of a 'third industrialisation' supported by the Basque Country-Ebro Valley-Catalonia-Valencia axis, which absorbed many resources.[17]

When the crisis hit, the Basque Country suffered another drain: the 'años de plomo' (years of intense terrorism by Euskadi Ta Askatasuna, the Basque separatist group, hereafter ETA). Many businessmen and professionals were subject to threats, extortion, the demand for a 'revolutionary tax', kidnapping and also murder. In January 1973, the businessman Felipe Huarte Beaumont, son of the builder Félix Huarte, had been kidnapped. On 7 July 1976, the businessman Ángel Berazadi was murdered. The letter that ETA had sent a year earlier to fifty businessmen was then publicised: 'The development of the struggle for national and social liberation that our people are carrying out requires an increasingly greater availability of material resources. The policy applied up to now by our organisation has been to recover, by way of expropriations, part of the capital gain that the capitalist class – and therefore you, as an important member of that class – is stealing from Basque workers. ETA wanted them to pay two million pesetas (1976 value), a smaller quantity, it was said, than the sum of taxes the businessmen paid the Spanish government, the oppressor of the Basque people.

On 20 May 1977, four individuals kidnapped Javier de Ybarra y Bergé from his home. They demanded a ransom of one thousand million pesetas, probably convinced it would be easy to get, given that Javier Ybarra belonged to the family that controlled the board of the Bank of Vizcaya. But there were problems getting the ransom. The family went to France, where these payments were negotiated. The final quantity was much smaller. ETA insisted and the family resisted. On 22 June 1977, Javier Ybarra was found dead with a shot in the back of his neck. For some, this was the beginning of the end for the big families of Neguri (a wealthy neighbourhood in Vizcaya). These families abandoned their industries and invested their money in banks. In 1980, Juan Alcorta, president of the firms Koipe and Savin, published a letter confronting ETA. Nothing happened, and he retired two years later in a multitudinous ceremony attended by several representatives of the business community, members of the government, the *lehendakari* (president of the Basque regional government), Garaikoetxea, and the secretary of the Basque socialists, Txiki Benegas. But two years later, ETA agents set fire to the Koipe bottling warehouse in Martutene, putting the company in dire straits. According to an opinion survey carried out by the Association of Basque Businessmen in 1984, 64 percent of those interviewed said they were persecuted, 74 percent felt threatened and 53 percent coerced. José María Vizcaíno, the president of the Association, regretted that it took so long to conclude it was bad to pay and to be convinced that not paying did not make one less *abertzale* (patriotic). In those years, being a businessman in the Basque Country was doubly penalised, and there was a great scattering of entrepreneurs and qualified professionals who moved to other parts of the country, taking their businesses with them. On one bank of the estuary, the factories were closed; on the opposite bank, the houses of the important families were abandoned. With the *Concierto Económico* (Basque tax system) reinstated, over the following years the Basque and central Governments negotiated reconversion and modernisation plans which contained the region's economic woes. In the latter half of the 1980s, industrial employment was maintained because new jobs in small and medium firms compensated for those lost in the big companies. The new and surviving firms produced goods similar to those from before, but on a different scale, with more modern technology and increased productivity. Furthermore, they managed to establish a wide range of export markets. As of 1990, the exodus of businessmen from the Basque Country stopped. Many of those who stayed decided to pay their 'taxes' and shut up.[18]

But let us back up. When the socialists came to power in 1982, they took the trouble to meet with entrepreneurs, bankers, the presidents of big banks, and the CEOE. Not only did they want to assure them of their intentions to dispel any fears of nationalisation or State intervention, they also sought their approval of the policy they planned to implement to keep the crisis in check. The President of the Government, Felipe González, and the Minister of Finance, Miguel Boyer, were the intermediaries. The selection of the economic ministers by Felipe González was carefully planned. Boyer, the son of an exile, had degrees in physics, economics and business. He had worked in the Departments of Studies of the Bank of Spain and the INI. He had been the director of strategical planning at Explosivos Riotinto and also the National Institute of Hydrocarbons. He had known Felipe González since the late 1960s. The radical amendment of the economic strategy approved by the first legal congress of the PSOE in 1976 led him to break with them and join the more liberal

Social Democratic Party. However, he always remained close to Felipe González, who he advised on economic matters, while being opposed by the more radical socialist, Alfonso Guerra. But González had put all his trust in him, and fully agreed with his goals. On 29 December 1982, when he was Minister of Finance, Boyer published a Royal Decree of urgent measures regarding budgetary, financial and lending issues. The passivity towards the economic situation had come to an end. Their absolute majority permitted the socialists to do what the UCD had been unable to do. As Boyer explained before the Chamber of Deputies a month later, his goal was to reestablish macroeconomic balances. Spain had been living beyond its means and the big problems had been company earnings and employment. It was necessary to 'tighten the belt': devaluate the peseta – done on 5 December – increase fiscal pressure through the definitive implementation of tax reform, and toughen monetary policy by raising interest rates and restricting loans, with the aim of halting the growth of domestic demand and the public deficit. Moreover, the minister favoured the gradual increase of oil prices, although this would make it difficult to fight inflation. In short, it was a policy of drastic measures, and at the same time, of structural reforms. Not everyone within the Socialist Party shared the same opinions, and the debate over the budget raised the protest of those who expected an economic reactivation through public spending and openly criticised the restrictive monetary policy that was, in their opinion, more typical of the right. Felipe González tried to settle the internal controversy once and for all, but his suggestion of appointing Miguel Boyer as vice-president of the Government produced such an angry reaction from Alfonso Guerra that Boyer resigned and left the Government for good in 1985.[19]

The atmosphere of the country changed radically at this point. The second half of the decade was wonderful. The economic crisis ended and a cycle of considerable growth began, in part thanks to the previous adjustments and overhaul, and also because of the positive situation abroad and Spain's definitive entry into the European Economic Union, although the fall of oil prices was the main reason for the bonanza. Fears of new competition arisen from the incorporation into Europe quickly disappeared, although many businessmen were already financially ruined. The structural changes in the industrial sector had reduced its influence with respect to the entire economy. The energy sector had considerably more influence, to the detriment of manufacturers. There was also a reorientation towards higher-technology production, although in this aspect, Spanish industry still lagged well behind the rest of Europe. The incorporation into Europe and the subsequent increase in foreign contacts brought about a significant increase in imports and the loss of the traditional control of the domestic market by Spanish industry. Afterwards, although it took time, Spanish exports also increased. In short, the Spanish industrial supply became more diverse and modern, the presence of multinational firms in the most dynamic branches increased, and industrial firms backed with Spanish capital expanded abroad. However, the greatest expansion occurred in the service sector and banking. Foreigners jostled to sell their products in Spain and make large investments. The stability of the peseta, high interest rates and increased profitability obtained from these investments opened the door to a torrent of foreign currencies and increased the presence of foreign financial institutions. In the heat of the growth and with the abundance of money, being a businessman became fashionable for almost the first time in Spain. It is still shocking that the figure of the businessman as a creator of wealth was rehabilitated and admired, and that young people took an interest in the vocation, under a socialist government. Not everyone was pleased with the changes. As the new CEOE president José María Cuevas complained, those pendular movements, from loathing to adoration of money, could end up destroying the image of the businessman by confusing 'making money' with 'doing business'. One thing was being a businessman; another, very different thing was doing business and making money by 'trafficking' or profiting from privileged information. It was then that the Minister of Finance, Carlos Solchaga, made a supposed appeal to enrichment, adding his two cents to what was called the '*cultura del pelotazo*' (speculative practices). 'The phrase will accompany me to the grave', he lamented later in an interview. He uttered it in a meeting with members of the *Asociación para el Progreso de la Dirección* (Association for the Progress of Management). He had wanted to convince them that the economic crisis had truly passed, and that Spain had become a focus of investment which could earn more money in less time than in other countries.[20]

Carlos Solchaga was the other socialist who played a leading role in the big changes that occurred in the Spanish economy between 1982 and 1992. He had worked as an economist for the Bank of Spain, the INI and the Bank of Vizcaya in their respective Departments of Studies. His political calling from early on led him to join the PSOE in 1974 and its executive committee in 1978. He was a minister and representative of the Basque Government in 1980, and the Minister of Industry and Energy in the first socialist Government. In the early stages of his term in office, he had to confront the industrial crisis and the public sector's role in view of the crisis. As we have seen, at the end of the 1970s, the INI group constituted the country's main industrial corporation and one of the biggest in Europe, which might have made it a possible mechanism to combat the crisis. Back when the UCD was in power, the directors of the Institute firmly believed public industrial policy had to be profitable. However, there was little they could do. The INI had specialised in 'mature, weak-demand' sectors. Moreover, it had to 'help' different companies from which private capital was 'withdrawn'. Two such firms were Altos Hornos de Vizcaya and Altos Hornos del Mediterráneo, the most important private iron and steel companies. After the second oil crisis, the National Institute of Hydrocarbons (INH) split from the INI. All the energy companies were eventually grouped under the INH, and almost all of them were profitable. As such, the INI's industrial profile changed dramatically. Its patrimonial structure deteriorated and the balance for 1983 showed two hundred thousand million pesetas in losses. Seventy percent of the INI group's deficit pertained to companies that were 'socialised' between 1977 and 1982, the hardest years of the economic crisis. The Institute was most harshly criticised because of its huge bureaucracy and its links to the Franco dictatorship. However, the INI could not simply shut down. Solchaga affirmed the usefulness of public companies as an instrument of reconversion and promotion of new activities and energy policies. Yes, it was necessary to contain rising costs and in the medium term transform investment and business strategy. After presenting his goals in the Chamber of Deputies, he told all the directors and presidents of the Institute's companies that a change of attitude was essential. It was necessary to sacrifice jobs and salaries, because it was unacceptable that public companies had losses in sectors where private companies earned profits.[21]

From 1985 to 1989, the INI underwent a profound change. Some companies were closed and others were resized, as had occurred in the private sector. Competitiveness increased through the purchase of technology and the perfection of productive processes. A financial overhaul was carried out and a corporate strategy was designed. It was neither easy nor cheap. It cost more than 100,000 jobs and two thousand million pesetas of public funds, an expense which revived the controversy. In 1988, the INI was transformed by law into a public entity corporation with full legal capacity and character dissociated from State budgets. At the time, some firms were already being privatised, because it was a cheap, fast solution that would guarantee the survival of the group. Companies that had interests abroad or which were profitable but had no strategic interest were privatised. The most important sale was that of Seat to Volkswagen in 1985. In the following years, before the socialists left power, shareholdings of companies in more strategic sectors were placed for sale on the stock market. The Government, however, wanted to maintain control of these shareholdings. Some examples of the shareholdings were 15 percent of Telefónica and 20 percent of Endesa in 1988, 80 percent of Repsol from 1989 to 1995, and 91 percent of Enagas in 1991. Behind these privatisations were a collection of varying motives, from the need to finance the public deficit, to European pressure to streamline industry, to expectations to participate in privatisations created in the big national or international financial capitals. With these privatisations began one of the processes that had the greatest impact on the transformation of Spanish firms.[22]

What some socialists considered an unforgivable dismantlement of the public sector company also fuelled complaints about the government's economic policy. Despite the excellent economic situation, or precisely because of it, these complaints culminated in an unprecedented conflict at the end of the 1980s. The upward cycle of the world economy and entry into the European Community sparked an increase in consumption, investment and growth of company earnings. The unemployment rate fell thanks to increased flexibility of the labour market and the expansion of temporary hiring. The tax burden continued to grow, as did the public deficit. The socialists had proposed to establish a modern welfare state – retirement pensions, health and education. This, along with growing unemployment benefits, required a lot more revenue than the government was collecting. Actual public expenditures accounted for more than a third of yearly budget expenditures, but public services did not improve in proportion to this spending. Monetary policy became stricter and Solchaga insisted it was necessary to contain pay raises and increase labour market flexibility. But the socialist trade union, UGT, believed that, with the worst of the crisis over, it was time to step in and have their say about economic policy. From that point, relations between the government and the trade unions began to sour. The pension plan reform in May of 1985 had ignited heated confrontations, and in the Chamber of Deputies, the secretary general of the socialist trade union, Nicolás Redondo, voted against the measure. Two years later, he quit his post, and at the Thirty-First Congress of the PSOE, he refused to accept the party presidency that Felipe González offered him. The UGT's loss of ground to the *Comisiones Obreras* in the trade union elections of 1986 had led it to think that its policy of dialogue and moderation was responsible for the failure, and decided to break from it and openly confront the Government. On 14 December 1988, the two unions convened a general strike which was a complete success. The big cities were paralysed for twenty-four hours, which showed there were more than union workers voicing their discontent. Felipe González, in an emergency Cabinet meeting, considered it had been a total defeat for the government, and even announced his willingness to resign. The cause of the strike had been the youth employment plan, seen as another step closer to the deterioration of the labour market, but it was a strike against the entire social policy. It was not a revolutionary strike, as past general strikes had been. It was a political strike. The enemy was not management but rather the socialist government, and the CEOE understood it as such. The traditional relation between the socialist party and the socialist trade union was broken for a long time. Nicolás Redondo attributed the break to the fact that some socialist ministers had succumbed to the spells of neoliberalism and the 'aristocratic embrace' of the socio-economic elites. Carlos Solchaga wanted to convince González that elections should be held immediately for citizens to decide whether they wanted a government conditioned by the unions. But at the time, Spain held the European presidency, and the elections were delayed until October 1989. For the first time, the UGT did not endorse the socialists. The PSOE won again, but lost many votes.[23]

The PSOE tried to reach an agreement with the UGT but failed because the union felt their offer was insufficient. More social measures were passed by decree. Solchaga thought they were 'extremely dangerous', because they entailed an increase in unemployment benefits, retirement pensions and other social aid packages. The Government's new spending commitments coincided with the end of the cycle of economic growth and the advent of a new recession, hastened by the Gulf War and the reunification of Germany. The creation of a single European market by the end of 1992 and the subsequent adjustment and increased competition also contributed to the change in the situation. The unemployment rate, softened in previous years by temporary employment that was too dependent on the growth of the 1980s, rose again. In June 1989, the peseta had entered the European Monetary System greatly overvalued. In 1991, Spain signed the European Union Treaty of Maastricht, and with it, the commitment to fulfill the obligations of convergence and monetary union. A 'social pact of progress' was signed with unions and employers, but the failure to moderate salaries and stop the growth of the deficit led to the enactment of the so-called *decretazo* (an important decree) in April 1992, a law that significantly cut unemployment benefits. The unions called for a general strike again, but it had much less impact, and the Government boldly proposed a new reduction of unemployment benefits the following year. Meanwhile, the 'fluctuations' in the

European monetary system and the attack on the currencies of the weak countries, which was the case of the peseta, led to three successive devaluations over the final months of 1992 and the first months of 1993. Not even the splendour of the Olympic Games in Barcelona and the World's Fair in Sevilla could hide the deterioration of the situation.[24]

The happy relationship between the socialist government and economic forces had ended, too. On 30 and 31 January 1992, over three thousand businessmen gathered in Madrid's Palace of Congresses, convened by the CEOE to talk about 'Spanish enterprise in the new Europe'. The function was inaugurated by the King and the president of the CEOE, José María Cuevas. Cuevas affirmed that Spain's integration in the new Europe should be considered an 'authentic governmental issue'. In the last six years, he said, Spanish entrepreneurs had carried out the biggest process of investment and renovation in Spain's recent history, but the new challenges were tremendously important. Different leaders of European business organisations and Carlos Ferrer Salat, then president of the Confederation of Industry and of Businessmen of Europe, also expressed their opinions. Several ministers gave speeches. Different politicians spoke, on and off the record. José María Aznar, the recently elected leader of the conservative Popular Party, made a sterling defence of small and medium business owners against those big companies and banks with 'majestic losses' involved in strange situations, perhaps preferring policies different from those which his party proposed. 'In the first place, I want to thank José María Cuevas, president of the CEOE, for his words', said Aznar informally at the luncheon in which he spoke. 'Now that nobody can hear us, I'll say that Cuevas and I have shared many ideas for a long time, and moreover, as everyone knows, we are united by a good and deep personal friendship'.[25]

The Banking Transition

The crisis and reconversion of the late 1970s also affected the 'most select club' in Spain at the beginning of the transition, the club of the presidents of the seven biggest banks: the Spanish Credit Bank, the Central Bank, the Hispano Americano Bank, the Bank of Bilbao, the Bank of Vizcaya, the Santander Bank and the Popular Bank. The club was led at the time by José María Aguirre Gonzalo, president of the Spanish Credit Bank, the bank with the greatest volume of deposits. The presidents had been meeting periodically since 1971 in the dining room on the twelfth floor of Banesto's headquarters. They always held a luncheon at the restaurant Jockey and followed a strict protocol according to the importance of the respective banks when it was time to sit down at the table and speak in the conversation. In those meetings, they spoke about the economic and political situation, offered opinions and argued. They also reached agreements on their banking and financial strategies. With the beginning of the transition, the most important politicians and other noteworthy figures began to be invited to these luncheons. When the Central Bank passed Banesto in deposits, its president, Alfonso Escámez, believed it was time to substitute Aguirre as the host. He had to wait a bit, until 1983. Aguirre's replacement in the presidency of the Spanish Credit Bank with Pablo Garnica Mansi, descendant of one of the traditional banking families, allowed Escámez to receive the club at the headquarters of the Central Bank, right across from the Bank of Spain. Along with Escámez and Garnica, the members of that select club were the young Alejandro Albert, president of the Hispano Americano Bank, who had a brief and troubled presidency in which he was replaced by Claudio Boada in 1985; José Angel Sánchez Asiaín, president of the Bank of Bilbao and Ángel Galíndez, president of the Bank of Vizcaya, both of whom had revolutionised their respective banks while the traditional families stayed on the boards of directors with less power; Emilio Botín-Sanz de Sautuola y López, patriarch of the Bank of Santander, who three years later would turn over the post to his son, Emilio Botín-Sanz de Sautuola y García Ríos. The seventh member was Luis Valls Taberner, the 'Florentine' banker, as some called him, president of the Popular Bank. The transfer of the site of the traditional luncheons in 1983 was a small change in comparison to some that had already taken place in the financial sector and others that were still to come.[26]

It has been written that the 'banking transition', like the political transition, was largely a change of personnel. Most of the big and old bankers disappeared, giving way to new bankers who ran their businesses in very different ways. The club no longer exists today because the seven big banks no longer exist, but also because the financial system was one of the spheres of the Spanish economy that underwent the biggest changes. It had been a tightly controlled, scarcely competitive, inefficient system with almost no money markets or capital; it evolved into a system marked by a gradual liberalisation and reform of financial institutions, a growing complexity and expansion into markets, a reinforcement of monetary policy mechanisms and greater competitiveness. The change made advances and caused setbacks. It provoked crises and made banks and institutions disappear. It brought about much-debated expropriations and interventions, rumours and perhaps conspiracies, takeovers and mergers. And beyond its technical aspects, a great deal has been written about it. José Ángel Sánchez Asiaín, one of the catalysts of this history, explained that 'conventional' banking gave way to big financial conglomerates which were more flexible and capable of adapting to an increasingly complicated demand. Some bankers saw what was happening and took measures accordingly; others remained anchored in their inertia for a long time. The competition between them increased, but the control of the biggest bankers was not broken.[27]

Pressures resulting from Spain's economic, tax and financial situation and the gradual integration into the European monetary and financial system all came to bear on these changes, but their impulse and evolution were pushed by the will of a handful of individuals intent on reform. Some of these individuals had participated in the preparation of the 1959 Stabilisation Plan and continued their work mainly in the offices of the Bank of Spain and its Department of Studies, looking for interlocutors in the political class and agreements with bankers, directors and administrators of financial institutions. It was not the inevitable result of market trends, but rather a delicate operation whose final goal was the liberalisation and creation of a true financial market which did not exist. To do so, it was necessary not only to change public and private banks and institutions, but also place the Bank of

Spain in the position of a central bank; that is, eliminate its prior subordination to the Ministry of the Treasury and provide it the tools necessary to control a growing number of different assets and prevent inflation. That called into question the sources of liquidity and profits that banking was accustomed to. As a result, banks were obligated to implement important innovations in their sizes and their ways of doing business.[28]

Proposals to liberalise the financial market were included in the package of the Moncloa Accords in 1977. The vice-president for Economic Affairs, Enrique Fuentes Quintana, met with the presidents of the national banks, the governor of the Bank of Spain and the Minister of the Treasury to present the general terms of the reform. Only Rafael Termes, who came from the Popular Bank, and José Ángel Sánchez Asiaín, president of the Bank of Bilbao, were receptive to the plans. As such, Fuentes Quintana decided that Termes would be his candidate to the presidency of the Spanish Association of Private Banking (AEB) and that this association should become an important backer of his projects. Termes was a faithful supporter of liberalisation. Over the course of his prolonged presidency, he became a leading spokesman to convince the financial community of the need for reform, although he never failed to express his criticisms when he felt it was necessary. He also played this role in relations with political parties and institutions, and he tried to persuade public opinion that banking was not a closed oligarchy.[29]

The good reformist proposals were compromised by the banking crisis that came to light at the beginning of 1978 and which lasted at least until 1983. The crisis was the worst in the history of the country, affecting fifty-eight of the one hundred and ten existing banks. Five disappeared and the rest survived, although under different names and owners. The causes of this tremendous crisis can be traced to the euphoria of the 1960s. The earnings of banks obtained prior to the liberalisation of the financial system led to an excess creation of new banks and branches on the part of people who had neither experience nor professionalism, motivated only by the expectation of big profits. The rise of risky investments in a situation of inflation with recession, along with speculative activities that bordered on illegality, and a financial system that had no preventive regulations or effective resources to supervise and sanction these practices, ended up creating a dramatic situation. It is not surprising that twenty of the thirty-four banks created after the 1962 law were affected by the banking crisis from 1978 to 1983. José María López de Letona, then governor of the Bank of Spain, discovered the first case of the crisis, in the Bank of Navarra. He was alarmed to verify the lack of means with which to confront a situation that, in his opinion, required a political solution. It was decided in the Cabinet Meeting on 16 January 1978 that state intervention was necessary. Meanwhile, a press campaign fuelled by those affected led to estrange relations between politicians and bankers. The bankers were worried about the publication of a decree that authorised the Bank of Spain to temporarily suspend a bank's boards of directors.[30]

When Álvarez Rendueles assumed the government of the central bank, he received a horrifying report on the state of Spanish banking: eight banks were enduring 'serious difficulties' and eleven were in situations of 'lesser gravity'. The three commercial banks and two industrial banks of the Rumasa group deserve a chapter of their own. From among the causes that, according to the report, had led to the situation, the one cited as the most important was the 'abuse of granting loans in favour of companies linked to the bank itself and/or persons that administered them'. Poor management, unnecessary risks, the uncontrolled expansion and ignorance or intentional distortion of the banking business were much more important reasons than those stemming from the economic crisis. Mariano Rubio, the subgovernor of the central bank at the time, would prove to play a crucial role in solving the banking crisis. He confirmed all the 'pathological cases' and insisted on the urgency of facilitating the central bank with means of control and obligating banks to comply with determinate accounting regulations and private audits, issues that were unusual then in Spanish banking practice. All these manouevers by the Bank of Spain tripped over the reluctance of private banking. Banks unwillingly formed part of the Banking Corporation and then the Fund for Guaranteed Deposits, institutions created to take charge of entities in trouble, overhaul them and afterwards sell them. Banks that were doing well did not want to take control of overhauled banks, either. Two of these were sold to foreign banks, which heightened the alarm. The presidents of some of the big Spanish banks felt that the banks in trouble should be left to go bankrupt, but the Government and the Bank of Spain rightly feared the repercussions this could have.[31]

Relations between banks and the UCD governments were not easy, and when the socialists won the 1982 elections by an overwhelming majority, nationalisation was still part of their programme. The situations of the Catalan Bank and José María Ruiz Mateos's industrial and financial conglomerate, *Rumasa*, were critical when the socialists took over, immediately putting the proposals of the new governors to the test. The Rumasa case was of greater significance than the Catalan Bank case. The Bank of Spain was well aware of it, having detected unrecorded liabilities in the accounts worth forty-two thousand million pesetas and accumulated losses worth nine thousand million, apart from the debts with the Treasury, which totalled over twenty thousand million. Ruiz Mateos's holding company had been growing thanks to the export of wines and grew at a dizzying rate in the 1960s and 1970s, when it acquired a large number of companies from diverse sectors through banks that came to be controlled by the holding company. Rumasa was an unusual case in Spanish banking, not only because it was outside the seven big banks' sphere of influence, but also because it was more normal for banks to own companies, not vice-versa. At the onset of the crisis, the group's pressing needs of liquidity caught it up in a snowball effect via risky purchases and the acquisition of interbank loans which were increasingly more expensive. The burden of these conditions fell on the holding company's firms, which as such bore costs much higher than those of the market. The alarm in the Bank of Spain increased when Ruiz Mateos cancelled the audit by Arthur Andersen that he had promised the Fund for Guaranteed Deposits, calling in Price Waterhouse to do the job instead.

After a bitter public controversy between the Minister of Economy and the president of Rumasa, who said he was subject to 'unprecedented aggression', it was decided in the Cabinet Meeting on 23 February 1983 to expropriate. The Bank of Spain had recommended an intervention that could take various forms, one of them expropriation. At 10:30 p.m., a government spokesman interrupted the TV news to announce that 'the Government, with the objective of fully guaranteeing bank deposits, jobs and patrimonial rights of third parties it considers seriously threatened, has passed a decree to expropriate the banks and other companies of the Rumasa group'. It was a bombshell. For some it was the product of the socialists' fear that the matter would get out of hand; for others, it was an excess. Some even saw it as a complicit nod by left wingers to compensate for other economic policies. It was the most extreme solution and a bold action for the socialists shortly after taking over the government. That same night, Miguel Boyer phoned Carlos Ferrer Salat and Rafael Termes to guarantee them, as it had been publicly announced, that Rumasa's banks and firms would immediately be privatised. The AEB issued a statement lamenting the expropriation – which 'could make private firms think they were defenceless before the State'. Nonetheless, it accepted Minister Boyer's reasons and appreciated his declared proposal to return banks and firms back to private control, which private banking supported in full. Some felt the manoeuver was a plot between big banks and the Government to get rid of the competition that Rumasa posed and 'keep its leftovers'. There were also those who saw in the attitude of the AEB a renunciation of the out-and-out defence of the principle of free enterprise. This time private banking did agree to the privatisation because the crisis of the Catalan Bank had almost led to nationalisation. The seven big banks, in collaboration with medium banks, presented an offer which resulted in the sale of the Catalan Bank to the Bank of Vizcaya and the distribution of Rumasa's banks among the seven. Ruiz Mateos the business star had burned out and the expropriation as well as the privatisation of Rumasa's firms lent to all types of speculation.[32]

At the end of 1983, the banking crisis ended, although there were still many problems pending. The result was greater concentration: of the 134 existing banks, 65 formed part of the groups led by the seven big banks and accounted for 73 percent of total assets. In March 1984, the subgovernor of the Bank of Spain, Mariano Rubio, as president of the managing committee of the Fund for Guaranteed Deposits, presented a report of his measures taken against the crisis to the Commission of Economy in the Chamber of Deputies. For some time, Rubio had been the socialist candidate most likely to succeed Álvarez Rendueles as governor of the central bank. Rubio's management during the banking crisis ended up consolidating his professional career. On 18 July, he was appointed by the Cabinet, and on 24 July, he was inaugurated in a solemn act that took place in the meeting room of the Bank's executive council and became a political event. It was the first time the President of the Government, Felipe González, entered the building on Alcalá Street, accompanied by two ministers, Miguel Boyer and Carlos Solchaga. However, the Vice-President, Alfonso Guerra, did not attend. The dissent within the Socialist Party regarding economic policy was well-known. Guerra backed the critics of that liberalism that was so worried about inflation. The Government's economic ministers seemed to have implanted that ideology, which was sealed when Mariano

Rubio became president of the Bank of Spain. 'Happily, you have not made the mistake of confusing progressivism with demagogy', said the new governor to the president of the Government and the ministers in attendance, as if wanting to corroborate the accusations of the Vice-President. All the presidents of the seven big banks were there: Garnica, Escámez, Albert, Asiaín e Ybarra, Galíndez y Toledo, Botín and Valls.[33]

As of the early 1980s, first with Mariano Rubio as governor and continuing when Luis Ángel Rojo took over in 1992, the Bank of Spain became the decision-making centre with regard to monetary and financial policy. Both men had spent time in the Department of Studies and helped form a team of economists that constructed Spain's first macroeconomic model, brought national statistics up to date, made its publications leading references and established solid relations with international financial institutions. The goal of the central bank was to achieve monetary stability in a country with little regard for it and often in opposition to the aims and dictates of politicians, who were more concerned with the growth of the GNP even if that meant high inflation rates. To reach this goal, as Rojo pointed out to Minister Fernández Ordóñez in 1978, it was necessary to 'institutionalise the autonomy and professionalisation of the Bank beyond the daily ups and downs of policy and persons'. The Bank of Spain needed independence. It was difficult for the governments of the UCD to renounce a mechanism of intervention as important as the Bank of Spain. The so-called *Ley de Órganos Rectores*, finally passed in June 1980, was the beginning of a new phase for the central bank because it recognised the Bank of Spain as the central authority on monetary policy, although it would be the Government that established the ground rules. The greatest guarantee of that still-partial independence was the King's appointment of the governor for a four-year, renewable term, a stipulation requested by the Cabinet. It was not until 1994 that the Law of Autonomy of the Bank of Spain was passed, thereby fulfilling the requirement of the Maastricht Treaty for entry into the European Economic and Monetary Union. The new law, introduced by Luis Ángel Rojo, stated that neither the Government nor any other organisation could instruct the Bank of Spain on the aims or execution of monetary policy. It was one of the most important requirements demanded by the European Union. The application of this norm had already eliminated official stockbrokers and circles of privileged information – insider trading – in the capital market. The entry of the peseta into the European Monetary System in 1989 was accompanied by a drastic reduction of mandatory investments, which necessitated a total transformation of bank treasuries and the beginning of a free public debt market.[34]

Because of all the changes in the markets and challenges from abroad, banks and financial institutions had to be renovated, always beneath the watchful eye of the Bank of Spain. The banking crisis was over, but there were still problems that affected even some of the bigger banks. In December 1984, the Bank of Spain had prohibited the Hispano American Bank from distributing dividends. It was the first time this had ever happened to one of the big banks. The Hispano American Bank as well as the Spanish Credit Bank and the Central Bank endured difficult times because of the takeovers of other banks they were charged with at the beginning of the decade. In some cases, the motive had been the traditional race to occupy the top spots in the banking classification. In other cases, such as the takeover of the Urquijo Bank by the Hispano American Bank, the Government obligated the bank to absorb the losses of struggling entities that fell within its sphere of influence. In still others, as in what happened to Banesto with the Garriga Nogués Bank directed by the young Javier de la Rosa, it was suddenly discovered that unsuspected irregularities in the accounts were hiding a situation of bankruptcy. In all of these cases, one of the roots of the problems was a very deteriorated or very unorthodox management and administration of the banking business. The Bank of Spain 'recommended' implementing changes and changing personnel, who occasionally and reluctantly accepted. Pablo Garnica in Banesto did this, consenting to the vice-presidency of López de Letona, but as occurred with Escámez in the Central Bank, they ran up against stiff opposition.[35]

At the end of the summer of 1987, a study by Jack Revell from the European Institute of Finances at the University of Wales reported that there were perhaps too many big banks in Spain for the size of its economy, and at the same time, these banks were too small to keep up with foreign competition. Of the seven biggest banks, the four smallest (Bilbao, Vizcaya, Santander and Popular) were more efficient than the three largest (Banesto, Central and Hispano American). The governor of the Bank of Spain, Mariano Rubio, forthrightly told the banks they had to think about their 'current dimensions'. José Ángel Sánchez Asiaín, president of the Bank of Bilbao, fired the starting gun on 19 November when he announced to a bewildered José María López de Letona, vice-president of Banesto, his willingness to initiate a process of merger. The ambitious 'European operation', as the project was known in the Bank of Bilbao, had the blessings of the political and monetary authorities, but encountered resistance from Banesto. The process of banking mergers had begun, and it would be accompanied by important changes of presidents in the big banks.

From 1941 to 1981, banks had been subject to legal limitations on the distribution of dividends and had resorted to creating new shares for shareholders and distributing shares as a way to increase shareholder profits. The result was that the number of shares had grown excessively. No shareholder, nor even board members or traditionally powerful families in banks, now controlled the majority of shares. However, this policy had left open the possibility that someone could suddenly acquire a shares portfolio big enough to upset the balance on a board of directors. This is how the Kuwaitis bought 4.95 percent of the shares of the Central Bank from the KIO group and its representative in Spain, Javier de la Rosa. The two cousins Alberto Cortina and Alberto Alcocer, executives of the company Construciones y Contratas (CC), acquired an important stock portfolio of the Central Bank and afterwards created Cartera Central with the Kuwaitis. Cartera Central controlled 12 percent of the shares of this bank, whose president was Escámez. On the other hand, Juan Abelló and Mario Conde emerged in Banesto. These two had made many millions of pesetas selling the company Antibióticos to the Italian firm Montedison. They, as well as 'the Albertos', wanted to be on the boards of their respective banks. Banesto's president, Pablo Garnica, announced his imminent retirement, and the vice-president, José María López de Letona, aspired to take over the post when the proposal to merge the Bank of Bilbao arose. Because López de Letona resisted the merger, he lost his chance and retired. Mario Conde was appointed president of Banesto and he asserted his position by defending the bank's independence, and the merger failed once and for all.[36]

Mario Conde and 'the Albertos' rose to prominence in the financial world from the outside, in ways not normally seen in the most traditional world of Spanish banking, pursuing the new spirit of doing business that accompanied the boom of the 1980s. At the same time, the new president of the Bank of Vizcaya, Pedro de Toledo, another young man with a style of his own, emerged onto the scene. He was born in Bilbao, received a Jesuit education and earned a degree in Economy and Law from Deusto (a Jesuit university). He did not belong to the traditional Basque families, although he married into one. After a few years at General Eléctrica, he joined the Bank of Vizcaya and immediately hit it off with the president, Ángel Galíndez, who also came from the electric industry. Both implemented big changes in the bank. In the early 1980s, the Bank of Vizcaya purchased the Commercial Credit Bank, the Occidental Bank and the Meridional Bank; in 1983, it bought the Catalan Bank. Galíndez found the perfect successor in Pedro de Toledo, and prepared him for the presidency, which he would assume at the end of 1987, like Mario Conde in Banesto.

When the merger of the Bank of Bilbao with Banesto failed, Sánchez Asiaín felt so slighted that he had to look for new options. Pedro de Toledo saw an opportunity to continue the growth of the Bank of Vizcaya, now by way of a merger with the Bank of Bilbao. On 7 January 1987, he had lunch with José Ángel Sánchez Asiaín. The operation took place very quickly. Although it was not what the economic authorities were expecting, preferring the merger of one of the more efficient banks with another that had more problems, the merger was approved, and on 27 January, the protocol was signed. The declared aim of the merger was to take over the leadership of Spanish financial institutions and become the model for European and international banking. In fact, the new Bilbao-Vizcaya Bank became Spain's most important, the leader of another twenty banks and a number of important financial companies, as well as three hundred firms, most notably electric companies. The agreement included the existence of two co-presidents, Sánchez Asiaín and Toledo. The first would be *primus inter pares* for two years, and then the second would take over in this role for the following two. In this arrangement, Toledo would see his chance to occupy a single presidency. However, as predicted in the Bank of Spain, it was not easy to manage a co-presidency or integrate the two banks' organisations, which had very different views about banking. Thus began a period of tensions and confrontations which increased when, on the morning of 13 December 1989, Pedro de Toledo died in a U.S. hospital after a sudden illness. In fact, the merger was delayed and the new bank was paralysed in the midst of a merciless fight which saw both banks exercise all their political influences. Finally, when the deadline expired, the Bank of Spain issued a ruling in favour of a single presidency. Although it recognised Sánchez Asiaín's many merits, it awarded the post to Emilio Ybarra, with two vice-presidents transferred from the Bank of Vizcaya.[37]

The merger of the Bank of Bilbao and the Bank of Vizcaya, the tensions on the boards of the Central Bank and Banesto, and the will of the Government to continue pushing mergers created great uncertainties for a few months. In his fight against Cartera Central, Alfonso Escámez leaked news of a possible merger with the Hispano American Bank, on whose overhaul Claudio Boada worked, but the plan never materialised. A little later, in May 1988, it was the Central Bank and Banesto which announced a highly publicised agreement. The preparatory technical work was done, but the differences between Escámez and Conde were too great, and the conversations between the presidents ceased. Almost a year later, in April 1989, after various requisitions from the governor of the Bank of Spain demanding the two bank presidents to act consistently, it was clear that the pact was dead and buried. In January 1991, however, the new president of the Hispano American Bank, José María Amusátegui, managed to achieve what his predecessor had not, and with a speed that surprised the Bank of Spain: he reached an agreement with Escámez, made possible perhaps because, at the time, the two cousins Alcocer and Cortina, who had always been opposed to the mergers, left the Cartera Central. That was how the Central Hispano Bank was born. It was the second biggest bank after the merger of the Banks of Bilbao and Vizcaya. Perhaps it was not the most effective solution, but the unusual size of the new entity protected it from control by what were then called 'financial sharks'.

Two of the seven big banks had kept out of those stormy events. One of them was the Popular Bank. Headed by the brothers Luis and Javier Valls Taberner, in the 1970s it had opted for commercial banking, had pulled out almost all of its investments in industrial firms and risky countries, and had not entered the frenzied race for the top spots of the banking classification. However, it was a modern, very profitable bank, marked by the personality of Luis Valls, who knew how to adapt the bank to the new situation brought about by democracy and defend it against those who tried to acquire important stock portfolios. The Popular Bank was undoubtedly a tempting target for those seeking a merger, but it jealously maintained its independence, while Luis Valls publicly stated it would always be alert to any sign of this sort that came from the Government. The other bank that kept its distance from rumours of merger, and which was also marked by the personality of the family running it, was the Santander Bank of the Botín family. In 1986, when the Santander Bank was already fifth in the classification of Spanish banking and managed over 7 percent of all Spanish banking resources, Mr Botín gave way to his son, Emilio Botín-Sanz de Sautuola García Ríos. The younger Botín undertook a campaign to get new clients by offering new financial products. Among these were loans, whose fiscal opacity caused Botín serious problems, and the popularly called *super accounts*, in which the bank offered tempting interest rates to depositors used to receiving next to nothing in exchange for their money. In a few months, the Santander Bank doubled the number of its clients, obligating the rest of the banks to compete, which for some proved costly.[38]

For the general public, the fashionable banker was Mario Conde. He had reached the presidency of Banesto in the middle of the battle against the Bank of Bilbao at the end of 1987, and he took control of the board of administration, displacing the bank's old families. In 1989, Conde created the Banesto Industrial and Financial Corporation, a holding company consisting of the more than 120 firms that depended on the Banesto group and which was proposed for admission to quotation on the stock market. Conde's ambitions went far beyond this. Spanish bankers were powerful, but they were so because they were bankers. Mario Conde was a banker because he wanted power, and the bank was his launching pad. He was convinced that the important decisions that affected the country were not made in Parliament or in political parties, but in the intimate, quiet atmosphere of mansions or in the dining rooms of big restaurants. And Mario Conde cast out his net to establish contacts. He took care of all his relationships, from the closest ones in the business and financial world to the distant ones in the highest levels of political power. He used all the means and the luxury that his bank provided him to rub shoulders and be seen with the most influential members of society. He deployed his charms and the aura of a young winner at parties, on hunting trips and with invitations to his yacht. At the same time, he secured in every way imaginable public and private information, and especially confidential information, that could be useful to him at some future time. He immediately understood that, in his rise to power, it was essential to create himself a niche in the media. It created a stir when he entered this field, which he was not at all familiar with, and the thousands of millions of pesetas the media adventure cost Banesto did not produce the desired result.

At the beginning of June 1993, three days after the general elections, in which the socialists lost their absolute majority but the Popular Party (the conservative party) did not achieve the success it had hoped for, Mario Conde received an honorary doctorate from the Complutense University of Madrid. The act was presided over by the King, and Mario Conde made sure the guests befitted the honour of the ceremony. In attendance were José María Amusátegui, Emilio Ybarra and Francisco Luzón, president of Argentaria Bank, although Escámez, Botín and Valls were not there. Jesús de Polanco, Antonio Asensio, Guillermo Luca de Tena and Pedro J. Ramírez, leading figures in the media world, also attended. The presentation was made by the historian and former Israeli ambassador to Spain, Shlomo Ben-Ami, and Mario Conde gave a clearly political speech. He insisted on the role of civil society in contrast to political parties and spoke of the need for creative change capable of producing a genuine 'democracy of citizens'. A few months later, almost all those who attended the function gave explanations for their attendance, because on 28 December, the Bank of Spain intervened and dismissed Banesto's board of directors, with its president, Mario Conde, at the top.[39]

In reality, when the Complutense University opened its doors to Conde, Banesto was already in a very difficult situation. However, as was the case until the end, only a handful of well-informed individuals realised the extent of the problems. The economic crisis of the early 1990s had prevented the Banesto Industrial Corporation from appearing on the stock exchange, which Conde had counted on. Moreover, the competition of the Santander Bank's *super accounts* and the merger of the Central and the Hispano American banks had derailed the strategy of reckless growth that Banesto had deployed since its failed merger with the former. During an inspection in the middle of 1992, the Bank of Spain had discovered the existence of irregularities in the accounts totalling between 45 and 60 thousand million pesetas. Luis Ángel Rojo, still in his role as subgovernor, wanted to intiate an investigation and obligate Banesto's administrators to keep selling shares and moderate the rate of expansion. There was a shakeup within the Bank of Spain because the case of the firm Ibercorp was published in the daily *El Mundo*. Ibercorp was created by one of the governor's best friends and former trustee of the Madrid Stock Exchange. The name of Mariano Rubio as an investor in said company was hidden from tax office records. Felipe González swore in defence of the governor, and many thought that Mario Conde was responsible for spreading that news. Perhaps he wanted the Bank of Spain to ease up on its investigation, because at the same time, he needed its protection.

In the middle of 1993, Banesto embarked on an impressive operation to increase capital in three successive stages. The operation was given the green light by the Bank of Spain, and apparently had the commitment of the U.S. bank, J.P. Morgan. The urgency to consolidate this commitment was just one of a number of pressures accumulating on Mario Conde. He also needed to maintain good relations with certain firms and individuals that had acquired a large portion of the treasury stock and were unable to pay back the loans, and especially take care of the good will the Bank of Spain had demonstrated up to then. However, he did not give up the political ambitions that figures of power from very different circles encouraged him to pursue. Nor did he neglect his personal relationships, including his contact with Felipe González, with whom he secretly interviewed. But after the summer, things got out of control. J.P. Morgan conducted its own investigation of Banesto's situation, and the last phase that should have continued the increase of capital with the issue of 400 million dollars in convertible bonds was paralysed. The North American bank demanded more guarantees that only the Bank of Spain could provide. However, the central bank was not receiving any convincing signs that Banesto was willing to straighten its accounts, and symptoms were only growing more alarming. From mid-December, the interviews and meetings continued. The Minister of Finance and Felipe González himself were punctually informed. The figures the Bank of Spain had on Banesto's situation and the quantity of capital needed to get out of debt were rejected by Mario Conde. On 22 December, Luis Ángel Rojo heard it personally from the J.P. Morgan vice-president that his bank was not going to give any more money, not even a single dollar. Conde and his team made a lightning trip to New York and obtained a letter supporting his plan, but both trip and letter were useless. There would not be another dollar from J.P. Morgan.

On 24 December, Luis Ángel Rojo went to La Moncloa (the presidential palace) for a meeting that lasted long into the night. There he affirmed that there were only two solutions: the replacement of the board of directors with a group of administrators from other banks, or Banesto's entry into the Fund for Guaranteed Deposits. The first would rectify the situation; the second would be traumatic for the bank. The president of the Government requested that the less difficult solution be adopted. The governor mobilised the presidents of the big banks to prepare a replacement team. On the afternoon of 27 December, Rojo received Conde to show him the radical discrepancies between the plan that Banesto proposed and the numbers that had been crunched that same day by the executive council of the Bank of Spain. These discrepancies were written up by both men in an exchange of letters that immediately followed the meeting. The following day, Rojo attended another meeting with Conde at 9:15 a.m. If there was no new solution on the table by noon, the bank's executive council would have to proceed with the substitution of Banesto's board of directors. Mario Conde asked for three more days, until the end of the year, and the Bank of Spain accepted the request. But when the Madrid Stock Exchange opened amidst great rumours, Banesto's shares began to plummet. The president of the National Stock Exchange Commission phoned Conde and asked him for explanations. Afterwards, he phoned the governor of the Bank of Spain, who was meeting with the executive council. The governor asked him to come immediately to the bank's headquarters on Alcalá Street, where he told him about the situation and the three-day grace period granted to Conde. All the telephones began to ring. If the quotation of the shares was suspended, the Bank of Spain would have to intervene immediately. At 2:30 p.m., with the quotation now suspended, the bank took that step. The decision was supported by the recent Law of Discipline and Intervention of Credit Institutions, which did not exist when the expropriation of Rumasa occurred, because it was enacted on 29 July 1988. Luis Ángel Rojo left the meeting to see Mario Conde again at 4:00 p.m. and gave him the report of the decision. With the report in his possession, the dismissed president returned to Banesto's headquarters, where many of the board members were meeting. They were furious with him because he had not consulted them. They felt betrayed, many of them recalling their long family tradition of dedication to the bank.

Banesto's new team of administrators, agreed upon by the Bank of Spain and the big banks, was led by Alfredo Sáenz. Sáenz was a Deusto economist who began his career in industrial enterprise but consolidated it in the Bank of Vizcaya. He took charge of the Catalan Bank after its expropriation and purchase by the Bank of Vizcaya in 1983, and was one of the two vice-presidents of the Banco Bilbao-Vizcaya (BBV) after the merger. On 26 March 1994, meeting in an atmosphere of high hopes, Banesto's General Shareholders' Council approved the renovation plan. A month later, the Bank of Santander was awarded Banesto in the shares auction. Although the BBV and, more symbolically, Argentaria also placed bids, the Bank of Santander made the best offer. On 31 December 1994, Banesto's losses were more than its total capital and reserves. The bank and part of the shareholder's equity had been saved, although by means of reducing capital and reserving the right of shareholders to participate in future expansion. Mario Conde, the young millionaire who wanted to imitate Silvio Berlusconi, was never a banking professional, nor was he interested in learning the trade. Banesto financed all his image campaigns and his dazzling board of directors was nothing more than a front for increasingly irresponsible actions, eventually emptying the bank's coffers under the guise of liquidating its industrial portfolio. The abandonment of any discipline whatsoever in prices and the systematic manipulation of figures led some to deny the existence of huge discrepancies in the accounts and interpret the intervention in Banesto as a political manoeuver to remove a character that was becoming more threatening. Mario Conde's speeches before the parliamentary commission formed to investigate the case intended to complicate the affair but, as a result of the investigation, Banesto's former president lost the battle in the eyes of public opinion. On 14 December, Banesto's vice-president, Arturo Romaní, was sentenced to unconditional prison as a result of the lawsuit brought by the public prosecutor's office of the *Audiencia Nacional* (a special high court). On 24 December, the same court ruled against Mario Conde, who would spend thirty-nine days in the Alcalá Meco prison. In 1997, he was sentenced to six years in jail, and in 2000, to ten more years.[40]

The intervention in Banesto and its sale to the Bank of Santander afterwards produced certain changes in the bank rankings. The Bilbao-Vizcaya Bank, dropping slightly after the merger, later regained first place. The Central Hispano Bank continued to lose ground. In 1994, it occupied a lower position than that which would have corresponded to the sum of the Central and Hispano-Americano banks based on their situation in 1987, and was overtaken by the Santander-Banesto Bank, which came to occupy second place.

Scandals and the Media

The socialist decade, 1982–1992, had been a period of 'lights and shadows', of changes and evident achievements. However, it left a final aftertaste that made many forget what had been accomplished. Continuing unemployment, the increase in spending and the public deficit, tax pressure and the poor functioning of certain services weighed negatively in the balance against the reconversion and growth of the late 1980s, liberalisation and greater competitiveness, concentrations and mergers in key sectors, the internationalisation of business and the spectacular increase in foreign investments, the streamlining of the public sector and the beginning of the process of privatisation. The crisis of 1992–1993, despite the rapid recovery the following year, contributed to this aftertaste. There had been ten years of absolute majority and conviction in the socialist ranks that it was their responsibility, and only theirs, to raise Spain to the heights it deserved. They had held virtually uncontested power, a power that had grown proportionally to the growth of the State, and government institutions had multiplied with the consolidation of the decentralised system. The party itself grew in the same way. Its needs grew, and it created a dense network of clients. Everything seemed justifiable in view of the objective announced in 1982 – *cambio* ('change', the socialists' principal slogan) – but reality harshly spoiled the promises of full employment, equal redistribution of the wealth without endangerment of economic stability, and the construction of an efficient welfare state. The socialists – those who wanted to – discovered that the absolute majority did not allow them to mold society at their will. In the 1990s, the prevailing themes in the Western world centred on the welfare state's tax crisis and the urgency of more freedom, more market and less State.[41]

The accusations of wasteful spending and considering the Administration their own property trashed the images of honesty and austerity the socialists had sold to the public. They had pretended to link an unblemished past with a magnificent present. More than unemployment or a bias towards the upwardly-mobile over the working class, it was the explosion of accumulated scandals that truly shocked the electorate, including the ranks of a party that appeared to be deeply divided into two camps, the 'renovators' and the '*guerristas*' (reference to Alfonso Guerra, a classic left-wing politician compared to liberal socialists), squared off in a struggle for control. In the 1989 general elections, the PSOE had retained its absolute majority, but by a very narrow margin. Most curious, however, was the change in the profile of their voters. In the two previous elections, this profile was largely masculine, young, urbane, and highly educated; in 1989 it was predominantly feminine, older, rural and less educated. The trend was confirmed in the 1993 elections when the socialists lost their absolute majority, although they still obtained good results. They formed a government with the help of *Convergencia I Unió* (conservative Catalan nationalist party), confronting the Popular Party, which had been renovated with the rise of José María Aznar to the presidency.[42]

Corruption scandals proliferated in the 1990s, not only in Spain, but in other European countries as well, and they affected not only socialist or social-democratic parties, although these were the protagonists in Mediterranean Europe: Greece, Italy and Spain. There were cases in Belgium, Germany, the United Kingdom, and outside Europe, in Japan and different Latin American countries. Corruption, thought to be exclusive to self-acclaimed, dictatorial regimes, turned out to be a reality well-adapted to democracy. It was possible in Spain in the 1990s because of a peculiar combination of economic, cultural and political factors, some of which have already been mentioned: a significant increase in State intervention in the economy, which multiplied opportunities for corruption; a premodern economic ethic in many sectors of the population, which resulted in permissiveness and tolerance towards this kind of behaviour; and a concentration of political power in the hands of only one party which was very personalised and charismatic. The socialists deactivated all mechanisms of control. The 'super leadership' of Felipe González, the high percentage of members that swelled the socialist ranks immediately to occupy posts of responsibility, the lack of generational renovation and the moral superiority this bred, as well as the absolute subordination of the party to the Government, were relevant factors. Spanish society, as some pessimists wrote, was not overly shocked by the succession of scandals, because Spanish society itself was corrupt to the bone. Perhaps this is why corruption occasionally became the subject of sensational news and commentary in the media, great political battles for public opinion, or more or less consistent investigative journalism, but hardly gave rise to academic studies like those produced in other countries.[43]

At times, the financing of political parties has been considered the root of all evil. This subject was not a big preoccupation in Spain until 1984 and the *Flick affair*. In the parliamentary committee formed to investigate the case, it was demonstrated that, one way or another, all the political parties had received German financing during the transition. Given the low party membership, the State subsidies were crucial in covering ever-greater electoral expenses as well as permanent activities. The State awarded these subsidies on the basis of the number of votes and seats each party obtained. The subsidies totalled 1.651 thousand million pesetas in 1979 and 2.431 thousand million in 1983. Party membership dues and private donations were important sources in those parties whose members were people of wealth, but not in all cases. Moreover, public financing a posteriori obligated the parties to rely on loans, which perhaps gave banks a certain influence and obliged the parties to assume risks and financial burdens that, when electoral results did not live up to expectations, turned out to be insurmountable. Neither the increase of subsidies in 1985 and 1994 nor the new financing law of 1987 proved to be efficient in terms of solving the parties' growing needs.[44]

To solve this problem, the socialists had first resorted to the German formula of creating a network of firms whose profits could be converted into revenue for the party, but these efforts failed, so they resorted to the French and Italian strategy of creating another 'type' of company. The best-known case was that of Filesa, a company supposedly dedicated to drafting technical reports for firms or banks. Payment for the reports was made, but the reports did not exist. The scandal emerged in May 1991, and eventually forced the resignations of the party's secretary of administration and finance, Guillermo Galeote, the treasurer of the parliamentary group, Carlos Navarro, and the senator José María Sala. The case of the socialist trade union, UGT, was different. The UGT's secretary general, at odds with the party leadership, wanted to break from dependence on the government by creating a business network, too. Its name was Social Promotion of Housing (PSV) and it became the head of an important holding company whose biggest problem was terrible management. This problem eventually led it to bankruptcy and triggered a scandal that forced Nicolás Redondo to resign. There were many illegal ways to raise funds, with many different kinds of agents and intermediaries. Although the final destination was supposed to be the party account, the money did not always make it there, or was less than expected. This corruption, benefitting both public and private interests, distorted the functioning of those markets whereby payment or proximity to power became an essential requirement for obtaining a government contract. The qualification and requalification of real estate and the procurement of public service contracts were fertile grounds for these practices, which were not exclusive to socialists, but in fact frequent among any party that controlled a municipality or regional government. One example was the so-called Naseiro case, one of the first scandals of the 1990s, named after the treasurer of the Popular Party, Rosendo Naseiro. All political parties created collection mechanisms and networks of corruption, violating the laws of free supply and demand, but this was especially true of parties long settled into power, parties that tended to identify their interests with the general interest (read: Convergence and Union in Catalonia, the Basque Nationalist Party in the Basque Country). It all became even more serious when the extortion turned violent.[45]

In January 1990, the press had uncovered the case of Juan Guerra, the brother of the vice-president of the Government. As of 1982 Guerra had an office in Sevilla, in the regional headquarters of the Government of Andalusia. With no official appointment, he decided to work as an adviser and engaged in businesses which quickly made him rich. At the time, González defended his vice-president, but in January 1991, decided to replace him. The Juan Guerra affair strained relations between the socialist Government and the press to the limit. The good rapport the socialists had maintained with the newspapers as the opposition party ended shortly after they landed in the government. The tension between the socialists and the press was heightened by top party leaders' repeated claims of unfair treatment. According to them, this treatment should coincide with the verdict of the vote, which on several consecutive occasions had given them the absolute majority. Everything got worse when the press took a stance on the Filesa affair.[46]

The intervention in Banesto and subsequent trial of Mario Conde, as well as the trial of Javier de la Rosa as a result of the spectacular suspension of payments by the Torras Group in December 1993 and the audit of Gran Tibidabo, were much-publicised scandals, but they were of a different type. They put an end to speculative practices, and moreover, they sparked an offensive which was far more intense than anything seen up to that moment. Some of the scandals that broke then had a well-defined personal and institutional goal, as happened with the resurrection of the case of Ibercorp in May of 1994. This case was clearly directed against Mariano Rubio and the Bank of Spain itself, and also forced ex-minister Carlos Solchaga to quit as representative and head of the socialist parliamentary group. The socialists were being shot at, and they were providing easy targets. One of the cases which did the most damage was, undoubtedly, that of Luis Roldán, Director General of the Civil Guard. At the end of 1993, the press began to learn that Roldán was growing suspiciously wealthy. They discovered that he was charging commissions for building and service contracts for the Civil Guard, and even pocketed money paid by businessmen as an 'extraordinary tax' to the ETA terrorist group. Until then, Roldán had been an exemplary civil servant, but he was dismissed in December 1993. The news of his escape months later brought about the resignation of the Minister of the Interior. That same year, Gabriel Urralburu, ex-president of Navarra, was convicted for bribing eighteen construction companies and for cheating the regional tax office. These affairs of personal enrichment by civil servants added to the denunciations against businessmen who had come out of nowhere to do business thanks to their proximity to the highest government officials. They were called the 'PSOE entrepreneurs'.

The tense climate produced by that seemingly endless string of scandals became even more strained as a result of a very different sort of case. In this one, the wrongful use of authority was more important than the possible enrichment of the people behind the scandal, although reserve funds of the Ministry of the Interior were involved. It was the *GAL affair*. Judge Baltasar Garzón took advantage of the case of Segundo Marey's kidnapping to reveal the truth about the implications of the illegal antiterrorist groups (GAL) operating from 1983 to 1986 in the 'dirty war' against ETA. Segundo Marey's case was given much publicity as he was thought to be a member of ETA and the GAL did not release him when they discovered he was not. Garzón was back in the Supreme Court after an aborted political career he had perhaps hoped to start as a minister in the Socialist government of 1993. Julián

Sancristobal, former civil governor of Vizcaya and ex-director general of Security, coincided with Mario Conde in prison. Their conversations on the prison patio could become 'dynamite' for the State. And they did. Those conversations, and the ones Conde had with former CESID agent, Juan Antonio Perote, after getting out of prison, also led to the phone-tapping scandal in June 1995. State security had spied on and recorded conversations of politicians, businessmen, journalists, and even the King himself. Felipe González had to appear before the Chamber of Deputies, carrying with him the resignations of the Vice-President of Government and the Minister of Defence. Apparently, one veteran socialist privately recalled the sentence pronounced in the Chamber more than sixty years earlier: either the Republic finishes with Juan March, or Juan March will finish with the Republic. Conde was the Juan March of the 1980s.[47]

The war of scandals was a product of revenge on the part of certain individuals who had a lot of economic power, but it was also fertile ground for the political battle between a Popular Party that decided to exploit the corruption at any cost and a divided, severely weakened Socialist Party. There came a moment in which everything was valid and citizens could hardly distinguish between information and its perverted use. The battle was not played out on the parliamentary stage, but before readers' own eyes. It amounted to a media war which had two obvious protagonists: El País and El Mundo, whose director, Pedro J. Ramírez, held a grudge against the socialists in power. El País was part of an important business group led by Jesús de Polanco. This group had taken control of Prisa (Promotora de Informaciones, S.A.) ten years earlier. Polanco came from the world of publishing. In 1958, he had founded the publishing house Santillana, which first published law books and later educational texts, and quickly expanded to the Latin American market. Several publishers would join the group over the years that followed. Prisa was set up in 1972 and Polanco joined its board of directors in September of 1973. On the board were Darío Valcárcel and José Ortega Spottorno, son of the philosopher José Ortega y Gasset. It had been Ortega Spottorno's idea to found a newspaper which would be called El País. It is very likely that Ortega Spottorno was thinking about El Sol, the newspaper created by Nicolás María de Urgoiti in 1917, in which his father, along with many other great intellectuals, thinkers and writers from the time, played such an important role. In the 1960s, with the onset of the political transition, it was easy to imagine a similar project.

At the beginning of the 1970s, there were three kinds of media groups: those who upheld unconditional faith in the Franco regime, most notably, the press of the Movement, which suffered huge losses and political and informative sclerosis; those opposed to the dictatorship, with very few newspapers and numerous magazines; and newspapers that maintained a certain independence but avoided direct confrontations – ABC, La Vanguardia and Ya – with three private groups behind them: Prensa Española, the Godó group and Editorial Católica. Franco's death and greater public attention to the news created a general increase in print runs, a 'sweet moment' which was the prelude to important changes. The press of the Movement was eventually abolished in 1982. The remaining newspapers had to confront an economic crisis in the sector and overcome technical and administrative deficiencies of companies that made uncompetitive products at increasingly more expensive prices for a readership reduced by the competition of radio and television after the early stages of the transition. Some papers survived, others perished and new ones were born. The companies changed: some maintained their dedication primarily to daily press (Prensa Española, Recoletos, Godó) or periodicals (Grupo 16, Semana), with some investments in other media; others evolved towards the multimedia business (Prisa, Correo and Zeta).[48]

Prisa was one of the groups that enjoyed spectacular growth. It took *El País* three years to obtain permission to publish after filing the request in 1973. Its first issue appeared on 4 May, 1976. This paper defined itself as 'liberal, independent, socially supportive and European'. It was directed towards an essentially cultivated audience and its great ambition soon became apparent. Its first director, Juan Luis Cebrián, later wrote, 'It must be said that it did not come about as just any newspaper... Its business structure, its ideological orientation and its characteristics as a political project – in the broadest sense of the term – distinguished it from any other type in its class'. *El País* enjoyed almost immediate success with its circulation and established itself as *the* newspaper of the transition. After its shares changed hands many times and became concentrated in only a few, the biggest shareholder, Jesús de Polanco, was appointed president of the group.[49]

Around that time, the whole of the media world, not only the daily press, began to change, and Jesús de Polanco had given signs of his desire to expand into other types of media. He had ushered in a new entrepreneurial spirit in the sector. During the governments of the UCD, legal regulation of the media had been vague, especially the control of public television. Perhaps this was because Adolfo Suárez had been CEO of Televisión Española (TVE) from 1969 to 1973, and throughout his term as president of the Government, he was particularly fond of using this medium for his public appearances. In 1980, the Statute of Spanish Radio and Television (RTVE) was passed, and RTVE became a public entity with legal capacity, a board of directors appointed by Parliament and a CEO appointed by the Government but supposedly the product of political consensus. There was no effective decision about 'third channels' or private television. Some UCD politicians and entities like the employers' organisation CEOE were in favour of private TV. Socialists were less than thrilled with the idea and communists rejected it outright, fearing it would fall into the hands of the big financial groups. As for radio stations, the State, in addition to owning National Radio and Spanish Radio Channel, held 25 percent of the three most important private stations.[50]

During the Socialist Government, many pending measures and laws were passed. The *Cadena del Movimiento* (Franco's radio broadcasting group) was permanently dissolved. Shares that the State still held in private radio stations were sold. A new law aiding media companies was passed, along with several others: the Telecommunications Regulation Law, the Private Television Law in 1988, the Satellite Television Law in 1992 (amended and adapted in 1995), the Cable Telecommunications Law and the Local Television Law, both from 1995. The passing of some of these laws, and especially the decisions their application entailed, caused controversies of far-reaching impact. This happened in part because the media itself encouraged them, but also because the defence of freedom of opinion against the weight of state media turned out to be an effective political argument for the opposition. The awarding of new concessions for FM stations in 1989, supposedly to fulfill social needs, favoured public radio stations over private, the same way that the Law of the Third Channel served to diversify the public offerings in television, although the door was opened for the establishment of private TV channels. The Statute of Radio and Television was not amended in terms of appointing the CEO, which was still the Government's decision, although control by a parliamentary commission was considered but not applied. Successive projects and proposals of this type bogged down. The directors remained at the head of the public entity and conflicts continued to erupt over RTVE's manipulation of news and its funds, when it was proven that self-financing was impossible. In the final years of the socialist government, the deficit of TVE became a genuine scandal.[51]

The Prisa group developed rapidly during these years, taking advantage of the opportunities for growth in all spheres of communication. It became a shareholder of the *Ser* station in 1983 and took complete control on acquiring the State's share in 1994, which contributed to the renovation of the management and put its news programmes at the top of Spanish radio. In 1989, the awarding of concessions for private TV stations finally took place. According to the 1988 law, television was still a public service, which is why the acceptance of private channels was considered an indirect provision of this service although it was in private hands. This solution, along with other stipulations set by law, had led the opposition parties and the media to believe that private television would be established with many limitations. On 25 August 1989, the Cabinet ruled on the awarding of the three channels planned for *Antena 3, Telecinco* and *Canal+*. This last channel, a company promoted by the Prisa group and Canal+ France, was the only one that requested the concession of a pay channel. The decision raised a great stir. In short, at the beginning of the 1990s, the Prisa group stood out as the first among media groups and it had become an imposing business conglomerate. However, with success came setbacks. As much as *El País* had maintained a critical line towards the legislative measures that affected the sector, as well as towards issues related to the dirty war against ETA and other scandals, the Prisa group became the object of priority attack for those in the sector who competed against it, and, in connivance with them, those who aspired to displace the socialists from power.[52]

In March 1996, the Popular Party won the elections, putting an end to the long Socialist reign. Contrary to most predictions, it was not a political disaster for the socialists because the Popular Party did not obtain an absolute majority. The first months of the PP Government were difficult and tense. One of the objects of its attack was the Prisa group, blamed for supporting socialist interests. The new government wanted to counter Jesús de Polanco's group with another to create competition. The group would consist of the newspapers most recognised for their radical opposition to the Socialist Party, especially *El Mundo*, and would also include radio *Cope*, Teléfonica and public television. This was the foundation on which Vía

Digital was created. It was a company which was supposed to counter the announced start of broadcasting by *Canal Satélite Digital*, the company of the Prisa group. The government was not willing to allow the uncontested reign of Canal Satélite, the only company which had the means and resources to begin broadcasting. On 31 January 1997, the Cabinet passed a Royal Decree and a ruling on the Law of Satellite Telecommunications, according to which all companies had to register with the Ministry of Public Works before starting to broadcast, and to demonstrate that their digital decoder was compatible with those of other operators. The approval of the Royal Decree in the Chamber of Deputies gave rise to a noisy dispute between conservative and socialist representatives, while *El País* launched a frenzied campaign to denounce what it considered a planned attack against the Prisa group. By decree, the government had raised the value-added tax on pay television and established that operators could not profit from the subscription fees clients were charged. On 28 February 1997, the judge Javier Gómez de Liaño accepted a suit presented by a columnist for *ABC* against Jesús de Polanco and Juan Luis Cebrián, for supposed fraud and misuse of subscription fees, and both of them were prohibited from leaving the country. It was not until June 1998, after receiving extensive coverage in the press, that the Sogecable affair was closed. The judge Javier Gómez de Liaño was accused and later convicted on three counts of malfeasance. The digital war went on to force the resignation of the secretary general of the Department of Broadcasting.[53]

At the end of the century, the Prisa group was still the most important media group in Spain, but there were others. The Catalan group Godó functioned on a regional scale. Along with other publications, it printed *La Vanguardia*, the oldest newspaper among those still published in the country. *El Periódico* has the biggest circulation in Catalonia. Together with other regional newspapers like *La Voz de Asturias* and *El Diario de Córdoba* and successful magazines like *Interviú*, it belonged to the Zeta group. The Recoletos group was created in 1977 out of the magazine *Actualidad Económica*. Daily sports publications like *Marca* and economic dailies like *Expansión* became more important, with the share of the company Pearson Overseas. Recoletos bought 5 percent of Vía Digital, and the following year, Telefónica acquired 20 percent of the group. Finally, closing the circle, the Recoletos group purchased 30 percent of Unidesa, the publisher of the news daily *El Mundo*, in 1999.

Via very different routes, another group has reached impressive heights in the world of communication: the Correo group. It was founded on the Basque newspaper of the same name, and by the end of 2000, it was in charge of eleven regional newspapers, all of them important, with a total daily circulation of 550,000. A few of its papers are *El Diario Montañés, La Verdad, El Ideal de Granada* and *El Norte de Castilla*. Although it is essentially a print media group, it is creating regional multimedia companies based on the newspaper mastheads. Moreover, it has acquired 25 percent of the third biggest private television channel. On 18 September 2001, the group announced its merger with, or more accurately, its takeover of, one of the country's most important newspaper companies, Prensa Española, publisher of the daily *ABC*. This purchase entailed a leap of incalculable importance for the group, but it also forced it to delay its planned listing on the stock exchange.[54]

The Powers of the New Economy

The Popular Party rose to power on the promise of putting an end to the socialist governments' policy of uncontrolled spending and budgetary deficit, a policy the socialists had begun to control from Pedro Solbes' Ministry of Finance. The positive situations at home and abroad favoured economic growth from 1997 to 1999, which made it easier to fulfill that promise and the requirements for Spain's entry into the European monetary union. The Socialist Party and their minister Solbes had worked hard to achieve this status, and the Popular Party, after some initial hesitation, fully assumed this endeavour. Balancing the budget, lowering taxes and reducing interest rates were other tasks the PP worked on. The goals of deregulating markets still under government control and total, definitive privatisation of public companies also formed part of their liberal programme.

José María Aznar appointed Rodrigo Rato vice-president and Minister of Finance to set the economic programme in motion, and in a Cabinet meeting at the end of June 1996, a programme of 'modernisation of the State's public business sector' was approved. A year earlier, the socialists had liquidated the INI and divided its companies into two groups: economically viable companies which did not receive public funds and firms which still depended on state assistance. The former went on to join the *Sociedad Estatal de Participaciones Industriales* (SEPI), and the latter constituted the *Agencia Industrial del Estado* (AIE). Up to then, the privatisations carried out by the socialist Government – complete in some cases and partial in others – did not follow any systematic plan. Even talk of *privatisation* was avoided; the term preferred was 'divestment'. Even so, the public sector's proportion in the whole of the economy had fallen from 12 percent in 1985 to 7 percent in 1993. In 1985, it had been fundamental in twelve sectors; in 1993, it was fundamental in only five. Over the same period, the number of public sector firms had dropped from sixty-two to forty-five. As of 1995, the socialists approached privatisations as a global issue within a 'plan for streamlining and modernising the public business sector', which also aimed to reduce the deficit. Measures were also taken to guarantee the maintenance of public control in companies that changed to private hands. One such measure was known as the 'golden share', which would remain under State control for a certain time.[55]

This philosophy changed when the Popular Party took over the government. The message now was total privatisation. There was no longer any reason to have reservations about dismantling the public sector. Only through this dismantling would global efficiency of the national economy be reached. The privatisation plan had to be a political action coordinated directly by the Government, administered by the shareholding agencies and guided by the principles of transparency, publicity and concurrence. For all of this, the Advisory Board for Privatisations was created and 2001 was set as the deadline for privatising everything, with very few exceptions (Renfe, RTVE, Correos y Telégrafos, Hunosa and Figaredo). Four years later, most of the objectives were reached. The State got rid of all or almost all of its shares in companies that up to then had been public, completely disappearing from sectors it had played a crucial role in since the first years of the INI (oil, electricity, natural gas, iron and steel, and telecommunications). Consequently, public employment was drastically reduced. Most of the privatisations were carried out via public sales of shares, although there were some auctions, restricted tenders and other processes involved. At the end of 1996, the State had shares in 11 percent of all companies listed on the Spanish stock exchange. This percentage fell to 0.5 percent by the end of 2000. That year, the process of privatisations was put on hold as a result of general elections which gave the Popular Party an absolute majority. Even so, some privatisations were carried out, including the first two phases of the privatisation of Iberia. The process entailed average annual revenue of 1.6 thousand million pesetas, approximately 1.9 percent of the annual GNP.[56]

Privatisation also affected the financial system and contributed to increasing the concentration of banks. In 1998, rumours about new mergers multiplied. The Central Hispano Bank had not rectified its inefficiency, while the Bank of Santander continued the work of expanding its presence. The result was the merger of both into the Santander Central Hispano Bank, which led to another merger: that of BBV and Argentaria. Argentaria had been established in 1991 out of then Minister of Finance Carlos Solchaga's desire to modernise State banking. The union of the existing public banks, housed under the name Argentaria, intended to direct public banking towards operating in the free market. Once this was functioning, Argentaria would be privatised and listed on the stock exchange, a process that began in 1993. When the Popular Party won the elections in 1996, Argentaria occupied third place in the bank rankings. The Government replaced Argentaria's president, Francisco Luzón, who would be quickly recruited as Chief Executive Officer for the Bank of Santander, with Francisco González, a man close to the Minister of Finance, Rodrigo Rato. González's main mission was to complete the privatisation without the Government losing control of the entity. Once the task was achieved, Argentaria became an appealing target for future mergers. On 7 September 1999, Emilio Ybarra and Francisco González coincided at a conference organised by the CEOE. They talked about their respective banks' situations, and the result was the birth of the BBVA a little over a month later. Actually, the process had begun earlier, and had its rocky moments. Although both banks were convinced the merger was a good idea, some of the BBV's board members refused to accept the union as a merger of two equals. The Basque bank had triple the deposits of Argentaria, six times as many employees and profits of 139 thousand million pesetas compared to Argentaria's 66 thousand million. But the Government was very interested in the merger and had the means to be very persuasive. The resistance on the part of the BBV eventually proved useless, and on 19 October, after notifying the Government and the central bank, both banks' boards approved the foundations of the accord. The Bilbao-Vizcaya-Argentaria Bank would have two co-presidents, Emilio Ybarra and Francisco González until 2002, when González would assume sole possession of the charge.[57]

The success of the process of privatisations had its difficult and tense moments, its conflicts and critics, on scandalous occasions. We will omit the criticism of those who argue for and justify the necessity of a public business sector, question the a priori assertion that private enterprise is more efficient and more profitable, and point out the existence of many good businessmen in the history of Spain's public sector, some of whom moved back and forth between state companies and private enterprise. The most frequent, most publicised comments refer to the way some of the privatisations were carried out, the interests wrapped up in them and the people that directed or embodied them. One of the Popular Party's first measures was the dismissal of all the socialist-appointed presidents of 'privatisable' companies and their replacement with new people who made up part of the nucleus of businessmen and financiers personally close to José María Aznar and Rodrigo Rato: Alfonso Cortina, brother of Alberto Cortina, who was appointed president of Repsol; Francisco González, who became president of Argentaria; Juan Villalonga, who wound up in Telefónica; Miguel Blesa, in Cajamadrid; César Alierta, in Tabacalera; and Rodolfo Martín Villa, in Endesa. The Government declared that these people were selected for their technical and professional ability, as a group and individually. According to their biggest critics, they were 'friends of Aznar' or Rato. They constituted what some have called a new 'business class' that worked for the interests of the Popular Party. This class tried to bridge the gap that existed during the early stages of the conservative government between the politicians and the most important centres of economic power, essentially the big banks. The Popular Party was also suspicious of the *hard nuclei* of stable shareholders in the newly privatised companies. The socialists tried to nurture these shareholders to compensate for the withdrawal from the public sector in companies considered very important, like Telefónica or Repsol. In the opinion of the new government, these *hard nuclei* could act too independently, a danger it tried to avoid by appointing 'independent' board members and putting limits on the representation of new shareholders on the boards by way of 'protective measures'. The most serious problems arose when the presidents of these big new privatised companies resisted or rebelled against Government directives, causing scandalous conflicts.[58]

This was the case of Juan Villalonga. A friend of Aznar's from their childhood, Villalonga had worked as an executive in Miguel Blesa's office and also with the cousins Alberto Cortina and Alberto Alcocer. In June 1996, he was appointed president of Telefónica. He had experience as an administrator, but knew little about the business he was going to run. The changes in the management team were somewhat disconcerting, as he surrounded himself with a group of executives which remained rather aloof from the rest of the company. The public sale of the shares that were still under State control – 21 percent – took place at the beginning of 1997. It was the first big public company that was privatised. It had a *hard nucleus* of members that came from Argentaria, the BBV and the Catalan Savings House. The first was a natural ally, and in the creation of the board of directors, Villalonga surrounded himself with trustworthy independents to compensate for the intervention of the banks. Taking hesitant steps in the search for a technological partner, he broke a previous agreement with British Telecom, while embarking on the creation of a media group, a possible communications holding company: an affiliate of Telefónica purchased 25 percent of Antena 3 and Villalonga reached an agreement with the Recoletos/Pearson group. The enormous expense that this entailed was of little concern, because it could yield important political benefits and, moreover, the price of Telefónica's shares rose like scum to the surface of a pond.

Villalonga was an example of a young and successful businessman, risen to the crest of the wave in the world of communications and the new economy. However, soon he would make mistakes. The infamous *stock options* affair, in which about one hundred of the company's executives pocketed several thousand million pesetas, put the Government in a real predicament. Its leaders had to explain to the press that Telefónica was a private company free to make its own decisions, although everyone knew it was the government that fixed the company's rates. Rumours about Villalonga's indulgent lifestyle began to circulate and hurt his image. There were many questions about the exorbitant sums Telefónica paid to purchase companies like the Dutch firm Endemol, which cost the telecommunications company 900 thousand million pesetas. The straw that broke the camel's back was when Villalonga launched the so-called 'operation Veronica' to purchase 100 percent of Telefónica's affiliates in different Latin American countries. This entailed an important increase in capital of 3.5 billion pesetas, which reduced the banks to minority shareholders. Other affairs interfered with this operation: the strategic alliance that Villalonga pacted with the vice-president of the BBVA, Francisco González, a move which entailed the exchange of shares and also of vice-presidents. The image of concentration of power that this pact would have produced was not politically advisable, so the pact was aborted. But in his search for protection, Villalonga negotiated a merger with the Dutch company KPN. In terms of business, the merger probably would have been profitable for both companies, but the Government, after approving the idea of the initiative, used its *golden share* to block it because KPN held a large share of public capital. The operation broke down and the price of Telefónica's shares on the stock exchange plummeted. Moreover, this action coincided with Villalonga's approaching the Prisa group to study the possibility of a common communications company. For many reasons, Villalonga had become a deeply uncomfortable figure and a dangerous source of scandals. It was essential that he step down from the presidency of Telefónica. His removal had the consent of the company's *hard nucleus* and some of its independent board members. On 24 July 2000, in Miami, where he had transferred Telefónica's headquarters, Juan Villalonga quit the presidency of the company.[59]

More important has been the criticism of the lack of a previous policy of deregulation, liberalisation and fragmentation of public companies in certain sectors. Such a policy would guarantee competition once privatisation took place, as such preventing a simple transfer of monopolistic positions from public to private hands. That is, some privatisations would have occurred before an effective liberalisation in the respective sectors, as happened in the electric sector with the sale of Endesa, and in the telecommunications sector with the sale of Telefónica. The policy of the Popular Party was guided by the desire to develop a 'popular capitalism' through public sales of shares that effectively created a considerable number of small shareholders in the privatised companies, but shareholders who had no say in big decisions. This 'popular capitalism' was strengthened by the significant increase in the number and value of firms quoted on the stock market, which led to optimism and euphoria in the Spanish Stock Exchanges, as well as drastic changes in the behaviour of individuals. In the mid-1980s, the Stock Exchanges moved hundreds of thousands of millions of pesetas annually; in 2000, it moved more than thirty-five billion pesetas, eleven billion of which were laid out by individuals. Preference for the small shareholder in the processes of privatisation did not overshadow the numerous institutional investments that took place. In many cases, these were international investments or purchases of important stock portfolios by big banks. These purchases consolidated positions of power on company boards and reconstructed old relations between banking and industry. The *hard nuclei* that were eventually formed undoubtedly helped the decision-making process. However, investments by the big banks – Banco Bilbao Vizcaya Argentaria (hereafter BBVA) and the Catalan Savings House on the one hand, and Banco Santander Central Hispano (hereafter BSCH) on the other – in key sectors like electric, oil, natural gas and telecommunications discouraged competition between companies with common interests and disenchanted other types of investors. The exercise of the right of veto that the possession of the 'golden share' gave to the Government was also used to block certain investments or orient and direct processes of business merger.[60] The process of privatisation produced a 'drastic change' in the Spanish business structure. Studies indicate that the Spanish business scheme is still dominated by small and medium enterprise. These kinds of businesses accounted for 98 percent of the business census in the mid-1990s, a proportion significantly higher than the average of the other European economies. In theory, it would be reasonable to assume the existence of a structural obstacle to the productive efficiency of Spanish companies and the improvement of their technological resources. However, it is risky to assert this in general terms, because in some sectors the most productive companies in terms of revenue per employee were businesses with very few workers.

Moreover, from the point of view of ownership, family business has traditionally been important in Spain. Here we define family business as one or more families that maintain control because they are majority shareholders, which does not necessarily imply that the companies are small. In 1993, the Family Business Institute was created. It was another important lobby in the business world, uniting ninety of the biggest companies of this type, which turned over approximately 7 percent of the GNP and directly employed 500,000 people. At the time, 229 of the 1,000 firms with the biggest turnover were family businesses (23 percent) and turned over 12 percent of the total. Better control over decisions and less reluctance to reinvest profits with an eye toward long-term growth have been two of the biggest advantages these kinds of companies enjoy, advantages which have provided the basis for their successful development. One example from the building sector is Ferrovial, whose president was Rafael del Pino Moreno until June 2000, when his son Rafael del Pino Calvo Sotelo took over. This family is still the major shareholder, even after the company was listed on the stock exchange in 1999. An example from a very different sector, the clothing industry, is the Inditex group. The Inditex group was listed on the stock exchange more recently. In the mid-1990s, when it was expanding to foreign markets, its president and founder, Amancio Ortega, held 80 percent of the shares. The keys to his success, in addition to his original approach to business and his commercialisation, have been the refusal by shareholders to collect dividends and the reinvestment of practically all the profits, as well as the decision to embark on the search for foreign markets once the domestic market was saturated.[61]

However, only the bigger, more international family businesses seem to overcome the problems arising from the need to grow and find directors from successive generations that are prepared and willing to continue the family tradition. As such, in recent decades, the number of family businesses has diminished. Some have disappeared and others have lost the status of family business through purchase by foreign interests. At the beginning of the 1990s, foreign capital controlled a modest number of companies in the whole of the Spanish economy. However, half of them were among the largest, and their turnover accounted for 30 percent of the total added value. That is, their presence was qualitatively important. This is the result of one of the biggest challenges that Spanish entrepreneurs have had to confront: the gradual liberalisation of the economy and the subsequent internationalisation of firms. The tendency of Spanish firms to export has grown significantly – 7.5 percent annually from 1986 to 1998, although less than imports. This tendency started at a much lower level compared to other countries and still cannot compare to the highest. As we saw above, foreign investment in Spanish companies has also increased much more than direct investment by Spanish companies abroad. The foreign capital has originated from mid-sized manufacturing companies with advantages in technology and image, and has converted some Spanish companies into world leaders. These are the Spanish companies that have taken the initiative in investing abroad. The Spanish business revolution that has taken place after and out of the crisis of the 1970s has been impressive. It has been engineered by a business class unknown to the greater public because this class consists of people that stay out of the limelight. Nonetheless, the revolution has been habitually overshadowed by huge investments abroad, like Telefónica's in Latin America through Telefónica Internacional Sociedad Anónima.[62]

Politicians were preoccupied with the integration of the Spanish economy into Europe. There was also much concern among businessmen and bankers about the absence of big companies in Spain. Size seemed to become almost indispensable in order to take part in the new competition. It was also an issue that concerned economic historians. At the beginning of the 1990s, in reviewing the history of the past two centuries, they concluded that big industrial companies have not emerged in Spain for several reasons: the country was too poor when new technologies were introduced; the State had distorted market mechanisms that could have better allocated entrepreneurial talent; and Spain perhaps lacked comparative advantages for developing that kind of company. The historians did not believe that Spain would create big industrial companies in the future, excepting affiliates of multinational firms, but would perhaps establish big service companies. At the beginning of the 1990s, almost half of the country's one hundred biggest firms were public service companies – water, gas, electricity and telephone. There was an especially high concentration in the case of electric and telephone companies. In 1990, in a ranking of one thousand companies around the world, the biggest Spanish electric and telephone companies were ranked relatively high in relation to their sector: Endesa was twelfth out of sixty-seven and Telefónica twelfth out of twenty-seven. Repsol was ranked twelfth out of forty-three oil companies. In finance, another sector that tended to concentrate big companies, the BBV, the only merged bank at the beginning of the decade, was in thirtieth place out of 121. Ten years later, there was a ranking of companies in European countries belonging to the Euro Zone. Out of the fifty biggest companies according to floated capital, Telefónica was ranked high (around ninth). The BBVA and the BSCH were in the middle of the pack (around twenty-first and twenty-sixth, respectively). Nearer the bottom were Endesa (around thirty-eighth) and Repsol (around forty-first). These positions would be much lower if British or Swiss companies were included. In any case, it is significant that the firms cited above are two big banks formed by mergers in the last decade and three formerly public companies that are now permanently privatised.[63]

In view of the companies that are the largest in Spain today, it still makes sense that concerns revolve around two or three issues. These concerns are expressed from very different perspectives and with very different intentions. In some cases, the viewpoints are more academic; in others, they are more political. The first issue is whether the big mergers and processes of concentration were a result of economic efficiency implemented to adapt to the technological revolution and the globilisation of markets, or rather defensive strategies for ensuring greater control, which has little to do with efficiency and even less with consumer benefits. The second is who makes the decisions in the business world, within each company but also in the network created via investments and board representation. The third is how to consider the relations between political and economic power in an economy that is more open to foreign markets and domestically more liberalised, but also more concentrated, and in which political decisions have at least as much impact as in the days of state intervention and public enterprise. In recent decades, no Spanish business sector has escaped the impact of mergers and concentrations. All of them have blamed the appetite for foreign investment and the processes of internationalisation, and many have felt the great impact of privatisations. 'The fact is that Spanish business sectors hardly resemble what they were at the outset of democracy', as one recent article concluded. The public sector has been dismembered, but private firms have also changed completely, and throughout the process, the search for size in order to compete has been top priority. One can imagine a network in which big interests cross, as in past times. It is not a question of reviving the old ghosts of oligarchies that control the State or of those who manipulated political action, nor is it a question of demanding inefficient intervention to slow down the development of the market. It is a question of recognising that the relations between and mutual influences of political and economic interests do not disappear with the shrinking of the public sector or the mandate of laws and regulations, but rather make up an essential part of reality. To defend competition and avoid the perverse interference of the public realm with the private realm, there has to be, at the very least, a scrupulous and vigilant State, and governments of impeccable democratic vocation.[64]

Notes

1. The quotation from Calvo Sotelo, in Calvo Sotelo (1990: 163). A political biography of Calvo Sotelo, in Prego (1999: 126–139). Interview in Ferrer Salat (1978).
2. The economic crisis, in Rojo (1987); the economic crisis and political transition, in Serrano Sanz (1994). An explanation a posteriori of the Moncloa Accords by Fuentes Quintana himself, in Fuentes Quintana (1995) and (1999).
3. Fuentes Quintana's interpretation of the necessary adjustment, in Fuentes Quintana (1995: 35ff.).
4. A good and recent history of the transition, in Powell (2001); the surmounting of the obstacles of the 1930s, in Juliá (1991) and (1994). The negative image of businessmen, compiled by themselves, in Martínez Soler (1983); businessmen in the candidacy of the Popular Alliance, in López Nieto (1988: 91–92 and 108–109); economic ties of representatives and senators in the first Parliaments, in Equipo de Documentación Política (1977: 56–65).
5. The political class 'at a distance' and the scarcity of businessmen in the government, in Pérez Díaz (1985: 20) and (1987: 161–164). Biographies in Prego (1999) and Martín Aceña and Comín (1991: 478).
6. On the different types of businessmen, reduced to two, see Aguilar (1985: 60). The *Círculo de Empresarios* and its activities, in Rodríguez Braun (2002) and in their Annual Reports (1977–2000). The role of López de Letona in the founding of the Society, recognised on the tenth anniversary (Annual Report from 1987).
7. The different organisational initiatives, in Aguilar (1985). The Fomento del Trabajo Nacional and its role in employers' reorganisation, in Vidal Folch (1990); also in Ludeviv and Serlavós (1985). The appearance of the first 'employer of employers', in Cabrera and Rey Reguillo (1997).
8. The interview with Ferrer Salat, in Martínez Soler (1983: 150–157). For the CEOE, see Martínez and Pardo (1985), Martínez (1993), Pardo (1996) and Rijnen (1985). Also, CEOE (1987).
9. The evolution of the conflict and the characteristics and implications of the policy of dialogue, in Pardo (1996); the employers' attitude, also in Iglesias (1988); the trade union unrest and transition, in Soto Carmona (1996); the peculiarities of corporate policy, in Molins and Casademunt (1999).
10. On the CEOE as an employers' organisation and its political role, see Costas y Nonell (1996); on the catastrophic opinions, see Calvo Sotelo (1990: 164–165) and Fuentes Quintana (1995); Suárez's resistance, in Prego (1999: 263).
11. The Society of Economy, in Cercle de Economia (1983); biographies of Ferrer Salat, in Prego (1999: 260–265) and Puig Raposo and Cabrera (2000: 548–554).
12. Fomento's campaign and the following elections, in Ludeviv and Serlavós (1985: 135–138) and in Vidal Folch (1990).
13. The role of the CEOE in the UCD's crisis, in Aguilar (1985: 75–76); Huneeus (1985: 368); Mella (1992: 341); Powell (2001: 284–285). It is also recounted by Jaime García Añoveros, Minister of the Treasury with the UCD from 1979–1982, in *Memoria de la transición* (1995). The note about the CEOE in February 1981, in Calvo Sotelo (1990: 166–167).
14. The Fomento's manifesto, in Vidal Folch (1990).
15. The vote of businessmen in 1982, in Pérez Díaz (1987: 161); Calvo Sotelo's opinions, in Calvo Sotelo (1990: 166–171).

16. The transformation of the economic crisis into an industrial crisis, in Serrano Sanz (1994: 154); the businessmen's pessimism, in Torrero Mañas (1988); the opinions of Ferrer Salat and other businessmen, in Martínez Soler (1983).

17. The economic crisis, in Myro (1988); the regional evolution, in Cuadrado Roura (1988) and the crisis of the Cantabrian coast, in Vázquez (1988).

18. The close ties between private and public sector companies in the iron and steel industry, in Fraile Balbín (1992); the 'third industrialisation', in González Portilla (1997); the 'años de plomo', in Calleja (1999: 23–69). The kidnapping of Javier Ybarra and the end of the Neguri families, in Cacho (1990: 529–534). The new industries, in Fernández de Pinedo (2001: 118–121).

19. Boyer, in Martín Aceña and Moreno (1997).

20. The reorganisation of industry, in Buesa and Molero (1999); internationalisation, in Costa (1999); foreigners jostling, in Rodríguez Braun (1992: 58). The shock that was the rehabilitation of the figure of the businessman, in Torrero Mañas (1988). The words of Cuevas, cited by Rivasés (1991: 508). The words of Solchaga, in an interview in *Memoria de la transición* (1995).

21. For the INI, see Martín Aceña and Comín (1991).

22. The socialists and the privatisations, in Chari (1999).

23. The socialist rupture, in Juliá (1995b); texts by the protagonists compiled and discussed in Juliá (ed.) (1989); testimonies of Solchaga and Redondo, in Burns Marañón (1996); also in *Memoria de la transición* (1995). Analysis of the strike, in Powell (2001: 428–436).

24. Solchaga, in Rodríguez Braun (1997).

25. Powell (2001: 420–422). The business conference in January in the CEOE/CEPYME (1992).

26. A general picture of the changes in banking and their relation to political power, in González Urbaneja (1994). For the 'select club', see Rivasés (1991: 17–19). Sánchez Asiaín (1987).

27. For the 'banking transition', see Tortella (1995); an excellent summary of the changes in the financial system, in Rojo (2000); also, for the changes, see Ontiveros and Valero (1999).

28. The vicissitudes of the policy of deregulation and liberalisation, in Pérez (1997). The role of the Bank of Spain's Department of Studies, in Martín Aceña (2000).

29. Fuentes Quintana (1991); the quotation, in LXIII. Termes's work and opinions, in Termes (1991: 1669–1687 and 1914–1918).

30. For the banking crisis, Rojo (2000).

31. Rendueles's arrival at the Bank of Spain, the April report and Mariano Rubio's opinions, in Rivasés (1991: 215–226).

32. The history of Rumasa and its expropriation, in Díaz González (1983); for the unusual case, see Termes (1994: 190). Also, Martín Aceña and Moreno (1997: 218–221). The position of the AEB and the statement, in Termes (1991: 1513–1528).

33. The concentration of banks, in Termes (1991: 1519); the chronicle of Mariano Rubio's rise to the governorship of the Bank of Spain, in Rivasés (1991: 32–39).

34. The battle for the autonomy of the Bank of Spain, in Rivasés (1991: 269ff.). The Law of Autonomy and the new monetary policy, in Martín Aceña (2000: 300-308).

35. For the changes mentioned and those that follow, see González Urbaneja (1994). The situation of the banks, in Rivasés (1991); the case of Garriga Nogués, in Ekaizer (1994: 119–141).

36. All of these movements, in Rivasés (1988) and (1991).

37. The merger of the Bank of Bilbao and the Bank of Vizcaya, in Rivasés (1988: 99–151); the decision by the Bank of Spain, in Rivasés (1991: 471–478); Pedro de Toledo, in Cacho (1990).
38. The Santander Bank and the Popular Bank, in Rivasés (1988); the biography of Luis Valls, in Serrano Alcaide (2000) and the biography of Botín, in Hoyo Aparicio (2000).
39. The story of Mario Conde and the intervention, in Ekáizer (1994).
40. Ekaizer (1994). Banesto's balance, in Termes (1994: 206–208).
41. The 'lights and shadows' in Powell (2001: 456ff.). For the 'severe lesson' of reality, see Pradera (1992).
42. The end of the images of honesty and austerity, in Pradera (1992). The evolution of the socialist electorate, in Wert (1992: 97–98).
43. The causes of corruption in Spain, in Lamo de Espinosa (1997); the features of the Socialist Party as a cause of the corruption, in Powell (2001: 562–565); the corruption of society, in Nieto (1997).
44. The financing of the parties, in Castillo (1985).
45. An astonishing description and explanation of the networks and mechanisms of corruption, in Nieto (1997); Filesa and PSV, on Nieto (1997: 27–43).
46. Fernández and Santana (2000: 180–205).
47. The different cases of corruption, in Powell (2001: 528–539). The scandals, also in Pérez Díaz (1996: 87–133).
48. The three groups of media companies after the 1996 law and the print runs, in Chuliá Rodrigo (1997: 368–375). An account of the process in the mid-1980s, in Bustamante (1988) and also in Fernández and Santana (2000: 219–224).
49. The words of Cebrián, in Cebrián (1995); the changes in the shareholders, there and also in García Ruiz (2000b) and in Fernández and Santana (2000: 66–67).
50. For the policy of the successive governments regarding the media, see Fernández and Santana (2000). The groups in the radio stations, in Franquet (1988).
51. The socialists' news policy, in Fernández and Santana (2000: 169–354).
52. The concessions of private television channels, in Fernández and Santana (2000: 326–340).
53. The 'digital war', in Powell (2001: 610–612). A detailed, although biased, account of this war, in Cacho (1990); brief references in García Ruiz (2000b: 542) and Fernández and Santana (2000: 376–378).
54. Data about the groups, on their respective web pages.
55. Comín (2004).
56. Comín (2004). The data, in CEOE (2001).
57. The controversy and tension over the merger, in Mota (1998: 127–149) and (2001: 143–170).
58. The criticism of the privatisation process and the rise of a new business class, in Mota (1998) and (2001).
59. Mota (1998: 99–126) and (200: 171–194).
60. Fernández Ordóñez (1999) and Segura (1999) point out the privatisation before the liberalisation. Also, Comín (2004), who expands on everything else.
61. For the business scheme of the 1990s, see Ontiveros (1997) and Fariñas (1999); family business and ownership, in Casado (1997); also in Galve Górriz and Salas Fumás (1997) and Otaegui Murúa (1997). Ferrovial and the del Pino family, in Cabrera (2000b); Inditex, from an interview with José María Castellano, in Martínez Soler (1997).
62. Ontiveros (1997), Fariñas (1999); localisation and internationalisation, also in Costa (1999).

63. The data on the big companies at the beginning of the 1990s, in Carreras and Tafunell (1996); the Euro Stoxx 50, in any economic newspaper; the rankings of the Spanish firms cited correspond to the final days of November 2001.

64. For the processes of merger and concentration, see the articles included in No. 82 of *Economistas*, published in 1999 and dedicated to entrepreneurial scale and competition; the article cited is by Noceda (1999).

Bibliography

Aguilar, S. 1985. 'El asociacionismo empresarial en la transición postfranquista', *Papers*, 24, 53–83.

Aguilar Fernández, P. 1996. *Memoria y olvido de la Guerra Civil española*, Madrid: Alianza.

Alcaide Inchausti, J. 1988. 'La distribución de la renta', in J.L. García Delgado (dir.), *España. Economía*, Madrid: Espasa Calpe, 639–667.

Alonso Olea, E. J. 2000. 'Isidoro Delclaux Aróstegui', in E. Torres Villanueva (dir.), *Los 100 empresarios españoles del siglo XX*, Madrid: LID, 344–349.

Álvarez Rey, L. 1993. *La derecha en la Segunda República*. Sevilla: Publicaciones de la Universidad-Ayuntamiento de Sevilla.

Amsdem, J. 1974. *Convenios colectivos y lucha de clases en España*. París: Ruedo Ibérico.

Aparicio, M. Á. 1980. *El sindicalismo vertical y la formación del Estado franquista*. Barcelona: Eunibar.

Arana Pérez, I. 1982. *El monarquismo en Vizcaya durante la crisis del reinado de Alfonso XIII (1917–1931)*. Pamplona: Eunsa.

Archivo Histórico Nacional. Presidencia de Gobierno. Dossier 457.

Arranz, L. 1985. 'La ruptura del PSOE en la crisis de la Restauración: el peso del octubre ruso', *Estudios de Historia Social*, 33, 7–91.

Arranz, L. 1995. 'Modelos de partido', *Ayer*, 20, 80–110.

Arranz, L. and Cabrera, M. 1996: 'Parlamento, sistema de partidos y crisis de Gobierno en la etapa final de la Restauración, 1914–1923', *Revista de Estudios Políticos*, 93, 293–313.

Arranz, L., Cabrera, M. and Rey, F. 2000. 'The Assault on Liberalism, 1914–1923', in J. Álvarez Junco and A. Shubert (eds), *Spanish History since 1808*, London: Arnold, 91–206.

Aubert, P. 2000: 'Los intelectuales y la II República', *Ayer*, 20, 105–133.

Babiano Mora, J. 1995. *Emigrantes, cronómetros y huelgas. Un estudio sobre el trabajo y los trabajadores durante el franquismo (Madrid, 1951–1977)*. Madrid: Siglo XXI.

Baena del Alcázar, M. 1999. *Elites y conjuntos de poder en España (1939–1992)*. Madrid: Tecnos.

Bahamonde, Á., Martínez, J. and Rey, F. 1988. *La Cámara de comercio e Industria de Madrid, 1887–1987. Historia de una institución centenaria*. Madrid: Cámara de Comercio de Madrid.

Balfour, S. 1994. *La Dictadura, los trabajadores y la ciudad. El movimiento obrero en el área metropolitana de Barcelona (1939–1988)*. Valencia: Alfons el Magnanim.

Ballbé, M. 1983. *Orden público y militarismo en la España constitucional (1812–1983)*. Madrid: Alianza.

Ballestero, A. 1993. *Juan Antonio Suanzes, 1881–1977. La política industrial de la posguerra.* Madrid: LID.

Bañón Martínez, R. 1978. *Poder de la burocracia y Cortes franquistas (1943–1971).* Madrid: Instituto Nacional de la Administración Pública.

Barciela, C. 1986. 'Introducción', in R. Garrabou, C. Barciela, and J. I. Jiménez Blanco (eds), *Historia agraria de la España comtemporánea. 3. El fin de la agricultura tradicional (1900–1960).* Barcelona: Crítica.

Barciela, C., López Ortiz, M. I. and Melgarejo Moreno, J. 1996. 'La intervención del Estado en la agricultura durante el siglo XX', *Ayer*, 21, 51–96.

Barragán Moriana, A. 1990. *Conflictividad social y desarticulación política en la provincia de Córdoba, 1918–1920.* Córdoba: Publicaciones del Ayuntamiento de Córdoba.

Barrera, E. and San Román, E. 2000. 'Juan Antonio Suanzes, adalid de la industrialización', in A. Gómez Mendoza (ed.), *De mitos y milagros. El Instituto Nacional de Autarquía.* Barcelona, Universitat de Barcelona-Fundación Duques de Soria, 35–65.

Belford, N. 1979. 'El sistema bancario durante la Dictadura de Primo de Rivera', *Cuadernos Económicos de I.C.E.*, 10, 227–265.

Beltrán Villalba, M. 1990. 'La Administración pública y los funcionarios', in S. Giner, S. (dir.), *España. Sociedad y política.* Madrid: Espasa Calpe, 315–352.

Ben Ami, S. 1984. *La dictadura de Primo de Rivera (1923–1930).* Barcelona: Planeta.

Benavides, M. D. 1976. *El último pirata del Mediterráneo.* México: Roca.

Bengoechea Echaondo, S. 1994. *Organització patronal i conflictivitat social a Catalunya.* Barcelona: Publicaicons de l'Alabadia de Montserrat.

Bengoechea Echaondo, S. 1998. *El locaut de Barcelona (1919–1920). Els precedents de la dictadura de Primo de Rivera.* Barcelona: Curial.

Biescas, J. A. and Tuñón de Lara, M. 1980. *España bajo la dictadura franquista (1939–1975), vol. X de Historia de España.* Barcelona: Labor.

Bolloten, B. 1989. *La guerra civil española. Revolución y contrarrevolución.* Madrid: Alianza.

Bosch, A. 1983. *Ugetistas y libertarios. Guerra civil y revolución en el País Valenciano, 1936–1939.* Valencia: Alfons el Magnanim.

Bosch, A. 2001. 'La Segunda República y la Guerra Civil: conflicto rural y colectivización', in P. Preston and I. Saz (eds), *De la revolución liberal a la democracia parlamentaria. Valencia 1808–1975.* Madrid-Valencia: Biblioteca Nueva, 54–68.

Boyd, C. P. 1990. *La política pretoriana en el reinado de Alfonso XIII.* Madrid: Alianza.

Braña, J., Buesa, M. and Molero, J. 1984. *El Estado y el cambio tecnológico en la industrialización tardía. Un análisis del caso español.* Madrid-México: Fondo de Cultura Económica.

Bricall, J. M. 1985. 'La economía española (1936–1939)', in M. Tuñón de Lara et al. *La Guerra Civil española 50 años después.* Barcelona: Labor, 359–417.

Buesa, M. and Molero, J. 1999. 'La industria: reorganización y competitividad', in J. L.García Delgado (dir.), *España. Economía: ante el siglo XXI.* Madrid: Espasa Calpe, 151–173.

Burns Marañón, T. 1996. *Conversaciones sobre el socialismo.* Barcelona: Plaza y Janés.

Bustamante, E. 1988. 'Prensa: la concentración a mitad de camino' in E. Bustamante and R. Zallo (coords), *Las industrias culturales en España. Grupos multimedia y transnacionales.* Madrid: Akal, 21–61.

Bustamante, E. and Zallo, R. (coords). 1988. *Las industrias culturales en España. Grupos multimedia y transnacionales.* Madrid: Akal.

Caballero, J. 1972. 'Clase obrera y relaciones de trabajo', in S. del Campo (dir.), *La España de los años 70. Vol.I. La sociedad.* Madrid: Moneda y Crédito, 593–757.

Cabana, F. 1972. *Bancs y Banquers a Catalunya.* Barcelona: Edicions62.

Cabana, F. 1997. *La burgesia catalana. Una aproximació històrica.* Barcelona: Proa.

Cabana, F. 2000a. 'Lluís Carulla i Canals', in E. Torres Villanueva (dir.), *Los 100 empresarios españoles del siglo XX.* Madrid: LID, 403–405.

Cabana, F. 2000b. 'Eduard Recasens y Mercadé (1884–1940)', in E. Torres Villanueva (dir.), *Los 100 empresarios españoles del siglo XX.* Madrid: LID: 298–302.

Cabana, F. 2000c. 'Josep Suñol i Casanovas (1867–1945)', in E. Torres Villanueva (dir.), *Los 100 empresarios españoles del siglo XX.* Madrid: LID: 159–164.

Cabana, F. 2000d. 'Eusebi Bertrand i Serra (1887– 1945)', in E. Torres Villanueva (dir.), *Los 100 empresarios españoles del siglo XX.* Madrid: LID, 259–262.

Cabana, F. 2001. *37 anys de franquisme a Catalunya.* Barcelona: Pòrtic.

Cabrera, M. 1983. *La patronal ante la II República. Organizaciones y estrategia (1931–1936).* Madrid: Siglo XXI.

Cabrera, M. 1987. 'Las organizaciones patronales ante la conflictividad social y los Jurados Mixtos', in *La II república. Una esperanza frustrada.* Valencia: Alfons el Magnanim, 64–82.

Cabrera, M. 1991. 'La opinión ante la empresa pública (1898–1936)', in F. Comín and P. Martín Aceña (dirs), *Historia de la empresa pública en España.* Madrid: Civitas, 375–403.

Cabrera, M. 1994. *La industria, la prensa y la política. Nicolás María de Urgoiti (1869–1951).* Madrid: Alianza.

Cabrera, M. 1995. 'Las Cortes republicanas', *Ayer,* 20, 13–47.

Cabrera, M. (dir.) 1998. *Con luz y taquígrafos. El Parlamento en la restauración (1913–1923).* Madrid: Taurus.

Cabrera, M. 2000a. 'Los escándalos de la Dictadura de Primo de Rivera y las responsabilidades en la República: el asunto Juan March', *Historia y política,* 4, 7–30.

Cabrera, M. 2000b. 'Rafael del Pino Moreno (1920)', in E. Torres Villanueva (dir.), *Los 100 empresarios españoles del siglo XX.* Madrid: LID, 482–487.

Cabrera, M., Comín, F. and García Delgado, J. L. 1989. *Santiago Alba. Un programa de reforma económica en la España del primer tercio del siglo XX.* Madrid: Instituto de Estudios Fiscales.

Cabrera, M. and Rey Reguillo, F. 1997. *Corporativismo y articulación de intereses económicos en la España contemporánea, Working paper no. 396. Seminario de Historia Contemporánea.* Madrid: Instituto Universitario Ortega y Gasset.

Cabrera, M. and Rey Reguillo, F. 2000. 'La patronal y la brutalización de la política', in S. Juliá (dir.), *Violencia política en la España del siglo XX.* Madrid: Taurus, 235–288.

Cabrera, M. and Rey Reguillo, F. 2001. 'Los empresarios, los historiadores y la España del siglo XX', in A. Morales Moya (coord.), *Las claves de la España del siglo XX. La modernización social.* Madrid: Sociedad Estatal Nuevo Milenio, 291–313.

Cacho, J. 1990. *Pedro de Toledo. El desafío.* Madrid: Temas de Hoy.

Calvo, Á. 1990. 'El Foment del Treball Nacional davant d'un nou horizon', *L'Avenç,* 38, 54–58.

Calvo, Á. 1994. 'Frank Pearson y la Barcelona Traction Light and Power', in A. Sánchez (dir.), *Barcelona 1888–1929. Modernidad, ambición y conflcitos de una sociedad soñada.* Madrid: Alianza, 57–65.

Calvo Sotelo, J. 1974. *Mis servicios al Estado. Seis años de gestión. Apuntes para la historia.* 2nd edn. Madrid: Instituto de Estudios de Administración Local.

Calvo Sotelo, L. 1990. *Memoria viva de la transición.* Barcelona: Plaza y Janés-Cambio16.

Calleja, J. M. 1999. *La diáspora vasca. Historia de los condenados a irse de Euskadi por culpa de terrorismo de ETA.* Madrid: El País-Aguilar.

Campo, S. (dir.). 1972. *La España de los años 70. La sociedad*, vol. 1. Madrid: Moneda y Crédito.

Carr, R. 1979. *España 1808–1975*. Barcelona: Ariel.

Carr, R. and Carr, S. 1981 'La crisis del parlamentarismo', in *Historia General de España y América. Revolución y Restauración (1868–1931)*, vol. XVI (2). Madrid: Rialp, 465–522.

Carreras, A. 1990. *Industrialización española: estudios de historia cuantitativa*. Madrid: Espasa Calpe.

Carreras, A. and Tafunell, X. 1996. 'La gran empresa en la España contemporánea: entre el mercado y el Estado', in F. Comín and P. Martín Aceña (eds), *Historia de la empresa pública en España*. Madrid: Civitas, 73–90.

Casado, F. 1997. 'La empresa familiar en España', *Economistas*, 73, 82–85.

Casanova, J. 1985. *Anarquismo y revolución en la sociedad rural alavesa, 1936–1938*. Madrid: Siglo XXI.

Casanova, J. 1997. *De la calle al frente. El anarcosindicalismo en España (1931–1936)*. Barcelona: Crítica.

Casanova, J. (comp.). 1988. *El sueño igualitario: campesinado y colectivizaciones en la España republicana, 1936–1939*. Zaragoza: Institutción Fernando el Católico.

Casassas Ymbert, J. 1983. *La dictadura de Primo de Rivera (1923–1930). Textos*. Barcelona: Anthropos.

Castejón Rodríguez, M. 2000. *La patronal hullera asturiana y el bienio reformista*. Research paper. Madrid: UNED doctorate programme (unpublished).

Castillo, J. J. 1979. *Propietarios muy pobres. Sobre la subordinación política del pequeño campesino. La Confederación Nacional Católico Agraria 1917–1942*. Madrid: Ministerio de Agricultura.

Castillo, P. 1985. *La financiación de partidos y candidatos en las democracias occidentales*. Madrid: Centro de Investigaciones Sociológicas.

Catalán, J. 1989. 'Autarquía y desarrollo de la industria de fábrica durante la Segunda Guerra Mundial. Un enfoque comparativo', in J. L. García Delgado (ed.), *El primer franquismo. España durante la segunda Guerra Mundial*. Madrid: Siglo XXI, 35–88.

Catalán, J. 1995. *La economía española y la Segunda Guerra Mundial*. Barcelona: Ariel.

Cayon García, F. and Muñoz Rubio, M. 2000. 'José María de Oriol y Urquijo (1905–1985)' in E. Torres Villanueva (dir.), *Los 100 empresarios españoles del siglo XX*. Madrid: LID, 419–423.

Cazorla Sánchez, A. 2000. *Las políticas de la victoria. La consolidación del Nuevo Estado franquista (1938–1953)*. Madrid: Marcial Pons.

Cebrián, J. L. 1995. 'El País, un intelectual colectivo en la transición', in *Memoria de la transición*. Madrid: El Pais, 85–87.

Cenarro Lagunas, Á. 1997. *Cruzados y camisas azules. Los orígenes del franquismo en Aragón, 1936–1945*. Zaragoza: Prensas Universitarias de Zaragoza.

Ceoe. 1987. *Ceoe. 10 aniversario. 1977–1987*. Madrid: CEOE.

Ceoe. 2001. *Actualidad sectorial. Resumen del informe de actividades del año 2000 del Consejo consultivo de privatizaciones*. Madrid: CEOE.

Ceoe/Cepyme. 1992. *Conferencia empresarial 1992. La empresa española en la nueva Europa. Intervenciones, 30 y 31 de enero*. Madri: CEOE.

Ceoe/Cepyme, 1993. *Asamblea Empresarial Extraordinaria. En defensa de la Empresa y el empleo. Madrid, 26 de marzo. Palacio de Congresos y Exposiciones*. Madrid: CEOE.

Cercle de Economía. 1983. *Cercle d'Economia 1958–1983. Una trajectòria de modernització i convivència*. Barcelona: L'Avenç.

Cervera Gil, J. 1998. *Madrid en guerra. La ciudad clandestina, 1936–1939*. Madrid: Alianza.

Círculo de Empresarios. 1977–2000. *Memoria 1977 to Memoria 2000*. Madrid: Círculo de Empresarios.

Círculo de Empresarios. 1997. *XX años. XX temas. 1977–1997*. Madrid: Círculo de Empresarios.

Clavera, J., Esteba, J. M., Mones, M. A., Monserrat, A. and Ros Hombravella, J. 1973. *Capitalismo español: de la autarquía a la estabilización (1939–1959)*. Madrid: Edicusa.

Cobo Moreno, F. 2000. 'El voto campesino contra la II República. La derechización de los pequeños propietarios y arrendatarios agrícolas jiennenses, 1931–1936', *Historia Social*, 37, 119–140.

Comín, F. 1987. 'La economía española en el período de entreguerras (1919–1935)' in J. Nadal, A. Carreras and C. Sudrià (comps), *La economía española en el siglo XX. Una perspectiva histórica*. Barcelona: Ariel, 105–149.

Comín, F. 1988. *Hacienda y economía en la España contemporánea (1800–1936)*, 2 Vols. Madrid: Instituto de Estudios Fiscales.

Comín, F. 1991. 'Los monopolios fiscales' in F. Comín and P. Martín Aceña (dirs), *Historia de la empresa públicca en España*. Madrid: Espasa Calpe, 139–175.

Comín, F. 1996. 'Sector público y crecimiento económico en la dictadura de Franco', *Ayer* 21, 163–186.

Comín, F. 2004. 'Evolución histórica del sector público empresarial en España. Las transformaciones de la empresa pública durante la democracia 1977–2003', in *El papel del sector público en la economía. Privatización y promoción empresarial*. Madrid: Fundación Empresa Pública, 17–36.

Comín, F. and Martín Aceña, P. 1984. 'La política monetaria y fiscal durante la Dictadura y la Segunda República', *Papeles de Economía Española*, 20, 236–261.

Comín, F. and Martín Aceña, P. 1999. *Tabacalera y el estanco de tabaco en España, 1636–1998*. Madrid: Fundación Tabacalera.

Comín, F. and Martín Aceña, P. (dirs). 1991. *Historia de la empresa pública en España*. Madrid: Espasa Calpe.

Comín, F. and Martín Aceña, P. (eds). 1996a. *La empresa en la historia de España*. Madrid: Civitas.

Comín, F. and Martín Aceña, P. 1996b. 'Rasgos históricos de las empresas en España. Un panorama', *Revista de Economía Aplicada*, 12, 75–123.

Corcuera, J. 2001. *Orígenes, ideología y organización del nacionalismo vasco (1876–1904)*, Madrid: Taurus.

Costa, M. T. 1999. 'Estrategias empresariales: localización, internacionalización y globalización' in J. L. García Delgado (dir.), *España. Economía: ante el siglo XXI*. Madrid: Espasa Calpe, 431–454.

Costas, A. and Nonell, R. 1996. 'Organización de los intereses económicos, función empresarial y política económica en España. El caso de la CEOE' in F. Comín and P. Martín Aceña (eds), *La empresa en la historia de España*. Madrid: Civitas, 457–471.

Cotarelo, R. (comp.) 1992. *Transición política y consolidaicón democrática. España 1975–1986*. Madrid: Centro de Investigaciones Sociológicas.

Crespo Montes, L. F. 2000. *Las reformas de la Administración Española (1957–1967)*. Madrid: Centro de Estudios Políticos y Constitucionales.

Cruz, R. 1987. *El Partido Comunista de España en la II República*. Madrid: Alianza.

Cruz, R. 1997. '¡Luzbel vuelve al mundo! Las imágenes de la Rusia soviética y la acción colectiva en España' in R. Cruz and M. Pérez Ledesma (eds), *Cultura y movilización en la España contemporánea*. Madrid: Alianza, 273–303.

Cruz, R. 2001. 'Dos rebeliones militares en España, 1923 y 1936. La lógica de la guerra en la política', *Historia y Política*, 5, 29–53.

Cruz, R. and Pérez Ledesma, M. eds, 1997. *Cultura y movilización en la España contemporánea*. Madrid: Alianza.

Cuadrado Roura, J. R., 1988 'La crisis económica y la redefinición del mapa económico regional' in J. L. García Delgado (ed.), *España. Economía*. Madrid: Espasa Calpe, 745–764.

Cuesta, J. 1978. *Sindicalismo católico agrario en España (1917–1919)*. Madrid: Narcea.

Chari, R. S. 1999. 'Spanish Socialists, Privatising the Right Way?' in P. Heywood (ed.), London: Frank Cass Publishers, 163–179.

Chuliá Rodrigo, E. 1997. *La evolución silenciosa de las Dictaduras. El régimen de Franco ante la prensa y el periodismo*. Madrid: Instituto Juan March de Estudios e Investigaciones.

Díaz del Moral, J. 1979. *Historia de las agitaciones campesinas andaluzas. Córdoba*. Madrid: Alianza.

Díaz Gijón, J. R.; Fernández Navarrete, D.; González, M. J.; Martínez Lillo, P. A. and Soto Carmona, A. 1998. *Historia de la España actual: 1939–1996. Autoritarismo y democracia*. Madrid: Marcial Pons.

Díaz González, E. 1983. *Rumasa*. Barcelona: Planeta.

Díaz Hernández, O. 1998. *Los Marqueses de Urquijo. El apogeo de una saga poderosa y los inicios del Banco Urquijo, 1870–1931*. Pamplona: Eunsa.

Díaz Hernández, O. 2000. 'Estanislao (1872–1948), Juan Manuel (1879–1956) and Luis (1881–1956) Urquijo y Ussía' in E. Torres Villanueva (dir.), *Los 100 empresarios españoles del siglo XX*. Madrid: LID, 209–215.

Díaz Morlán, P. 1999. *Horacio Echevarrieta, 1870–1963. El capitalista republicano*. Madrid: LID.

Díaz Nosty, B. 1977. *La irresistible ascensión de Juan March*. Madrid, Sedmay.

Díez Cano, L. S. 1992. *Las Cámaras de Comercio durante el franquismo. El caso salmantina*. Salamanca: Universidad-Cámara de Comercio de Salamanca.

Dixon, A. 1985. *Señor monopolio. La asombrosa vida de Juan March*. Barcelona: Planeta.

Domínguez Jiménez, M. E. 1994. *Actitudes y estrategias de las Cámaras de Comercio ante la liberalización económica: respuesta al cuestionario del Gobierno. Enero 1959*. Working paper no. 9402. Madrid: Fundación Empresa Pública.

Echániz Ortúñez, J. A. 2000. 'Juan Tomás de Gandarias y Durañona (1870–1940)' in E. Torres Villanueva (dir.), *Los 100 empresarios españoles del siglo XX*. Madrid: LID, 186–191.

Ekaizer, E. 1994. *Banqueros de rapiña. Crónica secreta de Mario Conde*. Barcelona: Plaza y Janés.

Ekaizer, E. 1995. 'La expropiación del miedo' in *Memoria de la transición*. Madrid: El País, 377–383.

Equipo de Documentación Política. *1977 Radiografía de las nuevas Cortes*. Madrid: Sedmay ediciones.

Equipo Mundo. 1970. *Los 90 ministros de Franco*. Barcelona: Dopesa.

Elorza, A. 1978. *Ideologías del nacionalismo vasco*. San Sebastián: Haramburu.

Fariñas, J. C. 1999. 'La empresa española: características generales y comportamientos' in J. L. García Delgado (dir.), *España. Economía: ante el siglo XXI*. Madrid: Espasa Calpe, 409–429.

Fernández Clemente, E. 1997. 'Mariano Navarro Rubio' in E. Fuentes Quintana et al., *La Hacienda en sus ministros. Franquismo y democracia*. Zaragoza: Prensas Universitarias de Zaragoza, 53–90.

Fernández de la Mora, G. 1977. *El Estado de obras*. Madrid: Doncel.

Fernández Ordóñez, M. A. 1999. 'Privatización, desregulación y liberalización de los mercados' in J. L. García Delgado (dir.), *España. Economía: ante el siglo XXI*. Madrid: Espasa Calpe, 661–682.

Fernández de Pinedo, E. 2001. 'De la primera industrialización a la reconversión industrial: la economía vasca entre 1841 y 1990' in L. Germán, E. Llopis, J. Maluquer de Motes and S. Zapata (eds), *Hisotria económica regional de España, siglos XIX y XX*. Barcelona: Crítica, 95–124.

Fernández, I. and Santana, F. 2000. *Estado y medios de comunicación en la España democrática*. Madrid: Alianza.

Ferrer Guasp, P. 2000. Joan March. *Els inicis d'un imperi financer*. Mallorca: Edicions Cort

Ferrer Salat, C. 1978. 'Interview', *Cambio 16*, 01 Juin 1978.

Flaquer, Ll., Giner, S. and Moreno, L. 1990. 'La sociedad española en la encrucijada' in S. Giner (dir.), *España. Sociedad y política*. Madrid: Espasa Calpe, 19–74.

Foessa Foundation. 1976. *Estudios sociológicos sobre la situación social de España 1975*. Madrid, Fundación Foessa.

Fontana, J. (dir.) 1986. *España bajo el franquismo*. Barcelona: Crítica.

Fraile Balbín, P. 1991. *Industrialización y grupos de presión. La economía política de la protección en España, 1900–1950*. Madrid: Alianza.

Fraile Balbín, P. 1992. *Interés público y captura del Estado: la empresa pública siderúrgica en España, 1941–1981*, Working paper no. 9.203. Madrid: Fundación Empresa Pública.

Franquet, R. 1988. 'Radio: un oligopolio en transformación', in E. Bustamante y R. Zallo (coords), *Las industrias culturales en España. Grupos multimedia y transnacionales*. Madrid: Akal, 77–107.

Fuentes Quintana, E. 1988. 'Tres decenios de la economía española en perspectiva' in J. L. García Delgado (ed.), *España. Economía*. Madrid: Espasa Calpe, 1–75.

Fuentes Quintana, E. 1991. 'Prólogo' a R. Termes, *Desde la banca. Tres décadas de vida económica española*, Vol. 1. Madrid: Rialp, LI–XCVII.

Fuentes Quintana, E. 1995. 'Interview' in *Memoria de la transición*. Madrid: El País, 172–176.

Fuentes Quintana, E. 1999. 'La economía como profesión: una memoria personal' in J. L. García Delgado (dir.), *España. Economía: ante el siglo XXI*. Madrid: Espasa Calpe, 731–755.

Fuentes Quintana, E. et al. 1997. *La hacienda en sus ministros. Franquismo y democracia*. Zaragoza: Prensas Universitarias de Zaragoza.

Fusi, J. P. 1975. *Política obrera en el País Vasco (1880–1923)*. Madrid: Alianza.

Fusi, J. P. 1986. 'La reaparición de la conflictividad en la España de los años sesenta' in J. Fontana (ed.), *España bajo el franquismo*. Barcelona: Crítica, 160–169.

Fusi, J. P. and Palafox, J. 1997. *España: 1808–1996. El desafío de la modernidad*. Madrid: Espasa Calpe.

Galindo Vegas, P. 2000. 'José Meliá Sinisterra (1911–1999)' in E. Torres Villanueva (dir.), *Los 100 empresarios españoles del siglo XX*. Madrid: LID, 444–450.

Galve Górriz, C. and Salas Fumás, V. 1997. 'Propiedad y control en la empresa española', *Economistas*, 73, 70–77

García Añoveros, J. 1995. 'Interview' in *Memoria de la transición*. Madrid: El País, 420–423.

García Delgado, J. L. dir. 1988. *España. Economía*. Madrid: Espasa Calpe.

García Delgado, J. L. ed . 1989. *El primer franquismo. España durante la Segunda Guerra Mundial*. Madrid: Siglo XXI.

García Delgado, J. L. ed. 1991. *España entre dos siglos (1875–1931)*. Continuidad y cambio. Madrid: Siglo XXI.

García Delgado, J. L. dir. 1999. *España. Economía: ante el siglo XXI*. Madrid: Espasa Calpe.

García Delgado, J. L. and Jiménez, J. C. 1999. *Un siglo de España. La economía*. Madrid: Marcial Pons.

García Fernández, J. 1990. 'Política empresarial pública, 1973–1988' in P. Martín Aceña and F. Comín (eds), *Empresa pública e industrialización en España*. Madrid: Alianza, 217–250.

García Ruiz, J. L. 2000a. 'Eduardo Barreiros Rodríguez (1919–1992)' in E. Torres Villanueva (dir.), *Los 100 empresarios españoles del siglo XX*. Madrid: LID, 478–481.

García Ruiz, J. L. 2000b. 'Jesús de Polanco Gutiérrez (1929)' in E. Torres Villanueva (dir.), *Los 100 empresarios españoles del siglo XX*. Madrid: LID 538–543.

García Ruiz, J. L. 2000c. 'Andrés Moreno García (1895-1960)' in E. Torres Villanueva (dir.), *Los 100 empresarios españoles del siglo XX*. Madrid: LID 350–353.

García Venero, M. 1963. *Santiago Alba. Monárquico de razón*. Madrid: Aguilar.

García Venero, M. 1967. *Historia del nacionalismo catalán*. 2 Vols. Madrid: Editora Nacional.

Garitaonanindia, C. and Granja, J.L. (eds). 1987. *La guerra civil en el País Vasco. 50 años después*. Erandio: Servicio Editorial de la Universidad del País Vasco.

Garrabou, R., Barciela, C. and Jiménez Blanco, J. I. eds. 1986. *Historia agraria de la España contemporánea. 3. El fin de la agricultura tradicional (1900–1960)*. Barcelona: Crítica.

Garrido González, L. 1979. *Colectividades agrarias en Andalucía: Jaén (1931–1939)*. Madrid: Siglo XXI.

Garriga, R. 1976a. *Juan March y su tiempo*. Barcelona: Planeta.

Garriga, Ramón. 1976b. *La España de Franco*. 2 Vols. Madrid: G. del Toro editores.

Gay de Montellá, R. 1940. *Autarquía. Nuevas orientaciones de la Economía*. Barcelona: casa Editorial Bosch.

German Zubero, L. 2000. 'Antonio Beteré Salvador' in E. Torres Villanueva (dir.), *Los 100 empresarios españoles del siglo XX*. Madrid: LID, 380-383.

German, L., Llopis, E., Maluquer de Motes, J. and Zapata, S. (eds). 2001. *Historia económica regional de España, siglos XIX y XX*. Barcelona: Crítica.

Gil Andrés, C. 2000. *Echarse a la calle. Amotinados, huelguistas y revolucionarios (La Rioja, 1890–1936)*. Zaragoza: Prensas Universitarias de Zaragoza.

Gil Pecharromán, J. 1994. *Conservadores subversivos. La derecha autoritaria alfonsina (1913-1936)*. Madrid: Eudema.

Giménez Caballero, E. 1965. *El dinero y España*. Madrid: Afrodisio Aguado.

Giner, S. (dir.) 1990. *España. Sociedad y Política*. Madrid: Espasa Calpe.

Gómez Mendoza, A. 2000a 'De mitos y milagros' in A. Gómez Mendoza (ed.), *De mitos y milagros. El Instituto Nacional de Autarquía, 1941–1963*. Barcelona: Universitat de Barcelona-Fundación Duques de Soria, 17–34.

Gómez Mendoza, A. 2000b. 'La tercera vía, entre la dictadura eléctrica y la autorregulación, 1941–1944' in A. Gómez Mendoza (ed.). *De mitos y milagros. El Instituto Nacional de Autarquía, 1941–1963*. Barcelona: Universitat de Barcelona-Fundación Duques de Soria, 69–84.

Gómez Mendoza, A. (ed.). 2000. *De mitos y milagros. El Instituto Nacional de Autarquía, 1941–1963*. Barcelona: Universitat de Barcelona-Fundación Duques de Soria.

Gómez Navarro, J. L. 1991. *El régimen de Primo de Rivera*. Madrid: Cátedra.

Gómez Navarro, J. L., González Calvet, T. and Portuondo, E. 1979. 'Aproximación al estudio de las élites políticas en la Dictadura de Primo de Rivera', *Cuadernos Económicos de I.C.E.*, 10, 183–208.

Gómez Navarro, J. L., Moreno Luzón, J. and Rey Reguillo, F. 1998. 'La elite parlamentaria entre 1914 y 1923', in M. Cabrera (dir.), *Con luz y taquígrafos. El Parlamento en la restauración (1913–1923)*. Madrid: Taurus, 103–142.

Gómez Roda, A. and Saz, I. 2001. 'Valencia en la etapa franquista: política y sociedad' in P. Preston and I. Saz (eds), *De la revolución liberal a la democracia parlamentaria. Valencia 1808–1975*. Madrid-Valencia: Biblioteca Nueva, 255–283.

González Calbet, T. 1987. *La Dictadura de Primo de Rivera. El Directorio Militar.* Madrid: El Arquero.

González Calleja, E. and Rey Reguillo, F. 1995. *La defensa armada contra la revolución. Una historia de las guardias cívicas en la España del siglo XX.* Madrid: Consejo Superior de Investigaciones Científicas .

González Cuevas, P. C. 1998. *Acción Española. Teología política y nacionalismo autoritario en España (1913–1936).* Madrid: Tecnos.

González Cuevas, P. C. 2000. *Historia de las derechas españolas.* Madrid: Biblioteca Nueva.

González Cuevas, P. C. 2001. 'Antonio Goicoechea. Político y doctrinario monárquico', *Historia y Política*, 6, 161–189.

González González, M-J. 1979. *La economía política del franquismo (1940–1970).* Madrid: tecnos.

González Portilla, M. 1987. 'La economía de guerra en el País Vasco al servicio del Ejército de Franco' in C. Garitaonaindía and J. L. Granja (eds), *La guerra civil en el País Vasco. 50 años después.* Erandio: Servicio Editorial de la Universidad del País Vasco, 277–87.

González Portilla, M. 1997. 'Crisis industrial y nacionalismo a finales de siglo', *Cuadernos de Alzate*, 17, 21–36.

González Portilla, M. and Garmendia, J. M. 1988. *La posguerra en el País Vasco. Política, acumulación, miseria.* Donostia: Kriselu.

González Urbaneja, F. 1994. *Banca y poder.* Madrid: Espasa Calpe.

González Urbaneja, F. 2000. 'José María Aguirre Gonzalo (1897–1988)' in E. Torres Villanueva (dir.), *Los 100 empresarios españoles del siglo XX.* Madrid: LID, 368–373.

Gortázar, G. 1986. *Alfonso XIII: Hombre de Negocios.* Madrid: Alianza.

Güerri Martín, C. 1988. 'La licencias de caza, un nuevo barómetro de la conflictividad social durante la República' in *Actas del Primer Congreso de Historia de Castilla-La Mancha* Vol. X (2), Talavera de la Reina: Servicio de Publicaciones de la Junta de Castilla La Mancha, 155–162.

Guía del bolsista ... Años 1936–1940. 1940, Madrid, s. e.

Gutiérrez Molina, J. L. 2000. 'José Banús Masdeu (1906–1984)' in E. Torres Villanueva (dir.), *Los 100 empresarios españoles del siglo XX.* Madrid: LID, 424–427.

Hernández Andreu, J. 1986. *España y la crisis de 1929.* Madrid: Espasa Calpe.

Heywood, P. (ed.) 1999. *Politics and Policy in Democratic Spain.* London: Frank Cass Publishers.

Howson, G. 2000. *Armas para España. La historia no contada de la Guerra Civil española.* Barcelona: Península.

Hoyo Aparicio, A. 2000. 'Emilio Botín-Sanz de Sautuola y López' in E. Torres Villanueva (dir.), *Los 100 empresarios españoles del siglo XX.* Madrid: LID, 398–402.

Huneeus, C. 1985. *La Unión de Centro Democrático y la transición a la democracia en España.* Madrid: Centro de Investigaciones Sociológicas.

Iglesias, R. 1988. 'La concertación social desde la perspectiva de las organizaciones empresariales' in A. Zaragoza (comp.), *Pactos sociales, sindicatos y patronal en España.* Madrid: Siglo XXI, 145–179.

Jerez Mir, M. 1982. *Élites políticas y centros de extracción en España, 1938–1957.* Madrid: Centro de Investigaciones Sociológicas.

Jerez Mir, M. 1996. 'El régimen de Franco: élite política central y redes clientelares (1938–1957)' in A. Robles Egea (comp.), *Política en penumbra. Patronazgo y clientelismo políticos en la España contemporánea.* Madrid: Siglo XXI, 253–274

Jiménez, F. 2000. 'El caso Matesa: un escándalo político en un régimen autoritario', *Historia y Política*, 4, 43–68.

Juana López, J. 2000. 'Eulogio Gómez Franqueira (1917–1988)' in E. Torres Villanueva (dir.), *Los 100 empresarios españoles del siglo XX*. Madrid: LID, 472–477.

Juliá, S. 1984. Madrid, 1931–1934. De la fiesta popular a la lucha de clases. Madrid: Siglo XXI.

Juliá, S. 1987. 'Los objetivos políticos de la legislación laboral' in *La II República española. El primer bienio*. Madrid: Siglo XXI, 27–47.

Juliá, S. 1991. 'Sociedad y política', in M. Tuñón de Lara et al., *Transición y democracia (1973–1985). Historia de España*. Vol. X (**). Barcelona: Labor, 29–186.

Juliá, S. 1994. 'Orígenes sociales de la democracia en España', *Ayer*, 15, 165–188.

Juliá, S. 1995a 'Sistema de partidos y problemas de consolidación de la democracia', *Ayer*, 20, 110–139.

Juliá, S. 1995b 'Ruptura de familia' in *Memoria de la transición*, Madrid: El País, 437–439.

Juliá, S. 1997. *Los socialistas en la política española, 1879–1982*. Madrid: Taurus.

Juliá, S. 1999a. *Un siglo de España. Política y sociedad*. Madrid: Marcial Pons.

Juliá, S. 2000a. 'Ocho meses en la vida de Indalecio Prieto' in *La Hacienda desde sus ministros. Del 98 a la guerra civil*. Zaragoza: Prensas Universitarias de Zaragoza, 315–342.

Juliá, S. (ed.) 1989. *La desavenencia. Partidos, sindicatos y huelga general*. Madrid: El País-Aguilar.

Juliá, S. (coord.) 1999b. *Víctimas de la guerra civil*. Madrid: Temas de Hoy.

Juliá, S. (dir.) 2000b. *Violencia política en la España del siglo XX*. Madrid: Taurus.

Lacomba, J. A. 1970. *La crisis española de 1917*. Madrid: Ciencia Nueva.

Lamo de Espinosa, E. 1997. 'Corrupción política y ética económica' in F. Laporta and S. Álvarez (eds), *La corrupción política*. Madrid: Alianza, 271–290.

Laporta, F. and Álvarez, S. eds. 1997. *La corrupción política*. Madrid: Alianza.

León Ignacio, J. 1981. *Los años del pistolerismo en Barcelona*. Barcelona: Planeta.

Linz, J. J. 1972. 'Continuidad y discontinuidad en la élite política española: de la Restauración al régimen actual' in *Estudios de Ciencia Política y Sociología. Homenaje al profesor Carlos Ollero*. Madrid, 361–423.

Linz, J. J. 1988. 'Política e intereses a lo largo de un siglo en España, 1880–1980' in M. Pérez Yruela and S. Giner (eds), *El corporatismo en España*. Barcelona: Ariel 67–123.

Linz, J. J. and Miguel, A. 1966. *Los empresarios ante el poder público*. Madrid: Instituto de Estudios Políticos.

López Carrillo, J. M. 2000. 'Damián Mateu Bisa (1863–1935)' in E. Torres Villanueva (dir.), *Los 100 empresarios españoles del siglo XX*. Madrid: LID, 130–136.

López Nieto, L. 1988. *Alianza Popular: estructura y evolución electoral de un partido conservador (1976-1982)*. Madrid: Centro de Investigaciones Sociológicas.

López Novo, J. P. 1995 'Empresarios y relaciones labourales: una perspectiva histórica' in F. Miguélez and C. Prieto (dir. and coord.), *Las relaciones laborales en España*. Madrid: Siglo XXI, 131–146.

López Rodó, L. 1979. *La larga marcha hacia la Monarquía*. Barcelona: Plaza y Janés.

López Rodó, L. 1990. *Memorias*. Barcelona: Plaza y Janés/Cambio 16.

Lorenzo Espinosa, J. M. 1989. *Dictadura y dividendo. El discreto negocio de la burguesía vasca (1937–1950)*. Bilbao: Universidad de Deusto.

Ludeviv, M. and Serlavós, R. 1985. 'El Fomento del Trabajo Nacional', *Papeles de Economía Española*, 22, 122–138.

Llopis Agelán, E. and Fernández, R. 1997. *Índices provinciales y regionales de producción manufacturera, 1964–1977*, Documento de Trabajo Fundación Empresa Pública, no. 9706. Madrid: Fundación Empresa Pública.

Macarro Vera, J. M. 1985. *La utopía revolucionaria. Sevilla en la Segunda República.* Sevilla: Caja de Ahorros y Monte de Piedad de Sevilla.

Malefakis, E. 1972. *Reforma agraria y revolución campesina en la España del siglo XX.* Barcelona: Ariel.

Malo de Molina, J. L. 1988. 'Mercado de trabajo: empleo y salarios. Distorsiones y ajustes' in J. L. García Delgado (ed), *España. Economía.* Madrid: Espasa Calpe, 927–951.

Maravall, J. M. 1970. *El desarrollo económico y la clase obrera.* Barcelona: Ariel.

Marín i Corbera, M. 2000a. *Els ajuntaments franquistes a Catalunya. Política i administració municipal, 1938–1979.* Lleida: Pagés editors.

Marín i Corbera, M. 2000b. *Catalanisme, clientelisme i franquisme. Josep Maria de Porcioles.* Barcelona: Societat Catalana d'Estudis Històrics-Institut d'Estudis Catalans.

Martín Aceña, P. 1984. *La política monetaria en España 1919–1935.* Madrid: Instituto de Estudios Fiscales.

Martín Aceña, P. 1985 'Desarrollo y modernización del sistema financiero, 1844–1935', en N. Sánchez Albornoz (comp.), *La modernización económica de España, 1830–1930.* Madrid: Alianza, 121–146.

Martín Aceña, P. 1987. 'Economía y política durante el primer bienio republicano' in *La II República. El primer bienio.* Madrid: Siglo XXI, 119–134.

Martín Aceña, P. 2000. *El Servicio de Estudios del Banco de España 1930–2000.* Madrid: Banco de España.

Martín Aceña, P. 2001. *El oro de Moscú y el oro de Berlín.* Madrid: Taurus.

Martín Aceña, P. and Comín, F. 1990a. 'El Instituto Nacional de Industria: inversión industrial y especialización sectorial' in P. Martín Aceña and F. Comín (eds.), *Empresa pública e industrialización en España.* Madrid: Instituto Nacional de Industria, 117–136.

Martín Aceña, P. and Comín, F. 1991. INI. *50 años de industrialización en España.* Madrid: Espasa Calpe.

Martín Aceña, P. and Comín, P. (eds) 1990b. *Empresa pública e industrialización en España.* Madrid: Instituto Nacional de Industria.

Martín Aceña, P. and Moreno, B. 1997. 'Miguel Boyer Salvador' in E. Fuentes Quintana et al. *La Hacienda en sus ministros. Franquismo y democracia.* Zaragoza: Prensas Universitarias de Zaragoza, 205–227.

Martín Aceña, P. and Pons, M. Á. 1996. 'Estructura y rentabilidad de las empresas financieras en España, 1874–1975' in F. Comín and P. Martín Aceña (eds), *La empresa en la historia de España.* Madrid: Civitas, 325–345.

Martín Gaite, C. 1977. *El conde de Guadalhorce, su época y su labour.* Madrid: Colegio de Ingenieros de Caminos, Canales y Puertos.

Martín Rodríguez, M. 1988. 'Evolución de las disparidades regionales: una perspectiva histórica' in J. L. García Delgado (dir), *España. Economía.* Madrid: Espasa Calpe, 703–743.

Martínez, R. 1993. *Business and democracy in Spain.* London: Praeger, Westport.

Martínez, R. and Pardo, R. 1985. 'El asociacionismo empresarial español en la transición', *Papeles de Economía Española,* 22, 84–114.

Martínez Mesa, F. J. 1997. *El Consejo de Economía nacional. Un estudio sobre el origen de la representación de los intereses económicos en el Estado español,* Madrid.

Martínez Ruiz, E. 1994. *La intervención del INI en la industria de la defensa durante la autarquía,* Working paper Fundación Empresa Pública no. 408, Madrid.

Martínez Soler, J. A. 1983. *Los empresarios ante la crisis económica.* Barcelona-Buenos Aires-Mexico.

Martínez Soler, J. A. 1997 'José María Castellano', *Economistas*, 73, 118–126.

Martorell Linares, M. Á. 2000. *El santo temor al déficit. Política y Hacienda en la Restauración*. Madrid: Alianza.

Mateos, A. 1997. *La denuncia del Sindicato Vertical*. Madrid: Consejo Económico y Social.

Maura Gamazo, G. 1930. *Al servicio de la historia. Bosquejo histórico de la Dictadura*. Madrid: Morata.

Meaker, G. H. 1978. *La izquierda revolucionaria en España, 1914–1923*. Barcelona: Ariel.

Mella, M. 1992. 'Los grupos de interés en la consolidación democrática' in R. Cotarelo (comp.), *Transición política y consolidación democrática. España 1975–1986*. Madrid: Centro de Investigaciones Sociológicas, 327–342.

Memoria de la transición. 1995. Madrid: El País.

Miguel, A. 1975. *Sociología del franquismo. Analisis ideológico de los ministros del régimen*. Barcelona: Euros.

Miguelez, F. and Prieto, C. (dirs). 1995. *Las relaciones laborales en España*. Madrid: Siglo XXI.

Miralles, R. 1999. 'Una visión historiográfica: la dictadura franquista según Manuel Tuñón de Lara', in J. L. Granja (ed.), *Tuñón de Lara y la historiografía española*. Madrid: Siglo XXI, 55–68.

Molinero, C. and Ysàs, P. 1991. *Els industrials catalans durant el franquisme*. Vic: Eumo.

Molinero, C. and Ysàs, P. 1993. 'Los industriales catalanes y el primer "ventenio" franquista: ¿adhesión política y disidencia económica' in I. Sánchez, M. Ortiz Heras and D. Ruiz (coords), *España franquista. Causa general y actividades sociales ante la Dictadura*. Albacete: Univerdidad de Castilla la Mancha, 161–178.

Molinero, C. and Ysàs, P. 1998. *Productores disciplinados y minorías subversivas. Clase obrera y conflictividad laboural en la España franquista*. Madrid: Siglo XXI.

Molinero, C. and Ysàs, P. 1999. 'Modernización económica e inmovilismo político (1959–1975)', in J. A. Martínez (coord.), *Historia de España. Siglo XX*. Madrid: Cátedra, 129–242.

Molins, J. and Casademunt, A. 1999. 'Pressure Groups and Articulation of interests', P. Heywood (ed.), *Politics and Policy in Democratic Spain*. London: Frank Cass Publishers, 124–146.

Montero Gibert, J. R. 1977. *El catolicismo social y político en la II República*, 2 Vols., Madrid: Ministerio de Trabajo y Seguridad Social.

Montoya Melgar, A. 1992. *Ideología y lenguaje en las leyes laborales de España (1873–1978)*. Madrid: Civitas.

Moradiellos, E. 2000. *La España de Franco (1939–1975). Política y Sociedad*. Madrid: Síntesis.

Morales Moya, A. (coord.) 2000. *Las claves de la España del siglo XX. La modernización social*. Madrid: Sociedad Estatal España Nuevo Milenio.

Moreno Castaño, B. 2000a. 'Lluis Alfons Sedó i Guichard (1873–1952)' in E. Torres Villanueva (dir.), *Los 100 empresarios españoles del siglo XX*. Madrid: LID, 216–222.

Moreno Castaño, B. 2000b. 'José Entrecanales Ibarra (1899-1990)' in E. Torres Villanueva (dir.), *Los 100 empresarios españoles del siglo XX*. Madrid: LID, 384–390.

Moreno Castaño, B. 2000. 'Lluis Alfons Sedó i Guichard' (1873–1952)' in E. Torres Villanueva (dir.), *Los 100 empresarios españoles del siglo XX*. Madrid: LID, 216–222.

Moreno Fonseret, R. 1999. 'El régimen y la sociedad. Grupos de presión y concreción de intereses', *Ayer*, 33, 87–113.

Moreno Gómez, F. 1989. 'La Represión en la España campesina' in J. L. García Delgado (ed.), *El primer franquismo. España durante la Segunda Guerra Mundial*. Madrid: Siglo XXI, 189–207.

Moreno Lázaro, J. 2000. 'Juan Gómez Cuétara (1900–1998)', in E. Torres Villanueva (dir.), *Los 100 empresarios españoles del siglo XX*. Madrid: LID 2000: 391–397.

Mota, J. 1998. La gran expropiación. *Las privatizaciones y el nacimiento de una nueva clase empresarial al servicio del PP*. Madrid: temas de Hoy.

Mota, J. 2001. *Aves de raPPiña. Cómo se han apoderado los populares de empresas, medios de comunicación y organismos independientes*. Madrid: Temas de Hoy.

Moya, C. 1975. *El poder económico en España (1939–1970)*. Madrid: Túcar.

Moya, C. 1984. *Estado nacional y sociedad industrial: España 1936–1980*. Madrid: Alianza.

Moyano Estrada, E. 1984. *Corporatismo y agricultura. Asociaciones profesionales y articulación de intereses en la agricultura española*. Madrid: Instituto de Estudios Agrarios, Pesqueros y Alimentarios.

Muñoz, J. 1969. *El poder de la banca en España*. Madrid: ZYX.

Muñoz, J. 1978. 'La expansión bancaria entre 1919 y 1926. La formación de una banca "nacional"', *Cuadernos Económicos de ICE*, 6, 98–162.

Muñoz, J. 1988. *El fracaso de la burguesía financiera catalana. La crisis del Banco de Barcelona*. Madrid: Endymion.

Muñoz, J., Roldán, S. and Serrano, Á. 1978a. 'La vía nacionalista del capitalismo español. Documentación y selección de textos', *Cuadernos Económicos de ICE*, 7/8.

Muñoz, J., Roldán, S. and Serrano, Á. 1978b. *La internacionalización del capital en España, 1959–1977*. Madrid: Edicusa.

Myro, R. 1988. 'Las empresas públicas', in J. L. García Delgado (ed), *España. Economía*. Madrid: Espasa Calpe, 471–497.

Myro, R. and Ruiz Céspedes, T. 1999. 'Concentración de la producción y liderazgo en la industria española', *Economistas*, 82, 70–86.

Nadal, J., Carreras, A. and Sudriá, C. (comps). *La economía española en el siglo XX. Una perspectiva histórica*. Barcelona: Ariel.

Nadal, J. and Carreras, A. (dirs). 1990. *Pautas regionales de la industrialización española*. Barcelona: Ariel.

Nieto, A. 1997. *Corrupción en la España democrática*. Barcelona: Ariel.

Noceda, M. Á. 1999. 'Participaciones y núcleos duros', *Economistas*, 82, 151–158.

Olábarri Gortázar, I. 1978. *Relaciones laborales en Vizcaya (1890–1936)*. Durango: Leopoldo Zugaza editor.

Ontiveros, E. 1997. 'Las empresas españolas en el fin de siglo', *Economistas*, 73, 6–15.

Ontiveros, E. and Valero, F. 1999. 'Sistema financiero: cambios estructurales e institucionales' in J.L.García Delgado (dir.), *España. Economía: ante el siglo XXI*. Madrid: Espasa Calpe, 271–302.

Ortiz Heras, M. 1992. *Las Hermandades de Labradores en el franquismo. Albacete, 1943–1977*. Albacete: Instituto de Estudios Albacentenses.

Ortiz-Villajos, J. M. and Dantart Pitarch, A. 2000. 'Félix Huarte Goñi (1896–1971)' in E. Torres Villanueva (dir.), *Los 100 empresarios españoles del siglo XX*. Madrid: Lid, 361–367.

Otaegui Murúa, M. 1997: 'Es relevante la propiedad de la empresa', *Economistas*, 73, 78–81.

Pablo, S., Mees, L. and Rodríguez Ranz, J. 1999. *El péndulo patriótico. Historia del Partido Nacionalista Vasco, I: 1895–1936*. Barcelona: Crítica.

Pabón, J. 1952. *Cambó (1876–1918)*, Vol. I. Barcelona: Alpha.

Pabón, J. 1969. *Cambó (1918–1930)*, Vol. II. Barcelona: Alpha.

Palafox Gamir, J. 1991a. *Atraso económico y democracia. La Segunda República y la economía española, 1892–1936*. Barcelona: Crítica.

Palafox Gamir, J. 1991b. 'Atraso agrario y modernización económica (1874–1931)', in J. L. García Delgado (ed.), *España entre dos siglos (1875–1931)*. *Continuidad y cambio*. Madrid: Siglo XXI, 157–177

Pániker, S. 1969. *Conversaciones en Madrid*. Barcelona: Kairós.

Pardo, R. 1996. 'Organizaciones empresariales, sindicatos y relaciones industriales' in J. Tusell, E. Lamo de Espinosa and R. Pardo (eds), *Entre dos siglos*. *Reflexiones sobre la democracia española*. Madrid: Alianza, 469–518.

Paredes, J. 1997. *Félix Huarte, 1896–1971*. Barcelona: Ariel.

Payne, S. G. 1965. *Falange. Historia del fascismo español*. París: Ruedo Ibérico.

Payne, S. G. 1987. *El régimen de Franco, 1936–1975*. Madrid: Alianza.

Payne. S. 1993. *Spain's First Democracy. The Second Republic, 1931–1936*. Wisconsin: University of Wisconsin Press.

Pérez, S. A. 1997. *Banking on Privilege. The Politics of Spanish Financial Reform*. Ithaca and London: Cornell University Press.

Pérez de Armiñan, G. 1970. 'Apéndice. La Ordenación Bancaria de 1962 y la nacionalización del Banco de España', in F. Ruiz Martín et al., *El Banco de España. Una historia económica*. Madrid: Banco de España, 481–524.

Pérez Díaz, V. 1985. 'Los empresarios y la clase política', *Papeles de Economía Española*, 22, 2–37.

Pérez Díaz, V. 1987. *El retorno de la sociedad civil*. Madrid: Instituto de Estudios Económicos

Pérez Díaz, V. 1996. *España puesta a prueba 1976–1996*. Madrid: Alianza.

Pérez Ledesma, M. 1990. *Estabilidad y conflicto social. España, de los iberos al 14-D*. Madrid: Nerea.

Pérez Yruela, M. and Giner, S. eds. 1988. *El corporatismo en España*. Barcelona: Ariel.

Perucho, A. 1930. *Catalunya sota la Dictadura (dades per a la història)*. Barcelona: Proa.

Pinilla de las Heras, E. 1968. *Los empresarios y el desarrollo capitalista*. Barcelona: Edicions 62.

Pinilla de las Heras, E. 1996. *La memoria inquieta. Autobiografía sociológica de los años difíciles (1935–1959)*. Madrid: Centro de Investigaciones Sociológicas.

Pla, J. 1981. Francesc Cambó. *Materials per a una història, Obra completa*, Vol. XXV. Barcelona: Destino.

Plata Parga, G. 1991. *La derecha vasca y la crisis de la democracia española (1931–1936)*. Bilbao: Diputación Foral de Vizcaya.

Powell, Ch. 2001. *España en democracia, 1975–2000*. Barcelona: Plaza y Janés.

Pradera, J. 1992. 'Las pasiones del poder: el PSOE tras diez años de poder', in J. Tusell and J. Sinova, *La década socialista. El ocaso de Felipe González*. Madrid: Espasa Hoy, 265–283.

Prego, V. 1999. *Diccionario de la transición*. Barcelona: Plaza y Janés.

Preston, P. and Saz, I. (eds). 2001. *De la revolución liberal a la democracia parlamentaria. Valencia 1808–1975*. Madrid-Valencia: Biblioteca Nueva.

Prieto, I. 1975. *Dentro y fuera del gobierno*. México: Oasis.

Prieto, I. 1999. *Textos escogidos*. Asturias: Junta general de Principado de Asturias.

Puig Raposo, N. and Cabrera Calvo-Sotelo, M. 2000. 'Carles Ferrer i Salat (1931–1998)' in E. Torres Villanueva (dir.), *Los 100 empresarios españoles del siglo XX*. Madrid: LID, 548–554.

Puy, J. 1983. *Alfons Sala i Argemí. Industrial i polític, 1863–1945*. Terrassa: Arxiu Tobella

Recasens, F. 1956. *Escritos (1927–1936)*. Barcelona.

Reig Armero, R. 2000. 'Luis Suñer Sanchis (1910–1990)' in E. Torres Villanueva (dir.), *Los 100 empresarios españoles del siglo XX*. Madrid: LID, 439–443.

Rey Reguillo, F. 1983. 'Actitudes políticas y económicas de la patronal catalana (1917–1923)', *Estudios de Historia Social*, 24–25, 23–148.

Rey Reguillo, F. 1992. *Propietarios y patronos. La política de las organizaciones económicas en la España de la Restauración (1914–1923)*. Madrid: Ministerio de Trabajo y Seguridad Social.

Rey Reguillo, F. 1997. 'El empresario, el sindicalista y el miedo', in R. Cruz and M. Pérez Ledesma (eds.), *Cultura y movilización en la España contemporánea*. Madrid: Alianza, 235–272.

Rey Reguillo, F. 2000. 'José Calvo Sotelo (1893–1936). Del maurismo a la contrarrevolución' in *La Hacienda desde sus Ministros. Del 98 a la guerra civil*. Zaragoza, Prensas Universitarias de Zaragoza, 281–314.

Riera, I. 1998. *Els catalans de Franco*. Barcelona: Plaza y Janés.

Rijnen, H. 1985. 'La Ceoe como organización', *Papeles de Economía Española*, 22, 115–121.

Riquer i Permanyer, B. 1996. *L'últim Cambó (1936–1947): La dreta catalanista davant la guerra civil i el primer franquisme*. Vic: Eumo.

Riquer i Permanyer, B. 2000a. 'Francisco Cambó i Batlle (1876–1947)', in E. Torres Villanueva (dir.), *Los 100 empresarios españoles del siglo XX*. Madrid: LID, 239–244.

Riquer i Permanyer, B. 2000b. 'Pròleg' in M. Marín i Corbera, *Els ajuntaments franquistes a Catalunya. Política i administració municipal, 1938–1979*. Lleida: Pagés editors.

Rivasés, J. 1988. *Los banqueros del PSOE*. Barcelona: EdicionesB.

Rivasés, J. 1991. Mariano Rubio. *Los secretos del Banco de España*. Madrid: Temas de Hoy.

Robles, C. 1997. *José Maria Urquijo e Ybarra, Opinión, Religión y Poder*. Madrid: Consejo Superior de Investigaicones Científicas.

Robles Egea, A. (comp.) 1996. *Política en penumbra. Patronazgo y clientelismo políticos en la España contemporánea*. Madrid: Siglo XXI.

Rodríguez Braun, C. 1992. 'De la agonía a la agonía', in J. Tusell and J. Sinova et al., *La década socialista. El ocaso de Felipe González*. Madrid: Espasa Hoy, 51–66.

Rodríguez Braun, C. 1997. 'Carlos Solchaga Catalán', in E. Fuentes Quintana et al. *La Hacienda en sus ministros. Franquismo y democracia*. Zaragoza: Prensas Universitarias de Zaragoza, 229–262.

Rodríguez Braun, C. 2002. *25 años del Círculo de Empresarios*. Madrid: Círculo de Empresarios.

Rodríguez Jiménez, J. L. 1997. *La extrema derecha española en el siglo XX*. Madrid: Alianza.

Rojo, L. Á. 1987. 'La crisis de la economía española, 1973–1984' in J. Nadal, A. Carreras and C. Sudrià (comps), *La economía española en el siglo XX. Una perspectiva histórica*. Barcelona: Ariel, 190–200.

Rojo, L. Á. 2000. 'El sector financiero', typewritten text from the conference given at the Real Academia de la Historia on 18 December.

Rojo Cagigal, J. C. 2000. 'Tomás de Zubiría e Ybarra (1857–1932)' in E. Torres Villanueva (dir.), *Los 100 empresarios españoles del siglo XX*. Madrid: LID, 100–105.

Roldán, S. and García Delgado, J. L. (with the collaboration of Juan Muñoz) 1973. *La formación de la sociedad capitalista en España, 1914–1920*. 2 Vols. Madrid: Confederación Española de Cajas de Ahorro.

Rubio Gil, Á. 2000. 'Pablo de Garnica Echevarría (1876–1959)' in E. Torres Villanueva (dir.), *Los 100 empresarios españoles del siglo XX*. Madrid: LID, 245–249.

Rueda Laffond, J. C. 1991. 'Antonio Maura: las pautas inversionistas de un miembro de la elite política de la Restauración', *Historia Social*, 11, 125–144.

Ruesga Benito, S. M. 1995. 'La negociación colectiva', in F. Miguélez and C. Prieto (dirs), *Las relaciones laborales en España*. Madrid: Siglo XXI, 379–402.

Ruiz, D. (dir.) 1994. *Historia de Comisiones Obreras (1958–1988)*. Madrid: Siglo XX.

Ruiz Martin, F. et al. 1970. *El Banco de España. Una historia económica*. Madrid: Banco de España.

Sánchez, A. (dir.) 1994. *Barcelona 1888–1929. Modernidad, ambición y conflictos de una sociedad soñada*. Madrid: Alianza.

Sanchez, I., Ortiz Heras, M. and Ruiz, D. (coords.) 1993. *España franquista. Causa general y actividades sociales en la Dictadura*. Albacete: Instituto de Estudios Albaceteños.

Sánchez Albornoz, N. (comp.) 1985. *La modernización económica de España, 1830–1930*. Madrid: Alianza.

Sánchez Asiaín, J. Á. 1987. *Reflexiones sobre la banca. Discurso leído en el acto de su recepción en la Real Academia de Ciencias Morales y Políticas*. Madrid: Real Academia de Ciencias Morales y Políticas.

Sánchez Asiaín, J. Á. 1999. *Economía y finanzas en la Guerra Civil española (1936–1939)*. Madrid: Real Academia de la Historia.

Sánchez Soler, M. 2001. *Ricos por la patria. Grandes magnates de la dictadura, altos financieros de la democracia*. Barcelona: Plaza y Janés.

San Román, E. 1999. *Ejército e industria: el nacimiento del INI*. Barcelona: Crítica.

Sardá Dexeus, J. 1970. 'El Banco de España (1931–1962)', in F. Ruiz Martín. et al., El Banco de España. *Una historia económica*. Madrid: Banco de España, 419–479.

Sartorius, N. and Alfaya, J. 1999. *La memoria insumisa. Sobre la Dictadura de Franco*. Madrid: Espasa Calpe.

Schwartz, P. and González, M. J. 1978. *Una historia del Instituto Nacional de Industria (1941–1976)*. Madrid: Tecnos.

Seco Serrano, C. 1995. *La España de Alfonso XIII. El Estado y la política (1902–1931). Historia de España de Ramón Menéndez Pidal, Vol. XXXVIII*. Madrid: Espasa Calpe.

Segura, J. 1988. 'Intervención pública y política de bienestar: el papel del Estado' in J. L. García Delgado (dir.), *España. Economía*. Madrid: Espasa Calpe, 831–857.

Segura, J. 1999. 'Sector público: análisis económico y perspectiva general', in J. L. García Delgado (dir.), *España. Economía: ante el siglo XXI*. Madrid: Espasa Calpe, 303–325.

Selva, E. 1999. *Ernesto Giménez Caballero. Entre la vanguardia y el fascismo*. Valencia: Pre-textos.

Sellés y Quintana, M. 2000. *El Foment del Treball Nacional 1914–1923*. Barcelona: Publicacions de l'Abadía de Montserrat.

Serrano Alcaide, C. 2000. 'Luis Valls-Taberner Arnó (1926)', in E. Torres Villanueva (dir.), *Los 100 empresarios españoles del siglo XX*. Madrid: LID, 512–517.

Serrano Sanz, J. M. 1994. 'Crisis económica y transición política', *Ayer*, 15, 135–164.

Shubert, A. 1984. *Hacia la revolución. Orígenes sociales del movimiento obrero en Asturias, 1860–1934*. Barcelona: Crítica.

Sierra, M. 1992. *La familia Ybarra, empresarios y políticos*. Sevilla: Muñoz Moya y Montraveta.

Solchaga, C. 1995. 'Interview', in *Memoria de la transición*. Madrid: El País, 384–387.

Soto Carmona, A. 1989. *El trabajo industrial en la España contemporánea (1874–1936)*. Barcelona: Anthropos.

Soto Carmona, Á. 1996. 'Conflictividad social y transición sindical', in J. Tusell and A. Soto (eds), *Historia de la transición 1975–1986*. Madrid: Alianza, 363–408.

Soto Carmona, Á. 1998. 'Estructura social. Relaciones labourales y huelgas', in J. R. Díaz Gijón et al. *Historia de la España actual: 1939–1996*. Madrid: Marcial Pons, 193–222.

Sudrià, C. 1990. 'Los beneficios de España durante la Gran Guerra. Una aproximación a la balanza de pagos española, 1914–1920', *Revista de Historia Económica*, VIII (2), 363–393.

Tafunell, X. 1996. *Los beneficios empresariales en España (1880–1981): elaboración de una serie anual*, Documento de Trabajo Fundación Empresa Pública, no. 9601. Madrid: Fundación Empresa Pública.

Tamames, R. 1966. *La lucha contra los monopolios*. Madrid: Tecnos.

Tamames, R. 1977. *La oligarquía financiera en España*. Barcelona: Planeta.

Tamames, R. 1978. *Introducción a la economía española*. Madrid: Alianza.

Tamames, R. 1979. *La República. La Era de Franco*. Madrid: Alianza.

Tedde, P. 1996. 'De la primera a la segunda Restauración. El Sector Público y la modernización de la economía española, 1875–1975', *Ayer*, 21, 15–49.

Termes, R. 1991. *Desde la banca. Tres décadas de vida económica española*. 2 Vols. Madrid: Rialp.

Termes, R. 1994. 'Los últimos doce años del sistema bancario español', in *Historia de una década. Sistema financiero y economía español 1984–1994*. Madrid: AB Asesores, 185–220.

Tezanos, J. F. 1990. 'Clases sociales', in S. Giner (dir.), *España. Sociedad y política*. Madrid: Espasa Calpe, 109–141.

Thomas, J. M. 1999. *Lo que fue la Falange*. Barcelona: Plaza y Janés.

Titos, M. 2000. 'Manuel Rodríguez-Acosta González de la Cámara (1874–1960)', in E. Torres Villanueva (dir.), *Los 100 empresarios españoles del siglo XX*. Madrid: LID, 223–228.

Toboso Sánchez, P. 2000a. 'José Fernández Rodríguez (1891–1982)', in E. Torres Villanueva (dir.), *Los 100 empresarios españoles del siglo XX*. Madrid: LID, 328–333.

Toboso Sánchez, P. 2000b. 'Ramón Areces Rodríguez (1904–1989)', in E. Torres Villanueva (dir.), *Los 100 empresarios españoles del siglo XX*. Madrid: LID, 413–418.

Torrero Mañas, A. 1988. 'Una nota sobre el empresario en la economía española' in J. L. García Delgado (dir.), *España. Economía*. Madrid: Espasa Calpe, 595–600.

Torres Villanueva, E. 1998. *Ramón de la Sota, 1857–1936. Un empresario vasco*. Madrid: LID.

Torres Villanueva, E. 2000a. 'Torcuato Luca de Tena y Álvarez-Ossorio (1861–1929)', in E. Torres Villanueva, *Los 100 empresarios españoles del siglo XX*. Madrid: LID, 110–115.

Torres Villanueva, E. 2000b. 'Juan March y Ordinas (1880–1962)', in E. Torres Villanueva, *Los 100 empresarios españoles del siglo XX*. Madrid: LID, 268–277.

Torres Villanueva, E. 2000c. 'Juan Lladó y Sánchez-Blanco (1907–1982)', in E. Torres Villanueva, *Los 100 empresarios españoles del siglo XX*. Madrid: LID, 432–438.

Torres Villanueva, E. (dir.) 2000. *Los 100 empresarios españoles del siglo XX*. Madrid: LID.

Tortella, G. 1990. 'CAMPSA y el monopolio de petróleos, 1927–1947', in P. Martín Aceña and P. Comín (eds), *Empresa pública e industrialización en España*. Madrid: Instituto Nacional de Industria, 81–116.

Tortella, G. 1994. *El desarrollo de la España contemporánea. Historia económica de los siglos XIX y XX*. Madrid: Alianza.

Tortella, G. 1995. 'La transición bancaria', in *Memoria de la transición*. Madrid: El País, 388–391.

Tortella, G. 1996. 'La iniciativa empresarial, factor escaso en la España contemporánea', in F. Comín and P. Martín Aceña (eds), *La empresa en la historia de España*. Madrid: Civitas, 49–60.

Tortella, G. 2000a. 'Prólogo', in E. Torres Villanueva (dir.), *Los 100 empresarios españoles del siglo XX*. Madrid: LID, 13–18.

Tortella, G. 2000b. 'José Luis de Ussía y Cubas (1885–1952)', in E. Torres Villanueva (dir.), *Los 100 empresarios españoles del siglo XX*, 373–378.

Tortella, G. 2000c. 'Ignacio Villalonga Villalba', in E. Torres Villanueva (dir.), *Los 100 empresarios españoles del siglo XX*, 354–360.

Tortella, G., Ballestero, A. and Díaz Fernández, J. L. 2003. *Del monopolio al libre mercado. La historia de la industria petrolera española.* Madrid: LID.

Tortella, G. and Jiménez, J. C. 1986. *Historia del Banco de Crédito Industrial.* Madrid: Alianza-Benco de Crédito Industrial.

Tortella, G. and Palafox, J. 1983. 'Banca e industria en España, 1918–1936', *Investigaciones económicas*, 20, 33–64.

Townson, N. 2000. *The Crisis of Democracy in Spain. Centrist Politics under the Second Republic 1931–1936.* Sussex: Sussex University Press.

Tuñón de Lara, M. 1978. *Luchas obreras y campesinas en la Andalucía del siglo XX. Jaén (1917–1920). Sevilla (1930–1932).* Madrid: Siglo XXI.

Tuñón de Lara, M. et al. 1991. *Transición y democracia (1973–1985). Historia de España.* Vol. X (**). Barcelona: Labor.

Tusell, J. 1987. *Radiografía de un golpe de Estado. El ascenso al poder del general Primo de Rivera.* Madrid: Alianza.

Tusell, J. 1993. Carrero. *La eminencia gris del régimen de Franco.* Madrid: Temas de Hoy.

Tusell, J., Lamo de Espinosa, E. and Pardo, R. (eds). 1996. *Entre dos siglos. Reflexiones sobre la democracia española.* Madrid: Alianza.

Tusell, J. and Sinova, J. et al. 1992. *La década socialista. El ocaso de Felipe González.* Madrid: Espasa Hoy.

Tusell, J. and Soto, Á. (eds). 1996. *Historia de la transición 1975–1986.* Madrid: Alianza.

Ugarte Tellería, J. 1998. *La nueva Covadonga insurgente. Orígenes sociales y culturales de la sublevación de 1936 en Navarra y el País Vasco.* Madrid: Biblioteca Nueva.

Varela, S. 1978. *Partidos y parlamento en la Segunda República.* Barcelona: Ariel-Fundación Juan March.

Vázquez, J. A. 1988. 'Regiones de tradición industrial en declive: la Cornisa Cantábrica', in J.L. García Delgado (dir.), *España. Economía.* Madrid: Espasa Calpe, 765–796.

Velarde Fuertes, J. 1973. *Política económica de la Dictadura.* Barcelona.

Vidal-Folch, X. 1990. 'La patronal de la transició democràtica', *L'Avenç*, 138, 66–73.

Villa, L. E. and Palomeque, C. 1977. *Introducción a la economía del trabajo.* Madrid: Editorial Debate.

Viñas, Á. 1984. *Guerra, dinero, dictadura. Ayuda fascista y autarquía en la España de Franco.* Barcelona: Crítica.

Wert, J. I. 1992. 'La opinión pública en el decenio del cambio', in J. Tusell and J. Sinova et al., *La década socialista. El ocaso de Felipe González.* Madrid: Espasa Hoy, 77–100.

Winston, C. M. 1989. *La clase trabajadora y la derecha en España 1900–1936.* Madrid: Cátedra.

Ybarra y Bergé, J. 1947. *Política nacional en Vizcaya.* Madrid: Instituto de Estudios Políticos.

Ynfante, J. 1996. *Opus Dei. Así en la tierra como en el cielo.* Barcelona: Grijalbo.

Ynfante, J. 1998. *Los muy ricos. Las trescientas grandes fortunas de España.* Barcelona: Grijalbo.

Zaragoza, Á. (comp.) 1988. *Pactos sociales, sindicatos y patronal en España.* Madrid: Siglo XXI.

Index